ORGANIZATIONAL BEHAVIOR

AN EXPERIENTAL APPROACH

SEVENTH EDITION

Joyce S. Osland

UNIVERSITY OF PORTLAND

David A. Kolb

CASE WESTERN RESERVE UNIVERSITY

Irwin M. Rubin

TEMENOS, INC.

Prentice
Hall

Upper Saddle River, New Jersey 07458

Library of Congress Cataloging-in-Publication Data

Osland, Joyce.
    Organizational behavior: an experiential approach / Joyce S. Osland, David A. Kolb,
Irwin M. Rubin.—7th ed.
      p. cm.
    Revised ed. of: Organizational behavior / David A. Kolb, Joyce S. Osland, Irwin M.
Rubin. 6th ed. c1995.
    A companion book of readings is available to accompany this text.
    Includes bibliographical references and index.
    ISBN 0-13-017610-9
      1. Psychology, Industrial. 2. Organizational behavior. I. Kolb, David A., 1939-
Organizational behavior. II. Rubin, Irwin M., 1939- III. Title.

HF5548.8 .K552 2001
158.7—dc21

                           00-027648

Editor: David Shafer
Managing Editor: Jennifer Glennon
Editorial Assistant: Kim Marsden
Assistant Editor: Michele Foresta
Media Project Manager: Michele Faranda
Executive Marketing Manager: Michael Campbell
Managing Editor (Production): Judy Leale
Production Editor: Cindy Spreder
Production Assistant: Keri Jean
Production Manager: Arnold Vila
Associate Director, Manufacturing: Vincent Scelta
Permissions Coordinator: Suzanne Grappi
Design Manager: Patricia Smythe
Designer: Michael Fruhbeis
Interior Design: Jill Yutkowicz
Cover Design: Michael Fruhbeis
Cover Art/Photo: David Madison / Tony Stone Images
Associate Director, Multimedia Production: Karen Goldsmith
Manager, Multimedia Production: Christina Mahon
Formatter: Ashley Scattergood
Composition: Preparé, Inc.

10 9 8 7 6 5 4 3 2 1

ISBN 0-13-017610-9

▲▲

To Asbjorn, Jessica,
Michael, Katrina, Bergit, and Ellie
Alice and Jonathan
Beth, Steven, and Corey

▲▲

Contents

▲▲

Foreword

This book–or better, the body of experiences it proposes–seeks to communicate some knowledge of general psychological principles, and some skills in applying that knowledge to social and organizational situations. Science tries to illuminate concrete reality by disclosing the general laws and principles that make the reality what it is. The generalization gives meaning to the concrete instance, but the instance carries the generalization into the real world–makes it usable. Experiencing social situations and then analyzing that experience brings generalization and concrete reality into effective union.

In teaching undergraduate and graduate management courses, I have frequently encountered students who hold a magical belief in a real world, somehow entirely different from any world they had hitherto experienced, and different, too, from the world of their textbooks. In teaching experienced executives, I have as frequently encountered people who balked at the proposal to apply general psychological principles to the concrete experiences of their everyday world. If there are skeptics of either variety in a group that undertakes one of these exercises, they can conduct their own tests of the relevance of theory to experience and vice versa. That is what the exercises are about.

But are the exercises themselves "real"? Can you really simulate social or organizational phenomena in a laboratory? The answer hangs on what we know of people–of their readiness to take roles, or, more accurately, their *inability not* to take roles when they find themselves in appropriate social situations, but this in itself is a psychological generalization: people are role-takers. Like any generalization, it should be tested empirically; and the exercises do just that. Each participant can be his or her own witness to the reality–or lack of it–of what has gone on.

But the purpose of the exercises is not just to increase understanding of principles, or understanding of concrete situations in terms of principles. They can be useful also as a means of developing skills for group situations: skills of observing, skills of self-insight, skills of understanding the behaviors and motives of others, skills of adapting behavior to the requirements of a task and the needs of groups and persons.

There is no magic to it. Learning here, like all learning, derives from time and attention directed to relevant material. The exercises provide the material. The time, attention, and active participation must be supplied by those who take part in them.

Herbert A. Simon

Preface

This seventh edition of *Organizational Behavior: An Experiential Approach* is the latest improvement on an experiment that began over 30 years ago. The first edition of this book was developed at MIT in the late 1960s and was the first application of the principles of experience-based learning to teaching in the field of organizational psychology. Since then the field has changed, the practice of experience-based learning has grown in acceptance and sophistication, and we, the authors, have changed.

The field of organizational behavior has grown rapidly in this time period and is today a complex tapestry of historical trends, contemporary trends, and new emerging trends. In the Introduction that follows we will describe these trends in more detail.

In comparison with previous editions, more emphasis has been placed upon cross-cultural issues throughout the book and integrative cases have been added at the end. We made substantial revisions in every chapter, adding recent research findings, new information on companies, and, in some chapters, new exercises. As always, our objective was not to overwhelm students with a comprehensive array of theories and findings, but to provide them with the essential materials and experiences they need to become effective managers and good employees.

Since the publication of our first edition, a number of other experience-based texts have been published in organizational behavior and other management specialties, and experiential-learning approaches have become widely accepted in higher education, particularly in programs for adult learners. The value of educational approaches that link the concepts and techniques of academia with learners' personal experiences in the real world is no longer questioned. In this latest edition we have attempted to reflect the state of the art in the practice of experiential learning and to bring these approaches to bear on the latest thinking and research in the field of organizational behavior.

This book is intended for students and managers who wish to explore the personal relevance and conceptual bases of the phenomena of organizational behavior. There are two goals in the experiential learning process. One is to learn the specifics of a particular subject matter. The other is to learn about one's own strengths and weaknesses as a learner (i.e., learning how to learn from experience). Thus, the book is focused upon exercises, self-analysis techniques, and role plays to make the insights of behavioral science meaningful and relevant to practicing managers and students. Each chapter is designed as an educational intervention that facilitates each stage of the experience-based learning process. Exercises and simulations are designed to produce experiences that create the phenomena of organizational behavior. Observation schemes and methods are introduced to facilitate understanding of these experiences. Theories and models are added to aid in forming generalizations. And finally, the intervention is structured in a way that encourages learners to experiment with and test what they have learned either in class or other areas of their lives. Our purpose is to teach students how to learn so that they will become continuous learners, capable of responding to demands for change and new skills throughout their career. Learning is no longer a special activity reserved for the classroom, but an integral and explicit part of work itself.

In addition to teaching students to be life-long learners, the exercises and the order of the chapters are designed to facilitate self-knowledge and team work. Students should leave this course with a much clearer understanding of themselves and the effect their behavior has on others. Students work in the same learning groups throughout the course. In these groups, members share their experiences and provide support, advice, feedback, and friendship to each other. A by-product of this group approach is the creation of a class environment that facilitates learning.

A companion readings book, *The Organizational Behavior Reader, Seventh Edition*, is also published by Prentice Hall. Many footnotes in this seventh volume, what we call the workbook, make reference to articles that have been reprinted there. These are simply cited as "*Reader*" in the footnote entries.

A preface is a place to publicly thank the many people who have helped us. Our feelings of pride in our product are tempered by the great indebtedness we feel to many others whose ideas and insights preceded ours. It is a tribute to the spirit of collaboration that pervades our field that the origin of many of the exercises recorded here is unknown. We have tried throughout the manuscript to trace the origins of those exercises we know about and in the process we may, in many areas, fall short of the original insight. For that we can only apologize. The major unnamed contributors are our students. In a very real sense, this book could never have been completed without their active participation in our explorations.

We wish to thank James McIntyre, our coauthor in the first four editions of this book, for his generous and creative contributions. While much has changed and will continue to change through successive editions of this book, Jim's presence will always be there.

The many instructors who, as users of previous editions of our text, have shared their experiences, resources, insights, and criticisms; have been invaluable guides in the revision process. Suzanne Adams, Janet Bennett, Mathew Crichton, Bill Essig, Howard Feldman, Barbara Gayle, Tom Howe, Abigale Lane, Stephen Miller, Asbjorn Osland, Stella Ting-Toomey, and Judith White were very helpful in a variety of ways. The reviewers did an excellent, thorough job: John Dopp, Gene Hendrix, Avis Johnson, Stephen Miller, and Dennis O'Connor. Bruce Drake deserves a special mention for selflessly contributing his formidable editorial skills to this project.

Our greatest debt of gratitude goes to Susan Mann research assistant and editorial critic extraordinaire. The reference librarians at the University of Portland – Tony Greiner, Susan Hinken, Pam Horan, Torie Scott, Heidi Senior, as well as the director, Rich Hines, – all went well beyond the call of duty in tracking down articles and correct citations. Ron Hill, dean at the University of Portland's business school, and the Robert B. Pamplin Jr. Foundation provided support for this project. We're grateful to Gwynn Klobes and Michael Kuchler, and all the student workers at the University of Portland business school who lent a helping hand to this project. We owe a special debt to Melissa O'Neill for her cheerful efficiency in tackling an endless stream of details and research leads.

It was a pleasure, as always, to work with the Prentice Hall crew: David Shafer, Jennifer Glennon, Michele Foresta, Judy Leale, Kim Marsden, and the unflappable Cindy Spreder.

Joyce S. Osland
David A. Kolb
Irwin M. Rubin

REVIEWERS

John Dopp, San Francisco State University
Gene Hendrix
Avis Johnson
Stephen Miller, California State University-Hayward
Dennis O'Connor, Le Moyne College

Introduction to the Workbook

▲▲▲

I hear and I forget
I see and I remember
I do and I understand
CONFUCIUS

As teachers responsible for helping people learn about the field of organizational behavior, we have grappled with a number of basic educational dilemmas. Some of these dilemmas revolve around the issue of *how* to teach about this most important and intensely personal subject. The key concepts in organizational behavior (indeed, in social science in general) are rather abstract. It is difficult through the traditional lecture method to bring these ideas meaningfully to life. Other problems concern issues of what to teach, since the field of organizational behavior is large and continues to grow. Relevant concepts and theories come from a variety of disciplines, and no single course could begin to scratch the surface. Another dilemma is one of control. Who should be in control of the learning process? Who should decide what material is important to learn? Who should decide the pace at which learning should occur? Indeed, who should decide what constitutes learning? Our resolution of these and related dilemmas is contained within this book. The learning materials in this book are an application of the theory of experiential learning to the teaching and learning of organizational behavior. In this method, primary emphasis is placed upon learning from your own experience. Each of the chapters in the workbook begins with an introduction that raises key questions and provides a framework for your experiences in the unit. The core of each unit is an action-oriented behavioral simulation. The purpose of these exercises is to allow you to generate your own data about each of the key concepts to be studied. A format is provided to facilitate your ability to observe and share the personal reactions you have experienced, while the summaries at the end of each unit help to integrate the unit experiences and stimulate further questions and issues to be explored. If there is an overriding objective of the book, it is that you learn how to learn from all of your experiences and practice the skills required of effective employees.

LEARNING ABOUT ORGANIZATIONAL BEHAVIOR

It has been over 30 years since we first began developing and testing the feasibility of experiential learning methods for teaching organizational behavior. Our initial attempts to substitute exercises, games, and role plays for more traditional educational approaches were met in many quarters by polite skepticism and resistance. Today experiential learning approaches are an integral part of management school curricula and management training programs everywhere. During these years, the subject matter of organizational behavior has undergone much change as well. Some of this change has been subtle and quiet, involving the consolidation and implementation of trends that began years ago. Other changes have been more dramatic. New vital perspectives have come alive, reorganizing and redirecting research, theory, and teaching in the field. Still other trends loom on the horizon, as yet underdeveloped, pointing the way toward the future shape of the field.

As we began to work on this seventh edition, we felt that it was time to take stock of these changes so that we might faithfully, in new selection of topics and experiential exercises, portray the field of organizational behavior as it is today—a complex of vital themes enduring from the past, alive in the present, and emerging in the future. Such a stocktaking is difficult to achieve objectively. Organizational behavior is a vast field with indefinite boundaries overlapping sister disciplines of social psychology, sociology, and anthropology, and management fields such as operations research, business policy, and industrial relations. One could convincingly argue that any patterns one sees in such diversity and complexity lie more in the eye of the beholder than in objective reality. At the very least, where one stands in defining organizational behavior is greatly influenced by where one sits, by one's particular experience and orientation to the field. Recognizing that any organization of the field is constructed from a combination of objective reality and subjective preference, we nonetheless felt that there is value in making explicit our view of the field, since it was on the basis of that view that choices of topics and exercises were made. By understanding our view, you, as learners, may be better able to articulate your own agreements and disagreements, thereby helping to sort the actual state of the field from our individual viewpoints.

Table I-1 summarizes the changes we have seen in the field in the last 60 years in six general areas: the way organizational behavioral is defined, the way management education is conducted, the field's perspective on the nature of persons, its view as to how human resources are to be managed, its perspective on organizations, and the nature of the change improvement process. In each of these areas there are three kinds of trends: *historical foundations of trends*, previous historical development that is now widely influential in shaping the field; *contemporary trends*, current research and development that is capturing the excitement and imagination of scholars and practitioners; and *emerging trends*, new issues and concerns that seem destined to shape the future of organizational behavior in research and practice.

DEFINITION OF THE FIELD

Paul Lawrence[1] traces the origin of the field of organizational behavior back to the early 1940s. He cites as the first key contribution to the field the group climate experiments of Kurt Lewin and his associates in 1943. Early scholars in the field came from industrial and social psychology and later from sociology. Organizational behavior departments were housed administratively in business schools, but in general they maintained their separate identity from the profession of management. Today we see major changes in orientation as organizational behavior departments have become more integrated units within professional business schools. Most new faculty today have Ph.D.s in organizational behavior as opposed to basic disciplines, and interdisciplinary research around the managerial task has burgeoned. Concepts are now more often defined in managerial terms (e.g., work team development) as opposed to behavioral science terms (group dynamics).

Active developments in organizational behavior today involve the expansion of the field from an industrial-business focus to a wider application of behavioral science knowledge in other professional fields—health care management, law, public administration, education, and international development. Perhaps because of this expansion into more complex social and political institutions, an emerging trend is toward a focus on sociological and political concepts that increase our understanding of management in complex organizational environments. In recent years the issue of environmental determinism has been raised, an even more "macro" approach to organizations. The population ecologists study the rise and fall of organizations within an entire industry and maintain that it is the environment, rather than actions by humans, that influences organizations. There is an active intellectual debate in the field between those who see strategic leadership and choice as the determinant of organizational success and those who subscribe to the environmental determinist position.

PERSPECTIVE ON ORGANIZATIONS

Early work in organizational behavior took a somewhat limited view of organizations, being primarily concerned with job satisfaction and human fulfillment in work. The focus later expanded to include organizational productivity. For many years organizational research was aimed at internal functioning. This focus was broadened by the advent of open systems theory. Since organizations, to survive, must adapt to their environment, organizational functioning cannot be understood without examining organization-environment relationships. This led to the contingency theory of organizations, which states that there is no one best way to organize and manage; it depends on the environmental demands and corresponding tasks for the organization.

---

[1] Paul Lawrence, "Historical Development of Organizational Behavior," in Jay Lorsch (Ed.), *Handbook of Organizational Behavior* (Upper Saddle River, N.J.: Prentice Hall, 1987)

TABLE I–1 Thematic Trends in Organizational Behavior, 1940–2000

	HISTORICAL TRENDS		CONTEMPORARY TRENDS		EMERGING TRENDS	
1. Definition of the field	Behavioral science discipline orientation	to Professional orientation	Industrial business focus	to Management focus	Micro psychological emphasis	to Balance of macro and micro views; systems focus and environmental determinism
2. Perspective on organizations	Job satisfaction, human fulfillment	to Organization productivity	Internal organizational functioning	to Organization, environment adaptation	Organizations as dominant, stable structures	to Organizations as symbolic entities networked with industries, institutions, careers in a global economy; boundaryless organizations
3. Perspective on persons	Tender (communication, intimacy, growth)	to Tough (power and influence)	Socioemotional factors	to Cognitive problem-solving factors	Deficiency orientation (adjustment)	to Appreciation orientation (development); self-efficacy
4. Human resource management	Human Relations	to Human resources	Management of people	to Management of work	Organization development	to Career development; diversity; global leadership; work/non-work boundary
5. Change processes	Expert, content consultation	to Process consultation	Change created by change agents; Simple, global technologies	to Management of change by the system; Highly differentiated problem-specific technologies	Change via change intervention, action research	to Change via vision-based strategic transformation; learning organizations; self-directed work teams and empowerment
6. Management education	Academic	to Experiential	Creating awareness	to Skill building	Performance orientation	to Learning to learn orientation; team focus; distance learning

The open systems view of organizations leads to an important emerging trend in the study of organizations. In most research to date, the organization is the focal point of study, conceived as the dominant stable structure around which the environment revolves. Yet in many cases the organization is but a part of a more pervasive and dominant industry, institutional, or professional career structure. Utilities, for example, cannot be understood without understanding the impact of their relationship with governmental regulatory institutions. Medical organizations such as hospitals were dominated solely by the medical profession as a whole and particularly by the socialization and training of M.D.s until the emphasis upon cost controls increased the power of financial interests. Improvements in the effectiveness of these organizations can be achieved only by consideration of the system of relationships among the organization and the institutions and professions that shape it.

Interorganizational networks are replacing the traditional view of the organization as the primary entity. Quasi-firms, such as construction jobs, which consist of subcontracted work teams, are becoming more common. Now we talk about boundaryless organizations that work at eliminating or diminishing boundaries between both internal and external groups and constituencies. The influence of the global economy is felt everywhere. Current research portrays organizations as symbolic systems in which members interpret their shared social reality. In this approach, reality is what is agreed upon, rather than an objective fact. The importance of organizational culture and shared values has also become an important consideration in understanding organizational behavior, since much of the recent economic growth has occurred in smaller firms, there has been renewed attention to entrepreneurship.

PERSPECTIVE ON PERSONS

In their perspective on persons and human personality, organizational behavior scholars have added an emphasis on power and influence processes to an earlier concern with the more "tender" aspects of socioemotional behavior (e.g., communication, intimacy, and human growth). These concerns with the social-motivational aspects of human behavior are currently being expanded by many researchers to include cognitive processes-learning, problem solving, decision making, and planning-thus contributing to a more holistic view of human behavior. A more comprehensive perspective on human functioning has emerged from the work of adult development psychologists in personality development, ego development, moral development, and cognitive development. Researchers in these fields are providing frameworks for human functioning in organizations that emphasize developmental-appreciative processes as opposed to the deficiency-adjustment perspective that dominated much work on human behavior in organizations in the past. Recent research focuses upon self-efficacy and self-management.

HUMAN RESOURCE MANAGEMENT

The changes in perspectives on the person, which we have just discussed, have been mirrored in changes in philosophy about how human beings are to be managed. From our current historical vantage point, early approaches to management in organizational psychology seem defensive and vaguely paternalistic. People were involved in work decisions and attention was paid to "human relations" to keep workers happy and to avoid resistance to change initiated by management. Recently participative management has come to be viewed more as a positive tool for improving organizational functioning. People are involved in decision making not only to make them feel more satisfied, but also because the improved information and problem-solving capability resulting from a participative process is more productive and effective.

Current research takes a more systematic approach to human resource management, shifting the perspective from management of people and the social-motivational techniques of management style, organizational climate, management by objectives (MBO), and so on, to a management of work perspective. This perspective considers the whole person as he or she adapts to the work environment. Work is seen as a sociotechnical system, considering the content of jobs as well as the management process. Managing work involves designing technological systems, organizational arrangements, and jobs themselves to obtain effective organizational adaptation to the environment and maximum utilization of human resources and talents.

An important emerging trend in human resource management involves the addition of a career development perspective to the organization development perspective we have outlined. A host of trends are occurring in the labor market, including an older population, a more balanced male-female work force, a more culturally and ethnically diverse workforce, and increasing career mobility and change among workers through their work lives.

There is an emergent trend that encourages greater responsibility on the part of workers to develop their own careers. As a result of downsizing to leaner structures and the clog of baby boomers, many companies are making it clear to employees that they can no longer guarantee a lifelong career within the company. While companies may still manage the careers of those in the "fast track," career responsibility belongs primarily to workers themselves. At present, the topic of managing diversity, both the domestic and international variety is viewed as a strategic competitive advantage. Developing global leadership is an emerging trend. The increased demands placed upon workers has generated interest in the work/non-work boundary and the personal and the social costs of the way work is organized.

CHANGE PROCESSES

Concern with change and organization improvement has been central to organizational behavior from its inception. Kurt Lewin's research methodology has been a dominant approach to integrating knowledge generation and practical application following his dictum: "If you want to understand something, try to change it." In the last decade the specialized field of organization development (OD) has emerged from the Lewinian tradition as a powerful practical approach for using behavioral science knowledge to improve organizational effectiveness and human fulfillment in work. A major contribution of OD has been an understanding of the process of introducing change. Process consultation, an approach that helps the organization to solve its own problems by improving the problem-solving, communication, and relationship processes in the organization, has emerged as an alternative to expert consultation, the approach where outside consultants generate problem solutions and present them for consideration by the organization. Currently the technologies for introducing and managing change are expanding and becoming more sophisticated and problem-specific as OD programs are being initiated in organizations of all types. As change becomes a way of life in most organizations, there is a shift of focus from change as something created and managed by external consultants to a concern with the manager as change agent, who manages managing the change process as part of his or her job function. As a result there is less concern today with training OD professionals and greater concern with improving managers' OD skills.

Responsibility for change has also been pushed down the hierarchy in some organizations. Learning organizations, in particular, take time to develop and evaluate improvements, as do self-directed work teams. In recent years, some managers have shared information and the power to make decisions and changes with "empowered" employees. Pressure from a global economy, rapid technological advances, and deregulation often trigger organization change.

MANAGEMENT EDUCATION

From the beginning, the field of organizational behavior has been concerned with educational innovations, particularly those aimed at communicating abstract academic knowledge in a way that is helpful and meaningful to pragmatically-oriented professional managers and management students. The two dominant innovative traditions in this respect have been the development of the case method, particularly at the Harvard Business School, and the experiential learning approaches that have grown from Kurt Lewin's early work on group dynamics and the sensitivity training movement that followed. Both these traditions have developed educational technologies that are sophisticated in their application of theory to practice. Today, most management schools offer a mix of educational approaches—the traditional lecture, the case discussion, and experiential exercises, sometimes combining them in new and innovative ways, such as in computer-based business simulations and real business projects and distance learning. With these new educational technologies, management educators have begun to raise their aspirations from increasing student awareness and understanding to improving skills in interpersonal relations, decision making, managing change, and other key managerial functions. Yet the future poses an even greater challenge. The rapid growth of knowledge and increasing rate of social and technological change make specific skill training somewhat vulnerable to obsolescence. The answer seems to lie not just in learning new skills, but in learning how to learn and adapt throughout one's career. An emerging concern in management education and research is, therefore, how individuals and organizations learn.

In many ways, organizational behavior is a mature field with concepts that have been fairly thoroughly researched and widely disseminated. The Total Quality movement accelerated the acceptance of many aspects of group skills and participative management. At present there is a trend towards self-management and empowerment. With the diminished number of middle managers in many companies, self-directed work teams are now expected to develop analytical, team-building, problem-solving, and leadership skills. Responsibility and control are being pushed to lower levels in organizations, requiring more training for a different group of employees.

THE PLAN OF THIS BOOK

In choosing topics and exercises for this book, we have attempted to represent all three trends in organizational behavior: those that are mature and established, those that are the focus of current research excitement, and new ideas that suggest the future shape of the field. The book is organized into four parts progressing from a focus on the individual to the group, organization, and the organization-environment interface.

Part I examines the individual in the organization and presents some of the different mental maps that individuals possess. Chapters 1 and 6 consider the individual's relationship with the organization over time through the concepts of the psychological contract and career development. Chapter 2 reviews the principal theories of management and managerial functions. Chapters 3 and 4 focus, respectively, on the learning process and motivational determinants of human behavior in organizations. Chapter 5 centers on individual values and their effect on ethical decision-making.

Whereas the primary focus of Part I is self-awareness and the appreciation of individual differences, in Part II there is more emphasis on the skill-building needed to develop effective work relationships and teams. It begins with a grounding in interpersonal communication (Chapter 7) and progresses to perception and attribution in Chapter 8. Chapter 9 focuses on group dynamics and self-managed work teams, while Chapter 10 deals with problem management and creativity. Multigroup relations, conflict, and negotiation are addressed in Chapter 11. Managing diversity, both in the United States and abroad, is the topic of Chapter 12.

Part III focuses on the skills needed for leadership (Chapter 13) and the critical leadership functions in the managerial role—creating, maintaining, and changing organizational culture (Chapter 14), decision making (Chapter 15), power and influence (Chapter 16), coaching and empowerment (Chapter 17), and performance appraisal (Chapter 18).

Part IV is concerned with managing effective organizations. Chapter 19 looks at the key issues of organization structure and design. Chapter 20 describes the process of planned change and organization development.

YOUR ROLE AS A LEARNER

You will find as you work with this book that a new role is being asked of you as a learner. Whereas in many of your prior learning experiences you were in the role of a passive recipient, here you are given the opportunity to become an active creator of your own learning. This is an opportunity for you to develop new and different relationships with faculty members responsible for this course. As you may already have sensed, the experiential learning approach provides numerous opportunities for shared leadership in the learning process.

Part 1

▲▲▲

UNDERSTANDING YOURSELF AND OTHER PEOPLE AT WORK

Mental Maps

The goal of the first section is to help you become aware of your mental maps or models, as well as those of fellow participants in the course. Although the concept has existed since ancient times, the term *mental models* was invented in the 1940s by Kenneth Craik, a Scottish psychologist. This term refers to "the images, assumptions, and stories that we carry in our minds of ourselves, other people, institutions, and every aspect of the world. Like a pane of glass framing and subtly distorting our vision, mental models determine what we see and then how we act."[1] One way to understand our behavior is to make these usually tacit maps visible. In this section, you will have an opportunity to examine mental maps about psychological contracts, theories of management, learning styles, ethics, and values. We hope you'll finish the section with more self-knowledge and a greater appreciation for the differences you will see in other people.

[1] P. Senge, A. Kleiner, C. Roberts, R. Ross, and B. Smith, *The Fifth Discipline Fieldbook: Strategies and Tools for Building a Learning Organization* (New York: Currency, 1993), 235.

THE PSYCHOLOGICAL CONTRACT

OBJECTIVES After completing Chapter 1, you should be able to:

A. Define the terms *psychological contract* and the *self-fulfilling prophecy* and explain their importance.

B. Describe the external influences that affect workplace expectations.

C. Explain the *pinch model.*

D. Make a psychological contract with your professor.

E. List the characteristics of the field of organizational behavior.

THE YOUNG AND THE RESTLESS

They want money, status, and power—right now. Can you handle the management problems that 20-somethings pose? It's the generation gap all over again. Only this time the baby boomers are on the other side of the divide. Uneasily aware of echoing their parents, boomers complain that their Generation X employees have short attention spans and no work ethic, show no respect for their elders and want money and promotions handed to them on a platter—immediately.

Xers must really be threatening, since a cottage industry in unflattering statistics about them seems to have sprung up. Television has turned their brains to mush, say the critics, citing College Board figures showing that mean SAT scores dropped from 463 (verbal) and 493 (math) in 1969 to 422 and 474 in 1991. But did the students get worse, or did their schools? Another criticism pegs the Xers as apolitical. Sure enough, only 46 percent of potential voters 30 and under bothered going to the polls in 1992 compared with 63 percent of voters between 30 and 54, says the Census Bureau. Then again, under-30s weren't voting in 1972 either, as George McGovern found out.

Instead of reaching for the nearest stereotypes, maybe boomers should take a look at what Xers bring to the table, including a fresh perspective, effortless technoliteracy, and an easy adaptability to change. Sound like attributes that can help your business, don't they?

THE ROOT OF X

If you want to know why Xers, defined by *American Demographics* magazine as those born between 1965 and 1976, turned out the way they did, compare the times they grew up in with the boomers' prime years. In the Eisenhower 1950s, things were, if nothing else, predictable. Mom stayed home, the divorce rate was low and Dad knew that in time he'd move up a well-defined chain of command and retire to a comfy pension at 65. Generation X, by contrast, is the first generation to raise itself. Between 1975, when the oldest Xers were in grade school and the youngest in diapers, and 1985, when the first Xers were about to hit the job market, the percentage of working mothers with children under 18 rose from 47 percent to 62 percent, according to the Bureau of Labor Statistics. In addition, many Xers grew up in single-parent households. According to the Census Bureau, both the divorce rate and the percentage of children born outside of marriage almost doubled between 1968 and 1977.

As for work, neither the easy money of the 1980s nor the burnout and widespread layoffs of the 1990s have done much to convince Xers that patience and corporate loyalty are the keys to success. Many young workers have spent their entire careers under the threat of potential cutbacks. "My husband and I are always talking about how we can keep ourselves versatile enough to land another job," says Amanda Gamblin, 28, a bookkeeper with the St. Andrew Legal Clinic in Portland, Oregon.

Xers' sense of economic insecurity is only heightened by the massive deficit and reports that Social Security will be depleted when they reach retirement. And they blame their elders for their plight. "Our futures have been mortgaged," says Melanie Piersol, 26, an audience-development coordinator for *P.O.V.*, a documentary-film series on PBS in New York.

These attitudes often conflict with prevailing boomer norms. For example, while boomers expected to work their way up the ladder, Xers don't trust their employers enough to wait around for rewards. "I would be willing to pay my dues to a corporation, but only if they offered me job security," says Gamblin.

Xers are also less likely than boomers to identify themselves by the jobs they hold. "This generation wants more balance in their lives," says Claire Raines, 49, a Denver management consultant and author of *Twentysomething: Managing and Motivating Today's New Work Force.* In the 1980s, notes Raines, "The focus was on money and success. For this generation, the focus is on happiness. They want jobs that are satisfying and fulfilling."

Make no mistake, Xers are demanding employees. And if you're a boomer, you might be inclined just to stick with what you know and hire 40-somethings. But resist the temptation. If you can bear in mind what makes them tick—and what leaves them cold—the Xers you manage can make your company stronger.

- **Vary their assignments** Multitasking is second nature to most Xers. Rosie Grove, 32, Gamblin's boss at St. Andrew, says, "Amanda is able, while she's talking on the telephone, to input completely unrelated data into the computer and be thinking about the next project. An older employee with exactly the same job is much more methodical." Turn that to your advantage by assigning your Xers a variety of tasks.
- **Teach them new skills** Many Xers see themselves as self-employed entrepreneurs, even though they're on your payroll. If you can teach them a portable skill, you've won their gratitude by increasing their value to future employers. Says Piersol, "A very strong selling point for a job is the skills we learn."

  That's why cross-training goes over big with Xers. Michele Sjolander, 30, coordinator of registration and patient services at Coon Rapids Medical Center in Coon Rapids, Minnesota, turned her young staffers' boredom into a win-win situation by insisting they teach one another their jobs. They felt more challenged, and their ability to perform different tasks averted paperwork and patient bottlenecks.
- **Teach them some manners** You've probably already encountered the otherwise charming and savvy young employee who casually addresses your most straitlaced client by her first name, or who unthinkingly takes a seat at the head of the table at an important staff meeting. Believe it or not, you're dealing with a different style, not disrespect. "You see their behavior as a lack of social graces," says Margaret Regan, a principal with Towers Perrin in New York. "They see it as being honest." In their view, formal politeness is merely a disguise for one's true feelings, rather than a skill that lubricates everyday interactions.

  In any case, it's a problem you have to manage. Try framing any advice you give as a lesson in office politics, not a brushup in etiquette. "Couch your advice in terms of their best interest," says Raines. "Give them an example or two of an employee who didn't take politics seriously, as well as an example of an employee who did. If you compare how well these two employees have fared in your company, the Xer will get the message."

- **Keep them in the loop** Nothing alienates an Xer faster than excluding them from decisions that affect them directly. At Phoenix's Doubletree Hotels Corporation, where 80 percent of the workforce is 30 or younger, Xers work in teams, interview potential hires, and evaluate one another's work once a year. "Team members are in a perfect position to decide whether a new player exemplifies what they're looking for," says Executive Vice President Ann Rhoades, 50.

  Likewise, feedback, even the negative kind, is crucial. But don't equate expressing approval or disappointment with giving feedback. "I need to know exactly what my employer needs of me so I can deliver it," says Gamblin. "I don't just want to hear that I'm doing a good job."

- **Tie praise for a job well done to a concrete reward** Karen Ritchie, executive vice president and managing director of the Warren, Michigan, office of General Motors Mediaworks, which negotiates the cost and placement of advertising for the automaker, suggests handing out new titles as frequently as every six months to give employees a useful marker of progress. "Generation Xers need to see where they are in regard to everyone else," says Ritchie, 53.

- **Keep it fun** When Doubletree employees rate each other, they ask whether a coworker "plays well with others and shares toys." The language comes straight out of day care, but the attitude behind it comes from Xers' everyday concerns. "They want to come to work and enjoy it," says Rhoades, "or they're outta here."

Wait a second. Employees who want to be informed, challenged, treated fairly, and invited to weigh in on decisions affecting their future? Maybe these Xers aren't so different from the rest of us after all.

Source: Donna Brown Hogarty, "The Young and the Restless," *Working Woman*, July–August 1996 p 27(2).

PREMEETING PREPARATION

A. Read "The Young and the Restless" in the chapter's opening vignette.

B. Answer the following questions.

  1. Have you ever had a job experience that did not work out as you thought it would?

  2. What expectations of yours were not met?

  3. Were there any expectations on the part of your boss that were not met?

C. Read the Topic Introduction.

D. If your instructor has assigned the Robbins Self-Assessment Library, use "How Committed Am I to My Organization?"

TOPIC INTRODUCTION

The generation Xers in the opening vignette, as well as the baby boomers who often manage them, bring certain expectations to the workplace. When individuals join an organization, they form an unwritten, implicit or (less frequently) explicit, psychological contract with the organization. This contract consists of the mutual expectations employees and employers have of each other. Such contracts help predict both the type of outputs employers will get from employees as well as the rewards employees will receive for their efforts from the organization. The psychological contract is based on people's perception that they have been promised a future return for their contributions, thus creating an obligation for the other party to reciprocate.[1]

If a new employee is given the impression that hard work will be rewarded with a promotion and raise in the near future and neither are forthcoming, the psychological contract is broken because the organization has failed to meet the employee's expectations about both advancement and credibility. On the other hand, if an organization agrees to pay the cost of an employee's MBA program, the boss may expect the employee to work harder or be more loyal because the company is contributing more to him or her than to other employees.

Even though such expectations may never formally be stated, they do exist and they have a tangible impact on the relationship between employee and employer. When the expectations of either side are not fulfilled or when the contract is violated, intense emotional reactions such as outrage, shock, resentment, and anger result. The trust and good faith of the employer-employee relationship is destroyed and cannot easily be rebuilt. The disillusionment over broken psychological contracts affects employee job satisfaction, productivity, and desire to continue with the organization.[2] Violation of the psychological contract also reduces employee commitment.[3] A company staffed by employees who feel cheated or betrayed cannot expect to be a high-performance company.

Psychological contracts differ from employment contracts because they focus on a dynamic relationship that defines the employees' psychological involvement with their employer. The actions of both parties mutually influence the psychological contract. For example, high company expectations about what employees should contribute to the company can produce increased individual performance; when individuals perform at a high level, they come to expect more than just a paycheck. They may also expect respectful treatment, challenging jobs, training that will help them develop and grow, and a share in the financial profits their increased performance levels have made possible.

From the company's perspective, the key questions are, "How can we manage our human resources so that we can maximize individual contributions?" and "How can we socialize our members to accept our expectations and norms as legitimate?" For the individual, the questions are, "How can I get the satisfaction and rewards that I want from this organization?" "How can I manage my own career so that my socialization takes place in organizational settings that encourage my personal growth and development?" and "How can I fulfill the expectations of the organization and still have time for my personal life?"

More than half the employees in one study reported violations of their psychological contract in their first job upon graduating from college.[4] Such discrepancies between expectations and reality are, therefore, fairly common. Students can try to avoid disillusionment by gaining a more realistic idea about what to expect from organizations through internships and by asking more questions during the job interview process.

Certainly both prospective employees and employers would be better off if their expectations were made explicit from the beginning. But often we are not aware of our expectations until they have been disappointed. That's why mechanisms or forums that allow for continued discussions and renegotiations of the contract are so crucial throughout the term of employment. Effective managers understand that the psychological contract is important because it links the individual to the organization. They ensure that the mutual expectations that comprise the contract are both understood and fulfilled so the employee-employer relationship is carefully maintained.

THE SELF-FULFILLING PROPHECY

Another important concept that relates to expectations and new employees is the self-fulfilling prophecy, the phenomenon that occurs when people perform in accordance with a rater's expectations of them. A manager's expectations for an employee cause the manager to treat the employee differently; therefore, the employee responds in a way that confirms the manager's initial expectations. We have Rosenthal and his albino rats to thank for this particular contribution to organizational behavior. In an experiment, he gave the same strain of rats to different groups of students at Harvard.[5] The students' task was to teach their rats to run a maze. However, one group of students was told their rats were bright; the other group was told their rats were dull. Although there were no inherent differences between the two groups of rats, the so-called "bright" rats learned to run mazes better than the "dull" rats. Further inquiry revealed that the students found the "bright" rats more likeable and, therefore, had treated them differently. Intrigued, Rosenthal and Jacobson tried the same experiment with school children.[6] They randomly chose one child out of every five and told teachers that these children were "academic spurters." At the year's end, the "academic spurters" had improved their IQ by an average of 22 points. The teachers' expectations about these students affected the way they treated the children. The children's response to that treatment was to become "academic spurters." The critical variable in these examples is the teacher's (or rat handler's) expectation: Higher expectations were associated with higher learning. The children (and the rats) became what the teachers thought they were, which is a perfect example of self-fulfilling prophecy.

We find the same self-fulfilling prophecy at work with newly hired people. Studies indicate that new hires who are immediately given challenging jobs are more likely to show high performance later on in their careers.[7] Today, many large corporations formally label those employees for whom they have high expectations as "fast-trackers" or "high potentials." As part of their succession management programs, companies pay special attention to this group and provide them with the experiences and opportunities that will prepare them to take a top leadership role in the future. Such programs can be very effective, but one of their by-products may be resentment and complaints (both valid and invalid) by "non-fast-trackers" who feel that they too could shine if they received the special treatment that goes along with higher expectations of one's performance.

What is the practical significance in the workplace of understanding the self-fulfilling prophecy?

- Employees who are expected to do well will likely perform better than those who are not, even though there may be no differences between them.
- Supervisors and managers who have high expectations of their employees will be more likely to have their expectations met.

EXTERNAL INFLUENCES AND CHANGING EXPECTATIONS

The tremendous rate of change that businesses undergo as they try to adapt to a global economy and changing economic conditions has resulted in marked changes in workplace expectations and psychological contracts. We can observe the dynamic nature of psychological contracts in the change that has occurred with employer-employee loyalty in the last 20 years.

More and more jobs in Europe, North America, and some Asian countries have been transformed from full-time, ongoing work (for core employees) to contingent, temporary employment (for peripheral employees). Globalization, downsizing, technology, outsourcing and subcontracting of work, and relatively low union representation have changed the picture of employment. For employees, there has been a simultaneous loss of job security accompanied by increasing demands for performance, flexibility, and innovation. Massive terminations resulting from downsizing, reengineering, and mergers and acquisitions have driven home the message that psychological contracts have changed.

For example, the terms of the previous psychological contract between many Americans and their corporate employers were relatively simple. Employees were willing to work their way slowly up the corporate ladder in return for the promise of a sufficiently high promotion in their middle age to allow them to live comfortably during their retirement years. This contract was always somewhat unbalanced because the company was expected to be loyal to employees, while the employees could resign whenever they wished. Lifelong job security is now viewed as an unaffordable luxury, even in companies such as IBM and countries such as Japan that were noted for it until the last decade.

How do employees react to the broken psychological contracts that accompany corporate restructuring? Some employees modify their expectations and make whatever sacrifices are necessary to retain their jobs, while others give more importance to family and nonwork interests. Still others place more emphasis on developing their reputational capital (i.e., building their resumes so they are more attractive to other companies) than on institution-building activities that would benefit their current employer. The key question for managers and human resource professionals is, "How do organizations promote commitment on the part of employees who no longer trust in job security?" The current employment contract has changed from long-term employment relationships and paternalism to employment based on business needs. Employees are now rewarded for skills and performance, not tenure, and they, rather than the company, are responsible for maintaining their own employability via personal reskilling and retraining.

Another environmental change that affects the psychological contract as well as commitment in the United States is the switch from high- to low-unemployment conditions. There are fewer people available to hire in what is described as the tightest labor market since the late 1950s. Combined with a flourishing economy, this means that finding high-quality employees and keeping them is the major problem facing many companies. Although companies still downsize employees, primarily due to mergers or a need for different skill sets, terminated employees remain unemployed for less time than in the 1980s and early 1990s.

In order to attract and retain good talent in a tight labor market, some companies have moved beyond salary and traditional benefits (e.g., health insurance and pensions) to offer career-advancement and work-family programs. There are several ranked lists of "best companies to work for" (*Business Week, Fortune, Mother Jones, Working Mother*) that provide incentives such as valet service, dry cleaning, house sitters who wait for repairmen, on-site child care, and primary education. Companies that make it easier for employees to juggle work and family report greater commitment, higher productivity, increased job satisfaction, and lower turnover among their employees. These positive outcomes are also correlated with having a supportive supervisor and jobs that offer autonomy, meaning, and learning opportunities.[8]

Commitment is also fostered by teamwork that builds important social relationships at work, challenging jobs that develop employees and allow them to utilize their talents, and pride in their organization. Other answers to developing committed employees come from research on "healthy companies." The seven values found in such organizations are (1) commitment to self-knowledge and development (continuous learning), (2) firm belief in decency (fair treatment, equity), (3) respect for individual differences (celebration of diversity), (4) spirit of partnership (strong belief in community, shared effort, teamwork, widespread participation), (5) high priority for health and well-being, (6) appreciation for flexibility and resilience (change is managed well), and (7) a passion for products and process (concern for both what is produced and how that happens, balancing stakeholder interests—family support, community responsibility, and enviromnental protection).[9] Not all organizations believe in these dimensions or put them into practice, but they reflect the growing belief that the contribution of the workforce is the ultimate key to the success of any company and provides an idea of what many employees are coming to expect from their employer.

Another example of changing expectations concerns the way we do business and with whom we work. The ever-increasing demands for high performance, quality, customer service, and innovation have resulted in new organizational forms—from telecommuting to virtual global teams who have never met in person to organizational alliances between historically fierce competitors. The proliferation of small and midsize firms, spearheaded by pioneer-like entrepreneurs, has been responsible for impressive innovations as well as the absorption of many employees who were downsized from large firms.[10]

The nomadic nature and the changing complexion of the workforce will continue. The average high school or college graduate will hold 13 different jobs in their career, staying 3.5 years on each job.[11] By the year 2020, women will make up approximately half of the entire workforce. White non-Hispanics will account for 68 percent, Hispanics 14 percent, African Americans 11 percent, and Asians 6 percent. Due to their higher birth rates, Hispanics will overtake African Americans as the second largest ethnic group around 2006.[12]

Finally, the last example of shifting expectations relates to changing value trends.[13] In addition to differences in the values held by various generations, changing societal norms also affect our psychological contracts at work and home. For example, in the United States 60 percent of married couples have dual careers and only 28 percent of U.S. families consists of a working husband and a stay-at-home wife who cares for the children.[14] This departure from what used to be the norm forces us to rethink our expectations of what it means to be a good employee, spouse, and parent and to adapt our psychological contracts accordingly.

A MODEL FOR MANAGING PSYCHOLOGICAL CONTRACTS

Working with people from other cultures forces the realization that psychological contracts have a cultural flavor to them. The Japanese concept of lifetime employment is one of many examples of cultural differences. The European expectation that worker councils will participate in company decisions is another example. Yet another is the Latin American expectation that bosses will attend the family celebrations—baptisms, first communions, marriages, and funerals—of their employees. In multicultural settings it quickly becomes apparent that different cultures utilize different psychological contracts, and it is critical to understand these differences. However, given the changing expectations within our society and the varying expectations of different generations and groups in the workplace, we may do well to follow the cross-cultural model wherein one proceeds on the assumption that other people's expectations are not necessarily the same as our own. Therefore, in order to avoid misunderstandings and disillusionment, it is crucial to identify and share mutual expectations in an ongoing process.

Sherwood and Glidewell have developed a simple but powerful model, the pinch model, which describes the dynamic quality of psychological contracts and suggests ways of minimizing the potentially dysfunctional consequences of shifting expectations (Figure 1-1). It provides a framework for the continuous management of the psychological contract in the day-to-day work setting. The first stage of any relationship between two individuals and/or an individual and an organization is characterized by a *sharing of information and a negotiating of expectations*. Suppose that a manager interviewing job candidates informs them that they will be expected to attend frequent company social events after hours and on weekends. If this does not appear to be a reasonable expectation to some candidates, they will deselect themselves, the equivalent of a *planned termination* in the following model.

Assuming that both parties accept the other's expectations, they enter a stage of *role clarity* and *joint commitment*. In other words, both the new employees and the manager understand and accept the role the other party expects them to play and are motivated to meet those expectations. The employee and employer both expect to move into a period of *stability* and productivity, which allows them to focus their energies on work.

Even with the best intentions and full sharing of initial expectations, changes are likely to occur over time. One or both of the parties begin to feel a "pinch" as Sherwood and Glidewell call it. For example, an employee may have been more than willing to put in heavy overtime and cover weekend shifts when he or she was single and new in town. But a marriage involving certain expectations about the time a couple should spend together might change the employee's attitude toward demanding hours and the automatic assumption that this particular employee is available to work them. Sherwood and Glidewell suggest that a pinch like this can be used as an early warning sign to manage the psychological contract process before situations become disruptive. Discussing and renegotiating expectations at this point will lead to either a return to stability or, if the differences cannot be resolved, a planned departure. Employees sometimes respond to pinches by saying, "I don't have time to test this issue" or "If I raise this issue with my bosses, they'll think I'm just complaining so I'll ignore it." But pinches have a habit of growing into larger problems

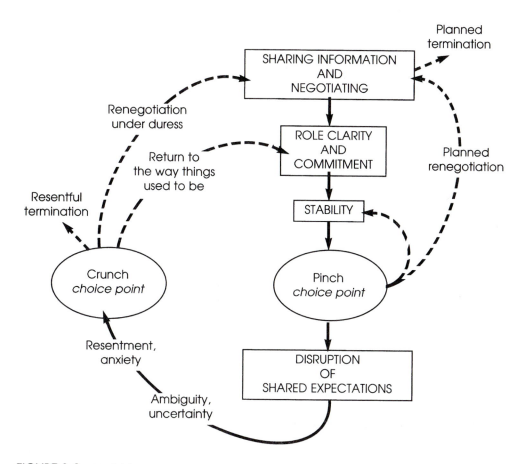

FIGURE 1-1   Model for Managing Psychological Contracts
Source: J. J. Sherwood and J. C. Glidewell, "Planned Renegotiation: A Norm Setting OD Intervention," *Contemporary Organization Development: Orientations and Interventions*, ed. W. W. Burke (Washington, DC: NTL Institute, 1972) 35–46.

if they are not handled in a planned manner rather than in the heat of emotion that accompanies the next stage, a *disruption of shared expectations*.

Since the "rules" that were accepted initially have been upset, one or both parties experience heightened *ambiguity and uncertainty*, which invariably result in *resentment and anxiety*. The situation may reach a crisis point, or *crunch*. People often refer to crunches as the straw that broke the camel's back (e.g., the boss who unfairly accuses a dedicated employee of not working hard because the boss is misinformed, or a job promotion that goes to another employee who is clearly less qualified). Crunches force people to choose among three alternative actions. A common outcome is an effort to *return to the way things used to be*. The parties apologize for the misunderstanding, smooth over the conflict, and attempt to renew their commitment to one another under the terms of the old contract. Another possibility is that the two parties *renegotiate under duress* by again sharing information and negotiating their expectations. The final possibility is that little or no discussion occurs and the result is some form of *resentful termination*. The termination may be either psychological ("I'll be darned if I'm going to do any more than I'm required to on this job" or "That's the last thing I ever do for that employee") or physical (absenteeism, tardiness, quitting, or firing).

In the classroom, the psychological contract is also very important. Generally only one of the parties makes their expectations explicit. Teachers begin a course by stating their requirements of students. Students are rarely asked to reciprocate, but woe to the teacher who fails to meet students' unstated expectations! The purpose of this unit is to introduce you to the concept of the psychological contract as it exists in the learning organization you are about to enter. In this way you will be able to move as quickly as possible to a period of stability and productivity (learning) and set in motion the processes of communication needed to deal with any subsequent pinches that may develop. We encourage participants to state their expectations in the following exercise because it is the first step in taking responsibility for one's own learning in this course.

PROCEDURE FOR GROUP MEETING: INSTRUCTOR/PARTICIPANT INTERVIEWS

The purpose of the exercise is to model how an explicit psychological contract can be set in the classroom. In the first phase, the instructor learns about the participants' expectations for the course by interviewing group representatives. In the second phase, group representatives interview the instructor to discover his or her expectations of students.

STEP 1. The total group should divide into small discussion groups, four or five people per group, and introduce themselves.

STEP 2. Each group should select a representative of the team who will be interviewed by the instructor.

STEP 3. Unless your instructor provides different questions, discuss the general question areas in the accompanying Instructor's Interview Guide. Your instructor will want to hear all the different views expressed in your discussion, so there is no need to come to a group consensus on each question.

STEP 4. All representatives must be able to accurately reflect their group members' views in response to the instructor's questions (you may want to jot these down on the guide that follows).
(Time allotted for steps 1–4: 20–30 minutes)

INSTRUCTOR'S INTERVIEW GUIDE

Few instructors ask group members to articulate their expectations for a class. During the ensuing interview, the instructor will try to gain an understanding of your views in the following general areas:

1. What are your goals for this course? To increase self-awareness? To learn theories? To fulfill a requirement? To get a grade? To apply learning in your job? Something else?

2. How can the instructor best help you achieve your goals? Lectures, examinations, seminar discussions (think back to excellent professors/courses you've experienced)?

3. What, if anything, have you heard about this textbook and/or this course from others?

4. What reservations, if any, do you have about this course?

5. What is the best thing that could happen in this course? What is the worst thing?

6. What are your resources for this course (prior work experience, courses in psychology, etc.)?

7. What norms of behavior or ground rules should we set to ensure that the course is success-ful (mutual respect, only one person talks at a time, punctuality, etc.)?

INSTRUCTOR'S INTERVIEW

STEP 5.   The representatives, one from each team, sit in the front of the room with the in-structor. The instructor will interview them (using the Instructor's Interview Guide) to understand their expectations for the course. The remainder of the class acts as ob-servers, paying particular attention to the instructor's questions and the areas that seem most salient.
(Time allotted for step 5: 20 minutes)

Participants' Interview of Instructor

STEP 6.   The class should form into the same small discussion groups as in step 1.

STEP 7.   Each group should select a member (other than the person it selected in step 2) as its team representative who will interview the instructor.

STEP 8.   Using the guide provided as a starting point (Participants' Interview Guide), groups should discuss any questions that they would like their representatives to pose to the instructor. Please feel free to ask questions that do not appear in this guide.

STEP 9.   Representatives should make certain that they understand the group's concerns so that they can accurately translate these concerns into questions to be posed to the instruc-tor (you may want to jot these down on the guide provided).
(Time allotted for steps 6–9: 10–20 minutes)

PARTICIPANTS' INTERVIEW GUIDE

You will have the opportunity to ask the instructor any questions you feel are relevant to effective learning during this course. (Note: It is important that you ask questions that are of real concern to you at this point. Only in this way can potentially important problems or conflicts be identified and managed.) You probably have many ideas of your own and the questions asked by the instructor during the first interview may suggest others to you. Be sure to ask specific questions.

Some areas you may want to discuss are the following:

1. The instructor's objectives for the course—what does he or she hope to accomplish?

2. The instructor's theory of learning (i.e., how do people learn?).

3. The instructor's opinion on the question of evaluation.

4. The instructor's expectations of you.

5. The instructor's role in the class.

6. Anything else you think is important.

Participants' Interview

STEP 10. Representatives interview the instructor to understand the instructor's expectations of them and the course. The remainder of the group acts as observers, paying particular attention to the following areas:

    a. In what ways do your (groups') expectations agree or disagree with the contributions the instructor feels he or she can make?

    b. In what ways do the instructor's expectations agree or disagree with the contributions you feel you can make?

    c. In looking back over your group discussions, how much diversity was there within the group concerning expectations?
(Time allotted for step 10: 20–30 minutes)

Comparison of Interviews and Identification of Potential Pinches

STEP 11. The total group should develop a list of (1) areas of difference that became apparent during the previous two interviews and (2) possible future conflicts—pinches—that will be important to watch for.
(Time allotted for step 11: 10 minutes)

    a. To the extent possible, differences that will influence the learning process should be discussed further, with an eye toward a mutually acceptable negotiated resolution.

    b. With respect to potential future pinches, the group should discuss its expectations concerning

        (1) Whose responsibility it will be or should be to raise a pinch if and when it develops.

        (2) The mechanisms to be used for raising pinches (e.g., written comments, informal discussions at the end of meetings).

STEP 12. Instructor and participants should discuss their feelings about beginning a course in this fashion and assess the value of this method.

    a. What differences do you see when you compare this method to the traditional way other courses begin?

    b. What is the impact of this exercise on you as a student?
(Time allotted for step 12: 10 minutes)

FOLLOW-UP

Although we do not often view the processes in the same terms, entering a classroom environment for the first time is very much like the first day on a new job. The typical orientation program in a company is usually very one-sided. Most company communication flows from the organization to the individual, "These are our policies, procedures, expectations."

One effect of this one-sided process is to cause new employees to feel that the organization is much more powerful than they are as individuals and may create a situation in which new employees, when asked their expectations, try to second-guess the company's expectations. Instead of trying to formulate and articulate their own expectations, the new employees (participants) often repeat what they *think* the organization (instructor) wants to hear. Another effect is the organization's tendency to oversocialize new members. This can result in a feeling of powerlessness and even greater passivity on the part of the employee.

Recall your last job interview. Remember how you tried to "look good" to the organization— to guess what it wanted. How much time did you spend telling the interviewer what your expectations were and asking what the organization could contribute to your needs? Probably very little and then very cautiously. Our studies on individuals' entries into organizations and our work with orientation and training programs have led to the conclusion that, upon entering an organization, nearly everyone experiences feelings of helplessness and dependency on the organization. From a functional point of view, this dependency seems necessary so that the organization can begin to socialize the incoming member to meet its norms and values, its way of doing things. Yet our observations have led us to conclude that most organizations overdo this—they tend to oversocialize their members. For example, placing too much emphasis on the organization's expectations of newcomers may result in conformity and passivity. In contrast, new members who are challenged by the tasks they face and are encouraged toward responsibility can move toward success and mastery.

The organization often reads passivity as a sign that new employees want and need more direction and control—they want to be told exactly what to do. This situation can create a feedback cycle (a vicious circle in this case) that, in the long run, operates to the detriment of both the individual and the organization. The organization needs people who are innovative, creative, and independent thinkers to survive and remain productive in a rapidly changing environment. Individual growth and satisfaction also demand these same kinds of behavior. Often, however, the new employee's first contact with the organization sets in motion a cycle that acts in direct opposition to these long-range goals and needs.

There is another way in which we can view the process of organizational socialization and the notion of the psychological contract. In approaching any new organization, an individual makes two classes of decisions: a decision to join and a decision to participate.[15] In some cases, such as being drafted into the military or taking required courses, individuals have no control over their own decision to join.

The process by which we join an organization has implications for the second class of decisions—the decision to participate. This particular decision refers to whether or not a person chooses to play an active role in the organization or is content with merely being physically present. At work, employees who have made a decision to participate are involved and working hard to contribute. Those who have decided not to participate are simply marking time, putting in their hours. In the classroom, those who choose to participate take an active role in the course and become involved in their own learning process. In contrast, those who decide not to participate either sit passively or don't attend and work just enough to get by and fulfill the organization's requirements for a grade. Their own expectations for learning, involvement, and stimulation go unsatisfied because they never made such expectations explicit when they joined.

Our purpose in encouraging students to participate in a joint expectation-setting exercise is to provide you with an opportunity to decide whether you want to join and participate in this course. Some educational systems and programs often unwittingly encourage passivity in students when learners are not expected to take responsibility for their own learning. They are much more accustomed to instructor's assuming full responsibility. Thus, when confronted with a genuine opportunity to participate in the learning process, they often became confused ("What kind of way is this to start a class?") or suspicious ("I wonder what the instructor is trying to do.").

When asked to articulate expectations, learners tend to be very vague and general, which is frustrating to everyone involved. Expectations are much more likely to be satisfied when a set of realistic, concrete goals can be developed. Instructors must realize that learners who are not used to controlling their own education will have to learn to accept that responsibility. The point is that *both* participants and instructor have a share of the responsibility for the learning process.

This point is an important one to reemphasize. Confusion sometimes, develops as a result of this initial contracting session, along the lines of: "Why all this talk about our expectations and stuff? You [the instructor] already have the course laid out, the syllabus typed, and the schedule planned!" As is true in any organization, the general thrust or goals are given. This is not a course in art or engineering. It is a course in organizational behavior, but there are many areas of flexibility: what *specific* goals you as a participating learner set within the general objectives, how you relate to peers and staff, who takes what responsibility for *how* goals are achieved. Differences might exist around these issues, and they need to be explored during the initial socialization process.

Clearly, within the context of a first class session of a few hours, all the possible conflicts that can arise will not be anticipated nor can all those identified be solved. More important than any concrete conclusions that may come out of this expectation-setting exercise is a series of norms for dealing with conflicts. As a result of this contract exploration process, the legitimacy of conflict or differences can be established, the right to question each other and particularly the instructor can be demonstrated, and a decision-making process of shared responsibility to resolve conflicts can be introduced.

The next two sections focus on what we mean by organizational behavior (OB) and the authors' objectives in designing this course.

CHARACTERISTICS OF ORGANIZATIONAL BEHAVIOR

One of the criticisms sometimes leveled at organizational behavior is that it is just "common sense." In fact, many common-sense truisms are actually paradoxical—for example, "Nothing ventured, nothing gained" as opposed to "Better safe than sorry" or "Two heads are better than one" versus "Too many cooks spoil the broth." The interesting question is, "If so much of organizational behavior is common sense, why is it not common practice?" Effective managers and organizations are more the exception than the norm. One of the aims of this course is to find answers to the question, "What does it take to get common sense into common practice?"

Organizational behavior is characterized by the following traits. It is a relatively young *multidisciplinary field* that pulls from the disciplines of psychology, sociology, anthropology, political science, and economics. It consists of three levels of analysis: *individual*, *group*, and *organizational*. One of the basic tenets of organizational behavior is that behavior is a function of the person and the environment, $B = f(P)(E)$.[16] For didactic purposes, the following equation is perhaps more helpful. Behavior is a function of the person (P), the group to which he or she belongs (G), and the organization (O) with its own unique culture, and the external environment (E), or $B = f(P)(G)(O)(E)$. *Environmental forces* have a major impact on behavior within organizations. The external changes (global economy, industrial and economic conditions, the labor market, and societal change) that affect our expectations and psychological contracts are examples of environmental impact.

Knowledge in the field is accumulated by using the *scientific method*, which means that theories and relationships are tested to see whether they can actually predict behavior. Much of the research looks at *performance* at all three levels of analysis. Researchers are constantly trying to determine what makes for success in organizations and what's the most effective way to do things. Therefore, organizational behavior is an *applied science*—its purpose is to develop knowledge that is useful to managers and employees. Because of the emphasis on performance and application, it comes as no surprise that OB is a *change-oriented discipline*. Strategies for improving performance or modifying behavior have always been important to the field, particularly the subfield of organizational development (OD).

Because of the variety and complexity of human behavior, there are few simple answers to questions about organizations. Organizational behavior scholars and consultants often respond to questions with "It depends," followed up by many questions about the particular situation and maybe even a request to observe what's going on. To managers looking for quick answers, such a response may seem evasive; however, the management literature abounds with examples of companies that made policy and management decisions based on a small fragment of the entire picture and lived to regret it. That's why this course is designed to broaden your appreciation of the complexity of organizational behavior.

COURSE OBJECTIVES

We hope that you will not only learn the basic organizational behavior theories and concepts, but that you will be able to use them to understand human behavior. As a result of the course, we'd like you to perceive organizations through new lenses that capture greater complexity. Organizations are like puzzles that need to be decoded.

We study organizational behavior because it helps us function more effectively in organizations. Regardless of our position in the hierarchy, it helps us understand what is occurring around us. It also teaches us the necessary skills to be an effective employee, team member, or manager. Many people reach a plateau in their careers because they have risen as far as their technical skills allow. Good "people skills" are usually a prerequisite for higher management jobs. As one professor stated in an attempt to sell his OB course to students, "The difference between understanding organizational behavior and not understanding it is the difference between a six-figure and a five-figure salary." We can't promise you a six-figure salary if you master everything in this course. But, if you do your part, you should finish the course with a greater understanding about who you are, more people and group skills, and a new way of looking at organizations.

LEARNING POINTS

1. The psychological contract is an individual's beliefs, shaped by the organization, regarding the terms and conditions of a reciprocal exchange agreement between individuals and their organization.

2. Psychological contracts are important because they are the link between individuals and the organization. If the contract is violated, disillusionment can affect employee satisfaction, productivity, commitment, and their desire to continue with the company.

3. The phenomenon of the self-fulfilling prophecy occurs when people perform in accordance with a rater's expectations of them. Managers with high expectations of employees are more likely to have their expectations met.

4. External influences, such as adapting to a global economy, economic and employment conditions, demographics, and societal change, affect workplace expectations and psychological contracts.

5. The diverse nature of the U.S. workforce will increase according to predictions for the year 2020. Women will make up 50 percent of the workforce. White non-Hispanics will constitute 68 percent, Hispanics, 14 percent, African Americans, 11 percent, and Asians, 6 percent.

6. The pinch model is a way to avoid major disruptions by heeding early warning signs that expectations about the psychological contract have changed and need to be reconsidered.

7. In approaching any new organization, an individual makes two classes of decisions: a decision to join and a decision to participate.

8. Organizational behavior has the following characteristics:
   a. Multidisciplinary nature
   b. Three levels of analysis: individual, group, organizational
   c. Acknowledgment of environmental forces
   d. Grounded in the scientific method
   e. Performance orientation
   f. Applied orientation
   g. Change orientation

FOR MANAGERS

- Provide realistic job previews during the hiring process so that new employees have accurate expectations. Don't oversell the job or your organization just to reel in new hires who will later become disillusioned and perhaps leave when they discover the truth.

- Set aside time to discuss and establish explicit expectations early on and then continue to do so on a frequent basis with new hires.

- Check to ensure that you and your employees perceive and interpret expectations in the same way. This is especially important when cultural differences exist. Unless there is a shared perception of obligations, an employee might believe there has been a contract violation simply because he or she perceives the contract in a unique manner.

- Provide clear and immediate feedback to employees who are not meeting the expectations set for them.

- Earn your employees' trust; employees react less strongly to violated contracts if they trust their employer and have good relationships with their work group.

- Pay special attention to expectations during a change process. Explain why the psychological contract has to change and acknowledge that it has been violated.[17]

- Be sensitive to the values and expectations of different generations in the workplace. Help these groups understand one another to prevent generational clashes.

- Remember that psychological contracts are very likely to change over time; therefore, make opportunities to check whether the contract is still viable and renegotiate if necessary. Managers or leaders who take the initiative to do this checking are greatly appreciated because it is sometimes difficult for subordinates to bring pinches to their boss's attention.

- Pinches are easier to handle than full-blown breakdowns in expectations.
- Sample questions for checking out expectations are:
  - What do you like/dislike about your job (or this relationship)?
  - Why do you continue with it?
  - Is there one thing that, if it were changed, would make you quit your job?
  - What are your expectations of me?
  - Do you think I am meeting them?
  - Is there any way I can help you do your job better?
  - What kind of supervision do you like best, or (for employers) what type of supervision do you prefer to use with employees?
  - Does the organization or do I hinder you in completing your work?
  - Is there anything you would like to see changed?
- Some people use the following matrix to judge whether mutual expectations are fairly balanced and reasonable. The contributions that individuals or organizations give should be balanced, more or less, by what they get. This matrix can be a good basis for discussion, but bear in mind that good human relationships are not based on a tit-for-tat mentality but on a flexible give-and-take approach.

	Expect to Get	Expect to Contribute
Individual (You)		
Organization or Group		

PERSONAL APPLICATION ASSIGNMENT

The following assignment is modeled after Kolb's adult learning cycle, which appears in Chapter 3. Please respond to the questions and submit them at next week's class. Each section of the assignment is worth 4 points that will be assigned according to the criteria that follow.[18]

The topic of this assignment is to think back on a significant incident when you experienced a pinch in a psychological contract. Pick an experience about which you are motivated to learn more; that is, there is something about it that you do not totally understand, that intrigues you, that makes you realize you lack certain skills, that is problematical or very significant for you. It could have taken place at school, in a work relationship or a social one (with a club or group), or within a personal relationship.

A. *Concrete Experience*

    1. *Objectively* describe the experience (who, what, when, where, how). (2 points)

    2. *Subjectively* describe your feelings, perceptions, and thoughts that occurred during (not after) the experience. What did others seem to be feeling? (2 points)

B. *Reflective Observation*

    1. Looking back at the experience, what were the perspectives of the key actors (including you)? (2 points)

    2. Why did the people involved (including you) behave as they did? (2 points)

C. *Abstract Conceptualization*

    1. Relate concepts or theories from the assigned readings or the lecture to the experience. Explain thoroughly how they apply to your experience. Please apply at least two concepts or theories and cite them correctly. (4 points)

D. *Active Experimentation*
1. What did you learn about psychological contracts from this experience? (1 point)
2. What did you learn about yourself? (1 point)
3. What action steps will you take to be more effective in the future? (2 points)

E. *Integration, Synthesis, and Writing*
1. Did you integrate and synthesize the four sections? (1 point)
2. Was the personal application assignment well written and easy to understand? (1 point)
3. Was it free of spelling and grammar errors? (2 points)

ENDNOTES

[1] D. M. Rousseau, *Psychological Contract in Organizations: Understanding Written and Unwritten Agreements* (Newbury Park, CA: Sage, 1995).

[2] S. L. Robinson, and D. M. Rousseau, "Violating the Psychological Contract: Not the Exception but the Norm," *Journal of Organizational Behavior 15* (1994): 245–59.

[3] R. A. Guzzo, K. A. Noonan, and E. Elron, "Expatriate Managers and the Psychological Contract," *Journal of Applied Psychology 79*, no. 4 (1994): 617–26; and R. Schalk, C. Freese, and J. Van den Bosch, "Het Psychologisch Contract Van Part-Timers en Full-Timers," *Gedrag en Organisatie 8*, (1995): 307–17.

[4] Robinson and Rousseau, "Violating the Psychological Contract: Not the Exception but the Norm."

[5] R. Rosenthal and K. L. Fode, "The Effect of Experimenter Bias on the Performance of the Albino Rat," *Behavioral Science 8* (1968): 183–89.

[6] R. Rosenthal and L. F. Jacobson, "Teacher Expectations for the Disadvantaged," *Scientific American 218* (1968): 19–23.

[7] D. W. Bray, R. J. Campbell, and D. L. Grant, *Formative Years in Business: A Long-Term AT&T Study of Managerial Lives* (New York: John Wiley, 1974) and D. E. Berlew and D. T. Hall, "The Socialization of Managers: The Effects of Expectations on Performance," *Administrative Science Quarterly 11*, no. 2 (September 1966): 207–33.

[8] J. T. Bond, E. Galinsky, and J. E. Swanberg, *1997 National Study of the Changing Workforce.* (Denver, CO: Families and Work Institute, 1998).

[9] R. H. Rosen with L. Berger, *The Healthy Company: Eight Strategies to Develop People, Productivity, and Profits* (New York: Tarcher/Perigee, 1992).

[10] T. Petzinger, Jr., *The New Pioneers: The Men and Women Who Are Transforming the Workplace and Marketplace* (New York: Simon & Schuster, 1999).

[11] D. L. Birch, "Thinking About Tomorrow," *Wall Street Journal,* May 24, 1999, R-30.

[12] C. D'Amico, "Back to the Future: A Current View of Workforce 2000 and Projections for 2020," *Employment Relations Today* (Autumn 1997): 1–11.

[13] J. Conger, "How 'Genx' Managers Manage," *Strategy & Business 10* (First Quarter, 1998): 21–31.

[14] U.S. Bureau of Labor Statistics, *Monthly Labor Review,* November 1997.

[15] See J. G. March and H. A. Simon, *Organization* (New York: John Wiley, 1963), especially Chapter 4, for a fuller discussion of this conceptual scheme.

[16] K. Lewin, *A Dynamic Theory of Personality* (New York: McGraw-Hill, 1935).

[17] These suggestions are based on the research implications of E. M. Morrison and S. L. Robinson, "When Employees Feel Betrayed: A Model of How Psychological Contract Violation Develops," *The Academy of Management Review 22*, no. 1 (1997): 226–56. This article contains a more complex, comprehensive descendant of the pinch model.

[18] This guideline was originally developed by Don McCormick, Antioch University, Los Angeles.

Chapter 2

▲▲▲

THEORIES OF MANAGING PEOPLE

OBJECTIVES By the end of this chapter, you should be able to:

A. Describe six theories of management and their "ideal" manager.

B. Explain the competing values framework and what constitutes a master manager.

C. Explain why it's important to identify your personal theories about management and organizational behavior.

D. Describe your personal theory of management.

E. Identify the managerial skills you need in today's environment.

F. Distinguish between Theory X and Theory Y managers.

THE JACK AND HERB SHOW

For a nationwide satellite broadcast, GE CEO Jack Welch and Southwest Airlines CEO Herb Kelleher recently met with Fortune editors John Huey and Geoffrey Colvin. The subject: how to create great companies and keep them that way.

Jack, let's start with a basic question. You've been in this job 17 years, and yet you're still bursting with energy. How come? What makes you so energized?

Jack Welch: There are a thousand things, I think. I have the greatest job in the world. We go from broadcasting, engines, plastics, the power system—anything you want, we've got a game going. So from an intellectual standpoint, you're learning every day.

We get a great kick out of the fact that we have made this company think outside itself. We want people who get up every morning with a passion about finding a better way: finding from their associate in the office, finding from another company. We're constantly on the search. We brag about learning from Motorola, HP, Allied. Wal-Mart—we learned quick market intelligence from them. Toyota—asset management.

So we've designed a culture that gets people to look outside the company, and we've designed a reward system that's aligned with that. As Herb has said, the rewards of these jobs have to be in the soul and in the wallet.

I get a sheet every week of stock optionees who've cashed options. This year we will see $1.6 billion in employee gains in stock options; $1.2 billion of that will be below any senior-management level. Some 40 percent of our optionees make $70,000 or less. If they got a thousand shares each of the past five years, they would today have a gain of $800,000. In five years they've gotten about 12 times their annual salary. That's a kick.

Sam Walton used to say that it takes a week to two weeks for employees to start treating customers the same way the employer is treating the employee. Everybody who's ever flown Southwest Airlines notices a big difference in the way you get treated at Southwest. What are you doing to these people to make them treat us so well?

Herb Kelleher: It's clearly the charisma of the chief executive officer.

But, seriously, your employees act as if they're empowered to make decisions and break rules. How do you encourage fun in a business where you've got people's lives in your hands every day?

Kelleher: There's something we call professional terminalism. People who emphasize too strongly the fact that they're professionals usually are not very good at what they do. What really adds up to professionalism is being very good at what you do in a very modest way. That's the way our people are: They're results oriented. Whether it's the best safety record in the world, the best customer service record in the world, the youngest jet fleet, or lower fares, our people are really focused.

GE also has an informality, which belies the image that most people would have of a huge, massive, financially driven global company. How does that work?

Welch: Informality gives you speed. It takes the crap out of the business equation, the pontificating. I can remember 20 years ago in this company when you went to a meeting, the lights went down, you read a script, you gave your pitch, and you got the hell out of the room. That was the game. Today you're in there having an open dialogue with self-confident people, real exchanges about real things.

Giving people self-confidence is by far the most important thing that I can do. Because then they will act. I tell people, if this place is stifling you, shake it, shake it, break it. Check the system, because it wants to be a bureaucracy. And if it doesn't work, get the hell out. If GE can't give you what you want, go get it somewhere else.

Jack, there's a story that at some point you quit, saying the GE bureaucracy had broken your spirit and you were leaving.

Welch: Right. It was after one year. But my boss's boss came up the night before the going-away party and convinced me that things would change. So I stayed.

It was really about the absolute roteness of it all. I was in a group of seven in development engineering, and we all got our raise the same day, and we all got the same amount of money. And I thought I was a hell of a lot better than the other six. I didn't think it was a good deal.

Did your boss's boss make good?

Welch: Yes. He gave me a project where I was the only employee. I was able to call myself king, emperor, any title you wanted. And I hired one technician. And from that, we built a plastics business.

Well, that's self-confidence. You looked around, you decided you're worth more than everybody else, and quit.

Let's turn to another subject. Herb, the figures I have are that 100,000 people applied for a job last year, and you hired 3,000. What's your advice to someone who wants a job at Southwest?

Kelleher: My first advice would be not to go for my job. Beyond that, I would say that if you're an altruistic, outgoing person who likes to serve others and enjoys working with a team, we want you. If you're the kind of person who enjoys a more secure, more regimented, more inflexible, more rule-governed type of environment, that doesn't mean that you're a bad person, but we're probably incompatible. We shouldn't even get engaged, much less get married.

Is it true that you should be prepared to tell a joke in the job interview?

Kelleher: No, that's not true. But it is true that we will say to someone, tell us how humor helped you get around one of the more difficult situations in your life.

People think it's kind of crazy, Jack, but we had a pilot-applicant class one day and we said, we don't interview you in suits; put on some Southwest Airlines shorts. Now, you may think that that seems kind of quirky and aberrational—irrational, even. But the ones who were delighted to do it because they thought it was a lark—those were the ones we hired.

You both run huge companies. How do you renew a big organization, renew your own spirit, and, most important, renew the sense of purpose of your employees?

Kelleher: The way that we accomplish that is that we constantly tell our employees—and Jack and I were discussing this earlier—think small and act small, and we'll get bigger. Think big, be complacent, be cocky, and we'll get smaller.

One way we avoid complacency—and this may just be because I don't have a long attention span—is that we reject the idea of long-range planning. We say, do strategic planning, define what you are, and then get back together soon to define whether you need to change that. And have the alacrity of a puma. Because this plan about what we're going to do 10 years from now will almost certainly be invalidated in the next six months.

Welch: You need to believe that you are a learning institution and to constantly challenge everything you have. I was at Crotonville [the Connecticut site of GE's Leadership Development Center] on Monday night. I said, how many people can raise their hand and say they predicted the Asian crisis? Not one hand went up, including mine. I said, what does that tell you? All of this crap you planned for is meaningless, basically. What's important is that you're agile, in your thinking and in your action.

We were getting steel casings for turbines in Mexico, which was making them for 40 percent less than they make them for here. Within 45 days our team had moved those casings out of Mexico to Korea, which was 40 percent below Mexico. That took just 45 days.

You've also got to use the strength of a big company, and reduce its weaknesses. For example, a big company doesn't communicate as well as a small company. There's no chance. A big company moves more slowly. We think we're the fastest elephant at the dance, but we are an elephant.

So what does the big company do well? It can go to bat more often. I've made more mistakes in the 18 years I've been doing this job than probably any human being in America has made. Most of them, *Fortune* doesn't find out about, the *Wall Street Journal* doesn't find out about. (Of course. when I screw up Kidder Peabody, I get on the front page of everything.)

But if I make small mistakes, no one sees them. We've made $10 billion to $15 billion of acquisitions every year for the past five years. Most don't even make the papers. A billion here, a billion there, two billion here. That's what a big company's balance sheet allows it to do: keep playing.

Jack, you're doing a total-quality thing 10 or 15 years after the rest of corporate America did it. Why are you doing it, and why now?

Welch: There was only one guy in the whole country who hated quality more than me. I always believed quality would come from just operating well and fast, and all these slogans were nonsense.

The guy who hated quality more was Larry Bossidy. He hated quality totally. Then he left GE and went to AlliedSignal. In order to resurrect AlliedSignal, Larry went out, saw Motorola, and did some stuff on Six Sigma. And he called me one day and he said, "Jack, this ain't b.s.—this is real stuff, this is really great stuff."

We poll 10,000 employees every year. In 1995 they came back and said, we desperately need a quality issue. So Six Sigma was something we adopted then. The results are fantastic. We're going to get $1.2 billion of gain this year. For years our operating margin was never over 10. It's been improving, and it's going to be 16.7 this year. Our working-capital turns were four for 35 years. It will be nine this year.

Herb, you're a company founder. Many people think there can't be a Southwest without Herb Kelleher. How do you follow your act?

Kelleher: The way I look at it is the United States was strong enough to live through Millard Fillmore and Warren G. Harding. And if we should make a mistake and get a successor who didn't subscribe to Southwest's value system, there will probably be an insurrection. So I think the culture is stronger than any individual who might try to fly in the face of it or defy it.

Finally, what keeps you guys awake at night?

Kelleher: What keeps me awake are the intangibles. It's the intangibles that are the hardest thing for a competitor to imitate. You can get airplanes, you can get ticket counter space, you can get tugs, you can get baggage conveyors. But the spirit of Southwest is the most difficult thing to emulate.

So my biggest concern is that somehow. through maladroitness, through inattention, through misunderstanding, we lose the esprit de corps, the culture, the spirit. If we ever do lose that, we will have lost our most valuable competitive asset.

Welch: What do I worry about? I was in Hong Kong about a month ago when our stock crashed through 70 to 69 from a high of 96 [the stock is now at 88]. People don't realize that 10 percent of our company is owned by our employees, including production workers, who own $2 billion worth. It is an incredible feeling of responsibility to take their savings and their life and have something go wrong with it.

Source: "The Jack and Herb Show," *Fortune,* January 11, 1999, 163–66.

PREMEETING PREPARATION

A. Read "The Jack and Herb Show."

B. Fill out and score the questionnaire on the following page.

C. Answer the following questions.

    1. How would you describe the ideal manager?

    2. How did you arrive at this ideal—previous experiences, values, role models, education, training, reading, and so on?

    3. What values underlie your picture of the ideal manager?

4. What were the significant learning points from the reading?

D. Read the Topic Introduction that follows.

E. If your instructor has assigned the Robbins Self-Assessment Library, use "What's My View on the Nature of People?"

Leadership Styles Questionnaire

This instrument is designed to help you better understand the assumptions you make about people and human nature. There are 10 pairs of statements. Assign a weight from 0 to 10 to each statement to show the relative strength of your belief in the statements in each pair. The points assigned for each pair must total 10 in each case. Be as honest with yourself as you can and resist the natural tendency to respond as you would "like to think things are." This instrument is not a test. There are no right or wrong answers. It is designed to be a stimulus for personal reflection and discussion.

1. It's only human nature for people to do as little work as they can get away with.   _____ (A)

   When people avoid work, it's usually because their work has been deprived of its meaning.   _____ (B)
   10

2. If employees have access to any information they want, they tend to have better attitudes and behave more responsibly.   _____ (C)

   If employees have access to more information than they need to do their immediate tasks, they will usually misuse it.   _____ (D)
   10

3. One problem in asking for the ideas of employees is that their perspective is too limited for their suggestions to be of much practical value.   _____ (E)

   Asking employees for their ideas broadens their perspective and results in the development of useful suggestions.   _____ (F)
   10

4. If people don't use much imagination and ingenuity on the job, it's probably because relatively few people have much of either.   _____ (G)

   Most people are imaginative and creative but may not show it because of limitations imposed by supervision and the job.   _____ (H)
   10

5. People tend to raise their standards if they are accountable for their own behavior and for correcting their own mistakes.   _____ (I)

   People tend to lower their standards if they are not punished for their misbehavior and mistakes.   _____ (J)
   10

6. It's better to give people both good and bad news because most employees want the whole story, no matter how painful.   _____ (K)

   It's better to withhold unfavorable news about business because most employees really want to hear only the good news.   _____ (L)
   10

7. Because a supervisor is entitled to more respect than those below him or her in the organization, it weakens the supervisor's prestige to admit that a subordinate was right and he or she was wrong.   _____ (M)

   Because people at all levels are entitled to equal respect, a supervisor's prestige is increased when he or she supports this principle by admitting that a subordinate was right and he or she was wrong.   _____ (N)
   10

(continued)

8. If you give people enough money, they are less likely to be concerned with
   such intangibles as responsibility and recognition.   _____(O)

   If you give people interesting and challenging work, they are less likely to
   complain about such things as pay and supplemental benefits.   _____(P)
                                                                                          10

9. If people are allowed to set their own goals and standards of performance, they
   tend to set them higher than the boss would.   _____(Q)

   If people are allowed to set their own goals and standards of performance, they
   tend to set them lower than the boss would.   _____(R)
                                                                                          10

10. The more knowledge and freedom people have regarding their jobs, the more
    controls are needed to keep them in line.   _____(S)

    The more knowledge and freedom people have regarding their jobs, the fewer
    controls are needed to ensure satisfactory job performance.   _____(T)
                                                                                          10

Source: Adapted from M. Scott Myers, *Every Employee a Manager* (New York: McGraw-Hill Book Company, 1970).

Scoring Instructions

Record the number you assign to each of the following letters in the space provided and then total each column.

Theory X	Theory Y
A _____	B _____
D _____	C _____
E _____	F _____
G _____	H _____
J _____	I _____
L _____	K _____
M _____	N _____
O _____	P _____
R _____	Q _____
S _____	T _____
_____ (Total) Theory X Score	_____ (Total) Theory Y Score

Theory X Assumptions (Traditional)	Theory Y Assumptions (Emerging)
1. People are naturally lazy; they prefer to do nothing.	1. People are naturally active; they set goals and enjoy striving.
2. People work mostly for money and status rewards.	2. People seek many satisfactions in work: pride in achievement, enjoyment of process, sense of contribution, pleasure in association, stimulation of new challenges, etc.
3. The main force keeping people productive in their work is fear of being demoted or fired.	3. The main force keeping people productive in their work is desire to achieve their personal and social goals.
4. People remain children grown larger; they are naturally dependent on leaders.	4. People normally mature beyond childhood; they aspire to independence, self-fulfillment, and responsibility.
5. People expect and depend on direction from above; they do not want to think for themselves.	5. People close to the situation see and feel what is needed and are capable of self-direction.
6. People need to be told, shown, and trained in proper methods of work.	6. People who understand and care about what they are doing can devise and improve their own methods of doing work.
7. People need supervisors who will watch them closely enough to be able to praise good work and reprimand errors.	7. People need a sense that they are respected as capable of assuming responsibility and self-correction.
8. People have little concern beyond their immediate, material interests.	8. People seek to give meaning to their lives by identifying with nations, communities, churches, unions, companies, and causes.
9. People need specific instruction on what to do and how to do it; larger policy issues are none of their business.	9. People need ever-increasing understanding; they need to grasp the meaning of the activities in which they are engaged; they have cognitive hunger as extensive as the universe.
10. People appreciate being treated with courtesy.	10. People crave genuine respect from their fellow human beings.
11. People are naturally compartmentalized; work demands are entirely different from leisure activities.	11. People are naturally integrated; when work and play are too sharply separated both deteriorate.
12. People naturally resist change; they prefer to stay in the old ruts.	12. People naturally tire of monotonous routine and enjoy new experiences; in some degree everyone is creative.
13. Jobs are primary and must be done; people are selected, trained, and fitted to predefined jobs.	13. People are primary and seek self-realization; jobs must be designed, modified, and fitted to people.
14. People are formed by heredity, childhood and youth; as adults they remain static; old dogs don't learn new tricks.	14. People constantly grow; it is never too late to learn; they enjoy learning and increasing their understanding and capability.
15. People need to be "inspired" (pep talk) or pushed or driven.	15. People need to be released and encouraged and assisted.

Source: Douglas McGregor, *The Human Side of Enterprise* (New York: McGraw-Hill Book Company, 1960).

TOPIC INTRODUCTION

Just like Jack Welch and Herb Kelleher, two of today's most respected CEOs, we all have our theories about what makes successful managers and organizations. Over the years, there have been numerous and varied contributions to our knowledge about organizations. Each reflected the theorist's model of what made excellent organizations and managers within their sociohistorical context. Some of the major theories or schools of thought will be touched upon in the following paragraphs to set the stage for the study of organizational behavior.

Scientific Management   Frederick Taylor's *scientific management*,[1] the "one best way" of doing a job, which emerged in the late 1800s, emphasized the efficient division of labor into small, specialized, standardized jobs that were carefully matched with the capacities of workers. For the first time, Taylorism made it possible for engineers to research the most efficient way to do jobs. Taylor's goal was to develop workers to the best of their abilities and to convey the message that it was *cooperation* between capital and labor that resulted in success. By increasing profits, rather than arguing over their distribution, both labor and owners would prosper.

Taylor's name is often mistakenly associated with time-and-motion studies run amok and an inhumane emphasis on output. In fact, Taylor was concerned about both the proper design of the job *and* the worker. In Taylor's eyes, the ideal manager (perhaps with the aid of an engineer) scientifically determined the goals that needed to be accomplished, divided the work up in the most efficient way, trained workers to do the job, and rewarded them by wage incentives such as piecework. However, since foremen were cast as the "brains" who did planning rather than actual operations, workers came to be seen as little more than "a pair of hands." While that sounds pejorative, it was a perspective more easily understood when placed within the context of a country just beginning to industrialize. The labor force quite naturally consisted primarily of people from rural areas without prior factory experience. In that era, workers were viewed as one more resource, much like machines.

Administrative Theory   The next phase in management history was termed *administrative theory*. At that time, beginning about the late 1920s, managers were grappling with the problems of organizing larger and larger organizations and defining the emerging role of the professional manager. Administrative theory came up with answers to both issues. Fayol defined the functions of a manager as planning, controlling, organizing, and commanding and advocated the study of management as a discipline.[2] Weber contributed greatly to our understanding of the "ideal" bureaucracy and the different types of authority that were appropriate for it.[3] In those days, bureaucracy did not have the negative connotations it does today. Indeed, bureaucracy was then viewed as a solution to the nepotism, favoritism, and unprofessional behavior found in organizations of the day. During this era, people believed that if managers designed the organization correctly and followed the proven principles of management (e.g., having a limited number of people report to each supervisor, having only one boss for each worker, and engaging in merit-based selection of employees), the organization would succeed.

Human Relations School   The formula for organizational success was expanded by the famous Hawthorne studies[4] that took place in the late 1920s and 1930s. It was a time when the credibility of businesspeople was low due to the stock market crash, and feelings of exploitation fueled the union movement. Decreased immigration had made labor scarce, and, as a result, the needs of workers began to receive attention. The Hawthorne studies contributed the idea that worker output was affected by numerous, heretofore ignored, variables: how workers were treated; how they felt about their work, coworkers, and boss; and what happened to them outside of work.

The attention the workers received in the experiment, rather than the varied work conditions, caused them to work harder. This phenomenon has come to be known as the Hawthorne effect. The *human relations school* grew out of this research and acknowledged that workers had to be considered as more than "hands"; workers also had "hearts" (i.e., feelings and attitudes that affected productivity). And the norms or implicit rules of the work groups to which they belonged also affected productivity. Therefore, the effective manager was expected to pay attention to people's social needs and elicit their ideas about work issues.

Decision-Making School   March and Simon,[5] writing in the late 1950s, were proponents of the *decision-making school*. They added yet another layer of complexity to our understanding of organizations with their description of organizations as social systems in which individual decisions are the basis of human behavior. As mentioned in the previous chapter, employees make the decision to join an organization, but once hired, they also have another decision to make—whether or not to participate and work as hard as they can. The outcome of this decision depends on the employee's rational analysis of the situation and the rewards involved. Now managers also had to take into account workers' "minds." The effective manager set the premises for employee decisions and relied on their rationality to make choices that would be best for both themselves and the organization. For example, if a CEO of a company in which marketing was seen as the springboard into top management decided that more emphasis needed to be placed on operations, he or she would promote more rapidly from operations positions. Employees would then realize that operations was the area receiving top-level attention and ambitious workers would elect to work in that area. Manipulating the decision premises is an unobtrusive form of controlling the organization.

However, March and Simon also made the sobering observation that our decisions are limited by the number of variables our brains can handle, the time available, our reasoning powers, and so on; they called this bounded rationality. It means that we often "satisfice" (choose a solution that is merely good enough) rather than maximize or optimize (search and consider all the available information) when we make decisions. Routine work drives out nonroutine work, which explains why it seems so much harder to launch important new projects than it is to maintain routine tasks. For theorists of this school, managerial effectiveness consisted of a thorough understanding of decision making.

Contingency Approach   By the middle of the century, managers and scholars had identified many variables that were thought to be related to success such as job specialization, managerial principles, worker attitudes and human relations, and rational decisions made by workers. In the 1960s, many scholars converged on the idea that there was no "one best way" to manage. Instead, they tried to identify which variables would be successful for particular situations.

This is still one of the dominant perspectives in the field of organizational behavior and is referred to as the *contingency approach*.[6] The gist of this approach is that effectiveness varies according to the particular situation. We know now that individuals, groups, cultural groups, occupational subgroups, industries, types of technology, managerial styles, organizations, and external environments can all vary enormously. There are many examples of successful organizations that do things quite differently. For instance, ITT under Harold Geneen and Matsushita under Konosuke Matsushita are examples of extremely well-managed, but exceedingly diverse, companies.[7] As long as organizations fit their environment and their various building blocks—their strategy, structure, systems, staff, style, skills, and superordinate goals—*fit* together in a complementary fashion, very different types of organizations will still be effective. The particular building blocks in the previous sentence are known as the 7S model.[8]

Procter & Gamble[9] is an example of a company that has good "fit." Its management values about staffing are to (1) hire good people of high character, (2) treat them as individuals and develop their individual talents, and (3) provide a work environment that rewards individual achievement. The company is well known for its training programs and promotion from within. General managers are evaluated and rewarded for their success in terms of volume, profit, and people. P&G has developed systems (sometimes cumbersome) and skills (marketing, marketing research, and R&D) that reinforce its strategic goals. It has been very responsive to changing market conditions and demographics. Marketing strategies are customized for different ethnic groups, and it has made a major effort to integrate employees from diverse ethnic and cultural backgrounds. P&G has also experimented with various structures to help it compete more effectively both domestically and globally. Its success is due, in large part, to its ability to keep the 7S's in alignment and maintain the fit with its environment.

Open Systems Theory   According to open systems theory, which became popular due to the rapidly changing environment of the mid-1960s, an effective manager understood the interdependence among different parts of systems and recognized that organizations are embedded within the larger environment. Open systems theory maintains that organizations and all the subdivisions within them take in resources and transform them into a service or product that is purchased or utilized by a larger system. Dealing with external entities is a crucial role for many managers. In this view, organizational effectiveness is governed by three major factors: the individuals who make up the organization, the organization itself, and the environment in which the organization exists. Effective management of the interfaces between these factors—between the individual and the organization and between the organization and its environment—is central to organizational success. The relationship between the individual and the organization is often mediated or linked by a work group.

Looking back on these theories of organization, one is reminded of the parable of the blind men who each touched a different part of the elephant and assumed that they understood the entire animal. How is it that previous theorists only touched on one part of organizing? One answer lies in the bounded rationality of their social context; most popular theories reflect ideas whose time has come, along with the personal predispositions and biases of the theorists themselves. Another answer is the increasing popularity of the concept of "paradox" regarding the process of organizing. Previous theories emphasized only one side of the equation (change versus stability, production versus social needs, Theory X versus Theory Y, etc.) rather than the balancing act that managers actually perform between them.

Competing Values Framework   According to Robert Quinn,[10] four of the previously explained theories help us understand the paradoxical nature of management. "Master managers" know how to balance the competing values of the rational goal model (similar to Taylor's scientific management with extra emphasis on profit) with those of the human relations model, and the competing values of the internal process model (comparable to administrative theory) with the open systems model. Figure 2-1 summarizes the differences among these models. Both organizational success and managerial effectiveness are linked to the ability to balance[11] what at first blush appear to be the competing values of models that face one another diagonally in Figure 2-2, the rational goal model with the human relations model and the internal process model with the open systems model. Many of us (including theorists) have mental maps that cause us to see these models as mutually exclusive. Yet productivity and profit cannot be achieved without attention to the human resources responsible for productivity, and growth cannot be sustained if it is not also tempered by a certain degree of stability.

According to Quinn, none of these models is the one best way to organize or manage; in fact too much emphasis on any one model will lead to failure. Too much of a good thing pushes the organization from what he calls the positive zone into the negative zone as shown in Figure 2-2. Overemphasis on productivity and lack of attention and sensitivity to human resources result in

	Rational Goal	Internal Process	Human Relations	Open Systems
Criteria of effectiveness	Productivity, profit	Stability, continuity	Commitment, cohesion, morale	Adaptability, external support
Means-ends theory	Clear direction leads to productive outcomes	Routinization leads to stability	Involvement results in commitment	Continual adaptation and innovation lead to acquiring and maintaining external resources
Emphasis	Goal clarification, rational analysis, and action taking	Defining responsibility, measurement, documentation	Participation, conflict resolution, and consensus building	Political adaptation, creative problem solving, innovation, change management
Climate	Rational economic: "the bottom line"	Hierarchical	Team oriented	Innovative, flexible
Role of manager	Director and producer	Monitor and coordinator	Mentor and facilitator	Innovator and broker

FIGURE 2-1   **Characteristics of the Four Management Models in the Competing Values Framework**
Adapted from R. E. Quinn, S. R. Faerman, M. P. Thompson, and M. R. McGrath *Becoming a Master Manager: A Competency Framework* (New York: John Wiley & Sons, 1996), 10–11. Reprinted with permission of the publisher.

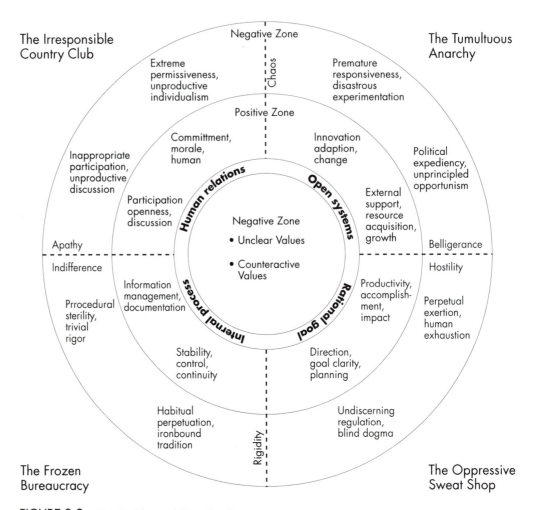

FIGURE 2-2   **The Positive and Negative Zones**
Adapted from Robert E. Quinn, *Beyond Rational Management* (San Francisco: Jossey-Bass, 1988), p. 7.

employee burnout and blind dogma—the oppressive sweatshop. In contrast, overemphasis on human resources and lack of attention to productivity result in extreme permissiveness, irrelevance, and inappropriate participation—the irresponsible country club. The other two poles are overemphasis on the external environment and change—the tumultuous anarchy—and excessive control and stability, which result in the frozen bureaucracy.[12]

IBM is an example of a company that found itself in the negative zone and later regained its balance. When Louis Gerstner took over as chairman in 1993, he identified IBM's strengths as world-class technology, extraordinary people, and loyal customers. He identified IBM's weaknesses as excessive costs, a preoccupation with internal processes, and slowness;[13] the company had losses of $18 billion in the previous three years. Most critics agree that IBM banked too heavily and too long on its mainframe business and market position. Thus, IBM overemphasized its internal processes at the expense of the open systems values; it should have focused more on customers and the market.

Gerstner's lack of experience in the computer industry, except as a customer, turned out to be an advantage. Since he thought like a customer, he encouraged IBM to develop data-processing solutions built around customer needs, not IBM's hardware. His mantra became: "The customer first, IBM second, and the business unit third." This strategy, made possible by the depth of IBM skills and talent and the breadth of its businesses, was also a good fit with the business environment. As one analyst stated, "The trends are with IBM for the first time in 15 years. It's service-led sales for them now, and that's appropriate because we are in a more solutions-oriented world."

IBM is once again operating in the black (1998 pretax profits of $9.7 billion) and viewed as a leader in its industry[14]—IBM is back in the positive zone.

All of us have theories about management, which then guide our behavior. For example, if manager A holds the belief that people are motivated primarily by money, he will see increased salary as a solution to low productivity. He may then see his role as little more than laying out the work that needs to be done and seeing that employees are well paid for doing it. In contrast, if manager B believes that people's attitudes affect their productivity, she will try to improve morale and see her managerial role as including mentoring and coaching. These examples indicate more than the ubiquitous presence of theories or models of behavior. They also show that our theories determine what we actually see in situations. Manager A may never consider the possibility that morale issues may be involved, while manager B may overlook the role of pay equity. Thus, our mental maps determine what we perceive when we look at situations and what role we are likely to take as a result of our theories of management. Look, for example, at the bottom of Figure 2-1 to see the various roles that go along with each model in the competing values framework.

The prework for today's lesson was assigned to help you clarify your personal theory about the role of effective managers.

PROCEDURE FOR GROUP MEETING: MANAGER OF THE YEAR ACCEPTANCE SPEECH

(Time allotted: 75 minutes)

STEP 1.   Divide into groups of five to seven participants.

STEP 2.   One of you (in each group) is about to receive the Manager of the Year Award. Your group can determine which member will receive this honor and the privilege of making a 5-minute acceptance speech. The entire group should help to craft the speech, which should come close to representing all your views. You can draw ideas from your prework assignment. The speech should include two subjects:
   a. A brief description of today's business environment.
   b. The qualities and skills essential to a manager's success in today's business world.
       (time allotted: 30 minutes)

STEP 3.   The award winner from each group presents a 5-minute speech to the entire class.
       (time allotted: 30–40 minutes)

STEP 4.   Listen for common themes about managerial success in the speeches. Try to categorize each quality and skill mentioned by the speakers in the appropriate quadrant of the competing values framework in Figure 2-1 and 2-2. For example, interpersonal communication would fit under the human relations model, while setting clear goals would fall into the rational goal model. In the following chart keep track (using hatch marks) of how many times each quality or skill is mentioned. We'll refer to these as *competencies*, a term that encompasses both qualities and skills.

STEP 5.   Discuss as a class the following questions:
   a. What were the common themes you heard in the speeches?
   b. What competencies did you place in the human relations quadrant? Open systems? Rational goal? Internal process?
   c. Which quadrant(s) had the most competencies? The most frequently mentioned competencies? Were there any quadrants that were not mentioned at all? What implications can we draw from this?
   d. Was anything mentioned that did not fit into the four quadrants? What can we learn from this?

Analysis of the Speeches

Write the qualities and skills that you hear in the speeches in the appropriate category and mark how many times the same item is mentioned.

Human Relations Model	Open Systems Model
Internal Process Model	**Rational Goal Model**

Items that cannot be categorized:

FOLLOW-UP

Another example of mental maps that people have concerning management is McGregor's Theory X and Theory Y concept.[15] McGregor described two ends of a continuum of assumptions about people and human nature. These assumptions appear on page 26. The Leadership Style Questionnaire that you filled out as part of the premeeting preparation is designed to help you assess the extent of your own Theory X versus Theory Y assumptions about people. Understanding these assumptions is of crucial importance because of the potential that exists for self-fulfilling prophecies. In other words, if you believe people are lazy and irresponsible (Theory X assumptions), you will most likely manage them in a way that is consistent with these assumptions (e.g., watch over their shoulders all the time). This behavior can cause your subordinates to feel that they really have no responsibility in their job, which could lead them to work hard only when you are watching them closely. A self-fulfilling prophecy has thus begun and will be continually reinforced.

In some cultures, we find a stronger tendency toward a Theory X or Theory Y orientation. One of the dimensions anthropologists use to differentiate cultures is their view of human nature. Is human nature good, evil, or neutral? Cultures that perceive humankind as innately evil tend toward a Theory X orientation (e.g., Latin countries). Cultures that perceive humankind as good are more likely to be characterized by a Theory Y orientation (e.g., Scandinavia). These generalizations do not mean that all managers in these cultures are similar but that we will find more aspects of Theory X or Theory Y in their organizations and managerial style. There are other dimensions along which management theories of other cultures differ. Therefore, it's important to understand indigenous management theories when working overseas. U.S. theories are written about most frequently due to the research emphasis of U.S. universities, but this does not mean that other important theories are not alive and well around the world.

The purpose of the group exercise was to identify still more of your own theories about managing and organizing. This is the first step in being able to evaluate when your theories are adequate and when you need to learn or borrow other theories that may be more appropriate to specific situations. Quinn argues that master managers are capable of utilizing competing theories, either sequentially or simultaneously, to master the paradoxes found in organizations.[16] Streufert and Swezey claim that there is a correlation between reaching the executive suite and high "cognitive complexity."[17] Cognitive complexity refers to the extent to which people are multidimensional in their thinking and to the number of different relationships they can make between different dimensions or concepts. Managers with high cognitive complexity can perceive how various management theories apply to situations and can, therefore, choose those that make the most sense in a given situation. Such managers have a variety of maps in their cognitive bank. However, they must also have the behavioral flexibility to perform the various roles that follow from each theory of management.

To be effective, today's managers must possess the capacity to analyze complex situations accurately and to choose appropriate responses. For example, do the individuals you supervise have a Theory X or a Theory Y orientation? Does this vary according to the tasks they are performing? What's the best way to manage them? Answering these questions successfully may mean introducing a different theory or going against one's natural way of doing things. Perhaps when life was less complex, it was sufficient for managers to espouse a "one best way" for managing and have a knee-jerk response to all situations. Today's environment, however, is too turbulent for routine responses, and today's global workforce is too diverse for just one theory of management.

What managers need now is a broad behavioral repertoire and the analytical skill to know what behaviors are most appropriate for each situation. Effectiveness also requires the self-control and self-discipline to do something other than "what comes naturally" when one's natural style would not work. The key then is learning—learning as many models or theories as possible, learning what's involved in different or changing situations, learning about different people and what makes them tick, and learning what works and what doesn't.

 ## LEARNING POINTS

1. Taylor's scientific management emphasized the efficient division of labor into small, standardized jobs that were matched to the capabilities of trained workers who received wage incentives.
2. Administrative theory focused on understanding the basic tasks of management and developed guidelines or principles for managing effectively.
3. The human relations school acknowledged the effect of the informal social system with its norms and individual attitudes and feelings on organizational functioning. This theory underlined the importance of employee morale and participation.
4. The decision-making school described organizations as social systems based on individual decisions and contributed the idea of bounded rationality. Managers could control employee behavior by controlling the premises of decision making.
5. The contingency approach contends that there is no one best way to manage in every situation. Managers must find the appropriate method to match a given situation.
6. Successful organizations are characterized by good "fit" among strategy, structure, systems, staff, style, skills, and superordinate goals. They must also fit their environment.

7. Open systems theory maintains that organizations and all the subdivisions within them take in resources and transform them into a service or product that is purchased or utilized by a larger system. All parts are interdependent, including the larger environment in which the organization is embedded.

8. In the competing values framework, master managers balance the paradoxes of four different models: rational goal model, internal process model, human relations model, and open systems model. Too much emphasis on any one model will lead to failure.

9. The first step in managing the paradoxes of organizational effectiveness is understanding one's own theories of management.

10. Our theories or mental maps determine what we see when we look at situations and determine the roles we perform.

11. Today's managers need to learn:
    a. how to analyze complex situations using a variety of models or theories.
    b. a broad repertoire of behaviors and knowledge about when to use them.
    c. how to adapt to rapidly changing environments.

12. Theory X is based on the assumption that humans are inherently lazy, dislike responsibility, and prefer to be led. Theory Y is based on opposite perceptions of human nature—that humans are responsible, motivated to work hard and develop skills, and capable of self-direction.

FOR MANAGERS

- The interdependence aspect of open systems theory means that changes in one part of the system will have repercussions elsewhere. Try to determine these consequences *before* making decisions and implementing changes.

- Interdependence within a system also means that problems are often rooted in other parts of the system. Train yourself to take a systems approach when looking at problems. At a minimum, ask yourself, "Have I thought about what's taking place on the individual, group, organizational, and environmental levels with regard to this particular situation?"

- People often look down on those whose theories are dissimilar to their own. One way to develop yourself is to seek out and work with people who have different beliefs. Doing so may involve a cost to you, but the payoff should be greater cognitive complexity and understanding of different mental maps.

- Gathering as many perspectives as possible about situations is helpful. Just as there is no one best way of managing, there is no one best way to see a situation. Managers who can count on others to help them "see" what's going on and give their opinions on what could be done are fortunate. If, however, you give the impression that you don't like to hear a different perspective or receive advice, you won't—until it's too late to do much about it.

- Strategies for developing yourself as a manager:
  - **Analyze yourself** To better understand yourself and your mental maps, fill out assessment instruments like the one at the beginning of the chapter. Ask other people to evaluate you, since this will provide another, perhaps more accurate, perspective. If you are surprised by their evaluations, discuss any differences in perception with an honest coworker or friend.
  - **Develop a change strategy** Select a specific area for improvement and set a goal that is possible to achieve in a particular time frame. You may want to keep a journal to record your questions, lessons, and progress. It is often helpful to work with a partner who provides the social support that makes it easier to change behavior.
  - **Learn about the skill you want to master** Educate yourself by reading books or attending workshops. Identify a good role model whom you can observe or who is willing to explain how to develop this skill. Ask someone to coach you on this skill.
  - **Practice the skill and request feedback** Put yourself in situations that require the skill you want to develop so that you can get the practice you need. Ask others for feedback on what you are doing well and what still needs to be improved.

PERSONAL APPLICATION ASSIGNMENT

A. What is your own theory of management? You can describe it in words or draw it as a model. (Keep a copy for yourself so that you can modify it as the course proceeds.)

B. Based on your theory of management and today's environment, answer the following questions:
  1. What blind spots could your theory lead you to have?

  2. What personal values seem to underlie your theory; that is, "people, managers, or organizations should/should not _____ (what?)."

  3. What implicit assumptions, if any, are you making about human nature or human motivation?

  4. What skills do you think are necessary to be a "master" manager?

5. Which of these do you already possess?

6. What skills would you like to work on during this course?

7. Write an action plan for learning these skills. How will you work on it? How will you know when your skills have improved?

ENDNOTES

[1] F. A. Taylor, *The Principles of Scientific Management* (New York: W.W. Norton, 1911).

[2] H. Fayol, *General and Industrial Management*, trans. C. Storrs (London: Sir Isaac Pitman, 1949).

[3] M. Weber, *The Theory of Social and Economic Organization*, trans. T. Parsons (New York: Free Press, 1947).

[4] F. J. Roethlisberger and W. J. Dickson, *Management and the Worker* (Cambridge, MA: Harvard University Press, 1939).

[5] J. March and H. Simon, *Organizations* (New York: John Wiley, 1958).

[6] For a famous example of research on contingency theory, see P. R. Lawrence and J. W. Lorsch, *Organization and Environment: Managing Differentiation and Integration* (Homewood, IL: Richard D. Irwin, 1969).

[7] R. Tanner Pascale and A. G. Athos, *The Art of Japanese Management* (New York: Simon & Schuster, 1981).

[8] The 7S framework appears in Pascale and Athos, *The Art of Japanese Management* and in R. H. Waterman Jr., T. J. Peters, and J. R. Phillips, "Structure Is Not Organization," *Business Horizons 23*, no. 3(1980): 14–26.

[9] C. A. Bartlett and S. Ghoshal, *Transnational Management* (Homewood, IL: Irwin, 1992).

[10] R. E. Quinn, *Beyond Rational Management* (San Francisco: Jossey-Bass, 1988).

[11] S. Hart, and R. E. Quinn, "Roles Executives Play: CEOs, Behavioral Complexity, and Firm Performance," *Human Relations 46* (1993): 115–42; and D. Denison, R. Joohiberg, and R. Quinn, "Paradox and Performance: Toward a Theory of Behavioral Complexity in Managerial Leadership." *Organization Science 6*, no. 5 (1995): 524–40.

[12] Quinn, *Beyond Rational Management*.

[13] J. H. Dobrzynski, "Rethinking IBM," *Business Week* (October 4, 1993): 86–97.

[14] D. Kirkpatrick, "IBM from Big Blue Dinosaur to E-Business Animal: *Fortune 139* (April 26, 1999): 116–17; and "Blue Is the Color," *The Economist 347*, no. 8071 (June 6, 1998): 65–69.

[15] D. M. McGregor, "The Human Side of Enterprise," *Management Review* (November 1957).

[16] Quinn, *Beyond Rational Management*.

[17] S. Streufert and R. W. Swezey, *Complexity, Managers, and Organizations* (Orlando, FL: Academic Press, 1986).

Chapter 3

▲▲

INDIVIDUAL AND ORGANIZATIONAL LEARNING

OBJECTIVES By the end of this chapter, you should be able to:

A. Describe the model of adult learning.

B. Identify individual learning styles and their characteristics.

C. Improve the learning organization in this course by sharing learning objectives, available resources for learning, and learning environment preferences.

D. Distinguish between adaptive and generative learning.

E. Describe the characteristics of a learning organization.

WHY DUMB THINGS HAPPEN TO SMART COMPANIES

Few people quarrel with the notion that companies must learn to invest in and manage knowledge if they hope to compete in an economy where, more than ever, knowledge is what we buy and sell. But how, they wonder, does one make the case for managing intellectual capital to CEOs and CFOs? And where do we start?

The two questions are cousins, since the best way to build support for any management effort is to start where you'll get early results. Mind you, the forgotten key to succeeding in management is not to stop there; quitting too soon condemns you to the hummingbird style of management, forever flitting and sipping from one blooming idea to another.

But you've got to start somewhere, and here's a way to figure out where: a list of nine symptoms of a "knowledge problem"—something wrong with how your company manages its brainpower. The list comes from David H. Smith, head of knowledge development for Unilever, the giant (1996 sales: $52 billion) maker of ice cream, soaps and detergents, frozen foods, and personal products. Smith, a witty Englishman who works in the Netherlands, has a background in both information technology and business. Nine months ago he was given the task of "helping Unilever act more intelligently"—that is, learn faster and leverage what it knows. You can reconstruct the conversation, since you've had the same one: "The solution to our problem isn't to work harder. We've got to learn to work smarter...." That, as Smith says, "is obviously true but also extremely trite." Besides, when your boss says, "Work smarter, Charlie," how, exactly, are you supposed to do that come Monday?

Like Lyme disease, knowledge problems have symptoms that sometimes mimic other problems, more benign or even more malign. But each of the following, says Smith, is a symptom that suggests that you don't manage knowledge well: People aren't finding it, moving it around, keeping it refreshed and up to date, sharing it, or using it.

The list is Smith's, the bells and whistles mine.

- **You repeat mistakes** "Your best teacher is your last mistake," Ralph Nader once told me. He, of course, has made a career out of publicizing companies that display this knowledge problem. It's rampant. Negligence lawyers don't wear Gucci loafers because companies make mistakes; they wear them because companies make the same mistake twice. The nature of icebergs being what it is, for every million-dollar lawsuit there must be tens of millions lost or wasted from repeated mistakes that are dumb but not tortious (actionable).

  Why does it happen? Fear, I'd guess, is the No. 1 reason: fear of being embarrassed, chewed out, or worse. Many people and companies are so busy trying to hide boners (from the boss, from stock analysts, from customers and competitors) that they tuck away the learning along with the evidence.

  You don't, obviously, want to encourage goofs just to learn from them. But the best way to avoid repeated errors is to study failure as assiduously as success. The history of medicine shows that you can learn as much from autopsies as you can from cures.

- **You duplicate work** "Reinventing the wheel" is the inevitable phrase, and most companies spend so much time doing it you would think they were suppliers to Schwinn. A classic example: You inspect the goods before you ship them, and your customer inspects them again after they arrive. Worse, you do the same thing in-house. Usually the underlying cause is a knowledge problem: Customer and supplier either don't know what each expects of the other, or they don't trust each other because they haven't shared processes or results.

  People fail to copy success for the same reasons that they succeed in copying mistakes: They're afraid or embarrassed to ask. Sometimes the problem is in systems and structures: They don't know where to look or looking takes too much time or they have no place to store corporate memory. Sometimes the problem is what one might call an overdeveloped engineer's mind: I know Eddie already did this, but I can do it better.

- **You have poor customer relations** If you're not selling schlock, why does a customer get peevish? Probably for one of three reasons, all knowledge problems. First, communication at the point of sale: Either he didn't understand what you were selling or you didn't understand what she was buying. Second, service: If I get the runaround when I have a problem, chances are the people who answer your 800 number are little more than switchboard operators, who don't know what they should.

  The third reason is subtler and more interesting. Knowledge work tends to be custom work, or at least customized. That changes the nature of the transaction. You don't sell janitorial services the same way you sell mops. Too often salespeople are in a hurry to hear "yes" so they can write up the order. (Too often their incentives encourage that practice.) Result: You talked about the sale but not the deal.

- **Good ideas don't transfer between departments, units, or countries** This is the most common knowledge problem of all: How do we get people to share ideas rather than hoard them, to accept ideas rather than reject them? There's no easy answer. Says Hewlett-Packard's, CEO, Lewis Platt: "Knowledge transfer is a problem that yields to ten different initiatives, not one." Here's a starter kit:

  Set an example: Great bosses love teaching; great teachers produce great students. Once, interviewing AlliedSignal CEO Larry Bossidy, I confessed not knowing what working capital was. Bossidy positively lit up, grabbed a sheet of paper, scooted around the table, and taught me; his pleasure in teaching turned an interview into a sharing of minds.

  Nudge: Nothing will get the troops to use the Lotus Notes database faster than a leader who asks at a staff meeting, "I'd like to hear everyone's thoughts on Kay's posting about the situation in Germany. Bill, let's start with you: What do you think we should do?"

  Create incentives: Says Robert Buckman, CEO of specialty-chemical maker Buckman Laboratories: "The most powerful incentives you have are salaries and promotions." Buckman makes sure—and makes it known—that he hands them out based substantially on how well people share and borrow ideas.

Benchmark: Be sure Phoenix knows it has twice as much bad debt as Dayton—and reward both if they close the gap.

Make it fun: When you return from a convention, which do you write up first, your expense account or your trip report? Which contains more creative thinking? Which is read more attentively? One group at Monsanto makes knowledge sharing fun by arming people with snazzy new Kodak digital cameras when they go on trips; when they get back, they show their pictures at the next staff meeting.

- **You're competing on price** No company wants to find itself in a commodity business. What makes the difference? Why could an executive in General Electric's lighting business—light bulbs, for Pete's sake—tell me, in a mock-serious tone, "Cutting prices is not a core value of the General Electric Co.," while some companies making computers—computers, for Pete's sake—are forced to do just that?

The answer is almost always knowledge, or the lack of it. Whatever you sell, you can get out of the price game if you and your customer ride the learning curve together. Everything you learn about a customer—from how he likes pallets stacked to what his plans are—is an opportunity to make it harder for competitors to horn in. The result: margin.

- **You can't compete with market leaders** Sometimes the big guys win because they've got something you ain't got, like prime-rate loans or Super Bowl–size ad budgets. But don't blame your problems on scale until you have explored this question: What do they know that we don't know? Toyota, Wal-Mart, and Southwest Airlines are just three examples of formerly small companies that outwitted bigger competitors.

- **You're dependent on key individuals** Remember the old Allan Sherman song?

Oh, salesmen come and salesmen go
And my best one is gone I know
And if he don't, come back to me
I'll have to close the factory . . .

Nothing's more dangerous than depending on a few key people. Usually this signals too little teamwork or an absence of ways to encourage star performers to reveal the secrets of their success.

Note, though: The fault may not lie in your stars. Sometimes people have greatness thrust upon them because others are unwilling to achieve it themselves. HP's Lew Platt says, "You've got a knowledge problem when decisions are made too high in the organization." When things come to Platt's desk that shouldn't, he takes it as a sign that people lack knowledge that would let them think for themselves.

- **You're slow to launch new products or enter new markets** It's obvious that being slow to market is a knowledge problem. But diagnosing its cause can be tricky; as with referred pain, the source may be far from the symptom. It could be a weak lab, a sludge-slowed commercialization process, a rigid budget bureaucracy, failure of competitor and market intelligence, or something else.

- **You don't know how to price for service** Do you build the cost of service into your price? Sell a service contract? Bill by the hour, the day, the job? Let someone in the distribution channel handle it? Can you clearly explain why you do what you do, or are you just following industry practice?

Of all the symptoms on Smith's list, this intrigues me most because the underlying knowledge problem is least self-evident. Here it is: If you don't know how to price for service or why to charge one way versus another, it's a sign that you don't fully understand what your customers do with whatever you sell them. Some customers just buy on price. More often, however, they are buying the solution to a problem. They don't want drills; they want holes. One adhesive company, Smith says, knew a way to help customers speed up assembly lines with the added benefit (for customers) of using less glue. But its sales force had no idea how to value and price this knowledge; worse, the reps were paid by the pound. If you know what customers are really paying for, you'd know better who should pay what.

Smith's list is diagnostic, not prescriptive. But each item on it is a knowledge problem with real business consequences that even a skeptical boss will want to fix. It's a start.

Source: Thomas A. Stewart, "Why Dumb Things Happen to Smart Companies." *Fortune*, June 23, 1997, *135*, no. 12, 159–60. Reprinted with permission of the publisher.

PREMEETING PREPARATION

(Time Allotted: 1 Hour, 30 Minutes)

A. Read "Why Dumb Things Happen to Smart Companies."

B. Answer the questions that follow concerning a real learning situation that you have recently faced or are currently facing (e.g., learning to use a new computer program, play an instrument, understand the income tax laws, master a new management technique, give a speech, play a new sport).

1. Describe what you were (or are) trying to learn.

2. How did you go about learning to do it? What sequence of steps did you follow?

3. What was the outcome?

4. What was the best group learning experience you ever had? What was good about it?

5. What was your worst group learning experience? What made it that way?

6. In your opinion, what conditions promote adult learning?

7. What are the significant learning points from the reading?

C. Complete the Learning Style Inventory that follows.

D. Score the Learning Style Inventory.

E. Read the entire unit *after* completing the Learning Style Inventory.

F. If your instructor has assigned the Robbins Self-Assessment Library, use "What's My Basic Personality?"

THE LEARNING STYLE INVENTORY

This survey is designed to help you describe how you learn—the way you find out about and deal with ideas and situations in your life. Different people learn best in different ways. The different ways of learning described in the survey are equally good. The aim is to describe how you learn, not to evaluate your learning ability. You might find it hard to choose the descriptions that best characterize your learning style. Keep in mind that there are no right or wrong answers—all the choices are equally acceptable.

> *There are nine sets of four descriptions listed in this inventory. Mark the words in each set that are most like you, second most like you, third most like you, and least like you. Put a "4" next to the description that is most like you, a "3" next to the description that is second most like you, a "2" next to the description that is third most like you, and a "1" next to the description that is least like you (4 = most like you; 1 = least like you). Be sure to assign a different rank number to each of the four words in each set; do not make ties.*

Example

_4_ happy	_3_ fast	_1_ angry	_2_ careful

Some people find it easiest to decide first which word best describes them (4 happy) and then to decide the word that is least like them (1 angry). Then you can give a 3 to that word in the remaining pair that is most like you (3 fast) and a 2 to the word that is left over (2 careful).

1. ___	discriminating	___	tentative	___	involved	___	practical
2. ___	receptive	___	relevant	___	analytical	___	impartial
3. ___	feeling	___	watching	___	thinking	___	doing
4. ___	accepting	___	risk taking	___	evaluative	___	aware
5. ___	intuitive	___	productive	___	logical	___	questioning
6. ___	abstract	___	observing	___	concrete	___	active
7. ___	present oriented	___	reflective	___	future oriented	___	pragmatic
8. ___	open to experience	___	observative	___	conceptual	___	experimental
9. ___	intense	___	reserved	___	rational	___	responsible
___	CE	___	RO	___	AC	___	AE

Source: Copyright 1976 by David A. Kolb

Scoring Instructions

Total the numbers in the shaded blanks for each column and write your answer in the empty blank at the bottom.

The four columns of words correspond to the four learning style scales: concrete experience (CE), reflective observation (RO), abstract conceptualization (AC), and active experimentation (AE).

To compute the two combination scores, subtract CE from AC and subtract RO from AE. Preserve negative signs if they appear.

AC   CE   AE   RO

AC-CE: ☐ – ☐ =   AE-RO: ☐ – ☐ =

To interpret the meaning of these scores, read the Topic Introduction.

TOPIC INTRODUCTION

Learning became a business issue in the past two decades once companies realized its importance to survival. "We understand that the only competitive advantage the company of the future will have is its managers' ability to learn faster than their competitors. So the companies that succeed will be those that continually nudge their managers towards revising their views of the world."[1] This was one of the lessons Arie de Geus, senior planner, learned from Shell's efforts to analyze long-term corporate survival. Many companies, such as Asea Brown Boveri (ABB), 3M, Ford Motor, GE, FedEx, Motorola, and Johnsonville Foods, have worked hard to transform their companies into learning organizations. A *learning organization* is an organization skilled at creating, acquiring, and transferring knowledge, and at modifying its behavior to reflect new knowledge and insights.

Learning organizations succeed, in part, when individuals make explicit their knowledge and contribute it to the institutional collection of mental models and lessons. The structure and culture of the organization will then determine how quickly individual learning spreads, as seen in this analogy from nature. Titmice travel in flocks and intermingle extensively; in contrast robins have carefully defined boundaries and work hard and belligerently at keeping other robins out of their territory. When titmice learned to pierce the aluminum seals of the milk bottles delivered to U.K. doorsteps, that knowledge quickly spread throughout the species. Although individual robins may have learned this trick, their knowledge will never be disseminated to the species as a whole because they lack the capacity for institutional learning.[2] Much like territorial managers and departments, the robins' focus on turf, and their competitive relationships result in hoarding, rather than sharing, knowledge.

Both companies and employees are being pressured to increase their learning capacity by the "white water" nature of today's business environment. According to Peter Vail, who coined this metaphor, managers in the past could paddle their canoes wherever they wanted on calm, still lakes. Now they are forced to learn to deal with a seemingly endless run of "white water," the rock-strewn, turbulent, fast-moving water in which canoeists struggle to stay afloat and unharmed. White water is exhilarating, but only if you possess the necessary skills. In a turbulent environment where a person's career will average 13 different jobs,[3] no course or program of education can provide students with all the skills and knowledge they will need for the rest of their career. Our best response is to teach you *how* to learn so you can become a lifelong learner.

This book is designed to create the learning environment that is most responsive to the unique needs of adult learners by addressing five characteristics of that environment. First, it is based on a *psychological contract of reciprocity*, a basic building block of human interaction. It is well documented that relationships that are based on a mutual and equal balance of giving and getting thrive and grow; those based on unequal exchange very quickly decay. Academic learning is often conceived as a process of getting rather than giving. Teachers give and students get. Yet in adult learning both giving and getting are critical. In getting, there is the opportunity to incorporate new ideas and perspectives. In giving, there is the opportunity to integrate and apply these new perspectives and to practice their use.

A second characteristic of an adult learning environment is that it is *experience based.* Ideally the motivation for learning comes not from the instructor's dispensation of rewards and grades but from problems and opportunities arising from the learner's own life experience. Experience shows adults what they need to learn and also allows them to contribute to the learning of others.

Third, the adult learning enviromnent emphasizes *personal application.* Since adults' learning needs arise from their own experience, the main goal of learning is to apply new knowledge, skills, and attitudes to the solution of the individual's practical problems.

Fourth, the learning environment is *individualized and self-directed.* In addition to their unique experiences, each person also brings different learning goals and styles. This means that learning enviroments have to be flexible and attempt to meet the needs of different students. Learners, however, must also be willing to take responsibility for achieving their learning objectives and alert the group or instructor if problems arise.

A final characteristic of an adult learning environment is that it *integrates learning and living.* There are two goals in the learning process. One is to learn the specifics of a particular subject matter. The other is to learn about one's own strengths and weaknesses as a learner (i.e., learning how to learn from experience). This understanding helps in "back-home" applications of what has been learned and provides a framework for continuing learning on the job.

A MODEL OF THE LEARNING PROCESS

Adults are often motivated to learn by a problem. A manager who has employees who habitually come late to work starts to chew on the problem. In addition to her individual reflections, she may consult management books or other managers who have solved this problem. Eventually, she will develop a mental model that explains her theory of tardiness: Employees come late to work because _____ (e.g., there are no negative consequences for doing so, employees rely on public transportation that is not dependable, late employees are not committed to the organization, etc.). Based on this model, she will take action to solve the problem (negative sanctions, company transportation, beginning the disciplinary process for some employees). If her interventions are successful, she will have gained knowledge about late employees. *Knowledge* is defined as the condition of knowing something through experience. If, on the other hand, employees still come late, this sets the learning cycle in motion all over again.

By examining this learning process we can come closer to understanding how it is that people generate from their experience the concepts, rules, and principles that guide their behavior in new situations, and how they modify these concepts to improve their effectiveness. This process is both active and passive, both concrete and abstract. As shown in Figure 3-1, it can be conceived of as a four-stage cycle: (1) concrete experience is followed by (2) observation and reflection, which lead to (3) the formation of abstract concepts and generalizations, which lead to (4) hypotheses to be tested in future action, which in turn lead to new experiences.

There are several observations to be made about this model of the learning process. First, this learning cycle is continuously recurring. We continuously test our concepts in experience and modify them as a result of our observation of the experience.

Second, the direction that learning takes is governed by one's felt needs and goals. We seek experiences that are related to our goals, interpret them in the light of our goals, and form concepts

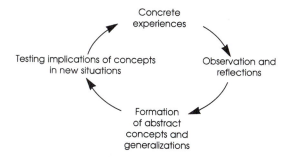

FIGURE 3-1   **The Learning Process**

and test implications of these concepts that are relevant to these felt needs and goals. The implication of this fact is that the process of learning is erratic and inefficient when personal objectives are not clear.

Third, since the learning process is directed by individual needs and goals, learning styles become highly individual in both direction and process. For example, a mathematician may come to place great emphasis on abstract concepts, whereas a poet may value concrete experience more highly. A manager may be primarily concerned with active application of concepts, whereas a naturalist may develop exceptional observational skills. Each of us develops a learning style that has some weak points and strong points. We may jump into experiences but fail to observe the lessons to be derived from these experiences; we may form concepts but fail to test their validity. In some areas our objectives and needs may be clear guides to learning; in others, we wander aimlessly.

INTERPRETING YOUR SCORES ON THE LEARNING STYLE INVENTORY

The Learning Style Inventory (LSI)[4] is a simple self-description test, based on experiential learning theory, that is designed to measure your strengths and weaknesses as a learner in the four stages of the learning process. Effective learners rely on four different learning modes: *concrete experience (CE), reflective observation (RO), abstract conceptualization (AC)*, and *active experimentation (AE)*. That is, they must be able to involve themselves fully and openly, and without bias in new experiences (CE); they must be able to reflect on and observe these experiences from many perspectives (RO); they must be able to create concepts that integrate their observations into logically sound theories (AC); and they must be able to use these theories to make decisions and solve problems (AE).

The LSI measures your relative emphasis on the four learning modes by asking you to rank order a series of four words that describes these different abilities. For example, one set of four words is *feeling* (CE), *watching* (RO), *thinking* (AC), *doing* (AE). Combination scores indicate the extent to which you emphasize abstractness over concreteness (AC-CE) and the extent to which you emphasize active experimentation over reflection (AE-RO).

One way to understand better the meaning of your scores on the LSI is to compare them with the scores of others. The "target" in Figure 3-2 gives norms on the four basic scales (CE, RO, AC, AE) for 1,933 adults ranging from 18 to 60 years of age. About two-thirds of the group are men and the group as a whole is highly educated (two-thirds have college degrees or higher). A wide range of occupations and educational backgrounds is represented, including teachers, counselors, engineers, salespersons, managers, doctors, and lawyers.

The raw scores for each of the four basic scales are listed on the crossed lines of the target. **By circling your raw scores on the four scales and connecting them with straight lines you can create a graphic representation of your learning style profile.** The concentric circles on the target represent percentile scores for the normative group. For example, if your raw score on *concrete experience* was 15, you scored higher on this scale than about 55 percent of the people in the normative group. If your CE score was 22 or higher, you scored higher than 99 percent of the normative group. Therefore, in comparison with the normative group, the shape of your profile indicates which of the four basic modes you tend to emphasize and which are less emphasized. No individual mode is better or worse than any other. Even a totally balanced profile is not necessarily best. The key to effective learning is being competent in each mode when it is appropriate. A high score on one mode may mean a tendency to overemphasize that aspect of the learning process at the expense of others. A low score on a mode may indicate a tendency to avoid that aspect of the learning process.

The LSI does not measure your learning style with 100 percent accuracy. Rather, it is simply an indication of how you see yourself as a learner. You will need data from other sources if you wish to pinpoint your learning style more exactly (e.g., how you make decisions on the job, how other see you learn, and what kinds of problems you solve best.) Be aware of stereotyping yourself and others with your LSI scores. Your scores indicate which learning modes you emphasize in general. They may change from time to time and situation to situation. Think

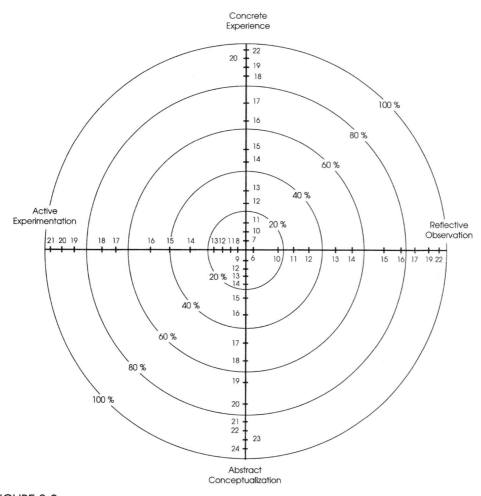

FIGURE 3-2 **The Learning Style Profile Norms for the Learning Style Inventory**
(Copyright 1976 by David A. Kolb)

back to the learning experience you wrote about in the prework. Which of the following modes best describes your approach?

An *orientation toward concrete experience* focuses on being involved in experiences and dealing with immediate human situations in a personal way. It emphasizes the perception of feeling, focusing on the uniqueness and complexity of present reality as opposed to theories and generalizations—an intuitive, "artistic" approach as opposed to a systematic, scientific approach to problems. People with a concrete experience orientation enjoy and are good at relating to others. They are often skilled intuitive decision makers and function well in unstructured situations. People with this orientation value relating to people, being involved in real situations, and an open-minded approach to life.

An *orientation toward reflective observation* focuses on understanding the meaning of ideas and situations by carefully observing and impartially describing them. It emphasizes understanding as opposed to practical application, a concern with what is true or how things happen as opposed to what is practical—an emphasis on reflection as opposed to action. People with a reflective orientation enjoy thinking about the meaning of situations and ideas and are good at seeing their implications. They are good at looking at things from different perspectives and at appreciating different points of view. They like to rely on their own thoughts and feelings to form opinions. People with this orientation value patience, impartiality, and considered, thoughtful judgment.

An *orientation toward abstract conceptualization* focuses on using logic, ideas, and concepts. It emphasizes thinking as opposed to feeling, a concern with building general theories as opposed to understanding intuitively unique, specific areas—a scientific rather than to an artistic approach to problems. A person with an abstract conceptual orientation enjoys and is good at systematic planning, manipulation of abstract symbols, and quantitative analysis. People with this orientation value precision, the rigor and discipline of analyzing ideas, and the aesthetic quality of a neat, conceptual system.

An *orientation toward active experimentation* focuses on actively influencing people and changing situations. It emphasizes practical applications as opposed to reflective understanding, a pragmatic concern with what works as opposed to what is absolute truth—an emphasis on doing as opposed to observing. People with an active experimentation orientation enjoy and are good at getting things accomplished. They are willing to take some risk to achieve their objectives. They also value having an impact and influence on the environment around them and like to see results.

IDENTIFYING YOUR LEARNING STYLE TYPE

It is unlikely that your learning style will be described accurately by just one of the four preceding paragraphs. This is because each person's learning style is a combination of the four basic learning modes. It is, therefore, useful to describe your learning style by a single data point that combines your scores on the four basic modes. This is accomplished by using the two combination scores, AC-CE and AE-RO. These scales indicate the degree to which you emphasize abstractness over concreteness and action over reflection, respectively.

The grid in Figure 3-3 shows the raw scores for these two scales on the crossed lines (AC-CE on the vertical and AE-RO on the horizontal) and percentile scores based on the normative group on the sides. By marking your raw scores on the two lines and plotting their point of intersection, you can find which of the four learning style quadrants you occupy. These four quadrants, labeled *accommodator, diverger, converger*, and *assimilator*, represent the four dominant learning styles. If your AC-CE score were −4 and your AE-RO score were +8, you would fall squarely into the accommodator quadrant. An AC-CE score of +4 and an AE-RO score of +3 would put you only slightly in the converger quadrant. The closer your data point is to the intersection where the lines cross, the more balanced is your learning style. If your data point is close to any of the four corners, this indicates that you rely heavily on one particular learning style.

The following is a description of the characteristics of the four basic learning styles based both on research and clinical observation.

The *divergent* learning style has the opposite strengths of the convergent style and emphasizes concrete experience and reflective observation. The greatest strength of this orientation lies in imaginative ability and awareness of meaning and values. The primary adaptive ability in this style is to view concrete situations from many perspectives and to organize many relationships into a meaningful gestalt. The emphasis in this orientation is on adaptation by observation rather than by action. This style is called "diverger" because a person of this type performs better in situations that call for generation of alternative ideas and implications, such as a brainstorming idea session. Divergers are interested in people and tend to be imaginative and feeling oriented. They generally have broad cultural interests and tend to specialize in the arts. This style is characteristic of individuals from humanities and liberal arts backgrounds. Counselors, organization development specialists, and personnel managers tend to be characterized by this learning style.

In *assimilation*, the dominant learning abilities are abstract conceptualization and reflective observation. The greatest strength of this orientation lies in inductive reasoning, in the ability to create theoretical models and in assimilating disparate observations into an integrated explanation. As in convergence, this orientation is less focused on people and more concerned with ideas and abstract concepts. Ideas, however, are judged less in this orientation by their practical value. Here it is more important that the theory be logically sound and precise. This learning style is more characteristic of individuals in the basic sciences and mathematics rather than the applied sciences. In organizations, persons with this learning style are found most often in the research and planning departments.

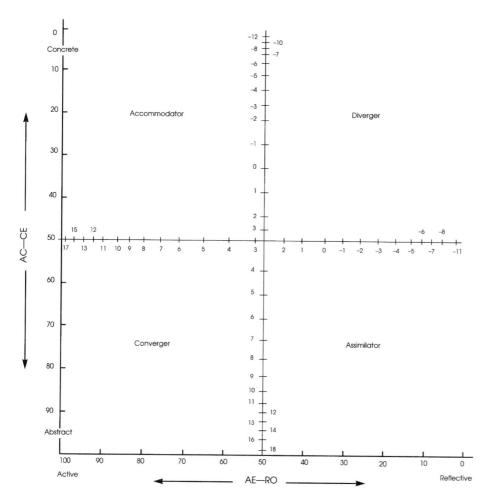

FIGURE 3-3 **Learning Style Type Grid**
Source: Copyright 1976 by David A. Kolb

The *convergent* learning style has the opposite strength of the diverger style. It relies primarily on the dominant learning abilities of abstract conceptualization and active experimentation. The greatest strength of this approach lies in problem solving, decision making, and the practical application of ideas. We have called this learning style the "converger" because a person with this style seems to do best in such situations as conventional intelligence tests where there is a single correct answer or solution to a question or problem. In this learning style, knowledge is organized in such a way that, through hypothetical-deductive reasoning, it can be focused on specific problems. Research on individuals with this style of learning shows that convergent persons are controlled in their expression of emotion.[5] They prefer dealing with technical tasks and problems rather than with social and interpersonal issues. Convergers often specialize in the physical sciences. This learning style is characteristic of many engineers and technical specialists.

The *accommodative* learning style has the opposite strengths of assimilation, emphasizing concrete experience and active experimentation. The greatest strength of this orientation lies in doing things, in carrying out plans and tasks, and in getting involved in new experiences. The adaptive emphasis of this orientation is on opportunity seeking, risk taking, and action. This style is called "accommodation" because it is best suited for those situations in which one must adapt to changing immediate circumstances. In situations in which the theory or plans do not fit the facts, those with an accommodative style will most likely discard the plan or theory. (With the opposite learning style, assimilation, one would be more likely to disregard or reexamine the facts.) People with an accommodative orientation tend to solve problems in an intuitive trial-and-error manner, relying on other people for information rather than on their own analytical ability. Individuals with accommodative learning styles are at ease with people but are sometimes seen as impatient and "pushy." Their educational background is often in technical or practical fields such as business. In organizations, people with this learning style are found in action-oriented jobs, such as marketing, sales, or management.

LEARNING STYLES AND MANAGEMENT EDUCATION

Differences in learning styles need to be managed in management education. For example, managers who return to the university in midcareer experience something of a culture shock. Fresh from a world of time deadlines and concrete, specific problems that they must solve, they are suddenly immersed in a strange slow-paced world of generalities, where the elegant solution to problems is sought even when workable solutions are at hand. One gets rewarded here for reflection and analysis rather than concrete goal-directed action. Managers who "act before they think—if they ever think" meet the scientists who "think before they act—if they ever act." Research on learning styles has shown that managers on the whole are distinguished by very strong, active experimentation skills and very weak reflective observation skills. Business school faculty members (and professors in general) usually have the reverse profile. To bridge this gap in learning styles, the management educator must somehow respond to pragmatic demands for relevance and the application of knowledge, while encouraging the reflective examination of experience that is necessary to refine old theories and to build new ones. In encouraging reflective observation, the teacher often is seen as an interrupter of action—as a passive "ivory tower" thinker. This is, however, a critical role in the learning process. Yet if the reflective observer role is not internalized by the learners themselves, the learning process can degenerate into a value conflict between teacher and student, each maintaining that theirs is the right perspective for learning.

Neither the faculty nor student perspective alone is valid. Managerial education will not be improved by eliminating theoretical analysis or relevant case problems. Improvement will come through the *integration* of the scholarly and practical learning styles. One approach to achieving this integration is to apply the experiential learning model directly in the classroom. This workbook provides simulations, role plays, and exercises (concrete experiences) that focus on central concepts in organizational behavior. They provide a common experiential starting point for participants and faculty to explore the relevance of behavioral concepts for their work. In traditional management education methods, the conflict between scholar and practitioner learning styles is exaggerated because the material to be taught is filtered through the learning style of faculty members in their lectures or presentation and analysis of cases. Students are "one down" in their own analysis because the data are secondhand and already biased. In the experiential learning approach, this filtering process does not take place because teacher and students alike are observers of immediate experiences that they both interpret according to their own learning style. In this approach to learning, the teachers' role is that of facilitators of a learning process that is basically self-directed. They help students to experience in a personal and immediate way the phenomena in their field of specialization. They provide observational schemes and perspectives from which to observe these experiences. They stand ready with alternative theories and concepts as students attempt to assimilate their observations into their own conception of reality. They assist in deducing the implications of the students' concepts and in designing new "experiments" to test these implications through practical, real-world experience.

LEARNING AND CULTURE

Another learning style difference that must be managed in the classroom relates to cultural diversity. For example, in some cultures professors are perceived as experts with all the answers. They dispense their knowledge to students who are socialized not to interrupt or question but to act respectfully with teachers in or out of class. In many U.S. classrooms (but not all), students are encouraged, expected, or even forced to participate in class. Asking questions that may reflect badly on the professor's expertise, while not necessarily politic, is not taboo in the American milieu. Students in Asian classrooms are seldom expected to speak and would never say anything to embarrass a professor in public. In general, Latin American students are less comfortable with unstructured, participative classes, and they expect professors to be more dramatic and expressive. Experiential learning may come as a shock to students who have been socialized to have more traditional expectations about learning and classroom roles. There is no question that some people will be more comfortable, at least in the beginning, than others in an experiential course. As a group, we should seek to understand and discuss the differences in our expectations and, when possible, make allowances for them.

THE LEARNING ORGANIZATION

It was Woodrow Wilson who said, "I not only use all the brains that I have but all that I can borrow." Using all the available brainpower, knowledge, and wisdom is one of the basic premises of a learning organization. Some of the essential characteristics of learning organizations are:[6]

- *Systematic problem solving.* Employees are taught to solve problems using the scientific method, which focuses on data rather than assumptions and requires the use of simple statistical tools.
- *Experimentation.* Employees are encouraged to take risks and experiment with continuous improvements to ongoing programs or to test innovative ideas using pilot or demonstration projects. The results of these experiments are shared with the rest of the organization and guide decision making.
- *Learning from past experience.* Companies take time to reflect on and evaluate their successes and failures. They summarize and quickly disseminate the lessons learned.
- *Learning from others.* Companies look outward to find and adopt good ideas from other organizations. They visit and benchmark (study) excellent companies and learn from "best practices" and are not reluctant to implement ideas that were "not invented here" within their own company.
- *Transferring knowledge.* Learning organizations have mechanisms for quickly sharing knowledge among their members.

The popularity of learning organizations has given rise to numerous tools to help managers surface their assumptions and mental models, develop creative strategies for the future, resolve problems utilizing cross-functional teams (action-learning and total quality management groups), continuously improve work processes, and analyze possible scenarios for the future.[7] As with any innovation, these tools do not succeed unless the other building blocks are in place, such as reward systems, management style, systems, and a culture that fosters organizational learning. In the following passage, Jack Welch, CEO of GE, describes the learning culture in his organization.[8]

> *GE is unique in that it is ... a very large, multi-business company with a learning culture that has transformed the diversity of its businesses and its size—from what is sometimes perceived as a handicap—into a tremendous competitive advantage .... At the heart of this culture is an understanding that an organization's ability to learn, and translate that learning into action rapidly, is the ultimate competitive business advantage. This appetite for ideas, this lust for learning, was born in the 1980s in a simple ritual called "Work-Out." Work-Out was nothing more complicated than bringing people of all ranks and functions—managers, secretaries, engineers, line workers, sometimes customers and suppliers—together into a room to focus on a problem or an opportunity, and then acting rapidly and decisively on the best ideas developed, regardless of their source. This simple process, and the growing reverence for the better idea that is spawned, is now in the cultural bloodstream of the Company. It is reflected every day in the sharing and learning that goes on constantly among GE businesses and between our businesses and other companies. This Boundaryless Learning culture killed any view that assumed the "GE way" was the only way or even the best way .... GE is a bubbling cauldron of ideas and learning—with tens of thousand of people playing alternate roles of teacher and student.*

PROCEDURE FOR GROUP MEETING: THE LEARNING STYLE INVENTORY

SHARING INDIVIDUAL LEARNING STYLES, OBJECTIVES, AND RESOURCES

(Time Allotted: 1 Hour)

STEP 1.   Individual self-assessment. (5 minutes) Group members should individually review their Learning Style Inventory scores in the light of what they now know about learning styles and their own personal experiences in learning (e.g., their educational background, current job function, and positive and negative learning experiences).

   a.   With this broader perspective, individuals should alter their position on the learning style type grid (Figure 3-3) to reflect their current best judgment as to the learning style that best describes them. *Do this by placing an X on the grid spot that best defines your learning style.* You may agree with the position indicated by your LSI score. If so, place the *X* on top of the point of intersection you calculated earlier with the AC-CE and AE-RO scores. Or you may feel you are really farther away from or closer to the center or even in a different quadrant. If so, move the *X* accordingly.

STEP 2.   Visual representation of class learning styles. (10 minutes)

   a.   Using masking tape for the axes, a learning style grid (see Figure 3-3) large enough for the entire class to stand on should be laid out on the floor of an open area.

   b.   Individual group members should stand on this floor grid in the position corresponding to *X* position they marked in step 1.

   c.   Look around and see how students are distributed on the grid.

STEP 3.   Group discussion on Learning Styles. (20 minutes)

   a.   With their closest neighbors on the grid, students should form small groups of five to six people with homogeneous learning styles.

   b.   Discuss the following questions, ensuring that all members have an opportunity to share their opinions. Please answer questions 2 and 3 based on your personal experience rather than the workbook content. Take notes on the answers so a group representative can report your thoughts to the class as a whole.

   1.   Do your learning profile scores seem valid to you? How do you characterize the way in which you learn? Does your learning style profile relate to the way you went about the recent learning situation you described in the prework assignment?

   2.   What do you think is your greatest strength as a learner?

   3.   What is your greatest weakness?

STEP 4.   Reports to the total group. (25 minutes) A representative of each small group should briefly report to the total group:

   a.   Where each group stood on the grid.

   b.   The main points of each group discussion—the *content* of the meeting.

   c.   Observations about the *process* of the group meeting. How did it feel to be in a group of individuals who had learning styles similar to yours? Was the group's learning style reflected in the way the meeting ran? Do you prefer being in a group with similar or mixed learning styles?

   d.   What connection can you make between this exercise and the readings for today's class?

CREATING A LEARNING COMMUNITY

(Time Allotted: 75 minutes)

STEP 1.   Form learning groups of approximately six members. Diversity should be the criterion for group composition because this will maximize your learning. Try to have at least one person from each of the four learning styles and people of different ages, sexes, races, occupations, and majors. (15 minutes)

STEP 2.   In your learning group discuss your answers to the premeeting question. (25 minutes)
    a. What was your best group learning experience? What was good about it?
    b. What was your worst group learning experience? What made it that way?
    c. In your opinion, what conditions promote adult learning?
    d. How could we turn this classroom into a learning organization?

STEP 3.   The group chooses one or more spokespersons who report the results of the group's discussion of questions c and d.

STEP 4.   The class and the instructor come to a consensus on how they will develop a learning organization in the classroom. (20 minutes)

FOLLOW-UP

One might assume that universities and their classrooms would be prime examples of learning organizations. Most universities, however, focus mainly on individual learning and incremental improvements in the programs they offer students. Distance learning is an exception, an innovation wherein students learn primarily from a professor and fellow students on the Web. It is an example of a new (and controversial) mental model about how students learn. The founders of distance learning questioned the basic assumption that students have to be physically present in a classroom; thus, distance learning is an example of generative learning, which is explained in the following section.

ADAPTIVE AND GENERATIVE LEARNING

For years Chris Argyris has studied the reasoning that underlies our actions and the relationship that exists with learning.[9] He concluded that we have two types of theories: *espoused theories* that we profess to believe ("Do as I say, not as I do") and *theories in action* that actually guide our behavior. We seldom examine the assumptions on which these theories are based. Indeed, we insulate them in defensive routines that prevent us from questioning their validity. An example of a defensive routine is smoothing over the conflict that arises on a team without ever looking carefully at the reasons for the conflict, thereby perpetuating the status quo.

This discovery led Argyris to describe two types of learning. Single-loop learning is like tracking the temperature on a gauge and responding to the feedback that it is too high or too low. An example of single-loop learning, now commonly referred to as *adaptive* learning, can be taken from the personal computer, (PC) industry. Most companies followed the traditional practice of selling through the retail channel (computer stores such as CompUSA and retailers that sell computers) and have since focused on a coping approach—measuring what they were currently doing and improving it incrementally.

They did not, however, question their theories or mental models about the PC business. This is what distinguishes single- and double-loop learning. In double-loop learning, people question the assumptions that underly their theories and ask themselves hard questions. Double-loop learning is currently known as *generative* learning. Generative learning consists of continuous experimentation and feedback in an ongoing analysis of how organizations define and solve problems.[10] As a result, it is a creative response rather than a coping response.

Michael Dell, founder and CEO of Dell Computer Corporation, did not have the option of using the retail channel when he started making and selling computers at age 19 in his college dorm room. Instead, he advertised in PC publications and sold custom-built computers through the mail. Customers saved money because Dell's prices did not include the middleman markup of 10 percent to 15 percent. Dell's direct-sales model is frequently cited as one of the most successful innovations in the PC industry. The company's mental model for doing business is based on maximum efficiency, a cash conversion cycle, meeting customers' needs, and providing excellent service. Most PC companies would agree that these goals are important, but not all of them turn this espoused theory into a theory in action as Dell did. For example, Dell makes each machine to order and maintains only 12 days of inventory. The company's competitors average 30 days of inventory with another 40 days in the distribution channel, which increases their inventory depreciation. Dell's Texas factory can build and pack a computer, complete with software, from scratch to finish in eight hours from the time an order is placed! Its direct link to customers provides the company with extensive firsthand information on customer needs. Dell was the first to sell computers on the Web, and its Web page was geared to a global market at a time when some of its competitors had nothing more than an 800 number on their Web pages. Dell's structure is segmented by customer sets, which are further subdivided when a unit grows too large so as not to lose focus. As Morton Topfer, Dell's vice chairman, states, "Some people still measure themselves by how many people work for them or how many dollars they generate. At Dell success means growing so fast that we take half your business away. It's a different mind set."[11] While the company has had its share of missteps, it has been quick to learn from them and get back on track. Dell's generative learning and mental models have resulted in performance measures that are higher than the industry averages.[12]

Organizations must be careful not to rely on "old programming," obsolete mental maps, and adaptive learning. Companies that are unlikely to survive in a rapidly changing environment not only limit themselves to adaptive learning, they may even punish generative learning. There are numerous examples of employees who leave large, unresponsive corporations to form successful, competing companies where they can put their knowledge and ideas to work. Organizational cultures that stifle creativity and innovation are sometimes accused of playing the "whack the gopher game."[13] People who stick their necks out by asking questions that threaten defensive routines or by making radical suggestions get "whacked."

MANAGING THE LEARNING PROCESS

Some organizations employ parallel learning structures. These are defined as part of the organization that operates alongside the normal bureaucracy with the purpose of increasing organizational learning by creating and/or implementing new thoughts and behaviors. Parallel learning structures consist of "a steering committee and a number of small groups with norms and operating procedures that promote a climate conducive to innovation, learning, and group problem solving" that is not possible within the larger bureaucracy.[14] For example, one fast-growing semiconductor company created a parallel learning structure that focused on organizational adaptation to a competitive and stagnant market. The parallel structure came up with solutions that the larger organization then implemented.

To conclude, let us examine how managers and organizations can explicitly manage their learning process. We have seen that the experiential learning model is useful not only for examining the educational process but also for understanding managerial problem solving and organizational adaptation. But how can an awareness of the experiential learning model and our own individual learning style help improve individual and organizational learning? Two recommendations seem important.

First, learning should be an explicit objective that is pursued as consciously and deliberately as profit or productivity. Managers and organizations should budget time to learn from their experiences. When important meetings are held or important decisions are made, time should be set aside to critique and learn from these events. All too few organizations have a climate that allows for free exploration of such questions as, "What have we learned from this venture?" Usually, active experimentation norms dictate: "We don't have time; let's move on."

This leads to the second recommendation. The nature of the learning process is such that opposing perspectives—action and reflection, concrete involvement, and analytical detachment—are all essential for optimal learning. When one perspective comes to dominate others, learning effectiveness is reduced. From this we can conclude that the most effective learning systems are those that can tolerate differences in perspective. This point can be illustrated by the case of an electronics firm that we have worked with over the years. The firm was started by a group of engineers with a unique product. For several years they had no competitors, and when some competition entered the market, they continued to dominate and do well because of their superior engineering quality. Today it is a different story. They are now faced with stiff competition in their original product area, and, in addition, their very success has caused new problems. They are no longer a small intimate company but a large organization with several plants in the United States and Europe. The company has had great difficulty in responding to these changes because it still responds to problems primarily from an engineering point of view. Most of the top executives in the company are former engineers with no formal management training. Many of the specialists in marketing, finance, and personnel who have been brought in to help the organization solve its new problems feel like "second-class citizens." Their ideas just don't seem to carry much weight. What was once the organization's strength, its engineering expertise, has become to some extent its weakness. Because engineering has flourished at the expense of the development of other organizational functions such as marketing and the management of human resources, the firm is today struggling with, rather than mastering, its environment.

The following chart (Figure 3-4) shows the strengths of the four learning styles and the steps people can take to develop each style. In the "Excess" and "Deficiency" categories, the chart describes what tends to occur when there is too little or too much of a particular learning style in an organization or work unit.

LEARNING POINTS

1. The rapid degree of change in today's business environment means that the ability of a company's managers to learn faster than their competitors is a key competitive advantage. Continuous learning is, therefore, a necessity for both individuals and organizations.

2. A learning organization is an organization skilled at creating, acquiring, and transferring knowledge, and at modifying its behavior to reflect new knowledge and insights.

3. Adult learning
   a. Is based on reciprocity.
   b. Is based on experience.
   c. Has a problem-solving orientation.
   d. Is individualized and self-directed.
   e. Integrates learning and living.
   f. Needs to be applied.

4. The adult learning process is a cycle composed of the following modes: concrete experience, reflective observation, abstract conceptualization, and active experimentation. The process is both concrete and abstract, both reflective and active.

5. Individuals usually see themselves as having a predisposition or a learned facility for one of the four styles in Kolb's learning model: divergence, assimilation, convergence, and accommodation.

Concrete Experience

Accommodator

Strengths: Getting things done
              Leadership
              Risk taking

Excess: Trivial improvements
              Meaningless activity

Deficiency: Work not completed on time
              Impractical plans
              Not directed to goals

To develop Accommodator learning skills,
practice:

- Committing yourself to objectives
- Seeking new opportunities
- Influencing and leading others
- Being personally involved
- Dealing with people

Diverger

Strengths: Imaginative ability
              Understanding people
              Recognizing problems
              Brainstorming

Excess: Paralyzed by alternatives
              Can't make decisions

Deficiency: Lack of ideas
              Can't recognize problems and
              opportunities

To develop Diverger learning skills, practice:

- Being sensitive to people's feelings
- Being sensitive to values
- Listening with an open mind
- Gathering information
- Imagining the implications of uncertain
  situations

Active
Experimentation ————————————————————— Reflective
Observation

Converger

Strengths: Problem solving
              Decision making
              Deductive reasoning
              Defining problems

Excess: Solving the wrong problems
              Hasty decision making

Deficiency: Lack of focus
              No testing of ideas or theories
              Scattered thoughts

To develop Converger learning skills, practice:

- Creating new ways of thinking and doing
- Experimenting with new ideas
- Choosing the best solution
- Setting goals
- Making decisions

Assimilator

Strengths: Planning
              Creating logical models
              Defining problems
              Developing theories

Excess: Castles in the air
              No practical application

Deficiency: Unable to learn from mistakes
              No sound basis for work
              No systematic approach

To develop Assimilator learning skills, practice:

- Organizing information
- Building conceptual models
- Testing theories and ideas
- Designing experiments
- Analyzing quantitative data

Abstract Conceptualization

FIGURE 3-4   **Characteristics of the Four Learning Styles**

6. Learning communities and organizations profit from having members with different learning styles because each style has its own particular strengths.

7. Some of the essential characteristics of learning organizations are systematic problem solving, experimentation, learning from past experience, learning from others, and transferring knowledge.

8. Argyris claims we have two types of theories: espoused theories that we profess to believe and theories in action that actually guide our behavior.

9. People develop defensive routines that prevent them from questioning the validity of the assumptions underlying espoused theories and theories in action.

10. Adaptive learning (single-loop learning) has a *coping* orientation and focuses on solving problems or making incremental improvements in the current way of doing business. It involves refining the prevailing mental model.

11. Generative learning (double-loop learning) has a *creative* orientation and involves surfacing and reviewing the underlying assumptions about the prevailing mental model. Generative learning involves continuous experimentation and feedback in an ongoing analysis of how organizations define and solve problems.

12. Parallel learning structures are part of the organization that operate alongside the normal bureaucracy with the purpose of increasing organizational learning by creating and/or implementing new thoughts and behaviors.

 **FOR MANAGERS**

- Be aware of your personal learning style so that you understand how you approach work issues and how you react to others who have different styles.

- When you are training others (even if it's only breaking in a replacement), remember that people have a tendency to assume that everyone learns the same way they do. Since this is not true, find out how the trainee learns best and adapt your instruction accordingly.

- Ensure that people with different learning styles are valued for their strengths. If you find yourself in a situation where this is not the case, you may want to give the work team or the management group the Learning Style Inventory so that the differences can be understood in a positive manner. The LSI is often used as an opening exercise in team-building efforts. Most project teams benefit from an understanding of the learning cycle—divergence, assimilation, convergence, and accommodation—and a somewhat orderly progression through it. This prevents the frustration that occurs when teams jump ahead or loop back too often.

- In order to create a learning organization, managers should[15]
  - Make time to reflect on work events and assume the stance, "What can we learn from this?" for both themselves and their employees.
  - Treat failure as a natural part of the learning process, which then leads to improvement. Employees should not be afraid to experiment and fail.
  - Avoid allowing an elite group or single point of view to dominate organizational decision making.
  - Create a climate of openness and supportiveness so that employees feel enough psychological safety to raise questions and generate new ideas.
  - Encourage the expression of conflicting ideas and train employees in conflict resolution.
  - Share with employees the data on performance, quality, consumer satisfaction, and competitiveness, so they can reflect on the company situation and make informed decisions.
  - Use cross-functional teams to benefit from different approaches and expertise.
  - Create norms that encourage people to question assumptions and challenge the status quo.
  - Focus on systems thinking by looking for interrelationships, examining entire work processes, and looking beyond symptoms for root causes.

PERSONAL APPLICATION ASSIGNMENT

Please respond to the following question in the upcoming week. Each section of the assignment is worth 4 points, which will be assigned according to the criteria shown.

The topic of this assignment is to think back on a previous learning experience that was significant to you. Choose an experience about which you are motivated to learn more; that is, there was something about it that you do not totally understand, that intrigues you, that made you realize that you lack certain skills, or that was problematical or significant for you. It may have been an academic or a nonformal educational experience (e.g., tennis camp, a seminar, on-the-job training program).

A. *Concrete Experience*
   1. *Objectively* describe the experience (who, what, when, where, how) (2 points).
   2. *Subjectively* describe your feelings, perceptions, and thoughts that occurred *during* (not after) the experience. What did others seem to be feeling? (2 points)

B. *Reflective Observation*
   1. Looking back at the experience, what were the perspectives of the key actors (including you)? (2 points)
   2. Why did the people involved (including you) behave as they did? (2 points)

C. *Abstract Conceptualization*

   1. Relate concepts or theories from the assigned readings or the lecture to the experience. Explain thoroughly how they apply to your experience. Please apply at least two concepts or theories and cite them correctly). (4 points)

D. *Active Experimentation*

   1. What did you learn from this experience? (1 point)
   2. What did you learn about yourslf? (1 point)
   3. What action steps will you take to be more effective in the future? (2 points)

E. *Integration, Synthesis, and Writing*

   1. Did you integrate and synthesize the four sections? (1 point)
   2. Was the Personal Application Assignment well written and easy to understand? (1 point)
   3. Was it free of spelling and grammar errors? (2 points)

ENDNOTES

[1] A. de Geus, "Planning as Learning…At Shell, Planning Means Changing Minds, Not Making Plans," *Harvard Business Review*, 66, no. 2 (1988) 70–75.

[2] J. S. Wyles, J. G. Kunkel, and A. C. Wilson, "Birds, Behavior and Anatomical Evolution," *Proceedings of the National Academy of Sciences, USA*, July 1983.

[3] D. L. Birch. "Thinking About Tomorrow," *Wall Street Journal*, May 24, 1999, R-30.

[4] The Learning Style Inventory is copyrighted by David A. Kolb (1976) and distributed by McBer and Co. 137 Newbury St., Boston, MA 02116. Further information on theory, construction, reliability, and validity of the inventory is reported in *The Learning Style Inventory: Technical Manual*, available from McBer and Co. The theory and its implications are found in Kolb's book, *Experiential Learning: Experience as the Source of Learning and Development* (Upper Saddle River, NJ: Prentice-Hall, 1984).

[5] H. Liam, *Contrary Imaginations* (New York: Schocken Books, 1966).

[6] D. Garvin, "Building a Learning Organization," *Harvard Business Review*, 71, no. 4, (1993) 78–92. M. A. Gephart, V. J., Marsick, M. E. Van Buren, M. S. Spriro, and P. Senge. "Learning Organizations Come Alive," *Training & Development* 50, no. 12 (December, 1996): 34–46.

[7] P. Senge, A. Kleiner, C. Roberts, R. Ross, and B. Smith. *The Fifth Discipline Fieldbook: Strategies and Tools for Building a Learning Organization* (New York: Currency, 1993); and R. M. Fulmer, P. Gibbs, and J. B. Keys. "The Second Generation Learning Organizations: New Tools for Sustaining Competitive Advantage," *Organizational Dynamics* 27, no. 2 (Autumn 1998): 6–21.

[8] J. F. Welch, "*A Learning Company and Its Quest for Six Sigma*." an executive speech reprint, presented at the General Electric Company 1997 Annual Meeting, Charlotte, North Carolina, April 23, 1997, 2–3.

[9] C. Argyris, *Reasoning, Learning, and Action* (San Francisco: Jossey-Bass, 1982).

[10] M. E. McGill, J. W. Slocum, Jr., and D. Lei, "Management Practices in Learning Organizations," *Organizational Dynamics* (Summer 1992): 5–17.

[11] L. M. Fisher, "Inside Dell Computer Corporation: Managing Working Capital," *Strategy & Business* (First Quarter, 1998) 68–75.

[12] Ibid.: and "Michael S. Dell: Nerdy Like A Fox," *Business Week*, January 11, 1999, 74.

[13] This metaphor is attributed to Peter DeLisi of Digital Equipment Corporation in E. H. Schein's article, "How Can Organizations Learn Faster? The Challenge of Entering the Green Room," *Sloan Management Review* (Winter 1993): 85–94.

[14] G. R. Bushe and A.B. Rami Shani, *Parallel Learning Structures: Increasing Innovation in Bureaucracies* (Reading, MA: Addison-Wesley, 1991), pp. 9–10.

[15] These suggestions are taken primarily from R. Tanner Pascale, *Managing on the Edge* (New York: Simon & Schuster, 1991), 236–37 and the works cited in this chapter: Senge's *The Fifth Discipline*; McGill's et al., "Management Practices"; Schein's "Organizations Learn Faster"; and Garvin's "Building a Learning Organization."

Chapter 4

▲▲▲

INDIVIDUAL AND ORGANIZATIONAL MOTIVATION

OBJECTIVES By the end of this chapter, you should be able to:

A. Explain the basic theories of motivation.

B. Understand and recognize McClelland's three needs.

C. Gain insight into your own motive patterns.

D. Explain how managers can direct employee motivation.

E. Identify job characteristics related to motivation.

F. Describe five methods of job redesign.

EMPLOYEE MOTIVATION: CREATING A MOTIVATED WORKFORCE

How do you create a motivated workforce? This question has bedeviled managers and HR professionals for decades.

Some say money is the answer—"Pay 'em more and they'll be motivated." Others say recognition is the key—"Give 'em pats on the back, awards and gifts when they achieve business objectives, and they'll be motivated."

Those with a more Machiavellian view of human nature believe that people are motivated not so much by material rewards but by a desire to increase their power and prestige in the corporate hierarchy. Still others say that the work environment is critical—that providing employees with interesting work and treating them with respect will motivate them.

Each of these theories has some truth to it, of course. But no single theory adequately explains all human motivation. The fact is, human beings are complex creatures. They are not purely economic animals. Nor are they purely political or psychological beings. Most people have a complex set of needs and desires—part material, part social, part emotional—that must be met if they are to be motivated. The answer is never as simple as, "Give them more money" or "Give them more interesting work."

AN URGENT QUESTION

The question of what motivates workers is more urgent today than ever before for at least two reasons.

First, workforce morale is at a low ebb. Rocked by downsizings and job instability, American workers are in a funk. According to a recent survey of 905 workers by Kepner Tregoe Inc., a Princeton, New Jersey–based management consulting firm, only one third (37 percent) feel that their bosses know what motivates them. "We would guess that these individuals are probably less motivated than they were in the past," says T. Quinn Spitzer, CEO of Kepner Tregoe. "They're more concerned, more apprehensive."

Second, the old methods of motivating people—through command-and-control—are no longer viable options. Organizations no longer have layers of management to hover over workers and push them. If companies are to succeed today—in the delayered, service-oriented economy—they must have motivated workers. "We need to motivate people to want to satisfy customers and solve problems, and use more of themselves, which is not just performing a task, but actually being motivated to care about the business and its success," says Michael Maccoby, author of *Why Work? Motivating the New Workforce*.

THE REAL WORLD

Given the limits of the various theories of human motivation, it is useful to turn our attention to the real world and some examples of what is working. Southwest Airlines Co., AptarGroup Inc., and Chick-fil-A Inc. are three companies known to have highly motivated workforces, evidenced by their low turnover rates, high employee productivity, and consistent profitability. Each, it should be noted, puts a high priority on selecting motivated people to begin with.

CHICK-FIL-A

In an industry where turnover rates of 300 percent are the norm—the fast-food industry—Chick-fil-A Inc., the Atlanta-based chicken chain, enjoys a turnover rate of 40 percent. Why so low? According to Huie Woods, vice president for human resources, the following factors make Chick-fil-A a very pleasant place to work.

- **Strong corporate culture** Chick-fil-A's corporate culture is rooted in the biblical principles of its founder. "That doesn't mean we cater to any one class of people or denomination," says Woods. "We just emphasize certain general business practices—fair play, pleasing the customer, a willingness to go the extra mile, hard work ... things you would find in a lot of different places."

  Trust is a critical part of the culture. Employees and store operators are not closely supervised at Chick-fil-A. "As long as you do your job, they're going to leave you alone," says Woods. This lack of "bossy bosses," as Woods calls them, motivates people.
- **A stable work environment** Chick-fil-A has never laid anyone off. It has been able to avoid furloughs because it has successfully pursued a strategy of gradual growth. "We don't grow that fast," says Woods. "We don't add a bunch of employees and then cut back a bunch." Providing a stable work environment has helped Chick-fil-A rid its workplace of one of the worst demotivators: employment insecurity.
- **Good pay** Employees at the home office of Chick-fil-A earn competitive salaries and enjoy company-paid benefits, a pension plan, and profit sharing. Notable but unremarkable. The most interesting aspect of the compensation system—in terms of motivation—is the arrangement with operators. Under the arrangement, the company builds the store for the operator, leases it to her and then splits the profits with her. All that is required financially of the operator is $5,000 in startup capital. "The $5,000 is a token amount," says Woods. "We'll put them in business and split the profits with them. What a tremendous incentive that is!" This pay structure has allowed Chick-fil-A operators to earn twice as much income as operators at some other fast-food establishments.

- **Good perqs** As a private company, Chick-fil-A can offer some perquisites to its employees that would be difficult for a public company to offer. Every year, for instance, the company takes its entire 225-person home office staff—plus their spouses—to the company convention, free of charge. Last year the event was in Bermuda. Next year it will be in Orlando, Florida.

  Chick-fil-A also gives away cars to store operators who increase sales by 20 percent in one year. Last year the firm gave away 18 cars. And store employees—most of whom are high school or college students—can get $1,000 scholarships from the parent company. To qualify, all they need is a recommendation from the store operator and proof of their enrollment in an accredited institution.

SOUTHWEST AIRLINES

Southwest Airlines, Dallas, prides itself on being a fun place to work, having an "amazingly low" turnover rate (7.5 percent) and a highly productive workforce. "We have the most productive workforce in the industry," boasts Sherry Phelps, director of corporate employment. The reason: Its workers are highly motivated. And here's why, according to Phelps.

- **Strong company culture** Southwest is a company that encourages its people to express their individuality. "We don't tell anyone: 'You have to be an entertainer in your job' but, if that is your natural bent, then you can use any creativity and talent that you have to get your job done," says Phelps.

  That is why flight attendants at Southwest have been known to sing the safety instructions and why pilots have been known to tell jokes over the PA system. "Every time that happens, the crowd loves it," says Phelps.

  Southwest's culture also deemphasizes hierarchy. "Elitism isn't looked upon very highly here," says Phelps. "Titles are not that important." She adds, "If somebody in the field has a great idea for something, they can go directly to that department head and say: 'Have you ever thought about this?'"
- **Job stability** Like Chick-fil-A, Southwest Airlines has pursued a strategy of steady growth. "We've never wanted to be the biggest," says Phelps. "We just want to be the best, in the markets we serve."

  And also like Chick-fil-A, that strategy has allowed the company to offer job security. In its 25-year history, Southwest Airlines has never furloughed anyone. "We won't staff up for peak and then furlough people once the peak season is over," says Phelps. Employees have been known to forgo higher pay at other airlines in exchange for more security and a better work environment at Southwest.
- **Opportunities for growth** Because employment at Southwest Airlines is relatively stable, employees can be reasonably sure that they will have the time—and the opportunities—to grow at the firm. Pilots, for instance, can look forward to a steady stream of promotions over the years—from flight engineer to first officer to captain—provided they acquire the requisite skills and flying experience.

  Other employees, likewise, can advance their careers by attending classes at the "university for people," run by Southwest's "people department." The university offers a wide variety of classes designed to "help people reach their personal best," according to Phelps.
- **Incentives** Because Southwest is an airline, it can offer employees one particularly attractive incentive: discounted or free travel.

  Those employees with no absences or late arrivals over a three-month period, for instance, receive two free, space-available airline tickets from the company. They can use these tickets any way they wish, even give them away to a friend. "That is a very valuable incentive," says Phelps. "It costs us nothing, because it's space available. But the value to our people is enormous."
- **Compensation** Southwest Airlines is 83 percent union, so most of its salary and wage structure is determined by union contract. In that respect it is quite similar to the pay structures of other airlines and, therefore, unremarkable.

What is unique about Southwest is its profit-sharing plan. When the company is profitable, as it has been in each of the past 24 years, a certain percentage of that profit is put into the company's profit-sharing fund. That money is initially invested in Southwest stock but, after five years of service, each employee of the company is fully vested and may direct the money into several different funds.

As a result of the investments—and Southwest's excellent financial performance over the years—a number of employees have become millionaires after 18 or 20 years of service.

AptarGroup Inc.

Few employees leave AptarGroup Inc., the Crystal Lake, Illinois–based manufacturer of aerosol valves, finger pumps, and other caps for shampoo and suntan lotion bottles. The turnover rate at the firm is about 10 percent, half the local average, a clear indication of a highly motivated workforce.

What's more, many of those individuals who do leave the firm actually return fairly quickly. "It is very common to see people reapplying to the firm within a year," says Rob Revak, director of human resources at Seaquist Perfect Dispensing, one of Aptar's divisions. Why do they return? Well, there are many reasons, some of which are outlined below.

- **Employment security** While it does not have a formal policy on job security—doing so could "get us into difficulties," according to Larry Lowrimore, vice president, HR—it does have a long track record of providing steady employment.

  When business slows down, as it does from time to time, Aptar prefers to ask people to voluntarily take time off rather than cut jobs. Generally, enough people opt for voluntary time off to tide the company over until business picks up again.
- **Communication and employee involvement** Aptar management believes that open communication and employee involvement in the workplace are central to motivating its workforce. The efforts to achieve these goals occur regularly.

  Each quarter, for instance, the president of each division holds a staff meeting to which all division employees are invited. At the meeting, the president discusses the financial state of the division and assesses how much progress has been made toward business goals. He or she also presents customer feedback that has been collected and asks for employee feedback on business issues. "Our employees know what's going on," says Revak.

  Aptar employees also participate in work teams. "Each team sets its own goals and reports on its progress to senior management," says Revak.

  "That, I think, has helped to motivate the workforce," he adds, "because they set their goals, strive toward them, and are very proud when they achieve them and can present their accomplishments to top management."
- **Recognition** The quarterly staff meetings at AptarGroup also provide an arena for publicly recognizing outstanding employee performance. At each meeting, one "quality employee of the quarter" is selected. The winner receives a couple of awards and some words of congratulation from his or her manager.

  While awards of this kind might not motivate all workers, they certainly do motivate some. "I've seen employees stand up and say, 'Thank you, this is the greatest award I've won in my life,'" recalls Lowrimore. "So, it means something to these people."

  Aptar also offers less formal perqs like pizza parties, extended lunch hours, and brief work shutdowns to show that it appreciates outstanding work.
- **Compensation** Aptar pays competitive salaries and offers a competitive benefits package. "We do an annual salary survey, and we are usually right near the top in terms of average wage," says Revak.

  But in addition to paying good wages, AptarGroup allows employees—all employees—to earn bonuses as well. The formulas used to calculate the bonuses vary from division to division, of course. Some are based on financial results, some on quality measures, and some on safety measures. But they all send the same message, namely: When the company does well, the workers also do well. This is motivating.

- **Opportunities for advancement** In addition to offering above-average compensation, Aptar also offers people opportunities to advance within the company. "I once did a little study of how many people had been promoted in the preceding three years," says Revak. "And although I can't remember the exact percentage, it was an amazing number. So, there is a great deal of opportunity within our company, and I think people realize that."

CONCLUSION

It is interesting to note that none of these companies rely heavily on elaborate new incentive plans or high base salaries to motivate employees. Pay is competitive at all the firms—and there are opportunities for individuals to augment their salaries with bonuses, stock, and profit sharing—but money is not at the center of the motivation strategy.

Rob Revak of AptarGroup may have come the closest to summarizing the consensus of these companies on the issue of motivating when he said, "Money is important, but if I had to rate it on a list of ten items that motivate people, I would put it somewhere in the middle .... Once pay is at a respectable level, then I think those other things, like a good work environment, a safe place to work, a feeling of security, opportunities to progress in the company, and how management treats employees, would be weighed by the average person much more than money."

Source: Donald J. McNerney, "Employee Motivation: Creating a Motivated Workforce," *HR Focus 73*, no. 8 (August 1996): 1(4).

PREMEETING PREPARATION

A. Read "Employee Motivation: Creating a Motivated Workforce."

B. Read the following Instructions for the Test of Imagination.[1]

C. Write stories on four pictures of your choice on the pages following those pictures. Do not take more than five minutes per story. Do this before reading the Topic Introduction.

D. Read the *entire* chapter.

E. What were the significant learning points from the readings?

F. If your instructor has assigned the Robbins Self-Assessment Library, use "What's My Attitude Toward Achievement?" "What Rewards Do I Value Most?" "What's My Job Motivating Potential" and "Do I Want an Enriched Job?"

TEST OF IMAGINATION

Please read the following instructions carefully before turning the page.

An important asset in the world is imagination. This test gives you an opportunity to use your imagination to show how you can create ideas and situations by yourself. In other words, instead of presenting you with ready-made answers from which you choose one, it gives you the chance to show how you can think things up on your own. On the following pages, write out four stories that you make up. To help you get started, there is a series of pictures that you can interpret and around which you can build your stories. When you have finished reading these instructions, turn the page, look at the first picture briefly, and write a story suggested by the picture. To help you cover all the elements of a story plot in the time allowed, you will find four questions spaced out over the page:

1. What is happening? Who are the people?
2. What has led up to this situation? That is, what has happened in the past?
3. What is being thought? What is wanted? By whom?
4. What will happen? What will be done?

Please remember that the questions are only guides for your thinking and need not be answered specifically in so many words. That is, your story should be *continuous and not just a set of answers to these questions*. If you limit yourself to brief answers, there will not be enough material to analyze. Please write a story that fills up the entire page. Do not take more than 5 minutes per story. You should complete the whole test no more than 20 minutes after you begin, although you may finish in less time.

There are no right or wrong stories; any kind of story is acceptable. You have a chance to show how quickly you can imagine and write a story on your own. Do not simply describe the pictures; write a story about them. They are vague and suggestive of many things on purpose and are just to help give you an idea to write about. Try to make your stories interesting and dramatic. Show that you have an understanding of people and can make up stories about human relationships.

If you have read these instructions carefully and understand them, turn the page, look at the picture, and then write your story. Then choose another picture, write out the story it suggests, and so forth.

Just look at the picture briefly (10 to 15 seconds) and write the story it suggests.

Work rapidly; do not spend more than 5 minutes on this story.

1. What is happening? Who are the people?

2. What has led up to this situation? That is, what has happened in the past?

3. What is being thought? What is wanted? By whom?

4. What will happen? What will be done?

When you have finished your story or your time is up, turn to the next picture.

Just look at the picture briefly (10 to 15 seconds) and write the story it suggests.

Work rapidly; do not spend more than 5 minutes on this story.

1. What is happening? Who are the people?

2. What has led up to this situation? That is, what has happened in the past?

3. What is being thought? What is wanted? By whom?

4. What will happen? What will be done?

When you have finished your story or your time is up, turn to the next picture.

Just look at the picture briefly (10 to 15 seconds) and write the story it suggests.

Work rapidly; do not spend more than 5 minutes on this story.

1. What is happening? Who are the people?

2. What has led up to this situation? That is, what has happened in the past?

3. What is being thought? What is wanted? By whom?

4. What will happen? What will be done?

When you have finished your story or your time is up, turn to the next picture.

Just look at the picture briefly (10 to 15 seconds) and write the story it suggests.

Work rapidly; do not spend more than 5 minutes on this story.

1. What is happening? Who are the people?

2. What has led up to this situation? That is, what has happened in the past?

3. What is being thought? What is wanted? By whom?

4. What will happen? What will be done?

When you have finished your story or your time is up, turn to the next picture.

Just look at the picture briefly (10 to 15 seconds) and write the story it suggests.

Work rapidly; do not spend more than 5 minutes on this story.

1. What is happening? Who are the people?

2. What has led up to this situation? That is, what has happened in the past?

3. What is being thought? What is wanted? By whom?

4. What will happen? What will be done?

When you have finished your story or your time is up, turn to the next picture.

Just look at the picture briefly (10 to 15 seconds) and write the story it suggests.

Work rapidly; do not spend more than 5 minutes on this story.

1. What is happening? Who are the people?

2. What has led up to this situation? That is, what has happened in the past?

3. What is being thought? What is wanted? By whom?

4. What will happen? What will be done?

When you have finished your story or your time is up, turn to the next page.

TOPIC INTRODUCTION

Concern over productivity levels raises the question of how well companies can compete in both the domestic and global marketplace. One of the key factors that affects productivity is motivation. Motivation has always been an issue of concern for managers; it has long been recognized as one of the classic managerial functions—planning, motivating, coordinating, controlling, and organizing. There persist, however, some commonsense notions about motivation that are misleading and just plain wrong. First among these notions is the idea that there are persons who are not motivated. This is incorrect. Every living human being is motivated. What managers really mean when they say that a worker is not motivated is that the worker is not motivated to do what the manager wants the worker to do. The same "lazy" employee who just goes through the motions at work may stay up all night working with great intensity on a sports car or devote many hours outside of work to the Girl Scouts. While it is true that some people are more energetic than others, the most important factor to consider is how this energy is directed—toward what goals and objectives. The prime task for managing motivation, therefore, is channeling and directing human energy toward the activities, tasks, and objectives that further the organization's mission.

A second erroneous idea about motivation is that managers "motivate" workers and that motivation is something you do *to* someone else. Motivation is an *internal* state that directs individuals toward certain goals and objectives. Managers cannot directly influence this *internal* state; they can only create expectations on the part of employees that their motives will be satisfied by doing the organization's work and provide the rewards that satisfy the employee's needs.

This distinction may appear subtle, but it is important because failure to understand it often leads managers to attempt to use motivation to manipulate employees. Manipulation is a very inefficient way of managing motivation because it requires that you as a manager maintain control of the carrot and stick. As a result you must spend time scheming about how you will motivate those you supervise on a day-to-day basis. A more effective way of managing motivation is through understanding. If you understand the needs and objectives of those whom you supervise, you can work with them to develop an equitable psychological contract that recognizes their particular desires and creates conditions where these motives can be satisfied in the work setting. The same is true of your own motivation. By becoming more aware of your own motives and desires, you can better organize your work and life activities to achieve satisfaction and productivity.

Our understanding of human motivation has increased substantially over the past few decades. Simplistic theories arguing that people worked primarily for money or primarily for social gratification have been replaced with more complex theories of human nature. Even so, no single theory is adequate to explain human motivation. Effective managers have an understanding of the various theories in this chapter (and the *Reader*) and rely upon those that are most helpful in a given situation. Some of these theories are *content* theories because they attempt to identify the factors unique to an individual that energize, direct, sustain, and stop behavior. Content theories focus on the specific internal needs that motivate people.

MASLOW'S HIERARCHY OF NEEDS

Maslow based his theory on two beliefs concerning human motivation.[2] First, human needs can be viewed in a hierarchical fashion—from physiological, to security, to social belonging, to self-esteem, and finally to self-actualization. Lower-order needs (physiological and security needs) must be satisfied to some extent before higher-order needs (social belonging, self-esteem, and self-actualization) become activated. Second, a satisfied need is no longer a motivator of behavior.

Maslow's hierarchy is not accepted as a universal theory that applies to all cultures; it reflects the U.S. cultural background of Maslow and his subjects.[3] Since culture partially determines an individual's needs, it is not surprising that international research using Maslow's hierarchy yields conflicting results.[4] While the order of the hierarchy is the same in some cultures, it varies for others. For example, the security need is more important than self-actualization in Greece and Japan. Social needs are more important in collectivist African countries than the self-esteem and self-actualization needs that are more figural in an individualistic culture like the United States. Social needs are also more important in the Scandinavian countries where quality of life is generally more highly valued than career success. In a study of eight different countries, however, self-actualization was more important and security was less important to highly educated people than to their less educated colleagues.[5] When working with people from another culture, managers should be aware that needs and their relative importance may differ. Even though Maslow's theory is not universal, it is a good starting point for understanding the various needs people bring to the workplace and a reminder that not everyone has the same needs we do.

HERZBERG'S TWO-FACTOR THEORY

Herzberg refined Maslow's ideas and suggested that dissatisfaction and satisfaction are two separate continuums.[6] The fact that demotivators are absent does not mean that people will be motivated. *Hygiene factors*—extrinsic factors such as the supervisor, attractiveness of the physical facilities, salary, company policy and administration, working conditions, and interpersonal relations—create dissatisfaction if they are absent. Their presence, however, does not create positive motivation. A second set of intrinsic factors—*motivators* such as the work itself, achievement, challenge, responsibility, advancement, growth, and recognition—are necessary to stimulate positive motivation.

Once we have met a person's hygiene needs, "more of the same" yields marginal benefits. Some studies indicate that providing extrinsic rewards actually takes the intrinsic pleasure out of performing a task.[7] Money is very motivating to people who have none; once people's income level is satisfactory, however, pay cannot be the only motivator. In a survey of 1,800 American workers, the following items were ranked more highly than pay as major motivators for employees: recognition of the importance of personal and family time, organizational direction, opportunities for personal growth, ability to challenge the way things are done, satisfaction from everyday work, and employee participation in planning organizational change.[8]

Herzberg's theory is not universal; research in other countries did not produce the same results as in the United States. In New Zealand, for example, supervision and interpersonal relationships were viewed more as motivators than hygiene factors.[9] While Herzberg's point is valid that removing demotivators is not enough to motivate employees, what constitutes demotivators and motivators will vary across cultures.

McCLELLAND'S THEORY OF NEEDS

Psychologists, most notably David McClelland, have made a great deal of progress over the past 40 years in scientifically measuring and defining human motives.[10] McClelland began by looking not at external action but at the way a person thinks and feels. He used the Thematic Apperception Test (TAT), which you completed in the premeeting preparation section, to record thought samples that could then be studied and grouped according to the dominant concerns, or themes, expressed in the stories. He and his coworkers were able to group the responses into three broad categories, each representing an identifiable human motive: need for affiliation (n-Aff), need for power (n-Pow), and need for achievement (n-Ach).

Most people, McClelland found, have a degree of each of these motives in their thoughts but seldom in the same strength. A person may be high in the need for affiliation, low in the need for achievement, and moderate in the need for power. Such people would tend to think more about friendship than about doing a good job or controlling others. Their motivation to work will be of a different order than that of the employee who is high in achievement motivation and low in affiliation and power motivations.

McClelland states that these motives are learned from our parents and our culture. He discovered different motive patterns for different cultures. For example, the power motive is very pronounced in Latin America where power and control are dominant cultural themes. Because of its projective nature, the TAT test can be readily used with people from different cultures and has been used successfully in various cultures. Nevertheless, Hofstede notes that the word *achievement* is not readily translated into all languages, and the need to achieve requires a certain tolerance of risk and concern with career success that is not found equally in all cultures.[11]

n-Power

The need for power is defined as "the need to influence and lead others, and be in control of one's environment." A high need for power is very common among middle- and upper-level managers because, by definition, their job is to influence people and organizations. A strong need for power can be satisfied by working in professions and positions that allow people to influence others, such as executives, politicians, labor leaders, police officers, military officers, and lawyers. There are two faces of n-Power. The positive face is *socialized power*, which is used for the good of others. People motivated by this need seek power to make their club, department, or organization function better so that others (members, customers, and employees) benefit. Characteristic actions that allow this group to satisfy their need for power are playing competitive sports as an adult and occupying officer roles in the organizations to which they belong. They tend to be more emotionally mature than people with a need for personalized power and are more hesitant to use their power in a manipulative fashion. They are less defensive and selfish, are more willing to take advice from experts, have a longer-range view, and accumulate fewer material possessions. They are more likely to use a participative coaching style; rather than creating dependence in their followers, they empower them.[12]

The negative face is *personalized power*, an unsocialized concern for personal dominance. People with a personalized power concern have little inhibition or self-control, and they exercise power impulsively. According to McClelland and Burnham, U.S. subjects with a high need for personalized power tend to drink too much and become nasty drunks, engage in casual sexual exploitation (scoring), and collect prestige symbols like expensive cars and large offices. They satisfy their needs vicariously by watching contact sports or violent television shows or films, and using alcohol, drugs, or mystical rituals in a way that makes them feel more powerful.[13] Dictators and people who establish fiefdoms at work are motivated by this type of n-Power.

A manager's effectiveness depends not only on his or her need for power but also on the other values he or she brings to the job. John Andrew's study of two Mexican companies is striking in this regard.[14] Both companies had presidents who scored high in n-Power, but one firm was stagnating whereas the other was growing rapidly. The manager of the growing company, although high in n-Power, was also high in n-Achievement and was dedicated to letting others in the organization satisfy their own needs for achievement by introducing improvements and making decisions on their own. The stagnant company, although well capitalized and enjoying a favorable market, was constantly in turmoil and experienced a high rate of turnover, particularly among its executives. In this company, the president's high n-Power, coupled with highly authoritarian values, led him to make all the decisions himself, leaving no room for individual responsibility on the part of his personnel. A comparison of motivation scores of upper-level managers of the two companies showed that the dynamic company's managers were significantly higher in n-Achievement than were those of the stagnant company, who tended to be more concerned with power and compliance than with individual responsibility and decision making.

The results of research have shown that a manager needs a reasonably high n-Power to function as a leader.[15] Whether he or she uses it well depends in large part on the other values and motives the individual holds. Being high in n-Power does not automatically make one autocratic or authoritarian. Good leadership may indeed be a function of the manager's ability to understand his or her need for power and to use it in creative, satisfying ways.

n-Affiliation

The need for affiliation (n-Aff) is "the desire for friendly and close interpersonal relationships." People high in n-Affiliation prefer cooperative situations to competitive situations, and they seek relationships involving a high degree of mutual understanding. As with the power motive, there are two faces of this need. The positive face of n-Affiliation, *affiliative interest*, is a concern for interpersonal relationships but not at the expense of goal-oriented behavior. People with this need value good relationships and work at maintaining them, but their concern with relationships does not prevent them from giving negative feedback or making tough decisions.

The negative face of n-Affiliation is *affiliative assurance*, a concern with obtaining assurance about the security and strength of one's relationships and avoiding rejection. According to Boyatzis,[16] managers with a strong need for affiliative assurance look for proof that others are committed to them and avoid issues and conflicts that might threaten the stability of the relationship. They seek approval from others and devote more energy to maintaining relationships than to achieving work goals. They worry about being disliked.

Although a high need for affiliation is found more often in supervisors than high-level leaders, people with a need for affiliative interest make a valuable contribution by creating a friendly, cooperative atmosphere at work. High n-Affiliation managers spend more time communicating with others than do managers high in either n-Power or n-Achievement[17] and are good at creating the networks that are crucial for success in many organization.[18]

n-Achievement

The need for achievement (n-Ach) is "a need to accomplish goals, excel, and strive continually to do things better." Whereas a high need for achievement seems absolutely necessary for entrepreneurs, it is not always functional for managers to be extremely high in this motive. Executives high in n-Achievement tend to have fewer meetings than other executives and tend to want to work alone, despite the fact that many organizational problems would be better solved by collaborative effort.[19] As with executives high in n-Power, their effectiveness as managers depends more on their other values than on their motivation alone.

Persons high in n-Achievement want to take personal responsibility for their success or failure, like to take calculated (moderate) risks, and like situations in which they get immediate, concrete feedback on how well they are doing. Their need for feedback keeps them from getting too involved in open-ended exploratory situations with no concrete goal and no benchmarks along the way. Their sense of personal responsibility will keep them from delegating authority unless they value developing subordinates. They will be task oriented, but the kind of climate they create in an organization will be healthier if their strong n-Achievement is balanced by moderate needs for power and affiliation.

Managerial Profiles

Successful managers of large organizations exhibit self-control and a strong need for power that is greater than their need to be liked.[20] These managers use their power to achieve organizational goals, practice a participative coaching style when they interact with subordinates, and do not spend much time developing close relationships with others.[21] In AT&T's longitudinal study of managers, people with this high n-Power and low n-Affiliation profile were promoted to a higher level than managers with other profiles. In small or decentralized companies, however, success depends more on a high need for achievement than a high need for power. The nature of such companies with their focus on constant improvement and cost-efficient growth is a better fit for people with a high need for achievement.[22] However, a high need for both power and achievement has been found in effective low- and middle-level managers.[23]

People have very different mental maps when it comes to motivation. But this is not the only factor that determines their behavior. Behavior is also a function of the person and the environment. McClelland's theory interacts with the environment in the following way: $T = M \times E \times R$.[24] T is the tendency to act in these three ways (to fulfill needs for power, affiliation, or achievement). M is the strength of the individual's motivation for power, affiliation, and achievement). E is the individual's perceived expectation that action in terms of one or more of these motives will be rewarded. R is the reward value of the power, affiliation, and achievement rewards that he or she expects to get. Thus, individuals act to maximize their satisfaction. While M refers to the individual's motivation, E and R refer to the individual's perception of the environment.

The equation in the preceding paragraph is based on the assumption that employees make conscious choices about their behavior at work. They calculate whether a certain level of effort will result in a particular goal; they determine whether the reward is worth the effort, and they also compare whether their efforts and rewards are comparable to those of other people. These decisions, which are based on employees' perception of the environment and previous experiences, affect their behavior and level of productivity.

These are the assumptions that underlie the second category of motivation theories, *process* theories that attempt to describe how personal factors and environmental factors interact and influence each other to produce certain kinds of behavior. Examples of these theories are expectancy theory, equity theory, reinforcement theory, and goal setting.

EQUITY THEORY

The equity that people perceive in their situation also influences motivation. If they discover that another employee who does the same job or produces the same results is paid more highly, they are likely to reduce their effort. According to equity theory,[25] employees perceive what they receive from a job (outputs such as pay, bonuses, job security, promotions, recognition, etc.) in relation to what they contribute (inputs such as time, skills, creativity, effort, etc.). They compare their own input-output ratio with (1) relevant others, (2) system policies and precedents, and (3) criteria related to the "self," such as previous jobs or family commitments. When inequity exists and they are either overrewarded or underrewarded, people will attempt to correct this situation. Those who are overrewarded will increase production or the quality of their work; those who are underrewarded will decrease production or quality, increase absenteeism, and perhaps even resign. When compensation systems are perceived as equitable, employees report greater levels of job satisfaction, organizational commitment, and trust in their supervisors.

EXPECTANCY THEORY

Expectancy theory assumes that motivation is a function of three linkages: (1) the effort-performance expectation that if a person makes an effort, it will result in good performance, (2) the performance-outcome expectation that good performance will result in a particular outcome or reward, and (3) the valence (value) of the reward to the person. If a student believes that studying 10 hours for a test will make it possible for her to do extremely well on an exam, she will be more motivated to study than if she has no previous experience with hard work paying off in the classroom. Her professor's exams cannot be so difficult that students think their efforts will be worthless. Our student must also believe that her good performance on an exam will be fairly graded and will yield an A outcome. If her professor has a reputation for being a biased, careless grader, our student will not put forth much effort because the payoff is uncertain. Finally, she has to think an A is a good thing, a reward that's worth her effort. If all these linkages are in place, she will be motivated. Note how much the professor's actions affect the students. The same is true in the workplace, which is why this theory has great practical value.[26]

SOCIAL REINFORCEMENT THEORY

Social reinforcement theory is another process theory that is useful for managers. This theory ignores internal motives and focuses on learned behavior. People learn to continue behavior that is rewarded and to suppress behavior that is punished. It is important for managers to understand the effect of their behavior and policies on subordinates and to know whether it is perceived as a reward or a punishment. For example, highly productive employees are sometimes "rewarded" only by being assigned extra work that less responsible employees are not completing. When this occurs, the productive employee may perceive this as working more for the same salary (i.e., a punishment), while irresponsible employees are "rewarded" by having less work to do. As a result, managers sometimes lose their high performers due to burnout or equity complaints. The main tenets of reinforcement theory are that managers should reinforce desired behavior and extinguish (by ignoring) or punish undesirable behavior.[27]

GOAL-SETTING THEORY

One of the easiest ways to spur motivation is through goal setting. Goals provide direction and a sense of how much effort is needed to be successful. There are several important lessons about goal setting: (1) specific goals increase performance, (2) compared to easy goals, difficult goals that are accepted by employees result in higher performance, (3) feedback leads to higher performance than nonfeedback,[28] and (4) people are more committed to goals that are made public and that they themselves set.[29]

PROCEDURE FOR GROUP MEETING: TAT MOTIVE ANALYSIS

The purpose of this exercise is to help you identify (but not score in detail) the motivational themes you expressed in your TAT stories. (Time Allotted: 1 Hour)

STEP 1.   Form trios, preferably with people in your learning group. Have one member read his or her first story to the other two members. Search the list of criteria that follows to determine which of them are present. Score the imagery in the story and record it on the accompanying Individual Scoring Form for Test of Imagination. Discuss the criteria matching the imagery in the story as a trio once the person finishes reading ("I marked power because the story matched criteria 3 when the boss was giving the subordinate the third degree and trying to catch her in a lie"). The second member reads his or her first story, and the process is repeated until all stories of each trio member have been scored and recorded on the form. Budget your time so all stories are heard. (40 minutes)

In approaching the task, you should keep several things in mind. It is possible for a story to contain none or all of McClelland's three motives, as well as other motivational themes such as sex, aggression, hunger, and so forth. The TAT pictures and your responses are meant to be stimuli for reflection and discussion, not necessarily an absolute measure of your motives. In addition, you are not expected to become expert scorers but to become familiar with general patterns. Finally, be wary of the pressure to reach consensus in your trio meetings. Each listener will, in fact, hear another's story through his or her own motivational filter. For example, a person high in the need for affiliation may well "see" considerable affiliation imagery in someone else's story. Only the achievement motive can be inferred; criteria for the other two motives have to be explicitly stated. Be careful not to read too much into the stories—either it explicitly meets the criteria or don't score the imagery.

The point of this exercise is that people do have different needs and that they do consequently see the world in different ways. A manager's task is to become aware of and effectively integrate these real differences.

Achievement motivation is present in a story when any one of the following occurs:

1.   Someone in the story is concerned about a *standard of excellence*. The individual wants to win or to do well in a competition. The person has self-imposed standards for a good performance or is emotionally involved in attaining an achievement goal. Standards of excellence can be inferred by the use of words such as *good* or *better* or similar words when used to evaluate performance.

2. Someone in the story is involved in a *unique accomplishment*, such as an invention or an artistic creation. Here the standard of excellence can be inferred and need not be explicitly stated.

3. Someone in the story is involved in a *long-term goal*, such as an invention or an artistic creation. Here the standard of excellence can be inferred and need not be explicitly stated.

Power motivation is present in a story when any of the following occurs:[30]

1. People *describe actions in which they express their power*. For example, strong, forceful actions that affect others, such as assaults, attacks, chasing or catching, verbal insults, threats, accusations, reprimands, crimes, sexual exploitation, and gaining the upper hand all indicate the presence of the power motive.

2. There are statements about someone *giving help, assistance, advice, or support that has not been solicited* by the other person.

3. There are statements that indicate that someone is *trying to control another person through regulating his or her behavior, or through searching for information* that would affect another person's life or actions. Examples of the last category are searching, investigating, and checking up on someone.

4. Someone is *trying to persuade, influence, convince, bribe, make a point, or argue* with another person, but not with the motive of reaching agreement or understanding. Mention of a disagreement is not sufficient to score the power motive here; there must be action or a desire for action that has the objective of changing another's opinion.

5. Someone is *trying to impress* another person or the world at large. Or someone in the story is described as being concerned about his or her reputation or position. Creative writing, publicity, trying to win an election or identifying closely with another person running for office, and seeking fame and notoriety can all be scored for power.

6. Someone does something that *arouses strong positive or negative emotions* in others, such as pleasure, delight, awe, gratitude, fear, respect, jealousy, and so forth.

Affiliation motivation is present when any of the following occurs:

1. Someone in the story is concerned about establishing, maintaining, or restoring a *positive emotional relationship* with another person. Friendship is the most basic kind of positive emotional relationship, and to mention that two characters in the story are friends would be a minimum basis for scoring imagery. Other relationships, such as father-son or lover-lover, should be scored *only* if they have the warm, compassionate quality implied in the definition given.

2. There is a statement that *one person likes or wants to be liked* by someone else or that someone has some similar feeling about another. Moreover, if a close interpersonal relationship has been disrupted or broken, imagery can be scored if someone feels sorrow or grief or takes action to restore the relationship.

3. Also score if the story mentions such *affiliative activities* as parties, reunions, visits, or relaxed small talk as in a bull session. However, if the affiliative nature of the situation is explicitly denied in the story, such as by describing it as a business meeting or an angry debate, imagery is not scored. Friendly actions such as consoling or being concerned about the well-being or happiness of another person are scored, except when these actions are culturally prescribed by the relationship (e.g., father-son). In other words, there must be evidence that the nurturing activity is not motivated solely by a sense of obligation.

STEP 2. Discuss motive scores. (20 minutes)

When your trio has finished scoring your stories, please discuss the following questions:

1. How much similarity or difference was there in your group concerning the dominant motivational concerns expressed in the stories? Of what significance is this similarity or difference? Does it affect the way your group functions?

2. In what ways did the motivational concerns you expressed in the stories agree or disagree with the image you held of yourself *before* you took the test? Of what significance are any differences?

3. What kinds of things cause one person to express affiliation concerns, another person to express power concerns, and a third to express achievement concerns in response to the same picture? Consider immediate (e.g., "He hadn't had anything to eat all day") as well as historical (e.g., "She flunked math in high school") factors.

4. Were there any particular reasons that you chose the four pictures you did? In other words, you chose not to respond to two pictures in particular—why? Did others choose the same pictures as you?

5. What motives do you think are relevant or important within the context of a job?

6. Of what value, if any, do you feel are projective techniques such as the TAT in assessing human motivation? What other alternatives might be feasible or better?

7. What connections can you make between this exercise and the readings?

Individual Scoring Form for Test of Imagination

Make a hatch mark every time you hear imagery that matches a criteria in the left column.

Criteria	Stories for Person A	Stories for Person B	Stories for Person C
Story Number			
Criteria for Scoring			
Achievement Imagery			
Concern with standard of excellence			
Unique accomplishment			
Long-term goal			
Power Imagery			
Forceful actions expressing power			
Unsolicited help, advice			
Controlling			
Persuading, influencing, etc.			
Impressing			
Arousing strong emotions			
Affiliation Imagery			
Working toward a positive emotional relationship			
Liking or wanting to be liked			
Affiliative activities			
Other Motives Present (specify)			

Summary	Person A	Person B	Person C
Number of stories with:			
Achievement			
Power			
Affiliation			

85

THE MOTIVATED CLASSROOM

The preceding chapter contained a group exercise devoted to transforming your class into a learning organization. To make that a reality, we also need to think about the role motivation plays in a learning organization. The purpose of this exercise is to apply the lessons of motivation theory and practice to this course by devising a motivation program.

STEP 1.   Divide into groups of five to six (your learning groups). Each group will be assigned at least one (depending on the number of groups) of the following topics to discuss and apply. (20–30 minutes)
   a. Maslow's Hierarchy
   b. Herzberg's Two-Factor Theory
   c. McClelland's Need Theory
   d. Goal-Setting Theory
   e. Equity Theory
   f. Expectancy Theory
   g. Social Reinforcement Theory

Please answer these questions:

1. How does this theory relate to the classroom and the learning organization we want to create?

2. Are there any practices that companies are successfully using to create a motivated workforce that you think we should borrow?

3. Based on the discussion so far, brainstorm some ways to motivate yourself and your classmates. Decide on your top recommendation. Use these criteria to help you decide: Remember that the instructor should not be the sole source of motivation and make sure your recommendation is feasible and easy to implement.

STEP 2.   A representative from each group briefly explains how the group's theory applies to the classroom and presents the group's recommendation. (20–30 minutes)

STEP 3.   The class and the professor decide which recommendation(s) they want to adopt. (15 minutes)

 **FOLLOW-UP**

There is a variety of methods companies can use to influence employees, as we saw in the chapter vignette. Their effectiveness varies with different levels and different types of employees so it is important that the program fit the people. The "carrots" that most of them hold out are recognition, participation, quality of worklife, or money. Companies cannot compete without motivated employees. CEO Howard Schultz attributes Starbucks' growth and success to sharing company profits in the form of stock options (Bean Stock) and health insurance benefits for both full- and part-time workers. To Schultz's knowledge, no other company provides benefits like these, but the payoff for Starbucks is low turnover and high productivity. "If people relate to the company they work for, if they will form an emotional tie to it, and buy into its dreams, they will pour their hearts into making it better."[31]

Managers cannot influence employee motivation unless they understand what motivates the individual employees. This is easier said than done. One study asked workers and supervisors to rank 10 job factors in order of their importance to the workers. Those factors that the workers ranked first, second, and third—appreciation for their work, being in on things, and sympathy for personal problems—were ranked eighth, ninth, and tenth by their supervisors! The supervisors mistakenly assumed that good wages, job security, and promotion were most important to the workers. People often hold mistaken assumptions about what motivates others.

While individuals come to organizations with previously learned motive patterns and unique needs, managers can affect how employees perceive their environment. They shape and direct motivation by establishing expectations and rewards that tap into employee motives and further the organization's goals. The manager's task is to make sure there is a fit and a direct link—between employee needs and rewards, between performance and rewards, and between employees and jobs. The better the fit, the higher employee motivation.

The intrinsic motivation of employees is very important, but job motivation is also affected by the situations in which workers find themselves, and, in particular, the way in which their jobs are designed. Based on what we know about motivation, alienation and worker/commitment, job situations that motivate people have the following characteristics:

1. **Skill variety** The degree to which a job requires a range of personal competencies and abilities in carrying out the work.
2. **Task identity** The degree to which a job requires completion of a "whole" and identifiable piece of work, that is, doing a good job from beginning to end with a visible outcome.
3. **Task significance** The degree to which the job is perceived by the employee as having a substantial impact on the lives of other people, whether those people are within or outside of the organization.
4. **Autonomy** The degree to which the job provides freedom, independence, and discretion to the employee in scheduling the tasks and in determining the procedure to be used in carrying out the task.
5. **Job feedback** The degree to which carrying out the job related tasks provides the individual with direct and clear information about the effectiveness of his or her performance.[32]

Skill variety, task identity, and task significance are geared towards increasing the sense of meaningfulness that is threatened whenever jobs are divided into small, repetitive segments. Granting employees autonomy over their jobs encourages them to feel responsible (powerful and in control) for the outcome of their work and reduces legalistic approaches to work, for example, "That's not my job" or "If they're gonna give me a robot's job to do, I'm gonna do it like a robot! Anyway, it just lowers my production record to get up and point out someone else's error."[33] Job feedback allows employees to receive immediate feedback from the work itself, not from a supervisor. This relates to one of the conditions McClelland found to be most favorable for people with high needs for achievement—immediate concrete feedback that allows them to adjust their performance to meet their personal and/or organizational goals. Jobs that involve dealing with others and have friendship opportunities are ways of encouraging social belonging and combating social isolation.

Jobs with these characteristics are termed "enriched." In their Job Characteristics Enrichment Model, which appears in Figure 4-1, Hackman and Oldham[34] show that the positive outcomes of job enrichment characteristics are high internal work motivation, high-quality work performance, high satisfaction with the work, and low absenteeism and turnover. However, these outcomes occur at maximum level only when all three of the critical psychological states are experienced: (1)

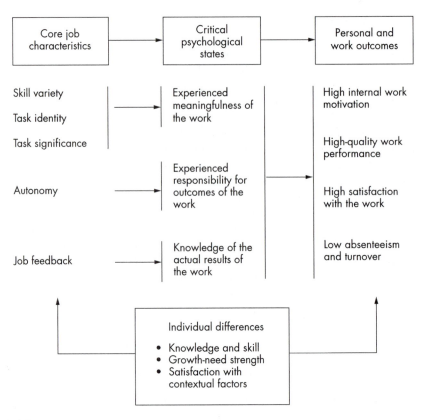

FIGURE 4-1   Job Characteristics Enrichment Model
Source: J. R. Hackman and G. R. Oldham, *Work Redesign* (Reading, MA: Addison-Wesley Publishing Co., Inc., 1980). Adapted from p. 90. Reprinted with permission of the publisher.

experienced meaningfulness of the work, (2) experienced responsibility for the work outcomes, and (3) knowledge of the actual results of the work. Hackman and Oldham also note that there are three types of individual differences that must be taken into consideration when planning job redesign projects. The first is the *knowledge and skill of the employee*—is the employee capable of performing an enriched job? The second is *growth-needs strength*, which refers to the individual's personal need for learning, self-development, and challenge. People with low growth needs may well prefer repetitive jobs to enriched ones. The final individual difference is *satisfaction with contextual factors*. Job redesign efforts are unlikely to be successful if employees are dissatisfied with other conditions at work.

Ensuring that the work situation is one that employees find motivating and involving is a major, ongoing task of managers. Because of the close relationship between well-designed jobs and productivity, it is an area that managers and organizations cannot afford to overlook. It is possible to design jobs that are more congruent with human needs and motivation. The major ways of doing so are briefly described as follows:

1. *Job rotation programs* that move people from one job to another to decrease their boredom and allow them to learn different skills.
2. *Job enlargement policies* increase the number of tasks performed by an individual. In an assembly-line example, a worker would perhaps install an entire door panel rather than securing only one part of the door. Herzberg called the addition of interrelated tasks "horizontal job loading."[35]

Job enlargement can meet employees' motivational needs because it allows more ownership over a product or process and decreases monotony. It also provides an opportunity for workers to feel more competent, since they may get to use more of their skills. Being responsible for a larger task may increase the meaningfulness of the job in the worker's eyes.

However, remember the comment of one critic, "You combine seven boring jobs and what do you get?"

3. *Job enrichment* methods attempt to change the nature of the job by broadening responsibilities, giving more autonomy for decision making, creating client systems and direct feedback systems, and generally enlarging the scope of jobs. Herzberg called this type of job design "vertical job loading" because it also includes tasks formerly performed by someone at a higher level—planning and control functions.[36] For example, a sales support clerk who formerly handled only one piece of the paperwork for the entire sales staff is now given responsibility for all paperwork in one district. He is encouraged to deal directly with the sales staff and quickly becomes an important resource for them. He also has discretionary control over the scheduling of his work and the responsibility for making sure he has made no errors. A feedback system is established so he can gauge both the quality and quantity of his output. Both contact with the sales staff and the monitoring of his work were formerly performed by his supervisor.

What is motivating about job enrichment? It resolves the problems of meaninglessness, powerlessness, and isolation factors that cause worker alienation[37] rather than commitment.

Job enrichment not only has the same motivational advantages as job enlargement, but the effects of job enrichment are stronger, and enrichment has the added benefit of granting workers autonomy. Autonomy allows people to utilize even more skills and to exercise their creativity and capacity to learn and develop. Research on work redesign programs indicates that they do reduce absenteeism and turnover; however, there are mixed results on productivity. Some job enrichment efforts result in higher productivity, while others do not.[38]

4. *Sociotechnical system* interventions attempt to match the necessary technology of the job with the social needs of the employees. Their goal is to produce a fit or integration of these two components. It's noteworthy that the basic unit of work design here is usually the group rather than the individual. Job rotation, enlargement, and enrichment focus upon individual rather than group needs.[39]

The most common example of sociotechnical systems are autonomous work teams. Such teams are totally responsible for assigning the work, determining the work schedule, work process, quality control procedures, reward structure, and so on. One of the most famous examples of autonomous work teams was found in the Volvo plant in Uddevalla, Sweden.[40] Instead of using an assembly line, the cars remained stationary while teams of eight to ten workers assembled three entire cars a day. This job design reduced tedium because the workers did a variety of jobs that required expanded skills. Furthermore, the workers experienced both greater task identity and control over their work.

The team approach at Uddevalla resulted in increased quality and satisfaction, but productivity and absenteeism were still a problem.[41] The teams required fifty labor hours to build a car, which is twice the hours needed at Volvo's Belgium plant. The Japanese can build a car in less than twenty hours. Volvo decided to shut down the Uddevalla plant and their Kalmar plant, which also used autonomous work teams, in order to cut costs. Many car manufacturers are utilizing some form of work teams, but they vary in terms of how many tasks they are responsible for and how much autonomy is granted to the teams.

Sociotechnical systems have the advantages of all the previous design systems plus the added benefit of group membership. Interdependent work teams anchor people firmly within a social system, thus avoiding isolation. Furthermore, groups are more creative and productive than are individuals when it comes to complex technology.

5. *Self-managed work teams*, highlighted in Chapter 9, share many similarities with sociotechnical systems. Both emphasize skill variety, task identity, task significance, autonomy, job feedback, and the social belonging that comes from group membership. In sociotechnical systems, however, more attention is specifically concentrated on balancing technical and human systems. Self-managed work teams decide how they will accomplish the goals for which they are responsible and allocate the necessary tasks. They are responsible for planning, scheduling, organizing, directing, controlling, and evaluating their own work process, which is usually an entire process or product. Some teams select and evaluate their own members.

None of the work redesign programs described in this section should be seen as a quick fix for organizations. Some programs succeed while other do not. The reasons for failure sometimes have more to do with the way programs are implemented than with the particular merits of the program in question. When implemented successfully, however, the workplace environment fosters and rewards employee motivation.

LEARNING POINTS

1. Motivation is not something that is "done" to other people. It is an internal state that directs individuals toward certain goals.
2. Individuals are motivated by different needs. Managers sometimes have mistaken assumptions about what motivates their employees.
3. The manager's job is to understand and channel the motivation employees already possess and direct it toward tasks that further the organization's objectives.
4. Maslow developed a hierarchy of needs—physiological, security, affiliation, self-esteem, and self-actualization. Lower-order needs must be satisfied before higher-order needs become motivators. Once a need is satisfied, it no longer motivates behavior.
5. Herzberg identified the extrinsic factors that cause dissatisfaction if they are absent. He called them hygiene factors (supervisor, attractiveness of the physical facilities, salary, company policy and administration, working conditions, and interpersonal relations). Intrinsic factors, which he called motivators, are necessary to stimulate positive motivation (the work itself, achievement, challenge, responsibility, advancement, growth, and recognition).
6. McClelland's theory of motivation focuses on three needs that are learned from one's culture and family: affiliation, achievement, and power. Almost everyone has these needs in varying degrees.
7. We can measure need strength and motive pattern (scores for affiliation, power, and achievement) with the Thematic Apperception Test (TAT). Job performance is affected by people's motive patterns as well as by the values that individuals hold.
8. There are two faces, positive and negative, to n-Power (socialized and personalized) and n-Affiliation (interest and assurance).
9. According to McClelland, high achievers
   a. Like to set their own goals.
   b. Tend to avoid either extremely difficult or extremely easy goals.
   c. Prefer tasks that provide immediate feedback on their performance.
10. In addition to internal need states, motivation is also affected by the environment. $T = M \times E \times R$, where T = tendency to act, M = strength of motive, E = expectation that motive will be rewarded, and R = reward value.
11. Equity theory maintains that employee motivation is affected by the perceived fairness of what people contribute and receive.
12. According to social reinforcement theory, people learn to use behaviors that are rewarded and to suppress behaviors that are punished or ignored.
13. According to research on goal setting, higher performance results when goals are specific, difficult (but accepted by employees), and when employees receive feedback on their progress. Publicly stated goals are more likely to be accomplished than private ones.
14. Managers can create an environment in which goal-oriented behavior is encouraged and rewarded by making sure there are fits between employee needs and rewards, between performance and rewards, and between employees and jobs.
15. Jobs that are motivating have the following characteristics:
   a. Skill variety
   b. Task identity
   c. Task significance
   d. Autonomy
   e. Job feedback

16. Methods of job redesign and motivating employees are
    a. Job rotation—switching different jobs.
    b. Job enlargement—horizontal job loading, which combines related tasks.
    c. Job enrichment—vertical job loading, which increases job scope by including planning and control functions formerly held by supervisors. It also includes in client contact and direct output feedback.
    d. Sociotechnical systems—integration of the needs of both people and technology. The basic work unit is usually the group rather than the individual. Autonomous work teams are an example.
    e. Self-managed work teams decide how they will accomplish the goals for which they are responsible and allocate the necessary tasks. They are responsible for planning, scheduling, organizing, directing, controlling, and evaluating their own work process, which is usually an entire process or product.
17. Job redesign efforts have been found to improve both satisfaction and productivity in some cases. However, job enrichment programs are also contingent upon the individual worker's (1) knowledge and skill; (2) need for growth, self-development, and challenge; and (3) satisfaction with contextual factors.

 **FOR MANAGERS**

- Managers often misdiagnose employees' motives for the following reasons:
  - They assume that everyone is motivated by the same factors that motivate them.
  - They hold stereotyped views about employees or make attributions about individual employees that prevent them from actually investigating motive patterns.
  - They overlook the individual and cultural differences in employee motive patterns.
  - They fail to comprehend that employee motives change over time.
- Figuring out what motivates employees is not always a simple matter of asking them. Learning about employees' nonwork activities, observing what they do with discretionary time at work, and determining what type of work or projects they enjoy are indirect methods of gauging their motive patterns. The yearly performance appraisal provides a good opportunity to check whether the manager's assumptions about what motivates an employee are accurate. There is a close relationship between understanding what motivates your workers and negotiating and renegotiating an effective psychological contract with them.
- Set challenging but attainable goals, establish clear work objectives and standards of good performance, and provide appropriate feedback to encourage achievement among employees.
- Link rewards to performance and ensure that rewards are equitably distributed; people who produce more should receive greater rewards. Reward employees for behaviors that promote the organization's goals. Be sure that the reward is one that the individual employee finds valuable or motivating.
- Whenever you are contemplating changes in the organization, make sure you have taken motivation patterns into consideration. For example, a secretary with a very boring job that is redeemed only by a central location that allows her to satisfy a high need for affiliation will not be as excited as you are about a new workstation placed in a remote location. The easiest way to avoid making errors of this sort is to understand what makes the job challenging or at least palatable for each employee and discuss possible changes with him or her before they are made.
- Put people in jobs they will find rewarding and recognize their contributions. Managers who always have their eyes on the next step of the career ladder often disparage workers who are content to remain in dead-end jobs. Doing a boring job well is just as great a contribution to an organization as doing any other job well.
- Remove demotivators that frustrate employees and sap their energy and morale. Common demotivators to eliminate: politics and favoritism, unclear expectations, unproductive meetings,

hypocrisy (saying one thing and doing another), constant change, withholding information, and low-quality standards that prevent employees from taking pride in their work.[42]

- Gain-sharing, another way to encourage motivation, is receiving a good deal of attention. In gain-sharing, the organization establishes a base period of performance. When performance gains occur, a formula is used to share the financial gains with all employees. Gain-sharing focuses attention on cost savings, continuous improvement, and higher performance from everyone, including managers.

- The key to success in redesigning work often lies in the way changes are implemented. Therefore, it's important to pay attention to implementation and the "fit" between the new design and other aspects of the organization.

- Whenever a new system of work design is implemented, it is realistic to expect that production may drop until employees master the new system and work their way up the learning curve.

- Job enrichment cannot take the place of decent pay and job security. Bear in mind Maslow's hierarchy, which states that pay and security are lower-level needs that must be satisfied before the higher-level needs met by job enrichment come into play.

- Conditions that affect the success of work design interventions are organizational culture, technology, union support or lack thereof, and the nature of the workforce itself.

PERSONAL APPLICATION ASSIGNMENT

The topic of this assignment is to think back on a motivation experience that was significant for you. Choose an experience that intrigues you and that you want to learn more about.

A. *Concrete Experience*

1. *Objectively* describe the experience (who, what, when, where, how) (2 points)
2. *Subjectively* describe your feelings, perceptions, and thoughts that occurred during (not after) the experience. What did others seem to be feeling? (2 points)

B. *Reflective Observation*

1. Looking back at the experience, what were the perspective of the key actors (including you)? (2 points)
2. Why did the people involved (including you) behave as they did? (2 points)

C. *Abstract Conceptualization*

1. Relate concepts or theories from the assigned readings or the lecture to the experience. Explain thoroughly how they apply to your experience. Please apply at least two concepts or theories and cite them correctly. (4 points)

D. *Active Experimentation*

1. What did you learn about motivation from this experience? (1 point)
2. What did you learn about yourself? (1 point)
3. What action steps will you take to be more effective in the future? (2 points)

E. *Integration, Synthesis, and Writing*

1. Did you integrate and synthesize the four sections? (1 point)
2. Was the Personal Application Assignment well written and easy to understand? (1 point)
3. Was it free of spelling and grammar errors? (2 points)

ENDNOTES

[1] This test is a variation of the standard six-picture Thematic Apperception Test cited in J. Atkinson, ed., *Motives in Fantasy, Action, and Society* (Princeton, NJ: D. Van Nostrand, 1958).

[2] A. Maslow, *Motivation and Personality* (New York: Harper & Row, 1970).

[3] G. Hofstede, "Motivation, Leadership and Organization: Do American Theories Apply Abroad?" *Organizational Dynamics 9*, no. 1 (1980): 42–63 and F. Trompenaars, *Riding the Waves of Culture* (London: The Economist Books, 1993).

[4] N. A. Adler, *International Dimensions of Organizational Behavior* (Cincinnati, OH: South-Western, 1997).

[5] H. J. Reitz, "The Relative Importance of Five Categories of Needs Among Industrial Workers in Eight Countries," *Academy of Management Proceedings* (1975): 270–73.

[6] F. Herzberg, B. Mausner, and B. Snyderman, *The Motivation to Work* (New York: John Wiley, 1959).

[7] A. Kohn, "Why Incentive Plans Cannot Work," *Harvard Business Review* (September–October 1993): 54–63.

[8] D. S. Campbell, "Firms Try to Adjust for Worker's New Career Expectations," *Knight-Ridder/Tribune Business News*, October 6, 1998.

[9] G. H. Hines, "Achievement, Motivation, Occupations and Labor Turnover in New Zealand," *Journal of Applied Psychology 58*, no. 3 (1973): 313–17.

[10] D. C. McClelland, *The Achieving Society* (Princeton, NJ: D. Van Nostrand, 1961), and D. C. McClelland, *Human Motivation* (Glenview, IL: Scott, Foresman, 1985).

[11] G. Hofstede, *Culture's Consequences* (Beverly Hills: Sage, 1980). See also "Motivation, Leadership, and Organization: Do American Theories Apply Abroad?" for Hofstede's critique of the major theories mentioned in this chapter.

[12] McClelland, *Human Motivation*.

[13] Ibid.

[14] J. D. Andrews, "The Achievement Motive in Two Types of Organizations," *Journal of Personality and Social Psychology 6* (1967): 163–68.

[15] H. A. Wainer and I. M. Rubin, "Motivation of Research and Development Entrepreneurs: Determinants of Company Success," *Journal of Applied Psychology 53*, no. 3 (1969): 178–84.

[16] R. E. Boyatzis, "The Need for Close Relationships and the Manager's Job," *Reader* (1991).

[17] K. Noujaim, "Some Motivational Determinants of Effort Allocation and Performance" (Ph.D. thesis. Sloan School of Management, Massachusetts Institute of Technology, 1968).

[18] G. A. Yukl, *Leadership in Organizations* (Upper Saddle River, NJ: Prentice-Hall, 1994).

[19] Noujaim, "Motivational Determinants."

[20] D. C. McClelland, *Power: The Inner Experience* (New York: Irvington, 1975). D. McClelland, Retrospective Commentary to "Power Is the Great Motivator." In S. Kerr, (ed.), *Ultimate Rewards* (Cambridge, MA: Harvard Business Review Books, 1997) 81.

[21] D. C. McClelland and D. H. Burnham, "Power Is the Great Motivator," *Harvard Business Review* (March–April 1976): 100–10; "Good Guys Make Bum Bosses" article in the *Reader* (1991).

[22] D. McClelland, Retrospective Commentary to "Power Is the Great Motivator."

[23] A. M. Harrell and M. J. Stahl, "A Behavioral Decision Theory Approach for Measuring McClelland's Trichotomy of Needs," *Journal of Applied Psychology* (April 1981) 242–47; M. J. Stahl and A. M. Harrell, "Evolution and Validation of a Behavioral Theory Measurement Approach to Achievement, Power, and Affiliation," *Journal of Applied Psychology* (December 1982): 744–51; and M. J. Stahl, "Achievement, Power, and Managerial Motivation: Selecting Managerial Talent with the Job Choice Exercise," *Personnel Psychology* (Winter 1983): 775–89.

[24] J. Atkinson, *An Introduction to Motivation* (Princeton, NJ: D. Van Nostrand, 1964), and J. Atkinson and N. T. Feather, *A Theory of Achievement Motivation* (New York: John Wiley, 1966).

[25] J. S. Adams, "Inequity in Social Exchanges," in L. Berkowitz (ed.), *Advances in Experimental Social Psychology* (New York: Academic Press, 1965), 16–23.

[26] V. H. Vroom, *Work and Motivation* (New York: Wiley, 1964). Please see the Nadler and Lawler article in the *Reader* on expectancy theory.

[27] F. Luthans and R. Kreitner, *Organizational Behavior Modification and Beyond: An Operant and Social Learning Approach* (Glenview, IL: Scott, Foresman, 1985). For excellent compilations of the research on this theory, see F. Andrasik, "Organizational Behavior Modification on Business Settings: A Methodological and Content Review," *Journal of Organizational Behavior Management*, no. 1 (1989): 59–77; and G. A. Merwi, Jr., J. A. Thomason, and E. E. Sanford, "A Methodology and Content Review of Organizational Behavior Management in the Private Sector: 1978–1986," *Journal of Organizational Behavior Management*, no. 1 (1989): 39–57.

[28] E. A. Locke, and G. P. Latham, *A Theory of Goal Setting and Task Performance* (Upper Saddle River, NJ: Prentice Hall, 1990); and P. C. Early, G. B. Northcraft, C. Lee, and T. R. Lituchy, "Impact of Process and Outcome Feedback on the Relation of Goal Setting to Task Performance," *Accademy of Management Journal 33*, no. 1 (1990): 87–105.

[29] M. E. Tubbs, "Commitment as a Moderator of the Goal-Performance Relation: A Case for Clearer Construct Definition," *Journal of Applied Psychology 78*, no. 1 (1993): 86–97.

[30] These categories were developed by D. G. Winter, *The Power Motive* (New York: Free Press, 1973), 251–55.

[31] L. Harman, "Starbucks' Schultz Reveals How Firm Keeps Perking," *San Diego Business Journal 18*, no. 39, September 29, 1997, p. 4.

[32] This list is composed of factors identified by J. R. Hackman and G. Oldham, *Work Redesign* (Reading, MA: Addison-Wesley, 1980) 77–80.

[33] Garson, *Luddites in Lordtown*, p. 235.

[34] J. R. Hackman and G. R. Oldham, "Development of the Job Diagnostic Survey," *Journal of Applied Psychology 60* (1975): 159–70.

[35] F. Herzberg, "One More Time: How Do You Motivate Employees?" *Harvard Business Review* (January-February 1968).

[36] Ibid.

[37] M. Seeman, "On the Meaning of Alienation," *American Sociological Review 24* (1959), 783–91; and "Alienation Studies" *Annual Review of Sociology 1* (1975): 91–123; and R. Blauner. *Alienation and Freedom: The Factory Worker and His Industry* (Chicago: University of Chicago Press, 1964).

[38] R. W. Griffin, "Effects of Work Redesign on Employee Perceptions, Attitudes, and Behaviors: A Long-term Investigation," *Academy of Management Journal* (June 1991): 425–35.

[39] An entire issue of the *Journal of Applied Behavioral Science 22*, no. 3 (1986), edited by W. Pasmore and W. Barko, is devoted to sociotechnical systems and includes information about autonomous work teams.

[40] J. Kapstein, "Volvo's Radical New Plant: The Death of the Assembly Line?" *Business Week*, August 28, 1989, 92–93.

[41] S. Prokesch, "Edges Fray on Volvo's Brave New Humanistic World," *New York Times*, July 7, 1991, C5.

[42] D. Spitzer, "The Seven Deadly Demotivators." *Management Review 84*, no. 11 (November 1995): 56–61 and *SuperMotivation* (New York: Amacom, 1995).

Chapter 5

▲▲▲

VALUES AND ETHICS

OBJECTIVES By the end of this chapter, you should be able to:

A. Describe how organizations foster unethical behavior.

B. Explain how organizations can promote ethical behavior.

C. Define ethics and values.

D. Better articulate your own values.

E. Distinguish between ethical and nonethical values.

F. Explain and recognize the stages of moral reasoning.

G. Describe five different ethical models.

RAY ANDERSON AND THE NATURAL STEP

A few years ago Ray Anderson, founder of a commercial carpet company called Interface Inc., had an epiphany. It came during a period of soul searching that was triggered when his company slipped from the number 1 slot. An employee gave Anderson the "Ecology of Commerce," a book by Paul Hawken who believes that companies need to control the creation of harmful waste rather than focus solely on waste disposal.[1] After reading about rapidly depleting natural resources and toxins that accumulate in the human body and pass on to the next generation, Anderson thought of his own grandchildren and wept. He realized that his company was guilty of consuming a disproportionate amount of hydrocarbons as well as producing harmful toxins.[2]

Anderson developed a new mission for Interface—create zero pollution with zero oil consumption while simultaneously advancing the interests of everyone involved in the company's endeavors (investors, employees, and customers). With the help of environmental consultants and The Natural Step format, his employees examined their work processes and designed less wasteful ways of producing carpet. For example, Interface originated the idea of installing carpet tiles under a "perpetual lease" program: for a monthly rental fee Interface removes deteriorated individual tiles and recycles them into new carpet. This is less wasteful than the general industry practices of replacing an entire carpet that is only worn in heavy traffic areas and failing to recycle old carpet. Interface also considers its employees a part of nature. In an industry noted for poor working conditions, Interface's mill is relatively quiet, odor-free, and sunny.[3]

As a result of Interface's new environmental mission, the company has saved $43 million to date.[4] Furthermore, many other businesses want to buy carpet from a "green" (environmentally concerned) vendor, so Interface's market share increased. The company is once again the leader in its industry.[5]

Anderson has become one of the leading U.S. proponents of The Natural Step, a not-for-profit environmental education organization founded by Dr. Karl-Henrik Robèrt. Robèrt, a Swedish pediatric oncologist, was motivated by an anomaly he observed in his work with children suffering from cancer. The parents of these children frequently vowed to do anything they could to save their children, including sacrificing their own lives. Yet Sweden as a whole was fairly complacent about taking steps to eradicate the environmental causes of cancer. As Robèrt noted "After a time of pulling drowning bodies out of a river, the intelligent person wants to go upstream to see if he can't prevent them falling in in the first place." Robèrt began a process of dialogue and consensus building about sustainability with scientists; fifty scientists, after numerous iterations, agreed on four basic, non-negotiable system conditions for sustainability. Due to his extraordinary networking skills, Robèrt succeeded in sending a booklet and an audiotape on these Natural Step principles to every household and school in Sweden.[6]

Sustainability is defined as meeting the needs of present generations without compromising the ability of future generations to meet their own needs. The moral basis for sustainability is the ethical position that destroying the future capacity of the Earth to support life is wrong. The Natural Step program promotes sustainability because it encourages people in organizations to consider the following four system conditions whenever they make decisions.

1. **Substances from the earth's crust must not systematically increase in the ecosphere.** This means that fossil fuels, metals and other minerals must not be extracted at a faster pace than their slow redeposit and reintegration into the Earth's crust. This requires a radically reduced dependence on mined minerals and fossil fuels. Businesses must ask themselves this question: "Which materials that are mined from the Earth's surface do we use (e.g., metals, fuels) and can we use less?"

2. **Substances produced by society must not systematically increase in the ecosphere.** Nature cannot withstand a systematic buildup of substances produced by humans, which means that substances must not be produced at a faster pace than they can be broken down and integrated into the cycles of nature or deposited into the Earth's crust. The question for business is: "Which unnatural substances does our organization depend on (e.g., plastics, chemical compounds) and can we use less?"

3. **The physical basis for productivity and diversity of nature must not be systematically diminished.** Nature cannot withstand a systematic deterioration of its capacity for renewal. In other words, societies cannot harvest or manipulate ecosystems in such a way that productive capacity and biodiversity systematically diminish. This requires that all people critically examine how they harvest renewable resources and adjust consumption and land use practices to be well within the regenerative capacities of the planet's ecosystems. The question for businesses is: "Does our organization depend on activities that encroach on productive parts of nature (e.g., over-fishing) and can we decrease these activities?"

4. **For the three previous conditions to be met, there must be fair and efficient use of resources with respect to meeting human needs.** Satisfying basic human needs must take precedence over the provision of luxuries, and there should be a just resource distribution. This will result in the social stability and cooperation required to make the changes that will eventually ensure sustainability. The question for businesses is: "Is our organization economically dependent on using an unnecessarily large amount of resources in relation to added human value (e.g., cutting down forests inhabited by indigenous people whose way of life is thereby threatened) and can we lessen this dependence?"

The Natural Step has gained widespread popularity in Swedish municipalities and multinationals such as IKEA, Electrolux, OK Petroleum, and Scandi Hotels. The program has also spread to other countries. According to early adopters of The Natural Step, the program has helped companies to achieve the following benefits:[7]

- Reduce operating costs.
- Stay ahead of regulatory frameworks and protect long-term investments.
- Enhance the organization's standing among stakeholder groups including customers, suppliers, and employees.

- Incorporate environmental concern into the culture of the workplace.
- Spark creativity among employees, especially those in product and process design.
- Differentiate their products and services and build brand image.

Ray Anderson and Interface became more successful as a result of incorporating The Natural Step system conditions, but it's not simply a question of profit for Anderson. His introduction to the importance of sustainability came "as a spear in the chest for me, and I determined almost in an instant to change my company.... Sometimes it seems very rapid; other times it's slow— but it began, frankly, in the heart, not in the mind. And I suspect that that's where the next industrial revolution has to begin—in the hearts of people—to do the right thing."[8]

Adapted from J. S. Osland, B. H. Drake and H. Feldman, "The Stewardship of Natural and Human Resources." In C. J. Dempsey and R. A. Butkus (eds.) *All Nature Is Groaning* (Collegeville, MN: Liturgical Press, 1999): 168–192.

PREMEETING PREPARATION

A. Read "Ray Anderson and The Natural Step."

B. Fill out the Rokeach Values Survey and score it.[9]

C. Complete the Moral Judgment Interview.

D. Read the Topic Introduction.

E. What were the significant learning points from the readings?

F. If your instructor has assigned the Robbins Self-Assessment Library, use "How Do My Ethics Rate?"

Rokeach Values Survey								
Please rate each value in terms of its importance to you, by circling the appropriate number (1 = of lesser importance, 7 = of greater importance). Think about each value *in terms of its importance to you, as a guiding principle in your life.* Is it of greater importance to you, or of lesser importance, or somewhere in between? As you work, *consider each value in relation to all the other values listed in each section.* Work slowly and think carefully about the importance you assign to all the values listed there.								

Terminal Values	Of Lesser Importance			Of Greater Importance			Weight	
A comfortable life	1 2 3 4			5 6 7			× 5 = _____	
An exciting life	1 2 3 4			5 6 7			× 4 = _____	
A sense of accomplishment	1 2 3 4			5 6 7			× 4 = _____	
A world at peace	1 2 3 4			5 6 7			× 5 =	_____
A world of beauty	1 2 3 4			5 6 7			× 3 =	_____
Equality	1 2 3 4			5 6 7			× 5 =	_____
Family security	1 2 3 4			5 6 7			× 1 = _____	
Freedom	1 2 3 4			5 6 7			× 1 = _____	
Happiness	1 2 3 4			5 6 7			× 4 = _____	
Inner harmony	1 2 3 4			5 6 7			× 5 = _____	

(continued)

Mature love	1	2	3	4	5	6	7	× 4 = _____	
National security	1	2	3	4	5	6	7	× 5 =	_____
Pleasure	1	2	3	4	5	6	7	× 5 = _____	
Salvation	1	2	3	4	5	6	7	× 3 = _____	
Self-respect	1	2	3	4	5	6	7	× 5 = _____	
Social recognition	1	2	3	4	5	6	7	× 3 = _____	
True friendship	1	2	3	4	5	6	7	× 4 = _____	
Wisdom	1	2	3	4	5	6	7	× 5 = _____	

$$\frac{P\ Total}{53} = P \qquad \frac{S\ Total}{18} = S$$

$$P \quad - \quad S \quad = \quad T \quad \text{(Terminal Values)}$$

$$\underline{\quad} \quad - \quad \underline{\quad} \quad = \quad \underline{\quad}$$

P Total   S Total

Scoring Instructions for Terminal Values

1. For all items, multiply the number you circled by the weighted value that appears under the heading "Weight." Write the total in the blank to the right.

2. Sum the numbers in the first column and write the total at the bottom where it says "P Total." Next divide this total by 53. Your new score should be a value between 1 and 7. This is your P score. P stands for Personal Values.

3. Sum the numbers in the second column and write the total at the bottom where it says "S Total." Next, divide this total by 18. Your new score should be a value between 1 and 7. This is your S score. S stands for Social Values.

4. Subtract S from P to find your **Terminal Values Score**. A positive sum indicates a "personal" orientation, while a negative sum indicates a "social" orientation.

Instrumental Values	Of Lesser Importance				Of Greater Importance			Weight	
Ambitious	1	2	3	4	5	6	7	× 5 = _____	
Broadminded	1	2	3	4	5	6	7	× 2 = _____	
Capable	1	2	3	4	5	6	7	× 5 = _____	
Cheerful	1	2	3	4	5	6	7	× 4 =	_____
Clean	1	2	3	4	5	6	7	× 3 =	_____
Courageous	1	2	3	4	5	6	7	× 2 =	_____
Forgiving	1	2	3	4	5	6	7	× 5 =	_____
Helpful	1	2	3	4	5	6	7	× 5 =	_____
Honest	1	2	3	4	5	6	7	× 2 =	_____
Imaginative	1	2	3	4	5	6	7	× 5 = _____	
Independent	1	2	3	4	5	6	7	× 5 = _____	
Intellectual	1	2	3	4	5	6	7	× 5 = _____	
Logical	1	2	3	4	5	6	7	× 5 = _____	
Loving	1	2	3	4	5	6	7	× 5 =	_____
Obedient	1	2	3	4	5	6	7	× 1 =	_____
Polite	1	2	3	4	5	6	7	× 3 =	_____
Responsible	1	2	3	4	5	6	7	× 4 = _____	

C Total   M Total

$$\frac{C\,Total}{36} = C \qquad \frac{M\,Total}{30} = M$$

$$C \quad - \quad M \quad = \quad I \quad \text{(Instrumental Values)}$$

$$\underline{\qquad} \quad - \quad \underline{\qquad} \quad = \quad \underline{\qquad}$$

Scoring Instructions for Instrumental Values

1. For all items, multiply the number you circled by the weighted value that appears under the heading "Weight." Write the total in the blank to the right.
2. Sum the numbers in the first column and write the total at the bottom where it says "C Total." Next divide this total by 36. Your new score should be a value between 1 and 7. This is your C score. C stands for Competence Values.
3. Sum the numbers in the second column and write the total at the bottom where it says "M Total." Next divide this total by 30. Your new score should be a value between 1 and 7. This is your M score. M stands for Moral Values.
4. Subtract M from C to find your **Instrumental Values Score**. A positive sum indicates a "competence" orientation, while a negative sum indicates a "moral" orientation.

Plot your Terminal Values Score on the horizontal axis and your Instrumental Values Score on the vertical axis of Figure 5-1 on page 103. Mark the point of intersection between the two scores.

MORAL JUDGMENT INTERVIEW[10]

Roger worked for a small accounting firm and was conducting an annual audit of a machinery manufacturer when he found that the firm had received a large loan from the local savings and loan association. It is illegal for savings and loan associations to lend money to a manufacturing firm; they are restricted by law to mortgages based on residential real estate.

Roger took his working papers and a copy of the ledger showing the loan to his boss, the partner in charge of the office. His boss listened to Roger and then told Roger, "I will take care of this privately. We simply cannot afford to lose a client of this status. You put the papers you have through the shredder."

Roger wonders what he should do.

Please answer the following questions as if you were Roger. Put yourself in his shoes and express your own personal opinion. There are no "correct" answers. Please explain why you might choose one action over another. Very short answers cannot be coded so be sure to elaborate fully. Even if you give a long description of what you think is right or what you think should be done, it is of no help if you do not explain why you think it is right or why you think it should be done.

1. Should Roger shred the papers? _____ (yes or no)
   Why or why not?

2. Does the illegality of the loan and Roger's duty as an auditor make a difference in Roger's decision to shred the papers? Explain.

3. If Roger had been advised by one of his peers to shred his papers, should Roger shred his papers? Why or why not?

4. Is it important for people to do everything they can to follow their conscience? Explain.

5. Shredding papers is against the AICPA (American Institute of Certified Public Accountants) Code and covers up an illegally made loan. Is Roger morally wrong if he shreds his papers? Explain.

6. If Roger's career was threatened if he refused to shred his papers, should Roger shred them? Why or why not?

7. Should people do everything they can to further their own careers? Explain.

TOPIC INTRODUCTION

Although business has always occupied a central role in U.S. society, Americans have often been ambivalent about business, money, and success.[11] In books and movies, businesspeople are usually portrayed in a negative light. As a profession, business has experienced alternating stages of low prestige and high prestige. Medicare fraud on the part of insurance and health care companies, tobacco company dishonesty about the link between smoking and cancer, Archer Daniel's price fixing, Prudential's defrauding of clients, and Astra's sexual harassment antics are merely the latest in a long string of scandals. The United States does not have a corner on the scandal market. In Singapore, a greedy British financial trader in his late twenties was jailed for fraud and forgery, bringing about the collapse of Barings Bank, Britain's oldest merchant bank. The largest criminal fine to date was levied on the Swiss-based F. Hoffman-LaRoche and the German-based BASF A.G. for fixing prices in the vitamin market they dominate.

The very nature of business means that managers may be confronted with more ethical questions than most other professions. Companies confront internal issues such as employee safety, discrimination and sexual harassment, theft of company property, and irregular accounting practices. In addition, companies have struggled with a host of external ethical dilemmas such as balancing profit with environmental protection and consumer safety and doing business in cultures where bribes are commonplace.

Ethics refers to "standards of conduct that indicate how one should behave based on moral duties and virtues arising from principles about right and wrong."[12] There is a mistaken perception that firms that act ethically have lower profits.[13] This may be true in the short term, but companies that engage in unethical practices make themselves vulnerable to lawsuits, boycotts, governmental restrictions and regulations, and loss of reputation—all of which can endanger profits. There is growing evidence that good corporate citizenship correlates with higher financial performance. Companies that look beyond maximizing wealth and profits and are driven by values and a sense of purpose outperform companies that focus only on short-term gain. Ethical practices pay off in the long run since trusting relationships with employees, stockholders, and well-satisfied customers are the basis of business success. Hartley contends that:

> The interests of a firm are best served by scrupulous attention to the public interest and by seeking a trusting relationship with the various publics with which a firm is involved. In the process, society also is best served.... Such a trusting relationship suggests concern for customer satisfaction and fair dealings. The objective is loyalty and repeat business, a durable and mutually beneficial relationship, which is contrary to the philosophy of short-term profit maximization, corporate self-interest, and coercive practices with employees and dependent suppliers.[14]

There are many ethical businesspeople who prosper in large part because of their integrity. In recent years, we have seen an increase in companies that define themselves as socially responsible companies in their mission statement. For example, Levi Strauss voluntarily set up Global Sourcing Guidelines to carefully select contractors in overseas factories and ensure that their products are not made in sweatshops by children.[15] Organizations like Anita Roddick's Body Shop and Ben and Jerry's Ice Cream donate part of their profits to "good works," such as human rights groups, community development projects, environmental groups, and peace programs.

Nevertheless, there have always been and always will be unethical people for whom money and power take precedence over all else. The key question is whether they are perceived as heroes or villains.[16] This is determined by societal values and by the ethical climate and norms created by each organization. In one study, 92 percent of the managers agreed that the ethical tone of their firm is determined by the behavior of those in charge, and one-third felt their bosses engage in unethical behaviors and are less concerned with ethics than they are.[17] Some companies place employees in positions that force them to choose between their careers and their personal sense of ethics.

Factors that lead to questionable practices in business are

1. overemphasis on both individual and firm performance;
2. mission statements, evaluation systems, and organizational cultures that focus on profit as the organization's sole objective;
3. intense competition among firms, departments, and individuals;
4. management concern for the letter of the law rather than the spirit;
5. ambiguous policies that employees interpret as "window dressing" for outsiders rather than clear expectations for ethical behavior;
6. inadequate controls so that managers get away with violating standards, allowing them to pursue greater sales and profits for personal benefit;
7. expediency and indifference to the customers' best interest;
8. management's failure to comprehend the public's ethical concerns;
9. custom ("let the buyer beware"); and
10. a "groupthink" mentality that fosters group decisions that individual members would not support.[18]

Companies that want to encourage ethical behavior need to (1) communicate their expectations that employees will behave ethically and define what that means; (2) hire top executives who set an example of moral behavior; (3) reward ethical behavior and punish unethical behavior; (4) teach employees the basic tools of ethical decision making; and (5) encourage the discussion of ethical issues.[19]

Ethical mistakes are responsible for ending careers more quickly and more definitively than any other errors in judgment or accounting.[20] Nevertheless, one of the factors that inhibits the discussion of ethics in the workforce is a reluctance on the part of managers to discuss the moral aspects of their decision making, even when they are acting for moral reasons.[21] Managers give several reasons for avoiding moral talk. First, people do not like to appear judgmental or intrusive, or lay themselves open to countercharges of wrongdoing. As a result, they often avoid confronting others who are not behaving ethically. Second, moral talk threatens efficiency when it simply muddies the waters and distracts attention from problem solving. Managers worry that it may be self-serving, simplistic, inflexible, or inexact. Finally, some managers fear that the esoteric and idealistic nature of moral talk is not in keeping with the image they want to convey, and they are leery about exposing their lack of training in ethics. Therefore, we find a norm in many businesses to justify decisions on the basis of organizational interests, practicality, and sound economic sense, even when moral considerations play an important role. Although managers struggle individually with ethical problems, they seldom discuss them in groups of managers, which gives rise to the term *the moral muteness* of managers. The purpose of this chapter is to provide you with a rudimentary understanding of ethical terms and principles so you can take part in ethical discussions.

VALUES

Both individuals and organizations have codes of ethics that are based on their values. One of the first steps in teaching ethics is to help people identify and articulate their own values. Values are *core beliefs or desires that guide or motivate attitudes and actions.* Whereas the study of ethics is concerned with how a moral person *should* behave, values concern the various beliefs and attitudes that determine how a person *actually* behaves. People do not always act in accordance with their espoused values. Our values are fixed early in life; we learn them from our parents, friends, teachers, church, and the culture that surrounds us. As adults, we often seek environments that are compatible with the values we learned as children. For example, values help determine what companies we are attracted to and how long we stay with them. They also affect how motivated we are at work; people who share the same values as the organization are more committed to the organization than those who do not.[22]

Employees choose to work in environments that match their ethical preferences. The better the ethical fit, the more likely employees are to continue with the organization and be committed to it.[23] Whenever people make decisions or talk about what constitutes appropriate behavior

Terminal Values

	Personal Values		Social Values
		+7 +6 +5 +4 +3 +2 +1	
Competence Values	Preference for Personal-Competence Values		Preference for Social-Competence Values
Instrumental (C minus M)	+7 +6 +5 +4 +3 +2 +1 0	0 −1 −2 −3 −4 −5 −6 −7	
		−1 −2 −3 −4 −5 −6 −7	
Moral Values	Preference for Personal-Moral Values		Preference for Social-Moral Values

FIGURE 5-1   **Personal Values Orientation Typology.**

at work, we can observe the impact of values, or even conflicts between different values. For example, when companies consider whether to employ temporary or permanent employees, which values are more important—saving money for the company or providing benefits and job security to employees?

Within our personal value system, some values are more important than others. The exercise in the premeeting preparation allows you to see which of the most common American values have the greatest significance for you. (In the following chapter on career development, you can see the link between values and career planning in the premeeting preparation exercise.)

Rokeach,[24] who developed the list of values that you rated, believes that people possess a relatively small number of values that they hold to varying degrees. He classified these key values into two types. *Terminal* values are desirable end states of existence or the goals that a person would like to achieve during his or her lifetime. Terminal values can be subdivided further into two categories: *personal* values (a comfortable life, freedom, happiness, salvation) and *social* values (world peace, equality, national security).

Instrumental values are preferable modes of behavior or the means to achieving one's terminal values. There are two types of instrumental values: *moral* values and *competence* values. Moral values (cheerful, courageous, helpful, honest) tend to have an interpersonal focus; when they are violated, we feel pangs of conscience or guilt. Competence values (ambitious, capable, intellectual, responsible) have a personal focus. When they are violated, we feel ashamed of our personal inadequacy rather than guilty about wrongdoing.

Rokeach looked for a relationship between terminal and instrumental values and found that all combinations are possible, as shown in Figure 5-1. The personal-competence value orientation is most commonly preferred by managers. The personal-moral and social-moral value orientations are the least common for managers and a majority of Americans.[25] When we compare individual values of managers with those of the population at large, we find that "sense of accomplishment," "self-respect," "a comfortable life," and "independence" are more highly valued by managers.[26]

ETHICAL VERSUS NONETHICAL VALUES

When ethical issues arise, we have to distinguish between *ethical* and *nonethical* values. The former are values that directly relate to beliefs concerning what is right and proper (as opposed to what is simply correct or effective) or that motivate a sense of moral duty. Core ethical values that transcend cultural, ethnic, and socioeconomic differences in the United States are (1) trustworthiness; (2) respect; (3) responsibility; (4) justice and fairness; (5) caring; and (6) civic virtue and citizenship.[27] The effort to identify these values is part of a trend toward character building as a remedy for the breakdown in societal values that is taking place in many countries. It is difficult for adults to act ethically if they have not been inculcated with ethical values when they were growing up.

Nonethical values simply deal with things we like, desire, or find personally important. Examples of nonethical values are money, fame, status, happiness, fulfillment, pleasure, personal freedom, and being liked. They are ethically neutral. One of the guides to ethical decision making is that *ethical values should always take precedence over nonethical values.*

MORAL REASONING

Values alone do not determine our actions. Our behavior is also influenced by our moral reasoning, organizational culture, the influence of significant others, the type of harm that could result from a decision involving ethics, and who might be harmed.[28] The first factor, moral reasoning, is the process by which we transform our values and beliefs into action. This reasoning affects the way managers make decisions.[29]

Kohlberg[30] conducted a longitudinal study of the moral reasoning reported by male subjects at various ages. He identified three different levels of moral development which we will call *self-centered*, *conformity*, and *principled*. Kohlberg uses different labels here (*preconventional*, *conventional*, and *postconventional*), but we think it is easier for you to remember titles that describe the major characteristic of each level.[31] The progression through these levels can be summarized as moving from (1) a self-centered conception of right and wrong to (2) an understanding of the importance of conformity and social accord and (3) universal principles of justice and rights. As shown in Figure 5-2, each level has two stages, the second of which is more advanced.[32]

Self-Centered Level (Preconventional)   This level of moral reasoning has a personal focus and an emphasis on consequences. It is usually found among children who see moral issues in the black and white terms of "good and bad" and "right and wrong." Actions are judged either by their consequences (punishment, reward, exchange of favors) or in terms of the physical power of those who lay down the rules.

This level is divided into two stages:

Stage 1: The Obedience and Punishment Orientation.   The physical consequences of an action determine its goodness or badness. An avoidance of punishment and unquestioning deference to power are valued but not because the individual believes in the importance of a moral order supported by punishment and authority.

Stage 2: Instrumental Purpose and Exchange (Instrumental Relativist Orientation).   Interest in satisfying one's own needs is the most important consideration. Elements of fairness, reciprocity, and equal sharing are present, but they are always interpreted in a physical or pragmatic way. For example, reciprocity is a matter of "you scratch my back, and I'll scratch yours" rather than loyalty, gratitude, or justice.

Conformity Level (Conventional)   At this level, there is a group focus and an emphasis on social harmony. People are concerned with meeting the expectations of their family, group, or nation. They have moved beyond a preoccupation with consequences to focus on conformity and loyalty to the social order. They support, justify, and identify with the existing social order or with the people or group(s) involved in it. Like the self-centered individuals, this group also sees rules and laws as outside themselves, but they obey them because they have accepted them. At this level, we find the following two stages.

Stage	What is Considered to be Right
Level One–Self-Centered (Preconventional)	
Stage One—Obedience and Punishment Orientation	Sticking to rules to avoid physical punishment. Obedience for its own sake.
Stage Two–Instrumental Purpose and Exchange	Following rules only when it is in one's immediate interest. Right is an equal exchange, a fair deal.
Level Two–Conformity (Conventional)	
Stage Three-Interpersonal Accord, Conformity, Mutual Expectations	Stereotypical "good" behavior. Living up to what is expected by peers and people close to you.
Stage Four-Social Accord and System Maintenance	Fulfilling duties and obligations of social system. Upholding laws except in extreme cases where they conflict with fixed social duties. Contributing to the society, group.
Level Three–Principled (Postconventional)	
Stage Five-Social Contract, Individual Rights	Being aware that people hold a variety of values; that rules are relative to the group. Upholding rules because they are the social contract. Upholding nonrelative values and rights regardless of majority opinion.
Stage Six-Universal Ethical Principles	Following self-chosen ethical principles of justice and rights. When laws violate principles, act in accord with principles.

FIGURE 5-2   **Three Levels of Moral Development According to Kohlberg**
Source: Linda K. Trevino, "A Cultural Perspective on Changing and Developing Organizational Ethics," in *Research in Organizational Change and Development* (eds.) W. A. Pasmore and R. W. Woodman (Greenwich, CT: JAI Press, 1990), 198.

Stage 3: Interpersonal Accord, Conformity, Mutual Expectations (The "Good Boy–Nice Girl" Orientation). Good behavior is defined as behavior that pleases or helps others and is approved by them. Conformity to stereotypical images of what is "natural" behavior (i.e., behavior that is characteristic of the majority of people) is a common guide. People are concerned with maintaining mutually trusting relationships with people. The Golden Rule, "Do unto others as you would have others do unto you," is common at this stage of moral reasoning. Judging behavior by its intention, for example, "she meant well," is also found for the first time at this stage.

Stage 4: Social Accord and System Maintenance (The Law and Order Orientation). At stage 4, the individual takes the perspective of a member of society. The individual perceives the social system as a consistent set of codes and procedures (legal, religious, societal) that applies impartially to all members in a society. There is an emphasis upon "doing one's duty" and showing respect for authority and maintaining the social order for its own sake.

Principled Level (Postconventional)   At this level, individuals have a more universal focus that emphasizes internalized ethical standards, rights, or duties. Individuals at this level examine society's rules and laws and then develop their own set of internal principles. These internalized principles take precedence over rules and laws.

Stage 5: Social Contract, Individual Rights (The Social Contract Legalistic Orientation). At this stage, the individual realizes that there is an arbitrary element to rules and the law. Right is relative and perceived as a matter of personal values and opinion. For the sake of agreement, the individual agrees to procedural rules such as respect for contracts and the rights of others, majority will, and the general good.

Stage 6: The Universal Ethical Principles Orientation. Right is defined by decisions of conscience, in accord with self-chosen ethical principles that are logically comprehensive, universal, and consistent. These principles are abstract and ethical, such as justice, the reciprocity and equality of human rights, and respect for the dignity of human beings.

The research of Kohlberg and others concluded that:[33]

1. People's reasoning tends to reflect one dominant stage, although they may occasionally be either one stage lower or higher than the dominant stage.
2. Most adults in Western urban societies reason at stages 3, 4, and 5. Stage 4 reasoning is the most common. Development can stop at any stage. Many prison inmates never get beyond stage 2 reasoning.
3. People develop moral maturity gradually, moving from step to step; they do not skip stages.
4. Development is not governed by age. Some young people reason at a higher stage than their elders. While cognitive development (which normally occurs during adolescence) is a necessary condition for abstract reasoning, it does not guarantee moral maturity.
5. Empathy, the capacity to feel what others are feeling, is also a necessary but not sufficient condition for moral development.
6. Managers whose values are categorized as social-moral in Figure 5-1 demonstrated a higher level of moral reasoning.[34]
7. Ethical decision making and intended ethical behavior generally increase as individuals utilize higher stages of moral reasoning.[35]

The major criticisms of Kohlberg's theory follow:

1. The highest stages of reasoning are based on abstract principles of justice rather than social considerations. Since women are more socialized than men to make care-based judgments (how will the people involved be affected?), Gilligan argued that the test was biased against women.[36] Originally Kohlberg only studied men, a common practice before researchers came to appreciate gender differences, but he later incorporated women. The controversy is not settled, although there is evidence that women and men do not reason differently when confronted with real-life dilemmas.[37]
2. Since Kohlberg's test consists of hypothetical dilemmas, the results might be different when people confront real-life ethical dilemmas. In Argyris's terms, their test answers might reflect their espoused theories rather than their theories-in-use.[38] In fact, research on real-life dilemmas showed that people reason at various stages, depending on the specific dilemma involved.[39] This contradicts Kohlberg's belief that people reason consistently at the highest possible level unless they are transitioning to a higher stage.
3. The theory is culturally biased. The roots of the model are Western European and North American, and the higher stages of the scale reflect individualism rather than an understanding of the demands faced in collectivist cultures. The Chinese, for example, do not seek universal norms for all situations and balance respect for the individual with the individual's subordination to society and the state.[40]

Although Kohlberg's theory of moral development has been the target of various criticisms, it has been refined and clarified in response and is still the most widely accepted model of moral development.

Both personal values and moral reasoning affect the way people make decisions. The group exercise provides an opportunity to discuss an ethical dilemma and identify different types of moral reasoning and value considerations.

PROCEDURE FOR GROUP MEETING: THE ROGER WORSHAM CASE[41]

STEP 1.   Read the extended version of the Roger Worsham Case individually. (10 minutes)

Arnold Abramson and Company is a regional accounting firm, with offices in Michigan and northern Wisconsin. It was founded in 1934 to provide auditing and tax services and, despite the depression, was immediately successful due to the economic growth of the area. The southern offices of Arnold Abramson and Company, in Flint and Detroit, competed directly with the large, national CPA firms, the "Big Five." They were able to operate successfully until the mid-1960s by providing more personalized services and by charging somewhat lower fees. However, competition sharply increased in the late 1960s and early 1970s as the tax laws became more complex, the auditing procedures more rigorous, and the bookkeeping more automated. The "Big Five" firms were able, through their extensive training programs and their continual staff additions, to provide more extensive help and assistance to their clients on tax changes and data processing procedures. Many of the small and medium-sized companies that had been customers of Arnold Abramson for years switched to one of the national firms. It was eventually necessary to close the Detroit office and to reduce the size of the staff at Flint.

Some of the partners of the company recommended a merger with one of the national CPA firms, but the founder, Mr. Arnold Abramson, was not only still living but was still active, and he and his two sons were uncompromising in their opposition to any sale or merger.

The old gentleman was 84 when I joined the firm, and he simply was not going to surrender to Arthur Andersen or Price Waterhouse. And, you know, he had a point; there is room left in the world for the more personal approach, even in auditing. The old man was adamant about this. I understand that at the partners' dinner this year he laid it right on the line to the other members of the firm. "You are to keep the local banks, retail stores and manufacturers as your clients; if you lose your clients to those people from Detroit, we'll shut down your office." He always referred to representatives of the Big Five firms as "those people from Detroit" even though they might be from offices in Lansing, Grand Rapids, or Milwaukee. (statement of Roger Worsham)

Roger Worsham was 32 years old when he graduated from the M.B.A. program at the University of Michigan. He had majored in accounting but had found it difficult to obtain employment at the large national CPA firms. He had interviewed with eight of the largest companies and had been rejected by all eight. The director of placement at the School of Business Administration had explained that this was due to his age, and that the Big Five firms were exceedingly hesitant to hire anyone over 28 to 30 years of age because they felt that the older entrants were unlikely to stay with the firm over the first few years of auditing, which some people found to be dull and tedious.

Roger, however, felt that perhaps his personality was more at fault than his age. He found it difficult to converse easily in the interviews, and he was afraid that he projected himself as a hesitant, uncertain individual. He had worked for six years as a science teacher in a primary grade school after graduating from college. Interviewers always asked about his decision to change professions and always seemed to imply that he was not certain about his objectives in life or his commitment to accounting.

At the suggestion of a faculty member who taught the small business management course at the business school, Roger applied to some of the smaller CPA firms in the state and was almost immediately accepted by Arnold Abramson and Company.

I met Mr. Abramson, Jr., and he talked about what I wanted to do in accounting, not what I had done in teaching. That interview went really well, and I knew when he asked me if my wife and I would mind living in a small town that he was going to offer me a job. It does not pay as much as working for some of the other firms, but I can get my CPA (in Michigan, two years of auditing experience is required after passing the written examinations) and then I assume they'll pay me more, or I can move into industry. (statement of Roger Worsham)

Roger was assigned to one of the northern offices, and he moved his wife and two children to the area and started work immediately after graduation. He had interesting, enjoyable work and his family enjoyed the area in which they were living. He felt that his life was beginning to take on a direction and purpose. But then he found clear evidence of fraud, and encountered a situation that threatened his newly found security and employment.

We were doing the annual audit for the machinery manufacturer. This company had not been doing well. Sales had been declining for four or five years, losses had been reported for each of those years, and the financial position of the company had steadily deteriorated. I was going through the notes payable, and found that they had a loan, and a large one, from the savings and loan association in our town.

Now, in the first place, it is illegal for a savings and loan association to make a loan to a manufacturing firm. They are restricted by law to mortgages based on residential real estate. But, even more, I knew this loan was not on the books of the savings and loan since I had been the one to audit the loan portfolio there. I had looked at every loan in the file. I had not statistically sampled from the file (which is the usual practice) but had checked each loan to see that it was supported by a properly assigned mortgage and a currently valid appraisal. The only thing I had not done was to add up the total for the file to check with the reported total, since the usual way is to sample, and you don't get a total when you sample. I still had my working papers back at our office, of course, so I went back and ran the total. Sure enough, it was off by the amount of the loan to the manufacturing company.

It was obvious what had happened. Someone had taken the folder covering the illegal loan out of the file prior to our audit. It became obvious who had done it: the president of the savings and loan association was a lawyer in the town who, I found by checking the stockholder lists, was the largest owner of the manufacturing company. He was also on the board of directors of the local bank and reputedly was a wealthy, powerful person in the community.

I took my working papers and a Xerox copy of the ledger showing the loan, and went to see the partner in charge of our office the next morning. He listened to me, without saying a word. When I finished, he told me, "I will take care of this privately. We simply cannot afford to lose a client of the status of (the name of the lawyer). You put the papers you have through the shredder."

I was astonished! The AICPA Code of Ethics and generally accepted auditing standards both require that you either resign from the engagement or issue an adverse opinion when you find irregularities. This was not a small amount. The loan was not only illegal, it was in default, and would adversely affect the savings and loan association.

I hesitated because I was surprised and shocked. He told me, "I will not tell you again. You put those papers through the shredder or I'll guarantee that you'll never get a CPA in Michigan or work in an accounting office in this state for the rest of your life."

I didn't know what to do. (statement of Roger Worsham)

STEP 2. In your learning group, discuss what Roger should do and why he should take this action.

STEP 3. If possible, come to a group consensus. What values can you identify in this discussion?

STEP 4. Using Figure 5-3, what stage of moral development is reflected in the reasoning behind your group decision? What stage of reasoning is reflected in your individual decision in the premeeting preparation? (Steps 2–4: 30–40 minutes)

STEP 5. General Debriefing Questions. (30–40 minutes)
1. What was your group decision? Describe the reasoning on which it was based.
2. Did having more information change your individual reasoning about the case? Why or why not?

Action Recommended	
Shred the Papers	**Do Not Shred the Papers**
Stage	
1 There is no reason for Roger to be a hero and risk losing everything.	Roger can avoid the worst penalty of all, which would be a criminal charge against him.
2 This would enable Roger to acquire the two years of auditing experience needed to get his CPA.	Shredding the papers could ruin Roger's credibility and stand in the way of a promotion or a future job.
3 Roger would be acting as a "team player" within the firm and his boss would appreciate that.	This course of action is better for Roger, the firm, and the stockholders of the savings and loan.
4 There is an obligation for every employee to be loyal to the employer. This is essential for the operation of any firm.	If we ignore accepted written laws within our society, there would be a breakdown of the system.
5 The partner has a right to run his office in the manner he deems necessary. He may have other information that may justify his actions for the greater good of all involved.	Roger should not compromise his perceived ethical code for a business.

FIGURE 5-3   **Representative Examples of Reasoning at Each Stage**

Source: James Weber and Sharon Green, "Principled Moral Reasoning: Is It a Viable Approach to Promote Ethical Integrity?" *Journal of Business Ethics 10*(1991): 328.

3. What values were evident in your group discussion? Was anyone thinking of different values when you made your individual decision prior to class? Which values took precedence—ethical or nonethical?

4. Did your decisions pass the Ethics Warning System? In other words, does it fit the Golden Rule? (Do unto others as you would have them do unto you)? Would you care if the newspaper published your decision? Would you be happy with the decision if your children were watching perched on your shoulder?

5. Who are the stakeholders in this decision? What harm could come to them as a result of Roger's decision?

6. What would you have said to the partner if you were in Roger's shoes?

7. Quickly read the following descriptions of the ethical models in the beginning of the Follow-Up section. Which of these approaches—utilitarian, rights and duties, justice, caring, or environmental ethics—did you and your group utilize in your discussion?

 FOLLOW-UP

Another conceptual framework that helps us understand the different ways we look at ethical issues are models of ethics, most of which come to us from the study of philosophy. Following are the basic approaches that people use to make decisions.[42]

1. **Utilitarian approaches** In utilitarian ethics, behavior is judged in terms of its effects on the welfare of everyone. A moral act produces the greatest good for the greatest number. Therefore, the good of the group takes precedence over consideration for individuals. Actions,

plans, and policies are judged by their consequences. This approach is quite common in business decisions. For example, when managers maximize profit, or opt for efficiency and productivity, they can argue that they are obtaining the greatest good for the greatest number. A disadvantage of this approach is that the rights of minority groups can be easily overlooked. The utilitarian orientation is often used with environmental issues.

2. **Approaches based on rights and duties** Unlike utilitarian ethics, these emphasize the personal entitlements of individuals. Examples are a person's right to privacy, free speech, and due process. Most rights have corresponding duties. For example, if a person has the right to be paid for an eight-hour day, he or she is also obligated to contribute a "fair day's work" for a "fair day's pay." Business contracts reflect this approach, which is commonly used with occupational health and safety problems. A negative consequence of rights-based ethics is that it engenders a self-centered, legalistic focus on what is due the individual, especially if the focus on duties is lost.

3. **Approaches based on justice** In these approaches, people are guided by fairness, equity, and impartiality when treating both individuals and groups. Fairness is the criterion for distributing the benefits and burdens of society, the administration of rules and regulations, and sanctions. This approach is appropriate for issues such as employment discrimination. One disadvantage of a justice ethic is that it encourages a sense of entitlement.

4. **Approaches based on caring** The focus in this approach is the well-being of another person. An ethical person is aware of the needs and feelings of others and takes the initiative to respond to that need. The criteria used to judge behavior is, "Who will be harmed and what will happen to existing relationships?"[43]

5. **Approaches based on environmentalism** While the preceding approaches concern person-person or person-society relationships, the environmental ethic extends the boundary to include the person-land relationship. A greater understanding of the interdependent relationship between humankind and the continuing sustainability of the earth has resulted in a growing acceptance of an environmental ethic.[44] The basis for sustainability is the belief that people have an obligation and a duty to act as stewards who protect the earth and its resources and keep them intact for future generations. Many U.S. businesses have "gone green" due to their leaders' personal values, government regulations, or their agreement with some strategy gurus that environmentalism is a strategic competitive advantage.

ETHICAL DECISION MAKING

How can managers ensure that they are taking an ethical approach to decision making? Nash devised 12 questions for examining the ethics of a business decision.[45]

1. Have you defined the problem accurately? What are the factual implications of the situation rather than a biased perspective that reflects your loyalties?
2. How would you define the problem if you stood on the other side of the fence?
3. How did this situation occur in the first place? What is the historical background of events leading up to this situation?
4. To whom and to what do you give your loyalty as a person and as a member of the corporation?
5. What do you want to accomplish in making this decision?
6. How does this intention compare with the probable results?
7. Whom could your decision or action injure?
8. Can you discuss the problem with the affected parties before you make your decision?
9. Are you confident that your position will be as valid over a long period of time as it seems now?
10. Could you disclose without qualms your decision or action to your boss, your CEO, the board of directors, your family, and society as a whole?
11. What would this decision symbolize for others if they interpret it correctly? What could it symbolize if the decision is misinterpreted by others?
12. Under what conditions would you allow exceptions to your stand?

INTERNATIONAL ETHICS

The difficulty of making ethical decisions is exacerbated in international business due to different value systems and practices. Bribery, which is frowned upon in many cultures, is a daily way of life in others. It is illegal for U.S. businesses to give bribes and kick-back payments in order to win contracts in other countries. However, this prohibition does not apply to competitors from countries that view bribery as a normal aspect of doing business.

While bribing is an ancient custom, there is a growing movement to curb this practice. The World Bank and the International Monetary Fund are attacking corrupt practices that prevent some countries from digging themselves out of poverty and joining the global economy. At the urging of the United States, the industrialized nations signed a treaty in 1997 that banned bribes and made bribes by businesses to foreign officials a crime.

One of the common dilemmas in international business is whether or not to subscribe to cultural relativism. Does one accept the values of the local culture (when in Rome, do as the Romans) or continue to observe or even impose one's own values? Do you promote women and minorities in international subsidiaries where there is little or no concern for diversity issues? Do you sell the pesticide that has been banned in the United States as a hazardous product to a lesser-developed country that has no environmental or consumer safety laws? Many of these issues and their legal ramifications are extremely complex. It's important to identify the cultural values, historical precedents, and legal requirements that are involved. It's also helpful to consult with various people from the other culture to make sure you understand the foreign viewpoint.

The ethics and values the owners of Kingston Technology Corporation brought with them from Taiwan and Shanghai have resulted in spectacular growth. Based in Los Angeles, John Tu and David Sun sell add-on memory modules for personal computers. In a cutthroat business, they treat their employees, suppliers, and customers like family. They pay their employees, two-thirds of whom are ethnic minorities, higher than average salaries and have promised them one to two years of salary if the business fails. They do multimillion-dollar deals with a handshake. They don't pressure suppliers on price, but they do pay them ahead of schedule if possible and never cancel orders. Their philosophy of making customers, workers, and suppliers happy has translated into one of the highest revenue per employee figures anywhere.[46]

LEARNING POINTS

1. Ethics refers to standards of conduct that indicate how one should behave based on moral duties and virtues arising from principles about right and wrong.
2. Ethical practices pay off in the long run since trusting relationships and well-satisfied customers are the basis of repeat business.
3. Companies create an environment in which unethical practices are more likely when they focus solely on profit and intense competition, when top management gives lip service only to ethical behavior and fails to establish clear policies and adequate controls, and when they are insensitive to the customer's best interests and public concerns about ethics.
4. Companies that want to encourage moral behavior (1) communicate their expectations that employees will behave ethically and define what that means; (2) hire top executives who set a good example; (3) reward ethical behavior and punish unethical behavior; (4) teach employees the basic tools of ethical decision making; and (5) encourage the discussion of ethical issues.
5. Values are core beliefs or desires that guide or motivate attitudes and actions.
6. Rokeach developed a list of the most common American values, which people hold to varying degrees.
7. Terminal values are desirable end states of existence or the goals people want to accomplish in their lifetime. Terminal values are either personal or social.

8. Instrumental values are preferable modes of behavior or the means to achieving one's terminal values. There are two types: moral and competence.

9. Ethical values directly relate to beliefs concerning what is right and proper and motivate a sense of moral duty (trustworthiness, respect, responsibility, justice and fairness, caring, and civic virtue). Nonethical values are things we like, desire or find important. Ethical values should always take precedence over nonethical values.

10. Kohlberg's theory of moral development consists of three levels: self-centered, conformity, and principled. Individuals move through these stages from a self-centered conception of right and wrong to an understanding of social contracts and internalized principles of justice and rights.

11. The five ethical models are utilitarian, rights and duties, justice, caring, and environmental ethics.

12. The difficulty of making ethical decisions is intensified in international business due to different value systems and business practices.

FOR MANAGERS

- Know your own personal values and those of the organization. Can you articulate them? Are they compatible?

- The top management of an organization sets the moral tone of the company. If they consistently behave in an ethical manner and set clear expectations that their subordinates should behave ethically, it is less likely that violations will occur. Some of the standards of moral behavior that are commonly expected of employees are (1) keeping one's promises, (2) not harming others, (3) helping others in need, (4) respecting others and not treating them merely as means to your own ends, and (5) not using company resources for one's own purposes.

- Managers should encourage and promote the discussion of ethical dilemmas. Employees should not be punished for questioning a decision on moral grounds. However, one of the difficulties of discussing ethics at work is that some people take the "moral high road" and criticize those who do not share their values. This makes it difficult to have reasoned discussions and often results in polarized views. Work at identifying and understanding the different perspectives on an issue and discuss the consequences of alternative actions that might be taken.

- Use the Ethics Warning System when you make a decision:[47]
    - **Golden Rule** Are you treating others as you would want to be treated?
    - **Publicity** Would you be comfortable if your reasoning and decision were to be publicized (i.e., how would it look on the front page of tomorrow's papers)?
    - **Kid on your shoulder** Would you be comfortable if your children were observing you? Is your behavior an example of ethical behavior?

- Whistle blowing is legitimate (1) when it would benefit the public interest; (2) when the revelation is of major importance and very specific; (3) when the facts have been checked and rechecked for accuracy; (4) when all other avenues within the organization have been exhausted; and (5) when the whistle blower is above reproach and has no personal advantage to gain by revealing the information.[48]

- Some companies utilize peer review systems to analyze their own ethics programs and find out what other companies are doing.[49]

PERSONAL APPLICATION ASSIGNMENT

Think back over the last few years and try to recall a specific event or situation at school, work, or home when you were confronted with an ethical dilemma or a difficult situation that called for a socially responsible action. Some examples might be taking something that did not belong to you, observing someone else's dishonest behavior, or having to decide between looking out for yourself and possibly harming another person.

1. In writing, describe the situation in some detail. Who else was there besides yourself? What were they doing? What were you doing? If you were on the receiving end of an unethical act, how were you treated? What were the issues involved?

2. What were the conflicts or dilemmas for you in this situation?

3. Why were they conflicts?

4. What did you do?

5. Why did you do that? Were there extenuating circumstances that affected your decision?

6. What were the results of your actions?

7. At the time of the situation, did you think you did the right thing?

8. Now, looking back, what if anything would you do differently?

9. What conclusions or lessons can you draw from this reflection?

ENDNOTES

[1] P. Hawken, *The Ecology of Commerce: A Declaration of Sustainability.* (New York: HarperBusiness, 1993).

[2] T. Petzinger, "Business Achieves Greatest Efficiencies When at Its Greenest," *Wall Street Journal*, July 11, 1997, B1.

[3] Ibid.

[4] H. Bradbury and J. A. Clair, "Promoting Sustainable Organizations with Sweden's Natural Step," *Academy of Management Executive*, 13, no. 4 (1999): 63–74.

[5] Petzinger, op. cit.

[6] Bradbury and Clair, op. cit.

[7] *The Natural Step: From Consensus to Sustainable Development* (Sausalito, CA: The Natural Step, 1997).

[8] Bradbury and Clair, op. cit., p. 72.

[9] The authors would like to thank Bruce Drake, James Weber, and Judith White for their contributions to this chapter. The instructions for scoring this version of the Rokeach Value Survey were developed by James Weber, "Managerial Value Orientations: A Typology and Assessment," *International Journal of Value Based Management 3(2)* (1990): 37–54, and adapted by Bruce Drake.

[10] This exercise was developed and copyrighted (1988) by James Weber, director of the Beard Center for Leadership in Ethics, Duquesne University. It is reprinted here with his permission.

[11] P. Steidlmeir, *People and Profits: The Ethics of Capitalism* (Upper Saddle River, NJ: Prentice-Hall, 1992).

[12] M. Josephson, *Making Ethical Decisions* (Marina Del Rey, CA: The Josephson Institute of Ethics, 1993), 4.

[13] R. F. Hartley, *Business Ethics: Violations of the Public Trust* (New York: John Wiley & Sons, 1993). This book describes ethical scandals and how companies handled them.

[14] Hartley, *Business Ethics*, 1 and 323.

[15] R. D. Haas, "Ethics—A Global Business Challenge," *Vital Speeches of the Day* (1994): 506–09.

[16] M. Josephson, *Ethical Obligations and Opportunities in Business: Ethical Decision Making in the Trenches* (Marina Del Rey, CA: Josephson Institute of Ethics, 1990).

[17] B. Z. Posner, and W. Schmidt, "Values and the American Manager: An Update Updated," *California Management Review* (Spring 1992): 80–94.

[18] Hartley, *Business Ethics*, 5; and G. F. Cavanagh, *American Business Values* (Englewood Cliffs, NJ: Prentice-Hall, 1984), 159.

[19] M. J. Baasten and B. H. Drake, "Ethical Leadership," *Social Sciences Perspectives Journal* (March 1990).

[20] R. C. Solomon, *Ethics and Free Enterprise in the Global 1990s* (Lanham, MD: Littlefield Adams, 1993).

[21] F. B. Bird and J. A. Waters, "The Moral Muteness of Managers," *California Management Review* (Fall 1989): 73–88.

[22] R. E. Boyatzis, and F. R. Skelly, "The Impact of Changing Values on Organizational Life," *The Organizational Behavior Reader* (Upper Saddle River, NJ: Prentice Hall, 1995).

[23] R. L. Sims, and E. G. Kroeck, "The Influence of Ethical Fit on Employee Satisfaction, Commitment and Turnover," *Journal of Business Ethics 13* (1994): 939–47.

[24] M. Rokeach, *The Nature of Values* (New York: The Free Press, 1973).

[25] J. Weber, "Exploring the Relationship Between Personal Values and Moral Reasoning," *Human Relations 46* (4) (1993): 435–63 and "Managerial Value Orientations: A Typology and Assessment," *International Journal of Value Based Management 3* (2) (1990): 37–54; and G. F. Cavanagh, *American Business Values.*

[26] D. A. Clare and D. G. Sanford, "Mapping Personal Value Space: A Study of Managers in Four Organizations," *Human Relations 32* (1979): 659–66.

[27] These core ethical values were developed by a diverse group of 30 national leaders. M. Josephson, *Making Ethical Decisions*, 9.

[28] Weber, "Personal Values and Moral Development," 459.

[29] L. K. Trevino and S. A. Youngblood, "Bad Apples in Bad Barrels: A Causal Analysis of Ethical Decision-Making Behavior," *Journal of Applied Psychology 75* (1990): 378–85.

[30] L. Kohlberg, "Stages of Moral Development as a Basis for Moral Education," in C. M. Beck, B. S. Crittenden, and E. V. Sullivan (eds.), *Moral Education: Interdisciplinary Approaches* (New York: Newman Press, 1971); and A. Colby and L. Kohlberg, *The Measurement of Moral Judgment, Vol. 1: Theoretical Foundations and Research Validations* (Cambridge, MA: University Press, 1987).

[31] These titles are taken from D. A. Whetton and K. S. Cameron, *Developing Managerial Skills* (New York: HarperCollins, 1991), 60.

[32] The more descriptive stage names are taken from L. K. Trevino, "A Cultural Perspective on Changing and Developing Organizational Ethics," in *Research in Organizational Change and Development* (eds.), W. A. Pasmore and R. W. Woodman (Greenwich, CT: JAI Press, 1990) pp. 195–230.

[33] L. Kohlberg, *Essays in Moral Development, Vol. I: The Philosophy of Moral Development* (New York: Harper & Row, 1981); and R. Duska and M. Whalen, *Moral Development* (New York: Paulist Press, 1975).

[34] Weber, "Personal Values and Moral Reasoning," p. 454.

[35] Ibid, 441.

[36] C. Gilligan, *In a Different Voice* (Cambridge, MA: Harvard University Press, 1982); C. Gilligan, and J. Attanucci, "Two

Moral Orientations: Gender Differences and Similarities," *Merrill-Palmer Quarterly 34* (1988): 223–37.

[37] G. R. Wark, and D. L. Krebs, "Gender and Dilemma Differences in Real-Life Moral Judgment," *Developmental Psychology 32*, no. 2 (1996): 220–31.

[38] C. Argyris, *Overcoming Organizational Defences: Facilitating Organizational Learning* (Boston: Allyn and Bacon, 1990).

[39] R. S. Snell, "Complementing Kohlberg: Mapping the Ethical Reasoning Used by Managers for Their Own Dilemma Cases," *Human Relations 49*, no. 1 (1996): 23–50.

[40] S. K. Lau, and H. C. Kuan, *The Ethos of the Hong Kong Chinese* (Hong Kong: Chinese University Press, 1988) and C. C. Ji, "Collectivism in Moral Development," *Psychological Review 80*, no. 3, (1997): 967–76.

[41] This case was originally prepared by Professor LaRue Tone Hosmer as a basis for class discussion. The names of all individuals and names and locations of all firms have been disguised. The case is copyrighted (1978) by the Regents of University of Michigan and is reprinted here with the author's permission.

[42] The first four ethical models are described in Cavanagh, *American Business Values*, pp. 139–45 and G. F. Cavanagh, D. J. Moberg, and M. Velasquez, "The Ethics of Organizational Politics," *Academy of Management Review 6* (3) (1981): 363–74 and "Making Business Ethics Practical," *Business Ethics Quarterly 5*, 3 (1995): 399–18.

[43] C. Gilligan, *In a Different Voice* (Cambridge: Harvard University Press, 1982).

[44] G. Dutton, "The Green Bottom Line," *Management Review 87*, no. 9 (1998): 59–64; C. Merchant, "Environmental Ethics and Political Conflict," *Environmental Ethics 12*, no. 1 (1990): 45–68; A. Miller, *Gaia Connections* (Savage, MD: Rowman and Littlefield, 1991); R. A. Buchholz, *Principles of Environmental Management: The Greening of Business* (Upper Saddle River, NJ: Prentice Hall, 1998).

[45] Adapted from L. L. Nash, "Ethics Without the Sermon," *Harvard Business Review* (November–December 1981): 79–90.

[46] "Doing the Right Thing," *The Economist 335*, no. 7915 (1995): 64.

[47] Josephson, *Making Ethical Decisions*, 40.

[48] S. Bok, "Whistleblowing and Professional Responsibilities," in *Ethics Teaching in Higher Education*, ed. D. Callahan and S. Bok (New York: Plenum Press, 1980), 277–95.

[49] *Business Ethics: Generating Trust in the 1990s and Beyond* (New York: The Conference Board, 1994), 8.

Chapter 6

▲▲▲

CAREER DEVELOPMENT AND WORK STRESS

OBJECTIVES By the end of this chapter, you should be able to:

A. Describe the characteristics of adult development.

B. Explain Levinson's concept of life structures.

C. Recognize career anchors and their significance.

D. Describe the functions that mentors perform.

E. Identify trends in career management and planning.

F. Explain the transactional model of career stress.

G. Assess your current life-career situation and develop a plan for the future.

OVERLOAD

Workloads never set out to hurt anybody. But doesn't it seem like over the past couple of years, someone named "Mr. Overload" muscled his way into all of our workplaces, sat down in our chairs and took over our lives? Both the increased speed and complexity of work these days is leaving everyone from the executive suite to the factory floor throbbing from a massive migraine just trying to get all their work done.

Why this has happened, and why no one seems to be talking about it intelligently, let alone doing something constructive about it—is even more puzzling.

WHAT'S CAUSING OVERWORK AND WHY IS IT A PROBLEM?

You guessed it. Most employees don't just sign up to get overworked because they enjoy it. Economic, technological and business factors such as downsizing, the skills shortage and low unemployment have forced those American workers who were left sitting in the hot seat to give 150 percent (or more) just to stay on top of their workloads. Now, U.S. business leaders have come to expect and rely on this accelerated pace. What were once considered crises-mode workloads have now become business as usual. After all, the more people get done, the more our companies profit, right? True, the United States certainly *is* enjoying economic nirvana, but at what price? Collective burnout? Of course, burnout isn't new, but what *is* new is the way in which job overload—causing burnout—has elbowed its way into most of our work lives, sometimes without our even realizing it's a problem.

Take Jennifer Johnson, for instance. Johnson, who's now the principal strategist for Johnson & Co. in Santa Cruz, California, is a classic example of a fast-tracker who was headed for burnout, but jumped off the train before she crashed. "I was a corporate warrior for about 15 years," says Johnson. "When I first left college, I immediately began working 80-hour weeks in my first job at Novell in Provo, Utah." As a 22-year-old editor, she turned the company's in-house newsletter into an international consumer magazine that Novell sold three years later to The McGraw-Hill Companies for $10 million. She recalls nights when she'd stay at the office until 2 A.M., and was back in the office by 8 o'clock the next morning. "I realized it was the dues-paying time of my life and I actually thrived on the fast pace," Johnson admits.

After she took a job in advertising at another firm, got married and had kids, the pace became dizzying. She vividly remembers her breaking point 19 months ago when life and work clashed in the extreme. "My husband Scott, who headed the marketing function for one of 3Com's international-business units, was returning from a trip to Japan. The plan was for me to hand off the kids to him at the airport, and then I was going to catch a plane for the East Coast." It turns out her husband's plane was 20 minutes late. The moment he arrived, she threw the kids to him and sprinted to her own plane, luggage in tow.

In flight and exhausted, Johnson found herself writing a resignation letter. "I was laughing out loud as I wrote it because it was so obviously what I needed to do," she says. Johnson then started her own company—a virtual marketing organization that teams 17 contractors, mostly women, from across the country. Many of them were as desperate to balance their lives as she was. "I saw a lot of women who were forced to make the choice of either working or taking care of their families because their companies wouldn't be flexible," says Johnson. "I'm now seeing a world in which employees, after being downsized and rightsized, are turning the tables and they're *my-sizing* their jobs."

Workers who feel trapped in jobs in which they're powerless to do something about it tend to burn out faster. Ironically, those employees who are in fast-track careers are often the first ones to crash and burn, according to Beverly Potter, a workplace consultant and author of *Overcoming Job Burnout: How to Renew Enthusiasm for Work* (Ronin Publishing, 1998).

Although Johnson admits when she was a 22-year-old she actually liked being what she calls a "fast burner," it wore her out after a while. Right before she left Novell the second time (she returned there after the ad agency job), she asked to be able to telecommute two days a week. "It really surprised me that they were unwilling to let me do that, even though they're a technology company," says Johnson. She found during her second maternity leave that she often got a lot more done working at home than when she was in the office—and having to contend with meetings, interruptions and mountains of extraneous information. "If HR and business line managers could start thinking outside the box about what *really* needs to get done, I think it would help relieve a lot of people's workloads."

If we can call it the bright side, all this overtime is helping push the recent surge in American workers' productivity. After growing at a brisk 2.9 percent annual rate in the 1960s and early 1970s, productivity slowed to a miniscule 1 percent from 1974 through 1995. Since then, it has been growing at around a 2 percent rate. That growth has led some economists to speculate that the economy has embarked on a new era of productivity growth, driven by computers and other high-tech innovations.

With the influx of technology, such as cellular phones and the Internet, workers are wired to the office 24 hours a day and are expected to achieve mind-boggling workloads. The *Associated Press* reported last May that the average business manager receives 190 messages per day.

Hundreds are quitting Corporate America daily because they're tired of the empty promises about companies helping them "balance their lives." The HR questions are: Have jobs grown too big for most workers? And what are companies really doing about it?

REENGINEERING JOBS TO FIT EMPLOYEES

One of the running jokes at Redmond, Washington-based Microsoft Corp. is you can work any 18 hours a day you want. Although it's well known that Microsoft employees reap hefty rewards for their intense productivity in terms of comp, benefits, stock options and the like, making overwork the corporate requirement can have its drawbacks. Many companies recognize the problem, and many think they've already solved it. But they should take another look at their solutions.

According to Terry Alan Beehr, professor of psychology at Central Michigan University in Mount Pleasant, Michigan, and an authority on organizational psychology, job stress is too often treated with medication or counseling rather than by making changes in the workplace and in workloads.

Companies need to take stock of where they're really at with their workloads and how those workloads piled up to where they are today. "This is a time when work needs to be trimmed just as firmly as the workforce has been trimmed," says William Bridges, consultant and author. He explains that companies have cut people out of the workforce (downsized) with razor-sharp accuracy, but haven't trimmed the workloads of the people who've remained with the same vigor. As a consultant, he has noticed there's a great deal of unnecessary work being done in U.S. companies. "Justifying work is very important," Bridges adds. It's a matter of figuring out what work is necessary and what isn't. It's essentially reengineering workloads. "I know that reengineering has a bad name," says Bridges, "but we need to take a close look at what we're making workers do." However, unlike reengineering, he says this is something workers themselves have to be very involved in.

For example, the HR leaders at Merck & Co., the giant pharmaceutical company based in Whitehouse Station, New Jersey, realized after hearing workers' complaints about overwork, inadequate training, schedule changes, poor new-hire screening and lack of communication, among other things, that they needed to respond—quickly. In a major work redesign effort, Merck's management team assigned employees to teams that were devoted to solving these problems. Work was analyzed, dissected and reorganized so that workers felt like they had more control over their workloads and schedules. "We focused on the things that are really important to our customers," says Michelle Peterson, senior director of work/life flexibility, who oversaw the effort.

In one area of the company, payroll employees weren't happy with the large amount of overtime they had to put in. During a series of meetings, team leaders realized that most of their work was more critical earlier in the week than toward the end of the week. Solutions included reducing peoples' commute time by allowing them to work at home more often, and giving them compressed work weeks. They provided technology so payroll workers could input data at home. Solutions to the most difficult problems were implemented within three months and turnover slowed from 45 percent to 32 percent, and is still dropping. In addition, overtime costs and absenteeism plummeted. And for the employees, overtime and commute time were slashed.

HR managers should also be willing to suggest that managers outsource tasks that are unnecessary, or could be done more effectively by a third party. "Who should do the work?" is the question every manager should ask about every bit of work. "And you may find some of the work could go outside, and you readjust what's left so it isn't so overwhelming," says Bridges.

Dell Computer Corp.'s direct-to-customer business model, for example, takes outsourcing to a new level. The firm doesn't just outsource a few tasks; it actually turns over three-quarters of its work to non-employees, particularly field service and manufacturing.

FOCUS ON WHAT'S MOST IMPORTANT

According to an article in the *Salt Lake Observer* in October 1998 called "The Zen of Managing Transition," one expert reminds us that you get what you focus on.

These days, in a 24-hour-a-day, global marketplace that moves faster than the speed of e-mail, it's important for HR managers to help their firms' management groups figure out what's most important to get done.

For example, this strategy has been a big focus at San Francisco-based AirTouch Communications Inc. this year. Tracey Borst, who heads the firm's HR team, says although she hears rumblings about overwork from time to time, the "noise level" about it hasn't gotten in the way lately. To nip the problem in the bud, the senior management team has been trying to get better at prioritizing work throughout the company by letting employees know which company goals are most important. "Even if we had all the money in the world, we still wouldn't have enough people and would have to let some things fall by the wayside," says Borst. "There's a limited number of resources to maintain customers and to create new products, so you have to focus on what's most important and create a balance."

Still, even with all the tweaking of processes and technological advances, why is it that companies are scrupulous about maintaining their inert equipment, but don't pay as much attention to giving their human assets workload tune-ups? Machines regularly get oiled, cleaned and tuned. But when it comes to workers, we just expect they'll handle ever-increasing amounts of work without regard to regular check-ups.

When you come right down to it, perhaps we can't prevent "Mr. Overload" from coming to our offices altogether. But we can learn to work with him more consciously and intelligently. There are some new tools and ideas HR professionals can use to alleviate the work overload problem. Recognizing the problem exists and that it can be destructive is a good first step.

Source: Excerpted from Jennifer Laabs, "Workforce Overload," *Work Force 78* (January 1999): 30–37.

PREMEETING PREPARATION

A. Read "Overload."

B. Read the entire chapter.

C. Complete the Life Goal Inventory.

D. What are the significant learning points from the readings?

E. If your instructor has assigned the Robbins Self-Assessment Library, use "What's My Locus of Control?" "Am I a Type-A?" "Am I Likely to Become an Entrepreneur?" "How Heavy is My Workload?" "Am I Experiencing Work-Family Conflict?" "How Stressful is my Life?" and "Am I Burned Out?"

LIFE GOAL INVENTORY

1. The purpose of the Life Goal Inventory is to give you an outline for looking at your life goals in a more systematic way. Your concern here should be to describe as fully as possible your aims and goals in all areas of your life. Consider goals that are important to you, whether they are relatively easy or difficult to attain. Be honest with yourself. Having fun and taking life easy are just as legitimate life goals as being president. You will have a chance to rate the relative importance of your goals later. Now you should try to just discover *all* the things that are important to you. To help make your inventory complete, we have listed general goal areas on the following pages. They are:

   - Career satisfaction
   - Status and respect
   - Personal relationships
   - Leisure satisfactions
   - Learning and education
   - Spiritual growth and religion
   - Material rewards and possessions

These categories are only a general guide; feel free to change or redefine them in the way that best suits your own life. The unlabeled area is for those goals that do not seem to fit into the other categories.

First fill in your own goals in the various sections of this inventory, making any redefinitions of the goal areas you feel necessary. Ignore for the time being the three columns on the right-hand side of each page. Directions for filling out these columns are on page 124.

Career Satisfaction

General Description: Your goals for your future job or career, including specific positions you want to hold.

Individual Redefinition:

Specific Goals	Importance (Hi, Med, Lo)	Ease of Attainment (Hi, Med, Lo)	Conflict with Other Goals (Yes or No)
1.			
2.			
3.			

Status and Respect

General Description: To what groups do you want to belong? What are your goals in these groups? To what extent do you want to be respected by others? From whom do you want respect?

Individual Redefinition:

Specific Goals	Importance (Hi, Med, Lo)	Ease of Attainment (Hi, Med, Lo)	Conflict with Other Goals (Yes or No)
1.			
2.			
3.			

Personal Relationships

General Description: Goals in your relationships with your significant other, colleagues, parents, friends, and people in general.

Individual Redefinition:

Specific Goals	Importance (Hi, Med, Lo)	Ease of Attainment (Hi, Med, Lo)	Conflict with Other Goals (Yes or No)
1.			
2.			
3.			

Leisure Satisfactions

General Description: Goals for your leisure time and pleasure activities—hobbies, sports, vacations, and interests you want to develop.

Individual Redefinition:

Specific Goals	Importance (Hi, Med, Lo)	Ease of Attainment (Hi, Med, Lo)	Conflict with Other Goals (Yes or No)
1.			
2.			
3.			

Learning and Education

General Description: What would you like to learn more about? What skills do you want to develop? What formal education goals do you have?

Individual Redefinition:

Specific Goals	Importance (Hi, Med, Lo)	Ease of Attainment (Hi, Med, Lo)	Conflict with Other Goals (Yes or No)
1.			
2.			
3.			

Spiritual Growth and Religion

General Description: Goals for peace of mind, your search for meaning, your relation to the larger universe, religious service, and devotional life.

Individual Redefinition:

Specific Goals	Importance (Hi, Med, Lo)	Ease of Attainment (Hi, Med, Lo)	Conflict with Other Goals (Yes or No)
1.			
2.			
3.			

Material Rewards and Possessions

General Description: What income level are you aiming for—upper class, middle class, voluntary simplicity?* What possessions do you want?

Individual Redefinition:

Specific Goals	Importance (Hi, Med, Lo)	Ease of Attainment (Hi, Med, Lo)	Conflict with Other Goals (Yes or No)
1.			
2.			
3.			

* Voluntary simplicity, both an inner and outer condition, is gaining popularity in the United States. It means deliberately organizing one's life around a purpose and avoiding exterior distraction and clutter, such as possessions that are irrelevant to one's chief purpose in life. Some people who practice voluntary simplicity set a goal of earning only enough income to support a pared-down lifestyle, which allows them to work less than 40 hours a week. They then take the freed-up time and devote it to whatever purpose they have chosen for themselves.

Open

Definition:

Specific Goals	Importance (Hi, Med, Lo)	Ease of Attainment (Hi, Med, Lo)	Conflict with Other Goals (Yes or No)
1.			
2.			
3.			

Directions for Rating Goals

2. *Goal importance:* Now that you have completed the inventory, go back and rate the importance of each goal according to the following scheme:

Hi (High)   Compared with my other goals, this goal is very important.

Med (Medium)   This goal is moderately important.

Lo (Low)   A lot of other goals are more important than this one.

Ease of goal attainment: According to the following scheme, rate each goal on the probability that you will reach and/or maintain the satisfaction derived from it.

Hi (High)   Compared with my other goals, I could easily reach and maintain this goal.

Med (Medium)   I could reach and maintain this goal with moderate difficulty.

Lo (Low)   It would be very difficult to reach this goal.

Goal priorities: Select the goals from the inventory that seem most important to you at this time. Do not choose more than eight. Rank order them in terms of their importance. (1 = High, 8 = Low)

1.

2.

3.

4.

5.

6.

7.

8.

3. *Anticipating conflicts:* One of the major deterrents to goal accomplishment is the existence of conflict among goals.

People who ignore the potential conflicts between job and family, for instance, may end up abandoning goals because of the "either/or" nature of many decisions. Or years later they may come to regret sacrificing family needs for the sake of career demands or vice versa.

In the order you prioritized in the preceding step, list your goals on both axes of the following matrix. Write your first goal where it says "Goal 1" on both axes, your second goal where it says "Goal 2," and so forth. Next, estimate the potential impact of the vertical goal statements you've written along the side of the chart on the horizontal goal statements you've written along the top. Please use the following symbols:

(+) for a helpful impact ("working on goal 1 will help me with goal 3")

(−) for a hindering impact ("working on goal 2 will make it more difficult to accomplish goal 5")

(0) for no impact of any kind

THE CROSS-IMPACT MATRIX

	GOAL 1	GOAL 2	GOAL 3	GOAL 4	GOAL 5	GOAL 6	GOAL 7	GOAL 8
GOAL 1	✕							
GOAL 2		✕						
GOAL 3			✕					
GOAL 4				✕				
GOAL 5					✕			
GOAL 6						✕		
GOAL 7							✕	
GOAL 8								✕

List conflicts in order of importance:

1.

2.

3.

4.

5.

Note: The Personal Application Assignment for this chapter is a continuation of this exercise.

TOPIC INTRODUCTION

One of managers' most important tasks concerns the personal growth and career development of their employees and themselves. Theories of adult development provide insight into our personal experience and help us to understand the developmental phases and challenges facing our colleagues at work.

Theorists generally agree on the following characteristics of adult development.[1]

1. Personality development occurs throughout the life cycle as a succession of fairly predictable phases.

2. Each stage is characterized by a cycle of intensity and quiescence. The equilibrium of the

former stage is disrupted, initiating intense coping efforts and activity that often result in life changes. This is followed by another period of equilibrium.

3. The disequilibrium of each stage is caused by a focal conflict or dilemma, which is created by internal forces, environmental demands, or both.

4. People cope with these focal conflict or dilemmas either positively through growth or negatively through defensiveness and regression.

5. Personal growth results from mastering the developmental tasks required to resolve the focal dilemma, satisfying both personal needs and social responsibilities.

Figure 6-1 portrays the stages three different researchers have identified. Gould[2] concentrates on the inner subjective experiences of individuals forming each period; his view asserts that we grow up with a mythical idea of adulthood and that, as we age, we need to let go of the myth and accept ourselves and the reality of our lives. Levinson, on the other hand, describes the developmental tasks that must be mastered before one can successfully move on to the next stage of development.[3]

Sheehy's stages reflect the current trends of taking longer to grow up and become full-fledged adults and longer to grow old. In the provisional adulthood of the "tryout twenties," the central task is to choose a life course. In first adulthood the focus on proving oneself and surviving gives way to mastery and a search for meaning in the first part of second adulthood. The final years of life are devoted to integrating the different parts of one's life.[4]

Age	Roger Gould	Gail Sheehy	Daniel Levinson
16	Escape from parental dominance	Provisional adulthood	Leaving the family
18			
20	Substitute friends for family		
22			
24	Aspiring builders of future		Getting into the adult world
26			
28	What am I doing and why?	First adulthood	
30			
32	A sense of urgency to make it		
34			
36			Transition period
38			Settling down and becoming one's own person
40			
42			
44	On terms with self as a stable personality		
46		Second adulthood	
48		Age of mastery	
50	Mellowing of friendships—valuing of emotions		
52			Midlife transition
54			
56			Restabilization and entering into middle age
58			
60			
62			Another transition
64			
66		Age of Integrity	
68			
70			
72			
74			
76			
78			
80			
82			
84			
86			

FIGURE 6-1   **Models of Adult Development**
Source: Dr. Eric Neilsen, *Case Western Reserve University*, Cleveland, Ohio.

Levinson developed his theory of adult development from biographical interviews with 40 men; he later expanded his research to include women. One of the gender differences Levinson found was that young men more easily formed a dream about what they would become than did young women. Another difference was that men were more likely to have a family and a career simultaneously if they so desired. In contrast, the women in the study made an either/or choice about family and career and had fewer cultural role models to guide them.

Other differences have been found between male and female development.[5] Male development focuses on independence, self-sufficiency, and an emphasis on work and career. In contrast, female development emphasizes interdependence and a struggle to combine relationships and accomplishments. Generally speaking, development for men signifies increased autonomy and separation from others so that they can concentrate fully on their work. Whereas men gain their primary identity from their work, women are more likely to define themselves in relation to others, so they focus more on attachments than separation.

Levinson and his colleagues[6] concluded that both men and women face a recurring developmental task at different stages of their lives. They must establish a "life structure," which refers to the pattern or design of a person's life, that is appropriate for each era of life. Life structures last approximately six to eight years and constitute periods of stability. However, life structures become obsolete because no single structure could contain all aspects of the self or respond to the demands of different eras. For example, a man or woman who has been staying at home taking care of small children may no longer find this life fulfilling when the children become older and more independent. At this point, he or she may decide to return to work or develop an artistic side that was not possible given the previous child care demands. When a life structure no longer fits, people undergo a transition period that lasts four to five years. During this period, they reexamine their lives and eventually decide upon a new direction or life structure. The most widely recognized transition period is the midlife crisis when people age 38 to 45 reevaluate what they have accomplished in comparison with their ambitions and decide where they would like to place greater priority in the coming years. Transition periods are characterized by self-centeredness, introspection, and ambivalence about intimate relationships; during the periods of stability, people are more other-centered and dedicated to investing time and energy to key social relationships.[7]

The developmental challenge and dilemma facing people in their twenties (22 to 28) is to remain open enough to explore the world and stay committed enough to make something of themselves. Some people keep all their options open and make few commitments, while others marry young and/or invest in a serious career effort. Whatever options people build into their early adult life structure, they are likely to question these early decisions when they reach the age of 30 and have enough years of adult experience to reassess their dreams. Similar transitions occur around ages 40 and 50. It is during these transitions that people make changes in their lives and try to build a life structure that is more attuned to the person they have become and that allows them to place more priority on areas that are central to them and that they may have had to shortchange in their earlier life structure. There is some evidence that people who do not resolve these issues during one transition will eventually be forced to confront them in a later transition.

Whether or not these life transitions turn into full-blown crises depends on the individuals and their circumstances. For some people it's more a matter of reform than revolution. A crisis occurs when individuals find their current life structure intolerable but are not yet able to create a new one. How can managers help people through this process?

1. By expecting the phenomenon and seeing it as a normal stage of healthy adult development rather than a sign of instability.
2. By practicing active listening[8] or perhaps referring the individual to a professional counselor.
3. By being as flexible as possible regarding the changes the employee feels he or she needs to make.

CAREER ISSUES

In addition to a basic understanding of adult development, managers should also understand the key findings of career development research, which are presented in the following sections.

Career Anchors

In the beginning of one's career, the major psychological issue is figuring out a career direction that meets one's needs and interests. Schein developed one of the most helpful models for diagnosing career interests, which he termed *career anchors*. As Schein states, "Certain motivational, attitudinal, and value syndromes formed early in the lives of individuals apparently function to guide and constrain their entire careers."[9] When people stray too far from these key interests, they serve as an anchor that pulls people back to their original interest. Different types of career anchors are (1) technical/functional competence, (2) managerial competence, (3) security and stability, (4) creativity/entrepreneurship, (5) autonomy and independence, (6) service, (7) pure challenge, and (8) lifestyle. These anchors, along with the characteristics of people with these anchors and their typical career paths, appear in Figure 6-2.

Career Anchor	Characteristics	Typical Career Paths
1. Technical/functional competence	• Excited by work itself • Willing to forgo promotions • Dislikes management and corporate politics	• Research-oriented position • Functional department management job • Specialized consulting and project management
2. Managerial competence	• Likes to analyze and solve knotty business problems • Likes to influence and harness people to work together • Enjoys the exercise of power	• Vice-presidencies • Plant management and sales management • Large, prestigious firms
3. Security and stability	• Motivated by job security and long-term career with one firm • Dislikes travel and relocation • Tends to be conformist and compliant to the organization	• Government jobs • Small family-owned business • Large government-regulated industries
4. Creativity/entrepreneurship	• Enjoys launching own business • Restless; moves from project to project • Prefers small and up-and coming firms to well-established ones	• Entrepreneurial ventures • General management consulting
5. Autonomy and independence	• Desires freedom from organizational constraints • Wants to be on own and set own pace • Avoids large businesses and governmental agencies	• Academia • Writing and publishing • Small business proprietorships
6. Service	• Enjoys work that manifests own values • Having an impact, not money, is central • Expect management to share own values	• Consultants • Financial analysts • Non-profit organizations • Socially responsible firms
7. Pure Challenge	• Prove self • Seeks ever greater challenges • Enjoys competition and winning	• Strategy/management consultants • Naval aviators
8. Lifestyle	• Integrates needs of individual, family and career • Desires flexibility (part-time work, sabbaticals, maternity/paternity leaves, etc.) • Common with dual career families	• Consultants • Socially progressive companies

FIGURE 6-2   **Career Anchors**

Source: Adapted from the work of Edgar H. Schein, *Career Dynamics* (Reading, MA: Addison-Wesley, 1978), "Individuals and Careers," in Jay W. Lorsch (ed.), *Handbook of Organizational Behavior* (Upper Saddle River, NJ: Prentice-Hall, 1987): 155–71; and adapted by the authors and R. Dunham and J. Pierce, *Management* (Glenview, IL: Scott, Foresman, 1989): 857.

Balancing Dual Careers

One of the most challenging aspects of modern life is balancing the demands of dual careers and raising a family. Three out of five U.S. marriages are dual-career couples.[10] Although this results in higher income, stress is a common feature of many dual-career marriages when couples run up against relocation issues, child-rearing responsibilities, and demanding jobs that leave little time to take care of the home front. Working wives who still carry the major burden of household tasks experience a great deal of stress. Couples generally adopt one of the following strategies to manage dual careers.[11]

1. **Limiting the impact of family on work**   Parents can delay having children or subcontract the child-rearing to day care centers or domestic help.
2. **Taking turns**   Spouses trade off career opportunities and child care at different times.
3. **Participating in joint ventures**   Both spouses have the same career or different careers in the same organization.
4. **Choosing independent careers**   Both partners pursue their careers as fully as possible and learn to cope with long separations or commuter marriages.
5. **Subordinating one career to the other**   One partner may leave the workforce or accept a job that is less demanding so that the other partner can optimize his or her career opportunities.

All of these strategies have advantages and disadvantages. The disadvantages have to do with who pays the cost—the children, the marriage, or the partner who is sacrificing so that the other can maximize career opportunities, and so forth. If couples can agree on a strategy and align the rest of their lives accordingly, some of the stresses found in dual-career marriages are more manageable.

Mentoring

A mentor is a senior person within the organization who assumes responsibility for a junior person. Mentors help socialize newcomers or junior members. Mentoring relationships occur either naturally or as part of a company program to develop junior employees. AT&T Bell Laboratories assigns mentors to women and minority hires and "technical mentors" to help new employees master their jobs. Research has shown that having a mentor was one of the characteristics that differentiated female executives who made it to the top from those who did not.[12] A study of both men and women found that those who were extensively mentored received more promotions, were more highly paid, and reported higher job satisfaction than those who received little mentoring.[13]

What is it that mentors do for their protégés? Kram identified two functions: career and psychosocial functions.[14]

Career functions consist of:

1. **Sponsorship**   Actively nominating a junior manager for promotions and desirable positions.
2. **Exposure and Visibility**   Matching the junior manager with senior executives who can provide opportunities and giving the junior person chances to demonstrate his or her ability (e.g., letting the junior person make important presentations that are attended by key executives).
3. **Coaching**   Giving practical advice on how to accomplish objectives and achieve recognition.
4. **Protection**   Shielding a junior manager from potentially harmful situations or senior managers.
5. **Challenging Assignments**   Helping a junior manager develop necessary competencies through challenging job assignments and feedback.

The psychosocial functions are:

1. **Role Modeling**   Giving a junior manager a pattern of values and behavior to imitate. (This is the most common of the psychosocial functions.)
2. **Acceptance and Confirmation**   Providing mutual support and encouragement.
3. **Counseling**   Helping a junior manager work out personal problems, thus enhancing his or her self-image.
4. **Friendship**   Engaging in mutually satisfying social interaction.

Career Management and Planning

There have been numerous changes in the area of career planning. In career management the necessity of tying strategic planning to human resource management has gained greater acceptance, along with the expectation that managers should be trained to provide career counseling to employees.[15] Leaner management hierarchies and the baby boom cohort have made assessment of management potential and succession management more appealing. Flatter organizations have also focused attention on the need for nontraditional career paths that provide alternatives to promotion such as lateral or rotational moves, dual-career ladders, downward moves, and early retirement.

There is more emphasis on self-directed careers as a response to downsizing. The burden lies on employees to learn skills that are in demand to maintain their employability and reputational capital. Midcareer choice points seem to be occurring earlier due to the bulge of baby boomers in managerial jobs and the need for balance in dual-career families. Today's employees are more likely to question and reject transfers and even promotions. Opting for self-initiated career plateauing (a cap to upward mobility) due to family considerations or lack of desire to assume the burdens of greater management responsibility is becoming more common, although it is still seen as un-American in some companies. Partly due to the glass ceiling that limits both women and minorities from reaching senior positions, more and more women are forsaking the corporate career path to become entrepreneurs. Freedom and flexibility are other reasons women give for starting a business. Women-owned U.S. businesses increased 42 percent from 6.4 million in 1992 to 9.1 million in 1999.[16]

There is currently a growing emphasis in the United States upon spirituality and finding meaning at work.[17] According to John Renesch, editor and publisher of the New Leaders Business Press, "There is a core need within individuals to bring their entire selves to the workplace, not to turn off their heart and soul when they go to work."[18] "New Age" leaders like Tom Chappell of Tom's of Maine, Anita Roddick of the Body Shop, and Susie Tompkins of Esprit have designed companies "with soul" that respond to this need.

Because people can expect to have numerous jobs (13 jobs that will last an average of 3.5 years), numerous employers, and more than one career, they will face far more career decisions than their parents or grandparents. To make good decisions, self-awareness and an understanding of adult development in general are both helpful. The turbulent nature of today's careers also affects how we see ourselves. In earlier times, personal identity was maintained in a relatively stable environment of known expectations. Once on a life path, personal choice was primarily a process of affirming expectations. People obtained a college degree or M.B.A., gained experience, and worked their way up the organization. They were "managers" who also derived part of their identity from their employer ("I'm an IBMer"). In today's "future shock" world, environmental complexity and change have denied us the easy route to personal identity. Now, more than ever, identity is forged through personal choices. The challenge is to make the "right" choices and manage our careers wisely.

Goal setting is a critical aspect of personal growth and career development. The ability to conceptualize life goals and to imagine future alternatives for living can free us from the inertia of the past by providing future targets that serve as guides for planning and decision making. Research results from several areas—management, psychotherapy, and attitude change—all confirm the importance of goal setting for personal growth and achievement of one's goals.[19] The increased likelihood of change resulting from the setting and articulating of goals is illustrated, for example, by Kay, French, and Myer, who found that improvement needs among managers were accomplished only about one-fourth of the time when they were not translated into goals in performance appraisal interviews. When these needs were transformed into clearly stated goals, the likelihood of accomplishment increased to about two-thirds.[20] It is not enough just to think about how you would like to change. It is necessary to translate those visions into concrete goals.

The following exercises provide an opportunity to gain greater self-awareness and develop career planning skills.

MY LIFE LINE

PROCEDURE FOR GROUP MEETING: THE LIFE LINE, WHO AM I? AND THE PAST EXPERIENCE INVENTORY

SELF-ASSESSMENT AND LIFE PLANNING

(Time Allotted: 1 Hour, 25 minutes)

STEP 1. **Form trios for life planning (5 minutes)** The total groups should divide into groups of three for the purpose of sharing the Life Goal Inventory prework and working together on the life planning activities that follow.

STEP 2. **Life line exercise (10 minutes)** Each member of the trio should draw a line in the box on the preceding page to describe his or her view of his or her whole life from beginning to end.

Draw a line that corresponds to your own concept of your life line. Your life line can be any shape and can go in any direction. It could be a road, a river, a thread, a path, a graph line, or anything else you can imagine. Another way to think of it is as a route across a map. Place a mark on this line to show where you are right now. Discuss the feelings and thoughts you had in drawing the line and in placing your mark with others in your trio.

Notice that each life line has three distinct portions: your past, the place you are now (the *X*), and the portion of the line that represents your view of your future career path. These three portions represent the three basic perspectives for self-assessment and career planning.

The Past

Your unique experiences, acquired skills, and personal history.

- The past has happened; we cannot change it.
- Our past has a place in our current lives; we need to accept it and use it creatively but not be inhibited by it.
- The past, creatively used, yields insight about our unfulfilled potential.
- The past creates expectations for ourselves and can influence or limit the goals we set for the future.

The Present

The here-and-now of your life with all its joys and frustrations; your current priorities as they are embodied in your daily life situation and the way you spend your time.

- Individuals can consciously plan their lives by assessing themselves, their environments, and their resources in the present.
- You can choose where you would like to go on the basis of what satisfies you now.
- We need symmetry and wholeness in our lives. Often we make choices in the present that lead to a lopsided future (e.g., being too career oriented at the expense of a private life of fun, friends, and family).
- Each person has a reservoir of undeveloped potential in the present that suggests directions for future development.

The Future

Your fantasies, dreams, goals, hopes, and fears, as well as specific commitments and responsibilities you have undertaken.

- In large part, we can create our own future.
- Our future becomes self-determined to a large degree through the choices we make in the present.
- We can try to create the future by the process of:

By using the combination of these three perspectives on your life, it is possible to develop a more fulfilling life plan. By taking all three perspectives into account, a kind of triangulation occurs that identifies common themes from your past, your present, and your future.

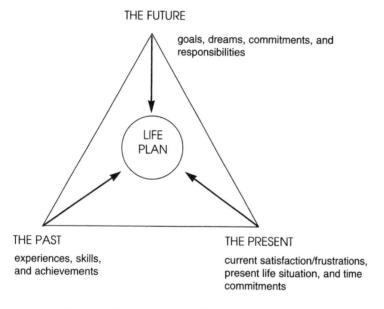

The next three exercises for your trio ask you to work together to assess yourselves from these three perspectives.

STEP 3.   **Who am I *now?* (20 minutes)**
- Write 10 separate short statements that answer the question, "Who am I?"
- Then rank these statements according to their importance to you.
- Discuss your answers and rankings with others in your trio.

Rank Order   Who Am I?

_____   1. I am _____

_____   2. I am _____

_____   3. I am _____

_____   4. I am _____

_____   5. I am _____

_____   6. I am _____

_____   7. I am _____

_____ 8. I am _____

_____ 9. I am _____

_____ 10. I am _____

STEP 4. **Past experience inventory** (30 minutes) Complete the following questions and discuss them in your trio.

Approximate
Dates

1. Who have been the most influential people in your life, and in what way have they been influential?

_____ _____

_____ _____

_____ _____

2. What were the critical incidents (events) that made you who you are?

_____ _____

_____ _____

_____ _____

3. What have been the major interests in your past life?

_____ _____

_____ _____

_____ _____

4. What were your significant work experiences?

_____ _____

_____ _____

_____ _____

5. What were the most significant decisions in your life?

_____ _____

_____ _____

_____ _____

6. What role have family, societal, and gender expectations played in your life?

_____ _____

_____ _____

_____ _____

7. Where do you feel fully alive, excited, turned on? Under what conditions does this occur?

_____ _____

_____ _____

_____ _____

8. Where do you feel dull, routine, turned off? What conditions produce that?

9. What are you really good at? What strengths do you have to build on?

10. What do you do poorly? What do you need to develop or correct?

11. What do you want to stop doing or do much less of?

12. What do you want to start doing or do much more of?

13. What do you want to learn or develop in yourself?[21]

STEP 5.   **My future goals (20 minutes)**   Share your Life Goal Inventory prework with each other. Your work on the previous exercise may suggest changes to you. If so, make them.

FOLLOW-UP

In cultures that believe in fate and destiny (e.g., Arab countries and Latin America), people are less proactive about planning their careers because "what will be will be." Cultures that believe people are the master of their own fate (such as the United States) place more emphasis on career planning. The disadvantage of the belief that humans control their destiny is that people blame themselves when they fail to achieve their career goals and ignore the role of luck. When economies undergo major restructuring, the careers of many people are disrupted through no fault of their own.

In recent years, reengineering, downsizing, and increased competition have been responsible for increased career-related stress. Obsolescence, midcareer transitions, job loss or threat of job loss, diminished upward mobility, forced early retirement, dual-career pressures,[22] increased workloads for the survivors in downsized companies, and lack of balance between work and nonwork are all sources of stress. The World Health Organization estimates the global price tag for job stress at more than $200 billion in absenteeism, tardiness, worker's compensation, and health care.[23]

Stress is defined as the nonspecific response of an organism to demands that tax or exceed its resources. There are three stages in the stress response: alarm, resistance, and finally,

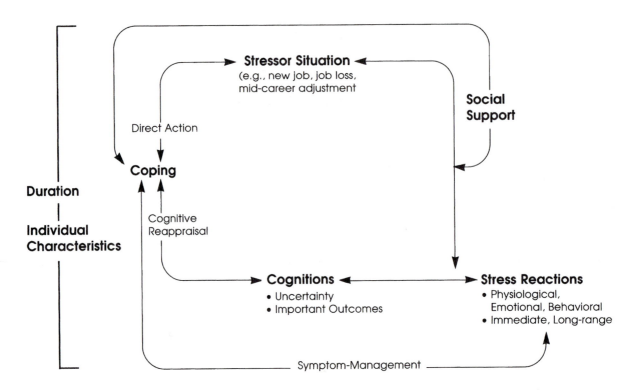

FIGURE 6-3 **Transactional Model of Career Stress**

exhaustion.[24] Stress is positive when it motivates us to work harder and negative when the stress level is greater than our coping abilities. In the latter instance, stress interferes with our ability to perform at work and can result in illness.

The transactional model of career stress is portrayed in Figure 6-3. We begin with a *stressor situation*, which can be either external, such as a new job or job loss, or internal, like a midcareer transition resulting from a shift in personal values. Stressors take the form of demands, constraints, or opportunities. A stressor does not result in a stress reaction unless it is first perceived as a stressor. What is stressful to one person may be merely challenging to another because people have different cognitions about stressor situations. *Cognitions* are "the individual's perceptions that the situation poses uncertainty about obtaining outcomes, and the perceived importance of those outcomes."[25] Thus, stress will be greater if people perceive that they have a lot at stake. For example, it is one thing to lose a job that you really enjoy with no other prospects in sight and no money in the bank. It is quite another to lose a job you dislike intensely when you have a sizable trust fund to fall back on.

The next category in the model is *stress reactions*. These can be physiological (e.g., pulse rate, blood pressure), emotional (e.g., anxiety, irritability), or behavioral (e.g., loss of sleep, weight gain). There are both immediate (e.g., job dissatisfaction) and long-term stress reactions (e.g., illness or job change).

Coping is the means by which individuals and organizations manage external or internal demands that tax or exceed the individual's resources. Coping strategies focus on (1) changing the situation (direct action), (2) changing the way we think about the situation (cognitive reappraisal), or (3) focusing on the stress reaction (symptom management). Not all coping mechanisms that focus on symptom management are positive. For example, drinking and overeating are harmful whereas meditation and exercise are positive. It is more effective to reduce or eliminate the source of stress (the stressor situation) than to treat its symptoms through stress management.[26] Coping mechanisms are an attempt to establish some degree of control over the situation and prevent a stress reaction.

Social support is another factor that can prevent stress. It is defined as receiving information that tells people they are loved, respected, valued, and part of a network of mutual obligations.[27] People who receive social support from their supervisors, coworkers, or families are somewhat buffered from the effects of stress.

The *duration* of the stressor situation also plays a role in this model. The longer the stressful situation lasts, the more likely that health problems will result. It is interesting that "daily hassles" may actually cause more stress than critical life events, such as divorce or the death of a loved one.[28] Stress is additive, which means that a seemingly innocuous stressor may be "the straw that breaks the camel's back" if the person has already been exposed to too many other stressors. This is another reason why the same stressful work event may impact individuals in different ways.

Individual characteristics also affect the stress process. For example, people who exhibit *Type A behavior who are quick to anger, mistrustful, and suspicious of other people* are more likely candidates for stress-related heart disease than both Type A personalities who are not hostile and people with Type B behavior.[29] The characteristics of Type A behavior are an obsession with achieving more and more in less and less time, inability to cope with leisure time, doing two or more things at once, impatience with the time it takes to make things happen, constant movement, and rapid walking and eating. Many workaholics exhibit this behavior, but only when it is accompanied by a hostile attitude is it harmful to the individual's health. Type B behavior is characterized by the absence of time urgency and impatience, no felt need to display or discuss achievements, and playing for fun and relaxation without an accompanying sense of guilt.

People with *external locus of control*, who believe that their lives are controlled by outside forces, also perceive situations to be more stressful than people who believe they control their own destiny. The latter condition is referred to as internal locus of control.[30]

Women and minorities in nontraditional careers, such as management, experience their own particular brand of work stress and career limitations like the glass ceiling. For example, African American career stress is referred to as a "Black Tax" that results from (1) having to prove their competence by being workaholics, (2) mutual feelings of distrust between African American executives, and (3) being involved with organizational policies that are not in the best interest of African Americans.[31]

Companies should be aware of the cost of excessive work stress, not only for minorities, but for all employees—decreased job satisfaction and performance, and increased absenteeism, alcohol and drug abuse, and illness.

Overwork is a potential source of stress as well as a detriment to personal satisfaction and family and community life, according to social critics. A recent study[32] found that the *average* number of hours in the U.S. workweek has not changed significantly since the 1970s (37 hours for women and 42 hours for men). There are, however, more individuals working either long or short weeks. Many of those working long weeks (who tend to more skilled and highly educated) would like to reduce their hours, while some employees working short weeks would prefer a regular 40-hour week with full benefits. The percentage of employees working at least 50 hours a week has increased to 25 percent of men and 10 percent of women. In one study, 45 to 50 percent of all workers (and 80 percent of those working over 50 hours a week) reported that they would like to have more free time; 25 percent of them would be willing to take a pay cut to work fewer hours.

Why haven't U.S. businesses responded and reduced work overloads? Many companies would rather overwork some employees and underwork others than pay costly benefits for more full-time employees. This practice may be beneficial to owners and stockholders in the short run; if we consider, however, the costs to a broader set of stakeholders—individual workers, their families, and their communities—the picture is less positive. Overworked people need time to nurture and maintain their families and relationships, to volunteer in their communities, and to replenish their energies and avoid burnout.[33] Finding a balance between work and nonwork is a personal challenge for many employees and an important HR issue for many organizations.

LEARNING POINTS

1. Adult development occurs in a succession of fairly predictable phases characterized by equilibrium and disequilibrium. The disequilibrium results from new psychological issues that arise from new internal forces and/or external demands or pressures.

2. According to Levinson, the developmental task for adults is to establish a life structure—the pattern or design of a person's life—that is appropriate for each stage of their lives.

3. People go through both stable and transitional periods. During the latter, individuals reevaluate and recreate their life structures. Transitions occur about the ages of 30, 40, and 50. If they are very turbulent, they are called crises.

4. Career anchors are motivational, attitudinal, and values syndromes formed early in life that function to guide and constrain people's careers.

5. The different career anchors are (a) technical/functional competence, (b) managerial competence, (c) security and stability, (d) creativity/entrepreneurship, (e) autonomy and independence, (f) service, (g) pure challenge, and (h) lifestyle.

6. The five strategies for managing dual careers are (a) limiting the impact of family on work, (b) taking turns, (c) participating in joint ventures, (d) choosing independent careers, and (e) subordinating one career to the other.

7. A mentor is a senior person within the organization who assumes responsibility for a junior person.

8. People who were extensively mentored received more promotions, were more highly paid, and reported higher job satisfaction than those who received little mentoring. Mentoring is especially helpful for women and minorities.

9. The career functions of mentoring are (1) sponsorship, (b) exposure and visibility, (c) coaching, (d) protection, and (e) challenging assignments.

10. The psychosocial functions of mentoring are (a) role modeling, (b) acceptance and confirmation, (c) counseling, and (d) friendship.

11. Current trends in career management include tying strategic planning to human resource management, training managers in career counseling, assessment of management potential, succession planning, and nontraditional career paths.

12. Current trends in career planning consist of self-directed careers, earlier midcareer status, more questioning/rejection of job moves and promotions, increased self-initiated career plateauing, and career planning as a mutual responsibility of the employee and organization. This results in greater employee need for information about career opportunities within the company.

13. People who set clearly stated career goals are more likely to achieve them.

14. Stress is defined as the nonspecific response of an organism to demands that tax or exceed its resources.

15. The transactional model of career stress consists of stressor situations, cognitions, and stress reactions. Social support and coping can prevent stress reactions. The stress process is also affected by the duration of the stressor and individual characteristics.

16. There are three types of coping mechanisms: direct action, cognitive reappraisal, and symptom management.

17. People who receive social support from their supervisors, coworkers, or families are somewhat buffered from the effects of stress.

18. Individual characteristics that are related to greater susceptibility to stress are hostile Type A behavior and external locus of control.

19. The cost of excessive work stress is decreased job satisfaction and performance, increased absenteeism, alcohol and drug abuse, and illness.

FOR MANAGERS

- Managers who sincerely try to help employees reach their career goals are usually rewarded with loyalty and commitment.
- Managers are more likely to provide effective counseling to employees if they themselves also receive it from their superiors. It should be modeled for them.
- Organizations that evaluate their managers on their ability to develop employees will generally see more positive results in this area. It's not enough to state that career development is important; measuring and rewarding it provides a clearer message that career development is valued.
- Personal growth or change is not a steady progression but rather a series of fits and starts.
- Once again, managers need to recognize that employees will have unique career goals and life situations. Too often managers who are single-mindedly pursuing a suite at the top find it difficult to value employees who are content to remain where they are. As long as employees perform their jobs well, lack of driving ambition should not be held against them.
- Managers need to bear in mind the different career stages of their employees. For example, a young "fast tracker" who may have many of the other skills needed for a managerial job may still be too involved in establishing his or her own career to mentor subordinates adequately. The best mentors are most likely to be found in the 40 to 60 age group because this coincides with a stage of adult development in which guiding the younger generation assumes greater importance. Individuals can also seek mentors outside their organization.
- Managers who drive their employees so hard that it is impossible for them to have a personal life usually have a higher degree of turnover.
- Take a careful look at workaholics. Sometimes working long hours is not a habit to admire but an indication of inefficient work habits and lack of social life outside of work. If this is the case, their need to socialize on the job may actually prevent other employees from getting their work done.
- Work schedules that change constantly do not allow employees to create a life outside of work. This is generally not healthy for an extended period. Most people need a balanced life to keep a perspective on problems and find a measure of contentment.
- Good time management skills can reduce stress.
- Make sure you are not a stress "carrier" who generates stress in subordinates by being disorganized, putting employees in double binds, making impossible demands, and so forth.
- Managers should understand that some kinds of stress at work cause people to resign while other types help retain employees. Examples of "bad stress" include office politics, red tape, and stalled careers. "Good stress" includes the challenges that accompany increased job responsibility, high-quality assignments, and time pressure. When employees perceive that stressful situations will result in money, new skills, or promotion, they are more likely to have a better attitude toward them and stay on the job.[34]
- When change is looming on the horizon or hits your organization or industry, try to adapt quickly rather than bemoaning the loss of "the way things were." Learn new skills or position yourself to weather such changes.

PERSONAL APPLICATION ASSIGNMENT

Eisenhower once said, "A plan is nothing; planning is everything." In career planning, too, the plan itself is not as valuable as the act of planning. Plans must give way to outside contingencies. But the process of planning—taking stock, devising objectives and possible means of reaching a goal, and then checking to see how one is faring and coming up with a new plan if necessary—is extremely valuable.

This assignment is the Goal Achievement Plan and Achievement Progress Record. It is designed to help you create a plan for attaining a goal you select to work on in the immediate future. The steps in the plan are based on the factors that research has shown to be characteristic of successful goal achievers. Following these steps should help you improve your ability to achieve your goals.

A. From the Life Goal Inventory that you completed in the premeeting preparation, pick the goal you most want to work on in the *next six months*. In choosing this goal you should consider the following issues. (See the ratings you made of goals.)

   1. Importance of the goal

   2. Ease of attainment

   3. Whether the goal is in conflict with other goals

B. The overall goal you choose to work on may include two or three of the goals you listed in the inventory. The main thing is to be clear about the future state you are striving for. To do this, complete the following Goal Definition form.

GOAL DEFINITION

   1. State as specifically as possible what goal you want to achieve *in the next six months*.

Now think about your goal in terms of the following questions.

   2. How important is it that you achieve your goal?

   3. What conflicts are there with other goals? How will you manage the conflicts?

4. How will you feel when you attain this goal? (Try to imagine yourself with the goal achieved. What are your feelings?)

5. How will you feel if you do not attain this goal? (Try to imagine again. What are your feelings?)

6. What do you think about your chances of succeeding? What will happen if you do succeed?

7. What will happen if you fail?

C. Now that you have defined your goal, the next step is to plan how to achieve it. There are two issues to be examined: the personal shortcomings and external obstacles that may prevent you from reaching your goal.

The questions on the accompanying Removing Obstacles and Planning Action form are designed to help you accomplish this.

REMOVING OBSTACLES AND PLANNING ACTION

What personal shortcomings might keep me from achieving my goal?

1.

2.

3.

4.

What external obstacles might keep me from achieving my goal?

1.

2.

3.

4.

What can I do to eliminate or lessen the effect of any of these obstacles or shortcomings? (Note that you need not eliminate the block entirely. Anything you can do to lessen the force of the obstacle will start you moving toward your goal.)

Obstacle	What I Can Do About It
_____	_____
_____	_____
_____	_____
_____	_____
_____	_____
_____	_____
_____	_____
_____	_____
_____	_____
_____	_____
_____	_____
_____	_____
_____	_____
_____	_____

What specific things can I do that will move me toward my goal?

1.

2.

3.

4.

5.

Circle the one that you are going to emphasize the most.

Who Can Help me Achieve my Goals?	What Will I Ask of them?
1. _____	_____
_____	_____
_____	_____
_____	_____
_____	_____
2. _____	_____
_____	_____
_____	_____
_____	_____
_____	_____
3. _____	_____
_____	_____
_____	_____
_____	_____
_____	_____
4. _____	_____
_____	_____
_____	_____
_____	_____
_____	_____

PROGRESS REPORT

Now that you have made your plan, the next task is to put it into effect. Figure out what steps you must take to reach your goal and how you will measure your progress. Plan out what you need to do each week and how long it will take to meet your goal. You may want to choose a partner who will help you monitor your progress. You can agree on a contract that stipulates how often you will check in with each other and what kind of help you want from your partner.

ENDNOTES

[1] D. M. Wolfe and D. A. Kolb, "Career Development, Personal Growth, and Experiential Learning," *Reader* (1991): 147.

[2] R. L. Gould, *Transformations* (New York: Simon and Schuster, 1979).

[3] D. J. Levinson, "A Conception of Adult Development," *American Psychologist 41*, no. 1 (January 1986): 3–13.

[4] G. Sheehy, *New Passages* (New York: Ballantine 1995); and *Understanding Men's Passages* (New York: Ballantine, 1999).

[5] This section is taken from J. V. Gallos, "Exploring Women's Development: Implications for Career Theory, Practice and Research." In M. Arthur, D. T. Hall, and B. S. Lawrence (eds.), *Handbook of Career Theory* (Cambridge: Cambridge University Press, 1989): 110–32.

[6] D. J. Levinson, in collaboration with C. N. Darrow, E. B. Klein, M. H. Levinson, and M. Braxton, *Seasons of a Man's Life* (New York: Ballantine, 1978), and ibid., 1986.

[7] D.C. Feldman, "Career Stages and Life Stages: A Career-Development Perspective," The 1987 Annual: *Developing Human Resources* (LaJolla, CA: University Associates, 1987): 231.

[8] For more details on active listening, see Chapter 7, *Interpersonal Communication* and Rogers and Farson's article entitled "Active Listening" in the *Reader*.

[9] E. Schein, *Career Dynamics: Matching Individual and Organizational Needs* (Reading, MA: Addison-Wesley, 1978): 133, and "Individuals and Career," in J. W. Lorsch (ed.), *Handbook of Organizational Behavior* (Upper Saddle River, NJ: Prentice-Hall, 1987): 155–71.

[10] J. A. Jacobs, and K. Gerson, "Who Are the Overworked Americans?" *Review of Social Economy 56* (1998): 442.

[11] E. H. Schein, *Career Dynamics: Matching Individual and Organizational Needs*; and L. Bailyn, "Involvement and Accommodation in Technical Careers: An Inquiry into the Relation to Work at Mid-Career." In J. Van Maanen (ed.), *Organizational Careers: Some New Perspectives* (New York: John Wiley, 1977).

[12] A. M. Morrison, R. P. White, E. Van Velsor, and the Center for Creative Leadership, *Breaking the Glass Ceiling: Can Women Reach the Top of America's Largest Corporations?* (Reading, MA: Addison-Wesley, 1987).

[13] G. Dreher and R. A. Ash, "A Comparative Study of Mentoring among Men and Women in Managerial, Professional, and Technical Positions," *Journal of Applied Psychology* (October 1990): 539–46.

[14] K. E. Kram, *Mentoring at Work: Developmental Relationships in Organizational Life* (Glenview, IL: Scott, Foresman, 1985), 22–39.

[15] M. B. Arthur, D. T. Hall, and B. S. Lawrence, *Handbook of Career Theory* (New York: Cambridge University Press, 1989); and D. T. Hall, *Career Development in Organizations* (San Francisco: Jossey-Bass, 1986).

[16] "Work Week," *Wall Street Journal*, June 8, 1999, A-1.

[17] J. Conger, *Spirit at Work: Discovering the Spirituality in Leadership* (San Francisco: Jossey Bass, 1994).

[18] G. Rifkin, "Finding Meaning at Work," *Strategy & Business* (Fourth Quarter 1996): 15–17.

[19] D. A. Kolb and R. E. Boyatzis, "Goal-Setting and Self-Directed Behavior Change," *Reader* (1984).

[20] E. Kay, J. R. P. French, Jr., and H. H. Meyer, "A Study of the Performance Appraisal Interview" (Management Development and Employee Relations Services, General Electric Co., New York, 1962).

[21] Questions 7–12 were adapted by D. M. Wolfe from the work of Herbert Shepard.

[22] Janina C. Latack, "Work, Stress, and Careers: A Preventive Approach to Maintaining Organizational Health," in M. Arthur, D. T. Hall, and B. S. Lawrence (eds.), *Handbook of Career Theory* (Cambridge: Cambridge University Press, 1989): 252.

[23] B. L. Seaward, "Job Stress Takes a Global Toll," *Safety & Health 151*, no. 1 (1995): 64–66.

[24] H. Selye, *The Stress of Life* (New York: McGraw-Hill, 1956); and "The Stress Concept: Past, Present, and Future," in C. L. Cooper (ed.), *Stress Research: Issues for the 80's* (New York: Wiley, 1983).

[25] Latack, *Work, Stress, and Careers*, 254.

[26] C. L. Cooper, and S. Cartwright, "Healthy Mind; Healthy Organization—A Proactive Approach to Occupational Stress," *Human Relations 47*, no. 4 (1994): 455–72.

[27] S. Cobb, "Social Support as a Moderator of Life Stress," *Psychosomatic Medicine 38* (1976): 300–14.

[28] R. S. Lazarus and A. DeLongis, "Psychological Stress and Coping in Aging," *American Psychologist 38* (1983): 245–54.

[29] R. Williams, *The Trusting Heart: Great News about Type A Behavior* (New York: Times Books, 1989).

[30] K. R. Parks, "Locus of Control, Cognitive Appraisal and Coping in Stressful Episodes," *Journal of Personality and Social Psychology 46* (1984): 655–68.

[31] D. L. Ford, "Job-Related Stress of the Minority Professional: An Exploratory Analysis and Suggestions for Future Research." In T. A. Beehr and R. S. Bhagat (eds.), *Human Stress and Cognition in Organizations* (New York: Wiley, 1985): 287–24.

[32] Jacobs and Gerson, "Who Are the Overworked Americans?," 442.

[33] J. S. Osland, B. H. Drake and H. Feldman, "The Stewardship of Natural and Human Resources," *All Nature Is Groaning*, C. J. Dempsey and R. A. Butkus (eds.) (Collegeville, MN: Liturgical Press, 1999): 168–92.

[34] "Good Stress, Bad Stress," *HR Focus 76* (April 1999): 4.

Part 2

▲▲▲

CREATING EFFECTIVE WORK GROUPS

In Part 2, we will focus on developing the key skills needed by effective managers and employees.

Chapter 7

▲▲

INTERPERSONAL COMMUNICATION

OBJECTIVES By the end of this chapter, you should be able to:

A. Understand the transactional model of communication.

B. List common sources of distortion in communication.

C. Identify gender differences in communication.

D. Describe and identify the five response styles.

E. Explain how to create a climate that encourages nondefensive communication.

F. Recognize assertive communication and utilize I-statements.

G. Improve your active listening skills.

COMMUNICATION MISTAKES ONLY REALLY SMART PEOPLE MAKE

When I first entered the workplace, I suffered the smugness shared by many young people who have had success in college. I could write well under the pressure of deadlines and felt comfortable speaking in public. I was quick to learn new skills and could solve technical problems that baffled more experienced colleagues. I had lots of energy, loved to work hard, and enjoyed succeeding at complex tasks. I was an up-and-coming star.

However, despite what I thought were my superior workplace skills, no one seemed to want to work with me. During meetings, my ideas were ignored. I was passed over for a promotion with the vague explanation that I needed to work on my interpersonal skills.

Although my technical skills were beyond reproach, I never seemed to progress in my career. My explanation: I wouldn't "suck-up" to the boss; I told the truth, particularly about the failings of my coworkers; and I intimidated other people with my intelligence and proficiency.

So I started the slow evolution into one of those bitter, sarcastic people I now see too often in the workplaces I visit. You probably know at least one.

I am one of the lucky ones. Because of the early intervention of several compassionate supervisors, I learned that the reason that I was not doing well had nothing to do with the jealousies or inadequacies of others.

To paraphrase one of my mentors, "The problem is not that you are so smart, Pat; the problem is that you are a jerk." ("Jerk" translates into "oblivious and/or unconcerned about how one's poor interpersonal skills impact others.")

Smart people are sometimes susceptible to "Jerkitude," because, if they are task oriented and have been rewarded only for measured success with computers, budgets, and other inanimate objects, they might ignore or even disparage the "soft" skills, such as negotiation, conflict management, and delegation. But, even if you are currently successful at building productive relationships, a change in your personal or professional situation can also change your behavior for the worse.

Here are some warning signs and prevention tips regarding three kinds of communication mistakes I have seen and heard in workplaces all over the United States, including universities, federal laboratories, high-tech companies, and research departments. Unfortunately, I am almost always there because the "jerk" factor is out of control, despite the fact that the majority of employees and administrators have postgraduate education and many years of experience. Being smart is not enough to protect you from these mistakes.

KEEPING IN THE BEST PERFORMANCE STATE

The first key to maintaining and improving excellent communication is to take your physical and emotional health seriously. How you feel, which is impacted by everything from the ugly situation with your daughter to the effects of the antibiotics you took for a gum infection, can impact your ability to assess accurately and respond effectively to situations in the workplace. You might not feel that your technical work has suffered, but did you slam that perfect budget report on the desk instead of handing it to the accountant with a smile?

At a radio station, one of the news anchors was coping with her mother, who was dying of cancer. Her way of dealing with the lack of control in her personal life was to become a raging perfectionist at work. When she realized what was happening, she asked a friend to give her a scorecard at the end of each day, particularly regarding her behavior during meetings with her producers and engineers. It took only two such scorecards for the news anchor to realize that she was not doing anyone a favor by staying on the job. She arranged a leave of absence, stayed with her family until her mother passed away, and then returned to work.

Of course, not everyone works for an institution where the policies allow for leeway during personal crises. And not everyone is fortunate to have honest and friendly coworkers. However, my experience is that you are deluding yourself if you think that willing away the effects of sadness, pain, and pharmaceuticals will ensure your workplace behavior is impeccable.

THE WRONG PROFESSIONAL ATTITUDE

Sometimes the cause of a smart person's behavior has nothing to do with a denial of the effects of stress. Sometimes an ineffective communication style is the result of years of conditioning, where the smart person is led to believe that being smart is the only measure of success, usually because he or she was rewarded for succeeding at taking tests or advancing through a hierarchical workplace, such as a university or large corporation. The smart person, in this case, thinks that all rank, authority, influence, and privilege in the workplace should be measured by "smart."

- "I have the most degrees, so I get to make the decisions for the group."
- "Only people who graduated from my prestigious college or its equivalent should be allowed into our program."
- "Hello, my name is Pat, and here is my IQ, as verified by a high-IQ organization. And what is your IQ? Oh, yes, and your name?"

My favorite story about ignoring rank comes from a pathologist, who ran a large laboratory. When a tissue sample defied diagnosis, he would recruit an ad hoc panel to comment on the problem. He always included young and relatively inexperienced lab technicians in the process. He had discovered that their fresh viewpoints were key to successfully analyzing the slides and specimens.

COMMUNICATION CLIMATE INVENTORY

The following statements relate to how your supervisor and you communicate on the job. There are no right or wrong answers. Respond honestly to the statement, using the following scale:

1. Strongly Agree
2. Agree
3. Uncertain
4. Disagree
5. Strongly Disagree

	Strongly Agree	Agree	Uncertain	Disagree	Strongly Disagree
1. My supervisor criticizes my work without allowing me to explain.	1	2	3	4	5
2. My supervisor allows me as much creativity as possible in my job.	1	2	3	4	5
3. My supervisor always judges the actions of his or her subordinates.	1	2	3	4	5
4. My supervisor allows flexibility on the job.	1	2	3	4	5
5. My supervisor criticizes my work in the presence of others.	1	2	3	4	5
6. My supervisor is willing to try new ideas and to accept other points of view.	1	2	3	4	5
7. My supervisor believes that he or she must control how I do my work.	1	2	3	4	5
8. My supervisor understands the problems that I encounter in my job.	1	2	3	4	5
9. My supervisor is always trying to change other people's attitudes and behaviors to suit his or her own.	1	2	3	4	5
10. My supervisor respects my feelings and values.	1	2	3	4	5
11. My supervisor always needs to be in charge of the situation.	1	2	3	4	5
12. My supervisor listens to my problems with interest.	1	2	3	4	5
13. My supervisor tries to manipulate subordinates to get what he or she wants or to make himself or herself look good.	1	2	3	4	5
14. My supervisor does not try to make me feel inferior.	1	2	3	4	5
15. I have to be careful when talking to my supervisor so that I will not be misinterpreted.	1	2	3	4	5
16. My supervisor participates in meetings with employees without projecting his or her higher status or power.	1	2	3	4	5
17. I seldom say what really is on my mind because it might be twisted and distorted by my supervisor.	1	2	3	4	5
18. My supervisor treats me with respect.	1	2	3	4	5
19. My supervisor seldom becomes involved in employee conflicts.	1	2	3	4	5
20. My supervisor does not have hidden motives in dealing with me.	1	2	3	4	5
21. My supervisor is not interested in employee problems.	1	2	3	4	5
22. I feel that I can be honest and straightforward with my supervisor.	1	2	3	4	5
23. My supervisor rarely offers moral support during a personal crisis.	1	2	3	4	5
24. I feel that I can express my opinions and ideas honestly to my supervisor.	1	2	3	4	5
25. My supervisor tries to make me feel inadequate.	1	2	3	4	5
26. My supervisor defines problems so that they can be understood but does not insist that his or her subordinates agree.	1	2	3	4	5
27. My supervisor makes it clear that he or she is in charge.	1	2	3	4	5
28. I feel free to talk to my supervisor.	1	2	3	4	5
29. My supervisor believes that if a job is to be done right, he or she must oversee it or do it.	1	2	3	4	5
30. My supervisor defines problems and makes his or her subordinates aware of them.	1	2	3	4	5
31. My supervisor cannot admit that he or she makes mistakes.	1	2	3	4	5
32. My supervisor tries to describe situations fairly without labeling them as good or bad.	1	2	3	4	5
33. My supervisor is dogmatic; it is useless for me to voice an opposing point of view.	1	2	3	4	5
34. My supervisor presents his or her feelings and perceptions without implying that a similar response is expected from me.	1	2	3	4	5
35. My supervisor thinks that he or she is always right.	1	2	3	4	5
36. My supervisor attempts to explain situations clearly and without personal bias.	1	2	3	4	5

COMMUNICATION CLIMATE INVENTORY SCORING AND INTERPRETATION SHEET

Place the numbers that you assigned to each statement in the appropriate blanks. Now add them together to determine a subtotal for each climate category. Place the subtotals in the proper blanks and add your scores. Place an X on the graph to indicate what your perception is of your organization or department's communication climate. You may wish to discuss with others their own perceptions and interpretations.

Part I: Defensive Scores

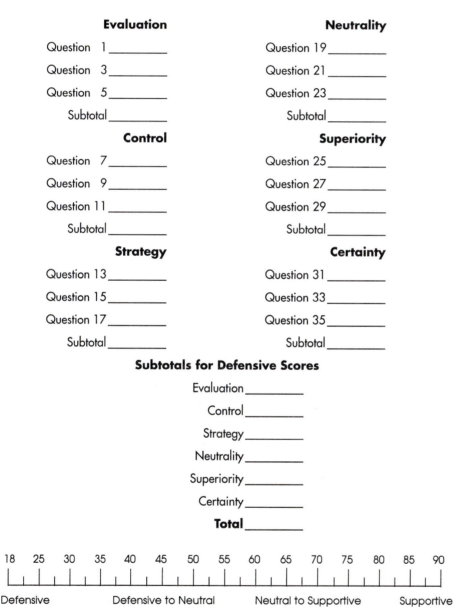

Evaluation

Question 1 _____

Question 3 _____

Question 5 _____

Subtotal _____

Neutrality

Question 19 _____

Question 21 _____

Question 23 _____

Subtotal _____

Control

Question 7 _____

Question 9 _____

Question 11 _____

Subtotal _____

Superiority

Question 25 _____

Question 27 _____

Question 29 _____

Subtotal _____

Strategy

Question 13 _____

Question 15 _____

Question 17 _____

Subtotal _____

Certainty

Question 31 _____

Question 33 _____

Question 35 _____

Subtotal _____

Subtotals for Defensive Scores

Evaluation _____

Control _____

Strategy _____

Neutrality _____

Superiority _____

Certainty _____

Total _____

18 25 30 35 40 45 50 55 60 65 70 75 80 85 90

Defensive   Defensive to Neutral   Neutral to Supportive   Supportive

Part II: Supportive Scores

Provisionalism

Question 2 _____

Question 4 _____

Question 6 _____

Subtotal _____

Empathy

Question 8 _____

Question 10 _____

Question 12 _____

Subtotal _____

Equality

Question 14 _____

Question 16 _____

Question 18 _____

Subtotal _____

Spontaneity

Question 20 _____

Question 22 _____

Question 24 _____

Subtotal _____

Problem Orientation

Question 26 _____

Question 28 _____

Question 30 _____

Subtotal _____

Description

Question 32 _____

Question 34 _____

Question 36 _____

Subtotal _____

Subtotals for Supportive Scores

Provisionalism _____

Empathy _____

Equality _____

Spontaneity _____

Problem Orientation _____

Description _____

Total _____

| 18 | 25 | 30 | 35 | 40 | 45 | 50 | 55 | 60 | 65 | 70 | 75 | 80 | 85 | 90 |

Supportive   Supportive to Neutral   Neutral to Defensive   Defensive

Note: See Jack Gibb's article on defensive communication in *Journal of Communication 11*, no. 3 (1961): 141–148 or in the *Reader* for an explanation of the framework underlying this instrument.

TOPIC INTRODUCTION

You can have brilliant ideas, but if you can't get them across, your brains won't get you any-where. . . . I hadn't yet learned what I know now—that the ability to communicate is everything.

Lee Iacocca, former CEO of Chrysler

Communication is an essential skill at all levels of business. It is the most important competency for entry-level job candidates, according to the managers who hire them.[1] At the M.B.A. level where technical proficiency is assumed, the top three selection criteria of recruiters from Fortune 500 companies are strong interpersonal skills, communication skills, and team-oriented skills.[2] As an experienced executive recruiter noted, "There are lots of brilliant people who can't relate with others—we replace that kind of person every day."[3]

Mintzberg's ground-breaking study on the nature of managerial work identified communication as the most frequent and important of managerial activities.[4] He described the manager's work as essentially that of communication. Mintzberg claimed that many managers spend 80 percent of their time in verbal communication.[5]

And even when managers are not trying to communicate, their actions (or lack thereof) are taken as messages. It's impossible to not communicate; rather the question for managers is, "Am I communicating effectively?" The definition of communication is *the process by which information is exchanged between communicators with the goal of achieving mutual understanding.*

To better understand this complex process of interpersonal communication, let's examine the basic model of communication that follows.

THE COMMUNICATION MODEL

The Greeks believed that the god Mercury plucked ideas from the brain of the speaker, impaled the ideas on the end of a spear, and plunged them into the listener's brain. Today communication is viewed as a transactional process.

The model shown in Figure 7-1 has two communicators who participate equally and sometimes simultaneously in the communication process.[6] While Person A sends a message, Person B listens and responds, verbally or nonverbally, sending a message of his or her own. Thus, as Person A speaks, he or she is also "listening" and receiving a message from Person B. This is called

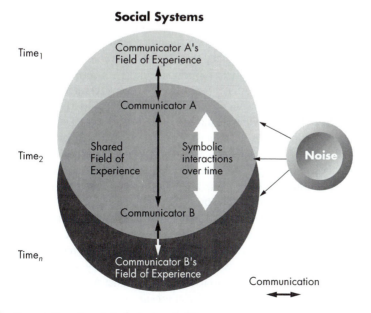

FIGURE 7-1   **Transactional model of communication**
Source: J. T. Wood, *Communication in Our Lives* (New York: Wadsworth, 1997): 21. Reprinted with permission.

a transactional model because it acknowledges that our responses to speakers' messages lead them to modify what they say next. Furthermore, the different *time* periods reflect the changing nature of communication over time, depending on what transpires between people. For example, we might communicate in a formal manner with a new boss (Time 1), more informally if we become good friends with the boss (Time 2), and even more formally and infrequently if we have a serious argument or falling out (Time 3).

Communication occurs within social systems, and each communicator has a personal context, a *field of experience* (e.g., family, religious associations, friends). Our individual backgrounds and personality cause us to encode and decode messages in a unique fashion. This makes mutual understanding more challenging and explains why the two communicators must find a *shared field of experience* (e.g., shared town, culture, organization). Both the personal and shared fields of experience can change over time.

The model also includes *noise*, defined as anything that interferes with the intended communication. There are three types of noise that prevent effective listening: (1) environmental (e.g., hot rooms, lawnmowers, etc.), (2) physiological (e.g., headaches or hunger pangs), and (3) emotional (e.g., worry, fear, anxiety). We can see how emotional states create noise in the following example: The employee who arrives late for an 8:30 A.M. meeting because of a domestic skirmish is unlikely to capture all the messages coming his or her way.

The potential for distortion in the communication process is very large. First, the way Person A encodes the message may not accurately reflect the message he or she wants to transmit. "No, that's not what I meant," frequently accompanies communication attempts.

Second, the way Person B decodes the message is strongly related to his or her individual background and personality. A feminist decodes a male boss's reference to "you girls" differently than a more traditional older woman. The recently hired low-level employee interprets a memo from the company president differently than a vice president. The most effective communicators are "receiver oriented" because they gear their messages to the receiver. They ask themselves, "If I were the receiver, how would this message strike me? How would I interpret it?"

Both encoding and decoding are heavily influenced by personal factors such as education, personality, socioeconomic level, family and child rearing, work history, culture, personal experience, and organizational role. It is a fact of communication that people perceive messages differently; thus, meaning lies in people, not in words. Chapter 8, "Perception and Attribution," focuses more on the individualistic interpretations made in communication. The better one knows another person and understands his personal context, the easier it is to read his communications accurately.

Gender is another factor that influences how we encode and decode communication. According to Tannen[7], women as a group are more concerned with maintaining the relationship with the person to whom they are speaking. They focus on seeking and giving confirmation and support, and they try to gain consensus. Men as a group are more concerned with status and trying to achieve or maintain the upper hand in a conversation. Whereas women try to create intimacy in conversations, men focus on establishing their independence.

Gender also affects the way we transmit messages and converse. Communication experts usually interpret gender differences in conversation as a reflection of power differences between men and women. For example, men and people with higher status speak more than women and people of lower status, invalidating a common stereotype that women are more talkative than men. Men are more likely to interrupt others who are talking, and women are interrupted more often than men. Men are more likely to control the topic and redefine what women say ("What you mean is..."). Some of the characteristics of female communication are attributed to their lower power status. For example, women are more likely than men to soften their statements by the use of *qualifiers* such as "maybe, perhaps, sort of, I guess, kind of." When men use qualifiers, they are perceived as warm and polite; when women use qualifiers, they are perceived as weak and unassertive. Women are also more likely to use *disclaimers* that weaken their position ("I'm not really sure about this, but..." "This probably doesn't mean anything, but..."). Because women are socialized to be more *polite* than males, they tend to phrase orders more politely ("Please finish the report" as opposed to "Get that report done"). Women are also more likely to frame orders as questions ("Can you meet me at my office?" rather than "Come to my office"). Compared to men, women use more *intensifiers*, adverbs that exaggerate the strength of an expression ("I am so-o-o-o hungry," "It was a very, very productive meeting"). As a result, female speech is sometimes perceived as overemotional in the workplace.[8]

Because the communication process is fraught with potential for distortion, the feedback aspect of communication is crucial. In this case, feedback refers to Person B's attempts to ensure that the message he or she decoded is what the sender really meant to convey. Asking for clarification and paraphrasing the sender's words ("Let me see if I have understood you correctly. Do you mean. . .?") are feedback methods. Senders can also check to see if their message got across. Managers often ask employees to paraphrase instructions to see if they are clear. The purpose of communication is *mutual understanding*. Unless we check with people, we may mistakenly assume that communication occurred when it did not.

The normal result of an attempt to communicate is a partial misunderstanding because of the uniqueness of the sender and receiver. Feedback and active listening are ways to avoid communication failures. When communication does break down, people often waste time and energy figuring out who is at fault, provoking a defensive reaction that further inhibits mutual understanding. However, if we accept misunderstandings as a basic reality of communication, we can stop looking for blame and start seeking better ways to communicate. A more effective response to breakdowns is, "How can we arrive at a level of mutual understanding that will allow us to accomplish our objectives?" and "How can we prevent a breakdown like this from happening again?"

Defensiveness is one of the most common barriers to good communication. Once people become defensive, they have difficulty hearing the sender's message because they are too caught up in protecting or justifying themselves. Defensiveness is usually caused by the sender's poor communication skills or by low self-concept of the receiver. The following section shows the relationship between different responding styles and defensiveness.

RESPONDING STYLES

Most of our response styles (80 percent according to some experts) fall into five categories:

1. **Evaluative** "What a great report!" "That idea will never work." An evaluative response indicates that the listener has made a judgment of the relative goodness, appropriateness, effectiveness, or rightness of the speaker's statement or problem. With this type of response, the listener implies what the sender should do.
2. **Interpretive** "You're just saying that because you lost the account." The interpretive response indicates that the listener's intent is to teach, to tell the sender what his or her statement or problem really means, and how the sender really feels about the situation. With this type of response, the listener implies what the sender should think.
3. **Supportive** "Don't worry, it'll work out." A supportive response indicates that the listener's intent is to reassure, to pacify, and to reduce the sender's intensity of feeling. The listener in some way implies that the sender need not feel as he or she does.
4. **Probing** "Why do you think you're going to be fired?" A response that indicates the listener's intent is to seek further information, provoke further discussion along a certain line, and question the sender. With this response, a listener implies that the sender needs to develop or discuss a point further.
5. **Understanding** "So, you think your job's on the line and you're pretty upset about it?" An understanding response indicates that the listener's intent is only to ask the sender whether the listener correctly understands what the sender is saying, how the sender feels about the problem, and how the sender sees the problem. With this response, the listener implies nothing but concern that the sender's message is accurately received.

Our natural tendency as listeners is to evaluate and judge what others say to us. The most common responses are evaluative, even though they are not always the most effective type of response to employ. Groups seeking creative solutions or resolution to a conflict are two examples of situations in which evaluative responses are clearly counterproductive.

These response styles communicate not only words but a message about the relationship between the two communicators. With the first four response styles, the responders put themselves in a one-up position in relation to the speaker. When we evaluate others, we assume the one-up position of a judge. The same is true when we interpret what others have said (as if we know best) or try to pacify them (as if they were children who shouldn't feel as they do), and even to some degree when we probe (as if they have not thought everything through). In contrast, the understanding response communicates that listeners have positioned themselves on the same level as the speaker, an egalitarian approach. This is the type of response that is used in active listening, which is explained later in the chapter. None of the responses described are appropriate for all situations. No response style can be said to be innately good or bad, but there are times when a certain type of response would be more appropriate or effective than another. A good communicator is aware of the type of response that is called for in each situation.

Carl Rogers, the famous psychologist, found that defensive communication in therapy sessions could be avoided by being descriptive rather than evaluative and by assuming an egalitarian rather than a superior stance.[9] Gibb contributed four more ways to avoid provoking defensive communication: (1) assuming a problem-solving orientation rather than trying to control the situation, (2) being spontaneous rather than strategic, (3) showing empathy rather than neutrality, and (4) being provisional rather than certain.[10]

An example of being certain rather than provisional is the manager who tears into employees when an error has been made before he or she has ascertained the facts of the situation. It's hard to repair the supervisor-employee relationship when this occurs because it signifies a lack of trust and respect for the employee and an unwillingness to give the employee the benefit of the doubt. The Communication Climate Inventory you filled out as part of the premeeting preparation measures the behaviors that create defensive and nondefensive climates.

ASSERTIVENESS

Communication that is perceived as overly aggressive can also provoke a defensive reaction. An assertive style, neither too aggressive nor too passive, is most likely to produce the desired results when we need to stand up for ourselves, express honest feelings, or exercise our rights. Assertiveness is the ability to communicate clearly and directly what you need or want from another person in a way that does not deny or infringe upon the other's rights. New supervisors often have difficulty finding the right balance in the nonassertive-assertive-aggressive continuum. Figure 7-2 provides a helpful description of the differences among these three styles. One characteristic of an assertive style is the use of I-statements, which are described in the following paragraph.

An I-statement is a feedback format designed to produce dialogue rather than defensiveness. I-statements have three components: (1) a specific and nonblaming description of the behavior exhibited by the other person, (2) the concrete effects of that behavior, and (3) the speaker's feelings about the behavior. Please look at the following examples of I-statements.

Behavior	Effects	Feelings
When you come late to our project meetings,	we have to use valuable time bringing you up-to-date, and others end up doing your share of the work,	and I resent that.
When you interrupt me,	I lose my train of thought and don't get to make my point,	and that makes me angry.

I-statements differ from you-statements, such as "You are lazy and irresponsible," "You never pull your weight around here," or "You're rude and inconsiderate." More often than not, you-statements provoke a defensive response and an argument. I-statements are more likely to encourage an open dialogue because they are descriptive rather than evaluative, and they focus on communicating the speaker's feelings and needs to the other person. In some cases, simply becoming

	Nonassertive (No Influence)	Assertive (Positive Influence)	Aggressive (Negative Influence)
Verbal	Apologetic words. Veiled meanings. Hedging; failure to come to the point. Rambling; disconnected. At a loss for words. Failure to say what you really mean. Qualifying statements with "I mean," "you know."	Statement of wants. Honest statement of feelings. Objective works. Direct statements, which say what you mean. "I" statements.	"Loaded" words. Accusations. Descriptive, subjective terms. Imperious, superior words. "You" statements that blame or label.
Nonverbal General demeanor	Actions instead of words, hoping someone will guess what you want. Looking as if you don't mean what you say.	Attentive listening behavior. Generally assured manner, communicating caring and strength.	Exaggerated show of strength. Flippant, sarcastic style. Air of superiority.
Voice	Weak, hesitant, soft, sometimes wavering.	Firm, warm, well modulated, relaxed.	Tensed, shrill, loud, shaky; cold, "deadly quiet," demanding; superior, authoritarian.
Eyes	Averted, downcast, teary, pleading.	Open, frank, direct. Eye contact, but not staring.	Expressionless, narrowed, cold, staring; not really "seeing" others.
Stance and posture	Leaning for support, stooped, excessive head nodding.	Well balanced, straight on, erect, relaxed.	Hands on hips, feet apart. Stiff, rigid. Rude, imperious.
Hands	Fidgety, fluttery, clammy.	Relaxed motions.	Clenched. Abrupt gestures, fingerpointing, fist pounding.

FIGURE 7-2   **A Comparison of Nonassertive, Assertive, and Aggressive Communication**
Source: Mastering Assertiveness Skills: Power and Influence at Work, ©1983 Elaine Zucker. Published by AMACOM, a division of the American Management Association. All rights reserved. Reprinted with permission of the publisher.

aware of the effects of one's behavior and the feelings it provokes is enough to make people change negative behaviors.

Congruent Communication

Learning to communicate in a congruent fashion is another key skill of effective communicators. The first step is being able to distinguish between thoughts and feelings. *Thoughts* are the products of our minds. We experience thoughts as perceptions, ideas, reasons, and rationales. *Feelings,* on the other hand, are the emotional reactions to our own thoughts or to others' thoughts, actions, and feelings. They are the affective part of interpersonal communications. In communication, thoughts and feelings are often intertwined, and the ability to differentiate between the two and articulate both is an important skill. For example, our understanding of another person's communication may be incomplete if we do not also understand the feelings accompanying the words. Furthermore, even when we are not discussing feelings, they may seep into the discussion by influencing *how* we communicate. Feelings can affect our words and nonverbal gestures ("Why are you so vociferous in turning down this proposal?" "Why do you roll your eyes every time the boss makes a suggestion?").

Much important communication is expressed via nonverbal means. A recent article on this topic concluded, "in spite of human garrulousness, perhaps as little as 20 percent of the communication among people is verbal. ...While people meander the earth through thickets of verbiage (theirs and others), many, perhaps most, do pay more attention to wordless signals and are more likely to be influenced and governed by nonverbal messages."[11] Generally speaking, our nonverbal signals relate to the feeling level of what (the content) is being communicated. And even when words are used, more meaning is taken from nonverbal signals. Mehrabian and Weiner found that words account for only 7 percent of the meaning we make out of communications; 55 percent of the meaning comes from facial expressions and posture, while 38 percent comes from vocal intonations and inflection.[12] This means that managers who continue doing paperwork while their employees are trying to talk to them are severely handicapping the communication process.

Effective communicators pay close attention to nonverbal clues when others communicate and make sure their own nonverbal communication conveys what they intend. To be congruent, both the verbal and nonverbal signals we send need to accurately reflect the thoughts and/or feelings we are experiencing inside ourselves and be consistent with one another. The classic example of incongruent communication is the beet-red person pounding his fist on the table while stating he is not angry.

ACTIVE LISTENING

When executives are asked to rank the communication skills they find most critical to their success on the job, they consistently place listening at the top of the list.[13] Executives spend 45 to 65 percent of their day listening, and this skill is related to higher performance, increased job satisfaction, and improved interpersonal relationships.[14] Listening is especially important when dealing with people from other cultures. In addition to the lack of a common native language, there are other filters that affect listening such as attitudes, biases, values, previous experiences, organizational roles (e.g., paying closer attention to what superiors say than to subordinates), and poor listening skills. These filters are minimized in active listening because people do not sit quietly like a bump on a log waiting patiently for the other person to finish speaking. Instead, the listener takes personal responsibility to ensure that the messages sent are accurately received. If any distortions are uncovered, they are clarified before proceeding with the conversation.

Humans have a physiological excuse for being less than excellent listeners. The rate of speech is 100 to 150 words per minute, whereas our brains are capable of thinking at a rate of 400 to 500 words per minute. People often use this slack time to daydream, to judge what the sender is saying, or to prepare what they want to say next. In contrast, active listeners use this slack time to concentrate fully on the sender's message. Active listening involves a greater level of attending to the speaker.

The skills of active listening are demanding,[15] but they can be learned using the guidelines in the paragraphs that follow. Some of the behaviors suggested may seem awkward and forced at first, but with practice they will feel more natural. It is difficult to respond with patience, understanding, and empathy when the other person is expressing ideas that strike you as illogical, self-deceiving, or even morally wrong. However, the behaviors suggested will, if practiced faithfully, generate attitudes of tolerance and understanding that will make empathy and nonevaluative acceptance of the other person come more easily.

Being Nonevaluative

Active listening includes a variety of verbal and nonverbal behaviors that communicate to the speaker that he or she is heard and understood, that the feelings that underlie the words are appreciated and accepted, that regardless of what the individual says or thinks or feels, he or she is accepted as a person by the listener. The object is to communicate that whatever the qualities of the ideas, events, attitudes, and values of the person who is talking, the listener does not evaluate the person or his or her ideas or feelings. The listener accepts the person for what he or she is without making judgments of right or wrong, good or bad, logical or illogical.

Paraphrasing the Content

When we paraphrase the content, we put what the speaker has said in our own words and repeat it to the speaker to test whether we have understood correctly. The content includes both the thoughts and feelings manifested by the speaker. These phrases are used in paraphrasing.

As I understand it, what you're saying is…
Do you mean that…?
So your feeling is that…
If I try to summarize what you've said…

The key to paraphrasing is that one has to listen intently to what the other is saying. If we spend the time when the other is talking thinking of what we are going to say next, or making mental evaluations and critical comments, we are likely not to hear enough of it to paraphrase it accurately.

The emphasis at this level is comprehending the stated or manifest content, that which is explicitly communicated verbally and/or nonverbally. The more indirect the content, the more important are the next two active listening skills.

Reflecting the Implications

This requires going a bit beyond the manifest content of what the other is saying and indicating to the speaker your appreciation of where the content is leading. It may take the form of building on or extending the ideas of the speaker, using such phrases as

I guess if you did that, you'd then be in a position to…
So that might lead to a situation in which…
Would that mean that…?
Are you suggesting that we might…?
Would that help with the problem of…?

It is important in reflecting the implications to leave the speaker in control of the discussion. When this technique is used to change the direction of the speaker's thinking or to show how much more clever the listener is by suggesting ideas the speaker has not thought of, it ceases to build trust and becomes a kind of skillful one-upmanship. When, however, this technique is genuinely used to help the speaker, it communicates very strongly that the listener has really heard and understood the drift of his or her thinking.

Reflecting Underlying Feelings

This technique goes still farther beyond the overt feelings content of what is said and brings into the open some of the underlying feelings, attitudes, beliefs, or values that may be influencing the speaker to talk in this way. One tries to empathize, to put oneself in the place of the speaker, to experience how it must feel to be in his or her situation. Then the listener *tentatively* expresses the feelings, using such phrases as

Does this make you anxious?
If that happened to me, I'd be upset. Are you?
Times when I've been in that sort of situation, I've really felt
    I could use some help.
If I achieved that, I think I'd feel rather proud of myself.
Sounds like that was very satisfying.

In reflecting the underlying feelings, delicacy is required so as not to overexpose the speaker or press him to admit to more than he would like to reveal. It is also important to avoid suggesting to the speaker that the feeling you reflect back is what she ought to feel in such a situation. This would tend to make the speaker feel evaluated, when what you are trying to do is to communicate acceptance of the underlying feelings. Often acceptance is communicated more by the manner and tone of the listener than by the words used.

Inviting Further Contributions

When one hasn't heard or understood enough yet to follow up with indications of understanding, empathy, and acceptance, one can at least communicate interest in hearing more. Phrases such as the following are useful.

Tell me a bit more about that.
How did you feel when...?
Help me understand...
What happened then?

This differs from the probing response style described earlier because these questions are motivated solely by a desire to clearly understand what the speaker is trying to communicate. Specific requests for information may constitute a unilateral demand for openness on the part of the speaker. To maintain balance, questions should not be used exclusively but should be followed after a bit by rephrasing or reflecting. Generally, open-ended questions create a more supportive, trusting climate than do pointed questions fired in machine-gun-like fashion.

Using Nonverbal Listening Responses

Active listening is often communicated as much by one's posture and nonverbal movements as it is by what one says. Nonverbal listening responses may vary from one culture to another. In the United States, these responses communicate interest and understanding: consistent eye contact, open body posture, leaning toward the speaker, head nodding, and receptive signals such as "um-hum."

When implemented in a climate of genuine concern and acceptance, the active listening skills described in this section help both parties understand as fully as possible the thoughts and the feelings in an interpersonal exchange. If, however, the listener is not being authentic—is not genuinely curious and caring—active listening will be perceived as just another technique to manipulate people.

 # PROCEDURE FOR GROUP MEETING: ACTIVE LISTENING EXERCISE

STEP 1.   Form groups of four. In this exercise, everyone should have an opportunity to be an expresser, active listener, and observer who performs the following roles.

   a. An *expresser* gets a chance to enhance his or her ability to express thought and feelings in a congruent, clear manner.

   b. An *active listener* practices listening and paraphrases what the expresser states. It is particularly critical that the active listener resists the temptation to give advice or try to solve the problem for the expresser.

   c. Two *observers* watch the interaction silently, use the observer sheet on page 164, and provide feedback afterward.

Each participant should have the opportunity to play each of the three roles. Participants can either choose a current topic that is controversial or one of the scenarios described on the following pages.

For each scenario there will be (1) a stage-setting statement, (2) a scripted set of *words* to start the interaction, and (3) a suggested set of feeling states. The scenarios are listed from easy to hard as determined by the range and intensity of feelings associated with the scenario. Here's an example.

1. **Setting the stage**   You are speaking with an outside consultant, brought in by your boss. The consultant has just delivered a copy of his or her final report.

2. **Script** I want to know why I wasn't consulted on that report! You were researching my territory and the decision will impact my people.
3. **Suggested feeling states** Bothered, insulted, left out, angry.

The roles needed in this scenario would be:

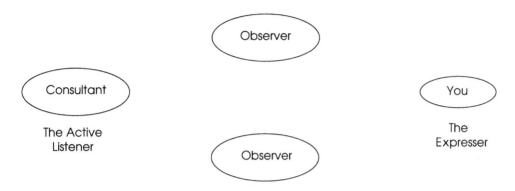

- "You" would communicate the first line as scripted, for example, "I want to know why...." In so doing, you would try to express some or all of the suggested feeling states (insulted, left out, etc.). "Consultant" would practice the *active listening* skills described in the introduction. "Observers" would watch the interaction carefully and critique it using the Observer Sheet.
- As the "Consultant" (in the scenario) actively listens, "you" would carry on and add to the conversation in a manner consistent with the thoughts and feelings reflected in the original scripted opening. Carry on the communication at least five minutes.

Your first task is to read over the suggested scenarios and pick a scenario that, as the expresser (not the active listener),
   a. Seems *real* to you (i.e., you have been or could imagine yourself actually being in that situation).
   b. Involves some suggested feeling states you would like to practice expressing that will stretch you but not immobilize you.

While this is meant to be a play-acting situation, it is also intended to be a serious opportunity to develop your interpersonal communication skills as *both* expressers and active listeners.

STEP 2. **Role plays (10 to 15 minutes each round)** Each role play should take 10 to 15 minutes and consist of:
   a. 5 to 8 minutes conducting the role-play scenario.
   b. 8 to 10 minutes of feedback discussion initiated by the observers and then expanded by the expresser and the active listener.

During the feedback discussion, people should try to link insights gained from playing the different roles. For example, as an expresser, I *may* find out that I am more likely to give off mixed or confusing messages around high-intensity negative feelings than anything else. As the active listener, I *may* find that I am less likely to hear and pick up on high-intensity positive feelings.

Suggested Scenarios

1. **Setting the stage** You are speaking with an outside consultant, brought in by your boss. The consultant has just delivered a copy of his or her final report.

   Script I want to know why I wasn't consulted on that report! You were researching my territory and the decision will impact on my people.

   Suggested feeling states Bothered, insulted, left out, angry.

2. **Setting the stage** You and a colleague are talking in your office. You are about to tell your colleague about an interaction you had with Ted, corporate vice president.

Script After the meeting, I was walking down the hall, and Ted stopped me and said, "You did a really great job on that account!" (smiling) I thought so too!

Suggested feeling states Proud, happy, contented, a sense of accomplishment.

3. **Setting the stage** You are reporting to the boss on the status of your group. You know that in the boss's opinion the group just has not been pulling its weight.

   Script We finally had a breakthrough in that contract. After all the hours I spent researching the market, I finally got an idea that the client liked (longish sigh). For a while I thought that the group would lose another one.

   Suggested feeling states Relieved, good, accomplished, productive, uncertain, scared.

4. **Setting the stage** You are a secretary whose boss feels that you have more promise and can utilize your talents better and move ahead. You are about to speak to your boss.

   Script Last week you mentioned that I could read those articles and compose an annotated bibliography. I know that you want to make my job more interesting. Maybe you even think that I'm bored. But, really, I just don't want to be challenged any more. I guess that I like things as they are.

   Suggested feeling states Embarrassed, scared, resentful, frustrated.

5. **Setting the stage** You have just been offered a middle-management position of considerable prestige. You are talking to your boss about it.

   Script Frankly, I'm just not sure whether or not to accept the promotion. I should be overjoyed with the opportunity. It's a chance to influence some policy. Most people around here don't understand why I haven't left already. But parts of this job are very exciting. Marketing is always a challenge. So I just don't know.

   Suggested feeling states Ambivalent, uncertain, frustrated, unfulfilled, afraid of success and/or failure.

6. **Setting the stage** You are the first and only female member of your audit team. You had hoped the marked increase in travel would not be a problem because you love the work and do it very well. You are talking to your boss.

   Script I know I said I would have no problem with the travel aspects of the job. I thought I would enjoy it. But I find that two to three weeks is too long. I'm not really happy when I'm traveling, and my husband and children are complaining.

   Suggested feeling states Dissatisfied, concerned, uncomfortable, worried, nervous.

7. **Setting the stage** You have just had an interaction with the division head, Ms. Sanchez who is your boss's boss. You are now telling your boss about it.

   Script What was I going to say to her anyway? Ms. Sanchez—the division head!—pats me on the back and tells me how concerned she is for my image. I knew this place was pretty straight, but that's the most ridiculous thing that I ever heard—that I can't have my own painting in my office. Why does everything here have to be designer perfect?

   Suggested feeling states Adamant, determined, angry, resistant, feeling pressured to fit into a mold.

8. **Setting the stage** You and your boss have a lot of trouble agreeing on how things should be done and on priorities. Here we go again!

   Script No! This is not a smoke screen for something else! Look, I really don't understand why I have to analyze the reports that way. I want to do an excellent job and I will. However, I'd like a little latitude in bringing some of my ideas into action.

   Suggested feeling states Annoyed, confused, frustrated, unchallenged.

9. **Setting the stage** Given the problems you and your spouse have been having, it has been amazing to you that you've been able to function at all. Your boss has just called you in and read you the riot act.

   Script Don't you think that I know that my work has been poor? Holy smokes, nobody is cooperating around here. I just… look… so I haven't been too pleasant. But I'm doing the best I can under the circumstances.

   Suggested feeling states Exasperated, strung out, as if the "bottom has dropped out," tense, as if you have to keep up a front.

10. **Setting the stage** Your long-time friend and colleague, Todd, has come to chat about his future career plans and long-term growth with the company. Your own career has been very much on your mind for months, so you almost interrupt Todd in midstream.

    Script Todd, you sound like I did about 15 years ago. I'm 50 years old, Todd. I'm one of, maybe, a hundred middle managers. I've been working my tail off to become a CEO. Nothing was more important to me than my career. Yeah, I'm good, but my wife and kids—they're strangers to me—and I'm not going to become a CEO. Look at the years I wasted working for a goal I'll never reach.

    Suggested feeling states Regret, frustration, bitterness.

STEP 3. **Class Discussion (15 minutes)** Answer the following questions:
   a. What was it like to practice active listening?
   b. What did you learn about yourself and others by doing this exercise?
   c. When should you use active listening?
   d. When would it be a mistake to use active listening?
   e. What connections can you make between this exercise and the readings?

OBSERVER SHEET

Your role is an important one. You should silently observe the interaction and note specific examples of effective and ineffective communication as you see them. These data will be important in the feedback discussion.

Active Listening Behaviors	Examples Where It Was Effectively Used by The Active Listener	Places Where It Could Have Been Used And/Or Was Used Ineffectively*
1. Being nonevaluative		
2. Paraphrasing the content		
3. Reflecting possible implications		
4. Reflecting the underlying feelings		
5. Inviting further contributions		
6. Using nonverbal listening responses		

*The observations you note in this column will give you the chance to provide feedback to both the listener and to the expresser: (1) thoughts and feelings you heard expressed that the listener did not hear or pick up on and (2) mixed messages you observed being expressed (incongruence between words and nonverbal communication).

FOLLOW-UP

A rational mechanical view of the process of communication could be depicted in the following manner:

Person A  Person B

In other words, A says something to B and B hears what A said. Were it so simple, we would never experience what has been labeled the "arc of distortion," which follows.[16] A communicates something to B that was *not intended*. B reacts to this *unintended* communication, and this response confuses A, as well it would, since A is unaware of part of the message sent. *All behavior* communicates some message—it is a form of communication. In the broadest sense, therefore, when we study the concept of interpersonal communication, we are dealing with interpersonal relationships. Communication is the process vehicle through which relationships form, are managed, and, occasionally, dissolve.

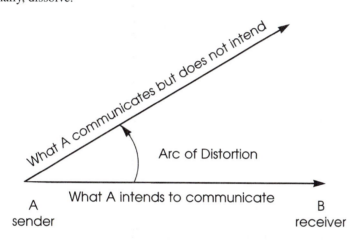

Communications must be understood within the context of the interpersonal relationship. If two people have been involved in an ongoing, bitter argument over a business decision, it will be more difficult for them to hear the other's messages without distortion. We communicate in a different, more effective manner with people who are supportive than with people who are not. Poor relationships and poor communication go hand in hand when trust is lacking. Covey explains this in terms of an Emotional Bank Account that exists for each relationship.[17] We make deposits and build up a reserve when we are kind, courteous, honest, and dependable in our interactions with the other person. This results in a high level of trust that allows the other person to overlook our communication errors and give us the benefit of the doubt. However, when we treat the other person in ways that indicate a lack of consideration (e.g., discourtesy, ignoring them, being arbitrary, etc.), our Emotional Bank Account with them becomes overdrawn. The level of trust is so low that each word must be chosen with great care so that the other person does not misinterpret the meaning and assume the worst. In reality, most people say many things that were better left unsaid or were better stated in a different manner. In the context of good relationships, such communications are tolerated and forgiven, and mutual understanding is much more likely to be achieved.

LATIN AMERICAN COMMUNICATION PATTERNS

Each culture has specific, learned communication patterns that must be deciphered for real understanding to occur. Unfortunately, we often make incorrect interpretations and negative attributions about cultural differences in communication. Although there are country differences in communication within Latin America, the following list summarizes the general characteristics of Latin American and Latino patterns of communication.[18]

- Emphasis on politeness and warm interpersonal relationships
- Use of indirect language to maintain harmonious social relations
- Use of affective style (process oriented and receiver focused), which avoids putting people in uncomfortable situations and relies more on nonverbal and intuitive meaning
- Use of the elaborate style, which involves a relatively high quantity of talk, great detail, repetition, and colorful language
- Value given to eloquence and expressive use of language
- Communication is high context, which means people convey more meaning through gestures, nonverbal communication, and reading between the lines and are less explicit than North Americans and Northern Europeans
- Frequent use of gestures
- Close proximity between people in face-to-face encounters
- Frequent touching, which is done in specific ways for specific occasions and relationships
- Preference given to personal, face-to-face communication over impersonal methods
- Respect may be shown to teachers by breaking eye contact and lowering the eyes

Based on this list, it is easy to see why people from this region may perceive the speech patterns of North Americans as too direct, too blunt, and too plain. Learn to decipher and acknowledge the differences when communicating with people from a different culture, region, or gender without evaluating them, and adapt your own style to theirs.

 LEARNING POINTS

1. Communication is a major portion of a manager's job and an essential skill for anyone working in business.
2. Communication is the process by which information is exchanged between communicators with the goal of achieving mutual understanding.
3. The transactional model of communication consists of two communicators who participate equally from their own personal context or field of experience. To communicate, they must find a shared field of experience. Over time, the nature of their communication may change as well as their fields of experience. Noise can interfere with their intended communication.
4. There is much potential for distortion in the communication process due to personal differences in encoding, decoding, and perception. Therefore, it's best to assume that any communication also involves a partial misunderstanding. Requesting and giving feedback on the message is one way to ensure that the message received is the intended message. Active listening is another way to minimize distortion.
5. Meaning lies in people, not in words.
6. Men and women communicate in different ways, primarily due to their different roles in society.
7. Defensiveness is a common barrier to communication because the energy devoted to defending oneself prevents attention to the message. Therefore, managers should learn to communicate in a manner that does not arouse defensiveness.
8. There are five common response styles:
   a. Evaluative
   b. Interpretive
   c. Supportive
   d. Probing
   e. Understanding
   Evaluative responses are most common. These styles also contain a message about the relationship between the two parties. Only the understanding response reflects an egalitarian stance rather than a one-up position.
9. A nondefensive climate is created when people are descriptive, egalitarian, focused on problem solving, spontaneous, empathic, and provisional.
10. Assertiveness is the ability to communicate clearly and directly what you need or want from another person in a way that does not deny or infringe upon the other's rights.

11. I-statements (behavior, effects, feelings) are an effective way to provide feedback to others.
12. In communication, thoughts and feelings are often intertwined, and the ability to differentiate between the two and articulate both is an important skill. Feelings often influence how we communicate—our choice of words and nonverbal gestures.
13. More meaning is taken from nonverbal signals and vocal intonation and inflection than from words themselves.
14. Both parties in an interpersonal exchange have the personal responsibility to use their active listening skills to ensure mutual understanding.
15. The components of active listening are:
    a. Being nonevaluative
    b. Paraphrasing the content
    c. Reflecting implications
    d. Reflecting underlying feelings
    e. Inviting further contributions
    f. Using nonverbal listening responses
16. The arc of distortion is the difference between what the sender intended to communicate and what the receiver understood the message to be.
17. Each culture has specific, learned communication patterns that must be deciphered and adapted to for real understanding to occur.

FOR MANAGERS

- There are several principles of communication that are helpful to managers:[19]
  - Give other people confirmation or validation by acknowledging their presence and indicating acceptance of them and their ideas.
  - Do not exclude others or resort to in-group talk. Include everyone present in the interaction.
  - Avoid talking about yourself too much. Even if you see yourself as "the center of the universe," remember that it's hard for others to stay interested in monologues.
  - Avoid both excessive criticism and undeserved praise. Instead, give an honest appraisal in a gentle manner.
  - Use language that neither offends nor demeans other people.
- The nonverbal cues that signify that you are attending to what another person is saying are facing them squarely with an open posture (no limbs crossed), leaning forward, and maintaining eye contact and a relaxed posture. Studies have shown that more information is shared when people come out from behind their desks and sit closer to their visitors.
- Take for granted that communication is a flawed process and try to eliminate as many pitfalls as possible. It's a good idea to ask employees to paraphrase your instructions (i.e., "Would you please put the instructions in your own words so that I can see if I communicated them clearly?") and to paraphrase for them the problems or requests that they bring to you (i.e., "Let me see if I've understood the problem correctly...").
- Some managers give written instructions along with verbal instructions to avoid both misunderstandings and later consultations.
- Before you communicate at work, ask yourself the following questions: What do I want to accomplish as a result of the following questions? Based on my knowledge of the receiver(s), how should I word this message and how should I transmit it? Am I the best person to communicate this message or does someone else have greater credibility or a better relationship with them? Will there be any likely resistance to the message that I need to take into consideration?
- Communication is a learned behavior, which means that people usually send messages that maximize rewards and minimize punishment. Managers who are guilty of the "kill the messenger" syndrome will be told only the "good news" even though the bad news may be crucial to the organization's survival.
- Self-concept serves as a filter through which we see all communication. People with low self-concepts present the greatest communication challenge because they can become defensive

with little or no provocation. The specific content of your message is less important than what you are communicating to them about your relationship with them; if it's anything less than fully supportive, they become defensive.

- Active listening is the appropriate response to use with people in a conflict situation. It's difficult to maintain anger when the listener is making a concerted effort to understand both your point and your feelings.

- Some managers deplore the power of the grapevine, the informal communication network. However, all organizations have grapevines, and some managers use the grapevine for their own purposes, for example, floating trial balloons to see how people react. The power of the grapevine can be decreased by more open sharing of information through formal channels. In a bureaucracy, information is often synonymous with power. Providing greater access to information means that employees will devote less energy to hoarding it or ferreting it out.

- Most organizations are characterized by top-down information flows. Unless managers make a concerted effort to seek information from employees, they will remain in the dark on many issues. For senior managers, it is not always enough to talk only with the layer of people immediately beneath them because this group may have a vested interest in presenting only positive information or self-serving interpretations of situations. This is why the concept of "managing by walking around" is so important.

PERSONAL APPLICATION ASSIGNMENT

At the beginning of this chapter you filled out an inventory in which you evaluated the type of communication climate your supervisor established. That question was based on Gibb's characteristics of defensive communication. This assignment is to gain insight into the type of communication climate you create. Choose one of the following ways to begin this assignment.

1. If you supervise employees, ask three of them to fill out a copy of the same questionnaire *anonymously*. If you're surprised at the results, discuss them and ask for clarification or examples from someone in your organization who you know will give you good, honest feedback. Take into consideration that your employees may be uncertain (or even terrified) about how you will accept feedback on your communication habits. Make sure they don't have to pay a price for their honesty.
2. Have a discussion on a controversial topic with someone (preferably someone difficult so you can test out the skills you practiced in this chapter). Try to create a supportive climate according to Gibb's framework. Afterward, evaluate the conversation. If it's possible, get the other person's evaluation of the conversation.

After you've completed (1) or (2), write up the experience in the usual format.

A. *Concrete Experience*
   1. *Objectively* describe the experience (who, what, when, where, how) (2 points)
   2. *Subjectively* describe your feelings, perceptions, and thoughts that occurred during (not after) the experience. What did others seem to be feeling? (2 points)

B. *Reflective Observation*
   1. Looking back at the experience, what were the perspectives of the key actors (including you)? (2 points)
   2. Why did the people involved (including you) behave as they did? (2 points)

C. *Abstract Conceptualization*
   1. Relate concepts or theories from the assigned readings or the lecture to the experience. Explain thoroughly how they apply to your experience. Please apply at least two concepts or theories and cite them correctly. (4 points)

D. *Active Experimentation*
  1. What did you learn about communication from this experience? (1 point)
  2. What did you learn about yourself? (1 point)
  3. What action steps will you take to be more effective in the future? (2 points)

E. *Integration, Synthesis and Writing*
  1. Did you integrate and synthesize the four sections? (1 point)
  2. Was the Personal Application Assignment well written and easy to understand? (1 point)
  3. Was it free of spelling and grammar errors? (2 points)

ENDNOTES

[1] J. D. Maes, T. G. Weldy, and M. L. Icenogle, "A Managerial Perspective: Oral Communication Competency Is Most Important for Business Students in the Workplace," *The Journal of Business Communication 34*, no. 1 (1997): 67–81.

[2] K. R. Kane, "MBA: A Recruiter's-Eye View," *Business Horizons 36* (1993): 65–68.

[3] K. Sandholz, "Do You Have What It Takes?" *Managing Your Career* (Fall 1987): 10.

[4] H. Mintzberg, *The Nature of Managerial Work* (New York: Harper & Row, 1973).

[5] Ibid., 171.

[6] J. T. Wood, *Communication in Our Lives* (New York: Wadsworth, 1997).

[7] D. Tannen, *You Just Don't Understand: Women and Men in Conversation* (New York: Ballantine, 1990) and *Talking from 9 to 5* (New York: William Morrow, 1994).

[8] The findings in this paragraph are reported in L. P. Arliss, *Gender Communication* (Upper Saddle River, NJ: Prentice-Hall, 1991); J. C. Pearson, "Language Usage of Women and Men," in J. Stewart's *Bridges Not Walls* (New York: Random House, 1986), 283–300; and D. Borisoff and L. Merrill, *The Power to Communicate: Gender Differences as Barriers* (Prospect Heights, IL: Waveland Press, 1992).

[9] C. R. Rogers, and R. E. Farson, *Active Listening*, (Chicago: Industrial Relations Center, University of Chicago, 1975) or *The Reader*.

[10] J. Gibb, "Defensive Communication," *Journal of Communication 11*, no. 3 (1961): 141–48 or *The Reader*.

[11] "Why So Much Is Beyond Words," *Time*, July 13, 1981, 74.

[12] A. Mehrabian and M. Weiner, "Decoding of Inconsistent Communications," *Journal of Personality and Social Psychology 6* (1967): 109–14.

[13] J. Brownell, "Preparing Students for Multicultural Environments: Listening as a Key Management Competency," *Journal of Management Education 16* (December 1992).

[14] Ibid.

[15] For an in-depth look at active listening, see D. Stone, B. Patton, and S. Heen, *Difficult Conversations: How to Discuss What Matters Most* (New York: Viking, 1999).

[16] H. Baumgartel, W. N. Bennis, and N. R. De (eds.), *Reading in Group Development for Managers and Trainers* (New York: Asia Publishing House, 1967), 151–56.

[17] S. R. Covey, *The 7 Habits of Highly Effective People* (New York: Simon and Schuster, 1989), 188–202.

[18] R. D. Albert, "A Framework and Model for Understanding Latin American and Latino/Hispanic Cultural Patterns." In D. Landis and R. Bagat (eds.), *Handbook of Intercultural Training* (Thousand Oaks, CA: Sage, 1996), 327–48; and W. Gudykunst, and S. Ting-Toomey, *Culture and Interpersonal Communication* (Newbury Park, CA: Sage, 1988).

[19] J. A. De Vito, *The Interpersonal Communication Book* (New York: Harper & Row, 1989): 197.

Chapter 8

PERCEPTION AND ATTRIBUTION

OBJECTIVES By the end of this chapter, you should be able to:

A. Define perception and explain the perceptual process.

B. Identify the sources of misinterpretation in cross-cultural interactions.

C. Understand both the benefits and the drawbacks of the perceptual process.

D. Recognize common perceptual errors.

E. Describe the Johari window.

F. Explain attribution theory.

G. Understand the relevance of perception and attribution for managers.

THE BLIND MEN AND THE ELEPHANT

JOHN GODFREY SAXE

It was six men of Indostan
To learning much inclined,
Who went to see the Elephant
(Though all of them were blind),
That each by observation
Might satisfy his mind.

The first approached the Elephant,
And happening to fall
Against his broad and sturdy side,
At once began to bawl:
"God bless me! but the Elephant
Is very like a WALL!"

The second, feeling of the tusk,
Cried, "Ho! what have we here
So very round and smooth and sharp?
To me 'tis mighty clear
This wonder of an Elephant
Is very like a SPEAR."

The third approached the animal,
And happening to take
The squirming trunk within his hands,
Thus boldly up and spake:
"I see," quoth he, "the Elephant
Is very like a SNAKE!"

The fourth reached out an eager hand,
And felt about the knee
"What most this wondrous beast is like
Is mighty plain," quoth he:
"'Tis clear enough the Elephant
Is very like a TREE!"

The fifth, who chanced to touch the ear,
Said: "E'en the blindest man
Can tell what this resembles most;
Deny the fact who can,
This marvel of an Elephant
Is very like a FAN!"

The sixth no sooner had begun
About the beast to grope,
Than seizing on the swinging tail
That fell within his scope,
"I see," quoth he, "the Elephant
Is very like a ROPE!"

And so these men of Indostan
Disputed loud and long,
Each in his own opinion
Exceeding stiff and strong,
Though each was partly in the right,
And all were in the wrong!

PREMEETING PREPARATION

A. Read "The Blind Men and the Elephant."

B. Read the Topic Introduction.

C. What are the significant learning points from the readings?

TOPIC INTRODUCTION

In the first part of the book, we studied various individual differences and mental maps. Yet another way in which people differ is the way we perceive the world. It is tempting to assume that human behavior is a response to an objective reality but, as the comedienne Lily Tomlin noted, "Reality is nothing more than a collective hunch." The same stimuli may be present in our environment, but what we do with that stimuli is affected by individual differences. For example, if you talk with a rabid Republican and a fanatical Democrat the day after a U.S. presidential debate, it may be difficult to believe they both watched the same debate. Each claims his or her candidate "won" and the other candidate was a disaster. This same thing can happen at work. We might see two managers with completely different impressions of an employee's performance; one manager wants to promote the employee while the other recommends firing. How do we end up with such diverse and even contradictory impressions? Chalk it up primarily to individual differences in perception. *Perception is the process by which we select, organize, and evaluate the stimuli in our environment to make it meaningful for ourselves.* It serves as a filter or gatekeeper so that we are not overwhelmed by all the stimuli that bombard us. The three stages of the perceptual process are explained next.

Selection   A key aspect of the perceptual process is selective attention. We simply do not see or hear everything that goes on around us. For example, when you live in another country and have reached a moderate level of fluency in that language, you occasionally stumble on a new word that you have never heard before. Once you master the word, you realize to your chagrin that it is in fact a very common word—you just weren't "hearing" or attending to it before.

Both internal and external factors determine what sensory impressions we pay attention to. Internal factors that affect perception are motives, values, interests, attitudes, past experiences, and expectations. For example, hungry people are more attuned to references to food than people not currently motivated by the hunger need. Hungry people may even "hear" the word *candy* when the speaker says *caddy* because we often hear what we want to hear. People tend to pick up only that stimuli that interests them or supports what they are looking for. Studies of both low-level supervisors and middle-management executives revealed that these individuals perceived only those aspects of a situation that related to the goals and activities of their own departments.[1] Information that conflicts with what we believe is often ignored or distorted to conform to our preconceptions. Selective attention explains why two people can attend the same meeting or event and have contradictory stories about what occurred. The diehard political supporters mentioned in the opening paragraph heard and saw only what they wanted to hear (great points made by their candidate, indications of strong leadership potential, etc.) and blocked out the strengths of the opposing candidate. In this way, their preconceived attitudes about the debate affected their perception and interpretation of the actual event.

The external factors that influence perception are characteristics of the target we perceive. Our attention is drawn by motion, intensity, size, novelty, and salience. Salience is the extent to which a given object or event stands out from the others around it. The salient object or event is the "figure" that dominates what we see; the rest is "ground" or background. What do you see in the picture below. What is figural to some people is merely background to others? Furthermore, our perceptions tend to remain constant; once a perceived object is fixed in our minds, it is difficult to reinterpret the stimuli.

Source: Circle Limit IV by M. C. Escher. ©1999 Cordon Art–Baarn–Holland. All Rights Reserved.

Organization   The second stage in the perceptual process is the *organization* of the stimuli that has been perceived. Our thought processes automatically structure stimuli into patterns that make sense to us. One example of such patterns are cause-and-effect relationships. It is easier to see cause-and-effect relationships in the physical world than it is with social interactions and human behavior. Nevertheless, we organize stimuli in the same patterns. For example, if an organization is successful, people tend to attribute this success to the leader whether or not the leader really had an impact.[2]

According to social cognition theory, we organize stimuli into schemas.[3] Schemas are mental maps of different concepts, events, or types of stimuli that contain both the attributes of the concept and the relationship among the attributes. Like geographical maps, schemas are representations of reality, but not reality itself. Everyone's maps are different. For example, each of us has a schema about "leadership" that includes the traits that we think describe a good leader. We tend to see these traits as a package deal; if someone has a few of these traits, we assume they also possess the other traits. Our leader schema might include attributes such as trustworthy, directive, courageous, enthusiastic, and value driven. If we see a leader who is trustworthy and directive, we may mistakenly assume he or she is also courageous, enthusiastic, and value driven. Once schemas have been established, they affect how we handle future information because they determine what we attend to and what we remember. We are less likely to notice and remember free-floating stimuli than stimuli that fits into existing schemas.

Evaluation   The third stage in the perceptual process is *evaluation* or inference. We interpret the stimuli in a subjective rather than objective fashion. Our conclusions are biased by our individual attitudes, needs, experiences, expectations, goals, values, and physical condition at the time. Not only do interpretations differ from person to person, but the same person can have diverse perceptions of the same stimuli at different points in time. When large organizations are involved in major change efforts, it is easy to see examples of differential interpretations of the same stimuli in the diverse reactions to announcements about upcoming innovations. No matter how carefully such announcements are worded, employees reach vastly different conclusions, and harmful rumors are commonplace. People who are frightened about the changes are more likely to make negative inferences about the announcements than people who are looking forward to the innovation.

Nowhere is it more obvious that different groups see and interpret the world in different ways than when we deal with people from different cultures or ethnic groups. For example, there is a West African tribe that lives in round houses and, as a result, does not perceive perpendicular lines. The way the Japanese bow and present their business cards conveys meaningful cues that are not even perceived much less correctly interpreted by most non-Japanese. Perceptual patterns are both learned and culturally determined.[4] They are also a barrier to effective cross-cultural communication when we fail to pay attention to cues that are important to another culture or when we misinterpret the behavior of a person from another culture.

Adler has identified three sources of misinterpretation in cross-cultural interaction:[5]

1. **Subconscious cultural blinders** We use our own cultural assumptions to interpret the events and behavior of a foreign culture.
2. **Lack of cultural awareness** We are unaware of our cultural values and norms and the way that other cultures perceive us. Without understanding our own culture, we cannot adapt our behavior so that it is perceived more accurately by others.
3. **Projected similarity** We assume that people from other cultures are more similar to us than they really are or that situations are similar when they are not. This is based on the ethnocentric view that there is only one way to be—like me.

A common danger that may result from our perception of people who are somehow different from us is stereotyping. *Stereotyping occurs when we attribute behavior or attitudes to a person on the basis of the group to which the person belongs.* Much of the cynicism in organizations is expressed in terms of stereotypes about other groups, such as "Top management cannot be trusted," or "You'll never get those employees to participate and work harder." The current emphasis on managing diversity should cause people to challenge the incorrect stereotypes they hold about different groups in the workforce. One fairly common stereotype is that older workers contribute less than younger workers. This stereotype is prevalent in Europe and Central America where older workers have no recourse or legal protection from discrimination. In reality, U.S. studies show that older workers are less likely to be absent, have half the accident rate of younger employees, and report higher job satisfaction.[6] Furthermore, researchers have found no evidence that older U.S. workers are less productive than younger workers.[7]

According to research, stereotypes are based on relatively little information, resistant to change even in light of new information, and rarely accurately applied to specific individuals.[8] For this reason, stereotyping is often viewed negatively as a source or excuse for social injustice. Nevertheless, the process of stereotyping is "a neutral, subconscious cognitive process that increases the efficiency of interpreting environmental information."[9] Stereotypes can be helpful *if* they are used effectively. According to Adler, helpful stereotypes are consciously held, descriptive rather than evaluative, accurate, and viewed as a "first best guess" about a group or person, which means they are subject to modification once we have firsthand experience with people.[10]

The drawbacks to perception are that it prevents us from taking in everything we should, makes our interpretations open to question, and promotes stereotypes. However, perception is an extremely useful process. It helps us to make sense of a world full of stimuli in three ways: first, by limiting the amount of information that enters our mind to prevent overload; second, by selecting what input we will attend to; and, third, by organizing and classifying the input we receive so we do not waste valuable time trying to make sense of behavior and situations that are in fact similar.

PERCEPTUAL DISTORTIONS

Stereotyping is one of several examples of distortion in the perceptual process. Another distortion, the *halo effect*, occurs when our evaluation of another person is dominated by only one of his or her traits. For example, a U.S. army study showed that officers who were liked were evaluated as being more intelligent than those who were disliked.[11] The halo effect does not always work to an employee's advantage. A perceived negative trait such as sloppiness can prevent a boss from seeing the other positive characteristics an employee may have.

Central tendency is a perceptual distortion that occurs when a person avoids extreme judgments and rates everything as average. We see this when managers rate all their employees as "3s" on a five-point scale, in spite of the fact that some employees really deserve a "5" or a "1." *Contrast effects* are present when our evaluations are affected by comparisons with other people we have recently encountered who are either better or worse in terms of this characteristic. For example, if a student has two of her university's best professors in the same semester, she may rate her other professors (who in reality are good professors) as only average or poor because she is comparing them with the excellent professors.

Another type of perceptual distortion is *projection*. This refers to the tendency to attribute one's personal attitudes or feelings to another person, thereby relieving one's own sense of guilt or failure. Projection is a defense mechanism that protects people from confronting their own feelings. It is most common in people who have little insight into their own personalities.[12] Multinational corporations (MNCs) have been reluctant to transfer female executives abroad on the grounds that a woman could not be effective in a traditional, male-dominated culture. In some cases, the MNC management is simply projecting upon the foreign culture its own feelings and prejudices about female managers. In reality, research has shown that female U.S. expatriates have been successful all over the world.[13]

The final source of perceptual distortion is known as the *perceptual defense*. These defenses act as a screen or filter, blocking out that which we do not want to see and letting through that which we wish to see.[14] The closer we get to schemas concerning our self-perceptions (self-image) and our relationships with important others, the more likely we are to call on these defensive screens.[15] These defenses help to create self-fulfilling or circular perceptual processes like the ones shown in the following examples.

Example 1
A Gender Stereotype

1. As a woman, I believe that men prefer women who are passive and unassertive.
2. Since I would like to develop meaningful relationships with men, I behave in a passive and unassertive manner.

3. I tend to develop relationships with men who expect women to be passive and unassertive.	or	3. I do not approach and/or am not approached by men who expect a woman to be active and assertive.
4. I am confirmed in my belief that men prefer women who are passive and unassertive.	or	4. I do not have the opportunity to develop my own assertiveness.

Example 2
A Managerial Dilemma

1. As a manager, I believe that subordinates are basically lazy and dislike work.
2. I assume, therefore, that to get the most out of subordinates I must watch over their every move.
3. I behave in a strict manner, delegating little responsibility, and demanding that everything be cleared through me first.
4. My subordinates react to this parentlike stance by acting like rebellious teenagers. I have to lean on them all the time, or they'll never do what I tell them.
5. Consequently, my original belief is confirmed; subordinates are basically lazy and dislike work.

The underlying pattern in these processes is one of (1) assumption or belief, (2) leading to behavior that is congruent with the assumption, followed by (3) observation of consequences, which, to the extent that selective perception is occurring, leads to (4) confirmation of the original assumption or belief. Testing the validity or desirability of this conceptual pattern is difficult for several reasons.

One important reason is that normal social interaction is basically conservative—social norms operate to preserve existing interaction patterns and perceptions. Sociologist Erving Goffman[16] has described the tendency of people to preserve the "face" that others present to them. When people act "out of character," social pressures are mobilized to force them back into their role. In social situations we tend to act in such a way that we maintain our own self-image and the self-image we see others presenting. We resist telling someone that they have egg on their chin because we assume that this is not part of the image they want to present and we do not want them to "lose face" and be embarrassed. This conservative interaction norm tends to decrease the accuracy of interpersonal perception by relinquishing opportunities to test the accuracy of our perceptions of ourselves and others. The norm dictates that we cannot frankly tell others our impressions of them if these impressions differ from the face they are presenting. It also acts as an obstacle to our testing with others whether or not we are projecting the kind of self-image we think we are. "Do you see me the way I see myself?" When people present themselves as leaders, it is hard to tell them you do not feel like following. Thus, we are denied information about others' true thoughts and feelings by the face we present.

A theoretical conceptualization of this process is depicted in the following matrix, called the Johari window.[17] This is an information processing model that consists of four regions determined by whether information about oneself is known or unknown to oneself and others.

	Known to Self	Not Known to Self
Known to others	Arena	Blindspot
Not known to others	Façade	Unknown

Arena	This cell includes information that I and others know about me—mutually shared perceptions. In other words, people see me the way I see myself (e.g., I feel confident, and people see me as confident).
Façade	This cell contains information that I know about myself but hide from others (e.g., I feel insecure, but I strive to project the image of a very secure person). In other words, people see a "false me," and I must always be on guard to prevent them from seeing the "real me."
Blindspot	This cell consists of information or characteristics that people perceive in me but that I do not see in myself (e.g., others see that my anxiety reduces my effectiveness, but I do not see—or will not admit to myself—that I am anxious). In other words, people know certain things about me that they may not tell me (like the old deodorant commercial, "Even your best friends won't tell you.")
Unknown	This cell is made up of information and characteristics that neither I nor others see in myself. Psychoanalysis might be necessary to unearth this type of information.

When a person's arena is very small, communication is greatly hindered. The more we know ourselves and allow others to know us, the greater the potential for effective communication. There are two ways to increase our arena—self-disclosure and feedback from others. Self-disclosure means sharing information about oneself, which moves information from the façade to the arena. Feedback from others about information in our blindspot also moves information into the arena. Trust and psychological safety are prerequisites for both self-disclosure and feedback. We instinctively hold back personal information from people we do not trust, and it is too risky to give feedback to people who might react defensively or angrily.

One of the basic competencies of effective managers is self-awareness. This requires an ability to both seek feedback from others and to disclose one's own feelings and thoughts. The following exercise is designed to help you develop these skills.

PROCEDURE FOR GROUP MEETING: HOW I SEE MYSELF AND OTHERS

SELF-PERCEPTIONS: INDIVIDUAL WORK

(Time Allotted: 20 minutes)

The first part of this unit is designed to help you sharpen your understanding of the image and perceptions you believe you communicate to others. During the second part, you will have the opportunity to explore how others believe they see you.

STEP 1.   As you think about the *image you have of yourself*, list in the appropriate spaces provided in the first column of the perception matrix on page 180:
   a. The first five or six words that come to your mind
   b. An animal
   c. A musical instrument
   d. A food

It is important that you work quickly. Let your first thought be the one you record.

STEP 2.   The words you have just listed are, at best, simplified cues or indicators of how you see yourself—your self-image. It is your own interpretation of what these words mean to you that contributes to your self-image. In this step you are asked to (a) interpret the meaning of those words and (b) decide whether or not each element of your self-image (known to self) is a part of your arena or your façade. Use the following space provided to record these points.
   a. Elements of my self-image that I believe are in my arena (i.e., known to me and known to others):

   b. Elements of my self-image that I believe are in my façade (i.e., known to me but not known to others):

STEP 3.   Each of us behaves in ways designed to allow various aspects of our self-image (known to self) to be known to others—an arena. Similarly, we behave in ways to keep various aspects of our self-image in our façade (not known to others).

a. In the space provided, jot down examples of how you communicate to others important elements of your arena. (For example, if you feel confident and believe people see you as confident, how do you behave to communicate confidence?)

b. In the space provided, jot down examples of how you behave to keep elements of your self-image (known to self) in the façade. (For example, if you feel insecure but try to project an image of confidence, how do you behave to "cover" your feelings of insecurity?)

TESTING SELF-PERCEPTIONS: SMALL-GROUP SHARING

(Time Allotted: 40 to 60 minutes)

In this part of the unit, you will have the opportunity to get a glimpse of how others see you. This will be a real test of your interpersonal skills. Giving and receiving feedback in a productive manner is difficult but important.

STEP 1. In your learning group, fill out the Perception Matrix form on page 180 for others in your group. It is important in filling out the Perception Matrix that you work quickly. Let your first thought be the one you record. It is helpful if there is no communication during this step.

STEP 2. (Read this paragraph to yourself.) The sharing process you are about to begin may not be an easy task. As was pointed out in the Topic Introduction, normal social interaction is basically conservative—social norms operate to preserve existing interaction patterns and perceptions. During this sharing process, you are, in effect, being asked to operate with an atypical set of social norms to share and discuss your impressions of one another.

In the discussions you have, it is important to remember that there is no one reality or truth. You have perceptions of yourself. Others have perceptions of you. Some of these perceptions will be shared—held in common. Others will be different. The issue is *not* whose perception is right or whose is wrong.

If I have a perception of someone and he or she does not share that perception of himself or herself, this discrepancy can serve as an important learning opportunity for *both of us*.

a. If I am the one being perceived, I may learn something about my blindspot or façade.

b. If I am the perceiver, I may learn something about the perceptual filters I use (e.g., I assume all big people are confident). I may learn that I tend to see in others elements of how I see myself.

All of us can learn something more about our own circular self-fulfilling perceptual processes. This awareness is only a first step. Whether or not a person chooses to alter these perceptual patterns is clearly a matter of individual choice.

STEP 3.   People should share the perceptions they have of each other as recorded on their Perception Matrix. Go around the circle, sharing all the perceptions (words through food) for one person before moving on to the next person. You can record these on page 181.

STEP 4.   Groups should now discuss their perceptions using the following suggestions to guide their discussions.
    a. What can you infer about your schemas (the concepts or categories you most often use in perceiving other people) from the words you listed for each person in your group?
        1. Did you list mostly adjectives (which tend to be evaluative or difference oriented, e.g., good versus bad, big versus small) or nouns (which tend to be neutral or nondifference oriented, e.g., man, student) or verbs (which are behavior oriented as opposed to trait or characteristic oriented)?
        2. Did your lists of words differ for each person or did your lists reflect similar concepts?
    b. Was your perception of some people generally closer to the ways they saw themselves than was true of your perception of other people? To what do you attribute any differences? Do some people project clearer self-images? Length of time or context within which you knew the person? Similarity to yourself?
    c. Where two or more people saw the same person in substantially different ways, they should try to understand how these differences arose.
    d. Based on the individual work you did in the beginning of this unit, some of you may have found:
        1. Elements that you thought were in your open arena were not known to others (i.e., they were in your façade).
        2. Elements that you thought were in your façade were known to others (i.e., they are in your arena).
        3. New perceptions from your blindspot.
        In exploring these "surprises," it is most important that you listen to and understand others' descriptions of how you behave. What lead them to form the impressions they have of you?
    e. It is very likely that you will uncover some typical circular perceptual defenses such as those discussed in the Topic Introduction. The group may want to outline a few of their own processes.
        1. What does a person gain or achieve through the pattern?
        2. What costs are incurred or opportunities forgone by maintaining the pattern?
        3. What steps could be taken to change the nature of these circular patterns?
    f. What connections can you make between this exercise and the readings?

PERCEPTION MATRIX OWN PERCEPTIONS

Member / Category	How You See Yourself	How You See A	How You See B	How You See C	How You See D	How You See E
5–6 Words						
Animal						
Musical Instrument						
Food						

PERCEPTION MATRIX OTHERS' PERCEPTIONS*

How I Am Seen by

Member / Category	A	B	C	D	E
5–6 Words					
Animal					
Musical Instrument					
Food					

* You may wish to use this space to record others' perceptions of yourself.

FOLLOW-UP

The most pertinent aspect of perception in terms of organizational behavior is social perception—how we perceive and judge other people. Our behavioral responses to others are based on our inferences about their behavior. According to attribution theory, when people observe behavior, they attempt to determine whether it is internally or externally caused.[18] For example, if a male group member does not pull his weight on a project, other group members may attribute his behavior to internal reasons that are under his control, such as "he's irresponsible and lazy." Or they may attribute it to external reasons, such as "he has too much other work to do a good job on this project." These attributions then determine the way peers and managers behave toward the person. If the employee is deemed irresponsible, his manager might take disciplinary measures or try coaching behavior. If the external cause is accepted, his manager might reorganize his work assignments, send him to time management courses, or negotiate with his other project leaders for more release time.

We use three types of information to help us make causal judgments about others:

1. *Consensus* refers to the extent to which others behave in the same manner.
2. *Consistency* is the extent to which the person acts in the same manner at other times.
3. *Distinctiveness* is the extent to which this person behaves in the same manner in other contexts.

Let's take the example of a human resources (HR) manager who is trying to figure out whether an employee complaint about his boss's managerial style is valid. The HR manager will consider whether other employees have also complained about this particular manager (consensus). She will also consider whether the employee has complained about this same boss on previous occasions (consistency) and whether the employee has a habit of complaining about all his bosses (distinctiveness). If no one else has complained about the boss, and the employee's evaluation of the boss has been inconsistent (sometimes positive, sometimes negative), and if the employee is a habitual whiner, the HR manager will probably conclude that the problem lies within the employee (internal attribution) rather than the manager (external attribution). If other employees have also complained about the boss, the employee's complaints about this boss have been consistent over time, and the employee never complained about previous bosses, she is more likely to conclude that it is time to take steps to help the boss improve her style.

There are biases that distort our attributions about success and failure. The Chinese usually attribute personal success to luck and failures to personal failings.[19] In contrast, when Americans succeed, they attribute it to personal, internal factors (e.g., hard work, intelligence, initiative). However, when Americans fail they are more likely to blame it on external factors (such as tough competition, poor leadership, interdepartmental problems). This is called the *self-serving bias.* When U.S. managers evaluate their employees, the opposite occurs; they are more likely to attribute low performance to the subordinates' personal failings, and they underestimate the influence of external factors upon subordinate performance. This is known as *fundamental attribution error.*[20]

Given these natural tendencies, managers should make an extra effort to ensure that their attributions about employees are accurate. Bertrand Russell, British scholar and mathematician, showed his understanding of human nature when he proposed the following conjugation of "irregular verbs."

> *I am firm.*
> *You are obstinate.*
> *He is a pig-headed fool.*

Perception plays a major role in communication and decision making in the workplace, particularly in the areas of hiring and firing, performance appraisals, promotions, and work assignments. Effective managers acknowledge that their own perceptions may be uniquely biased and work hard at gathering and understanding the perceptions of other people so there is a greater chance of approximating "reality."

It is as difficult for humans to understand the impact of their own perceptual schema as it is for a fish to understand the concept of water. Yet our perceptual maps and the fish's water are equally important for survival. Without a conceptual system to simplify and order our experiences, we would become overwhelmed by stimuli. However, failure to recognize that our perceptions are to some extent our own creation can leave us closed, defensive, and unable to profit from new experiences. In the following Personal Application Assignment, an engineer analyzes his reactions to the perception chapter and struggles to understand his own way of perceiving others.

STUDENT PERSONAL APPLICATION ASSIGNMENT

Again it seems I am going to write a paper about myself rather than the suggested topic. Whenever I reflect on the subject matter we study, I can directly relate it to myself. I have always considered myself "free of hangups"; however, there are many things I do that I do not completely understand. Previously I have never taken the time to question myself, but now, being forced to think about a concept, I can see how I have been influenced by that concept and can attempt to explain, but not always justify, the way I feel toward many things. Well, here goes!

I am the perfect example of a person blinded by his own perception of the world. Not all of the time, mind you, but mainly in one case—the case being when I become "snowed" by a girl. I'll begin by relating my current project in this area—at least I think the project is current, although I'm not sure as of this moment because of a possible misperception on my part. Being alone in a new city, I engaged in the well-known game of mixer this autumn in the hope of meeting someone interesting. I accomplished my goal without any difficulties, and here is where my problem began—I committed my unpardonable sin of becoming snowed.

I do not have many difficulties with first perceptions. I think I am pretty objective and usually make good judgments. First impressions are almost solely objective! As long as I do not become emotionally involved, that is, as long as there is no filter between what I see and how I perceive what I have seen, I am quite able to understand what is communicated. However, once I am personally involved with the reason behind the attempted communication, my vision of what is actually happening is, I believe, distorted.

This weekend, for example, I did not take Mary (a fictitious name) out because of our last date and a phone call I made after the date. Even though I wanted to take her out, I didn't. Consequently, I have been asking myself all weekend what motivated me not to ask her out; and I do not have a specific answer—but I know it stems from how I perceived how she feels. However, maybe that's not how she really feels, and I do not let myself comprehend that there may be a difference between these two versions of the same feelings. I guess I feel that my logical reasoning of what a particular look or remark means is the correct idea. I completely leave out the possibility that everyone does not (thankfully) think about everything the same way I do.

Zalkind and Costello, in their article on perception, give five reasons why a person misperceives.[21] These are:

1. You are influenced by cues below your own threshold (i.e., the cues you don't know you perceived).
2. You respond to irrelevant cues to arrive at a judgment.
3. You are influenced by emotional factors (i.e., what is liked is perceived as correct).
4. You weigh perceptual evidence heavily if it comes from a respectable source.
5. You are not able to identify all factors (i.e., not realizing how much weight is given to a single item).

I feel I am guilty, if one can be "guilty," of most of the mentioned means of misperception. However, I feel that rather than imposing a perceptual defense on myself, I project a perceptual offense, and this greatly compounds my misperception. Rather than looking for favorable acts of communication and not allowing unfavorable perceptions, I am forever (when I become emotionally involved with a girl) on the lookout for any signs of displeasure. And at the slightest hint, my mind begins to work on such questions as "What if that means. . . ?"

For example, to the question, "Did you have a good time?" I got the reply, "Yeah, I guess so." I did not perceive this as a positive statement. My perceptual offense was quickly in play and I have since been analyzing that statement. I don't know Mary well enough to say what anything she says really means, but because I was afraid the reply meant "I had a bad time," that is what I have convinced myself that she meant (although nothing else that was said even hinted at that idea; and to the friend who doubled with me, the opposite was obviously true). I didn't ask her out this weekend for reasons mainly based on this one perception of how she feels about dating me. Looking back on my action, I see I have committed three of the Zalkind-Costello misperception errors.

- **No. 2** I may have responded to an irrelevant cue—her remark probably just came out and didn't really have any deep meaning behind it.
- **No. 3** I was influenced by a (negative) emotional factor—I was so worried that she was not enjoying herself, with the repercussions that would have to my emotional happiness, that my perception might have been distorted.
- **No. 5** I did not realize how heavily I weighted this single cue.

Being apprehensive of how she felt, I ended up analyzing every little remark she made. I did not take time to think that my ways of comprehending a perception may be inaccurate—the thought never seemed to enter my mind. The handout on perception states, "These defenses act like a screen or filter ... blocking out that which we don't want to see and letting through that which we wish to see." I, however, feel that I block out that which I want to see and let in that which I don't want to see. This is a definite problem, but one that I never thought of before. And to compound matters, the perceptions I let in are my own personal version of what is perceived and may be the opposite of what is being communicated.

I do not have this problem until I begin to like a girl. Trained as an engineer, I think I am able to cope with objective matters; but when I try to understand another person, I seem to fail—especially when my perceptions pass through an emotional filter.

To take a statement out of context, Zalkind and Costello say, "A little learning encourages the perceiver to respond with increased sensitivity to individual differences without making it possible for him to gauge the real meaning of what he has seen." Well, I have had only a little learning about perception, and their statement applies to me perfectly. I try to play psychologist without knowing the first thing about what I am looking for. This is a habit I have gotten myself addicted to, and one I will have to break down in order to have a better understanding of the people around me. Right now the unknown (i.e., the human unknown—what people are thinking) confronts me and I am frustrated by it. In response to this frustration, I set up a perceptual defense (I guess my perceptual offense is nothing but a type of perceptual defense—there is an old football theory that the best offense is a good defense), which only adds to my frustration. Thus, to move from the unknown to perceptual understanding, I must first realize that I am reacting defensively to what is being communicated to me.

It seems I am now coming back to a familiar theme in all the topics we have covered so far. Zalkind and Costello say, "The person who accepts himself is more likely to be able to see favorable aspects of other people." I feel this is especially true of myself. If I stop and realize that my date is probably thinking of the same things that I am (at the initial stages of human relations, most of the time is spent in the unconscious, hidden, and blind areas of perception), then I may prevent my perceptual defense from operating at its current level. If I continually look at weak points and never strong points, and do not realize that I am doing this, I am not really aware of myself and, therefore, not aware of how others perceive me.

I feel I can improve myself in a number of ways. First, I must accept my own feelings and not worry or analyze them. As is stated in the workbook, "Each of us has both his tender and tough emotions." Second, I should stop analyzing logically—it's hard for me to accept the fact that all of my world is not logical. Third, I should experiment more in the giving and receiving of perceptual feedback. I spend too much time analyzing a date's behavior and not enough time giving her feedback, thus blocking the understanding between us. Finally, the fourth area of improvement, and the factor that this paper has led me to explore, is increasing my own awareness and understanding of the causes of emotion. I hope I can put these steps into action and then build on them.

LEARNING POINTS

1. Perception is the process by which we select, organize, and evaluate the stimuli in our environment to make it meaningful for ourselves.
2. Selective attention means that people perceive only some of the stimuli that is actually present.
3. Both internal factors (motives, values, interests, attitudes, past experiences, and expectations) and external factors (motion, intensity, size, novelty, and salience) affect what we perceive.
4. Perceived stimuli is organized into patterns such as cause-and-effect relationships and schemas.
5. Schemas are cognitive frameworks that represent organized knowledge about a given concept, event, or type of stimulus. Once established, they determine what stimuli we attend to and remember.
6. People evaluate and interpret the stimuli they perceive in a subjective fashion.
7. Three sources of misinterpretation in cross-cultural interactions are (1) subconscious cultural blinders; (2) lack of cultural self-awareness; and (3) projected similarity.
8. Stereotyping occurs when we attribute behavior or attitudes to a person on the basis of the group or category to which the person belongs.
9. The drawbacks to perception are that it prevents us from taking in everything we should, makes our interpretations open to question, and promotes stereotypes.
10. On the positive side, the process of perception limits, selects, and organizes stimuli that would otherwise overwhelm us.
11. There are numerous perceptual distortions to avoid: stereotyping, the halo effect, central tendency, contrast effects, projection, and self-fulfilling perceptual defenses.
12. The Johari window consists of four quadrants: the arena, blindspot, façade, and unknown. It is an information processing model that distinguishes among information about oneself that is either known or unknown to the self or the other in a social interaction. Good communication is most likely to occur when both parties are operating from their arena.
13. Attribution theory contends that when people observe others' behavior, they attempt to determine whether it is internally or externally caused. We look for information about consensus, consistency, and distinctiveness to decide on causation.
14. The self-serving bias occurs when people attribute their success to personal qualities while blaming their failure on external factors.
15. Fundamental attribution error is the tendency to overestimate the influence of personal failings and underestimate the influence of external factors when judging others.

FOR MANAGERS

- As W. I. Thomas stated, situations that are perceived to be real are real in their consequences. Managers must deal with misperceptions, no matter how ridiculous they seem at times. It is not enough to ignore misperceptions with the comforting thought that they are untrue. For example, if employees perceive that their employer does not respect them or care about their welfare, there may well be tangible consequences in the form of high absenteeism, low productivity, and turnover.
- The most important lesson to be learned from perception is that no one's perceptions are ever totally accurate. Arguing about what different people really saw or heard is often futile. For this reason, it's best to take a provisional approach that allows for different perceptions:

    Not: "I know I'm right; I heard him with my own ears!"
    But: "I thought he said that, but perhaps I'm mistaken."

    Not: "I'm positive the staff decided to approve my budget just as it is."
    But: "Well, if we have different perceptions about the outcome of the decision, we'd better check it out with the rest of the staff. We both may have heard only what we wanted to hear."

- Rephrase what is said to you so you're sure you really understand the message.
- Question the validity of your conclusions about others and check your perceptions with other people.
- When people give you feedback, remember that their view of you may be distorted by their perceptions. It's a good idea to check out feedback with more than one person to make sure it is accurate.
- Once again, knowing yourself is useful in managing perceptions. If you suspect you have a bias in regard to certain people or issues, you can make a special effort to use active listening to keep your mind from leaping to conclusions, and check out your perceptions with an objective person.
- People who have a greater degree of self-understanding are less likely to view the world in black-and-white terms and to make extreme judgments about others.[22]
- Our own characteristics affect the characteristics we are likely to see in others. Traits that are important to us are the ones we look for in others. The truism that we see in others that which we most dislike in ourselves applies to perception. People who are self-critical are more likely to criticize others.
- Make sure there are no promotional barriers for minorities in your organization that are based on stereotypical assumptions.
- Trying to put yourself in the other person's shoes—empathizing with them—prevents distortion and improves communication.
- Self-disclosure is like a bell-shaped curve. Too much disclosure scares people off and makes them nervous. Too little disclosure doesn't give others enough information about the person to form a relationship with that person.

PERSONAL APPLICATION ASSIGNMENT

The topic of this assignment is to write about an experience that involved perception or attribution. Choose an experience that was significant to you and one about which you are motivated to learn more.

A. *Concrete Experience*
1. *Objectively* describe the experience (who, what, when, where, how). (2 points)
2. *Subjectively* describe your feelings, perceptions, and thoughts that occurred during (not after) the experience. What did others seem to be feeling? (2 points)

B. *Reflective Observation*
1. Looking back at the experience, what were the perspectives of the key actors (including you)? (2 points).
2. Why did the people involved (including you) behave as they did? (2 points)

C. *Abstract Conceptualization*
1. Relate concepts or theories from the assigned readings or the lecture to the experience. Explain thoroughly how they apply to your experience. Please apply at least two concepts or theories and cite them correctly. (4 points)

D. *Active Experimentation*
1. What did you learn about perception or attribution from this experience? (1 point)
2. What did you learn about yourself? (1 point)
3. What action steps will you take to be more effective in the future? (2 points)

E. *Integration, Synthesis, and Writing*
    1. Did you integrate and synthesize the four sections? (1 point)
    2. Was the Personal Application Assignment well written and easy to understand? (1 point)
    3. Was it free of spelling and grammar errors? (2 points)

ENDNOTES

[1] D. Dearborn and H. Simon, "Selective Perception: A Note on the Departmental Identification of Executives," *Sociometry 21* (1958): 142, and A. Kofman, "Selective Perception Among First Line Supervisors," *Personnel Administrator 26* (September 1963).

[2] J. R. Meindl and S. B. Ehrlich, "The Romance of Leadership and the Evaluation of Organizational Performance," *Academy of Management Journal 30* (1987): 91–109.

[3] S. T. Fiske and S. E. Taylor, *Social Cognition* (Reading. MA: Addison-Wesley, 1984).

[4] N. J. Adler, *International Dimensions of Organizational Behavior* (Cincinnati, OH: South-Western, 1997).

[5] Ibid., 78–84.

[6] W. Keichel III, "How to Manage Older Workers," *Fortune*, November 15, 1990: 183–86.

[7] G. M. McEvoy and W. F. Cascio, "Cumulative Evidence of Relationship Between Employee Age and Job Performance," *Journal of Applied Psychology* (February 1989): 11–17.

[8] D. Christensen, and R. Rosenthal, "Gender and Nonverbal Decoding Skill as Determinants of Interpersonal Expectancy Effects," *Journal of Personality and Social Psychology 42*, (1982): 75–87; and C. McCauley, C. L. Stitt, and M. Segal, "Stereotyping: From Prejudice to Prediction," *Psychological Bulletin 29* (1980): 195–208.

[9] L. Falkenberg, "Improving the Accuracy of Stereotypes Within the Workplace," *Journal of Management 16*, no. 1 (1990): 108.

[10] N. J. Adler, *International Dimensions of Organizational Behavior.*

[11] S. S. Zalkind and T. Costello, "Perception: Implications for Administration," *Administrative Science Quarterly VII* (September 1962): 218–35.

[12] Ibid., 226.

[13] N. Adler and D. N. Izraeli. *Women in Management Worldwide* (Armonk, NY. M. E. Sharpe, 1988); and M. Jelinek and N. Adler, "Women: World Class Managers for Global Competition," *Academy of Management Executive 2*, no. 1 (1988): 11–19.

[14] M. Haire and W. F. Grunes, "Perceptual Defenses: Processes Protecting an Organized Perception of Another Personality," *Human Relations 3* (1950): 403–12; and M. Rokeach. *The Open and Closed Mind* (New York: Basic Books, 1960).

[15] For two excellent collections of material relevant to this point, see W. G. Bennis et al., *Interpersonal Dynamics*, rev. ed. (Homewood, IL: Dorsey Press, 1968), and R. Wylie, *The Self Concept* (Lincoln: University of Nebraska Press, 1965).

[16] E. Goffman, "On Face Work: An Analysis of Ritual Elements in Social Interaction," *Psychiatry 18* (1955): 213–31.

[17] J. Luft, "The Johari Window," *Human Relations and Training News* (January 1961): 6–7.

[18] H. H. Kelley, "Attribution in Social Interaction," in E. E. Jones et al. (eds.), *Attribution: Perceiving the Causes of Behavior* (Morristown, NJ: General Learning Press, 1972).

[19] L. Pye, *Chinese Negotiating Style* (Cambridge, MA: Oelgeschlager, Gunn, & Hain, 1982).

[20] L. Ross, "The Intuitive Psychologist and His Shortcomings," in L. Berkowitz (ed.), *Advances in Experimental Social Psychology 10* (Orlando, FL: Academic Press, 1977): 174–220; and A. G. Miller and T. Lawson, "The Effect of an Informational Option on the Fundamental Attribution Error," *Personality and Social Psychology Bulletin* (June 1989): 194–204.

[21] Zalkind and Costello, "Perception."

[22] E. Weingarten, "A Study of Selective Perception in Clinical Judgment," *Journal of Personality XVII* (1949): 369–400.

Chapter 9

▲▲

GROUP DYNAMICS AND WORK TEAMS

OBJECTIVES By the end of this chapter, you should be able to:

A. List the benefits of self-managed teams.

B. Identify what organizational requirements must be in place to set the stage for successful work teams.

C. Describe two models of group development.

D. Distinguish between group content and group process.

E. Explain and diagnose group process behaviors that either help or hinder group effectiveness.

F. Describe and recognize task and maintenance behaviors.

A FAIR DAY'S WORK

For 18 years Ginny, had been doing about the same thing: packing Expandrium fittings for shipment. She was so well practiced that she could do the job perfectly without paying the slightest attention. This, of course, left her free to socialize and observe the life of The Company around her. Today, however, Ginny was breaking in a new packer.

"No, not that way. Look, Jim, if you hold it that way, well, then you have to twist your arm when you pack this corner, see. This way it's easier."

"But that's the way Claude Gilliam [the Methods Engineer] said we had to do it."

"Sure he did, Jim. But he's never had to do it eight hours a day like me. You just pay attention to what I say."

"But what if he comes around and says I should pack the other way?"

"Oh, that's easy. When he's here you do it his way. Anyway, after a couple weeks you won't see him again. And slow down, you'll wear yourself out. No one's going to expect you to do 80 pieces a week anyway."

"But Mr. Gilliam said 90."

"Sure, he did. Let *him* do it. Look, here's how to pace yourself. It's the way I was taught, and it works. You know the *Battle Hymn of the Republic*?" (Ginny hummed a few bars.) "Well, just work to that, hum it to yourself, use the way I showed you, and you'll be doing 80 next week."

"But what if they make me do 90?"

"They can't. Y'know, you start making mistakes when you go that fast. No, 80 is right. I always say, a fair day's work for a fair day's pay."

Source: Reprinted and adapted with permission from *The Ropes to Skip and the Ropes to Know* by R. Richard Ritti (New York: John Wiley, 1998): 78.

How Lynn Mercer Manages a Factory That Manages Itself

The skeptics persist in doubting the potential for self-direction in the workplace. They think workers lack initiative and that bosses will never give up control.

If you're among the naysayers, please meet Phillip Dailey and Lynn Mercer of Lucent Technologies.

Mr. Dailey works on an assembly line here. He strings cables inside a steel box the size of a refrigerator—a digital transmitting station for cellular-phone systems. While studying a bottleneck along the line, Mr. Dailey realized that with 25 percent more staff his team could increase output by 33 percent. He proved the concept by recruiting temporary workers from other teams—then clued in the bosses.

Ms. Mercer, for her part, is the plant manager here, content with broad goals and measurements. She distributes authority three levels downward for the same reason her bosses do. "I know how to do my job better than the guys three levels above me," she says.

In the brutal global market for digital cellular base stations, high speed and low cost are everything. So how does this self-directed workforce of 480 stack up? In two years it hasn't missed a single delivery deadline. And total labor costs represent an exceedingly low 3 percent of product cost.

Lucent employs no formulas or fixed methods here; constant change is the only constant. But a few simple principles were evident during my visit.

1. Hire attitude over aptitude.

The work is technical but teachable. What isn't teachable is initiative, curiosity and collegiality—the hallmarks of the self-directed workforce. So Ms. Mercer puts applicants through tests intended to weed out loners and curmudgeons. People come in as contractors, anointed as employees only after proving they're self-starters and team players.

Teams elect their own leaders to oversee quality, training, scheduling, and communication with other teams. Richard Denning, a quality leader, swears he has more say-so in this $21 billion-a-year company than he had in his father's electrical contracting business. "My friends and family don't believe how much people listen to me here," he says.

A well-hired workforce also polices itself: In the men's room during the shift change, I could hear one worker gently chiding another for missing a team meeting.

2. Create mission from above, methods from below.

The plant follows a one-page list of "working principles"—not some vague mission statement in a wooden frame but a contract signed by every employee committing them to speed, innovation, candor, deep respect for colleagues, and other plainly stated goals. People cite the document as if it were the Bill of Rights.

Though management establishes the mission, workers fulfill it. "If I give you an endgame," Ms. Mercer says. "You can find your way there." Teams continually alter the manufacturing process and even the product design itself. A senior engineer named David Therrien, who compiled the original assembly procedures, no longer recognizes them. "My instructions were nothing but a starting place," he says.

Engineers and assemblers constantly bat ideas around; the professional cubicles sit next to the assembly cells, mixing potted plants and power drills. "We solve problems in hallways rather than conference rooms," says production manager Steve Sherman. The process is so fluid that none of the manufacturing equipment is bolted to the floor.

What, then, prevents anarchy in the place?

3. Foster feedback.

Any complex adaptive system—a hive, an immune system, an economy—balances itself through sophisticated internal communication, magnifying the good changes and shutting off the bad ones.

In this plant every single procedure is written down—but any worker can propose changing any procedure, subject to ratification by those whose work it affects. When a new process takes hold, a worker logs into a network to write it into the law of the plant. "There are plenty of checks and balances," Ms. Mercer says.

Operating statistics are displayed everywhere; where performance trails a goal, the chart hangs behind a sheet of blood-red, see-through plastic. People with a few spare minutes consult an "urgents board" listing orders that are behind schedule, jumping in where most needed.

4. Unite the inside and the outside.

That means putting employees next to customers. Assemblers know the destination of every product they touch. When a completed product rolls off the line, the assemblers sign an inside panel. Dozens of entry-level technicians know the customers personally because Ms. Mercer sends them to trade shows and installation sites. Workers conduct the customer tours.

5. Reward teamwork.

The yearly bonus, equivalent of 15 percent of regular pay in 1996, is based equally on individual achievement and team performance. Ms. Mercer also fights elitism to nurture an all-for-one atmosphere; when a shipment of faulty wire crimps came in, managers throughout the plant jumped into the inspections.

But the greatest motivator may be the shaping of a giant enterprise. "This business has been handed to us," says technician Tom Guggiari. "This business is ours."

Source: Thomas Petzinger Jr., "How Lynn Mercer Manages a Factory That Manages Itself," *Wall Street Journal*, March 7, 1997, B1.

PREMEETING PREPARATION

A. Read "A Fair Day's Work" and "How Lynn Mercer Manages a Factory That Manages Itself."

B. Then read the Topic Introduction.

C. Answer the following questions.

    1. Focus on an effective group to which you belong (or belonged).

        a. List the norms (unwritten rules of conduct) of this group.

        b. How do you think the group developed these norms?

2. Now think about a poorly functioning group to which you belong(ed).
   a. List its norms.

   b. How do you think they developed?

3. How would you go about changing the norms in a poorly functioning group?

4. What are the norms in your learning group or class? How do they hinder or promote learning?

5. What are the significant learning points from the readings?

D. If your instructor has assigned the Robbins Self-Assessment Library, use "Am I a Team Player?" and "How Good Am I at Building and Leading a Team?"

 TOPIC INTRODUCTION

One of the most significant trends in business is the move toward teamwork. According to a recent study, 73 percent of U.S. companies are utilizing work teams and this number is expected to grow.[1] The impetus for incorporating teams into organizational structures comes from the need for speed and flexibility. Downsizing strategies have eliminated supervisors and middle managers and delegated many of their functions to self-managed or self-directed teams. When they function well, such teams allow their members to make a greater contribution at work and constitute a significant competitive advantage for the organization. Research shows that self-managed teams were rated as more effective in terms of productivity, costs, customer service, quality, and safety than traditionally managed teams. Other company benefits are reduced absenteeism, lower turnover, and increased employee motivation.[2] In terms of employee benefits, members of self-managed teams reported greater growth satisfaction, social satisfaction, and trust than did the members of traditionally managed groups.[3]

Self-managed work teams have the following characteristics. The teams determine how they will accomplish the goals they must achieve and how they will allocate the necessary tasks. Usually they are responsible for an entire product or process. The work teams take responsibility for planning, scheduling, organizing, directing, controlling, and evaluating their own work process. Some teams also select their own members and evaluate members' performance. Leadership varies in these teams—some have no formal leader, others elect a leader, while still others have a formal leader assigned by management.

Even though there is currently a tendency to see work groups as a panacea, they are not appropriate for every organization. In order to succeed, teams require a common purpose and specific goals. They also need a supportive context—top management, an organizational culture, and policies that all promote and support teamwork.[4] Furthermore, team members and supervisors must be trained in the necessary skills. It is difficult for supervisors or managers to make the transition from being a "boss" to being a coach or facilitator. They too need to be taught skills to ensure that teams are taken seriously and allowed to succeed.

Team members require technical, administrative, and social skills. They are often cross-trained so that they possess all the technical skills needed by the team; in some companies, people are paid more when they learn new technical skills. Team members need administrative skills to run meetings and comply with whatever administrative or data-gathering requirements the team has. Team members also need interpersonal skills in areas such as communication, conflict resolution, problem solving, and decision making. One of the key requirements for work teams is an understanding of the group dynamics and skills presented in this chapter.

In an individualistic society such as the United States, working in groups does not always come as naturally as it does in more collectivist societies in which people feel a stronger sense of loyalty to groups. We have phrases, such as "A camel is a horse put together by a committee," that reflect our reservations about group efforts. And in fact, Americans sometimes contribute less effort to group projects than when they work alone. This is known as *social loafing*. This phenomenon was not observed in a comparison study with Chinese groups, presumably because this behavior is less likely in a collectivist society.[5] Nor do we find this behavior in "turned-on" U.S. groups and teams that work well together and find their work more productive and enjoyable as a team. Group experiences can be extremely rewarding when all goes well and extremely frustrating when members lack the proper skills. Some people believe that working in groups is inevitably less efficient, more time consuming and frustrating, and that it creates conformity in thinking. Many of these deeply held beliefs are simply unsubstantiated or found to be less generally true than was originally believed. Stoner's work,[6] for example, on the riskiness of group versus individual decisions is a case in point. It is clear that, contrary to popular belief, under certain conditions groups make riskier decisions than do individuals.

When it comes time to acknowledge team accomplishments, outsiders, particularly in individualistic cultures, often insist on bestowing credit on individuals rather than groups.

"When New Zealander Sir Edmund Hillary's team climbed Mt. Everest for the first time in 1953, the whole team agreed not to speak about which individual reached the summit first. The important thing, they decided, was that the team reach the summit. They had, perforce, to travel in single file. No individual could possibly have made it without the team.

Then the journalists and nationalists in the United Kingdom and Nepal got into the act. The Nepalese feted Tenzing Norkay, the Sherpa who guided the group, parading him in a seat of honor atop the royal carriage. The rest of the team rode inside that carriage, not visible to the crowd. A U.K. newspaper was incensed at such behavior, insisting that Tenzing was only a servant/guide and that Hillary, the *real* leader, was the first to set foot on Everest's summit."[7]

The ensuing bickering damaged the friendship between the two men. Many of us have had personal experience with group members who try to grab the credit or who do not carry their fair share of the work. In spite of years of experience in various sorts of groups—families, clubs, sports teams, work teams—we don't always take the time to carefully observe what was going on in the group or reflect on why the members were behaving the way they were.[8] One of the factors that affects behavior is the group's developmental age. We act differently in a brand-new group than we do in a group that has been functioning for several years. Therefore, it is helpful to have an understanding of how groups typically develop, even though not all groups are exactly alike.

GROUP DEVELOPMENT

Most groups evolve through the same sequence of stages. Effective team leaders help the group successfully weather each stage in which members confront specific issues that affect their behavior. The most well-known model of group development follows.[9]

- **Forming** In this stage, members focus on accepting each other and learning more about the group and its purpose. This is a period of uncertainty, self-consciousness, and superficiality. Effective group leaders help orient members, clarify the purpose of the group, and work on establishing trusting relationships. By the end of this stage, members feel like they belong to the group.
- **Storming** Members confront the issues of how much individuality they must relinquish to belong to the group and who will control the group. Tension, criticism, and confrontation are typical of this stage. The group becomes polarized, subdivides into cliques, and challenges the leader and others. Effective leadership involves helping the group focus on a common vision, modeling constructive conflict management, and legitimizing expressions of individuality that do not hinder productivity. Skilled leaders ensure that the group is a safe place for all members. They also reassure members that storming is a normal stage in a group's development, which paves the way for later productivity (unless the group becomes stuck in destructive conflict).
- **Norming** Members develop shared expectations about group roles and norms. This stage is characterized by collaboration, commitment, increased cohesion, and identification with the group. Effective leaders continue to help set norms, provide positive feedback on the group's progress, and prevent groupthink. *Groupthink* is the tendency for members of a highly cohesive group to seek consensus so strongly that they fail to explore alternative courses of action.
- **Performing** At this point, the group focuses its energy on achieving its goals and being productive. There is increased cohesion, acceptance of individual differences, and mutual support during this stage. Skilled leaders help the group run itself at this point, foster the development of group traditions, and encourage the group to evaluate its effectiveness.
- **Adjourning** Temporary groups disband and focus less on performance and more on closure. In this stage, members struggle with holding on (nostalgia) and letting go (looking ahead to the future). Effective leaders encourage the group to reflect on and celebrate its achievements.

Another way to understand group development is the punctuated equilibrium model (see Figure 9-1). According to this model, the productivity of some groups can be described as periods of

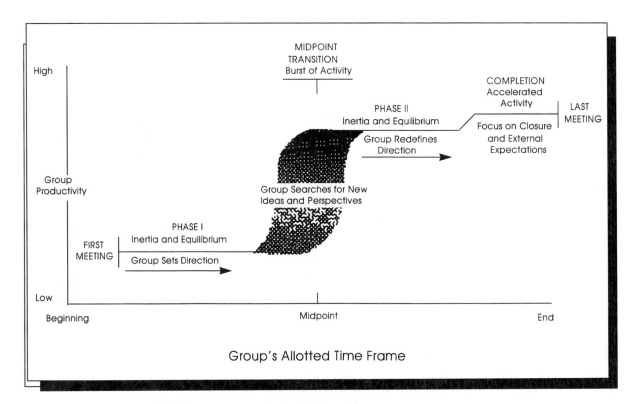

FIGURE 9-1   **The Punctuated Equilibrium Model of Group Development**

inertia or equilibrium that are punctuated by a transitional period of radical change that occurs at the midpoint of the group's calendar life.[10]

1. In the *first meeting*, the group sets its direction and does not reexamine it until the transition.
2. This is followed by *Phase 1*, a period of inertia and equilibrium.
3. When the group has used up half its allotted time, a *transition* occurs that includes a burst of activity and a search for new ideas and perspectives. The group redefines its direction at this point.
4. A second phase of inertia and equilibrium, *Phase 2*, follows the transition.
5. Accelerated activity takes place during the group's last meeting in the *completion* phase.

Regardless of how long groups have to accomplish their task, some of them do not "get serious" until half of their time has been used up.

CONTENT VERSUS PROCESS

In any group there are at least two classes of issues operating at any given point. One is the reason for the group's existence in the first place (e.g., to solve a particular problem). When we observe *what* a group is talking about, with regard to work that must be done, we are focusing on group *content* . When we try to observe *how* the group is functioning, we are talking about a second and equally important set of issues, group *process*.[11] There are two types of group process: task process and maintenance process. *Task process* focuses on how groups accomplish their work, including setting agendas, figuring out time frames, generating ideas, choosing techniques for making decisions and solving problems, and testing agreement. *Maintenance process* concerns how groups function with regard to meeting group members' psychological and relationship needs. It includes issues such as leadership, membership, norms, communication, influence, conflict management, and dealing with difficult members and dysfunctional behaviors.

Effective group members pay attention to both group content and process, so they can intervene when necessary in an appropriate manner. Although work groups spend most of their time on content, a failure to address process issues usually prevents a group from reaching its maximum potential and accomplishing its task in a timely manner. Effective facilitators focus on both productivity and commitment. The following sections focus on process issues that help us understand how groups function.[12]

COMMUNICATION

One of the easiest aspects of group process to observe is the pattern of communication:

1. Who talks? For how long? How often?
2. At whom do people look when they talk?
    a. Individuals, possibly potential supporters
    b. The group
    c. Nobody
3. Who talks after whom, or who interrupts whom?
4. What style of communication is used (assertions, questions, tone of voice, gestures, etc.)?

The kind of observations we make gives us clues to other important things that may be going on in the group, such as who leads whom and who influences whom.

Group decisions are notoriously hard to undo. When someone says, "Well, we decided to do it, didn't we?" any budding opposition is quickly immobilized. We can undo the decision only if we reconstruct and understand how we made it and test whether this method was appropriate or not.

Some methods by which groups make decision follow.[13]

1. The *plop:* "I think we should appoint a chairperson." ... Silence.
2. The *self-authorized agenda:* "I think we should introduce ourselves. My name is Jane Allen. . .".
3. The *handclasp:* Person A: "I wonder if it would be helpful to introduce ourselves?" Person B: "I think it would; my name is Pete Jones."

4. The *minority decision:* "Does anyone object?" or "We all agree, don't we?" Agreement or consensus may not be present, but it's difficult for others to object sometimes.
5. *Majority-minority voting:* "Let's vote and whoever has the most votes wins."
6. *Polling:* "Let's see where everyone stands. What do you think?"
7. *Consensus seeking:* Genuine exploration to test for opposition and to determine whether the opposition feels strongly enough to refuse to implement the decision. It's *not* necessarily unanimity but essential agreement by all. Consensus does *not* involve pseudo-"listening" ("Let's hear Joe out") and then doing what you were going to do in the first place ("OK, now that everyone has had a chance to talk, let's go ahead with the original decision").

TASK, MAINTENANCE, AND SELF-ORIENTED BEHAVIOR

Behavior in the group can be viewed in terms of what its purpose or function seems to be. When a member says something, is the intent primarily to get the group goal accomplished (task) or to improve or patch up some relationship among members (maintenance), or is the behavior primarily meeting a personal need or goal without regard to the group's problems (self-oriented)?

As the group grows and members' needs become integrated with group goals, there will be less self-oriented behavior and more task or maintenance behavior. Types of behavior relevant to the group's fulfillment of its task are the following:[14]

1. **Initiating** For any group to function, some person(s) must be willing to take some initiative. These can be seemingly trivial statements such as "Let's build an agenda" or "It's time we moved on to the next item," but without them, little task-related activity would occur in a group. People would either sit in silence or side conversations would develop.

2,3. **Seeking or giving information or opinions** The clear and efficient flow of information, facts, and opinions is essential to any task accomplishment. Giving-type statements—"I have some information that may be relevant" or "My own opinion in this matter is..."—are important to ensure decisions based on full information. Information-seeking statements not only help the seeker but the entire group.

4. **Clarifying and elaborating** Many useful inputs into group work get lost if this task-related behavior is missing. "Let me give an example that will clarify the point just made" and "Let me elaborate and build on that idea" are examples of positive behaviors in this regard. They communicate a listening and collaborative stance.

5. **Summarizing** At various points during a group's work, it is very helpful if someone takes a moment to summarize the group's discussion. This gives the entire group an opportunity to pause for a moment, step back, see how far they have come, where they are, and how much further they must go to complete their work.

6. **Consensus testing** Many times a group's work must result in a consensus decision. At various points in the meeting, the statement "Have we made a decision on that point?" can be

Source: Reprinted by permission of the Chicago Tribune-New York News Syndicate.

very helpful. Even if the group is not yet ready to commit itself to a decision, it serves to remind everyone that a decision needs to be made and, as such, it adds positive work tension into the group.

7. **Reality testing** Groups can take off on a tangent that is very useful when creativity is desired. However, there are times when it is important to analyze ideas critically and see whether they will hold up when compared to facts or reality. This helps the group get back on track.

8. **Orienting** Another way of getting a group back on track is through orienting behavior that helps the group to define its position with respect to goals and identify points of departure from agreed-upon directions. When questions are raised about the direction the group is pursuing, everyone is reminded of the group goal and has an opportunity to reevaluate and/or recommit to meeting it.

The following behaviors are necessary to keep a group in good working order. These *group maintenance* roles help create a climate that permits maximum use of member resources:

1. **Gatekeeping** Gatekeeping, directing the flow of conversation like a traffic cop, is an essential maintenance function in a group. Without it, information gets lost, multiple conversations develop, and less assertive people get cut off and drop out of the meeting. "Let's give Joe a chance to finish his thought" and "If people would talk one at a time, I'd find it easier to listen and add to our discussion" are examples of gatekeeping behavior.

2. **Encouraging** Encouraging also ensures that all the potentially relevant information the group needs is shared, listened to, and considered. "I know you haven't had a chance to work it through in your mind, but keep thinking out loud and we'll try to help." "Before we close this off, Mary, do you have anything to add?"

3. **Harmonizing and compromising** These two functions are very important but tricky because their overuse or inappropriate use can serve to reduce a group's effectiveness. If smoothing over issues (harmonizing) and each party's giving in a bit (compromise) serve to mask important underlying issues, creative solutions to problems will be fewer in number and commitment to decisions taken will be reduced.

4. **Standard setting and testing** This category of behavior acts as a kind of overall maintenance function. Its focus is how well the group's needs for task-oriented behavior and maintenance-oriented behaviors are being met. All groups will reach a point where "something is going wrong" or "something doesn't feel right." At such points, effective groups stop the music, test their own process, and set new standards where they are required. "Is the way we're tackling the problem working for everyone?"

5. **Using humor** The use of humor to put people at ease and reduce tension is an important maintenance function. However, the inappropriate use of humor can prevent groups from reaching their goals quickly and stop them from tackling uncomfortable issues that need to be resolved.

For a group to be effective, both task-oriented behavior and maintenance-oriented behavior are needed.

EMOTIONAL ISSUES: CAUSES OF SELF-ORIENTED EMOTIONAL BEHAVIOR

The process described so far deals with the work-facilitating functions of task and maintenance. But there are many active forces in groups that disturb work, which represent a kind of emotional underground or undercurrent in the stream of group life. These underlying emotional issues produce a variety of self-oriented behaviors that interfere with or are destructive to effective group functioning.[15] They cannot be ignored or wished away, however. Rather, they must be recognized, their causes must be understood, and as the group develops, conditions must be created that permit these same emotional energies to be channeled in the direction of group effort. What are these issues or basic causes?

1. The problem of identity: Who am I here? How am I to present myself to others? What role should I play in the group?
2. The problem of control and power: Who has the power in the situation? How much power, control, and influence do I have in the situation? How much do I need?
3. The problem of goals: Which of my needs and goals can this group fulfill? Can any of my needs be met here? To which of the group's goals can I attach myself?
4. The problem of acceptance and intimacy: Am I accepted by the others? Do I accept them? Do they like me? Do I like them? How close to others do I want to become?

Self-oriented behaviors tend to be more prevalent in a group at certain points in the group's life. In a new group one can expect to see many examples of self-oriented behaviors. Members are unfamiliar with one another and a certain amount of "feeling out" is to be expected. Sometimes this takes place in after-hours social situations—"Why don't we get together after work for a drink?" Self-oriented behaviors can also be observed when a newcomer joins an already established group. It is not unlike the dynamics that develop when a new sibling arrives in a family. Everyone else may be sincerely happy with the newcomer ("We really need her resources"); nonetheless, this is now a "new" group. The old equilibrium has been changed and a new one must take its place.

The potential destructiveness of self-oriented behaviors is highest just when the group most needs to be effective—when it is under stress. Groups, like individuals, sometimes regress to previous stages of development in times of stress. Effective leaders try to predict difficult transitions or events and minimize their effect. Ford's global teams refer to stressful periods and cultural tension points as "bumps" (e.g., when team members transfer in or out and when the team moves from planning to implementation).

Types of emotional behavior that result from tension and from the attempt to resolve underlying problems follow.

1. Tender emotions: love, sympathy, desire to help, need for affiliation with others
   a. Supporting and helping others
   b. Depending on others
   c. Pairing up or affiliating with others
2. Tough emotions: anger, hostility, self-assertiveness
   a. Fighting with others
   b. Punishing others
   c. Controlling others
   d. Counterdependency
3. Denial of all emotion
   a. Withdrawing from others
   b. Falling back on logic or reason

Individuals have different styles of reducing tension and expressing emotion. Three "pure types" have been identified:

1. The "friendly helper" orientation: acceptance of tender emotions, denial of tough emotions— "Let's not fight, let's help each other"—can give and receive affection but cannot tolerate hostility and fighting.
2. The "tough battler" orientation: acceptance of tough emotions and denial of tender emotions—"Let's fight it out"—can deal with hostility but not with love, support, and affiliation.
3. The "logical thinker" orientation: denial of all emotion—"Let's reason this thing out"—cannot deal with tender or tough emotions; hence, shuts eyes and ears to much going on around him or her.

BUT...

Friendly helpers will achieve their world of warmth and intimacy *only* by allowing conflicts and differences to be raised and resolved. They find that they can become close with people *only* if they can accept what is dissimilar as well as what is similar in their behavior.

Tough battlers will achieve their world of toughness and conflict *only* if they can create a climate of warmth and trust in which these will be allowed to develop. Logical thinkers will achieve their world of understanding and logic *only* if they can accept that their feelings and the feelings of others (both tough and tender) are also facts and contribute importantly toward our ability to understand interpersonal situations. Table 9-1 portrays the different orientation and characteristics of each type. These three, as described, are clearly pure types; the average person has some elements of each. What differentiates people is their predisposition toward a particular type.

We can learn to use emotional resources more appropriately by:

1. Accepting our own feelings and acknowledging that each of us has both tender and tough emotions.
2. Understanding group behavior at the feeling level as well as at the logical level, since feelings are also part of the group's reality.

TABLE 9-1   Orientation of the "Pure Types"

1. Friendly Helper	2. Tough Battler	3. Logical Thinker
Best of All Possible Worlds		
A world of mutual love, affection, tenderness, sympathy	A world of conflict, fighting, power, assertiveness	A world of understanding, logic, systems, knowledge
Task-Maintenance Behavior Demonstrated		
Harmonizing Compromising Gatekeeping by concern Encouraging Expressing warmth	Initiating Coordinating Pressing for results Pressing for consensus Exploring differences Gatekeeping by command	Gathering information Clarifying ideas and words Systematizing Procedures Evaluating the logic of proposals
Constructs Used in Evaluating Others		
Who is warm and who is hostile? Who helps and who hurts others? Who is nice and who is not?	Who is strong and who is weak? Who is winning and who is losing?	Who is bright and who is stupid? Who is accurate and who is inaccurate? Who thinks clearly and who is fuzzy?
Methods of Influence		
Appeasing Appealing to pity	Giving orders Offering challenges Threatening	Appealing to rules and regulations Appealing to logic Referring to "facts" and overwhelming knowledge
Personal Threats		
That he or she will not be loved That he or she will be overwhelmed by feelings of hostility	That he or she will lose his or her ability to fight (power) That he or she will become "soft" and "sentimental"	That his or her world is not ordered That he or she will be overwhelmed by love or hate

3. Increasing our awareness through observation and analysis of the causes of emotions. By learning to recognize which events in the here-and-now trigger emotions, we can gain better control of ourselves in a given situation and behave more appropriately.
4. Experimenting with expressing emotion differently and asking for feedback.

GROUP NORMS

Another issue that must be addressed with respect to group process is group norms. *A norm is an unwritten, often implicit rule that defines what attitudes and behaviors characterize a "good" group member versus a "bad" group member.* Norms are the group's shared beliefs about appropriate behavior, attitudes, and perceptions concerning matters that are important to the group. For example, in the opening vignette, "A Fair Day's Work," Ginny made sure Jim the newcomer learned the rules—that doing 80 pieces was good. Doing 90 would be bad because then the boss might pressure everyone to maintain that rate. Ginny was socializing Jim, teaching him the ropes. By doing so, she pointed out the difference between formal rules—those set by bosses and that may or may not be obeyed—and informal rules—norms that employees enforce among themselves. If a member does not comply with important group norms, the other members will pressure him or her to do so. If he or she still does not comply, the rest of the group may well ostracize the offending group member. If Jim were to insist on making 90 pieces, he would soon be labeled a rate buster and given the cold shoulder.

All groups create norms as they develop and mature. In and of themselves, norms are neither good nor bad. The important point is whether or not the norms that exist support the group's work or act to reduce effectiveness. In this way, group norms control the behavior of members and make group life more predictable.

Let's take a real-world example. The president of a multimillion-dollar multinational corporation wanted to make a major change in the way he and his three vice presidents functioned. The general pattern of behavior was such that each vice president would argue for decisions that would benefit his or her particular department. Turf battles and tunnel vision were standard fare during group meetings.

It was the president's desire to create what he called the "Office of the Presidency." When he and his vice presidents met, he wanted everyone to look at the issues before them from an executive perspective. In other words, he wanted everyone to focus on the corporation as a whole, looking at decisions through the "eyes" of a president.

Clearly a host of group norms would have to change dramatically. Historically, no meeting ever began until the president arrived. After all, it was "his meeting." If the new philosophy was to be taken seriously, the "Office of the Presidency" had to function *irrespective* of who—as an individual—was present or absent.

One Monday morning the three vice presidents arrived for their normally scheduled meeting. But one "small" problem had arisen: a devastating weekend snowstorm caused the president to be stranded 1,000 miles away. Still, several critical topics were on the agenda. After considerable anxious grasping for solutions (conference calls, private jets, and even prayer) and much nervous laughter, they bit the bullet. The "Office of the Presidency" was called to order. An old norm had been changed.

The pinch point occurred Tuesday morning at 8:00 A.M., only now it was the president who felt the anxiety. To his credit, he asked to be *informed* as to the decisions taken by the Office of the Presidency in his absence. Any other behavior on his part, such as reopening decisions he personally did not like, would have violated and made a game of the new normative expectations.

Fortunately, this president was aware of the importance of norms. Too many groups operate under the norm: "In this group, no one ever dares to question or suggest that we examine our norms." As a result, there is an absence of standard setting and testing and an implied punishment for anyone who engages in such behavior. Such a "Catch-22" norm is unlikely to facilitate the development of an effectively functioning group.

The following exercise provides an opportunity for you to observe group norms in action as well as other content and process issues we need to monitor.

PROCEDURE FOR GROUP MEETING: THE INNER-OUTER EXERCISE

The purpose of this exercise is to provide an opportunity to experience and study group dynamics and discuss effective work groups.[16]

STEP 1.   Divide the class into an even number of groups of 8 to 10 people by counting off. Choose an observer from each group and ask them to go outside the classroom to read their instructions on page 203. The groups will be paired (the Ones paired with the Twos, the Threes paired with the Fours, etc., depending on how many participants there are in the class). The paired groups will sit in two concentric rings of chairs, forming an inner circle (the odd-numbered groups) surrounded by an outer circle (the even-numbered groups) with both groups facing inward. When the observers return, they will sit outside the outer circle at opposite points so each observer has a clear view of a different part of the inner circle.

STEP 2.   Each group has the same two tasks and the same amount of time to complete the tasks—four periods of 4 minutes each for a total of 16 minutes (or whatever time periods your instructor chooses). You are allowed to work on the two tasks only when your group is seated in the inner circle. At this time, you should act as if the other group is not present. When your group is seated in the outer circle, your role is to act as observers and potential consultants to the other group. Therefore, you should observe carefully how the other group functions. Try to identify what they are doing that either impedes or facilitates their accomplishment of the two tasks. Please write down your observations, *but do not talk with the other members of your group while you are in the outer circle* because it will distract the other group.

To start, the Ones, for example, seated in the inner circle will have 4 minutes to work before time is called. They immediately switch seats with the Twos and observe them at work for 4 minutes. Switch seats quickly because the clock starts running for the following group as soon as time is called. The paired groups may borrow ideas from each other, but the goal is for each group to develop its own product.

The two tasks are:
a. Be the most effective group you can; and
b. Create a list of the 10 characteristics of effective groups and rank order them.
To summarize, your group has two roles: "problem solvers" when you are seated in the inner circle and "observers" when you are seated in the outer circle.

STEP 3.   Observers read the Observer Instructions on page 203.

STEP 4.   After the second round, members of the group in the inner circle will turn around to face the members of the other group who are seated directly behind them. Both people should act as consultants to the other group. Tell the other person what you saw occurring in his or her group and give some advice about how the other group could function more effectively. The idea is for everyone to listen carefully to someone who has observed his or her group and take back to that group suggestions for improvement. Thus, members of both groups have the opportunity to both give and receive advice during a 4-minute period. Then complete the final rounds of the exercise.

STEP 5.   Each group presents its list of the characteristics of effective groups or posts them on the wall if using flip charts. What are the similarities and differences? (5 minutes)

STEP 6.   Everyone counts off by four forming new heterogeneous groups. Each group will discuss a different aspect of group process that has a major impact on the life of any group or team. Our goal is to figure out what behaviors either hindered or helped group effectiveness.

a. **Group One's task** (all the number Ones) is to explore the concept of "goals" as they have influenced the life of the developing groups. You should look at goals from the perspective of those that were imposed on the group by the instructor, and those that evolved as the real group goals, which may or may not have anything to do with those established by the instructor. Did you see any individual goals that differed from the general goals of the group? Please develop specific examples of how individual and group goals influenced the life of the groups and helped determine their success. How can groups handle the problem of disparate goals?

b. **Group Two's task** (all the Twos) is to look carefully at the "membership" criteria that prevailed in the groups. Membership in this case is equivalent to what behaviors were acceptable or not acceptable in terms of gaining entry to the group. During this exercise, some individuals gained greater membership than others because of their behavior. What kinds of behavior or circumstances made some people less than "full" members? Why? The group must understand not only what these criteria were but also how they influenced the feelings, motivation, and morale of the group itself. Please give examples of each of the criteria that you develop and examples of how they influenced the life of the groups. What can a group do to make everyone feel like a full member?

c. **Group Three's task** is to take an in-depth look at the behavioral norms, the implicit or explicit "rules of the game," that influenced the life of each group. How did the groups handle conflict and stress, make decisions, listen, generate ideas, allow certain language to prevail, and so on? Be sure that with every norm that you identify you note specific examples and make comparisons among the groups when it is obvious that some of the norms differed radically. What can groups do to ensure that they develop norms that help rather than hinder group effectiveness?

d. **Group Four's task** is to explore the kinds of leadership that developed in the groups—who had it, who took it, to whom it was given, and who if anyone was able to establish and maintain a real presence of leadership? What different kinds of behaviors did leaders demonstrate? What behaviors resulted in either resistance or a loss of leadership? Decision making is of specific importance here—how were decisions made, who made them, and how did this influence the group? The names of individuals are not important but specific behaviors are because we can then begin to understand how the life of each group was influenced. If you observe different types of leadership, what were the pros and cons of each leadership style? What can a group do to promote the type of leadership that is most effective for that group?

You will all have 20 to 30 minutes to develop an understanding of your particular concept and prepare a presentation.

STEP 7.   Each of the four groups presents its findings and examples.

STEP 8.   General Debriefing Questions
   a. Did your group act out all the characteristics on your list? Why or why not?
   b. How would you describe the relationships between the paired groups?
      Did you see any evidence of competition? If so, from where did the competition come? Did the groups learn from watching each other? Why or why not?
   c. What was the result of the consultation period? Why did this result(s) occur?
   d. What did you learn about the way you behave in groups?

STEP 9.   The observers present their communication feedback to the group they observed. What are the implications of the communication pattern that emerged? What are the consequences of talking a lot in a new group and talking very little? (10 minutes)

OBSERVER INSTRUCTIONS

Your task is to unobtrusively chart the communication that takes place in one of the groups, using the Observer Chart on the following page. Please don't talk or distract the group in any way.

1. Write down the names of the people in your group in the same order they are seated, both horizontally and vertically.
2. When a person speaks to another group member, please code who is speaking to whom and how often by putting a mark in the box that intersects the speaker's name on the side with the target of the communication, whose name is listed along the top. If it is a statement, write down a hatch mark. If it is a question, write down a question mark.

    The way to tell to whom a remark or question is addressed is to watch the eyes of the speaker. If the speaker is clearly making an effort to make eye contact with the whole group while talking (scanning) or is not looking at anyone when speaking, count the target as the "group" as a whole (the first column). Otherwise, count it as a communication directed at the person whom the speaker is looking at *when he or she finished talking*. That person is usually the one we are trying to influence or looking to for support. So even if the person has looked at other people while talking, code the communication in the box of the last person the speaker looked at.
3. Write down any observations you have about the way the group is communicating or functioning on the bottom of the Observer Chart. Does anyone seem left out of the discussion and, if so, why? Is there a dominant person or subgroup that is controlling the communication? Is anyone exhibiting task behavior? Is anyone exhibiting group task or maintenance behaviors?
4. Add up the marks and prepare your feedback for the group. Remember to deliver it in a nonevaluative and noninterpretive fashion so that no one becomes defensive.

 ## FOLLOW-UP

The distinction made in the inner-outer exercise between content issues and process issues can be important in understanding how groups function. Most of us assume that if a group of people is called together to perform a task, nothing but the task is important or relevant. This assumption rests on the belief that it is not only feasible but essential that we separate our emotional self (needs, wants, motives) from our intellectual, rational, problem-solving self. This is impossible. When people enter a group situation, they bring their total selves, the emotional as well as the intellectual. In fact, certain aspects of our emotional selves will become more salient because we are in a group situation. Attempts to bury, wish away, or ignore the interpersonal aspects of group interaction is much like sweeping dirt under the rug—sooner or later the pile gets big enough that someone will trip over it.

In some ways, the appointment of a chairperson or moderator recognizes that groups do not always "stay on track." While appointing a leader is often useful, there are two potential problems with this approach. First, seldom do the group members spend any time discussing *why* they are "off track." More often the chairperson will say something like "We're getting off the main track, let's get back to it!" and that's all that happens. It is extremely important to realize that if people are having difficulty staying on track, there are reasons for the behavior and simply saying "Let's get back to it" does nothing to eliminate the basic causes. Worse than that, this kind of behavior ("Let's quit wasting time and get to the task") may further accelerate the underlying reasons for lack of involvement and make the situation worse.

Second, there is no inherent reason that only one person in a group should have the responsibility for worrying about how the group is progressing. Everyone can and should share this responsibility. To delegate this function or role to just one individual is often a highly inefficient utilization of resources. People can learn to be skilled participant-observers in groups. In effective groups, *anyone* who feels that something is not right can and should raise the issue for the total

Observer Chart—Who Speaks to Whom?

Target

Speaker	Group	1	2	3	4	5	6	7	8	9	10	Total
1												
2												
3												
4												
5												
6												
7												
8												
9												
10												
Total												

Code: Statements ⊞ Questions ???

Observations:

group to examine. Anyone who observes a need for a particular kind of task or maintenance behavior can help the group. In a well-functioning group (working on something other than a routine programmable task), an observer looking in from the outside might not be able to pick out the formal leadership. The "leadership function" passes around according to the group's need at a particular point. It is important, in other words, to distinguish between leaders as persons and leadership as a function. For example, summarizing or gatekeeping when the group needs it is performing an important act of leadership. To see the need and fail to respond can be viewed as a failure to fulfill one's membership responsibilities.

It is often argued that "We don't have the time to worry about people's feelings or to discuss how the group is working." Sometimes this is perfectly true, and under severe task pressure a different kind of process is necessary and legitimate. People can accept this, however, if they know from past experience that this situation is temporary. More often, however, lack of time is used as a defense mechanism to avoid the discussion completely. Furthermore, if a group is continually under severe time pressure, some time ought to be spent examining the effectiveness of the group's planning procedures.

A group that ignores individual members' needs and its own process may well find that it meets several times to make the same set of decisions. The reason for this is that the effectiveness of many decisions is based on two factors[17]—logical soundness and the level of psychological commitment among the members to the decision made. These two dimensions are not independent; in fact, some people who are uncommitted (often because of process issues) may withhold, on a logical basis, information necessary to make the soundest decision. In any event, the best decision (on a task or logical level) forged at the expense of individual commitment is not a very good decision at all.

Finally, what can be done to learn to use self-oriented emotional resources more appropriately? As a first step, it is important to accept our own feelings and to realize that everyone has both tender and tough emotions. Within some American companies, managers (and particularly males) are expected to be tough, hard, and aggressive. Any sign of "tender emotions" (warmth, affection) may be perceived as a sign of weakness. However, feelings do not go away simply because we ignore them, and there is no question that emotions can affect group decisions. Given the opportunity to experiment with and get feedback on our emotional behavior (and a climate that supports such behavior), we can become more aware of when it is appropriate to be tough, tender, or neither.

It is foolhardy to assume that simply because a group of people assembles to perform a task, it will somehow automatically know how to work together effectively.[18] A comparison between the behavior of a football team and the behavior of a management team highlights the essence of this paradox. The football team spends untold hours practicing teamwork in preparation for the 60 minutes each week that its members' performance as a team really counts. In contrast, most management teams do not spend even 60 minutes per week practicing teamwork in spite of the fact that for 40 or more hours every week their behavior as a team really counts. For this reason, in recent years both management groups and work teams have undergone team-building training.[19]

Most team-building efforts encourage members to (1) establish their goals and priorities, (2) define the roles that need to be performed, (3) examine and determine the procedures the group uses or should use, and (4) examine the team's interpersonal relationships and norms.[20] Common complaints about personality problems in teams often have their root in the failure to clarify goals, roles, and procedures, so the order in which teams tackle these issues is very important.

As society and the global economy become more complex and as technology continues to advance, more and more of organizational life will revolve around a team or group structure. The "information explosion" will guarantee that no one person can expect to have all the facts necessary to make many decisions. "Temporary systems" in which a group of people join for a short-term task and then disperse to form new and different task groups to tackle other problems have become more prevalent. Virtual teams, in which members are geographically dispersed and seldom work face-to-face, have become more common. "Unlike conventional teams, a virtual team works across space, time, and organizational boundaries with links strengthened by webs of communication technologies."[21] Their popularity has necessitated a new term to distinguish virtual teams from conventional teams—*collocated teams*. The global nature of many virtual teams has also made cross-cultural skills a requirement for team members. Teams play an important role in organizational life today, and every indication points toward their increased importance in the future.[22] Teams work best when they share common methods of problem solving, decision making, and conflict management—topics that are addressed in subsequent chapters.

INTERNATIONAL EXAMPLE OF GROUP NORMS— A CONCRETE EXPERIENCE AND REFLECTIVE OBSERVATION

As we saw in the exercise, norms vary from group to group. They also vary from culture to culture. The following vignette relates the "concrete experience" of one expatriate professor who taught overseas in Latin America.

I sat back in my chair, glancing around the handsome room with its graduation photographs of faculty members in full academic regalia, including some remarkably fetching scarlet robes and exotic headgear from a Spanish university. Finding it difficult to break an unconscious habit of punctuality, I have spent many moments alone in this room, waiting for colleagues to arrive. As a result, I have learned to bring along small projects to occupy my time while waiting for those who live by a different internal clock. By now, other faculty members, all males except for myself, are dribbling in, responding to the external summons of a telephone call from on high, the Rector's (president's) secretary. They enter with a lot of good-natured greetings and jokes and, as always, it is a pleasure to see them.

In today's meeting, the dean is trying to get faculty support and compliance with policies and procedures that will improve academic standards and quality. As usual, I am intrigued by the norms in these meetings. Even though there are only 10 people present, the dean jots down the names of the professors who wish to speak in the order in which they signal him. This order is respected in the beginning but becomes more difficult to maintain when people want to respond immediately to the comments. At this point they are reminded by the dean or others that there are several people ahead of them in the queue. Occasionally, a senior faculty member is allowed to break in and make his comments without being reprimanded for being out of order. The result of the group's self-imposed structure is often a disjointed conversation with lots of looping back to previous points. There seems to be an unspoken expectation that everyone should speak at some point in the meeting, whether or not they are contributing a different opinion. The dean fields and reacts to each comment or question, immediately judging its worth. I am always surprised that one person, rather than the group, is granted the power to dispose of ideas that could possibly be developed and honed by more group discussion. If the communication pattern were graphed, it would show that a large majority of the comments are directed to and returned from a central hub, the dean. A much smaller percentage of the interactions occur laterally among the participants.

Since I agree with the policies and am already complying with the rules, my most fervent wish is to have the meeting end quickly so I can "return to work." I sense no similar urgency on the part of my colleagues; they are "at work." I decide to take advantage of the situation to clarify a practice I have never fully understood. I ask if students might not do better on future tests if their exams were returned to them. My suggestion is rapidly shot down with comments like, "This is the way it's always been done" and "Students would take advantage of the policy you are suggesting." Except for another expatriate, no one appears to find any merit in my suggestion and the discussion quickly moves on.

When the meeting ends, I head for yet another one with my departmental colleagues. I am immediately struck by the difference in atmosphere between the two meetings. Perhaps because we share many of the same values and because we have put in many hours and miles together, I feel more at ease, more listened to, and much more able to be myself in the second meeting. This group also has more experience working with women, so gender is not an issue. We are like a self-managed group in many ways. We begin a free-wheeling discussion in which everyone chimes in on a single topic until closure is reached, and then we move on to another point. We are tackling a topic that we chose ourselves—determining our regional strategy. Comments are directed to the entire group and everyone, including brand-new employees, apparently feels free to respond with his or her opinions, and even feelings. The group has a coordinator but not a formal leader. The coordinator helps keep the group on track at times but does not make the decisions. After vigorous discussion with clear differences of opinion, the group makes consensus decisions. It never occurs to me that I am a minority or an outsider in this meeting, even though I do not always agree with what my colleagues do or say. I don't find myself glancing at my watch in this meeting, and when we leave to return to our individual offices, I have a smile on my face.

When I reflect on this situation, I see numerous cultural differences between myself, an American, and the other faculty members who are primarily Latin American. Although not all individuals or organizations fit these stereotypes, the following cultural differences are generally acknowledged and appear to influence the norms in the first meeting. A major difference is a polychronic versus monochronic orientation. People in monochronic cultures tend to be punctual and do one thing at a time in a linear fashion. In polychronic cultures, people pay attention to several things at once; punctuality is less important than finishing other activities. In this example the monochronic American arrives on time and is disconcerted when one topic is not discussed until it is completed. The polychronic Latins arrive when it is convenient and easily track the various topics being discussed at once. For them, speaking out in the meeting may serve to maintain relationships and promote a sense of collegiality; in contrast, the norm that everyone should speak runs counter to a U.S. value of not wasting time.

Other differences are that Latins tend to respect tradition and resist policy changes while many Americans value change, sometimes for its own sake. Decision making is more centralized and leadership is generally more authoritarian in Latin America, which explains why people grant the dean the right to pass judgment on suggestions. In comparison, Americans tend to be more participative and egalitarian. The take-a-number-to-speak norm is not found in all Latin groups; it may be somewhat unique to the dominant organizational culture. Hierarchical power is much less important in the departmental meeting. In general, however, there is a greater emphasis on control and rules in Latin cultures, accompanied by attempts to get around these rules. People with high status or connections are more successful at evading rules, which explains why senior faculty are not always obliged to respect the queue. In U.S. universities, senior faculty are also privileged. What varies from school to school and country to country is the particular form that privilege takes.

In both meetings, there are norms that promote friendly relations and an institutional concern for excellence. Beyond these similarities, the two meetings are characterized by very different norms even though the cultural composition is fairly similar in both groups. Cultural differences are less significant in the departmental group than in the more formal faculty meeting. The smaller group is part of a cultural subgroup with values that are closer to my own and norms that I have helped create. As a result, only in the second group do I feel like a full-fledged member.

LEARNING POINTS

1. In order to set the stage for successful work teams, organizations require supportive top management, an organizational climate and policies that promote teamwork, teams with a common purpose and specific goals, and supervisors and team members who have the necessary skills to make teams function.

2. Self-managed work teams are not appropriate in all situations, but they can be more effective and satisfying than traditionally managed teams.

3. The five-stage model of group development consists of forming, storming, norming, performing, and adjourning.

4. The punctuated equilibrium model describes group productivity as periods of inertia or equilibrium that are punctuated by a transitional period of radical change that occurs at the midpoint of the group's calendar life. Productivity accelerates again right before the group's time is completed.

5. In any group there are two types of issues operating at any given time: content and process. Content issues refer to the task, "what" the group is working on. Process issues refer to "how" the group is functioning.

6. Task process focuses on how groups accomplish their work, including setting agendas, figuring out time frames, generating ideas, choosing techniques for making decisions and solving problems, and testing agreement.

7. Maintenance process concerns how groups function with regard to meeting group members' psychological and relationship needs. It includes issues such as leadership, membership, norms, communication, influence, conflict management, and dealing with difficult members and dysfunctional behaviors.

8. By observing communication patterns and decision-making procedures, we can understand better how a group functions.

9. Task behaviors contribute to accomplishing the group task or goal. They consist of initiating, seeking, or giving information or opinions, clarifying and elaborating, summarizing, consensus testing, and orienting.

10. Maintenance behaviors are geared toward creating a good climate for work and good relationships that permit maximum use of member resources. They are gatekeeping, encouraging, harmonizing and compromising, standard setting and testing, and using humor.

11. Groups need both maintenance and task behaviors to be effective. Groups that emphasize content and ignore their process are just as likely to fail as groups that emphasize process at the cost of task.

12. Self-oriented emotional behavior interferes with effective group functioning. Issues of identity, inclusion, power, acceptance, intimacy, and goal agreement occur and reoccur at various points in a group's development.

13. The "pure types" that represent the three different styles of reducing tension and expressing emotion are:
    a. The "friendly helper" (tender emotions)
    b. The "tough battler" (tough emotions)
    c. The "logical thinker" (denial of all emotions)
    However, each of these types can only create the type of climate in which they feel most comfortable by incorporating some of the perspectives of the other two types and accepting their dissimilarities.

14. We can learn to use our emotional resources better by:
    a. Accepting our personal feelings.
    b. Trying to understand the feelings that occur in a group.
    c. Trying to identify what causes our emotions to be triggered in a group.
    d. Experimenting with expressing emotion differently and asking for feedback.

15. Group norms are unwritten, often implicit, rules that define the attitudes and behaviors that characterize good and bad group members. All groups have norms. By making them explicit, a group can determine whether their norms help or hinder their group's effectiveness.

16. Ideally, all members of a group should be participant-observers so everyone can contribute to keeping the group on track and bringing up the need to discuss process issues that may be hindering the group. Group leadership should be performed by more than just the designated leader.

17. Groups that ignore their process often take longer to resolve content issues because process problems prevent commitment and full sharing of information.

18. It takes practice and effort to transform a group into an effective team.

FOR MANAGERS

- Groups of employees can have either positive or negative impact on productivity and the work environment, depending on the norms and stances they have taken. The more cohesive the group, the more likely the members are to take a unified position; cohesive groups aren't by definition more productive than noncohesive groups.
- Informal leaders of employee work groups are important communication links for getting input, sending out trial balloons, and disseminating information about upcoming plans or events.
- Understanding group behavior is especially important at meetings. Heightening people's awareness of the roles they play is often helpful. Rotating the responsibility for chairing the meeting gives everyone an opportunity to develop leadership skills and see, at the same time, how difficult it is to run a good meeting.
- Asking a work group to help establish norms can be very effective. It can be done by asking group members:

    What would be effective behaviors at work?
    How should we treat each other at work?
    How should we make decisions?
    How should we communicate?
    Do we have any norms that are keeping us from being effective?

- Teams need ready access to pertinent information if they are to succeed.
- If you want to avoid the problem of social loafing on a team, reward the team on the basis of its results and on the basis of individual contribution to those results.
- The characteristics of a productive team are:[23]
    - common agreement on high expectations for the team
    - a commitment to common goals
    - assumed responsibility for work that must be done
    - honest and open communication
    - common access to information
    - a climate of trust
    - a general feeling that one can influence what happens
    - support for decisions that are made
    - a win-win approach to conflict management
    - a focus on process as well as results

GUIDELINES FOR CONDUCTING GROUP MEETINGS:

- Prepare an agenda that is distributed beforehand so participants have time to prepare for the meeting
- Put difficult topics in the middle of the agenda
- Go over the agenda at the beginning of the meeting and clarify what the group wants to accomplish in the meeting
- Assign roles: scribe, timekeeper, secondary facilitator if needed
- Set ground rules with a new group about how the group will work and make decisions
- Start and end on time—some groups set time parameters for each issue on the agenda
- Guide but do not dominate the discussion
- Encourage participation and listen carefully to all members
- Encourage the open discussion of ideas and differences while discouraging personal attacks and insults
- At the end of the meeting summarize what was accomplished and prepare a responsibility chart that describes what needs to be done before the next meeting by whom and by when

PERSONAL APPLICATION ASSIGNMENT

The face-to-face group working on a problem is the meeting ground of individual personality and society. It is in the group that personality is modified and socialized; and it is through the workings of groups that society is changed and adapted to its times.

Herbert Thelen

The topic of this assignment is to think back on a group experience that was significant for you. Choose an experience that intrigues you and about which you want to learn more. (You may wish to write about one of the exercises your learning group did in this course.)

A. *Concrete Experience*
  1. *Objectively* describe the experience (who, what, when, where, how) (2 points)
  2. *Subjectively* describe your feelings, perceptions, and thoughts that occurred during (not after) the experience. What did others seem to be feeling? (2 points)

B. *Reflective Observation*
  1. Looking back at the experience, what were the perspectives of the key actors (including you)? (2 points)
  2. Why did the people involved (including you) behave as they did? (2 points)

C. *Abstract Conceptualization*

    1. Relate concepts or theories from the assigned readings or the lecture to the experience. Explain thoroughly how they apply to your experience. Please apply at least two concepts or theories and cite them correctly. (4 points)

D. *Active Experimentation*

    1. What did you learn about groups or teams from this experience? (1 point)

    2. What did you learn about yourself? (1 point)

    3. What action steps will you take to be more effective in the future? (2 points)

E. *Integration, Synthesis, and Writing*

    1. Did you integrate and synthesize the four sections? (1 point)

    2. Was the Personal Application Assignment well written and easy to understand? (1 point)

    3. Was it free of spelling and grammar errors? (2 points)

ENDNOTES

1 "Teams," *Training* (October 1996): 64.

2 C. C. Manz, and C. P. Neck, "Teamthink: Beyond the Group-think Syndrome in Self-Managing Work Teams," *Journal of Managerial Psychology 10*, no. 1 (1995): 7–16.

3 S. G. Cohen and G. E. Ledford, Jr., "The Effectiveness of Self-Managing Teams in Service and Support Functions: A Field Experiment." Paper presented at the Academy of Management annual meeting, San Francisco, August 1990. See R. A. Guzzo, and M. W. Dickson, "Teams in Organizations: Recent Research on Performance and Effectiveness," *Annual Review of Psychology 47* (1996): 307–39.

4 J. R. Katzenback and D. K. Smith, *The Wisdom of Teams* (Cambridge, MA: Harvard Business School Press, 1992).

5 P. C. Earley, "Social Loafing and Collectivism: A Comparison of the United States and the People's Republic of China," *Administrative Science Quarterly* (December 1989): 565–81.

6 J. A. F. Stoner, "Risky and Cautious Shifts in Group Decisions: The Influence of Widely Held Values," *Journal of Experimental Social Psychology*, no. 4 (1968): 442–59.

7 J. Lipman-Blumen, and H. J. Leavitt, *Hot Groups* (New York: Oxford, 1999), 25.

8 The literature on group dynamics has grown to enormous proportions. See J. R. Hackman, (ed.), *Groups that Work (and Those that Don't)* (San Francisco: Jossey-Bass, 1990); K. Fisher, *Leading Self-Directed Work Teams* (New York: McGraw-Hill, 1993); and A. Zander, *Groups at Work* (San Francisco: Jossey-Bass, 1977) and *Making Groups Effective* (San Francisco: Jossey-Bass, 1982).

9 B. W. Tuckman and M. C. Jensen, "Stages of Small Group Development Revisited," *Group and Organizational Studies,* December 1977, pp. 419–27; and M. F. Maples, "Group Development: Extending Tuckman's Theory," *Journal for Specialists in Group Work* (Fall 1988), pp. 17–23; J. D. Rothwell, *In Mixed Company: Small Group Communication* (Fort Worth, TX: Harcourt Brace Jovanovich, 1992); and M. F. Maples, "Group Development: Extending Tuckman's Theory," *Journal for Specialists in Group Work 13* (1988): 7–23.

10 C. G. Gersick, "Time and Transition in Work Teams: Toward a New Model of Group Development," *Academy of Management Journal* (March 1988): 9–41; and C. G. Gersick, "Marking Time: Predictable Transitions in Task Groups," *Academy of Management Journal* (June 1989): 274–309.

11 For a discussion of the differences between content and process issues, see E. H. Schein, *Process Consultation: Its Role in Organizational Development* (Reading, MA: Addison-Wesley, 1988).

12 Much of the following material has appeared in a variety of places and is a standard input into many training programs such as those conducted by the National Training Laboratory. This particular material was abridged with permission of the author from "What to Observe in Groups," from *Reading Book for Relation Training*, C. R. Mill and L. C. Porter (eds.) (Arlington, VA: NTL Institute, 1982), 28–30; and B. E. Collins and H. Guestzkow, *A Social Psychology of Group Processes for Decision Making* (New York: John Wiley, 1964).

13 This typology was developed by R. R. Blake.

14 K. D. Benne and P. Sheats, "Functional Roles of Group Members," *Journal of Social Issues 2* (1948): 42–47, and E. H. Schein, *Process Consultation* (Reading, MA: Addison-Wesley, 1988).

15 This section is based on Schein's *Process Consultation*. For another view of emotional behavior in groups, see W. C. Schutz, "Interpersonal Underworld," *Harvard Business Review 36*, no. 4 (July–August 1958): 123–25, and W. W. Liddell and J. W. Slocum, Jr., "The Effects of Individual Role Compatibility upon Group Performance: An Extension of Schutz's FIRO Theory," *Academy of Management Journal 19* (1976): 413–26.

16 Adapted from R. W. Napier and M. K. Gershenfeld, *Making Groups Work: A Guide for Group Leaders* (Boston: Houghton Mifflin, 1983), 114–20.

17 This dichotomy of a decision's quality is analogous to issues raised during the discussion of the concept of psychological contract in the introduction of Chapter 1. In that case, the dichotomy was the decision to join versus the decision to participate. See also Chapter 15, "Leadership and Decision Making," for more detail on effective decision-making styles.

18 One such process for learning how to work more effectively in groups is called broadly "laboratory training." For a full discussion of this and related educational techniques, see E. H. Schein and W. G. Bennis, *Personal and Organizational Change Through Group Methods: The Laboratory Approach* (New York: John Wiley, 1965).

19 For good description of team building, see W. G. Dyer, *Team Building: Issues and Alternatives* (Reading, MA: Addison-Wesley, 1987), and R. Fry, I. Rubin, and M. Plovnik, "Dynamics of Groups that Execute or Manage Policy," in *Groups at Work*, ed. by R. Payne and C. Cooper (New York: John Wiley, 1981), 41–57.

20 R. Beckhard, "Optimizing Team-Building Efforts," *Journal of Contemporary Business* (Summer 1972): 23–32.

21 J. Lipnack, and J. Stamps, *Virtual Teams* (New York: John Wiley & Sons, 1997): 7.

22 See J. Lipman-Blumen, and H. J. Leavitt, *Hot Groups* for an explanation and description of exciting, successful teams.

23 W. D. Hitt, *The Leader-Manager* (Columbus, OH: Batelle Press, 1988).

Chapter 10

▲▲

PROBLEM SOLVING AND CREATIVITY

OBJECTIVES By the end of this chapter, you should be able to:

A. Explain the four stages of problem solving.

B. Describe the red/green modes of problem solving.

C. Explain the different roles a manager plays during problem solving.

D. Identify what problem-solving stage a group is in and how to facilitate a group's progress.

E. Describe the creative process.

F. Explain the organizational conditions that promote creativity.

BEARS AND HONEY POTS

A small electric utility company located in a mountainous region of the Pacific Northwest was plagued by a problem it could not solve. Spring and fall ice storms coated the power lines with ice that was so heavy it often snapped the lines and cut off power to customers. Removing the ice, however, was a dangerous job for linemen who had to scale icy towers and poles to shake the wires with a long pole. A consultant brought together a diverse group of employees from different backgrounds to brainstorm a solution. There were linemen, accountants, secretaries, mailroom clerks, and supervisors in the group.

Several hours of brainstorming did not produce anything useful. During a break, the consultant overheard one lineman telling another that he really hated de-icing the lines. The last time out, a bear had chased him! When the group reconvened, the consultant related this tale in an effort to prod the group's thinking. A participant wondered if they could train bears to climb the poles; the bears' weight would shake the poles enough to knock off the ice. Once the group stopped laughing, someone suggested the group get back on task. But another lineman commented that the trick would be getting the bears to climb the poles sequentially so no poles would be overlooked. Someone else suggested they could get the bears to climb each pole by putting a honey pot at the top as a reward.

The group came up with several drawbacks to this idea. What would keep the bears from eating the honey in good weather rather than waiting for ice storms? What would keep raccoons or other animals from eating the honey? What if the bears eventually got tired of honey?

The tension level rose as conflict developed between two subgroups—the people who wanted to continue pursuing the bear-and-honey-pot idea and others who thought it was a dead-end and wanted to move on to more practical ideas. A cynical lineman recommended using the executive helicopter that transported company VIPs around to put honey pots on top of each pole after an ice storm. The mention of helicopters brought a secretary into the discussion for the first time. As a former nurse's aide in Vietnam, she remembered that the helicopters bringing in wounded soldiers had a tremendous down wash. Would helicopter down wash be strong enough, she asked, to knock off the ice?

Bingo! That turned out to be the magic solution. The company, however, never would have hit on this idea if it had not put together a diverse group capable of tolerating ambiguity, conflict, and seemingly off-the-wall, impractical ideas—all essential elements for group creativity.

PREMEETING PREPARATION

A. Read "Bears and Honey Pots" and the following "Cardiotronics, Inc." case.

B. Read the Topic Introduction.

C. What were the significant learning points from the readings?

D. Make a plan to conduct tomorrow's meeting of Assembly Unit D as if you were Marion Andrews. Prepare a list of questions or statements that Marion could use during each stage of the problem-solving process described in the Topic Introduction. For example, what kinds of questions would facilitate good problem solving during the valuing stage, the priority-setting stage, and so on?

Role Play Preparation:
Questions/statements leaders can use during each stage of the problem-solving process:

1. Valuing/Exploration

2. Priority Setting

3. Information Gathering

4. Problem Definition

5. Idea Getting

6. Decision Making

7. Participation

8. Planning

E. If your instructor has assigned the Robbins Self-Assessment Library, use "What's My MBTI Personality Type?" and "Do I Have a Creative Personality?"

CARDIOTRONICS, INC.

Cardiotronics, Inc., was started 17 years ago in a small New Hampshire town by two biomedical engineers whose goal was to produce a quality cardiac monitor (a device that continuously displays the wave pattern of the heart's function). The company originally produced customized monitors on a small scale. After five years the owners had perfected a quality monitor that was significantly less expensive than custom monitors, and they decided to mass produce it.

The company currently has just over 200 employees. It remains nonunionized, but the labor union in this old New England milltown has from time to time made efforts to win a union election.

For the past 11 years, the company has enjoyed a strong competitive edge and has gained a reputation for a quality product and prompt service. Recently, however, the company's top-management team has been informed that a similar monitor, reputed to be of equal or better quality than Cardiotronic's, will soon be introduced into the U.S. market by a large Japanese electronics firm.

Monitor Assembly Process   The cardiac monitors (excluding cables) are produced in four stages. In the first stage, circuit boards are produced largely by machine process. During the second stage, the circuit boards are placed by hand on a motherboard and are connected to one another. The final step in stage 2 is the attachment of the motherboard to the base panel. In the third stage, the casing is mounted by hand onto the base panel and external hardware and cables are placed. In the final stage, the monitors are tested for a week before shipping.

The Second-Stage Assembly Task   Four assembly teams are responsible for the second stage of monitor assembly, the manual assembly and the wiring of the motherboard. Each team consists of five workers operating in a U-shaped area. The motherboard is started at station 1. Each worker adds his or her circuit, connects it to the others, and passes it to the next worker. The assembly process requires some manual dexterity but is relatively easy to do. Each job on the line is of equal difficulty as determined by a recent industrial engineering study. The assembly arrangement for one of these teams, Team D, is as follows.

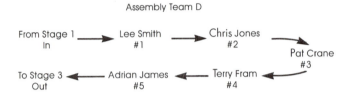

Assembly Team D

The following are the recently announced assembly team average daily production figures for the last month:

- Team A = 40 boards
- Team B = 32 boards
- Team C = 43 boards
- Team D = 35 boards

Your Problem as Marion Andrews, Supervisor of Team D   You are the new supervisor of Team D, Marion Andrews. You have been in the position for a month, having recently been promoted from the quality control section where you worked for five years. During your second week, you received a memo stating that to meet increased production requirements resulting from increased sales, all second-stage teams were to meet their minimum daily production rates. You informed the team in a brief meeting but had to leave for a week of supervisory training shortly thereafter. After returning from the training program, you note that the daily production has increased to 36 but that your team is still 4 units below the daily minimum rate of 40 units. In looking into the problem you note the following:

- Work accumulates at Pat Crane's station #3, and there are typically several motherboards waiting. Pat is 58 years old and has been with the company for 13 years. The supervisors of the other production teams do not consider Pat acceptable for transfer.
- Only one monitor from your team has been rejected in the past month by quality control.
- Assembly and test equipment is relatively new and in good working order.

Team D's assembly line will be closed for 30 minutes tomorrow, and you have decided to call a meeting for Team D.

How do you plan to conduct this meeting?

TOPIC INTRODUCTION

For many scholars who study organizations and management, the central characteristic of organizations is that they are problem-solving systems whose success is measured by how efficiently they solve the routine problems associated with accomplishing their primary mission—be it manufacturing automobiles or selling insurance—and how effectively they respond to the emergent problems and opportunities associated with survival and growth in a changing world. Kilmann's view is representative of this perspective:

One might even define the essence of management as problem defining and problem solving, whether the problems are well structured, ill structured, technical, human, or even environmental. Managers of organizations would then be viewed as problem managers, regardless of the types of products and services they help their organizations provide. It should be noted that managers have often been considered as generic decision makers rather than as problem solvers or problem managers. Perhaps decision making is more akin to solving well-structured problems where the nature of the problem is so obvious that one can already begin the process of deciding among clear-cut alternatives. However, decisions cannot be made effectively if the problem is not yet defined and if it is not at all clear what the alternatives are, can, or should be.[1]

In this view, the core task of management is problem solving. While experience, personality, and specific technical expertise are important, the primary skill of the successful manager is the ability to manage the problem-solving process in such a way that important problems are identified and solutions of high quality are found and carried out with the full commitment of organization members. The Y2K problem, concerning computers that were not designed to recognize the year 2000, is a large-scale problem that organizations had to resolve before the turn of the century.

Problem solving has received more attention in recent years due to the emphasis on employee involvement groups and total quality programs. As a result, the initiative and responsibility for problem solving has been pushed farther down in the organizational hierarchy. Problem-solving techniques are being taught at all levels in companies that have a continuous improvement orientation.[2]

THE NATURE OF PROBLEM SOLVING

This chapter describes a model of the problem-solving process[3] that defines the stages and tasks involved in such a way that managers can better manage their own and their organization's problem-solving activities. This model of problem solving is based on three premises: First, problem solving is basically a process of learning from experience; second, problem solving involves the manipulation and control of the external world through one's mental processes—mind over matter; and third, problem solving is by its nature a social process.

A Process of Learning from Experience

The experiential learning process presented in Chapter 3 identifies four phases: concrete experience, reflective observation, abstract conceptualization, and active experimentation. Common-sense notions of problem solving tend to focus on the phases of concrete experience and active experimentation—on the specific difficulties experienced in immediate situations and the actions taken to overcome them. Traditional educational ideas about learning, on the other hand, tend to focus on the phases of reflective observation and abstract conceptualization—emphasizing the gathering of information and development of general concepts. Just as the process of traditional education is improved when the concrete and active emphasis of problem solving is added, the effectiveness of problem solving is enhanced by the addition of the academic learning perspectives of reflection and conceptualization. In both cases, what results is a more holistic and integrated adaptive process. More specifically, by viewing problem solving as a process of experiential learning, more attention is given to finding the right problem to work on, problems are more adequately defined, better-quality solutions are found, and the implementation process is more effective.

Mind over Matter

The ability to solve complex problems is uniquely human, resulting from the structure of the human mind, first, in its dialectic ability to perceive experiences in the world and to comprehend these experiences through words and other symbols. Second, human self-consciousness provides a perspective on and control over this process. We can choose which aspects of our experience to attend to and discipline ourselves to pursue a line of thought or action. As Kaplan described it, "The manager gives form to a problem in the way a potter sees and then shapes the possibilities in a lump of clay. The difference is that managers practice their craft using an intangible medium: information."[4] Thus, problem solving is the process of using our minds to control the world around us.

It is literally the way we achieve the power of mind over matter. For centuries humans watched birds fly and dreamed that they, too, might fly. That vision of flight became a motivator of countless problem-solving efforts that have culminated today in flight achievements far beyond the dreams of our ancestors.

A Social Process

Problem solving is not just an activity of the mind; it is fundamentally a social process. Solutions to problems are inevitably combinations, new applications, or modifications of old solutions. From other people we get new dreams, new ideas, information, and help in getting things done. Language, communication, and conflict are central in problem solving. Particularly in organizations, it is difficult to conceive of a problem that does not in some way involve other people—in choosing the problem, supplying information about it, helping to solve it, or implementing the solutions. Given the social nature of problem solving, the effective management of problem solving involves four tasks:

1. The management of one's own and other's thinking processes to ensure an orderly and systematic process of analysis that determines the right problem or opportunity to work on, the most likely causes of the problem, the best solution given available alternatives and constraints, and a process for implementing the solution that ensures quality and commitment.
2. The proper organizational arrangements to promote cooperation among interdependent groups and assignment of problems to appropriate organizational units.
3. The management of relationships among people to ensure the appropriate involvement and participation of others.
4. The constructive use of conflict in an organizational climate that removes interpersonal and group barriers to information sharing and collaborative problem solving.

A MODEL OF PROBLEM SOLVING BASED ON THE THEORY OF EXPERIENTIAL LEARNING

The model of problem solving derived from the theory of experiential learning describes an idealized problem-solving process that is characteristic of the fully functioning person in optimal circumstances. Ineffective problem solving deviates from that normative process because of personal habits and skill limitations or because of situational constraints such as time pressure, the limited access to information that can result from one's position in the organization, or from mistrusting relationships with subordinates. The model consists of four analytic stages that correspond to the four stages of the experiential learning cycle: Stage 1, *situation analysis*, corresponds to concrete experience; Stage 2, *problem analysis*, to reflective observation; Stage 3, *solution analysis*, to abstract conceptualization; and Stage 4, *implementation analysis*, to active experimentation. These four stages form a nested sequence of analytical activities so that each stage requires the solution of a particular analytic task to frame the succeeding stage properly.

The four stages of problem solving and the basic questions each answers are presented in the paragraphs that follow.

Situation Analysis: What's the Most Important Problem?

The task of *situation analysis* is to examine the immediate situational context to determine the right problem to work on. While problem-solving activity is often initiated by urgent symptomatic pressures, urgency alone is not a sufficient criterion for choosing which problems to tackle. As every manager knows, the press of urgent problems can easily divert attention from more important but less pressing long-term problems and opportunities. Every concrete situation contains a range of problems and opportunities that vary in urgency and importance. Some of these are obvious, whereas others are hidden or disguised. Situation analysis requires exploration to identify the problem that takes precedence by criteria of both urgency and importance. This is what is meant by the popular saying, "Managers do things right; leaders do the right thing." Problem finding is equally as important as problem solving.

Problem Analysis: What Are the Causes of the Problem?

Given the appropriate choice of a problem, the task of *problem analysis* is to define the problem properly in terms of the essential variables or factors that influence it. Here the task is to gather information about the nature of the problem and evaluate it by constructing a model of the factors that are influencing the problem. This model serves to sort relevant from irrelevant information and guides the search for further information to test its validity. The result of problem analysis is to define the problem so that the criteria to be met in solving it are identified.

Solution Analysis: What's the Best Solution?

Once the problem is analyzed correctly, the third stage, *solution analysis*, seeks to generate possible solutions and to test their feasibility for solving the problem against the criteria defined in Stage 2. This is the most intensively studied stage of problem solving, given its emphasis on brainstorming.

Implementation Analysis: How Do We Implement the Solution?

The solution chosen in solution analysis is next implemented in the fourth stage of problem solving: *implementation analysis*. Tasks essential for implementing the solution must be identified and organized into a coherent plan with appropriate time deadlines and follow-up evaluations. Responsibility for implementing the plan is developed through participation of those individuals and groups not already involved in the problem-solving activity who will be directly affected by the solution. Implementation activities from Stage 4 are carried out in the situation identified in Stage 1 and, thus, modify that situation, creating new opportunities, problems, and priorities. Effective problem solving is, therefore, a continuing iterative cycle paralleling the experiential learning cycle. For example, when individuals affected by the solution participate in implementation analysis, new problems and opportunities may come to light as priorities for continuing problem-solving efforts. There is some evidence that the solution to one problem causes another, because solutions often have unanticipated consequences that problem solvers fail to predict.

THE DIALECTICS OF PROBLEM SOLVING

The process of problem solving does not proceed in a logical, linear fashion from beginning to end. Instead, it is characterized by wavelike expansions and contractions alternatively moving outward to gather and consider alternatives, information, and ideas and inwardly to focus, evaluate, and decide. These expansions and contractions have been variously labeled *green light/red light* and *divergence/convergence*.

Elbow's[5] description of "doubting" and "believing" games is another way to conceptualize the two different mind-sets required for problem solving. The first rule of the believing game is that people refrain from doubting or evaluating and instead focus on possibilities, how an idea *could* work. In contrast, the doubting game focuses on a reductive, structured, "objective" rationality. People with this orientation are constantly asking, "What's wrong with this?" As a result, they poke holes in ideas and arguments, torpedo assumptions, and probe in an analytical manner. Thus, problem solving is not the result of a single mental function such as logical thinking. Effective problem solving involves the integration of dialectically opposed mental orientations—red- and green-mode mind-sets.

The green-mode mind-set facilitates creative imagination, sensitivity to the immediate situation, and empathy with other people. The green-mode mind-set facilitates the expansion phases of problem solving—valuing, information gathering, idea getting, and participation. The red-mode mind-set, on the other hand, facilitates analysis, criticism, logical thinking, and active coping with

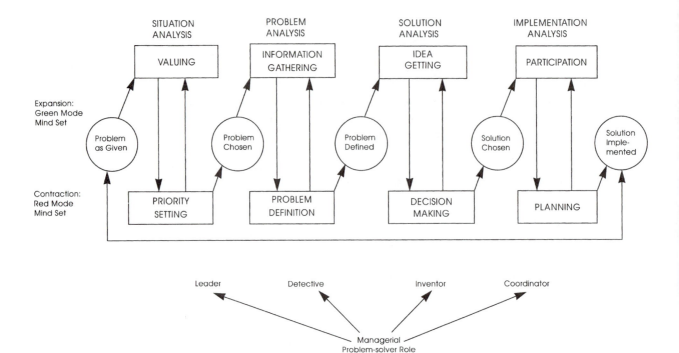

FIGURE 10-1   **Problem Solving as a Dialectic Process**

the external environment. The red-mode mind-set is, therefore, most appropriate for the contraction phases of problem solving—priority setting in situation analysis, problem definition in problem analysis, decision making in solution analysis, and planning in implementation analysis. Effectiveness in problem solving is enhanced by approaching the expansion/contraction phases of each problem-solving stage in the appropriate mind-set. For problem solvers to accomplish this matching of mind-set and problem-solving task, they must first become aware of when they are in the red or green mode of consciousness and then learn to shift from one mode to the other. With some practice, this can be accomplished quite easily, and usually practice in identifying and separating the two mind-sets has the effect of increasing the intensity of both. Managing the problem-solving process with groups of people requires the creation of a climate that stimulates and reinforces the appropriate mind-set in participants.

The problem-solving process is further guided by four roles that focus the dialectic interplay of red and green mind-sets on the relevant stage of the problem-solving process. In situation analysis, the problem solver adopts the role of a *leader*, focused on identifying goals and values in the situation in the green mode and setting priorities in the red mode. In problem analysis, the role is that of a *detective*, focused on gathering information in the green mode and building and evaluating models in the red mode. In solution analysis, the role is that of an *inventor*, generating ideas in the green mode and testing their feasibility in the red mode. In implementation analysis, the problem solver adopts the *coordinator* role, developing participation in the green mode and planning in the red mode. Conscious attention to these roles serves to focus attention on the priorities of each analytic stage and signals the transition from one stage to another. A diagram of this model is shown in Figure 10-1 and is described in the paragraphs that follow.

SITUATION ANALYSIS—VALUING AND PRIORITY SETTING

Most problem-solving activity begins with a problem as given—a specific circumstance, task, or assignment that demands attention. The task of situation analysis is to transform this problem as given into a problem that is consciously chosen to meet the dual criteria of urgency and importance.

Urgent structured problems in organizations are often the result of previous failures to address unstructured problems (e.g., the continued urgent need to replace bank tellers may result from the failure to address more unstructured problems of worker morale or career opportunities). Structured problems are repetitive and routine, and definite procedures are developed for dealing with them. Unstructured problems are novel and not covered by ready-made procedures because they occur infrequently or are very complex. In addition, for many organizations in rapidly changing environments, aggressive opportunity seeking is essential to maintain stability and growth. Careful situation analysis is, therefore, most critical in those cases in which long-term adaptation to a changing environment takes precedence over expedient action.

When people discuss problems, they devote time to talking about how they would like the situation to be. For example, the technique of visioning involves asking people to close their eyes and imagine their ideal organization. This reflects the green mode, whereas the exploration of current realities represents the red mode. The result is a menu of problems and opportunities in the situation from which one can be chosen that satisfies the criteria of urgency and importance. The process of articulating desired goal states is called *valuing*. To be successful, the valuing process must overcome barriers that exist in most organizational settings to open sharing of values. Foremost among these barriers is the organizational press to be realistic. Wishing, wanting, and valuing must be explored independently of reality for them to develop fully. Two other barriers to the valuing process are the fear of conflict and the threat of isolation.

Charles Lindblom[6] noted some time ago that it is easier to find agreement on a course of action than it is to get agreement on the goals for the action. Discussion of values accentuates human individuality and emotional commitment with a resulting increase in conflicting viewpoints. In the dialectic view, such conflict is essential for the discovery of truth. Many managers, however, shy away from conflict because it is unpleasant and they do not know how to use disagreement constructively. A related barrier to valuing is the threat of isolation that comes from holding values different from those of the majority. It is this barrier that gives rise to conformity and groupthink in problem finding.[7] A worker, for example, may suppress his or her genuine values for achievement and excellence so as not to violate group norms of mediocrity. For this reason an effective valuing process requires an environment that gives security and support for individuality.

The contrasting pole to valuing in the situation analysis dialectic is *priority setting*. As with any dialectic, valuing and priority setting mutually enhance one another—valuing gives direction and energy to priority setting and priority setting gives substance and reality to valuing. Every managerial decision reflects values; choosing one problem as a priority reveals the values of the decision makers. Priority setting has three specific tasks: (1) to explore the current situation for those features that facilitate or hinder goal achievement, (2) to test the feasibility of changing those features, and (3) to articulate reality-based goal statements that give substance to values and allow them to be realized. Priority setting is not a rational, analytic process of reflective planning. It is an active, intuitive process of trial-and-error exploration of what is going on in the situation. It involves "knocking on doors," listening to people, trying things out, and taking risks.

Taken as a whole, the central issue in situation analysis is leadership, and the basic social role of the problem solver is that of a leader whose responsibility is to guide the problem-solving attention of the organization to those problems and opportunities whose solution will be of maximum benefit to the long-run effectiveness of the organization. Someone once said that the key to successful leadership is to find out which way people are going and then run out in front of them. There is an element of truth in this, for the successful leader in situation analysis identifies the values and goals of those in the situation and then holds up those that are most important as priorities for action.

PROBLEM ANALYSIS—INFORMATION GATHERING AND PROBLEM DEFINITION

Problem analysis begins with the problem chosen in situation analysis and seeks to understand and define the problem in such a way that solutions to it can be developed. In the expansion mode, information about the concrete problem situation is gathered. The *information-gathering phase* of problem analysis is a receptive, open-minded phase in which all information associated with the problem is sought and accepted. This receptive stance has both a cognitive and interpersonal component. Cognitively, it is important in the information-gathering phase to avoid biases and preconceptions about the nature of the problem and its causes in favor of letting the data about the problem speak for themselves. Interpersonally, information gathering requires skills in the development of trusting relationships so that others do not hold back or modify information to say "what the boss wants to hear" or to avoid reprisals. In many organizations, these two components negatively interact with one another to produce a climate in which the gathering of accurate information is very difficult. Mistrust and threat cause workers to withhold information, and this forces management to rely on its own prejudgments as to the nature of the problems. By acting on these prejudgments, they sometimes reinforce worker mistrust and perpetuate a cycle that restricts accurate information exchange.

In the contraction mode of *problem definition*, the task is to define the problem based on the information gathered. Problem definition is basically a process of building a model portraying how the problem works—factors that cause the problem, factors that influence its manifestation, and factors mediating the application of solutions. Two skills are critical in building a model that defines a problem: causal analysis and imagery. Causal analysis uses the inductive logic of experimental inquiry to evaluate data and identify those invariant causal relationships that define the problem. It is a means of sorting relevant from irrelevant information. Imaging is a way of refining the problem definition by imagining its dynamics and subjecting them to "thought experiments." Stated simply, imaging is the process of creating in one's mind a model or scenario of how the problem occurs and then subjecting that model to various transformations to understand how the model operates and how the problem might be solved. Prince describes this process graphically:

> *Imaging is our most important thinking skill because it accompanies and facilitates all other thinking operations. I find it useful to think of my imaging as my display system or readout of my thinking processes.*[8]

With practice, imaging can create richly detailed problem scenarios and can portray large amounts of information in complex interrelationships. When concrete information is juxtaposed against a conceptual model, it serves to evaluate that model. Furthermore, the model guides the search for new and relevant information. In a sense, the problem solver in the problem analysis stage is in the role of detective—gathering clues and information about how the "crime" was committed, organizing these clues into a scenario of "who done it," and using that scenario to gather more information to prove or disprove the original hunch. The dialectic between information gathering and problem definition has synergistic power. By combining them, one can learn from what does *not* occur or has *not* happened as well as from what has. As in Sherlock Holmes's famous case, "The Dog Who Didn't Bark," a model suggests events that should occur if the model is true and, thus, their nonoccurrence in reality can invalidate the model.

The output of the problem analysis phase is a model of the problem validated through the interplay of information gathering and problem definition. The problem as defined describes the problem in terms of those essential variables that need to be managed to solve it.

SOLUTION ANALYSIS—IDEA GETTING AND DECISION MAKING

Solution analysis is achieved through the interplay between getting ideas about how the problem can be solved and decision making about the feasibility of the ideas generated. This two-stage process has been highly developed in brainstorming. The first step of solution analysis focuses on creative imagination, the green light stage of brainstorming, where the aim is to generate as wide a range of potential solutions as possible in an atmosphere that is free from evaluation and supportive of all ideas. Research on both communication and meeting behavior reveals that most responses are evaluative. Obviously, this does not promote either creativity or participation.

The second substage, the red light stage of brainstorming, focuses on evaluation, sorting through the ideas generated in the first substage and evaluating them systematically against the criteria that an effective solution must meet. This substage ends with the selection of the best solution. In the solution phase, the problem solver takes the role of inventor, creatively searching for ideas and then carefully evaluating them against feasibility criteria.

IMPLEMENTATION ANALYSIS—PARTICIPATION AND PLANNING

Implementation analysis is accomplished through the interplay of planning and the process of carrying out plans. Since implementation of solutions in organizational settings is most often done by or with other people, the critical expansion task is *participation*, enlisting the appropriate involvement of those actors in the situation who are essential to carrying out the problem solution. Three subtasks are involved here:

1. The anticipation of the consequences that will result from implementing the solution and the involvement of those who will experience these consequences in developing ways to deal with them.
2. The identification of those key individuals who by virtue of expertise and/or motivation are best qualified to carry out the various tasks in implementation.
3. Sometimes in the process of accomplishing subtasks 1 and 2, it becomes necessary to ask these key individuals to recycle through the problem-solving process to reevaluate whether the most important problem has been chosen, whether the problem is properly defined, and whether the best solution has been identified.

In the participation phase of implementation, the essential attitude to adopt is inclusion of others, receptivity, and openness to their concerns and ideas.

The *planning phase* of implementation analysis is an analytic process involving the definition of tasks to be accomplished in implementing the solution, the assignment of responsibility to qualified individuals, the setting of deadlines and planning for follow-up monitoring, and the evaluation of the implementation process. If the problem and its solution are very complex, planning may be quite complicated using network planning methods such as PERT (Program Evaluation Review Technique) or CPM (Critical Path Method) of analysis. Often, however, a simple chart listing key tasks, responsible individuals, and time deadlines is sufficient for planning and monitoring implementation.

As with the other three stages of our problem-solving model, there are two dialectically related processes involved in implementation analysis. The first involves developing plans for implementation and identifying the potential consequences of implementing these plans. An iterative process is often useful here—scout potential issues that may arise in implementation, develop a rough plan, share it with those involved in the situation to get reactions, and then modify the plan. The other dialectic can be termed the "who's" and the "what's." Managers appear to have distinct stylistic preferences about how they deal with this issue. Some prefer to define the "what's" first—the plan and tasks to be accomplished—and then assign these tasks to individuals to carry them out. Others begin with the "who's," seeking to identify qualified and interested individuals and then developing plans with them. While the best approach probably varies with the situation and task, beginning with the "who's" has the advantages of giving priority to often scarce human resources and maximizing participation and delegation. In synthesizing these dialectics, the problem solver in implementation analysis adopts the role of coordinator, working to accomplish tasks with other people.

Cultural differences can be seen in the way problems are solved in different countries.[9] Fatalistic cultures (e.g., Thailand, Indonesia, and Malaysia) are more likely to accept situations as they are; therefore, they may be slower to identify and resolve problems. In other cultures, such as the United States, managers are more likely to take a problem-solving approach to most situations and perceive problems as an opportunity to make improvements. Fixing problems is part of the American orientation toward action. That same predisposition toward action, however, can sometimes result in solutions that have not been thoroughly analyzed.

The alternative solutions developed in problem solving are also affected by cultural orientations toward time. Cultures that are oriented toward the past (England, Italy) tend to look for historical patterns and lessons. Future-oriented cultures (United States, Australia) are more likely to generate new alternatives because they are less bound to the past.

CREATIVITY

Another factor that affects the problem-solving process is the degree of individual and group creativity. *Creativity, the process by which individuals or small groups produce novel and useful ideas,* plays a role in how problems are defined and determines how many innovative solutions are generated. Because innovation in today's business environment is closely linked to organizational survival, creative thinking is an important skill and a competitive edge. For example, when Southwest Airlines needed 800 personal computers (PCs) for a new reservations center, the information systems group saved the company $1 million by purchasing parts from wholesalers and organizing an assembly line of employees to build the PCs themselves.[10]

3M is a company that is well known for its creative products and employees, as well as having an organizational culture and policies that foster innovation.[11] The company sets an annual goal to have close to a third of its sales come from products developed within the last few years. To make this happen, technical staff members at 3M are allowed to spend 15 percent of their time on any project they wish. Post-It Notes came about in part because a 3M employee, Spence Silver, took advantage of this autonomy and became interested in a light adhesive glue. However, it wasn't until he hooked up with another employee, Art Fry, who'd encountered a problem with bookmarks for his church hymnal, that a practical application was found for the glue. Fry took equipment home to his basement and made a machine to manufacture prototypes. Incidentally, the machine grew to such a size that he had to break a hole in the wall of his basement to return the equipment to 3M! Other scientists and marketing people were pulled in to help with the project. Post-It Notes failed 3M's market tests, but the marketing people broke the rules by personally visiting test sites and giving away free samples to customers, who quickly became addicted to Post-Its. Although it took years to get this invention to market, 3M fortunately had an organizational culture that allowed employees to persist in championing a new idea. As a result, the company has earned a half-billion dollars in annual revenue from Post-It Notes.[12]

The persistence of these 3M employees is just one characteristic of the creative personality.[13] Creative people also tend to be selfconfident, independent, attracted to complexity, tolerant of ambiguity, and intuitive. They are likely to have broad interests, high energy, and a concern with achievement. Highly creative people tend to be risk takers who love their work.

Studies of how creative people work have identified the following pattern of events. The catalyst is a problem or perceived need, which triggers these four stages in the creative process.[14]

1. **Preparation** This stage is akin to doing one's homework, and it requires a good deal of effort. People gather information and immerse themselves in everything that is known about the problem, often to the point of saturation.
2. **Incubation** This stage involves a process of reflective thought. The subconscious mind continues to mull over the problem, combining unrelated thoughts, even when people are no longer actively focusing on the problem.
3. **Illumination** Individuals have a flash of inspiration about the solution to the problem, often while engaged in an unrelated activity.
4. **Verification** The solution is tested by logic or experimentation and evaluated more rigorously to see whether it meets some standard of acceptability.

Although some people are naturally more creative than others, anyone can be trained in creative thinking. Many companies provide workshops on creativity. Among other things, employees learn to break mental sets and take new perspectives on problems. They learn divergent thinking, which generates multiple solutions to problems, as well as learning to use heuristics such as analogies and metaphors and making associations. They also learn to avoid making premature judgments that kill off ideas before they have time to be fully developed.[15]

The Creative Environment

It is not coincidental that some organizations possess more creative employees than others. Organizational conditions determine how much creativity is unleashed or repressed. For example, according to research, people are less creative when they are extrinsically rather than intrinsically motivated. Other "creativity killers" include focusing on how one's work will be evaluated, being under surveillance while working, competing with peers in a win-lose situation, and having one's limits dictated by superiors.[16] Organizations that successfully foster creativity set innovation goals, recognize and reward creativity, encourage autonomy and risk taking, have supportive peers as well as supportive supervisors and leaders who do not overcontrol employees, and promote internal diversity and interaction.[17] Such organizations also have flexible structures and participative decision making. Creative companies do not punish failure because they know that false starts are a normal part of the creative process. For this reason, a research and development company had Friday celebrations that included a hideous trophy that was jokingly awarded for the "Screw-Up of the Week."

PROCEDURE FOR GROUP MEETING: CARDIOTRONICS ROLE PLAY

PART 1.   ASSEMBLY TEAM D MEETING

(Time Allotted: 45 Minutes)

During the meeting, groups will have the opportunity to practice problem solving on a real work problem by means of a role play.

STEP 1.   In this role play each group of six class members will be Assembly Team D with individuals in your group assuming the role of Marion Andrews, Lee Smith, and so on. (In groups of five, combine the Lee Smith role with that of Chris; i.e., "Chris can speak for his or her friend Lee who is sick today." Groups larger than six should have observers. Observers should take notes on the group's problem-solving process during the role play using the Cardiotronics Case Review form on page 227.)

STEP 2.   Group members should choose roles. One person should play Marion Andrews and prepare to conduct the meeting. Role descriptions for the other team members are on the pages cited.

Lee Smith	page 229	Tear out the page describing
Chris Jones	230	your role and make a "name tent."
Pat Crane	231	
Terry Fram	232	
Adrian James	233	

LEE SMITH

role instructions on back

STEP 3.   Action.

Instructions for Team D workers

Place your name tent in front of you after you have read the role description and prepare to be the person described.

Instructions for Marion Andrews

The assembly line just closed and the five workers from Assembly Team D have gathered in your office. You have 30 minutes to conduct the problem-solving meeting before everyone goes back to work.

Four Tips on Role Playing:

- Be *yourself* as much as you can.
- Imagine yourself in that person's life.
- Don't "ham it up."
- Talk loudly enough for the observers to hear.

PART II. ANALYSIS

(Time Allotted: 50–60 minutes)

STEP 1.   After finishing the role play, write down the decision that was reached. (5 minutes)

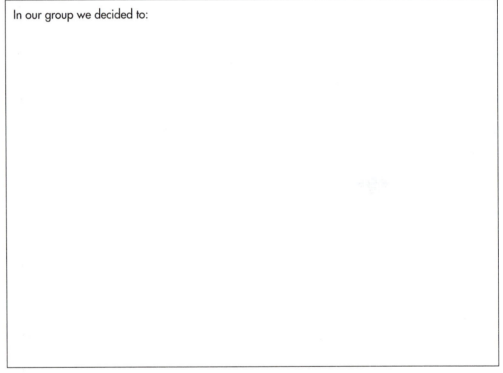

In our group we decided to:

STEP 2.   The group should prepare a group review of its problem-solving process by completing the Cardiotronics Case Review on page 227 (20 minutes).

STEP 3.   Results from each group can be summarized for discussion on a chalkboard or flip chart so the whole group can compare subgroup results. The Summary of Role-Play Results on page 228 gives one format for preparing this summary. The last row in this chart gives results for 10 groups of business executives for comparison purposes. (5 minutes)

STEP 4.   Everyone should read the summary. (5 minutes)

STEP 5.   Total group discussion. (20–30 minutes) Each group should share the solution it decided on and describe the highlights of the problem-solving process. Consider the following questions:
   a. What differences were there in the problem-solving process followed in each group?
   b. Were these differences related to the adequacy of the solutions arrived at (e.g., firing or removing Pat is not a particularly good solution since work would only pile up at Terry's position; realizing this requires green-mode information getting so that Terry feels free to share his or her role information)?
   c. What common obstacles to effective group problem solving came up? How were these dealt with by Marion Andrews? By other Team D members?
   d. How creative was your group's solution? Why?
   e. What connections can you make between this exercise and the readings?

CARDIOTRONICS CASE REVIEW

Describe How the Following Problem-Solving Activities Took Place	Approximate % of Total Problem-Solving Time Spent in This Activity	Sequence in Which Activity Took Place In Meeting (1 = First, 2 = Second, Etc.)
Valuing Examining the situation for opportunities and problems:		
Priority Setting Agreeing on the most important problem:		
Information Gathering Getting information on possible causes:		
Problem Definition Choosing most likely cause:		
Idea Getting Generating possible solutions:		
Decision Making Selection of the best idea:		
Participation Deciding how/when to involve others:		
Planning Constructing a plan:		

SUMMARY OF ROLE PLAY RESULTS

Group No.	Situation Analysis		Problem Analysis		Solution Analysis		Implementation Analysis		Solution Decided on by Assembly Team D
	Valuing "Examine Solution"	Priority Setting "Agree on Problem"	Information Getting "Information on Causes"	Problem Definition "Choose Cause"	Getting Ideas "Generate Ideas"	Decision Making "Select Idea"	Participation "Involve Others"	Planning "Construct Plan"	
1 Sequence									
% Time									
2 Sequence									
% Time									
3 Sequence									
% Time									
4 Sequence									
% Time									
Averages for 60 managers (1/2 female; 1/2 male; 10 Groups) Sequence (ave. rank)	1	3	2	4	5	7	6	8	
% Time	5.2%	6.2%	7.7%	5.2%	43.0%	12.9%	6.2%	14.0%	

STATION 1
LEE SMITH

You find you can easily do more work, but you have to slow down because Pat gets behind. So as not to make Pat feel badly, you hold back. You don't want to get Pat into trouble. Right now, the job lacks challenge and is boring.

STATION 2
CHRIS JONES

You and Lee work closely together, and you are usually waiting for the board from Lee. Waiting for the board is more prevalent in the latter part of the day than in the beginning. To keep busy, you often help out Pat who can't keep up. However, you are careful not to let the supervisor catch you helping Pat because Pat might be let go. Pat is a bit old for the pace set and feels the strain. For you, the job is easy, and you feel the whole job is slowed down too much because of Pat. "Why couldn't Pat be given less to do?" you ask yourself.

STATION 3
PAT CRANE

You work hard, but you just aren't as fast as the others. You know you are holding things up, but no matter how you try, you get behind. The faster you try to go, the more difficult it is to make correct connections. You feel quality is important, and you don't want to make mistakes. The rest of the workers are fine people and have more energy than you do at your age.

STATION 4
TERRY FRAM

You are able to keep up with the pace, but on your last assembly job, you were pressed. Fortunately, Pat is slower than you are, and this keeps that pressure off you. You are determined that Pat will not be moved off the job. Somebody has to protect people from speed-up tactics.

STATION 5
ADRIAN JAMES

You get bored doing the same circuit operations over and over. On some jobs you get variety by working fast for a while and then slowly. On this job you can't work fast because the boards aren't fed to you fast enough. Why can't the supervisor see that Pat is a problem and needs to be moved out of the group? It gets you down to keep doing exactly the same thing over and over in slow motion. You are considering getting a job someplace where they can keep a worker busy.

FOLLOW-UP

Most experienced managers tend naturally to follow a problem-solving sequence that is close to that described in the four-phase model of situation analysis, problem analysis, solution analysis, and implementation analysis. There are, however, significant differences in the amounts of energy devoted to each of these phases, which sometimes inhibit effective problem solving. Perhaps the most significant of these is the tendency to spend too little time defining the problem at hand before generating possible solutions. This tendency to be solution oriented often results in the treatment of symptoms rather than causes of the problem, and time is wasted working on solutions before relevant information is known. If this process is typical of an organization's problem solving, a crisis fire-fighting atmosphere develops where symptom-oriented solutions fail to resolve basic problems that recur over and over. This further reduces the time available for thoughtful situation and problem analysis.

Effective problem solving requires balanced attention to each phase of the problem-solving process and equal emphasis on the expansion/green-mode and contraction/red-mode mind-sets. We learned in Chapter 3, "Individual and Organizational Learning," that individual learning styles emphasize different aspects of the experiential learning cycle. There is a strong correlation between people's learning styles and the way they approach problem solving.

USING THE EXPERIENTIAL LEARNING MODEL TO ANALYZE PERSONAL APPROACHES TO PROBLEM SOLVING

Figure 10-2 overlays a model of the problem-finding and problem-solving process on the experiential learning cycle and identifies problem-solving activities that characterize different stages of the cycle. In this figure we can see that the stages in a problem-solving sequence generally correspond with the learning style strengths of the four major learning styles described earlier. The accommodator's problem-solving strengths lie in executing solutions and in initiating problem finding based on some goal or model about how things should be. The diverger's problem-solving strengths lie in identifying the multitude of possible problems and opportunities that exist in reality. The assimilator excels in the abstract model building that is necessary to choose a priority problem and create alternative solutions. The converger's strengths lie in the evaluation of solution consequences and solution selection.

The Guide for Analysis of Your Personal Problem-Solving Process, found on page 236, identifies more specifically the types of problem-solving activities that characterize the different phases of the learning/problem-solving process. Its purpose is to assist you in the analysis of problem situations and how you approach them. Activities that characterize the four learning style types are grouped together around the graph.

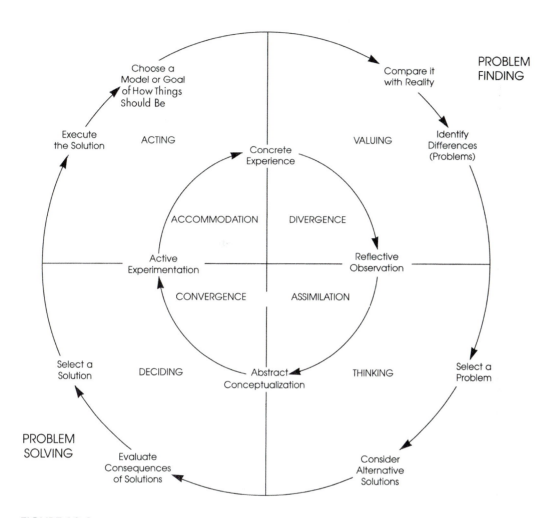

FIGURE 10-2   Comparison of the Experiential Learning Model and the Problem-Solving Process

GUIDE FOR ANALYSIS OF YOUR PERSONAL PROBLEM-SOLVING PROCESS

Briefly describe a problem you solved.

Rate on a scale of 1 to 7 how much each of the following activities were a part of your approach to the problem you were trying to solve.

Given your Learning Style Inventory scores in Chapter 3, does your problem-solving approach relate to your learning style?

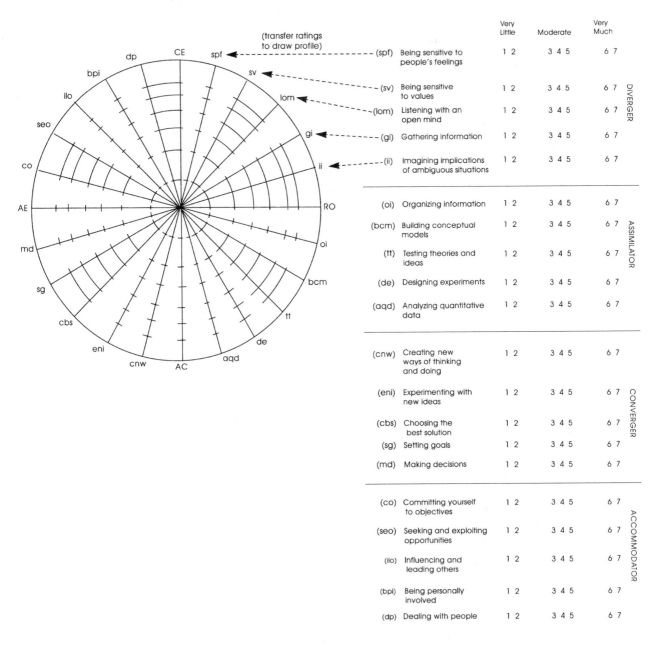

		Very Little	Moderate	Very Much	
(spf)	Being sensitive to people's feelings	1 2	3 4 5	6 7	DIVERGER
(sv)	Being sensitive to values	1 2	3 4 5	6 7	
(lom)	Listening with an open mind	1 2	3 4 5	6 7	
(gi)	Gathering information	1 2	3 4 5	6 7	
(ii)	Imagining implications of ambiguous situations	1 2	3 4 5	6 7	
(oi)	Organizing information	1 2	3 4 5	6 7	ASSIMILATOR
(bcm)	Building conceptual models	1 2	3 4 5	6 7	
(tt)	Testing theories and ideas	1 2	3 4 5	6 7	
(de)	Designing experiments	1 2	3 4 5	6 7	
(aqd)	Analyzing quantitative data	1 2	3 4 5	6 7	
(cnw)	Creating new ways of thinking and doing	1 2	3 4 5	6 7	CONVERGER
(eni)	Experimenting with new ideas	1 2	3 4 5	6 7	
(cbs)	Choosing the best solution	1 2	3 4 5	6 7	
(sg)	Setting goals	1 2	3 4 5	6 7	
(md)	Making decisions	1 2	3 4 5	6 7	
(co)	Committing yourself to objectives	1 2	3 4 5	6 7	ACCOMMODATOR
(seo)	Seeking and exploiting opportunities	1 2	3 4 5	6 7	
(ilo)	Influencing and leading others	1 2	3 4 5	6 7	
(bpi)	Being personally involved	1 2	3 4 5	6 7	
(dp)	Dealing with people	1 2	3 4 5	6 7	

LEARNING POINTS

1. Some scholars characterize organizations as problem-solving systems whose success depends upon how well they perform that process.
2. The problem-solving model presented is based upon three premises:
   a. Learning from experience
   b. Mind over matter
   c. Problem solving as a social process
3. The problem-solving model consists of four stages:
   a. Situation analysis
   b. Problem analysis
   c. Solution analysis
   d. Implementation analysis
4. The role of the manager is different for each stage and can be characterized as:
   a. Leader
   b. Detective
   c. Inventor
   d. Coordinator
5. Problem solving is not a logical, linear process. Instead, it is characterized by wavelike expansions and contractions alternately moving outward to gather and consider alternatives, information, and ideas and inwardly to focus, evaluate, and decide.
6. Each of the stages in the problem-solving model possesses two substages that reflect the two dialectics of problem solving: the expansion/green mode and the contraction/red mode.
7. Effective problem solving requires balanced attention to each phase of the problem-solving process and equal emphasis on the expansion/green and contraction/red mode mind sets.
8. Creativity is the process by which individuals or small groups produce novel and useful ideas.
9. Characteristics of creative people are persistence, self-confidence, independence, attraction to complexity, tolerance of ambiguity, and intuitiveness. Creative types have broad interests, high energy, a concern with achievement, and are risk takers who love their work.
10. The creative process, triggered by a problem, consists of four stages: preparation, incubation, illumination, and verification.
11. Organizations can foster creativity by setting innovation goals, recognizing and rewarding creativity, encouraging autonomy, risk taking, and participative decision making, encouraging supportiveness on the part of both peers and supervisors, promoting internal diversity and interaction, and establishing flexible structures.

FOR MANAGERS

- The management of group problem solving can be enhanced by avoiding the following common obstacles to effective group problem solving:
  ▶ *Preparation for the Meeting*
    Little or no preplanning.
    Low expectations.
    Failure to include the right people or inclusion of irrelevant people.
    Group's goal and function are ambiguous (e.g., is it advisory, information sharing, decision making?).
  ▶ *Managing the Meeting*
    Lack of clarity about:
        Procedures and ground rules
        Goals and agenda
        How decisions get made (by voting or by consensus, etc.).
        Roles (chairperson, recorder, etc.).

Group members do not follow an orderly problem-solving sequence together.

Failure to balance the discussion—dominance by high-status or aggressive members.

Conflict is either avoided or allowed to become personalized as opposed to problem focused.

Members do not understand what is being said but think they do.

▶ *Situation Analysis*

Urgent and structured problems take priority over important problems.

Symptoms are treated as the problem (e.g., often people as opposed to situations are seen as the problem).

Problems are accepted as given—reluctance to express hopes and dreams and to search for opportunities.

▶ *Problem Analysis*

Premature discussion of solutions.

Critical facts are not made known to all.

No distinction is made between facts and opinions.

▶ *Solution Analysis*

Generation and evaluation of ideas not kept separate.

Premature focusing.

Unproductive conflict and competition in evaluation.

Undue weight given to secondary decision criteria—the primary criterion is whether the solution solves the problem. Secondary criteria such as cost should not be allowed to overshadow the primary criterion.

▶ *Implementation Analysis*

Failure to gain commitment of those who will implement solutions.

Failure to assign clear responsibility to individuals for tasks.

Failure to follow up and monitor.

- Try to include people with different learning styles in problem-solving groups and see that their disparate skills are both valued and utilized.
- Feelings and perceptual biases influence the problem-solving process as do the mental ruts that prevent us from generating creative solutions. Discussing the situation with neutral outsiders or objective insiders is often helpful.
- Remember that problems are embedded within a system. For example, a scheduling problem can be related to a turf fight between department heads. It's important to consider all the system links, both to define the problem and to make sure that implementation obstacles don't arise.
- The successes of employee involvement groups and TQM groups has shown that employees are capable of solving problems that management either did not recognize or had not been able to resolve.

PERSONAL APPLICATION ASSIGNMENT

In this assignment you will write about an experience involving problem management or creativity. Choose an experience about which you want to learn more.

A. *Concrete Experience*

   1. *Objectively* describe the experience (who, what, when, where, how) (2 points)

   2. *Subjectively* describe your feelings, perceptions, and thoughts that occurred during (not after) the experience. What did others seem to be feeling? (2 points)

B. *Reflective Observation*

   1. Looking back at the experience, what were the perspectives of the key actors (including you)? (2 points)

   2. Why did the people involved (including you) behave as they did? (2 points)

C. *Abstract Conceptualization*

    1. Relate concepts or theories from the assigned readings or the lecture to the experience. Explain thoroughly how they apply to your experience. Please apply at least two concepts or theories and cite them correctly. (4 points)

D. *Active Experimentation*

    1. What did you learn about problem solving or creativity from this experience? (1 point)

    2. What did you learn about yourself? (1 point)

    3. What action steps will you take to be more effective in the future? (2 points)

E. *Integration, Synthesis, and Writing*

    1. Did you integrate and synthesize the four sections? (1 point)

    2. Was the Personal Application Assignment well written and easy to understand? (1 point)

    3. Was it free of spelling and grammar errors? (2 points)

ENDNOTES

[1] R. Kilmann, "Problem Management: A Behavioral Science Approach," *Management Principles for Non-Profit Agencies and Organizations*, ed. by G. Zaltman (American Management Association, 1979): 214–15.

[2] As a result of this trend, there are numerous books on problem solving, such as G. Nadler and S. Hibino's *Breakthrough Thinking: Why We Must Change the Way We Solve Problems, and the Seven Principles to Achieve This* (Rocklin, CA: Prima, 1990). Two workbooks that contain the team problem-solving techniques used in total quality programs are P. R. Scholtes, *The Team Handbook* (Madison, WI: Joiner Associates, 1988); M. Brassard, *The Memory Jogger Plus+* (Methuen, MA: GOAL/QPC, 1989); and G. K. Kanji, and M. Asher, *100 Methods for Total Quality Management* (Thousand Oaks, CA: Sage, 1996).

[3] The problem-solving model described here was developed in collaboration with Richard Baker and Juliann Spoth.

[4] R. Kaplan, "Creativity in the Everyday Business of Managing," *Issues and Observations* (Greensboro, NC: Center for Creative Leadership, 1983), and *Reader* (1990).

[5] P. Elbow, *Writing Without Teachers* (New York: Oxford University Press, 1973).

[6] C. Lindblom, "The Science of Muddling Through," *Public Administration Review 2* (1959): 78–88.

[7] I. L. Janis, "Group Think," *Psychology Today* (November 1971); *Reader* (1990).

[8] G. Prince, "The Mind Spring Theory: A New Development from Synetics Research," *The Journal of Creative Behavior 9*, no. 3 (1975): 159–81.

[9] N. J. Adler, *International Dimensions of Organizational Behavior* (Cincinnati, OH: South-Western College, 1997).

[10] K. Melymuka, "Sky King," *Computerworld 32*, no. 39, September 28, 1998, 68.

[11] R. M. Kanter, J. Kao, and F. Wiersema, *Innovation* (New York: Harper, 1997); and "Ten Commandments for Managing Creative People," *Fortune*, January 16, 1995, 135.

[12] P. R. Nayak, and J. M. Ketteringham, *Breakthroughs!* (New York: Rawson Associates, 1986).

[13] C. Martindale, "Personality, Situation, and Creativity," in J. A. Glover, R. R. Ronning, and C. R. Reynolds, (eds.), *Handbook of Creativity* (New York: Plenum, 1989), 211–32; F. B. Barron and D. M. Harrington, "Creativity, Intelligence, and Personality," *Annual Review of Psychology 32* (1982): 439–76; and M. Csikszentmihalyi, *Creativity: Flow and the Psychology of Discovery and Invention* (New York: HarperCollins, 1996); D. W. MacKinnon, "Assessing Creative Persons," *Journal of Creative Behavior 1* (1967): 303–04; E. Ransepp, "Are You a Creative Manager?" *Management Review 58* (1978): 15–16; and R. J. Sternberg, "A Three-Faced Model of Creativity," in R. J. Sternberg, (ed.), *The Nature of Creativity* (London: Cambridge University Press, 1988): 125–47.

[14] D. G. Marquis, "The Anatomy of Successful Innovations," *Managing Advancing Technology 1* (1972): 34–48; and J. F. Mee, "The Creative Thinking Process," *Indiana Business Review 3* (1956): 4–9.

[15] J. M. Higgins, "Creating Creativity," *Training and Development 48*, no. 11 (November 1994): 11–16. Two of the most well-read authors on creativity are R. von Oech, *A Whack on the Side of the Head* (New York: Warner, 1983); and E. de Bono, *New Think* (New York: Basic Books, 1968).

[16] T. Stevens, "Creativity Killers," *Industry Week 63*, January 23, 1995, 63; and T. M. Amabile, "Motivating Creativity in Organizations: On Doing What you Love and Loving What You Do," *Creativity Management Review 4*, no. 1 (1997): 39–58.

[17] A. Cummings, and G. R. Oldham, "Enhancing Creativity: Managing Contexts for the High Potential Employee," *Creativity Management Review 40*, no. 1 (1997): 22–38; T. M. Amabile, "Motivating Creativity in Organizations: On Doing What you Love and Loving What You Do"; R. M. Kanter, *The Change Masters* (New York: Simon & Schuster, 1983); and R. F. Lovelace, "Stimulating Creativity through Managerial Intervention," *R&D Management 16* (1986): 161–74.

▲▲

Chapter 11

CONFLICT
AND NEGOTIATION

OBJECTIVES By the end of this chapter, you should be able to:

A. Describe behaviors that characterize group conflict.

B. Identify common sources of conflict.

C. Explain the five conflict-handling modes.

D. Understand the functional and dysfunctional nature of conflict.

E. Differentiate between distributive and integrative bargaining.

F. Explain principled negotiation.

G. Describe how culture influences conflict.

COSTA RICA'S ALTERNATIVE TO LABOR CONFLICT—*SOLIDARISMO*

Once upon a time in Costa Rica, there was a great deal of conflict in the work environment. Many of the country's labor unions were viewed as radical or leftist, particularly by industry, government, and the ruling elite. Labor-management relations were often confrontational, and both sides took an adversarial approach. One large multinational shut down a major agricultural operation in the 1960s because they were tired of dealing with a communist labor union (many labor unions in Latin America are based on communist ideology). Company officials believed they could work more harmoniously in neighboring countries. One indication of the degree of mistrust that had evolved was the union's insistence that the company's threats to shut down were simply bluffs. As the story goes, the company had already stripped everything out of their buildings, including the toilets, but the union leaders were still maintaining this was all a ruse. The company's departure dealt a serious blow to the economy. Some Costa Ricans worried that other companies interested in foreign direct investment would be put off by the strongly adversarial nature of labor-management relations. As Roberto Rojas, former minister of the economy, industry, and commerce, stated, "During the 1950s and 1960s, unions were politically part of the communist movement and disruptive to our work environment. Society decided we did not want unions in Costa Rica." *

What many see as a win-win solution to this problem is credited to two Costa Ricans. In the late 1940s, Alberto Martén Chavarría began advocating a concept called *solidarismo* (solidarity).[†]

The idea caught hold in several companies but became even more widespread after a Catholic priest, Claudio Solano, founded an institute in 1963 that taught the principles of *solidarismo*. Its basic premises are that management and labor are interdependent and should share the common goal of making the organization succeed, and both would benefit.

In practice, both employers and employees contribute a percentage of employee salaries to their organization's *solidarismo* association fund. From their peers, employees elect a board of directors to manage the fund. Unlike a traditional union setup or management-driven benefits, each organization's association decides for itself how the money will be used. They may opt for loans, company cafeterias, recreation centers, transportation, education needs, housing assistance, or low-cost medical and dental care. Some of the funds are sometimes invested in company stock. These services are also supposed to benefit the families of employees.

Some companies include *solidarismo* membership as a job benefit in their newspaper advertisements. As of 1994, 200,000 of Costa Rica's 900,000 workers were members of *solidarismo*. According to a 1999 source, the membership totals about 43 percent of the working population.[‡] Most employers like *solidarismo* because it allows them to resolve labor disputes and negotiate work contracts without strikes or violent confrontations. *Solidarismo* is credited with the transformation from adversarial to collaborative relations in Costa Rica's labor environment. The payoffs, a high level of foreign business investment and labor peace, have been important factors in making Costa Rica's economy the most stable in Central America.

Not everyone, however, is a fan. The most vociferous critics have been international labor organizations. For example, the ILO (International Labor Organization) based in Geneva claimed *solidarismo* interferes with trade union activity. In 1994, the AFL-CIO made an unsuccessful request that the United States drop Costa Rica's favorable trading privileges. In their argument, the U.S. labor union claimed that *solidarismo* functions like a union and that membership is a requirement of employment. Both the ILO and the AFL-CIO have urged Costa Rica to provide more protection to workers who are trying to form trade unions. Nevertheless, for a country that highly values democracy and peace (Costa Rica has no armed forces), *solidarismo* has been an appropriate and innovative win-win solution.

[*] N. Sheppard, Jr., "AFL-CIO Asks U.S. Officials to Revoke Costa Rica's Special Trade Privileges," *The Journal of Commerce and Commercial 397*, no. 28035, August 10, 1993, 4A.

[†] Information for this vignette is taken from N. Sheppard, Jr., "AFL-CIO Asks U.S. Officials to Revoke Costa Rica's Special Trade Privileges," *The Journal of Commerce and Commercial 397*, no. 28035, August 10, 1993, 4A; O. Bejarano, "La Fuerza del Solidarismo," *La Nacion*, July 18, 1997; "Bananas," http://www.iuf.org/iuf/Ag/02.htm, October 20, 1999.

[‡] R. Jiménez Vega, "Solidarismo in Costa Rica," http://www. edyd.com/solidarismo/englishgeneral.htm, October 20, 1999.

PREMEETING PREPARATION

A. Read "Costa Rica's Alternative to Labor Conflict—*Solidarismo*."

B. Answer the following questions before reading the Topic Introduction.

   1. What was the worst experience you ever had with conflict? What was so bad about it?

2. What are some of the things that caused the conflict?

3. What would you like to learn about conflict?

4. What are the significant learning points from the readings?

C. Read the Topic Introduction.

D. If your instructor has assigned the Robbins Self-Assessment Library, use "What's My Preferred Conflict-Handling Style?"

 TOPIC INTRODUCTION

Conflict can play both a positive or negative role in organizational life and, therefore, needs to be understood and carefully managed. More and more companies and work teams are insisting that employees learn conflict management skills. Intel, for example, attempts to set the stage for healthy conflict by training employees in constructive confrontation. Questioning and arguing over ideas is encouraged—personal attacks and persisting after a decision or resolution has been made is not.

Conflict is a form of interaction among parties that differ in interests, perceptions, and preferences. Conflict is also defined as "the process that begins when one party perceives that the other has negatively affected, or is about to negatively affect, something that he or she cares about."[1]

The Sherifs' field experiment shows how easily behavior may be changed by putting individuals in a competitive, limited contact situation with another group.[2] Their research is called the Robbers Cave experiment, named after a summer camp at Robbers Cave, Oklahoma. A homogenous group of 22 boys was divided into two groups of 11. During the first stage of the experiment, the boys were unaware of the existence of the other group. Each group did a variety of cooperative tasks and developed their own group norms and leadership. During the second stage, the groups were informed they would be competing against each other in a week-long grand tournament. The counselors manipulated the scores so that the two groups were neck and neck until the last event. The groups became very antagonistic; there were several commando raids and the losing team robbed the winning team of their medals. When members of one group passed the other, they held their noses. In addition to this sound qualitative evidence of intergroup conflict, the researchers employed quantitative measures that proved that (1) the members of each group had an ethnocentric view of the other group, and strongly preferred "their own kind," (2) that each group overvalued the performance of its own members and devalued the performance of the other group, and (3) that each group stereotyped the other. One's in-group was "brave, tough, and friendly," while the out-group was comprised of "sneaks, stinkers, and smart-alecks." These adjectives and this story seem humorous, but one sees the same dynamics with union-management conflicts and in companies undergoing less than friendly mergers.

What caused the intergroup conflict at Robbers Cave? We-they feelings are very common but they don't always blaze into open conflict. The key variable in this instance was the competition with its scarce resources. The winning team would receive wonderful prizes, while the losing team would win nothing. Since both groups already thought more highly of themselves than of the other group, whichever team lost would think the tournament was unfair.

During the third stage of the experiment, the researchers tested two of the most effective methods for reducing intergroup tension: (1) noncompetitive contact in which the two antagonistic groups have equal status and (2) a superordinate goal that was important for all and attainable only by joint cooperation.[3] As the Sherifs suspected, the first solution, equal status contact, did not work with groups that had reached this level of antagonism. However, the superordinate goal technique was effective; the boys had to cooperate in finding a leak in their water supply, to pool their money to rent a movie, and to pull a broken-down bus. By the end of the third week, the boys had ceased hostilities, eaten meals together, and opted to share a single bus on the trip home. Furthermore, they had begun to treat each other as individuals and chose friends for reasons other than common group membership. (Incidentally, the boys had a wonderful time at camp.)

A test of stereotyping at the end of the research revealed that the boys thought the members of the other group had changed and become more like themselves. In fact, the only difference was due to an environmental change from competition to cooperation.

Characteristics of Conflict   From this study and others, we know that there are certain behaviors that are typical of conflict situations: stereotyping, overvaluation of one's own group, devaluation of the other group, polarization on the issues, distortion of perceptions, and escalation. "Escalation is reflected in such changes as increasing the number and size of the issues disputed, increasing hostility, increasing competitiveness, pursuing increasingly extreme demands or objectives, using increasing coercive tactics, decreasing trust, and enlisting other parties to take sides in the conflict."[4] Conflict is characterized by an unwillingness to give the other party the benefit of the doubt regarding their motives or actions.

Group Conflict   In the beginning example of the opening vignette, union and management exhibited these conflict behaviors. While the cause of this particular conflict was not solely related to competition over scarce resources, it was resolved in the same manner as in the Robbers Cave study. An overarching goal was determined—establishing a stable economy that provided both jobs and profits. To achieve this goal, they had to give up an ingrained adversarial relationship and perceive themselves as members of the same team.

The distinctive nature of group conflict is related to the effects of group membership on individual behavior. Many other studies have since confirmed and added to the body of knowledge about the effects of group membership on individual behavior.[5] Researchers have noted strong tendencies to believe whatever others in a strong reference group believe, even when it contradicts one's visual perceptions. Groups to which we belong, particularly the ones we value most, tend to affirm us in ways we cannot always do for ourselves. By accepting us, they let us know that we are "okay" and erase a lot of the doubts we may have about our identity. But with that acceptance often comes a series of pressures, subtle or overt, to conform to a set of values or behaviors that the group deems acceptable.

In organizations there are different functional groups, professional specialties, geographical groupings, hierarchical levels, ethnic groups, genders, and social class distinctions. Any or all of these can serve as focal points for the creation of strong reference groups that provide their members with a sense of acceptance and identity in exchange for group loyalty and commitment. To the individual, these reference groups are often the most immediate and tangible sources of a sense of belonging to the organization. As a result, these groups are a vehicle for gaining commitment to organizational goals and motivation to work.

Yet group loyalty and commitment lead group members to value their own priorities, goals, and points of view more highly than those of out-groups. This often leads to a competitive we-they atmosphere between groups, which further strengthens internal group loyalty and out-group hostility in a cycle of increasing intensity. Organizations may find this to be a major stumbling block in optimizing productivity and reaching the organization's goals. For example, the people in production see the marketing department as making inordinate demands on them for changes in products with insufficient lead time. Marketing, on the other hand, may see production as intractable, a group that does not understand the necessity of meeting the competition from other companies. In the resulting conflict the energy of both groups is being expended in defense of their own position as well as attacking the position of the other group, all at the expense of organizational goals. Furthermore, in many cases, conflict is a major source of stress for the individuals involved.

Is competition between groups always dysfunctional? Not necessarily. There are numerous examples in our society of the advantages of intergroup competition. In the sports world one team is always competing against another. This phenomenon produces much excitement for audiences since they have an emotional identification with one or the other team and feel actively involved in the battle. The competitive nature of the encounter produces excitement for the players and motivates or induces them to exert maximum effort to reap the rewards of winning. In the business world, companies compete with one another for a larger share of the consumer dollar. Competition between organizations often increases the excellence of the product and customer service.

Situations in which competition between groups is productive have several distinguishing characteristics. First, they usually involve entities (groups) that are not part of the same formal organizational structure. The Packers and the Vikings are a part of the NFL, but they represent independent and autonomous operating organizations. Deliberate intergroup competition has been used by many government contracting agencies within the framework of parallel projects. The same task (usually a feasibility study) is given to two or more different companies with the understanding that the best proposal will win the follow-up contract. The assumption underlying the strategy is that the higher quality of the final product resulting from such a competitive structure will justify the duplication of effort and expenditure of funds. A second distinguishing characteristic is that seldom do any of these competing organizations (groups) find it necessary to work together to solve a common problem or to reach a common goal. For example, when a group of baseball owners tries to elect a new commissioner, the competitive element that proved so beneficial in their other activities often gets in the way when they must collaborate. Disparate units of the same organization can compete without harming the overall organization only when there is no interdependence or need for collaboration between them.

In sum, competition is both functional and the essence of the marketplace when it results in greater team spirit and effort. It is dysfunctional when it siphons energy away from the overall mission of the organization.

Sources of Conflict   Conflict within organizations is inevitable and comes from several sources. In addition to we-they situations resulting from group membership, conflict is likely to occur anywhere in the organization where there are "joints" or interfaces between different functions. The current move toward "horizontal corporations" that organize themselves around core processes rather than functions is, in part, an attempt to avoid conflict between the "silos" of functional departments.[6] Other common causes of conflict are differences in values, interests, personalities, education, culture, perceptions, goals, and expectations. Conflict may also result from deficient information that causes misunderstandings. Ambiguity can cause conflict when people battle over power or turf that has not been clearly assigned. Competition over scarce resources in whatever form—recognition, money, or even offices with windows—is also a source of conflict. Whenever the work is structured in such a way that groups are interdependent and their output depends on that of another department, there is a potential for conflict.

To some degree the human factor determines whether conflict will actually occur at some of these interfaces. Individuals and different ethnic groups are comfortable with varying levels of conflict. In U.S. culture we receive two somewhat contradictory messages: (1) fight and stand up for yourself, but (2) only when it is acceptable. Part of being politically savvy is understanding when conflict is appropriate. Some people thrive on conflict and create it wherever they go; others go to great lengths to avoid it. Managers at either end of this continuum are likely to be less than effective in their jobs and in their ability to create a positive work environment for their employees.

THE FUNCTIONAL NATURE OF CONFLICT

In addition to blocking the achievement of organizational goals, dysfunctional conflict reduces productivity, morale, and job satisfaction and can cause heightened anxiety, absenteeism, and turnover. Functional conflict, however, plays an important role in organizations. Conflict forces us to articulate our views and positions, which usually results in greater clarification and understanding. It makes the values and belief system of the organization more visible and makes it easier to see organizational priorities. Conflict helps preserve groups when it serves as a safety valve that allows people to blow off steam and still maintain their relationship. When people band together in a conflict, group cohesiveness is increased. One of the most valuable contributions of conflict is the creativity that results when we are forced to find new ways to look at situations and seek innovative solutions and decisions.

Sometimes managers will instruct groups or individuals in conflict to go off and solve a conflict themselves. Unless the employees already possess good conflict resolution skills, this can result in more harm than good. If we want the diversity of ideas that results when organizations encourage healthy conflict, we have to give employees the skills they need to manage conflict in a positive way. Work teams, in particular, need to be trained in conflict management. When groups share norms about how conflict should be handled and possess the requisite skills, people are less likely to suppress conflict out of fear that the situation will blow up or become worse if they try to address the conflict.

CONFLICT-HANDLING MODES

Thomas developed a taxonomy of conflict handling modes, shown in Figure 11-1, that reflects a person's strategic intention in a conflict.[7] The two axes are (1) *assertiveness*—the degree to which the individual wants to satisfy his or her own concerns and (2) *cooperativeness*—the degree to which he or she wants to satisfy the concerns of the other party. The *competitive* orientation implies winning at the other's expense. This is an example of a win-lose power struggle. In contrast, the *accommodation* style represents appeasement or satisfying the other's concern without

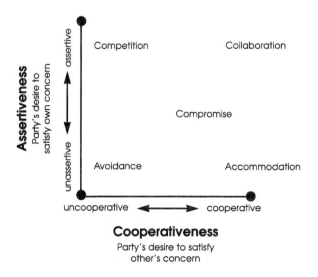

FIGURE 11-1   Five Conflict-Handling Modes

TABLE 11-1   Gains and Losses Associated with Conflict Styles

	Competition	Avoidance	Accommodation	Compromise	Collaboration
Gains	Chance to win everything Exciting, games-manship Exercise own sense of power	No energy or time expenditure Conserve for fights that are "more important"	Little muss or fuss, no feathers ruffled Others may view you as supportive Energy free for other pursuits	No one returns home empty-handed "Keeps the peace" May or may not encourage creativity	Both sides win Better chance for long-term solutions Creativity in problem solving Maintains relation-ship New level of under-standing of situation Improves quality of solution and commitment
Losses	Chance to lose everything Alienates others Discourages others from working with you Potentially larger-scale conflicts in the future (or more avoidance of conflict)	Less stimulation Less creative problem solving Little understand-ing of the needs of others Incomplete comprehension of work environment	Lowered self-assertion and possibly self-esteem Loss of power Absence of your unique contribution to the situation Others dependent on you may not feel you "go to bat" for them	Since neither side is totally satisfied, conflicts are likely to recur later Neither side realizes self-determination fully	Requires more time, in the short run Loss of sense of autonomy

Source: Adapted from the work of R. Fry, J. Florian, and J. McLemore, Department of Organizational Behavior, Weatherhead School of Management, Case Western Reserve University, Cleveland, Ohio, 1984.

taking one's own needs or desires into consideration. This is a lose-win situation (I lose—you win.) *Compromising* reflects the midway point between these two styles and involves give-and-take by both parties. Both parties gain and give up something they want. The *collaborative* orientation differs from compromising in that it represents a desire to satisfy fully the concerns of both parties. People search for solutions that are mutually beneficial, a win-win solution. The *avoiding* orientation implies lack of concern about the desire of either party, a lose-lose situation. As with any taxonomy, each conflict-handling mode has its advantages and disadvantages, which are shown in Table 11-1. Table 11-2 indicates when each mode is appropriate, according to 28 CEOs. Effective managers are capable of employing more than one mode and know which one to use in a given situation.

BARGAINING APPROACHES

At times intergroup conflicts are resolved through bargaining and negotiation. Most negotiation strategies are based on two types of bargaining. *Distributive bargaining* is the classical win-lose approach in which a fixed amount of resources is divided. For example, if a union fails to nego-tiate a favorable salary contract, management wins at the union's expense. If the union gains a large increase, management loses because its costs have increased accordingly. Distributive bargaining

TABLE 11-2 Appropriate Situations for the Five Strategic Intentions

Competing
- When quick, decisive action is vital (i.e., emergencies)
- On important issues in which unpopular actions need implementing (e.g., cost cutting, enforcing unpopular rules, discipline)
- On issues vital to company welfare when you know you're right
- Against people who take advantage of noncompetitive behavior

Avoiding
- When an issue is trivial, or more important issues are pressing
- When you perceive no chance of satisfying your concerns
- When potential disruption outweighs the benefits of resolution
- To let people cool down and regain perspective
- When gathering information supercedes immediate decision
- When others can resolve the conflict more effectively
- When issues seem tangential or symptomatic of other issues

Accommodating
- When you find you are wrong—to allow a better position to be heard, to learn, and to show your reasonableness
- When issues are more important to others than yourself—to satisfy others and maintain cooperation
- To build social credits for later issues
- To minimize loss when you are outmatched and losing
- When harmony and stability are especially important
- To allow subordinates to develop by learning from mistakes

Compromising
- When goals are important, but not worth the effort or potential disruption of more assertive modes
- When opponents with equal power are committed to mutually exclusive goals
- To achieve temporary settlements to complex issues
- To arrive at expedient solutions under time pressure
- As a backup when collaboration or competition is unsuccessful

Collaborating
- To find an integrative solution when both sets of concerns are too important to be compromised
- When your objective is to learn
- To merge insights from people with different perspectives
- To gain commitment by incorporating concerns into a consensus
- To work through feelings that have interfered with a relationship

Source: K. W. Thomas, "Toward Multi-Dimensional Values in Teaching: The Example of Conflict Behaviors," *Academy of Management Review 2*, (1977): 487. Copyright 1977 by *Academy of Management Review*. Reprinted by permission.

has a short-term focus on relationships because, like the competitive conflict management style in Thomas's model, it often results in winning the battle and losing the war. The resentful losers try to figure out a way to get back at the winners, which creates an adversarial relationship.

Integrative bargaining is a win-win approach that is more suitable to maintaining long-term relationships. It does not assume that there is a fixed amount of resources to be divided because the parties search for various settlements that would be agreeable to both parties.[8] The settlements in integrative bargaining often consist of creative solutions. Costa Rica's "better idea" in the opening vignette is an example of integrative bargaining because union and management recognized their interdependence and sought solutions that were mutually advantageous. This form of bargaining is akin to the collaborative conflict-handling mode in Thomas's model.

A BIAS TOWARD COLLABORATION

According to Thomas, there are many advantages to a collaborative approach to conflict.[9] It results in greater satisfaction and self-esteem and relationships characterized by trust, respect, and affection. From an organizational point of view, it also results in more open exchanges of information and better decisions. However, it is not appropriate in all situations. Collaboration does not work if there are competitive incentives and procedures already in place. It is also inappropriate when the two parties have insufficient problem-solving skills, do not trust each other, and when time is too short. Compromise or competition is more appropriate under these conditions.

However, collaboration is the direction in which modern businesses are moving. Even though we may be forced to use a competitive style in a given situation, Thomas recommends that we should try to change the context so that collaboration is possible in the future. The Standard Fruit Company wanted to improve its negotiations with union members in Costa Rica. They hired consultants to teach them the collaborative negotiation method presented in the following section. The consultants insisted and management agreed that the same training be given to the union representatives. In doing so, the company changed the situational context from one that promoted competitive negotiation to one that encouraged collaboration. The payoff was more positive outcomes and less time-consuming negotiations.

PRINCIPLED NEGOTIATION

The negotiating scheme presented in the next section is based on integrative bargaining and a win-win approach. Fisher and Ury observed that some people are too soft and accommodating when they negotiate while others are too hard and competitive.[10] As a result, they developed an alternative called "principled negotiation" that consists of four principles.

1. **People: Separate the People from the Problem**
   This relates to the need to maintain a relationship with the other party. They recommend being "soft on people and hard on the problem" and taking the stance of a partner working with the other side to solve the problem under negotiation. To do this, the negotiator should be empathetic with the other party and accept that human problems concerning perception, communications, and emotions will emerge in the negotiation process.

2. **Interests: Focus on Interests, Not Positions**
   When negotiators focus only on a predetermined position, it may be more difficult for them to achieve what they really want. The story that is often used to illustrate this point concerns two library patrons who were noisily arguing over the following positions. One wanted the window closed while the other wanted the window open. The librarian who came to investigate the ruckus asked the first man why he wanted the window open. He explained that he thought the library was too stuffy. In response to the same question, the other man explained that he had a cold and did not want to sit in a draught. The librarian thought for a moment and opened a window in an adjacent room. This solution pleased both the men because it allowed the first man to have more air circulating and prevented the second man from getting any sicker than he already was. Had they continued arguing about their positions, it is doubtful such a creative solution would have surfaced.

   When parties enter a negotiation (or conflict) with a set position, they may become locked into it and develop a vested interest in saving face by not backing away from that position. The parties should assertively present their own interests and mutually identify those that are shared, opposed, and simply different.

3. **Options: Invent Options for Mutual Gain**
   It is difficult to come up with optimal solutions in the pressure of a negotiation setting. Therefore, in this stage the parties brainstorm options that are favorable to both parties. This requires creativity and a commitment to joint problem solving.

4. **Criteria: Insist on Objective Criteria**
   Sometimes negotiators (and bosses, spouses, parents, etc.) take a hard line and insist on getting their way. To avoid a standoff, look for objective criteria, such as market value, expert opinion, custom, or law, that are agreeable to both parties. For example, a stalled salary negotiation moved forward after both parties agreed to use a salary survey of similar companies

as an objective standard of reference. The Blue Book of car values is another example of an objective criteria that can facilitate a negotiation over the price of a used car. When objective criteria exist, negotiators can resort to principles rather than pressure to reach agreements.

Another aspect to principled negotiation is the concept of BATNA. This acronym stands for *Best Alternative To a Negotiated Agreement.* Fisher and Ury recommend that negotiators arm themselves with an alternative in case the negotiation does not go as expected. For example, what alternative does a job candidate have if his or her salary negotiation does not turn out as planned? A BATNA in this case might be going to work in the family firm. Or what fall-back scheme can homeowners have if negotiations fail with a potential buyer? Their BATNA might be taking the house off the market and either remodeling it or renting it out. A BATNA liberates negotiators from thinking they have to reach an agreement at all costs because it provides the security of an alternative. During the important preparation period for a negotiation, people should determine their own BATNA as well as consider what the other party's BATNA might be.

In principled negotiation, three criteria determine whether or not a negotiation has been successful:

a. It should produce a wise agreement if agreement is possible.

b. It should be efficient and not waste time.

c. It should improve or at least not harm the relationship between the parties.[11]

The criteria for successful negotiations, as well as negotiating practices, vary from culture to culture. Table 11-3 shows national styles of persuasion that influence negotiation. It's crucial to do your homework on cultural differences before attempting an international negotiation.[12]

The purpose of the following exercise is to simulate a set of organizational relationships among groups. As you go through the exercise, try to be aware of your feelings about your group and other groups; there will be time after the exercise to reflect on your feelings individually and to discuss them with your group and the entire class.

TABLE 11-3   National Styles of Persuasion

	North Americans	Arabs	Russians
Primary negotiating style and process	Factual: Appeals made to logic	Affective: Appeals made to emotions	Axiomatic: Appeals made to ideals
Conflict: opponent's arguments countered with...	Objective facts	Subjective feelings	Asserted ideals
Making concessions	Small concessions made early to establish a relationship	Concessions made throughout as a part of the bargaining process	Few, if any, small concessions made
Response to opponent's concessions	Usually reciprocate opponent's concessions	Almost always reciprocate opponent's concessions	Opponent's concessions viewed as weakness and almost never reciprocated
Relationship	Short term	Long term	No continuing relationship
Authority	Broad	Broad	Limited
Initial position	Moderate	Extreme	Extreme
Deadline	Very important	Casual	Ignored

Source: Reprinted with permission from *International Journal of Intercultural Relations 1*, E. S. Glenn, D. Witmeyer, and K. A. Stevenson, "Cultural Styles of Persuasion." Copyright ©1984, Pergamon Press, Ltd.

PROCEDURE FOR GROUP MEETING: THE RED-GREEN GAME

The purpose of this exercise is to simulate the feelings and behaviors that may appear in a conflict situation.

STEP 1.   Divide the class into four groups composed of least three people and seat each group in separate corners of the room. Assign a number to each group from 1 to 4. Each group should take one piece of paper and tear it into eight pieces. Write your group number on each piece of paper.

STEP 2.   Read your instructions, which follow.

Your Task: Your objective is to win as many positive points as possible. Your team will have 2 minutes to decide whether to vote green or red in each round of the game. To indicate your votes, write an *R* (red) or *G* (green) on one of your pieces of paper with your team number. The game director (usually your instructor) will collect your votes but is not allowed to answer any questions. Before rounds 3, 4, 6, and 7, you may send a representative to discuss with the other team representatives in the center of room for 2 minutes. During this time, representatives should speak very loudly so others can hear their discussion, and the rest of the class should remain silent so as not to distract them. Your representative does not always have to be the same person. Whatever you earn in round 4 will be doubled; your score in round 8 will be multiplied by

Scoring Rules

GGGG	All teams win +50 points.
GGGR	The teams voting green lose 100 points. The team voting red wins 300 points.
GGRR	The teams voting green lose 200 points. The teams voting red win 200 points.
GRRR	The team voting green loses 300 points. The teams voting red win 100 points.
RRRR	All teams lose 50 points.

Scoring Chart

Rounds	Votes				Cumulative Scores			
	Team 1	Team 2	Team 3	Team 4	Team 1	Team 2	Team 3	Team 4
1								
2								
3R								
4R(2Xs)								
5								
6R								
7R								
8(10Xs)								

10. Remember, the purpose of the game is to win as many points as possible. The following chart indicates how the game will be scored. You have 2 minutes to decide on your vote for round 1.

STEP 3.   After the simulation (25–30 minutes), the class debriefing takes place. (30 minutes)

   a. Did conflict occur in this simulation? Why? What was the cause?

   b. What role does trust play in this simulation? What made you trust or distrust certain teams or individuals?

   c. What did the conflict look like? What were its characteristics?

   d. What was it like to be a representative in this simulation?

   e. Did you see any examples of effective leadership among the representatives?

   f. What's the relationship between ambiguity and conflict?

   g. What can we learn about conflict from this simulation?

   h. What can you learn about your own conflict-handling style? Which of the styles in the Thomas model did you use in this simulation?

   i. What connections can you make between this exercise and the readings?

NEGOTIATION EXERCISE—THE FILM-MAKING EQUIPMENT

The purpose of this exercise is to allow you to practice principled negotiation.
(time allotted: 80 minutes)

STEP 1.   Divide the class so they can negotiate in groups of five people: two representatives from Ivy League U. and two representatives from Intelligentsia U. and one observer. (You can use two observers if the number of students is not divisible by five.)

STEP 2.   Determine who will play each role. Read only the role description for your university; please do not read the other role description. The two pairs of representatives in each group should go off together and prepare their negotiating strategy. Identify the interests of both parties. Think about potential options for mutual gain and objective criteria. What might be the BATNA for both parties? (20 minutes)

Observers should read both roles and go over the observer worksheet on page 255. Fill out the worksheet as you are observing and write down any interesting, funny, and outrageous comments you hear during the negotiation session. Be prepared to describe the strategy of each team and its results.

STEP 3.   The negotiating session takes place between the two representatives from each university, under the careful eye of the observer. By the end of the time period your instructor assigns, be prepared to announce the details of the agreement you made with the other representatives. (20 minutes)

STEP 4.   Under the leadership of the observer, evaluate the negotiation that just occurred in your group of five students using the Observer Worksheet on page 255. (20 minutes)

STEP 5.   Discuss these questions as a class. (20 minutes)
   a. What outcome did your group reach? What strategy did you use?
   b. Was your group able to separate people from the problem? Did observers hear any interesting comments?
   c. What were the interests of Ivy League U.? Or Intelligentsia U.?
   d. How did you invent options? What were some creative options?
   e. What objective criteria did you use?
   f. What was the BATNA of Ivy League U.? Of Intelligentsia U.?
   g. How could you improve upon the negotiation?

Ivy League U. Role

A well-established university, Ivy League U., has a film-making department that it no longer wants. Its new president has decided to eliminate departments with small numbers of students and focus on more successful programs. Therefore, the department chair, Dr. Hitchcock (who fortunately had tenure and was switched to another department rather than fired) and Ivy League's business manager, Lou (the) Hatchet, have been ordered to sell the equipment quickly. They have only four weeks to remove the equipment so another department can take over the premises before the next semester begins. There is no space on campus to store the equipment, which is rather bulky. Hitchcock and Hatchet have succeeded in selling off some of the smaller equipment, such as lights, but the film-making department inventory still contains the following:

- 10 video cameras, two of which have never been used
- 2 television cameras
- 1 editing machine
- 3 computers that are two years old
- 1 nearly new computer that does state-of-the-art, digitized editing

The university paid a total of $75,000 dollars for this equipment when it was new, and it was all top-of-the-line quality. A secondhand store is willing to pay $35,000 for the lot. However, Hitchcock heard via the grapevine that a small, private, liberal arts school, Intelligentsia U., wants to set up a film department and is looking for equipment. Hitchcock and Hatchet have made an appointment with its representatives to see if they can get a better deal by selling to Intelligentsia. But, first, they will sit down and plan out their negotiating strategy.

Observer Worksheet

1. Which conflict handling styles in the Thomas model were individual negotiators using?

2. What was the effect of these styles?

3. What type of bargaining occurred during the role-play?
   Distributive   1   2   3   4   5   Integrative
   Why?

4. Did the negotiators separate the people from the problem?   Yes _____   No _____
   Examples?

5. Did they focus on interests rather than positions?   Yes _____   No _____
   Examples?

6. Did they invent options for mutual gain?   Yes _____   No _____
   Examples?

7. Did they insist on objective criteria?   Yes _____   No _____
   Examples?

8. How could the negotiation have been improved?

Intelligentsia U. Role

Intelligentsia U. is a small, relatively young, private liberal arts school that just became a university by adding on some different programs. It is hoping to increase its student body by offering more glamorous majors. Intelligentsia has decided to add a film-making department and is looking for equipment at a reasonable price. Since the school is still scrambling to establish itself, its resources are limited. Nevertheless, the chair of the new film-making department, Dr. Reel, wants to provide students with all the equipment they'll need to get a good background in film. An alumni donated some of the smaller equipment they require, but following is a list of things Reel needs to buy.

- 10 video cameras
- 2 television cameras
- 1 editing machine
- 1 computer that does state-of-the art, digitized editing

If the university bought this equipment new, it would cost $90,000. Another alternative is to buy used pieces of equipment, which would cost $40,000.

The facilities are not yet ready for the equipment. The film studio will not be completed for two months. But Intelligentsia U. has a large warehouse where equipment could be stored until the studio is ready.

Dr. Reel heard via the grapevine that Ivy League U. is trying to sell off its film-making equipment because it is closing down its department. Reel wants to meet with Ivy Leagues representatives, not only to buy their equipment but also to establish a good relationship. Intelligentsia wants to set up an exchange program so that its students can go to Ivy League for classes they can't get at their own school, and vice versa. Reel has asked Intelligentsia's business manager, Pat Spreadsheet, to go along to meet and negotiate with the representatives from Ivy League U. Spreadsheet agreed, so now they will sit down and plan out their negotiating strategy.

 FOLLOW-UP

Many organizations suffer from intergroup conflict. The results of intergroup conflict are usually very predictable. See if the following description, based on Schein's research, is similar to what happened in the conflict simulation.[13]

What Happens *Within* Groups?

The members of competing groups begin to close ranks and quickly experience increased feelings of group loyalty and pride. Each group sees itself as the best and the other group as the enemy. Under the pressure of time and task deadlines, the group willingly accepts more structure and autocratic leadership. The group climate is characterized by work, as opposed to play or fight; task, as opposed to maintenance. Conformity is stressed and there is little tolerance for individual deviation.

What Happens *Between* Groups?

Whatever interaction there was between the members of the two groups before the competition decreases and becomes more hostile. Whatever communication there is becomes very selective, each group hearing only comments that confirm its stereotype of the other and support its own position.

What Happens to the *Winners*?

The winning group climate can be called "fat and happy." Tension is released; there is little desire to get on to work. People would prefer to play and rest on their laurels. There is little motivation to explore earlier conflicts and possibly learn from them.

Generally, the winners not only retain their prior cohesion but become more cohesive. The exception is when the group really does not feel as if it won or when the decision is close and they did not win decisively. Under these conditions, winners often act like losers.

What Happens to the *Losers?*

The members deal initially with having lost in one of two ways. Some groups deny reality—"We didn't really lose. It was a moral victory." Other groups seek a scapegoat, someone other than themselves to blame for the defeat. The rules, for instance, are often blamed.

A losing group is, however, also a "lean and hungry" group. Tension increases, old conflicts are reexamined, and the group really digs in and learns a lot about itself in preparation for the next task.

What Happens to *Negotiators* Between Groups?

The negotiator often experiences significant role conflict between being a good judge and a good group member. Judges often find it difficult to ignore loyalties to their own groups and be completely neutral. If their group happens to be a loser, they experience much difficulty reentering, and often bear the brunt of much of the scapegoating behavior (often in a jocular fashion).

People seldom realize how much responsibility a person feels when asked to represent a group and the tension that results from being put in such a position. In addition, it is often unclear just how free a representative really is to be himself or herself as opposed to being what the group expects him or her to be. How flexible is the person to deviate from the group's mandate in response to changes in the situation? Finally, if the group loses, the representative often feels guilty and responsible.

Dysfunctional Conflict   Most of us have seen instances in which too much conflict has paralyzed groups. However, too little expressed conflict between groups can be just as dysfunctional.[14] Brown maintains that conflict will exist between groups by their very nature and that the task of the manager is not necessarily to eliminate conflict but to maintain it at a level appropriate to the task. Too much conflict can lead to defensiveness and an inability to work collaboratively toward organizational goals. Too little conflict can stifle ideas and innovation. Conflict is often repressed when there are relative differences in power between groups because the "low-power" group finds that expressing its views to the "high-power" group is much too risky.

The manager who wishes to manage conflict productively needs to develop skills in diagnosing dysfunctional situations at both extremes. Many conflicts in society (race, gender, age) require the effective manager to be aware of those larger conflicts, assessing as clearly as possible the extent to which his or her organization reinforces them, and to work to change those attitudes, behaviors, and structures that institutionalize them.

As we have seen in the exercise, intergroup conflict is easy to induce. Getting the conflicts in the open and managing them effectively is another matter. Generally, it has been found that intergroup conflict, once it begins, is extremely hard to reduce.[15] The strategy of locating a common enemy or a superordinate goal is useful, but much work must be done to overcome the negative consequences that have already developed before such strategies become feasible. Educational techniques exist and are being used with considerable success to help organizations deal with intergroup conflict that has dysfunctional consequences.[16]

Given the difficulties of reducing intergroup competition, Schein's strategies for eliminating it in the first place are very important. He suggests four steps that have proved to be effective in helping organizations avoid the dysfunctional consequences of intergroup conflict.[17]

1. Relatively *greater emphasis is given to total organizational effectiveness* and the role of departments in contributing to it; departments are measured and rewarded on the basis of their *contribution to the total effort* rather than on their individual effectiveness.

2. *High interaction and frequent communication* are stimulated between groups to work on problems of intergroup coordination and collaboration; organizational *rewards are given partly on the basis of help* that groups give each other.
3. There is frequent *rotation of members* among groups or departments to stimulate high degrees of mutual understanding and empathy for one another's problems.
4. *Win-lose situations are avoided.* Groups should never be put into the position of competing for the same organizational reward. Emphasis is always placed on pooling resources to maximize organizational effectiveness; rewards are shared equally with all the groups or departments.

CULTURE AND CONFLICT

Cultural assumptions about conflict affect our approaches to conflict as well as our expectations and behaviors in conflict situations. For example, Hall's concept of high- and low-context communication influences conflict styles.[18] Low-context communication refers to a communication system that utilizes explicit verbal messages. Examples of low-context cultures include Germany, England, Switzerland, and the United States. In contrast, high-context communication involves transmitting intention or meaning via the context (e.g., social roles, positions) and nonverbal communication (such as pauses, silence, tone of voice). The listener is expected to "read between the lines" of high-context communication. High-context cultures include Japan, China, Egypt, France, and Saudi Arabia.

According to Ting-Toomey, in low-context cultures, conflict is instrumental, which means the world is viewed in analytic, linear, logical terms.[19] Issues are viewed as separate from people, which makes it less threatening to address conflict. Conflict is more direct, disclosing, and likely to contain verbal messages that threaten the "face" of the other party. Face is defined as "upholding a claimed sense of positive public image in any social interaction."[20] In high-context cultures, conflict is indirect to preserve face and the relationship.

Another cultural aspect that influences conflict is the individualism-collectivism dimension.[21] In individualistic cultures (e.g., many Western European cultures such as France, Germany, and Scandinavia as well as Britain, Australia, and the United States), people are primarily concerned about themselves and their families. The individual, rather than the group, is important, and personal rights are valued. In collectivist cultures (e.g., many Asian, Mediterranean, Latino, Middle Eastern, and African cultures), people subordinate their personal interests for the good of the group and think in terms of "we" rather than "I."

Because harmonious relationships with the group are extremely important in a collectivist culture, conflict is approached more indirectly and face-saving behaviors are more common. In some collectivist cultures, the use of third-party mediators helps preserve the relationship between the two parties in conflict. In individualistic cultures, people are more likely to strongly assert their personal opinion, express personal emotions, and focus on individual rather than group accountability for problems. Conflict in individualistic cultures tends to center around violations of individual expectations ("I thought you would do your chores before the weekend"). Collectivistic conflict focuses more on violations of group norms or expectations ("You've let the extended family down with your behavior")[22] Barnlund described the cultural differences between Japanese and Americans with regard to conflict:[23]

> *Conflict is far less common in Japanese society for a number of reasons. First, the emphasis on the group instead of the individual reduces interpersonal friction. Second, an elaborate set of standards emphasizes "obligations" over "rights," what one owes to others rather than deserves for oneself. Third, the value attached to harmony cultivates skill in the use of ambiguity, circumlocution, euphemism, and silence in blunting incipient disputes. The ability to assimilate differences, to engineer consensus, is valued above a talent for argument.*

Individualists tend toward an outcome-oriented model of conflict—they want to resolve the conflict and quickly achieve tangible outcomes. For them, settling the conflict is more important than facework. In contrast, collectivists are process oriented—they take care of mutual face saving before they discuss outcomes. Issues related to face are pride, honor, insults, dignity, shame, disgrace, humility, trust, mistrust, respect, and prestige.[24]

Individualists also tend to be more self-oriented, controlling, and competitive than collectivists, who tend to use integrative and compromising styles. For example, Asians are more likely to use the avoiding and accommodation styles of conflict handling in the Thomas model and less likely to use the competitive style. Individualists may perceive collectivists, with their indirect style, as sidestepping the actual issues. On the other hand, collectivists may perceive individualists as pushy, rude, and overbearing.[25] In the Gulf War, it was very clear that the cultures involved did not understand each other's approach to conflict or their typical ways of dealing with conflict. Table 11-4 illustrates some of these differences. When engaged in conflict with people from other cultures, it is necessary to learn their unique style of handling conflict. And, of course, it is always helpful to understand one's own conflict style.

TABLE 11-4   Arab and Western Assumptions about Conflict Resolution

Virtues of Battle/Peace

Western: Battle is costly; peaceful resolution preferred.

Arab: War is not shameful; peace can be costly; struggle can be a progressive, invigorating, and purifying process.

Utilitarianism versus Pain

Western: Conflict brings discomfort that can be avoided or eliminated.

Arab: Discomfort and physical suffering are preferable to a loss of honor, loss of face, or perpetuation of an injustice.

Change: Optimistic or Pessimistic Outlook

Western: Change can be managed in ways that make people better off. Success comes through adaptation to or capturing of new technologies, market developments, and so forth. Joint gains are possible.

Arab: The forces of change lie outside one's control. Most changes have made Arabs worse off over time. Conflicts may be inherently unresolvable.

Scientific versus Moralistic World Views

Western: Conflicts can be reduced to objective problems that have objective solutions.

Arab: Conflict may reflect struggles between good and evil. Compromise may imply compromising on deeply held moral principles.

Interpersonal Styles

Western: Informality, personal self-revelation, openness to one's feelings, development of positive interpersonal relationships among parties are to be encouraged. Mediators must be trusted and need to develop informal relationships with the parties.

Arab: Formality and clarity of social roles are important for self-identity and maintaining relationships with negotiating partners and opponents. Authority figures make better mediators than peers or others lacking a formal role.

Agreements

Western: Agreements are to be enforced by law, convention, or specified procedures.

Arabs: Agreements tend to be broken; agreeing to an enforcement procedure implies giving up control over the future.

Source: Paul E. Salam, "A Critique of Western Conflict Resolution from a Non-Western Perspective," *Negotiations Journal 9* (1993): 361–69.

LEARNING POINTS

1. Conflict is a form of interaction among parties that differ in interests, perceptions, and preferences.

2. Groups in conflict tend to stereotype each other, see their own group as ideal, and overvalue the contributions of their own members, while devaluing those of the other group. Perceptions of the other group become distorted and hostilities tend to escalate.

3. The Sherifs' Robbers Cave experiment revealed that conflict behavior was induced by having two groups of boys compete for scarce resources—limited prizes. The hostility that resulted decreased greatly when the researchers introduced superordinate goals that were important to all the boys and required collaboration.

4. Two ways to resolve intergroup conflict are (a) noncompetitive contact in which the groups have equal status; and (b) establishing a superordinate goal that can only be attained through joint cooperation.

5. Organizations are full of reference groups that provide individuals with a sense of belonging and identity in exchange for loyalty and commitment. However, a we-they attitude often develops when these groups come into contact with each other.

6. We-they attitudes between internal groups can foster competition and a lack of collaboration that hinder productivity and achievement of the overall goals of the organization. In contrast, competition with external groups can be very productive.

7. Common sources of group conflict in organizations are we-they attitudes of reference groups, competition for scarce resources, ambiguous authority, interdependence, deficient information, and differences in values, interests, personalities, education, culture, perceptions, goals, and expectations.

8. While dysfunctional conflict siphons energy away from organizational goals, functional conflict plays an important role in organizations. One way to ensure that conflict is functional is to train employees in conflict management skills.

9. The five conflict-handling modes are based on a person's strategic intentions along two axes:
   a. Assertiveness—desire to satisfy one's own concerns
   b. Cooperativeness—desire to satisfy the concerns of the other party

10. The five conflict-handling modes are:
    a. Competition
    b. Avoidance
    c. Accommodation
    d. Compromise
    e. Collaboration

11. Effective managers use the mode that is appropriate to the situation.

12. There are two types of bargaining: distributive (win-lose) and integrative (win-win).

13. Fisher and Ury's scheme of principled negotiation consists of four steps:
    a. Separate the people from the problem.
    b. Focus on interests, not positions.
    c. Invent options for mutual gain.
    d. Insist on objective criteria.

14. Too much or too little conflict are both dysfunctional states. Dysfunctional intergroup conflict can be avoided when organizations emphasize the contribution of departments to total organizational effectiveness, stimulate frequent interaction among groups, rotate members among departments, and avoid win-lose situations.

15. It is easier to create conflict than resolve it.

16. Cultural dimensions, such as high- and low-context communication and individualism-collectivism, influence conflict approaches, expectations, and styles.

𝑇𝐼𝑃𝑆 **FOR MANAGERS**

- One way to avoid conflict is by clearly determining both authority and responsibility.
- Try to reframe conflict situations from a "we-they" position to a "we versus the problem" approach. For example, the manager of an auditing department realized her efforts to incorporate the auditing department of a recently merged smaller bank were not succeeding. In fact, hostility between the two groups was increasing. Rather than fighting over whose procedures were better, the manager wisely reframed the situation and asked the entire group to start from scratch and use the merger as an opportunity to devise the best possible procedures. Their final product was "ours," and in the process, the two departments became a cohesive unit.
- Look for mutual goals and values, or even a common enemy. Make sure common enemies are outside the company and not a person or group with whom it is important to have a collaborative relationship.
- Managing conflict may appear to be too time consuming in the short run, but conflicts that are allowed to fester can cause great harm and take up more time in the long run.
- Managers can sometimes decrease conflict by the use of a liaison or a buffer. Liaisons or boundary spanners absorb heat from both sides and try to interpret the actions of both groups to each other. Buffers can also be inanimate objects that prevent two groups from having to interact, for example, the order wheel in restaurants and automatic reordering systems in warehouses.
- Managers can set the stage for collaboration between departments or divisions by having a clear understanding of the contribution each group makes and continually communicating the importance of all groups.
- They can also show an interest in all groups and insist that they work together. The manager's attention is often one of the scarce resources in an organization. Therefore, managers who share their attention as equally as possible (or at least explain to the others why they are focusing on a certain area) are more likely to have a collaborative climate.
- Managers can make it clear that they welcome the existence of differences within the organization.
- When conflicts are brought to managers to be settled, they should:
  a. Listen with understanding rather than evaluation and recognize and accept the feelings of the people involved without judging them.
  b. Analyze the source of the conflict and make sure all parties understand the nature of the conflict from everyone's perspective.
  c. Suggest procedures and ground rules for discussing and resolving the differences:
     ○ Everyone will be treated with respect.
     ○ Although groups may be committed to their own position, they should still be open to other perspectives.
     ○ Avoid unproductive conflict strategies such as blaming, forcing, threatening, and manipulating.
     ○ Give all parties equal opportunity to present their views and arguments and ensure fair treatment.
     ○ Keep the focus on the current situation rather than past history that has no relevance.
     ○ Seek a win-win solution.
  d. Suggest problem-solving procedures, such as brainstorming and agreement on objective criteria, to judge solutions.
  e. Teach problem-solving skills so employees can resolve conflicts themselves in the future.

PERSONAL APPLICATION ASSIGNMENT

This assignment is to write about a situation involving conflict or negotiation. Choose an experience about which you want to learn more. When you address the Reflective Observation section, make a special effort to take the perspective of all parties.

A. *Concrete Experience*

    1. *Objectively* describe the experience (who, what, when, where, how) (2 points)

    2. *Subjectively* describe your feelings, perceptions, and thoughts that occurred during (not after) the experience. What did others seem to be feeling? (2 points)

B. *Reflective Observation*

    1. Looking back at the experience, what were the perspectives of the key actors (including you)? (2 points)

    2. Why did the people involved (including you) behave as they did? (2 points)

C. *Abstract Conceptualization*
1. Relate concepts or theories from the assigned readings or the lecture to the experience. Explain thoroughly how they apply to your experience. Please apply at least two concepts or theories and cite them correctly. (4 points)

D. *Active Experimentation*
1. What did you learn about conflict on negotiation from this experience? (1 point)
2. What did you learn about yourself? (1 point)
3. What action steps will you take to be more effective in the future? (2 points)

E. *Integration, Synthesis, and Writing*
1. Did you integrate and synthesize the four sections? (1 point)
2. Was the Personal Application Assignment well written and easy to understand? (1 point)
3. Was it free of spelling and grammar errors? (2 points)

ENDNOTES

[1] K. W. Thomas, "Conflict and Negotiation Processes in Organizations," in M.D. Dunnette and L. M. Hough (eds.), *Handbook of Industrial and Organizational Psychology*, 2nd ed. (Palo Alto, CA: Consulting Psychologists Press, 1991): 653.

[2] M. Sherif, and C. W. Sherif, "Ingroup and Intergroup Relations: Experimental Analysis," in *Social Psychology* (New York: Harper & Row, 1969); and M. Sherif, *Intergroup Relations and Leadership* (New York: John Wiley, 1962).

[3] M. Deutsch, "An Experimental Study of the Effects of Cooperation and Competition upon Group Process," *Human Relations 2* (1949): 199–231, and G. W. Allport, *The Nature of Prejudice* (Reading, MA: Addison-Wesley, 1954).

[4] Thomas, "Conflict and Negotiation," 697.

[5] For example, D. Cartwright and A. Zander, *Group Dynamics Research and Theory* (New York: Harper & Row, 1968); M. Deutsch, *The Resolution of Conflict* (New Haven, CT: Yale University Press, 1973); C. Alderfer and K. K. Smith, "Studying Intergroups Relation Embedded in Organizations," *Administrative Science Quarterly* (March 1982): 35–64; S. P. Robbins, *Managing Organizational Conflict* (Upper Saddle River, NJ: Prentice Hall, 1974); and D. W. Johnson, and F. P. Johnson, *Joining Together: Group Theory and Group Skill* (Boston: Allyn & Bacon, 1994).

[6] J. A. Byrne, "The Horizontal Corporation," *Business Week*, December 20, 1993, 76–81.

[7] K. W. Thomas, "Conflict and Conflict Management," in *Handbook of Industrial and Organizational Psychology*, edited by M. D. Dunnette (Chicago: Rand McNally, 1976): 889–935.

[8] R. J. Lewicki and J. A. Litterer, *Negotiation* (Homewood, IL: Irwin, 1985): 280.

[9] K. Thomas, "Conflict and Conflict Management," *Journal of Organizational Behavior 13* (1992): 265–74.

[10] R. Fisher and W. Ury, *Getting to Yes: Negotiating Agreement Without Giving In* (Boston: Houghton Mifflin, 1981); R. Ury, *Getting Past No: Negotiating Your Way from Confrontation to Cooperation* (New York: Bantam, 1993); and R. Fisher, W. Ury, and B. Patton, "Negotiation Power: Ingredients in an Ability to Influence the Other Side," in L. Hall (ed.), *Negotiation: Strategies for Mutual Gain: The Basic Text of the Harvard Law School Program on Negotiation* (Newbury Park, CA: Sage, 1993), 3–14. See B. McRae, *Negotiating and Influencing Skills* (Thousand Oaks, CA: Sage, 1998) for more detailed information on negotiation.

[11] Fisher and Ury, *Getting to Yes*, 4.

[12] For information on international negotiations, see N. J. Adler, *International Dimensions of Organizational Behavior* (Cincinnati, OH: South-Western College, 1997); S. E. Weiss, "Negotiating with 'Romans'—Part 1," *Sloan Management Review* (Winter 1994): 51–61; S. E. Weiss, "Negotiating with 'Romans'—Part 2," *Sloan Management Review* (Spring 1994): 85–99; and R. D. Lewis, *When Cultures Collide: Managing Successfully Across Cultures* (London: Nicholas Brealey, 1996).

[13] E. H. Schein, *Organizational Psychology* (Upper Saddle River, NJ: Prentice Hall, 1965): 80–86.

[14] L. D. Brown, "Managing Conflict Among Groups," In *The Organizational Behavior Reader*, D. Kolb, J. Osland, and I. Rubin (eds.) (Upper Saddle River, NJ: Prentice-Hall, 1995): 317–28.

[15] The reality of this is nowhere clearer than in our efforts to combat years of racial prejudice and discrimination.

[16] J. W. Anderson, M. Foster-Kuehn, and B. C. McKinney, *Communication Skills for Surviving Conflict at Work* (Cresswell, NJ: Hampton Press); J. P. Folger, M. S. Poole, and R. K. Stutman, *Working Through Conflict* (New York: Longman, 1997); and C. De Dreu, and E. Van De Vliert, (eds.). *Using Conflict in Organizations* (Thousand Oaks, CA: Sage, 1997).

[17] E. H. Schein, *Organizational Psychology*.

[18] E. T. Hall, *Beyond Culture* (Garden City, NY: Anchor Press/Doubleday, 1976).

[19] S. Ting-Toomey, "Intercultural Conflict Competence." In W. R. Cupach, and D. J. Canary, (eds.) *Competence in Interpersonal Conflict* (New York: McGraw-Hill, 1997): 121–47.

[20] Ibid., 132.

[21] H. C. Triandis, *Individualism & Collectivism* (Boulder, CO: Westview Press, 1995); G. Hofstede, *Culture's Consequences* (Thousand Oaks, Sage, 1980).

[22] Ting-Toomey, "Intercultural Conflict Competence."

[23] D. S. Barnlund, *Communication Style of Japanese and Americans: Images and Reality* (Belmont, CA: Wadsworth, 1989): 3.

[24] Ting-Toomey, "Intercultural Conflict Competence."

[25] Ibid.

Chapter *12*

▲▲▲

MANAGING DIVERSITY

OBJECTIVES By the end of this chapter, you should be able to:

A. Explain the advantages and disadvantages of culture.

B. Define ethnocentrism and stereotyping.

C. Describe six dimensions of cultural differences.

D. Explain what happens to tokens in organizations.

E. Explain why diversity is a business issue.

F. Understand how to manage diversity in organizations.

WHAT'S YOUR ECCENTRICITY QUOTIENT?

How weird can you be in a major corporation and still keep your job? Kathleen McDonald, organization development team leader who was responsible for a project on managing diversity at Exxon, devised an eccentricity model to help employees answer that very question.

According to McDonald, the employees' goal is to balance their *perceived competence* with their *perceived eccentricity* ($PC = PE$). She defines perceived competence as how you and your job performance are seen by others in your organization. But note that this perception can be different from reality; perceived competence is how good others in the organization "think" you are.

Perceived eccentricity refers to those parts of you or your actions that do not fit neatly into the profile of the "ideal organization person" as defined by your organization. As McDonald describes it, perceived eccentricity refers to the corners of the square peg as you work in an environment that rewards round pegs. Obviously, some of those corners can be worn down, while others are difficult, if not impossible, to remove. In the higher realms of most *Fortune* 500 companies, anyone who is female, foreign born, or a person of color is likely to have a higher perceived eccentricity score than a WASP male. Likewise, people with different lifestyles, vocal religious beliefs, or a unique style of dress, mannerisms, or speech may also be perceived as eccentric in some organizations. In technical environments, perceived eccentricity can also relate to the degree of risk and innovation you display.

How you manage the perceived eccentricity side of your equation has to do with how much acceptance you seek and what that acceptance represents. How much of an insider can you be? How much of an insider do you want to be? How much of yourself are you willing to leave at home or to censor at work? These can be tough issues, especially for minorities who feel the strain of struggling to fit an "ideal type" that bears little resemblance to them.

McDonald described the experience of a white man who moved from a plant to a technical service position. At the plant he and just about everyone else wore jeans. For his new job he upgraded his wardrobe to wear a sport coat with his jeans. Eventually word drifted back to him that the salespeople did not want to take him with them on customer calls because of his "eccentric" dress. He had a choice to make: he could work at raising his perceived competence so that his new colleagues would see him as an invaluable resource even in a burlap sack, or he could invest in a new wardrobe and decrease his perceived eccentricity. He went out and bought suits—a quicker if more expensive route to correcting an imbalance in the eccentricity model.

However, it's easier to change clothes than skin color. The African American female, who entered a predominantly white company and was assigned to a supervisor who was also brand new, had more difficulty in overcoming the perceived eccentricity of her race. Because the new supervisor couldn't inform her about the company's norms early on or interpret her competence to others in the organization, it took longer for the African American to establish her perceived competence.

McDonald says that you can be as eccentric as you are competent. And it's usually a good idea to establish your competence before you test the company's tolerance of eccentricity. How do you scope out your perceived competence and eccentricity? From performance appraisals, the rewards that come your way, and from feedback. And you may have to take an active role in seeking out feedback so you can decide how to manage yourself in the workplace. McDonald's eccentricity model is a good barometer for figuring out the consequences of your choices.

Examples of employees whose perceived eccentricity far outweighed their perceived competence come readily to mind. These are folks who are no longer around to tell their tale or who are continuously passed over for promotion. The danger of that kind of imbalance is clear. However, McDonald sees no advantage in the opposite kind of imbalance, even though there are typically many people in organizations who are perceived to be more competent than they are eccentric. The danger here is that employees will lose valuable opportunities to grow, both personally and professionally, by playing it safe. And organizations won't learn how to live with and profit from the diversity of their employees. So if your organization perceives you as more competent than eccentric, even up the equation and break out a little. Let those at work know how wonderfully weird or innovative you can be. You'll be doing everyone a favor.

Source: Adapted from an unpublished document by Kathleen McDonald.

PREMEETING PREPARATION

A. Read "What's Your Eccentricity Quotient?"

B. Read the entire chapter to become familiar with the topic and prepare for the group meeting. Do this first.

C. Complete the following exercises:
  1. Analysis of a Personal Experience of Being Different.
  2. Intensity of Differentness Rating.

D. What are the significant learning points from the readings?

E. If your instructor has assigned the Robbins Self-Assessment Library, use "How Well Do I Handle Ambiguity?" and "Am I Well-Suited for a Career as a Global Manager?"

ANALYSIS OF A PERSONAL EXPERIENCE OF BEING DIFFERENT*

The experience of being different from others can be frustrating, isolating, and even painful. In our desire to avoid these feelings of difference, we are often tempted to deny our individual uniqueness

---

* This exercise was developed by David Akinnusi, Lyda Detterman, Rafael Estevez, Elizabeth Fisher, Mary Ann Hazen, David Kolb, Dennis O'Connor, and Michelle Spain, a diverse group if there ever was one.

and to "fit in"—to adopt the superficial characteristics of the majority. But doing so is not good for us as individuals for we are denying part of ourselves, which can result in feelings of alienation. It is ineffective as well because our skills lie with who we are, not who we pretend to be. Nor is this denial of differences good for the organization, for without a variety of perspectives and alternatives for action, organizations become rigid and less effective.

Think of a recent experience you have had where you felt you were being treated as though you were "different," where others were not recognizing you as a unique person. It could be an experience in this course, at work, or anywhere. (Use another page if you need more space.)

1. Describe what happened in the situation.

2. How did you feel, think, and act?

3. How did others feel, think, and act?

4. What was the outcome of the situation?

5. What did you learn from the experience?

INTENSITY OF DIFFERENTNESS RATING

We are all unique individuals with unique cultural and subcultural backgrounds and identities. As a result, we all have experiences of being different, of being stereotyped and discriminated against. These feelings are most pronounced and intense:

- When the situation is very important (e.g., when a job is at stake, in personal relationships, or when physical safety is at risk).
- When our own cultural experiences are markedly different from the dominant culture around us.
- When these differences are visible to others (e.g., skin color, sex, age, language, manner of dress).
- When there are power differences between ourselves and the dominant culture (i.e., when we are "one-down" in influence or rank).

- When we are alone or isolated from others who share our culture or subculture.
- When others are stereotyping us in an obvious fashion.
- When we have strong emotional reactions of frustration, anger, or humiliation.

Look back over your description of the situation where you felt "different." Score it on the following issues:

Intensity of Differentness Scale

	Circle the Number that Applies		
1. How important was the situation to you?	0 Relatively unimportant	1 Important	2 Very critical
2. How different were you?	0 Very little difference	1 Some difference	2 Great difference
3. Were these differences visible to others?	0 No	1 A little	2 Obvious
4. Were there power differences?	0 I was one-up, in charge	1 Equal	2 I was one-down
5. Were you isolated from others similar to you?	0 I had several others like me for support	1 One other person like me	2 I was alone
6. Were you stereotyped?	0 I was treated as a unique individual	1 I felt stereo- typed	2 There was direct evidence of stereotyping
7. Did the situation cause you to react emotionally?	0 No emotional reaction	1 I felt slightly upset	2 I had a strong emotional reaction

Add the numbers circled to get your total intensity of differentness score: _____ .

TOPIC INTRODUCTION

As companies become more global and the workforce becomes more diverse, we find ourselves increasingly involved with coworkers who differ from us in their cultural or subcultural identities. Neither trend is likely to diminish. The markets with the most potential for growth, as well as the cheapest labor supply, are located around the globe. Without some degree of cross-cultural understanding and sensitivity, international business cannot succeed. Many companies are already trying to take advantage of a diverse workforce by learning to (1) appreciate and understand differences, (2) communicate and work with diverse groups, (3) develop an organizational culture that welcomes all groups and their unique contributions, and (4) allow all kinds of people to reach their full potential. The purpose of this chapter is to focus on both cross-cultural and domestic diversity issues.

CULTURE

A second grade teacher asked her students to solve this problem: "There are four blackbirds sitting in a tree. You take a slingshot and shoot one of them. How many are left?"

"Three," answered the seven-year-old European with certainty. "One subtracted from four leaves three."

"Zero," answered the seven-year-old African with equal certainty. "If you shoot one bird, the others will fly away."[1]

The difference between these answers is explained by diverse cultural orientations, a focus on task versus relationship. The European perceived the question as a hypothetical situation that required a literal answer (task). In contrast, the African focused on the relationship among the birds and the predictable behavior that would result from a shot (relationship). In some cultures, such as the United States, task is the primary focus, and people quickly get down to business. In many other cultures, such as in Italy, Senegal, and Ecuador, people expect to establish a relationship first so they can trust one another before doing business. Like the students' answers, one orientation is not better than the other; they are simply different and, therefore, have to be taken into consideration when working across cultures.

Culture causes humans to see the world differently through their cultural lenses and is also a major determinant of behavior. People are usually introduced to their own culture in the act of confronting another. One learns what it means to be an American, Japanese, or South African, and so on by rubbing up against other nationalities. And even then, one discerns mainly those aspects of one's own culture that come into conflict with those of the other culture. "What observers notice about the culture they visit will depend not only on the society they choose to study but also their own cultural background."[2] We don't notice similarities as quickly because our eyes are drawn first to differences. Another way to explain this phenomenon is to cast it into the Gestalt scheme of figure and ground. What is ground in one's own culture and country becomes figural when thrown up against the relief provided by another culture. Figure 12-1 presents a list of American cultural values.

The way humans react to the basic issues that confront all humankind is determined by culture. For example, old age and dying represent an inescapable problem for all societies, but the manner of approaching and resolving this problem derives primarily from particular cultural values and beliefs. The prestige and respect given to the elderly, beliefs about the afterlife, and economic values determine how a culture will handle the problem of old age and death.

Equality	People are created equal and should try to diminish real differences in status.
Informality	Interactions are casual and spontaneous rather than bound by rigid rules.
Rationality	Scientific reasoning is the best way to understand the world, and people think analytically about what they perceive as objective reality.
Time	Time is a commodity, like money, and should not be squandered.
Action	The emphasis is on "doing." Getting things done is worthwhile.
Materialism	Material comforts and convenience are important.
Achievement	People experience a need to prove themselves because part of their identity results from success and achievement.
Self-reliance	Independence is emphasized as well as being "self-made" and becoming one's own person.
Pragmatism	The focus is on getting things done and moving forward.
Progress	Progress is very desirable and people are optimistic that their efforts may create a better world. Change is positive.

FIGURE 12-1   **American Cultural Values**

Source: This chart is based on E. Stewart and M. Bennett, *American Cultural Patterns: A Cross-Cultural Perspective* (Yarmouth, ME: Intercultural Press, 1995).

Culture provides us with both ready-made solutions to basic human issues and a sense of identity. However, we must also acknowledge the cost.

> *But while humans gain so much from culture, they are also brainwashed, to some extent by the culture to which they are exposed from birth. Equipped with a collection of stereotypes with which to face the world, humans are apt to lose sight of possible alternative modes of behavior and understanding.[3]*

The concept of trade-offs is a useful one when studying different cultures. Traditional cultures with clear norms may be more confining and slower to change, but their members usually possess a strong sense of identity. Creativity and adaptability are often identified as by-products of American culture; however, the price Americans pay for allowing people the freedom to go their own way in a polyglot and highly mobile society is insecurity and rootlessness. All cultures have advantages and disadvantages when considered objectively. Human nature sometimes prevents us from appreciating the advantages or the good points of other cultures. This quality is referred to as ethnocentrism.

Ethnocentrism is defined as the "exaggerated tendency to think the characteristics of one's own group or race are superior to those of other groups or races."[4] Humans are preoccupied with the differences between their "own" kind and outsiders. Anthropologists have encountered many tribes whose name is literally translated as "the human beings"; this implies that those outside their tribe are not human and, therefore, not worthy of the same consideration.

Ethnocentrism is very obvious in the epithets used by countries at war, but it is not triggered only by military conflict. Within the United States ethnocentrism is reflected in racial issues and complaints about promoting minorities at work—all of which represent threats to the economic and social dominance of the white majority.[5] Because ethnocentrism in the United States seldom results in all-out warfare, we should not be lulled into overlooking its existence. Everyone possesses some degree of ethnocentrism. For anyone who deals with people who are different, the first step is to acknowledge one's ethnocentrism and try to curb the natural thought that one's own group, culture, gender is, by definition, better than others.

CULTURAL DIFFERENCES

The next steps in cross-cultural relations are gaining an understanding of your own culture, followed by a serious attempt to understand the other culture or subculture. Until we understand the internal logic of another culture, we can only interpret their behavior using our own cultural norms and assumptions. This leads to misperceptions and false attributions about their behavior. One dimension of cultural differences, the concept of individualism versus collectivism, provides us with a clue to some of the major differences we see both abroad and in our own countries.[6]

Individualism is a cultural pattern found in most northern and western regions of Europe and in North America. It is defined as the extent to which people are responsible for taking care of themselves and giving priority to their own interests. Collectivism is characterized by individuals who subordinate their personal goals to the goals of some collective. Individuals give their loyalty to a group and in return the group takes responsibility for the individual. Collectivism is common in Asia, Africa, South America, and the Pacific.

In individualistic cultures, people define themselves as an entity that is separate from the group. There is an emphasis on personal goals and less concern and emotional attachment to groups. Successes are individual successes whereas in collectivist cultures, successes are group successes. Competition is interpersonal in individualistic cultures; in collectivist cultures, it occurs between groups. People in collectivist cultures define themselves as part of a group. They are concerned for the integrity of the group and have an intense emotional attachment to the group. For example, the bond between a mother and son (Indo-European collectivist cultures) or father and son (East Asian collectivist cultures) will be stronger than the bond between a wife and a husband because the family group is the most important. Vertical relationships (parent-child, boss-subordinate) are more important in collectivist cultures, whereas horizontal relationships (spouse-spouse, friend-friend) are more important in individualistic cultures.

In-groups are also very important in collectivist cultures. In the previous family example, the extended family is the in-group. In-group members in collectivist cultures warrant very different treatment than out-group members who are often treated with hostility and distrust. In contrast, people in individualistic cultures tend to treat people more consistently because they see themselves as belonging to more and larger in-groups (for example, people like us in terms of social class, race, beliefs, attitudes, interests, or people from our region or state). The difference is that the individualists' ties are not as strong with all these groups.

There is an emphasis on harmony and face-saving in collectivist cultures. In contrast, people in individualistic cultures are more likely to value confrontation and "clearing the air." Individualistic cultures have more short-term relationships and use contracts in business dealings. Collectivistic cultures think in terms of long-term relationships, which makes the use of contracts less important.

Not everyone in an individualistic culture is individualistic; the same is true for collectivist cultures. In both types of cultures, one can find allocentric people who value social support and idiocentric people who value achievement. Individualistic cultures have higher gross national products, but they also have more social ills and higher heart attack rates. Collectivist cultures report lower degrees of loneliness, alienation, and social problems. However, they have more government corruption because in-group loyalty dictates that those in power will try to enrich their in-group rather than concern themselves with the country as a whole.

Individualism and collectivism affect how we structure organizations and how we expect people to act in the workplace. Hofstede concluded that American management techniques are not universally applicable because they reflect U.S. values (such as individualism).[7] He administered surveys to 166,000 employees of IBM to see whether or not there were cultural differences among them. Even though they worked for the same company and held similar positions, they varied along four different dimensions:

1. *Power distance*: The extent to which a society accepts the fact that power in institutions and organizations is distributed unequally.
2. *Uncertainty avoidance*: The extent to which a society accepts or avoids uncertain and ambiguous situations.
3. *Individualism*: The extent to which people are responsible for taking care of themselves and give priority to their own interests. Its opposite is collectivism in which individuals give their loyalty to a group and in return the group takes responsibility for the individual.
4. *Masculinity*: The extent to which the dominant cultural values are assertiveness, the acquisition of money and things—as opposed to its opposite, femininity, which refers to dominant values of caring for others, quality of life, and people.

Later on while working in China, Hofstede and Bond identified a fifth dimension, *long-term orientation* versus *short-term orientation*. The long-term orientation, found in China, includes a greater concern with the future and values thrift and perseverance. The short-term orientation, which characterizes Russia and West Africa, is more concerned with the past and present and values tradition and fulfilling social obligations.[8]

Hofstede's cultural dimensions, as well as other bipolar dimensions, are commonly used to compare and contrast cultures. They are helpful tools, but they fail to capture the complexity within a culture. For example, no culture is always individualistic or collectivist; how people behave depends in large part on the context. Therefore, we run the risk of stereotyping entire cultures with these bipolar dimensions unless we understand they are simply a helpful first step in decoding another culture and that we will no doubt run into what looks like paradoxical behavior.[9]

Americans, Hofstede found, value equality (low power distance), are individualists (extremely high individualism) who willingly tolerate uncertainty (low uncertainty avoidance), value achievement and striving more than nurturance and support (above average masculinity) and have a short-term orientation. American management techniques, he argues, are largely based on these values. As a result, they do not work as well in a culture, for example, that values the collective over the individual, that emphasizes feminine values, or that is comfortable with high power distance. For example, empowerment and servant leadership are management concepts originating in the United States that will not be easily transferred to cultures characterized by high power distance. Management practices need to be adjusted to the values and attitudes of the culture or subculture in question. This is true not only in cross-cultural management in other nations but in our day-to-day relationships with those who identify with different subcultures within our own country. The focus of this chapter is managing diversity in multicultural organizations. It underscores the importance of individual differences and seeks to develop skills in managing these differences.

STEREOTYPING

People entering organizations bring with them their own assumptions and preconceptions, and they use these ideas to form new impressions about other groups in the organization. When we act toward individual members of a group based on our assumptions about the group to which they belong, we are engaging in a stereotypic behavior. Aronson describes this as follows: "To stereotype is to assign identical characteristics to any people in a group regardless of the actual variation among members of the group."[10]

A stereotypic perception of individual differences is called a prejudice. Stereotypes abound in organizations. The common ones are based on gender, race, age, and professional groups. For example, as stated in the chapter on perception, there is no empirical evidence to support the stereotype that older workers are less productive.[11] In fact, research shows that job satisfaction, job involvement, internal work motivation, and organizational commitment increases with age.[12] Ageism may be responsible for the difficulty some people over the age of 55 have in finding jobs.

Figure 12-2 presents common stereotypical misinterpretations and the values that more accurately explain Asian American behavior. Stereotyping often results in misattributions about behavior.

Observed Behavior of Asian Americans	Common Stereotypical Misinterpretations	Possible Cultural Explanation
Nonconfrontational	Passive; does not care one way or another	Values harmony; sees disagreements as being in disharmony
Quiet; reserved	Has no opinions	Values opinions of others and fitting in with group
Agreeable; dependable follower	Unassertive; no leadership qualities	Values what is good for group; can be assertive and a leader if needed for the group
Industrious	Make good "worker bees"	Values carrying their share of work; believes hard work will be recognized and rewarded
Technically and scientifically competent	No management competence or leader-type charisma	Values science as universal language crossing cultural barriers; believes leadership comes in many forms
Deferential to others	Not committed to own opinions, judgments, or preferences	Values being respectful of others; believes in "saving face" for self and others; values age and wisdom
Very American behavior	Looks Asian; must be of different culture	Born in United States; values American heritage

FIGURE 12-2 **Asian Americans: Common Stereotypes and Corresponding Cultural Explanations**
Source: Reprinted with permission from NTL Institute from *Managing in the Age of Change*, edited by Roger A. Ritvo, Anne H. Litwin, and Lee Butler, 1995.

Racial stereotypes sometimes prevent organizations from realizing the potential of minority employees. They are also a source of difficulty and pain for minorities. Billie Jean King once asked another tennis star, Arthur Ashe who contracted AIDS via a blood transfusion while undergoing heart surgery. "What's the most difficult thing for you?" Ashe replied, "Most people would think it's HIV, AIDS, or my heart, but it's really being a black man. Every time I walk out the door, I know my day could be difficult because of prejudice."[13] Prejudice has tangible outcomes. More African Americans lost their jobs during the 1990–1991 recession than any other ethnic group.[14]

Stereotyping is partly responsible for the glass ceiling facing female executives. Although the U.S. workforce is close to 50 percent female and women hold 40 percent of the management positions, they hold only 5 to 6 percent of top-management positions.[15] In a study by Catalyst, a New York–based research organization, 52 percent of female executives (and 25 percent of male CEOs) surveyed responded that "male stereotyping and preconceptions about women" kept women from being promoted to executive positions. The second most frequently cited reason by the female executives, "exclusion from informal networks," was identified by 49 percent of the women (and 15 percent of the male CEOs). For the male CEOs in this study, the major reason for the lack of women at the top was their "lack of significant general management or line experience" (82 percent of the men and 47 percent of the female executives) and not having been "in the pipeline long enough" (64 percent of male CEOs and 29 percent of female executives). Furthermore, 49 percent of the male CEOs reported that opportunities for women had improved greatly, whereas only 23 percent of the women shared this view. These results confirm a common phenomenon—majorities and minorities often perceive the world differently.

Workplace stereotypes prevent people who are different from feeling accepted and living up to their full potential. They also deny individual uniqueness. When people are treated only as members of a group rather than as individuals with their own unique characteristics, difficulties in interpersonal communication and cooperation often result.

Another effect of stereotyping is that it blocks learning in organizations. If we view individuals and organizations as learning systems, then individual differences need to be fostered rather than suppressed if learning is to occur. Friedlander asserts that "for an organism to learn, it must be sufficiently heterogenous to contain differences. These are differences in perception, value, preferences, time orientations, plans, expectations, etc."[16] Therefore, the multicultural organization provides an excellent opportunity for individual and organizational learning because it accommodates people with unique differences and perspectives. For example, one occasionally sees references to the "feminine" values that are found in the management practices of certain successful companies. Presumably these companies tolerated the "deviance" of individual female managers and, in the process, discovered or learned that such practices had value. We know that culture constrains our ability to conceive of alternative behavior; therefore, seeking out different cultural and individual perspectives is a way of ensuring that we are not blindly pursuing solutions that would be better served by diverse views. Customers are themselves a diverse group. Minority employees can help companies understand and better serve their diverse customers if the company is willing to listen.

THE MINORITY EXPERIENCE

Organizations exist in a multicultural environment and cannot avoid this reality. People in organizations bring with them aspects of their cultural experience and, thus, organizations come to mirror issues facing society and the world. Brown, for example, reminds us that the minorities in a society that allows discrimination tend to be particularly sensitive to discriminatory behaviors within the organizations that employ them.[17] They perceive discriminatory intent in behaviors that may seem appropriate and nondiscriminatory to members of the dominant culture. As a result, members of the majority may feel insulted if accused of discrimination. They do not recognize that they are beneficiaries of institutional discrimination and do not understand why minorities are so sensitive about discrimination. People from different cultures or groups are likely to put outsiders through a testing period. Minorities who have had negative experiences with majority members or institutions are especially likely to watch for possible signs of discrimination or untrustworthiness in new relationships or settings and take longer to form relationships with majority members. This is sometimes mistakenly interpreted as standoffishness; in fact, it's merely a different timetable for forming relationships.

Minorities in both cultures and organizations often pay a high price for their "differentness." Feeling the need to represent one's entire race, gender, or culture is quite a burden. As one African American man, who was tired of fielding questions in an all-white group, stated, "I'm not putting on a charm school course on blacks for white folk." Kanter's study of "tokens" in a large corporation found that three perceptual tendencies occur when there is a small *number* of minorities. This phenomenon can be observed with any tokens, including white males when they constitute a small minority.[18]

1. Tokens receive *more attention* because they are more highly visible. In Gestalt psychology terms, the tokens become the "figure" rather than the "ground." (This concept was discussed in Chapter 8, Perception and Attribution.) As a result, the tokens are constantly in the public eye, and their behavior is scrutinized for symbolic content because they represent their entire group, not just themselves. Performance pressures are thereby magnified.
2. *Contrast* between the token and the majority group results in exaggeration and polarization of the differences between the two groups. Exposure to a minority makes the majority self-conscious and, therefore, uncomfortable and uncertain. As a result, the boundaries of the dominant group become even stronger and isolation of the tokens occurs.
3. *Assimilation* of the tokens occurs via stereotyping. A larger number of "token-type" people would allow the majority to perceive that there are, in fact, many individual differences among this group. However, due to their small numbers, tokens are forced into limited and caricatured roles, which Kanter refers to as "role encapsulation." Common stereotypes for tokens are mascot, cheerleader, sex object, and militant.

Sensitivity to the stress that accompanies tokenism can be partially alleviated by managers who understand the phenomenon. But the systemic answer to the problem is to hire and promote enough people from the minority group to make tokenism a moot point.

Networks

To some extent every cultural group, including any minority group in an organization, tends to develop shared meanings, values, frameworks, and languages among the members of the subculture. Such groups are likely to have common interests and to share needs that the formal organization seldom meets. As a consequence, these groups form their own networks in which they exchange the things they need and desire, such as support, advice, and collaboration.

Within an organization there exists a multiplicity of social networks that arise out of the many possible types of social relationships that tie people to one another. Researchers, however, show that kinship, ethnic, and minority ties are among the strongest links that hold together a network.[19] Each emergent network has its own social and functional logic, and it does not necessarily become part of one major structure that might be colled the informal organization. Such networks, however, can provide an alternative power base within an organization for its members.

PROCEDURES FOR GROUP MEETING: CROSS-CULTURAL COMPETENCY SKITS

The purpose of this exercise is to give you an opportunity to practice and recognize effective and ineffective cross-cultural or intercultural interactions.

(Time allotted: 1 to $1\frac{1}{2}$ hours)

STEP 1.   If yours is a diverse, multicultural classroom, divide into cultural groups with two to six members. If your class is not culturally diverse, divide into groups of four to six participants.

STEP 2.   Read the list of cultural competencies that follows. Then, as a group, make up a two-part skit that lasts no more than 8 minutes. The first part should portray an ineffective way to handle a cross-cultural or intercultural interaction that you might face at work. The second part should present effective handling of the same interaction, demonstrating cultural competencies. Be as creative as possible and have fun with your skit. Prepare to ask the rest of the class to analyze "what's right and wrong with this picture." (20–30 minutes)

STEP 3.   Each group presents its skit and asks the rest of the class to identify what was ineffective in the first part and effective in the second part.

Cultural Competencies

- Tolerance of differences
- Tolerance of ambiguity
- Patience
- Positive attitudes toward people and experiences
- Interpersonal sensitivity
- Empathy
- Good communication skills, including active listening
- Open-mindedness
- Sense of humility
- Capacity to learn
- Ability to handle conflict
- Ability to handle stress
- Behavioral flexibility
- Personal self-awareness

THE EMBASSY RECEPTION

(Time allotted: $1\frac{1}{2}$ hours)

The purpose of this exercise is to simulate a cross-cultural experience and the feelings that accompany it. It also provides a chance to "decode" another culture.

STEP 1.   Divide the class into two groups. One group is called the Embassy Crowd; the other group is the Host Country Nationals.

STEP 2.   The groups should meet in two different locations so they can discuss their strategy openly. Your task is to create a culture from scratch, using Hofstede's dimensions of national culture. Read the following instructions. (30 minutes)

THE EMBASSY RECEPTION INSTRUCTIONS

Your group task is to form your own culture. At the end of this planning period, you are invited to an embassy reception, hosted by the Embassy Crowd, where the two cultures can meet and get acquainted.

A culture is the totality of the norms, standards, and behaviors that operate in a society. These attributes distinguish a society's members, individually and collectively, from other societies and cultures. Hofstede's four dimensions of national culture are examples of cultural differences.

A. Read Figure 12-3, which shows some of the characteristics of each dimension.

Power Distance Dimension	
Low Power Distance	**High Power Distance**
Inequality in society should be minimized.	Inequality is acceptable and everybody has his or her rightful place in the hierarchy.
Superiors consider subordinates to be "people like me."	Superiors consider subordinates to be a different kind of people.
Subordinates consider superiors to be "people like me."	Subordinates consider superiors to be different from them.
Superiors are accessible.	Superiors are inaccessible.
Everyone should have equal rights.	Power holders are entitled to privileges.
Those in power should try to look less powerful than they are.	Those in power should try to look as powerful as possible.
People at various power levels feel less threatened and more prepared to trust people.	Other people are a potential threat to one's power and can rarely be trusted.
Examples: Israel, Austria, Denmark, Ireland, Norway, Germany, United States.	*Examples*: Spain, France, Japan, Mexico, Singapore, Brazil, Indonesia

Uncertainty Avoidance Dimension	
Weak Uncertainty Avoidance	**Strong Uncertainty Avoidance**
The uncertainty inherent in life is more easily accepted and each day is taken as it comes.	The uncertainty inherent in life is felt as a continuous threat that must be fought.
Conflict and competition can be contained on the level of fair play and used constructively.	Conflict and competition can unleash aggression and should, therefore, be avoided.
More acceptance of dissent is present.	A strong need for consensus is evident.
Deviance is more likely to be tolerated.	Deviance is threatening so intolerance holds sway.
There is more willingness to take risks in life.	There is great concern with security.
There should be as few rules as possible.	There is a need for written rules and regulations.
Examples: Denmark, Canada, Norway, Singapore, Hong Kong, Australia, United States	*Examples*: Israel, Austria, Japan, Italy, Argentina, Peru, France, Belgium

Individualism Dimension	
Collectivist	**Individualist**
In society, people are born into extended families or clans who protect them in exchange for loyalty.	In society, everybody is supposed to take care of himself or herself and his or her immediate family.
"We" consciousness holds sway.	"I" consciousness holds sway.
Identity is based on the social system.	Identity is based on the individual.
The emphasis is on belonging to organizations; membership is the ideal.	The emphasis is on individual initiative and achievement; leadership is the ideal.
Belief is placed in group decisions.	Belief is placed in individual decisions.
Examples: Colombia, Pakistan, Taiwan, Peru, Singapore, Japan, Mexico, Greece, Hong Kong	*Examples*: Australia, Great Britain, Canada, The Netherlands, New Zealand, United States

Masculinity Dimension	
Feminine	**Masculine**
Quality of life is important.	Performance is what counts.
You work in order to live.	You live in order to work.
People and the environment are important.	Money and things are important.
Interdependence is the ideal.	Independence is the ideal.
One sympathizes with the unfortunate.	One admires the successful achiever.
Examples: Norway, Sweden, Denmark, Finland	*Examples*: Japan, Austria, United States

FIGURE 12-3   **Characteristics of Cultural Value Dimensions**
Source: Based on G. Hofstede, *Culture's Consequences* (Thousand Oaks, CA: Sage, 1980).

B. In the following chart, choose a cultural pattern by deciding whether you want your culture to be high or low on the first two dimensions and by deciding which end of the continuum you want on the individualist and masculinity dimensions. For the right-hand column, invent norms that will manifest the cultural value pattern you chose. Don't tell the other group which cultural value pattern you chose.

C. Decide which norms and customs your group can develop to operationalize your cultural value pattern. For example, how would persons from a high uncertainty avoidance and low masculinity culture behave at an embassy reception? What would their conversation be like? Gestures, food rituals and habits, language, gender relationships, status differential, and leadership are some of the many areas for which your group can develop norms. Your group's task for this period is to discuss this matter fully so that these norms become a part of you. You may wish to practice them with the use of role playing, or you may suggest additional supporting behaviors such as signs and symbols for use among yourselves.

Your Cultural Value Pattern	High or Low	Norms Your Group Chose
Power Distance		
Uncertainty Avoidance		
Individualism		
Masculinity		

STEP 3.   The embassy reception will take place; each group observes its cultural customs while interacting with the other culture. (20 minutes)

STEP 4.   The entire class discusses the following questions:
  a. What words would you use to describe the other's group culture?
  b. What was it like to interact with them? How did you feel when you were talking to them?
  c. What norms did you observe for the *other* culture? For the Embassy Crowd? For the Host Country Nationals?
  d. Which cultural value patterns do you think the other culture chose? Why? For the Embassy Crowd? For the Host Country Nationals?
  e. What were the norms of your own culture?
  f. Which cultural values did you choose?
  g. What can you learn from this simulation?

 FOLLOW-UP

Diversity can be broadly defined as differences with respect to ethnicity, race, gender, age, functional and educational backgrounds, lifestyle preferences, tenure with the organization, personality traits, and ways of thinking.[20] Therefore, diversity efforts are not necessarily exclusionary. In the past, there were clearly moral and legal reasons for managing diversity well. Today, however, progressive corporations also see diversity as a business issue. One reason lies in the *benefits of having diverse viewpoints*.

Ernest Drew, CEO of Hoechst Celanese, became an advocate of diversity when he attended a company conference in 1990. Hoechst's 125 top officers, mostly white males, were joined by about 50 lower-level women and minorities. To tackle the questions of how the corporate culture affected the business and what changes were needed to improve results, problem-solving groups were formed. Some groups were composed only of whites and males; other groups were heterogeneous in terms of race and gender. When the groups presented their findings, Drew became a believer in diversity. "It was so obvious that the diverse teams had the broader solutions," he recalls. "They had ideas I hadn't even thought of. For the first time, we realized that diversity is a strength as it relates to problem solving. Before, we just thought of diversity as the total number of minorities and women in the company, like affirmative action. Now we knew we needed diversity at every level of the company where decisions are made."[21]

A second business reason is that a diverse workforce has a *better understanding of the needs of diverse customers*. Women make more than 85 percent of total household purchasing decisions.[22] Avon, for example, has been very successful at understanding minority customers because of its diverse employees.

A former CEO of Avon, James Preston, had his own epiphany regarding diversity in the late 1970s when the company's first female vice president, Patricia Neighbors, asked him if she could open a meeting of regional sales managers.[23]

> *She walked in, went to the podium and began greeting the assembled men. "Hello, Tom, you've changed your hairstyle, haven't you?" "Charlie, that suit looks great on you." "Jack, you're losing weight, aren't you?" She paused, Preston says, to let the astounded silence reign for a moment, and then said, "How do you feel?" Another pause. "That's how two thousand female sales reps feel when you talk to them in such an unprofessional way."*

When women and minorities feel uncomfortable and blocked from advancement at work, they may simply leave. Therefore, a third reason why diversity is a business issue has to do with the *turnover costs of losing women and minorities to the competition* after investing in their early career development. For nonunion employees, the turnover costs related to rehiring and training replacements are estimated to be between 90 to 150 percent of annual salary.[24]

And finally, organizations with a reputation for managing diversity well have a *competitive advantage in attracting and retaining well-qualified employees*. There are books and business magazines that rate companies as to how well they treat minorities; these companies naturally become "preferred employers" for talented women and minorities.

Organizations that want to "maximize the benefits and minimize the drawbacks of diversity, in terms of workgroup cohesiveness, interpersonal conflict, turnover, and coherent action on major organizational goals, must create multicultural organizations."[25] The characteristics of a multicultural organization are:[26]

1. It actively seeks to capitalize on the advantages of its diversity, rather than attempting to stifle or ignore the diversity, and to minimize the barriers that can develop as a result of people having different backgrounds, attitudes, values, behavior styles, and concerns.
2. Organizational resources (key jobs, income, perquisites, access to information, etc.) are distributed equitably and are not determined or affected by cultural characteristics such as race and gender.
3. The ability to influence decisions and the way they are carried out is shared widely, not differentially by cultural characteristics.
4. Minority group members are fully integrated in the informal networks of the organization.
5. The organizational culture (assumptions about people and groups, take-it-for-granted norms, the way work gets done) is pluralistic in that it recognizes and appreciates diversity and all cultural groups respect and learn from each other. The culture acknowledges both the need

for "being the same" in some ways to work together effectively and the need for "being different" in some ways to recognize individual and group interests, concerns, and backgrounds.

6. Institutional policies, practices, and procedures are flexible and responsive to the needs of all employees.
7. There is an absence of prejudice and discrimination.
8. Majority and minority members are equally identified with the organizational goals.
9. There is a minimum of intergroup conflict among diverse groups.

Developing these characteristics poses great challenges for employees and managers; among these are learning from their experiences and viewing differences as a challenge and an opportunity rather than a set of problems.

Diversity in group membership is advantageous when the task requires creativity and judgment. However, there are also difficulties with heterogeneous groups. When group members come from different functional areas, conflict over the task is more likely because people from each area have their own perspective and approach to work. However, this conflict over how to accomplish the task usually results in higher performance. In contrast, when group members differ in terms of race and tenure, there tends to be more emotional, rather than task, conflict in the group. This is especially true with new groups that are working on nonroutine tasks. However, emotional conflicts tend to diminish over time as the groups learn to work together.[27]

Given the increased emphasis on both globalization and work teams (particularly cross-functional teams), employees are being asked to work more often and more closely with other employees, who are more and more likely to be different from them. Thus, the ability to work with diverse people is becoming more and more essential. Today technical competence is a necessary but insufficient condition for success. Effectiveness depends on an ability to develop good interpersonal relationships that are built on an acceptance and appreciation of differences, respect for the cultural beliefs of others, and a willingness to learn from people who are different.

There is a general consensus that women and minorities are slowly making progress. For example, in 1999 minority directors were on the boards of 60 percent of U.S. Fortune 1000 companies, almost double the number reported in 1990.[28] However, up until 1998, when Franklin Raines became the CEO of Fannie Mae, no African American, Asian American, or Hispanic had ever been CEO of a Fortune 500 company. Persons of color had led other types of organizations—military, government agencies, universities, and large nonprofits—but scaling the heights of business organizations has proved more difficult. The odds of a person of color holding an executive position in a Fortune 500 corporation is 33 to 1 compared to those for whites.[29]

Minorities sometimes find themselves limited to "racialized" jobs—Equal Employment Opportunity oversight, community relations, government affairs, and ethnic markets—that do not lead to senior executive positions. Although many corporations hire minorities with the ability to advance, very few of them have the internal systems to ensure that people of color can rise through the ranks. Instead, most high-ranking minorities are hired from other firms. Thomas and Gabarro say the problem is not so much that minorities run into a glass ceiling but that the problems occur much farther down in the hierarchy. They blame "squishy floors" and "revolving doors" for preventing people of color from making it to the upper-middle-management jobs.[30]

When organizations fail to provide women and minorities with equal opportunities or an environment in which they are appreciated for themselves, they often quit. A recent survey of minority executives found that 50 percent were likely to leave their companies for more challenging positions. "A chronic issue for senior minority executives is that they feel underutilized," according to a managing director at the Korn/Ferry job search firm.[31]

More proof of Big Business failure in the diversity arena can be found in the swelling ranks of minority and female entrepreneurs. Of the women who founded businesses during the past 10 years, 22 percent cited a corporate glass ceiling as one reason they became entrepreneurs.[32] The most powerful career barriers that women face are found in Figure 12-4.

Nevertheless, we can see progress. There is a small but growing number of women and minority executives, and more companies are framing diversity as a business issue. In 1999, women headed up three of General Motors' six vehicle divisions. "There's a saying: If you looked at GM

- Negative assumptions in executive ranks about women, their abilities, and their commitment to careers
- Perceptions that women don't fit with the corporate culture
- Lack of career planning and the range of job experiences commensurate with the future needs of the organization
- Lack of core opportunities for female employees who have management potential
- Assumption that women will not relocate for career advancement
- Failure to make managers accountable for advancing women
- Management reluctance to giving women line (revenue-generating) experience
- Absence of, or too limited, succession planning
- "Negative mentoring" and self-selection where women move into staff areas instead of line positions
- Lack of mentoring and exclusion from informal career networks, where men have typically learned the unwritten rules of success
- Appraisal and compensation systems that are not uniform for men and women
- Corporate systems designed prior to women's large-scale infusion into the workplace, such as benefits systems and productivity measures that don't take into account new policies such as flexible work arrangements
- Other forms of "cultural discouragement," like a work enviromnent that values long hours over actual performance or that offers limited support for work-family initiatives and limited commitment to diversity programs in general
- Discrimination and sexual harassment

FIGURE 12-4   **Barriers to Retaining and Advancing Women**
Source: From S. W. Wellington, *Advancing Women in Business: The Catalyst Guide* (San Francisco: Jossey-Bass, 1998): xxi–xxii. Reprinted with permission.

in the past, it was run by 12 white guys from Cleveland," says Ronald Zarrella, president for GM's North American operations. "In today's world, 12 white guys from Cleveland are not going to make a successful, globally diverse company."[33]

LEARNING POINTS

1. Culture provides us with ready-made solutions for basic human problems and a sense of identity, but it also limits our ability to see and sometimes appreciate alternative behaviors.
2. All cultures have both positive and negative aspects and are best understood as a series of trade-offs.
3. Ethnocentrism is the tendency to think one's own group or race is superior to other groups or races.
4. Everyone possesses a degree of ethnocentrism, but it must be curbed to work effectively with people from other groups or races.
5. Cultural dimensions that help us compare and contrast cultures are task versus relationship, individualism-collectivism, power distance, uncertainty avoidance, masculinity-femininity, and long-term versus short-term orientation.
6. Hofstede claims that American management techniques reflect American cultural values—low power distance, high individualism, low uncertainty avoidance, and above average masculinity. As such, they are not always applicable in other countries or with people from different subcultures within the United States.
7. Stereotyping is assigning identical characteristics to any member of a group regardless of his or her individual differences. The prejudice that accompanies stereotypes prevents us from judging individuals fairly on their own merit.

8. Minorities in societies characterized by discrimination are especially sensitive to discriminatory behavior in the organizations that employ them.

9. Three perceptual tendencies and their results affect tokens:

   a. High visibility leads to performance pressures on tokens.

   b. Contrast that exaggerates differences between two groups leads the dominant group to heighten its cultural boundaries, which isolates tokens.

   c. Assimilation by stereotyping results in role encapsulation for the tokens.

10. These consequences, which cause stress for tokens, can be avoided by increasing the number of the minority group within the organization so minorities are perceived as individuals rather than tokens.

11. Minority groups often form networks within larger organizations to share common interests and meet needs that the formal organizations may not fill.

12. Managing diversity well (a) allows minorities and eccentric people to feel comfortable and contribute fully at work, (b) permits organizations to benefit from diverse viewpoints, (c) makes it easier to serve a diverse group of customers, and (d) helps the organizations attract and retain high-quality minority employees.

 **FOR MANAGERS**

- Guidelines for dealing with people from different cultures:
  - Know and understand your own culture. (Why do we value certain things and behave in certain ways?)
  - Know the other culture.
  - Make an effort to understand why members of the other culture hold the values they do and behave as they do.
  - Look for strengths in the other culture rather than focus on weaknesses or differences.
  - Respect the other culture and bear in mind that it's the ability to create relationships and work through others that leads to effectiveness.
  - Recognize the degree to which you are ethnocentric and keep it in check.
  - Listen actively so that people from the other culture can guide you and so the organization will benefit from its diversity.
  - Use management techniques or intervention strategies that will be appropriate for the given culture or subculture.
- Multicultural groups can be the source of learning and creativity but only when groups can be open about their differences and use them to enhance understanding.
- Some diversity training has pitted groups against each other, resulting in less rather than more understanding. A divisive approach (e.g., blaming white males) only causes hard feelings and a backlash against minorities. Diversity training should emphasize an appreciation of differences, a focus on similarities, and the ways in which diversity can be a competitive advantage.
- Companies that understand the business value of a diverse workforce have learned the following lessons:[34]
  - Get the CEO's commitment.
  - Make diversity a business objective.
  - Define diversity widely so all employees understand that they bring some diversity to the table.
  - Adopt a plan for addressing the concerns of white males.
  - Scrutinize compensation and career tracking for fairness.
  - Identify high-potential employees so they are developed and considered for promotions.
  - Avoid diversity training that is divisive.
  - Celebrate differences.
  - Improve the supply of diverse workers. College internships, for example, are a means of locating and attracting more minorities.

PERSONAL APPLICATION ASSIGNMENT

Quelle verité que ces montagnes burnent, qui est mensonge au monde qui si tient au dela?
[What kind of a truth is this that is bounded by a chain of mountains and is falsehood to the people living on the other side?]

(Montaigne, Essa is II, XII, p. 34)

The topic of this assignment is to think back on a diversity experience that was significant for you. Choose an experience that intrigues you and that you want to learn more about.

A. *Concrete Experience*
   1. *Objectively* describe the experience (who, what, when, where, how information) (2 points)
   2. *Subjectively* describe your feelings, perceptions, and thoughts that occurred during (not after) the experience. What did others seem to be feeling? (2 points)

B. *Reflective Observation*
   1. Looking back at the experience, what were the perspectives of the key actors (including you)? (2 points)
   2. Why did the people involved (including you) behave as they did? (2 points)

C. *Abstract Conceptualization*
    1. Relate concepts or theories from the assigned readings or the lecture to the experience. Explain thoroughly how they help describe your experience. Please apply at least two concepts or theories and cite them correctly. (4 points)

D. *Active Experimentation*
    1. What did you learn about diversity from this experience? (1 point)
    2. What did you learn about yourself? (1 point)
    3. What action steps will you take to be more effective in the future? (2 points)

E. *Integration, Synthesis, and Writing*
    1. Did you integrate and synthesize the four sections? (1 point)
    2. Was the Personal Application Assignment well written and easy to understand? (1 point)
    3. Was it free of spelling and grammatical errors? (2 points)

ENDNOTES

[1] "Cultural Diversity in Today's Corporation," *Working Woman* (January 1991): 45.

[2] J. S. Wiggins, K. E. Renner, G. L. Clore, and R. J. Rose, *The Psychology of Personality* (Reading, MA: Addison-Wesley, 1971): 109.

[3] V. Barnouw in R. Webber, *Culture and Management* (Homewood, IL: Irwin, 1969): 69.

[4] G. Hofstede, *Culture's Consequences: International Differences in Work-Related Values* (Beverly Hills, CA: Sage, 1977, 1980, 1984): 25.

[5] R. Webber, *Culture and Management* (Homewood, IL: Irwin, 1969).

[6] The following section is based on the work of H. C. Triandis, R. Bontempo, M. J. Villareal, M. Asai, and N. Lucca, "Individualism and Collectivism: Cross-Cultural Perspectives on Self-Ingroup Relationships," *Journal of Personality and Social Psychology 54*, 2 (1988): 323–38; and H. C. Triandis, R. Brislin, and C. H. Hui, "Cross-Cultural Training Across the Individualism—Collectivism Divide," *International Journal of Intercultural Relations 12* (1988): 269–89.

[7] G. Hofstede, "Motivation, Leadership, and Organization: Do American Theories Apply Abroad?" *Organizational Dynamics 9* (1980): 42–62.

[8] G. Hofstede, "Cultural Constraints in Management Theory," *Academy of Management Executive 7* (1993): 81–94; G. Hofstede, and M. H. Bond, "The Confucian Connection: From Cultural Roots to Economic Growth," *Organizational Dynamics 16* (1988): 4–21.

[9] J. Osland, and A. Bird, "Beyond Sophisticated Stereotyping: Cultural Sensemaking in Context," *Academy of Management Executive 14*, no. 1, (2000): 65–77.

[10] E. Aronson, *The Social Animal* (San Francisco: W. H. Freeman, 1976): 175.

[11] G. M. McEvoy, "Cumulative Evidence of the Relationship between Employee Age and Job Performance," *Journal of Applied Psychology* (February 1989): 11–17.

[12] S. R. Rhodes, "Age-Related Differences in Work Attitudes and Behavior: A Review and Conceptual Analysis," *Psychological Bulletin* (March 1983): 328–67.

[13] Quoted in *The Oregonian* (Monday, February 22, 1999) C-2 from Billie Jean King's acceptance speech for the Arthur Ashe Award for Courage.

[14] R. Sharpe, "Losing Ground," *Wall Street Journal* (September 14, 1993) A-1, col. 6.

[15] "The Global Glass Ceiling: Ten Women Who Broke Through It," *Fortune*, October 12, 1998, *138*(7): 102–04; the Catalyst data were reported in "He Said, She Said: Women Executives and the Gender Gap," *Parade*, October 20, 1996, p. 20. Also see S. W. Wellington, *Women in Corporate Leadership: Progress and Prospects* (New York: Catalyst, 1996); and B. R. Ragins,

B. Townsend, and M. Mattis, "Gender Gap in the Executive Suite: CEOs and Female Executives Report on Breaking the Glass Ceiling," *Academy of Management Executive 12*, no. 1 (1998): 28–42 and the *Reader*.

[16] F. Friedlander, "Patterns of Individual and Organizational Learning," in S. Srivastva & Associates, *The Executive Mind* (San Francisco: Jossey-Bass, 1983): 192–220.

[17] L. D. Brown, *Managing Conflict at Organizational Interfaces* (Reading, MA: Addison-Wesley, 1983).

[18] R. M. Kanter, *Men and Women of the Corporation* (New York: Basic Books, 1977): 206–42.

[19] J. P. Lafargue, "A Survival Strategy-Kinship Networks," *American Journal of Nursing 80*, no. 9 (1980): 480–95; M. F. Neitlin, L. Ann, and R. E. Ratcliff, "New Princes for Old? The Large Corporation and Capitalist Class in Chile," *American Journal of Sociology 80* (1974): 87–123; and R. D. Alba, "Ethnic Networks and Tolerant Attitudes," *Public Opinion Quarterly 42*, no. 1 (1980): 1–16.

[20] R. R. Thomas, Jr., *Beyond Race and Gender* (New York: AMACOM, 1991).

[21] F. Rice, "How to Make Diversity Pay," *Fortune 130*, no. 3, August 8, 1994, p. 78.

[22] *Advancing Women in Business: The Catalyst Guide* (San Francisco: Jossey-Bass, 1998).

[23] Ibid., p. 14.

[24] Ibid., p. xix.

[25] T. H. Cox and S. Blake, "Managing Cultural Diversity: Implications for Organizational Competitiveness," *Academy of Management Executive 5* (3) (1991): 52.

[26] J. Merevitch and D. Reigle, *Toward a Multicultural Organization* (Cincinnati, OH: Proctor & Gamble, January 1979) and T. H. Cox, "The Multicultural Organization," *Academy of Management Executive* (May 1991): 34–47.

[27] L. Pelled, K. Eisenhardt, and K. Xin, "Exploring the Black Box: An Analysis of Work Group Diversity, Conflict, and Performance," *Administrative Science Quarterly 44*, no. 1 (1999): 1–28.

[28] *Wall Street Journal*, Tuesday, June 8, 1999, p. A-1.

[29] D. A. Thomas, and J. Gabarro, *Breaking Through: The Making of Minority Executives in Corporate America* (Boston: Harvard Business School Press, 1999). This book describes how companies can successfully promote diversity and how people of color can break through to senior management levels.

[30] Ibid.

[31] "Work Week," *Wall Street Journal*, April 13, 1999, p. A-1.

[32] P. Thomas, "Closing the Gender Gap," *Wall Street Journal*, May 24, 1999, p. R12.

[33] T. Y. Jones, "Gender Motors," *Forbes*, May 17, 1999, p. 50.

[34] F. Rice, "How to Make Diversity Pay," pp. 78–84 and *Advancing Women in Business: The Catalyst Guide.*

Part 3

▲▲▲

LEADERSHIP AND MANAGEMENT

Part 3 focuses on the knowledge and skills required of effective leaders and managers.

▲▲

Chapter 13

LEADERSHIP

OBJECTIVES By the end of this chapter, you should be able to:

A. Define leadership.

B. Describe what followers expect of leaders.

C. Differentiate between leadership and management.

D. Identify the traits related to leader success.

E. Define initiating structure and consideration behavior.

F. Explain the meaning of a contingency theory of leadership.

G. Distinguish among transformational, transactional, and charismatic leaders.

H. Explain servant leadership.

ARROGANCE: THE EXECUTIVE ACHILLE'S HEEL

What makes potential management superstars fail to live up to their advance billing or not make the most of their careers? Wayne D. Calloway, chairman and CEO of PepsiCo Inc. and one of the nation's most admired corporate leaders, thinks he has some answers—at least why would-be superstars fell short of their mark in his $17.8 billion organization based in Purchase, New York. PepsiCo recently conducted an internal study to determine why executives and managers failed, and if the company was at fault. The study focused on young recruits, a lot of them M.B.A.'s—all bright and full of potential.

"By failure, I don't mean skid row," says Mr. Calloway. "I'm talking about the young gifted manager who is capable of being a division president but somehow doesn't get there—tops out as a vice president or director. Nothing to be ashamed of, but not up to his or her potential."

The results surprised him. The three major reasons why bright young people failed had nothing to do with intelligence, or where they went to school, or even how well they knew their jobs. All three reasons for failure were traceable to one core area—flawed values.

"To be specific, the single biggest reason for failure at PepsiCo was arrogance. There's nothing wrong with confidence, but arrogance is something else. Arrogance is the illegitimate child of confidence and pride. Arrogance is the idea that not only can you never miss (shooting) a duck, but no one else can ever hit one," explains Mr. Calloway.

Arrogance is an insurmountable roadblock to success in a business where the "team" is what counts. The flip side of arrogance is teamwork—the ability to shine, to star, while working within the group, believes Mr. Calloway.

Lack of commitment was the second biggest reason why executives failed at PepsiCo. "I don't mean they're not willing to work long hours or make personal sacrifices. I mean an unwillingness to commit to a goal that's bigger than they are—to keep coming at a problem even after failing, until they finally come up with a solution," observes Mr. Calloway.

"The failed superstars at PepsiCo were not willing to commit themselves in the manner of Thomas Edison, who tried an experiment 128 different ways before finding success. Instead, our failed superstars gave up after one frustration and they never moved ahead. They somehow failed to really commit themselves to a bigger idea, a bigger notion. They eventually quit," recalls Mr. Calloway.

PepsiCo found the third biggest reason for failure had (and has) to do with another human value—[lack of] loyalty. "In these days of mixed allegiance, loyalty has gone the way of poodle skirts and bobby socks in terms of publicity. But not in reality. I don't mean an unwillingness to question authority. I mean an unwillingness to put a larger cause—like the company or team performance—above your own interests. If an executive doesn't have this concept of loyalty, what eventually starts to (creep) through is pettiness, constant complaints and excuses, cutting down coworkers, and, finally, acrobatics to cover his (or her) backside so he (or she) doesn't get blamed for mistakes. It all adds up to mediocre performance at best—destructive behavior at worst."

The flip side of failure is success, and it turns out that winners at PepsiCo demonstrate teamwork, commitment, and loyalty in pretty large doses. "Keep in mind, we're not talking about a 'go-along-to-get-along environment' but a success-driven atmosphere packed with some of the most aggressive businesspeople you'll ever meet," observes Mr. Calloway.

The PepsiCo CEO contends that truly successful businesses are never dominated by arrogant, dishonest types for long. "They may succeed for a short time or in a specific situation, but over (a long) time victory goes to people who work hard, are consistent, fair, open, and candid," believes Mr. Calloway.

Source: Adapted from an article by Brian S. Moskal appearing in *Industry Week*, June 3, 1991, p. 19.

PREMEETING PREPARATION

A. Read "Arrogance: The Executive Achille's Heel."

B. Think of four leaders whom you have had occasion to observe or read about. If you have not observed a leader in a work setting, choose leaders from clubs, teams, neighborhoods, and so on.

_____ Leader 1 (Initials)   _____ Leader 2

_____   _____

_____   _____

_____   _____

_____   _____

_____   _____

_____ Leader 3   _____ Leader 4

_____   _____

_____   _____

_____   _____

_____   _____

C. Now write down the ways these leaders behave differently from each other. Be specific. For example, if one leader strikes you as being a better communicator than another, don't stop with "M.G. communicates well; B.D. communicates poorly." Write down the specific behavior that is different. For example, "M.G. makes expectations clear; B.D. doesn't explain what she wants us to do."

D. Return to the list of behaviors or characteristics you generated for C. Rank these characteristics according to how important they are in terms of a leader's effectiveness. The most important characteristics should be number one, the second most important should be number two, and so on.

E. What are your own strengths as a leader?

F. How would you rate yourself on the characteristics you previously identified?

G. Is there anything you could improve that would make you a better leader?

H. If your instructor has assigned the Robbins Self-Assessment Library, use "What's My Leadership Style?"

 # TOPIC INTRODUCTION

Thumb through U.S. business magazines and you'll find a great deal of print devoted to describing corporate leaders. Some people think we tend to romanticize leadership and either give leaders more credit than they deserve or expect them to work miracles when their hands are fairly well tied.[1] However, there is also strong evidence that leaders do in fact make a notable difference in organizations,[2] particularly those undergoing crisis, growth, and change. Not only do companies with effective leaders report higher net profits, but in times of increased competitive pressures and widespread demands for change, good leadership is not just a competitive advantage but an essential survival factor. The increased demand for leadership skills is not limited to people in executive suites. Given the flattened hierarchies in companies that have terminated middle managers and the move toward empowerment, teams, and networks, companies are looking for leadership from people at all levels.

Leaders are "individuals (1) who establish direction for a group, (2) gain the group members' commitment, and (3) motivate them to achieve goals to move in that direction."[3] An important aspect of this definition is that leaders make others "want" to follow them voluntarily. Leadership is generally held to be in the eye of the beholder because there are no leaders without followers. Zaleznik once wrote, "Leadership is based on a compact that binds those who lead with those who follow into the same moral, intellectual, and emotional commitment."[4]

We develop a schema concerning leaders that determines whether or not we perceive someone as a leader.[5] The characteristics you listed in the premeeting preparation should give you a better idea about your own leadership schema because these are the factors you notice about leaders.

FOLLOWER EXPECTATIONS OF LEADERS

According to U.S. research managers, followers expect four characteristics of their leaders, in descending order of importance.[6]

1. Honesty (truthful, trustworthy, consistent in word and deed, has character, has convictions)
2. Forward-looking (sense of direction and concern for the future)
3. Inspiring (enthusiastic, energetic, positive about the future)
4. Competence (capable, productive, effective)

In combination, these characteristics determine a leader's credibility. When employees perceive management to have high credibility and a strong philosophy, employees are more likely to:[7]

- Be proud to tell others they are part of the organization
- Have a strong sense of team spirit
- See their own values as consistent with those of the organization
- Feel a sense of ownership about the organization
- Feel attached and committed to the organization

In contrast, those who do not perceive management to be credible work primarily for money, produce only when watched, bad-mouth the organization in private, and would consider leaving the organization in rough times. In other words, there is a positive payoff for leaders and management teams that work hard at building and preserving their credibility with subordinates.

Leadership is closely related to organizational ethics. In a study of managerial values, 92 percent reported that "the behavior of those in charge is the principle determinant of the 'ethical tone' of my firm." To make matters worse, one-third of these managers felt their bosses engaged in unethical behaviors and were less concerned about ethics than they were.[8]

Our schemas of what constitutes good leadership vary from one culture to another. In the United States people value charisma in their leaders; in West Germany, charisma is distrusted because it reminds people of Hitler. We find more participative leadership and shared governance in cultures with small power distance (e.g., Scandinavia). In contrast, cultures characterized by large power distance tend to have autocratic leaders (e.g., Russia).[9] A Russian study found that participative management techniques decreased rather than increased productivity.[10] Therefore, expatriate managers who work abroad with a participative style may find that subordinates in a high power distance culture are, at least initially, uncomfortable when the leader does not call all the shots. Asking for advice may be interpreted as incompetence or weakness in cultures in which leaders are supposed to be omnipotent experts.

Villages in French West Africa have a different tradition of leadership. Villages have a "palaver" tree where the entire village meets to discuss important issues. Representatives from the elders, the young men, and the women express their opinions and talk until a consensus opinion is reached. When working with people from other cultures or ethnic groups, it is very important to understand their accustomed leadership style and to adapt one's own style accordingly.

Leadership schemas change over time. For example, Latin Americans have historically preferred authoritarian leaders and centralized decision making,[11] but recent studies have found more evidence of participative leadership.[12] U.S. citizens now expect their leaders to provide or help create a vision that encompasses both environmental threats and opportunities and an appropriate response to situations. For example, some political pundits maintain that George Bush, Sr. lost the 1992 presidential election primarily because he did not grasp the importance to U.S. citizens of what he called "the vision thing."

MANAGERS VERSUS LEADERS

Managers are in danger of making a similar mistake if they do not understand that being a good manager and a good leader are not necessarily synonymous. Much has been written about the differences between managers and leaders. Whereas leaders establish a vision, managers do planning and budgeting. While leaders focus on imaginative ideas, managers focus on processes and systems. Leaders spend time and effort aligning people so that they understand and accept their vision and strategies, while managers focus on organizing and staffing. While leaders motivate and inspire others, managers focus on control and problem solving. As a result, leaders tend to produce change while managers tend to produce order, predictability, and the key results expected by stakeholders.[13]

Obviously both leadership and management are important. Leaders should not ignore the organization's core competencies (a Japanese concept that refers to well-developed operating capabilities) to focus solely on an abstract vision.[14] And managers should not get so caught up in pushing the organization along that they lose sight of the broader picture or overlook the importance of providing a vision that motivates people. In recent years, the following phrase caught our attention, "managers do things right and leaders do the right thing." For most of us, however, it makes more sense to aim for both—to develop ourselves as leaders who also strive to be good managers with a thorough understanding of organizational functions.

Effective leadership helps provide employees with a sense of pride and with superordinate goals and values that take priority over individual interests; good leadership also makes it easier for employees to adapt to change.[15]

THE EVOLUTION OF LEADERSHIP THEORY

Our conceptions of leadership and the theories we use to explain it have evolved over time. Although there are more than 7,000, books and articles on leadership, no one theory is universally accepted. The rest of the chapter presents the practical highlights of leadership research: (1) leader traits; (2) behavior styles; (3) contingency theory; (4) transformational and charismatic leadership; and (5) self-leaders.[16]

The first leadership studies focused on the question of why some people become leaders and others do not. Years ago common wisdom held that leaders were born, not made, so researchers began by looking at leader traits. This attempt to figure out what characteristics distinguished leaders from nonleaders yielded limited results. However, a recent study of successful business leaders found they shared the following traits: drive, honesty and integrity, leadership motivation, self-confidence, cognitive ability, knowledge of the business, creativity, and flexibility.[17] There are only two leader traits, intelligence and high energy, that are inherited, which means there is at least some truth to the statement that leaders are born. However, one's childhood experiences play a more important role than genes in determining leadership potential.[18] Furthermore, leaders can be developed, primarily through work experiences, challenging job assignments, role models, mentors, and training.[19] Opportunity, luck, and the motivation to lead also determine who will become leaders.

Once researchers gave up on the idea that leaders were born, they started observing differences in behavior between leaders and nonleaders. Much of the early research identified two principle dimensions of leader behavior—a concern for task/production and a concern for people—defined next.

1. *Initiating structure*—leader behavior that organizes and defines what group members should be doing to maximize output.
2. *Consideration*—leader behavior associated with creating mutual respect or trust and that focuses on a concern for group members' needs and desires.

Research programs (Ohio State studies, University of Michigan studies, the Managerial Grid) reported that leaders who were rated as high on both these dimensions were generally more likely to have high subordinate performance and satisfaction. The results, however, were not conclusive because these studies did not take situational factors into consideration. Not every situation requires leaders who employ a high degree of both initiating structure and consideration. For example, highly skilled employees who are self-motivating require neither of these behaviors on the part of a leader.[20]

Once again, researchers and practitioners came to the conclusion that there is no "one best way" to lead; it depends on the situation. Effective leaders analyze the factors pertaining to the situation, task, followers, and the organization, and then choose the appropriate style. This is why several leadership theories serve as good examples of contingency theory.

Contingency theories of management include various leadership styles. One continuum, which appears in Figure 13-1, ranges from one extreme at which the manager has total freedom to make decisions to the other extreme at which managers and employees make joint decisions. In Chapter

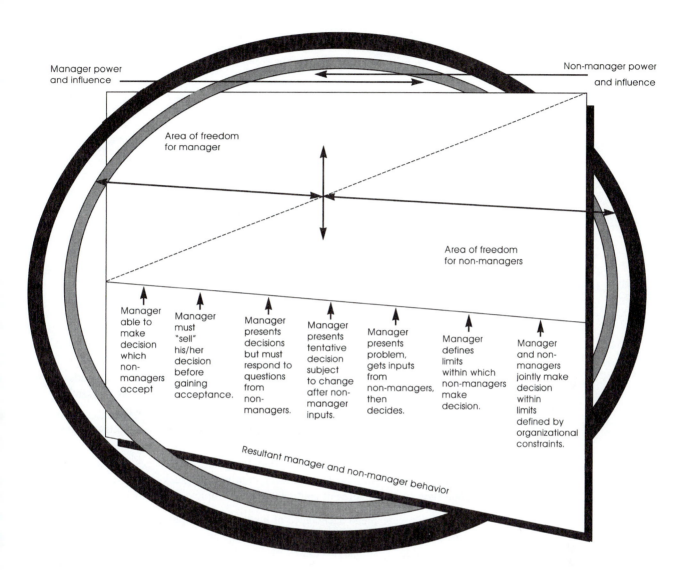

FIGURE 13-1   **Continuum of Manager-Nonmanager Behavior**
Source: Reprinted by permission of *Harvard Business Review*. An exhibit from "How to Choose a Leadership Pattern"
by Robert Tannenbaum and Warren H. Schmidt, (May–June 1973). Copyright ©1973 by the President and Fellows of
Harvard College; all rights reserved.

15, the Vroom model of leadership and decision making is another example of a contingency theory of leadership that includes an autocratic-consultative-participative continuum of leader styles.
Other theories go beyond decision-making behavior styles to include concepts such as initiating
structure and consideration behavior. For example, House's path-goal theory of leadership[21] (see
Figure 13-2) maintains that leaders motivate higher performance by helping subordinates attain
individual goals that are aligned with organizational goals. It is based upon expectancy theory
(effort → performance → outcome) and the effect leaders have on subordinate expectations.[22]
According to path-goal theory, leaders motivate employees when they (1) clarify the path that
will result in employee achievement, (2) provide the necessary guidance and support to get the job
done, (3) remove the obstacles that block the path to goal achievement, and (4) link rewards to goal
accomplishment. Leader behavior is acceptable if subordinates perceive it as a source of either immediate or future satisfaction. Depending on both *subordinate contingency factors* (locus of control, experience, perceived ability) and *environmental contingency factors* (task structure, formal
authority system, and work group), the leader employs one of the following four leadership styles,
which should result in employee performance and satisfaction.[23]

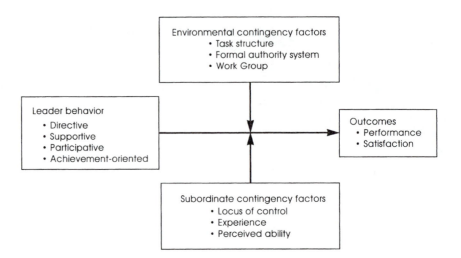

FIGURE 13-2   **The Path-Goal Theory**

Directive. The leader informs subordinates what is expected of them, sets performance standards, schedules activities, and provides specific guidance as to what should be done and how to do it. This is essentially the same as the "initiating structure" concept mentioned before.

Supportive. The leader is friendly and approachable and shows concern for the needs, status, and well-being of subordinates. He or she treats subordinates as equals. This is essentially the same as the "consideration" concept found in behavior theories of leadership.

Participative. The leader consults with subordinates, solicits their suggestions, and takes suggestions into consideration before making a decision.

Achievement oriented. The leader sets challenging goals, emphasizes excellence, expects subordinates to perform at their highest level, continuously seeks improvement in performance, and shows a high degree of confidence in the employee's abilities.

Although there is widespread acceptance of a contingency approach to leadership, no one theory contains all the possible contingencies. Some of the proven connections between specific situational factors and leadership styles follow.

- Subordinates benefit from a directive style when they are working with an unstructured or stressful task. When they know how to do a routine job, further instruction not only wastes time but may be perceived as insulting.
- When subordinates perform boring, repetitive, unsatisfying tasks, leaders should consider restructuring the job (see Chapter 4, Motivation) so it would meet more of the employees' needs. If that proves impossible, leaders should use a supportive style that allows employees to meet their social needs on the job.
- In highly formalized organizations where everything is standardized, there is little need for a task-oriented leader. Cohesive work groups with norms that heavily influence employees make both consideration and initiating structure leader behavior redundant.
- Subordinates who do not want to take responsibility at work prefer autocratic rather than participative leaders.
- Leaders behave differently with different followers, a basic tenet of the leader-member exchange model.[24] Highly motivated, skilled, and trustworthy subordinates, as well as subordinates who are similar to the leader in terms of personality, age, or gender, are sometimes given preferential treatment and constitute an in-group. The leader's favoritism consists of giving them more attention, resources, and recognition[25] and inflating their performance ratings when they underperform.[26] As one would expect, research has generally shown that in-group members perform better and are more satisfied at work;[27] they are also less likely to resign.[28] The increased mentoring in-group members receive also helps them be more successful in their

career.[29] Although it is very natural for leaders to treat their in-group members differently, this practice usually results in jealousy and resentment among out-group members and reduced cooperation and communication between the two groups.

One contingency factor that has generated a good deal of controversy in recent years is gender. The similarities between the way women and men lead outweigh the differences.[30] Once given a leadership role and legitimized by the organization, women and men do not act very differently. Women, however, prefer a more democratic leadership style than men.[31] Women encourage participation, share power and information, and attempt to enhance the self-worth of their followers. They use inclusion and rely on their charisma, expertise, contact, and interpersonal skills to influence others. Men are more likely to rely on the formal authority of their position to influence others and to use a command-and-control style. These differences are usually attributed to early socialization practices in which girls are expected to demonstrate care and consideration, whereas boys are expected to compete and perform. However, when women find themselves in situations that require a more autocratic style (e.g., working in a male-dominated or hypermasculine organization such as the military or the police), they tend to adapt their style accordingly.[32]

The following exercise allows us to look at the relationship between emergent leader behavior and the particular contingencies in a given situation.

PROCEDURE FOR GROUP MEETING: THE PERFECT SQUARE

The purpose of this exercise is to provide an opportunity to observe different types of leadership and followership. (Time allotted: 80–90 minutes)

STEP 1.   Form a circle with 8 to 18 people in a large area of empty space where you can spread out without running into chairs or walls.

STEP 2.   Ask for a volunteer(s) to be an observer. If your group is small, one observer will do. If your group has 18 people, you can have up to three observers. The observers should withdraw from the circle. The observer instructions are found on page 294. Please read them carefully.

STEP 3.   The members of the circle should blindfold themselves. If you wear glasses, place them in your pocket or give them to an observer to hold.

STEP 4.   The instructor (or student facilitator) will read you the instructions for the exercise found on page 299. The blindfolded group has 20 minutes to complete the assigned task. (25 minutes)

STEP 5.   Individual Reflection. Please answer the following questions without talking in the next 10 minutes. (10 minutes)
   a.   What different types of leadership emerged in this exercise? In your opinion, who were the leaders and why? What leader behaviors did they exhibit?
   b.   What occurred in the group to help you solve the problem?
   c.   What occurred in the group that hindered you from solving the problem or from solving it quickly?
   d.   What did you learn about leadership from this exercise?
   e.   What did you learn about yourself as a leader in this exercise?

STEP 6.   Group Discussion. Discuss these questions with your group. Ask the observers what they observed. Choose a representative to report to the entire class a summary of questions 1-4 steps. (20–30 minutes)

STEP 7. Plenary Debriefing Session. (20 minutes)

a. Have an observer from each group briefly and objectively describe what happened when his or her group did the blindfolded exercise. Next, the group representative presents his or her report.

b. Can you see any relationships between this exercise and the real world you experience at work or in other organizational settings?

c. What are the important contingencies in this particular situation? What type of leadership works best in a situation such as this? What leader behaviors are needed? What's the difference between a leader and a facilitator?

d. There are no leaders without followers. In this exercise, what were the characteristics of a good follower?

e. What did you learn about yourself as a leader in this exercise?

f. If you were to repeat this exercise, what would you do differently to be a better leader?

Observer Instructions

Please do not talk, laugh, or make any noises at all during the exercise so you do not disturb the group. Do keep an eye out for their safety; move any items that could trip them, and warn them if they are approaching the edge of a cliff. Otherwise, do not talk to them or to the other observers.

Please answer the following questions based on your observations.

1. Look for leadership behavior in the group. Who emerged as leaders and what exactly did they do to become leaders?
2. Please observe and describe the group's communication patterns and nonverbal language.
3. How did the group make decisions?
4. Be prepared to share these observations in your group discussion period.
5. Be prepared to give a very brief description of your group's strategy for resolving this problem and its degree of success during the plenary debriefing session.

FOLLOW-UP

In recent years, attention has shifted somewhat from contingency theories of leadership to *transformational* and *charismatic* leadership. Transformational leaders are value-driven change agents who make followers more conscious of the importance and value of task outcomes. They provide followers with a vision and motivate them to go beyond self-interest for the good of the organization. Given the difficult challenges currently facing business, the need for leaders who can transform organizations is understandable. In several studies, researchers have listened to effective transformational leaders describe how they lead others. Bennis and Nanus found that highly effective and charismatic leaders manage four areas: attention, meaning, trust, and self.[33] They manage attention by being highly committed to a compelling vision or outcome. They manage meaning by making ideas seem real and tangible for others, by means of both words and symbols. They manage trust by being reliable and congruent so that people know what they stand for. And, finally, they manage self by knowing and using their skills effectively, learning from mistakes, and focusing on success rather than failure. Kouzes and Posner asked leaders to describe their "personal best" leadership experience, a time when they accomplished something extraordinary in their organization.[34] From these critical incidents, they identified five leadership practices.

1. *Challenging the process* (questioning the status quo, seeking new opportunities to improve and grow, taking risks)
2. *Inspiring a shared vision* (envision an uplifting and ennobling future)
3. *Enabling others to act* (fostering collaboration and empowerment)
4. *Modeling the way* (setting a good example and planning small wins)
5. *Encouraging the heart* (recognizing individual contributions and celebrating team accomplishments)

Transformational leaders have been contrasted with transactional leaders, who get subordinates to perform using promises and rewards for good performance and using threats and discipline for poor performance. Transactional leaders are less effective than transformational leaders in making major organizational changes.[35]

Although charismatic leaders share some behaviors with transformational leaders, the former are seen as extraordinary or heroic leaders. Charismatic leaders have special relationships with their followers and elicit high levels of performance, loyalty, sacrifice, and enthusiasm. They develop a vision to which they are strongly committed that touches the emotions of their followers. Charismatic leaders take risks and act in unconventional ways. Such leaders are very self-confident and good at communicating.[36] Herb Kelleher, CEO of Southwest Airlines, and Mary Kay Ash, CEO of Mary Kay Cosmetics, are both examples of charismatic leaders.

There are two types of charismatic leaders. *Ethical charismatic leaders* use power to serve others, align their vision with their followers' needs and aspirations, accept and learn from criticism, encourage followers to think independently, work to develop followers into leaders, and rely on internal moral standards. In contrast, *unethical charismatic leaders* are motivated by personalized power, pursue their own vision and goals, censure critical or opposing views, encourage blind obedience, dependency, and submission in their followers, and lack an internal moral compass.[37]

An opposing view to charismatic leaders as an answer to the challenges of today's business world is the concept of "superleadership."[38] Sims and his colleagues contend that it is time to move beyond the notion of leaders as heroes to leaders as hero-makers who empower subordinates and teach them to be self-leaders.

We find the same normative trend in the argument that leaders should be stewards who choose service over self-interest.[39] In doing so, they are willing to be accountable for the well-being of the larger organization by operating to serve rather than control those around them. Servant leadership is rooted in spirituality, which is a growing trend in the United States. Shell encourages servant leadership among its employees and defines a servant leader as one who[40]

- recognizes that, as an individual, one does not have all the answers.
- is able to demonstrate a sense of humility and vulnerability.

- advances his or her own transformation, the personal transformation of others, and the transformation of the company.
- builds the capability of the company and the people in it.

Looking for strong leaders to "save us" localizes the responsibility, power, ownership, and privilege at the top of the organization. Instead, organizations should move from patriarchy to partnership. Thus, the organizational vision is not simply created and passed down from the top; each employee is responsible for articulating a vision for his or her own area of responsibility.

The concept of a leader as servant or coach is a far cry from the arrogance that tripped up the PepsiCo fast-trackers described in the opening vignette. M.B.A.'s are often accused of arrogance, a trait that produces little except resentment. It is a characteristic that we associate less and less with effective leadership and good work relationships.

Theories about leadership have evolved from the original emphasis on traits to behavior styles theory and situational theories, to fairly recent research on transformational and charismatic leadership, self-leadership, and leaders as stewards. This evolution reflects both the progress that has been made in understanding a complex concept and our changing expectations and conceptions about leaders.

LEARNING POINTS

1. Although Americans tend to romanticize leadership, there is evidence that leaders do make a notable difference in organizations, particularly organizations that are undergoing crisis, growth, and change.
2. Leaders are individuals who (a) establish direction for a group, (b) gain group members' commitment, and (c) motivate them to achieve goals to move in that direction.
3. Followers expect their leaders to be honest, competent, forward-looking, and inspiring.
4. Our schemas of what constitutes good leadership vary from one culture to another and from one era to another.
5. Not all managers are leaders. Leaders tend to produce change while managers tend to produce order, predictability, and the key results expected by stakeholders.
6. Successful business leaders possess the following traits: drive, honesty and integrity, leadership motivation, self-confidence, cognitive ability, knowledge of the business, creativity, and flexibility.
7. Although intelligence and high energy are inherited leader traits, it is definitely possible to develop and train people to become leaders.
8. Leadership styles are differentiated by leader behavior, such as initiating structure or consideration behavior, and the way the leader makes decisions (e.g., the autocratic-delegative continuum).
9. The leadership styles found in House's path-goal theory of leadership are directive, supportive, participative, and achievement oriented. The effectiveness of the style depends on both employee and environmental contingency factors.
10. Effective leaders analyze the factors pertaining to the situation, task, followers, and the organization, and then choose the appropriate leadership style.
11. According to the leader-member exchange model, leaders give preferential treatment to an in-group that is, therefore, more satisfied and more successful. However, the leader's favoritism results in less communication and cooperation between the in-group and out-group.
12. Other than preferring a more participative decision-making style, the managerial style of female managers does not differ significantly from male managers.

13. Transformational leaders are value-driven change agents who make followers more conscious of the importance and value of task outcomes. They provide followers with a vision and motivate them to go beyond self-interest for the good of the organization.

14. According to Kouzes and Posner, effective leaders (a) challenge the process; (b) inspire a shared vision; (c) enable others to act; (d) model the way; and (e) encourage the heart.

15. Transactional leaders exchange rewards for performance.

16. Charismatic leaders develop a special relationship with their followers that includes high levels of performance, loyalty, sacrifice, and enthusiasm. They are adept at communicating an inspiring vision.

17. Instead of relying upon hero-leaders, superleadership focuses on empowerment and turning employees into self-leaders.

18. Servant leaders are stewards who are responsible for serving, developing, and transforming the organization and its people.

 **FOR MANAGERS**

- Think of followers as volunteers who contribute their efforts, not because they are paid, but because their needs are met in the process. This prevents leaders from taking their followers for granted.
- Leaders need to have an in-depth and up-to-date understanding of what makes both their followers (including ones from diverse backgrounds) and their organization tick.
- Many initially successful leaders let power go to their heads. A measure of humility and the ability to accept negative feedback and admit mistakes can prevent this common occurrence.
- Consistency, honesty, and fairness all contribute to a leader's respect and credibility. When followers perceive that they are being manipulated by a leader or that the leader is motivated by self-interest rather than the good of the organization, it may be impossible for the leader to regain his or her credibility.
- Leaders should articulate a clear vision that appeals to followers, express confidence in their followers' capacity to achieve the vision, consistently serve as a good example, treat employees fairly and avoid favoritism, and celebrate successes and accomplishments.[41]
- Leaders cannot control what happens in their environment, but they can influence how it is seen. One of the symbolic roles of leadership is to frame meaning for followers, helping them to see the world the way their leaders do.[42]
- The leadership function is shared in many effective groups. Leaders rise to the occasion but return to follower status once their contribution is made. Such groups do not require a leader so much as a facilitator (rotating or fixed) who helps the group stay on track and allows people to be heard.
- Following are lessons from Korean parables of leadership.[43]
  a. Listen to the unheard—the hearts of followers, their uncommunicated feelings, unexpressed pains, and unspoken complaints—rather than listening only to superficial words of followers.
  b. Humble rulers with deep-reaching inner strength who bring well-being to their followers are more effective than vain rulers.
  c. A leader's commitment and willingness to work alongside his or her followers is a strong determinant of success.
  d. The wise leader earns the devotion of followers by placing them in positions that fully realize their potential and secures harmony among them by giving all of them credit for their distinctive achievements.

PERSONAL APPLICATION ASSIGNMENT

The topic of this assignment is to think back on a leadership experience that was significant for you. Choose an experience that intrigues you and that you want to learn more about.

A. *Concrete Experience*

   1. *Objectively* describe the experience (who, what, when, where, how information) (2 points)

   2. *Subjectively* describe your feelings, perceptions, and thoughts that occurred during (not after) the experience. What did others seem to be feeling? (2 points)

B. *Reflective Observation*

   1. Looking back at the experience, what were the perspectives of the key actors (including you)? (2 points)

   2. Why did the people involved (including you) behave as they did? (2 points)

C. *Abstract Conceptualization*

   1. Relate concepts or theories from the assigned readings or the lecture to the experience. Explain thoroughly how they help describe your experience. Please apply at least two concepts or theories and cite them correctly. (4 points)

D. *Active Experimentation*

   1. What did you learn about leadership from this experience? (1 point)

   2. What did you learn about yourself? (1 point)

   3. What action steps will you take to be more effective in the future? (2 points)

E. *Integration, Synthesis, and Writing*
  1. Did you integrate and synthesize the four sections? (1 point)
  2. Was the personal application assignment well written and easy to understand? (1 point)
  3. Was it free of spelling and grammatical errors? (2 points)

Facilitator Instructions for the Perfect Square
(For the Facilitator Only)

General Procedure. The groups should for a circle in a large empty area away from a wall or sidewalk they could use as a guide. Pass out the blindfolds. Ask for the number of volunteers your instructor has set and have them stand outside the circle. When the others are blindfolded and cannot see, read them the instructions below and pass out the rope. Do not let them see the rope beforehand—they shouldn't know how long it is. The last person to receive the rope should be the quietest person—take the slack (leftover rope) and lay it on the ground behind the last person so he or she has to search for the end. This is a test to see whether the group listens to quiet people. Identify the quietest person and give the first end of the rope to the person on his or her side and hand out the rope in that direction around the circle so you end with the quiet person. Don't tell the group there is leftover rope. Watch their group process as they work, but don't intervene unless someone is in danger of falling or hurting themselves. Don't talk at all during the exercise except to read them the instructions and give them a 5-minute warning. Note what time they start; when 15 minutes have passed, tell them they have 5 minutes left. When the 20 minutes are up, have them take off their blindfolds and answer individually the questions in Step 5. If they finish earlier, ask if they are satisfied with their square. If so, let them take off their blindfolds. Collect the blindfolds and the rope while they work on Step 5.

  1. Read the participants these instructions:
Please form a circle. Who would like to observe this exercise? Everyone else should put on a blindfold so you cannot see. I'll give you the rest of the instructions once everyone is blindfolded.

Your task is to form a perfect square utilizing all the rope that I am passing out. Here are the rules:
    1. Use all the rope so that your square is taut, with no slack.
    2. You must keep both your hands on the rope at all times.
    3. You have 20 minutes to form a perfect square.

I can repeat these rules if you like, but after that I cannot answer any question. Shall I repeat the rules?
  2. Notification of 5-minute warning (after 15 minutes have passed)
  3. Call time when 20 minutes are up and refer them to Step 5 on page 293.

ENDNOTES

[1] J. R. Meindl and S. B. Ehrlich, "The Romance of Leadership and the Evaluation of Organizational Performance," *Academy of Management Journal 30* (1987): 91–109; J. Pfeffer, "The Ambiguity of Leadership," *Academy of Management Review* (January 1977): 104–11; and A. B. Thomas, "Does Leadership Make a Difference to Organizational Performance?" *Administrative Science Quarterly* (September 1988): 388–400. Pfeffer's position is that leaders have limited power within their organizations and even less control over external factors. When something occurs within an organization, we attribute the cause to the leader regardless of his or her actual contribution.

[2] S. Motowidlo, "Leadership and Leadership Processes," in *Handbook of Industrial Organizational Psychology*, 2nd ed., ed. M. D. Dunnette (Palo Alto, CA: Consulting Psychologists Press, 1992).

[3] Adapted from J. Conger, *Learning to Lead* (San Francisco: Jossey-Bass, 1992): 18–19.

[4] A. Zaleznik, "The Leadership Gap," *Academy of Management Executive 4*, no. 1 (1990): 12.

[5] J. G. Hunt, *Leadership: A New Synthesis* (London: Sage, 1991).

[6] B. Z. Posner, and W. H. Schmidt, "Values and the American Manager: An Update Updated," *California Management Review* (Spring 1992): 80–94; and J. M. Kouzes, and B. Z. Posner, *The Leadership Challenge: How to Get Extraordinary Things Done in Organizations* (San Francisco: Jossey-Bass, 1995).

[7] Ibid., pp. 26–27.

[8] B. Z. Posner, and W. H. Schmidt, "Values and the American Manager: An Update Updated."

[9] G. Hofstede, "Motivation, Leadership, and Organization: Do American Theories Apply Abroad?" *Organizational Dynamics 9* (1980): 42–62.

[10] D. H. B. Welsh, F. Luthans, and S. M. Sommer, "Managing Russian Factory Workers: The Impact of U.S.-Based Behavioral and Participative Techniques," *Academy of Management Journal 36*, no. 1 (1993): 58–80.

[11] F. Quezada and J. E. Boyce, "Latin America," in *Comparative Management*, ed. R. Nath (Cambridge, MA: Ballinger, 1988): 247–69.

[12] J. S. Osland, L. Hunter, and M. M. Snyder, "A Comparative Study of Managerial Styles in Nicaraguan and Costa Rican

Female Executives," *International Studies of Management and Organization 28*, no. 2, (1998): 54–73; E. Kras, *Modernizing Mexican Management Style: With Insights for U.S. Companies Working in Mexico* (Las Cruces, NM: Editts, 1994).

[13] J. P. Kotter, *A Force for Change: How Leadership Differs from Management* (New York: Free Press, 1990).

[14] L. R. Sayles, "Doing Things Right: A New Imperative for Middle Mangers," *Organizational Dynamics* (Spring 1993): 5–14.

[15] A. Zeleznik, "The Leadership Gap."

[16] See G. Yukl's book, *Leadership in Organizations* (Upper Saddle River, NJ: Prentice-Hall, 1994) for a comprehensive, reader-friendly treatise geared for both academics and practitioners. C. Stiver's *Gender Images in Public Administration* (London: Sage, 1993) looks at leadership theory from a feminist perspective.

[17] S. A. Kirkpatrick and E. A. Locke, "Leadership: Do Traits Matter?" *Academy of Management Executive 5(2)* (1991): 48–60.

[18] Conger, *Learning to Lead*, pp. 22–24.

[19] J. Kotter, *The Leadership Factor* (New York: Free Press, 1988) details best practices of companies that create talented management teams.

[20] J. P. Howell, D. E. Bowen, P. W. Dorfman, S. Kerr, and P. M. Podsakoff, "Substitutes for Leadership: Effective Alternatives to Ineffective Leadership," *Organizational Dynamics* (Summer 1990): 21–38.

[21] R. J. House, "A Path-Goal Theory of Leader Effectiveness," *Administrative Science Quarterly* (September 1971): 321–38.

[22] See "Motivation: A Diagnostic Approach" by Nadler and Lawler, *Reader*, for an explanation of this theory.

[23] Adapted from R. J. House and T. R. Mitchell, "Path-Goal Theory of Leadership," *Journal of Contemporary Business* (Autumn 1974): 83.

[24] R. C. Liden and G. Graen, "Generalizability of the Vertical Dyad Linkage Model of Leadership" *Academy of Management Journal 23* (1980): 451–65.

[25] G. B. Graen, and M. Wakabayashi, "Cross-Cultural Leadership-Making: Bridging American and Japanese Diversity for Team Advantage," in H. C. Triandis, M. D. Dunnette, and L. M. Hough, eds., *Handbook of Industrial and Organizational Psychology* 2nd ed., vol. 4, (Palo Alto, CA: Consulting Psychologists Press, 1994): 415–66.

[26] N. T. Duarte, J. R. Goodson, and N. R. Klich, "How Do I Like Thee? Let Me Appraise the Ways," *Journal of Organizational Behavior 14* (1993): 239–49.

[27] R. J. Deluga, and J. T. Perry, "The Relationship of Subordinate Upward Influencing Behavior, Satisfaction and Perceived Superior Effectiveness with Leader-Member Exchanges," *Journal of Occupational Psychology 64* (1991): 239–52.

[28] G. R. Ferris, "Role of Leadership in the Employee Withdrawal Process: A Constructive Replication," *Journal of Applied Psychology 70* (1985): 777–81.

[29] T. A. Scandura, and C. A. Schriesheim, "Leader-Member Exchange and Supervisor Career Mentoring as Complementary Constructs in Leadership Research," *Academy of Management Journal 37* (1994): 1588–1602.

[30] G. N. Powell, *Women and Men in Management* (Thousand Oaks, CA: Sage, 1993).

[31] A. H. Eagley, and S. J. Karau, "Gender and the Emergence of Leaders: A Meta-Analysis," *Journal of personality and Social Psychology 61* (1991): 685–710; A. H. Eagley, M. G. Makhijani, and B. G. Klonsky, "Gender and the Evaluation of Leaders: A Meta-Analysis," *Psychological Bulletin 108* (1992): 3–22.

[32] Melamed, T. and N. Bosionelos, "Gender Differences in the Personality Features of British Managers," *Psychological Reports 72* (1992): 979–86.

[33] W. Bennis and B. Nanus, *Leaders* (New York: Harper & Row, 1985).

[34] Kouzes and Posner, *The Leadership Challenge*, p. 14.

[35] N. Tichy, and D. O. Ulrich, "The Leadership Challenge—A Call for the Transformational Leader," *Sloan Management Review* (Fall 1984): 59–68; B. M. Bass, "Does the Transactional-Transformational Leadership Paradigm Transcend Organizational and National Boundaries?" *The American Psychologist 52*, no. 2 (1997): 130–40.

[36] J. Conger and R. N. Kanungo, *Charismatic Leadership* (San Francisco: Jossey-Bass, 1988); and in a chapter in the same book by B. Bass, "Evolving Perspectives on Charismatic Leadership," pp. 40–77.

[37] J. Howell, "Two Faces of Charisma: Socialized and Personalized Leadership in Organizations," in J. Conger and R. Kanungo, eds., *Charismatic Leadership* (San Francisco: Jossey-Bass, 1988): 213–36 and J. Conger, "The Dark Side of Leadership," *Organizational Dynamics* (Autumn 1990): 44–55.

[38] C. C. Manz and H. P. Sims, "Superleadership: Beyond the Myth of Heroic Leadership," *Organizational Dynamics 19* (1991): 18–35.

[39] P. Block, *Stewardship: Choosing Service Over Self-Interest* (San Francisco: Berrett-Koehler, 1993). The founder of servant leadership is a Quaker, Robert Greenleaf, who wrote the original essay in the 1970s that sparked this movement. R. K. Greenleaf, *Servant Leadership: A Journey into the Nature of Legitimate Power and Greatness* (New York: Paulist Press, 1991).

[40] W. B. Brenneman, J. B. Keys, and R. M. Fulmer, "Learning Across a Living Company: The Shell Companies' Experience," *Organizational Dynamics 27*, no. 2 (1998): 61–71.

[41] Yukl, *Leadership in Organizations*.

[42] G. T. Fairhurst, and R. T. Sarr, *The Art of Framing: Managing the Language of Leadership* (San Francisco: Jossey-Bass, 1996). This book provides explicit advice on framing and communicating with employees.

[43] W. C. Kim and R. A. Mauborgne: "Parables of Leadership," *Harvard Business Review* (July–August 1992): 123–28.

Chapter 14

▲▲▲

ORGANIZATIONAL CULTURE

OBJECTIVES By the end of this chapter, you should be able to:

A. Define organizational culture and explain its function.

B. Explain how it evolves and is transmitted.

C. Describe the characteristics of a strong culture.

D. Explain the relationship between strong cultures and high performance.

E. Describe how leaders can manage culture.

F. Identify the four stages in the organizational life cycle.

SOUTHWEST:BACK TO THE FUNDAMENTALS

Linking human spirit and personal performance to training and corporate vision is the key to Southwest Airlines' success in the aviation industry. Now ranked No. 5 in size among all global carriers, Southwest has a unique recipe for personal and business success in a highly competitive industry.

It all begins with the Fundamentals, which are emphasized in every course offered at the University for People. The airline's corporate university trains 25,000 people per year.

FUNDAMENTAL 1: HIRE FOR ATTITUDE; TRAIN FOR SKILL

Employees must have a sense of humor and a desire to have fun at Southwest Airlines. The company deliberately looks for applicants with a positive attitude who will promote fun in the workplace and have the desire to "color outside the lines."

FUNDAMENTAL 2: DO IT BETTER, FASTER, CHEAPER

Cost control is a personal responsibility for employees at Southwest and is incorporated into all training programs. Employees know that lower operating costs means lower fares for customers, which is a hallmark of the airline's success.

FUNDAMENTAL 3: DELIVER POSITIVELY OUTRAGEOUS CUSTOMER SERVICE (POS) TO BOTH INTERNAL AND EXTERNAL CUSTOMERS

The customer comes second at Southwest. The Southwest philosophy? Put your employees first and they will take care of the customers. Taking care of company employees, according to CEO Herb Kelleher, automatically produces better care of the customers.

FUNDAMENTAL 4: WALK A MILE IN SOMEONE ELSE'S SHOES

Southwest employees are encouraged to spend some time learning other jobs within the company. The goal of such cross-training is to promote a better understanding of overall operations. How does the cross-training program work? While the program is not mandatory, and there is no incentive for taking part, employees do volunteer. For example, a pilot works with ramp agents for a full day; a reservationist works in the University for People; a customer service agent helps the skycaps. And Herb Kelleher frequently passes out peanuts and serves drinks on flights. He even helps the baggage handlers load and unload on holidays. The important thing to remember about this type of philosophy: It must come from the top.

FUNDAMENTAL 5: TAKE ACCOUNTABILITY AND OWNERSHIP

Hiring for attitude and training for skill places greater emphasis on personal accountability and teaches employees to think as if they own the company. A great value is placed on taking initiative, thinking for yourself, even if that means going against something in the policy manual. For instance, employees have been known to take stranded passengers back to their own homes in emergencies.

FUNDAMENTAL 6: CELEBRATE AND LET YOUR HAIR DOWN

Keeping employees motivated is a key concern for Southwest. Chili cook-offs, lavish Halloween productions, and Christmas parties in July are all tools for motivating people. Participation in such social exercises shows employees to look outside their immediate responsibilities, see the bigger picture, and look for different ways to do the job better. The reason? In study after study it has been shown that when people have fun on the job, their productivity and performance improve.

FUNDAMENTAL 7: CELEBRATE YOUR MISTAKES AS WELL AS YOUR TRIUMPHS

Southwest's philosophy is that humans make mistakes. We learn from our mistakes. Turning failures into personal growth is part of celebrating mistakes, a philosophy that encourages trying new ideas without the fear of repercussions.

FUNDAMENTAL 8: KEEP THE CORPORATE CULTURE ALIVE AND WELL

A unique element of Southwest's success is the result of the firm's culture committee headed up by Executive Vice President of Customers and Corporate Secretary Colleen Barrett. Members of the committee visit regularly at stations all across the country, infusing the corporate culture, reiterating the company's history, and motivating employees to maintain the spirit that made the airline great.

Source: Anne Bruce, "Southwest: Back to the FUNdamentals." Reprinted with permission. *HRFOCUS* (March 1997): 11.

PREMEETING PREPARATION

A. Read "Southwest: Back to the FUNdamentals."

B. Fill out the accompanying Organizational Culture Questionnaire for an organization to which you belong(ed).

C. Read the Topic Introduction and follow-up section.

D. Read the Ecoquest case, Part I, and prepare your individual analysis.

E. If your instructor has assigned the Robbins Self-Assessment Library, use "What's the Right Organizational Culture for Me?"

ORGANIZATIONAL CULTURE QUESTIONNAIRE

For each of the seven organizational culture dimensions described, place an (a) above the number that indicates your assessment of the organization's **actual** *position on that dimension and an (i) above the number that indicates your choice of where the organization should* **ideally** *be on this dimension.*

1. **Conformity**. The feeling that there are many externally imposed constraints in the organization; the degree to which members feel that there are many rules, procedures, policies, and practices to which they have to conform rather than being able to do their work as they see fit.

| Conformity is very characteristic of this organization. | 1 2 3 4 5 6 7 8 9 10 | Conformity is not characteristic of this organization. |

2. **Responsibility**. Members of the organization are given personal responsibility to achieve their part of the organization's goals; the degree to which members feel that they can make decisions and solve problems without checking with superiors each step of the way.

| No responsibility is given in the organization. | 1 2 3 4 5 6 7 8 9 10 | There is a great emphasis on personal responsibility in the organization. |

3. **Standards**. The emphasis the organization places on quality performance and outstanding production, including the degree to which the member feels the organization is setting challenging goals for itself and communicating these goal commitments to members.

| Standards are very low or nonexistent in the organization. | 1 2 3 4 5 6 7 8 9 10 | High, challenging standards are set in the organization. |

4. **Rewards**. The degree to which members feel that they are being recognized and rewarded for good work rather than being ignored, criticized, or punished when something goes wrong.

| Members are ignored, punished, or criticized. | 1 2 3 4 5 6 7 8 9 10 | Members are recognized and rewarded positively. |

5. **Organizational clarity**. The feeling among members that things are well organized and that goals are clearly defined rather than being disorderly, confused, or chaotic.

| The organization is disorderly, confused, and chaotic. | 1 2 3 4 5 6 7 8 9 10 | The organization is well organized with clearly defined goals. |

6. **Warmth and support**. The feeling that friendliness is a valued norm in the organization, that members trust one another and offer support to one another. The feeling that good relationships prevail in the work environment.

| There is no warmth and support in the organization. | 1 2 3 4 5 6 7 8 9 10 | Warmth and support are very characteristic of the organization. |

7. **Leadership**. The willingness of organizational members to accept leadership and direction from qualified others. As needs for leadership arise, members feel free to take leadership roles and are rewarded for successful leadership. Leadership is based on expertise. The organization is not dominated by, or dependent on, one or two individuals.

Leadership is not rewarded; members are dominated or dependent on hierarchical leaders; leadership attempts by others are resisted.

1 2 3 4 5 6 7 8 9 10

Shaded leadership based on expertise is accepted and rewarded.

8. What are the dominant values of this organization?

9. What are some of the behavioral norms of the organization that an outsider or a newcomer would quickly notice?

10. How do the leaders of the organization reinforce these values and norms?

11. How are newcomers socialized in this organization?

12. Does this culture help or hinder the organization in terms of performance?

13. What do you want to learn about organizational culture and socialization?

14. What are the significant learning points from the readings?

THE ECOQUEST CASE, PART I

Ecoquest is a Memphis consulting firm specializing in environmental analyses used by business-es and developers. Because the firm helps clients comply with environmental laws, its work has to be very reliable. If mistakes are made, both the firm and its clients could be sued. The company was founded two years ago by two women and a man with various backgrounds in environmental science and engineering. They had become friends while employed at a large firm in Atlanta with clients all over the Southeast. Fed up with the poor management and red tape at their former firm, they became convinced that they would do better on their own. A year after the founders launched Ecoquest, another environmental engineer bought into the company, making a total of four principals.

Due to the principals' reputation for giving clients what they want, Ecoquest quickly gained a respectable share of the market and no longer has to worry about bringing in enough business to survive. The firm has added on employees over time and currently employs 21 staff. The four principals work directly with clients and also supervise the work of 12 environmental experts and technicians, who form project teams. Three support staff are responsible for administrative work and the final preparation of client reports. Two part-time bookkeepers keep track of the firm's finances. Most of the staff are idealistic and very pleased to be working in the environmental field. What they like best about the company are its flexible work hours and knowledgeable, team-oriented colleagues. Given a tight labor market, the principals are concerned about both attracting and retaining good staff.

Preparing the analyses for clients involves a good deal of teamwork. The office becomes very hectic around deadlines because the work of several people must be pulled together and compiled into flawless reports. Each project is supervised by one of the principals. Given the liability concerns in the field, a second principal always reviews each report before it goes out the door to make sure there are no errors.

Ecoquest is housed on the first floor of a small office building on the fringe of downtown Memphis. Its quarters are cramped and utilitarian. In some offices, reports are stacked in formidable piles on the floor. One of the principals shares her office with two other employees. The CEO's office is slightly more elegant than the others but still fairly small. The lobby has one modest chair in close proximity to the receptionist's desk. Although the principals have offices with windows, the rest of the employees work in cubicles located in the center of the office. Employees have all the equipment they need, and the computer system and laboratory are state of the art. The only art work in the office are posters with environmental themes. Employee cubicle decor varies widely from family pictures to red chile pepper lights. The bulletin board by the coffeemaker is overflowing with announcements of training courses, outdoor recreational events, and cartoons poking fun at environmentalists. Casually dressed employees walk around quickly as if they are on deadline, but they take the time to tease each other as they go. The office is known for bantering and practical jokes.

When they planned the company, the principals wanted to create a firm that provided quality service to customers in a fun, participative workplace. They wanted their employees, all well-educated professionals, to feel empowered—something that was lacking in the large firm they came from. They also wanted to make more money, which has become a reality for the principals. At present, however, the firm is experiencing growing pains. They were not planning to grow so quickly, if at all, but it seemed foolish to turn down business. In addition to the outgrown office space, employees are starting to complain about unclear policies, lack of input into decisions, and not knowing whom to go to with certain requests. (Actually, the more savvy employees have figured out which principal is likely to say yes to which request.) It takes the principals longer to make decisions than employees think it should. Employees receive year-end bonuses based on a joint decision by the principals, but there is no formal performance evaluation process. The major problem facing Ecoquest, however, is the unexpected illness of its CEO, Chel (pronounced like "shell") Morrison.

Chel, the majority owner of the firm, is a dynamic environmental engineer in her late forties. She is extremely good with clients and goes all out to provide them with the service they want.

Some say she goes too far and asks for too many sacrifices on the part of both employees and the firm's bottom line to satisfy clients. For example, when legitimate extra expenses are involved in a project, Chel refuses to charge clients more than the estimated cost. Chel is popular with the staff. She wants them to enjoy their work, and she and the other principals are generous with benefits. Her major flaw is lack of delegation, which has turned into a vicious circle. Chel's excuse is that her employees do not have the experience or skills that she does, which is partly true. As a result, she works 80 to 100 hours a week and has no time to develop the employees. Last month, Chel was diagnosed with a serious autoimmune deficiency disease that is usually related to stress.

Chel's illness has thrown the company into turmoil. Someone else has to take over the CEO position because Chel's doctors do not think she will be able to return to work any time soon, if ever. The other three principals talked the succession issue over but could not agree which of them should be the CEO. All of them are interested in the position. Since the discussion looked as if it might turn into a divisive argument, the principals suggested that their two outside board members should make the decision with Chel's guidance. There may well be some hard feelings no matter who is chosen. However, the three principals have agreed to accept whatever decision is made and support the new CEO. They refuse, however, to consider bringing in an outsider to be CEO. Chel and the two outside board members have opted to hire a small business consulting firm (you) to help them select Chel's successor. Their goal is to choose a CEO who will contribute to the firm's continued success. The profiles of the candidates, the three principals, follow.

Mike Lewis

Mike is an environmental engineer in his early fifties. He is very knowledgeable and has a good reputation in his field. Mike bought into the firm a year later than the other principals because he was working overseas at the time. He is an exacting boss who is very detail oriented. He expects a lot of himself as well as others. Unlike the other principals who want as little structure and bureaucracy as possible, Mike likes to set up policies and track figures. Mike has often argued with Chel about overemphasizing client service at the expense of making a profit. He caused a ruckus in the office by distributing a ranked list of employees from the most to the least profitable. This was perceived as unfair by employees who did more administrative work or who worked on long-term projects that appeared less profitable than short-term projects in his rating system. Those at the bottom of the list were embarrassed or somewhat demoralized. Nevertheless, employees respect Mike and his expertise.

Anita Sanchez

Anita, a woman in her mid-forties, has a Ph.D. in environmental biology. She is good at developing employees, working on teams, and building a sense of community. Anita was the one who insisted on company outings, such as the annual "in-tents" camping trip. She has also been encouraging the other principals to create a mentoring program for employees. She and Chel have been good friends for 15 years. Since the firm's inception, they have worked together so closely in getting new business that it is difficult to know whether Anita is capable of bringing in business on her own. Anita is, however, a very hard worker. She has more people skills than financial skills. In the past, she has taken less interest in the financial side of the business, and the board does not know whether that is due to a greater preoccupation with projects or an inability to master that area. Recently Anita has been scuffling with Mike over his ranking system. She is afraid employees will start to cut corners on quality just to look good on paper and get a higher bonus.

Kent Chang

Kent, in his early forties, became disenchanted with his previous career as a tax lawyer. After going back to school to study environmental science, he now specializes in interpreting government environmental regulations for clients. Kent seems to have difficulty setting priorities and prefers to work on one project at a time. He is a great prankster and is well liked by the staff. Kent is also popular with clients and good at making contacts. Like Chel, he is not as used to delegating as are Mike and Anita. Kent has been opposed to growing the firm and had an upper limit of 12 employees in mind. To him, more employees mean more headaches and red tape. One of his goals in starting the company was to have some control over his lifestyle and work environment. Kent sees unlimited growth as a threat to these goals.

YOUR TASK

The concerns of succession and continuity are complex problems, and many factors are involved in successfully dealing with such problems. Please analyze this case by answering the following questions. Be prepared to back up your opinions in class when you will work with a team of consultants to prepare your final report for Ecoquest.

1. How would you describe the organizational culture of Ecoquest? List the firm's values and the evidence that supports your claim.

2. What do you see as the major strengths and weaknesses of the three candidates?

3. Which candidate would you recommend as the new CEO of Ecoquest?

4. What is your rationale for this choice? What kind of leadership style does the company need now?

5. How would you rank the other candidates?

6. A change of leadership is a good opportunity to make sure that all aspects of the organization are in alignment. Without this "fit," new leaders might fail or current problems may not be addressed. What organizational changes should be made to ensure that your recommended CEO candidate is successful?

7. What should the new CEO do to maintain or change Ecoquest's organizational culture?

TOPIC INTRODUCTION

Organizational culture has become an exceedingly popular topic in the last 20 years. The publicity given to successful companies with strong cultures has had several results.[1] Many companies have put more effort into developing strong cultures while others have paid more attention to maintaining a high-performance culture. Managers have also come to realize that cultural values sometimes impede the organizational changes they would like to make. Thus, we have seen an increased focus on the leader's role in creating, maintaining, and changing organizational culture.[2]

Schein defines organizational culture as:

Organizational culture is the pattern of basic assumptions that a given group has invented, discovered, or developed in learning to cope with its problems of external adaptation and internal integration, and that have worked well enough to be considered valid, and, therefore, to be taught to new members as the correct way to perceive, think, and feel in relation to those problems.[3]

In simple terms, organizational culture is the pattern of shared values and beliefs that lead to certain norms of behavior,[4] in other words, "the way we do things around here." The sources of an organizational culture are the values of the founders or strong leaders of the organization and the solutions to problems that other members have learned over time. Industry, environment, and national culture also influence the culture of an organization.

In a large organization, there is usually a dominant culture accompanied by various subcultures.[5] Subcultures usually share the dominant culture's core values as well as other values that characterize their own department, geographical unit, and so on. For example, an accounting department may value observing rules to a greater degree than do salespeople because rules make the accountants' job easier. See Schein's article. "Three Cultures of Management," in the *Reader* for a description of the occupational subcultures of executives, engineers, and operators and their impact on an organization's ability to learn and change.

A discussion of organizational culture raises once again the issue of "fit," both internally and externally. Two important aspects of culture are external adaptation and internal integration of new members. One of the functions of a culture is to ensure that its members fit the culture. This is very common with strong cultures, which have the following characteristics.[6] People in the organization can easily identify the dominant values. The selection processes target people who are likely to fit into the culture and find it satisfying. Socialization and training convey to newcomers the "ropes" they need to learn. Employees who do not fit the culture or produce in accordance with its values are sometimes fired. People within the company are rewarded for acting in accordance with the dominant values of the organization. By their behavior, leaders and managers send clear, consistent signals about desired values and norms. Managers measure and control what is important to the culture. Examples of organizations with strong cultures are McDonald's, Intel, Walt Disney, and General Electric.

The distinction between strong and weak cultures is that strong cultures are "thicker." They have core values and beliefs that are intensely held, more widely shared and more ordered. By this we mean that cultural members know which values are more important relative to other values. For example, the value of customer service trumps (is given priority over) a value like informality.[7]

Because of the intensity and consensus of shared values in a strong culture, the individual-culture fit is important. Employees are more likely to succeed is an organization that has values similar to their own. During the hiring process, both cadidates and the company should attempt to determine whether this fit is present. However, there are other important aspects of fit. Organizational effectiveness is more likely to occur when the following aspects are in alignment:

1. The *people* in the organization, their abilities, and motives.
2. The *organization's tasks* and the kinds of behavior needed to accomplish those tasks most effectively.

3. The *organization's external environment* and the demands it makes on the organization for creativity, flexibility, quality, and so on.
4. The *strategy* that dictates how an organization attempts to position itself in relation to its competitors.
5. The *organization's culture* as determined by the leadership styles of management and the organization's structure and values.

Stated simply, the goal of organization design is to match people with tasks that inspire them and best utilize their abilities and to design tasks and a strategy that can cope with environmental demands and opportunities. The organizational culture should reinforce these efforts. Culture serves as the glue that holds the organization together. Culture also provides members with a sense of identity, generates commitment to something larger than self-interest, and helps people make sense of what occurs in the organization and the environment. Furthermore, strong organizational cultures serve the same control function as the cultural rules we learn in childhood. When groups of people share the same behavioral norms, there is less need for external controls and close supervision.

Although organizational cultures result in control, alignment, and motivation, these contributions do not yield high performance unless there is a fit with the environment. This brings us to the second aspect of culture, external adaptation. Lack of external adaptation or fit was the impetus for some of the widespread restructuring that U.S. industry has undergone in recent years. In addition to outdated strategies, structures, technology, and employee skills, many companies had cultures that did not fit a rapidly changing global economy.

Because so many excellent companies had strong organizational cultures, there seemed to be a relationship between strong culture and high performance. Research has found that companies with strong cultures perform better than companies with weak cultures.[8] One study supports this assumption when leadership is also present. Kotter and Keskett found that corporate culture can in fact have a significant impact on a firm's long-term economic performance. Firms with strong cultures that focused on all the key constituencies (customers, stockholder, and employees) and that had leadership from managers at all levels outperformed other firms without these characteristics. "Over an 11-year period, the former increased revenues by an average of 682 percent versus 166 percent for the latter, expanded their work forces by 282 percent versus 36 percent, grew their stock prices by 901 percent versus 74 percent, and improved their net incomes by 756 percent versus 1 percent."[9] They predict that corporate culture will probably be an even more important factor in determining company success or failure in the next decade. Cultures, even strong ones, that are not adaptive or change oriented may not survive. Thus, the culture-environment fit warrants a good deal of attention.

In addition to high performance under certain conditions, the advantages of a strong culture include the following: clear sense of purpose, commitment and loyalty, pride in working for the organization, and values that serve as standards of reference for decision making. Strong corporate cultures are also difficult to copy, so they can constitute a competitive advantage, which is increasingly important to success.[10] However, strong cultures also have the disadvantages of resistance to change and conformity.[11] Strong cultures exert more pressure for conformity than weak cultures, which may decrease the tolerance for individual differences unless valuing diversity is one of the culture's values. Strong cultures run the risk of becoming obsolete if the company does not value learning and staying attuned to its environment and customers.

Many companies with strong cultures that were successful in the past failed to adapt as the environment changed. Their cultures became arrogant, inwardly focused, politicized, and bureaucratic. Managerial self-interest took precedence over concern for customers, stockholders, and employees when effective leadership was lacking. Previous success often led the companies to resist innovation and continue with strategies and policies that were no longer viable.[12] Employees who wanted to change such companies often became discouraged and quit because they did not fit the culture: Thus, the situation perpetuated itself.

Both AT&T and the banking industry had strong cultures, but when their external environments changed, these stable and inbred cultures became a threat to their survival. The survivors learned to play a different game and developed more competitive and innovative organizational cultures. IBM has always had a strong culture, complete with an extensive language all its own. Historically, IBM culture was seen as an advantage. However, its culture was criticized in the early 1990s for slowness and arrogance, which prevented IBM from adapting radiply to environment changes. Therefore, the company broke with tradition and hired an outsider as CEO, Lou Gerstner. He had the following reaction to IBM culture, "I have never seen a company that is so introspective, caught up in its own underwear, so preoccupied with internal processes .... People in this company tell me it's easier doing business with people outside the company than inside. I would call that an indictment.[13]" Fortunately, Gerstner and others have been successful in making the culture more cooperative and customer oriented.

If a culture is self-sealing and refuses to consider new assumptions, its very strength can become a weakness.

> *Many outstanding organizations have followed ... paths of deadly momentum—time-bomb trajectories of attitudes, policies, and events that lead to falling sales, plummeting profits, even bankruptcy.... Productive attention to detail, for instance, turns into an obsession with minutia; rewarding innovation escalates into gratuitous invention; and measured growth becomes unbridled expansion.[14]*

Organizations need people who question cultural values and suggest different assumptions. For this reason, it comes as no surprise that one study found that companies with well-organized workplaces and strong participative cultures performed better than did other firms.[15] Presumably, the value placed on participation would allow for the expression of different opinions and assumptions about the external environment. Another alternative is to hire managers from the outside who bring in fresh perspectives and are more likely to question cultural assumptions. One of the dilemmas in organizations is finding the right degree of stability and flexibility. Managers need to understand and respect past history while simultaneously ensuring that organizational learning and adaptation are taking place.

Leaders can affect an organizational culture, but they cannot unilaterally determine what that culture should be.[16] Culture emerges from a consensus held by people in a social system. Cultures take time to develop and are slow to change because cultural values are internalized and provide us with part of our identity. Thus, managers should not see cultural change as a quick fix. Nevertheless, it is possible to instill certain values and reward certain behaviors. Consistency is essential in managing culture. Too many companies have an official set of cultural values that does not represent the real values that are acted out in the organization. Employees quickly spot the hypocrisy when managers do not "walk the talk."

TRANSMITTING CULTURE

Culture is transmitted through various mechanisms: socialization, stories, symbols, jargon, rituals and ceremonies, and statements of principles.[17]

Socialization

Socialization is the systematic process by which organizations bring new members into their cultures. Socialization is the process of becoming a member of a group, learning the ropes, and being taught how to communicate and interact to get things done.

Strong cultures use a socialization process that consists of the following seven steps.[18]

1. **Careful selection of entry-level candidates** Candidates who do not fit the culture are encouraged to deselect themselves and apply elsewhere.
2. **Humility-inducing experiences that cause newcomers to question prior behavior, beliefs, and values** Boot camp performs this function in the military; businesses may put new employees through extensive and demanding training programs that leave them with no time

to do anything else. Other companies use upending experiences to induce the humility that allows newcomers to learn with an open mind. In one company, newly graduated engineers are given a problem to solve that does not conform to the theories learned in school. When they inevitably fail, they realize they still have more to learn at the company. The humility and self-examination triggered by experiences such as these make it more likely that newcomers will buy into the company's values.

3. **In-the-trenches training that leads to mastery of one of the business's core disciplines** Employees work their way up the ranks, and promotion depends on a proven track record.

4. **Meticulous attention given to rewards and control systems** The company's critical success factors (the limited number of factors that are central to a firm's performance) and corporate values are monitored. They are included in the performance appraisal system, and employees are rewarded and promoted for contributing to the success factors and behaving in accordance with cultural values.

5. **Careful adherence to the firm's core values** Managers ensure that their own decisions and actions are consistent with stated values. As a result, employees are more likely to make personal sacrifices for the organization.

6. **Reinforcing folklore** The company stories and legends told to newcomers always reinforce the values of the corporate culture. For example, there is a Procter & Gamble story about one of its best brand managers who was fired for exaggerating a product's features. The moral of this story is that making ethical claims is more important than making money.[19]

7. **Consistent role models** Cultural heroes and "winners" consistently exhibit the traits valued by the organization's culture. For example, the Morgan and Stanley employees identified as having high potential exhibit the energy, aggressiveness, and team play demanded by their culture.

The consistency and careful thought that characterize this socialization process make it possible to effectively transmit and maintain a strong organizational culture.

Stories

The importance of stories as reinforcing folklore was mentioned above previously. All organizations have stories that are repeated to newcomers. They often explain what's important in the culture and legitimize how the organization does things. To transmit its culture to newcomers, Hewlett-Packard has several stories that are told in various settings—training classes, management meetings, retirement parties, and newsletters. Some of the most common HP stories describe:[20]

- *How Bill and Dave (as Hewlett and Packard are commonly addressed) started the company with $538 in the garage behind Dave's rented house. Bill rented a spare room there.*
- *How they called their first instrument the 200A so that people would not know they were just starting out.*
- *How Bill Hewlett challenged HP labs to build a scientific calculator he could put in his shirt pocket, which led to the introduction of the world's first small scientific calculator and one of HP's most important business segments.*

Symbols

Symbols also transmit culture and convey meaning. Material objects such as the type of building and office decor often tell us something about a company's culture—whether it values, for example, informality, prestige, or frugality. The pink Cadillacs awarded to successful saleswomen symbolize Mary Kay Cosmetics' cultural values of determination and achievement. Company slogans also communicate the company's values.

Jargon

Organizations sometimes develop their own language or slang. Employees use a shorthand form of communication that identifies them as members of the culture. Microsoft employees use the term *dogfood* to indicate that a new product is being used and tested by Microsoft employees before it is sold to the public.

> *Apparently the term comes from that old advertising industry joke about the agency that just couldn't seem to come up with a successful campaign for a dogfood company. Punchline: "The dogs just didn't like the dogfood," meaning, no amount of effort can sell a lousy product. At Microsoft they like to say, "We eat our own dogfood."[21]*

Rituals and Ceremonies

These usually repetitive activities celebrate the values of a corporate culture. The Friday beer busts common in high-tech companies such as HP symbolize the informality and cross-fertilization valued in these cultures.

Statements of Principles

Many organizations create and distribute a list of their values and basic assumptions. It is not uncommon to see such principles displayed on office walls. Sometimes they are included in a firm's code of ethics. The vignette for this chapter is an example of Southwest Airlines' key values.

Maintaining a corporate culture that employees value is an important managerial task. Apple had a cultlike culture that recruited highly talented, creative people who were attracted to the "cause" of changing the world of computers. In the early days the culture was people centered; when the company's performance slumped, this focus changed. Apple downsized in what was perceived as a callous manner and cut many of the activities that had helped build and maintain its culture, such as the bagel-and-cheese get-togethers and project completion parties, to save money. Because of these and other management actions, some Apple employees assumed they were no longer valued and resigned.[22]

MERGERS

When companies are considering a merger or acquisition, they generally do careful analyses of the strategic and financial aspects of the deal. However, an audit of both organizational cultures is equally important because mergers often fail due to cultural clashes. The company doing the acquiring often dominates the smaller company, assuming it must know best because it is taking over. However, there have been many instances in which the imposed culture of the buyer does not fit the acquired company and results in serious problems. These problems become even more complex in international mergers that also involve cultural differences. Some experts recommend that companies considering a merger first work together on joint ventures to see whether their cultures are compatible.[23]

MANAGING ORGANIZATIONAL CULTURE

Changing an organizational culture is not a quick process because of all the fits within the organization. Often the first step in changing a culture involves a change to a more participative management style. This allows people to openly discuss the culture and its impact.

How do leaders create and transmit organizational culture? There are primary and secondary mechanisms that managers can use to create or modify culture.[24] The *primary mechanisms* follow.

1. **What leaders pay attention to, measure, and control on a regular basis.** If managers talk about the importance of continuous improvement (TQM) but show no interest in the improvements suggested by employee groups, employees correctly discern that quality is not a value of this organizational culture. In contrast, if managers monitor and evaluate quality improvements, this sends out the opposite message and reinforces the value of producing quality

products. Similarly, when the CEO visits the R&D lab the first thing every morning, this is a clear signal that innovation is a value of the organizational culture.

2. **The reactions of leaders to critical incidents and organizational crises.** What happens, for example, when the company faces a downturn in business or a cash flow problem? Does upper management immediately start firing lower-level employees or does everyone make sacrifices (e.g., four-day workweeks or across-the-board pay cuts for everyone) and start looking for creative solutions? The response shows employees what the company values.

3. **Observed criteria by which leaders allocate scarce resources.** How does the organization create its budgets? What gets funded? What are acceptable levels of financial risk? Budget decisions and the budget process itself reflect cultural values and beliefs. For example, a company that utilizes bottom-up budgets may do so because it values entrepreneurial managers. A top-down process may reflect a paternalistic culture that does not value participation.

4. **Deliberate role modeling, teaching, and coaching by leaders.** One international manager was a master at recreating the organizational culture in new overseas offices. Since he was the only person in the office with in-depth knowledge of how the organization functioned, he had new employees come to his office to review their work during the first month. He used this opportunity to correct their mistakes, teach them the finer points of their jobs, answer their questions, hear their suggestions, and explain how their work fit into the broader picture of the local office and the international organization. He told them stories about the organization's heroes and success stories from other countries. At the same time, he developed a personal relationship with them and gained their loyalty and commitment. As a result, they felt comfortable going to him in the future with their concerns and ideas, even after the office had grown much larger and he no longer supervised their work directly. By doing this, he transmitted to them the values of the international headquarters and created a strong culture.

5. **Criteria for allocating rewards and status.** We can analyze what type of behavior is rewarded to determine what the organization values. Are whistle-blowers who point out unethical practices congratulated and promoted, or are they shunned or even fired? Those who enact the key values of the organizational culture should be rewarded and respected. Otherwise, we cannot tell who are the cultural heroes whom we should try to emulate.

6. **Criteria for recruitment, selection, promotion, retirement, and excommunication.** The question of who fits and does not fit the organizational culture and who deserves to play a key role figures either consciously or unconsciously in these personnel decisions. Companies that are concerned with creating a strong culture devote time and energy to hiring and promoting only those people whose values are compatible with those of the company. It is very difficult, if not impossible and unethical, to change people's personalities. Service companies in particular find it easier to hire people who already have a service ethic. There is, however, a danger in trying to obtain a perfect person-culture fit with every employee. Cultural deviants often keep organizations "honest" by questioning the culture's dominant assumptions and behaviors. Too much conformity is not healthy, so organizations are wise to pay attention to deviant views. Excommunication takes the form of either firing or being given a less important job (perhaps kicked upstairs) and isolated.

Managers can also influence other aspects of the organization, called *secondary mechanisms*, to build or change a culture.

1. **The way in which the organization is structured and designed** (decision making, coordination, reporting, structure).
2. **Systems and procedures** (performance appraisal, information, control, decision support systems, etc.).
3. **Rites and rituals.**
4. **The design of physical space, facades, and buildings.**
5. **Anecdotes, legends, myths, and parables about people and events.**
6. **Formal statements of philosophy, creeds, and values.**

Managers can utilize many of these same mechanisms to change an organizational culture. It is not impossible to change a culture, but it is a difficult task and one that is not accomplished overnight. Some experts claim it is a four- to ten-year process. Successful cultural changes usually involve effective leaders with an outsider's perspective who take advantage of a propitious moment or crisis to mobilize support for a cultural change. Leaders create a new vision that they communicate with optimism and enthusiasm.[25] However, it is also important to "honor the past" and maintain some aspects of a culture for the sake of continuity.[26] According to Trice and Beyer, all cultural change is partial, and we cannot expect to completely eradicate a previous culture.[27]

We usually associate cultural change with a strong, visionary leader. However, cultural changes have also occurred from the bottom-up, when management has planted the seed and allowed workers the autonomy to make the necessary changes. Ford's focus on quality and customer service is an example of a bottom-up change effort.[28] Other change efforts, such as Corning Glass Works' switch to a total quality culture, have used widespread education and training programs as the catalyst.[29]

British Land Rover is both a positive and negative example of changing an organizational culture. At one point, the company was famous for bad management with high costs, poor labor relations, and low-quality products. Therefore, the company decided to transform themselves into a learning organization, via extensive workforce training, a total quality leadership program, and quality action teams. To encourage employees to learn, the company reimbursed them for any kind of educational course, whether or not it related directly to work. The company succeeded in changing its culture as well as its performance. The emphasis on continuous improvement and relying on employee groups to find better ways to work resulted in savings of 16 million pounds, increased production, and a 25 percent decrease in the time required to produce a vehicle. By changing the culture, British Land Rover decreased its costs while improving quality and labor relations. The company also began to attract executives who wanted to work in an innovative environment. This was a success story until BMW bought the company and imposed its own organizational culture. BMW changed the focus from participation to control, recentralizing training and limiting the power of employee teams. Once again, the company is characterized by adversarial labor relations.[30]

PROCEDURE FOR GROUP MEETING: THE ECOQUEST CASE

STEP 1. The class should divide up into learning groups (approximately five to six persons per group).

STEP 2. Each group should prepare a 5-minute summary analysis of the Ecoquest case to share with the total class. (25 minutes) Use the accompanying Ecoquest Case Summary form to write down your conclusions. This summary should touch on the following points:
   a. What do you see as the major strengths and weaknesses of the three candidates?
   b. Which candidate would you recommend as the new CEO of Ecoquest?
   c. What is your rationale for this choice?
   d. What other organizational changes would you recommend to help the new CEO be successful?
   e. How should the organizational culture be maintained or changed?

STEP 3. When the subgroups have completed their work in step 2, the entire class should reconvene for a summary discussion and analysis. (40 minutes)
   a. Each of the subgroups should share its analysis with the entire class. Others should ask clarification questions during the process to ensure understanding. (20 minutes)

STEP 4. *After* sharing these analyses, the class should take a few moments to read over the Ecoquest Case, Part II and discuss the additional questions raised at the end of the case. (20 minutes)

Ecoquest Case Summary

	Mike Lewis	Anita Sanchez	Kent Chang
Major Strengths			
Major Weaknesses			
Group Choice for the New CEO:			
Rationale for Group Choice:			
Organizational Changes to Help CEO Succeed:	Recommendations for Maintaining or Changing Ecoquest's Culture:		

ECOQUEST, PART II—THE AFTERMATH

(Please do not read until directed to do so during the class session.) The consultant team recommended promoting Mike Lewis to the CEO position on the grounds that he had the organizing skills needed at this point in the company's development.

Kent was quick to acknowledge that he did not really want the added responsibility of the CEO position, even though he had been tempted by the title. Anita, however, was disappointed that she was not chosen. She and Mike argued quite a bit in the first few months over the service-versus-profit issue and the need for more organization. Anita and Kent were still operating with the mind-set that policies and structure led straight to rigid bureaucracy. The conflict over these competing values began to spill over onto the rest of the organization when the principals started grousing about each other.

Mike established job descriptions and policies, but he did so without any input. Some policies had a nit-picky flavor, causing a mini-rebellion among staff. Morale dropped, some key employees quit, and a few clients started complaining about the service they received and Mike's "bean-counter" mentality. Finally, the board (and Chel from her sickbed) insisted that the principals resolve their differences.

After acknowledging that their arguments had taken much of the fun out of work, Anita, Mike, and Kent took a hard look at the business and what they needed to accomplish. In a long emotional meeting, Kent pointed out that both service and profit were important and had to be balanced. The principals agreed to monitor the firm's critical success factors and develop some guidelines about what they considered quality service. In a surprise move Mike resigned as CEO, saying he wasn't cut out for the job.

Anita replaced him and quickly put into place a mentoring program that made Ecoquest a preferred employer. Her people skills helped repair relations with staff and clients. Once the conflict and competition died down, both Anita and Mike realized that their differences could be complementary rather than divisive. Anita became more open to Mike's suggestions about clearer roles and policies. Anita and Kent agreed that they had grown to a point where more organization was needed. She asked a task force to revise the policies. Then Anita showed them to the entire staff and asked for their suggestions. The resulting, new-improved policies were accepted, and the firm ran much more smoothly. This success helped Kent accept growth as long as it was managed well and did not result in either chaos or bureaucracy. Over time, Mike took on more and more administrative functions, which allowed Anita to concentrate on bringing in new clients and managing and developing staff. In this way, the strengths of both Mike and Anita were available to the company. Mike's organizing abilities were essential to keep operations running smoothly, but Anita's values and skills were a closer fit with Chel's and the organizational culture. One of the most important lessons the principals learned, however, was to make sure they maintained the organizational culture that was so crucial to their early success. They became more skilled at recognizing decisions and behaviors that threatened their cultural values. They even put up a sign by the bulletin board as a reminder—"How to Avoid Becoming an Endangered Species—Quality Service, Fun, and Empowerment."

CLASS DISCUSSION QUESTIONS

1. What can you learn about leadership and succession from this case?

2. What type of leadership does Ecoquest need at this stage in their development? Where are they in the organizational life cycle?

3. What is your analysis of Ecoquest's organizational culture?

4. What threats to Ecoquest's organizational culture appeared in the case?

5. What connections can you make between this exercise and the readings?

ASSESSING THE ORGANIZATIONAL CULTURE OF THE CLASSROOM

(Time allotted: 1 1$\frac{1}{2}$ hours)

This exercise utilizes a technique known as the *nominal group technique*, developed by Andre Delbecq. It is designed to gather ideas or data quickly in a democratic fashion. The round-robin nature of this technique prevents influential people from controlling the air time or the vote. Once ideas are mentioned, they become the property of the group, not ideas advocated by specific individuals.

STEP 1.   Write three to five statements that describe the following: (15 minutes)
   a. The ideal state of the organizational culture of your learning organization—this course.
   b. The current state of this learning organization.
   c. The ideal state of your learning group.
   d. The current state of your learning group.

Note: *(1) It's not necessary to write complete sentences as long as your words or phrases will be understood by others. (2) For the "ideal state" questions, give yourself free rein here to be creative and think beyond the constraints of the current situation. (3) For the "current state" questions, try to think of both positives and negatives to "cover the waterfront." Don't limit yourself by merely reversing positive characteristics you may have identified for the ideal state.*

STEP 2.   The instructor will go around the room asking each participant to read out loud one statement from his or her list and write it on a flipchart or blackboard. Participants can "pass" when all the statements on their list have been recorded. (15 minutes)

STEP 3.   The class will examine the statements to see if all are comprehensible and that there are no duplicates. Some statements may need to be combined. (10 minutes)

STEP 4.   Participants mark the three statements that are most significant to them as individuals with a marker or chalk mark. Put a hatchmark beside or beneath the three statements. This is a way of quickly prioritizing group opinion. (10 minutes)

STEP 5.   The marks will be counted, identifying the major issues regarding the organizational culture in the class.

STEP 6.   The class as a whole can discuss the results, using the discussion questions that follow. (30 minutes)

Note: *Another option with this exercise is to break into learning groups and choose a student facilitator who will guide the group through the nominal group technique, using only c and d questions focusing on the ideal and current state of your learning group. Afterwards, each group can discuss how to close the gap between the two and improve the learning group.*

DISCUSSION QUESTIONS ABOUT ORGANIZATIONAL CULTURE

1. Does the culture of the learning organization fit your values and needs?
2. Is there a fit between the task of our learning organization and the other aspects of our organizational culture?
3. What steps can be taken to change the culture in this classroom to enhance the realization of the psychological contract or to bring the reality closer to the ideal state?

FOLLOW-UP

THE ORGANIZATIONAL LIFE CYCLE

The leader's role in managing culture varies according to the stages of organizational growth that are explained in the following paragraphs. Organizations (like people) go through stages of growth and development.[31] Although the time spent in each stage varies, most organizations evolve in a predictable sequence. The typical stages in the organizational life cycle are the entrepreneurial stage, the collectivity stage, the formalization stage, and the elaboration stage, as shown in Figure 14-1.

1. **Entrepreneurial Stage** This is the start-up phase, driven by an entrepreneur with vision, energy, and a strong desire to succeed. At this point, the organization seldom has a formal structure; people pitch in to help wherever they are needed. The goals are to create a product and survive. Communication is informal and face-to-face. The entrepreneur makes most of the decisions and there is little formal planning. In this stage, creativity and morale are often high because people enjoy the challenge of being in on the ground floor of a new venture.

2. **Collectivity Stage** If the organization survives this stage (and many do not), it moves to stage 2, collectivity. Some form of hierarchical authority has to be defined so employees know whom to go to for decisions and orders. Although some formal aspects of organization are beginning to appear, such as an initial division of labor, communication and control are still likely to be fairly informal. Employees identify with the organization and its mission. The name of this stage, collectivity, refers to this sense of a highy committed group that is working together to make the organization succeed. A more directive leadership style is needed in this stage.

   Organizations are often characterized by growing pains such as lack of coordination among newly created departments, missed deadlines, overrun budgets, poor or uneven quality

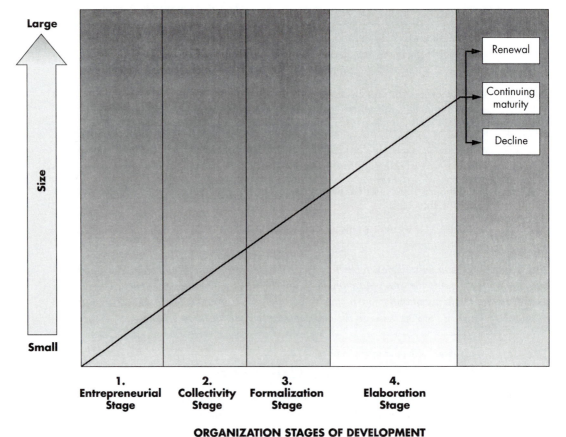

FIGURE 14-1 Organizational Life Cycle

control, and overworked CEOs and employees. If these normal stresses and strains are not managed effectively, the organization may find itself on a sharp downward spiral. While the forces are undoubtedly many and complex, a critical variable appears to be the organization's ability to reorganize and accept the fact that at different points in its life it needs different kinds of top-management motivation and leadership and a different organizational culture. These transitional issues are particularly disconcerting to the entrepreneur-owner. The organization is his or her "baby" and letting go in certain areas and recognizing the need for more teamwork and group problem solving and conflict resolution, for example, is by no means simple. Some entrepreneurs inherently dislike adding bureaucracy to their business, even though a certain degree of organization is necessary to support their growth. Many companies are "underorganized" during this stage, which sometimes results in conflict over issues that are "fought out" by employees rather than resolved by policies and hierarchical authority.

3. **Formalization Stage** A greater degree of formalized organization and bureaucratization, in the form of rules, policies, and control systems, is needed to sustain growth in this stage. The management style is less entrepreneurial and more professional, relying on analytical tools and focusing on efficiency. The morale and excitement, so high in the early years may start to disappear. That old feeling of personal contact and easy access to the boss begins to wane as the organization grows in size. Top management concentrates on strategy rather than operations, which is taken over by middle management. The leader in forced to delegate more authority to others, and the organization becomes more decentralized.

4. **Elaboration Stage** This is the mature stage of the organizational life cycle, evidenced by large size and bureaucratic systems. By this point, companies usually have multiple products or service lines. Communication has become very formal, and there are numerous rules and regulations concerning the planning process. Long-term planning is common. Too much bureaucracy is perceived as a major threat, so organizations in this stage often rely on decentralization and teams to maintain responsiveness. There is a focus on streamlining bureacracy and using social control and self-discipline rather than formal bureaucratic controls. Leadership is concerned with creating a complete organization and making sure the necessary coordination and controls and functioning.

The elaboration stage can result in continuing maturity organizational decline, or renewal. When organizations are not successful in balancing the right degree of bureaucracy with their need to learn, adapt and innovate, they may go into decline. *Decline* is characterized by rigid, top-heavy, and overly complex organizational structures. Communication breakdowns are common. There is often blind adherence to a "success formula," regardless of environmental changes that make this formula obsolete. Decision making emphasizes form rather than substance, and self-serving politics are the norm. There is an excess of conformity and compromise. There are nine early warning signals of organizational decline:[32]

1. Excess personnel
2. Tolerance of incompetence
3. Cumbersome administrative procedures
4. Disproportionate staff power
5. Replacement of substance with form (e.g., the planning process is more important than results)
6. Scarcity of clear goals and decision benchmarks
7. Fear of embarrassment and conflict prevents problem identification
8. Loss of effective communication
9. Outdated organizational structure

Experts say decline is almost inevitable unless management takes steps to avoid it. This is best done before the organization finds itself in difficulty. Some organizations manage to halt a decline and enter a renewal stage that allows the organization to shift itself back to a previous stage. To fight off organizational decline, reengineering efforts closely examine how the organization functions and then take action to streamline and improve processes and the structure.

Each stage requires a different type of leadership that is capable of tackling the major growth challenges. Leaders should also manage organizational culture differently in each stage.[33] In the entrepreneurial and collectivity stages, an organizational culture is often the glue that holds the organization together and makes growth possible. The leader should elaborate, develop, and articulate the cultural values. In the formalization stage, culture tends to be taken for granted. The culture often becomes more diverse as subcultures form in the different areas of the organization. Leaders can reward the subcultures whose values are in the organization's best interests. In the elaboration stage, the culture may become dysfunctional, and the leader's task is to change the culture and make it more adaptive.

Beatty and Ulrich suggest that the probability of renewal of mature organizations increases if four principles are understood and practiced.[34]

1. **Mature organizations renew by instilling a customer perspective and focusing on customer demands** This involves seeking a sustained competitive advantage that comes from understanding and meeting customer needs in unique ways. Companies question whether their mind-sets, or mental models, and practices really meet customer requirements and expectations.

2. **Mature organizations renew by increasing their capacity for change** Organizations have an internal clock about how long it should take to make decisions. In many cases, the challenge is to decrease the cycle time for decisions. Companies have to focus more on alignment so that all aspects of the organization are moving toward consistent and shared goals. Symbiosis is also emphasized so that companies can learn and benefit from removing boundaries both inside and outside the organization. Reflexiveness, the ability to learn from previous actions, is a necessity.

3. **Mature organizations renew by altering both the hardware and software within the organization** The hardware (strategy, structure, and systems) is where many renewal programs begin. However, hardware has to be supported by software (employee behavior and mental models).

4. **Mature organizations renew by creating empowered employees who act as leaders at all levels of the organization** Individuals have both responsibility and accountability in their areas.

 LEARNING POINTS

1. Organizational culture is defined as a pattern of shared values and beliefs that produces certain norms of behavior.

2. Organizational culture is formed by (a) the values of the founder or strong leaders and (b) learned solutions to problems over time.

3. Strong cultures have the following characteristics:
   a. People in the organization can easily identify the dominant values.
   b. The selection processes target people who are likely to fit into the culture and find it satisfying.
   c. Socialization and training convey to newcomers the "ropes" they need to learn.
   d. Employees who do not fit the culture or produce in accordance with its values are sometimes fired.
   e. People within the company are rewarded for acting in accordance with the dominant values of the organization.
   f. By their behavior, leaders and managers send clear, consistent signals about desired values and norms.
   g. Managers measure and control what is important to the culture.

4. Compared to weak cultures, strong cultures have core values and beliefs that are intensely held, more widely shared and more ordered.

5. There should be a fit among the people, the organization's task, environment, strategy, and culture.

6. Organizational culture provides members with a sense of identity, generates commitment, helps people make sense of what occurs in the organization and the environment, and serves as a control mechanism.

7. A strong culture does not guarantee good performance unless it focuses on all its key

constituencies (customers, stockholder, and employees) and has leadership from managers at all levels.

8. The advantages of strong organizational cultures are high performance under certain conditions, clear sense of purpose, more value-driven decision making, and employee commitment, loyalty, and pride. Two disadvantages of strong cultures are their pressure for conformity and resistance to change.

9. Culture is transmitted through socialization, stories, symbols, jargon, rituals and ceremonies, and statements of principles.

10. Leaders can affect an organizational culture, but they cannot unilaterally determine what that culture should be. The primary mechanisms a leader can use to create, transmit, or change culture are:

   a. what leaders pay attention to, measure, and control on a regular basis
   b. the reactions of leaders to critical incidents and organizational crises
   c. observed criteria by which leaders allocate scarce resources
   d. deliberate role modeling, teaching, and coaching
   e. criteria for allocating rewards and status
   f. criteria for recruitment, selection, promotion, retirement, and excommunication

11. Most organizations go through predictable stages of growth—the entrepreneurial stage, collectivity, formalization, and elaboration. Each stage requires a different type of leadership.

TIPS FOR MANAGERS

- Before you join an organization, try to read its culture and determine whether or not your values are compatible with those of the organization.
- Figure out your organization's cultural characteristics and use that understanding when making analyses and decisions. Awareness of the history of the organization can keep new managers from making errors.
- Respect the past, but make sure the culture is adapting and learning in the present.
- Establishing an effective organizational culture requires consistency. What managers do to reinforce culture is stronger than what they say.
- Don't assume that continuity will naturally occur in an organizational culture; it must be nurtured. If you don't need to change the organizational culture, work to maintain and strengthen the existing culture. Whenever decisions are made, people should ask the question, "Is this decision in keeping with our cultural values?"
- Encourage a certain degree of nonconformity. Although it is more difficult to handle people who don't fit the culture very well, they are often valuable in pointing out the assumptions that are guiding the dominant culture. Sometimes they see the need for change more clearly than others.
- One of the disadvantages of culture is that it blinds us to other values and other ways of doing things. Strategy decisions are affected, sometimes adversely, by the organizational culture.
- Helping a work group or organization to make its norms explicit identifies what values need to be reinforced or changed.
- Creating traditions and events that emphasize the cultural values you deem important help form a culture (e.g., the Glorious Booboo Award in the R&D lab, roasts for people who get promoted or retire, and Friday afternoon TGIF parties).
- Some companies utilize stories rather than policy manuals to transmit culture to employees. Stories and parables are easy to remember and help guide employee behavior. Managers can also analyze what's going on in the company by listening to the stories that are commonly told.
- The organization's culture must be taken into consideration whenever changes are planned, because culture can be a major impediment to change. Changes that utilize the culture, rather than fight against it, are more likely to succeed. Even so, cultural change is a slow, evolutionary process that requires patience.
- Cultures that promote ethical behavior were found to be high in both risk and conflict tolerance and have members who identify with the professional standards of their job.[35]

PERSONAL APPLICATION ASSIGNMENT

Your assignment is to analyze the culture of an organization you know well (a work setting, church, club, or even the school where you are taking this course).

1. What is the background of the founders?

2. What explains the organization's growth and survival?

3. What does the organization stand for? What is its motto?

4. What values does the organization talk about?

5. What values does the organization act out?

6. How do people get ahead? What does it take to do well in this organization? To stay out of trouble?

7. What kind of mistakes are not forgiven?

8. Who is considered deviant in the culture and why? How does the organization treat them?

9. How are good employees rewarded?

10. What are the main rules that everyone has to follow in this organization?

11. How does the company respond to crises?

12. What message is conveyed by the physical setting?

13. How do things get done in this organization?

14. How do people spend their time at work?

15. How does the company take in new members?

16. What kinds of stories are told about the organization?

17. Who are the heroes and why?

18. Is there anything that cannot be talked about?

19. How do people exercise power?

20. What is the organization's code of ethics?

Based on the answers to these questions, what is your analysis of this organizational culture?

ENDNOTES

[1] R. T. Pascale and A. G. Athos, *The Art of Japanese Management: Applications for American Executives* (New York: Simon and Schuster, 1981); T. Peters and R. H. Waterman, *In Search of Excellence* (New York: Harper and Row, 1982); T. Peters and N. A. Austin, *A Passion for Excellence* (New York: Random House, 1985); T. E. Deal and A. A. Kennedy, *Corporate Cultures: The Rites and Rituals of Corporate Life* (Reading, MA: Addison-Wesley, 1982); and J. P. Kotter and J. L. Heskett, *Corporate Culture and Performance* (Toronto: The Free Press, 1992).

[2] H. M. Trice and J. M Beyer, *The Cultures of Work Organizations* (Englewood Cliffs, NJ: Prentice Hall, 1993). This book is a compendium of what is known about organizational culture to date. See also *Gaining Control of the Corporate Culture*, ed. by R. H. Kilmann, M. J. Saxton, and R. Serpa and Associates (San Francisco: Jossey-Bass, 1986).

[3] E. H. Schein, "Coming to a New Awareness of Organizational Culture," *Sloan Management Review* (Winter 1984): 3.

[4] L. Smircich, "Concepts of Culture and Organizational Analysis," *Administrative Science Quarterly* (September 1983): 342.

[5] S. A. Sackmann, *Cultural Complexity in Organizations: Inherent Contrasts and Contradictions* (Thousand Oaks, CA: Sage, 1997).

[6] E. Schein, *Organizational Culture and Leadership* (San Francisco: Jossey-Bass, 1985).

[7] V. Sathe, "Implications of Corporate Culture: A Manager's Guide to Action," *Organizational Dynamics* (Autumn 1983): 5–23.

[8] J. C. Collins and J. I. Porras, *Built to Last* (New York: Harper-Business, 1994); D. R. Denison and A. K. Mishra, "Toward a Theory of Organizational Culture and Effectiveness," *Organization Science* (March–April 1995): 204–23.

[9] Kotter and Heskett, *Corporate Culture and Performance*, p. 11.

[10] J. Pfeffer; *The Human Equation: Building Profits by Putting People First* (Boston. MA: Harvard Business School Press, 1998).

[11] R. T. Pascale; "The Paradox of 'Corporate Culture': Reconciling Ourselves to Socialization," *California Management Review* (Winter 1985): 26–41.

[12] Kotter and Heskett, *Corporate Culture and Performance*, p. 142.

[13] J. H. Dobrzynski, "Rethinking IBM," *Business Week,* October 4, 1993, p. 88. See also G. Lewis, "One Fresh Face May Not Be Enough," *Business Week*, April 12, 1993.

[14] D. Miller, *The Icarus Paradox,* (New York: Harper Business, 1990): 3.

[15] R. D. Denison, "Bringing Corporate Culture to the Bottom Line," *Organizational Dynamics* (Autumn 1984): 5–22.

[16] Trice and Beyer, *Culture of Work Organizations*, pp. 356–57.

[17] J. S. Ott, *The Organizational Culture Perspective* (Chicago: Dorsey, 1989).

[18] R. Pascale, "The Paradox of 'Corporate Culture'."

[19] Ibid.

[20] R. O. von Wessowets, "Human Resources at Hewlett-Packard," Harvard Business School Case #482-125 (1982): 6.

[21] M. Kinsley, "Company Man," *The New Republic 215*, no. 10, (September 2, 1966): p. 42.

[22] Pfeffer, *The Human Equation.*

[23] S. Cartwright and C. L. Cooper, "The Role of Culture Compatibility in Successful Organizational Marriage," *Academy of Management Executive*, 7 (1993), 57–70.

[24] Schein, *Organizational Culture and Leadership*, 228–53.

[25] Kotter and Heskett, *Corporate Culture*, 147; and Trice and Beyer, *Culture of Work Organizations,* 399–413.

[26] A. L. Wilkins, *Developing Corporate Character* (San Francisco: Jossey-Bass, 1989). See J. Thorbeck's "The Turnaround Value of Values," *Harvard Business Review*, (January–February, 1991): 52–62 for a firsthand account by a manager who took company history into account and successfully revived company values.

[27] Trice and Beyer, *Culture of Work Organizations.*

[28] R. T. Pascale, *Managing on the Edge: How the Smartest Companies Use Conflict to Stay Ahead* (New York: Simon and Schuster, 1990).

[29] L. Schein, "A Manager's Guide to Corporate Culture," Research Report from The Conference Board.

[30] Pfeffer, *The Human Equation.*

[31] K. G. Smith, T. R. Mitchel, and C. E. Summer, "Top Level Management Priorities in Different Stages of the Organizational Life Cycle," *Academy of Management Journal* (December 1985): 799–820; R. E. Quinn and K. Cameron, "Organizational Life Cycles and Shifting Criteria of Effectiveness: Some Preliminary Evidence," *Management Science* 29 (1983): 33–51; and L.E. Greiner, "Evolution and Revolution as Organizations Grow," *Harvard Business Review* 76 (May-June 1998): 55–64; P. Lorange and R. T. Nelson, "How to Recognize and Avoid Organizational Decline," *Sloan Management Review* (Spring 1987): 41–48.

[32] Lorange and Nelson, "How to Recognize and Avoid Organizational Decline," 43–45.

[33] E. H. Schein, *Organizational Culture and Leadership* (San Francisco: Jossey-Bass, 1997).

[34] R. W. Beatty and D. O. Ulrich, "Re-Energizing the Mature Organization," *Organizational Dynamics*, 20, no. 1 (1991): 16–30.

[35] B. Victor. and J. B. Cullen, "The Organizational Bases of Ethical Work Climates," *Administrative Science Quarterly* (March 1988): 101–25.

Chapter 15

▲▲▲

DECISION MAKING

OBJECTIVES By the end of this chapter, you should be able to:

A. Explain why decision making is a social process.

B. Describe four models of decision making.

C. Explain groupthink.

D. Identify your personal approach to organizational decision making.

E. Apply the leader-participation model of decision making.

PAJAMA TALK

The Sleepytime Pajama factory was going great guns. Sales were up. The workforce was expanding. There was only one hitch. To remain competitive, factory managers were constantly adapting both work techniques and products. Workers were often transferred to different jobs or had parts of their job modified, either in the name of progress or as a result of high turnover and absenteeism. The biggest problem facing Sleepytime was worker resistance to these changes. As soon as they became proficient at one job, they'd be switched to another. They worked on a piece-rate incentive system, and it wasn't easy to work their way up to producing 60 units per hour, the standard efficiency rate. Some suspicious souls thought management just switched workers to new jobs when they had finally mastered their tasks and could begin to earn bonuses for producing more than 60 units. Even though workers received a transfer bonus that made up for the money lost learning new jobs, it didn't make up for the loss in status of being a "greenhorn" on a new task. Workers still hated to be transferred to a new job, and some quit rather than change. Others complained bitterly about management and fought with their supervisors and the time-study engineers. Statistics showed that experienced workers took longer to relearn new jobs and get up to speed than did new employees with no work experience! This convinced the company that the problem was really a question of motivation and resistance to change.

Mr. Sleepytime himself, Joe Berg, had the production people organize the output figures in relation to the changes that had been introduced during the last year. He was surprised to find that the work groups supervised by Kathy Johnson seemed to have fewer problems with changes. Her groups got back to speed more quickly after the changes and had a higher level of output than the others. She also had fewer terminations, even after the job transfers. So Berg sent his industrial relations expert out on the floor to figure out what was going on.

After observation, the expert discovered that the difference lay in how the supervisors handled the changes. Supervisors of the low-productivity groups simply announced to their employees that a job had to be changed, explained the new piece rate, and answered questions.

In contrast, Johnson used physical demonstrations with her workers in which she showed them samples of pajamas made using new and old techniques, explained the cost differential, and asked them if they could tell the difference between them. Or she'd bring in pajamas made by a competitor who was underselling them and show them why changes had to be made to respond to this challenge. Next, she'd ask the group how the new jobs should be designed. They'd come up with a blitz of ideas for improving the job, and then they worked with the time-study engineer to test out the innovations. Johnson let the workers do most of the talking and planning. She didn't have in her head a "one best way" to make the changes; she let them figure it out for themselves. As a result, they bought into the changes and became committed to making them work. Johnson made the factory workers participants in the change process rather than victims of it. And so it was that Berg learned that the sooner people are brought into a change effort and allowed to participate in the decision making, the better.

Source: Based on Lester Coch and John R. French, Jr., "Overcoming Resistance to Change," *Human Relations, 1* (1947): 512–31.

PREMEETING PREPARATION

(Time allotted: 30 minutes)

A. Read "Pajama Talk."

B. Read the descriptions of decision-making alternatives for individual and group problems in Table 15-1 and describe how you would handle each of the five decision-making cases that follow. Indicate whether the case describes an individual or group problem and which decision-making approach you would use. Choose your approach based on what you would do in each case and explain your rationale. This will allow a comparison between your decision-making style and the recommendations of the decision-making model described in this chapter.[1]

TABLE 15-1   Leadership Styles

AI	You solve the problem or make a decision yourself, using whatever facts you have at hand.
AII	You obtain any necessary information from those who report to you and then reach a decision alone. You may or may not tell them about the nature of the situation you face. You seek only relevant facts from them, not their advice or counsel.
CI	You consult one-on-one with those who report to you, describing the problem and asking for each person's advice and recommendations. The final decision, however, is yours alone.
CII	You consult with those who report to you in a meeting, describing the problem and requesting their collective advice and recommendations. The final decision, however, is yours alone and may or may not reflect your subordinates' influence.
GII	You share the problem with your subordinates as a group. Your goal is to help the group concur on a decision. Your ideas are not given any greater weight than those of others.

A = Autocratic Decision, C = Consultative Decision, G = Group Decision

C. After completing B, read the Topic Introduction and the Procedure for Group Meeting.

D. What are the significant learning points from the readings?

E. If your instructor has assigned the Robbins Self-Assessment Library, use "How Intuitive Am I?"

CASE 1: THE FINANCE CASE

You are the head of a staff unit reporting to the vice president of finance. The vice president has asked you to provide a report on the firm's current portfolio to include recommendations for changes in the selection criteria currently employed. Doubts have been raised about the efficiency of the existing system in the current market conditions, and there is considerable dissatisfaction with prevailing rates of return.

You plan to write the report, but at the moment you are quite perplexed about the approach to take. Your own speciality is the bond market, and it is clear to you that detailed knowledge of the equity market, which you lack, would greatly enhance the value of the report. Fortunately, four members of your staff are specialists in different segments of the equity market. Together they possess a vast amount of knowledge about the intricacies of investment. However, they seldom agree on the best way to achieve anything when it comes to investment philosophy and strategy.

You have six weeks before the report is due. You have already begun to familiarize yourself with the firm's current portfolio and have been provided by management with a specific set of constraints that any portfolio must satisfy. Your immediate problem is to come up with some alternatives to the firm's present practices and select the most promising for detailed analysis in your report.

How would you deal with this situation?

With a checkmark, indicate the style that most closely describes the action you would take.

	AI	You solve the problem or make a decision yourself, using whatever facts you have at hand.
	AII	You obtain any necessary information from those who report to you and then reach a decision alone. You may or may not tell them about the nature of the situation you face. You seek only relevant facts from them, not their advice or counsel.
	CI	You consult one-on-one with those who report to you, describing the problem and asking for each person's advice and recommendations. The final decision, however, is yours alone.
	CII	You consult with those who report to you in a meeting, describing the problem and requesting their collective advice and recommendations. The final decision, however, is yours alone and may or may not reflect your subordinates' influence.
	GII	You share the problem with your subordinates as a group. Your goal is to help the group concur on a decision. Your ideas are not given any greater weight than those of others.

Why would you use this style?

CASE 2:   INTERNATIONAL CONSULTING COMPANY

You are regional manager of an international management consulting company. You have a staff of six consultants reporting to you, each of whom enjoys a considerable amount of autonomy with clients in the field.

Yesterday you received a complaint from one of your major clients to the effect that the consultant whom you assigned to work on the contract with them was not doing his job effectively. They were not very explicit as to the nature of the problem, but it was clear that they were dissatisfied and that something would have to be done if you were to restore the client's faith in your company.

The consultant assigned to work on that contract has been with the company for six years. He is a systems analyst and is one of the best in that profession. For the first four or five years his performance was superb, and he was a model for the more junior consultants. However, recently he has seemed to have a "chip on his shoulder" and his previous identification with the company and its objectives has been replaced with indifference. His negative attitude has been noticed by other consultants, as well as by clients. This is not the first such complaint that you have had from a client this year about his performance. A previous client even reported to you that the consultant reported to work several times obviously suffering from a hangover.

It is important to get to the root of this problem quickly if that client is to be retained. The consultant obviously has the skill necessary to work with the clients effectively. If only he were willing to use it!

How would you as regional manager deal with this problem?

With a checkmark, indicate the style that most closely describes the action you would take.

	AI	You solve the problem or make a decision yourself, using whatever facts you have at hand.
	AII	You obtain any necessary information from those who report to you and then reach a decision alone. You may or may not tell them about the nature of the situation you face. You seek only relevant facts from them, not their advice or counsel.
	CI	You consult one-on-one with those who report to you, describing the problem and asking for each person's advice and recommendations. The final decision, however, is yours alone.
	CII	You consult with those who report to you in a meeting, describing the problem and requesting their collective advice and recommendations. The final decision, however, is yours alone and may or may not reflect your subordinates' influence.
	GII	You share the problem with your subordinates as a group. Your goal is to help the group concur on a decision. Your ideas are not given any greater weight than those of others.

Why would you use this style?

CASE 3: THE ENGINEERING WORK ASSIGNMENT

You are supervising the work of 12 civil engineers. Their formal training and work experience are very similar, permitting you to use them interchangeably on projects. Yesterday your manager informed you that a request had been received from an overseas affiliate for four engineers to go abroad on extended loan for a period of six to eight months. For a number of reasons, she argued and you agreed, this request should be met from your group.

All your engineers are experienced in and are capable of handling assignments such as this. From the standpoint of present and future work projects, there is no particular reason why any one should be chosen over any other. The problem is somewhat complicated by the fact that the overseas assignment is in what is generally regarded in the company as an undesirable location.

How would you deal with this situation?

With a checkmark, indicate the style that most closely describes the action you would take.

	AI	You solve the problem or make a decision yourself, using whatever facts you have at hand.
	AII	You obtain any necessary information from those who report to you and then reach a decision alone. You may or may not tell them about the nature of the situation you face. You seek only relevant facts from them, not their advice or counsel.
	CI	You consult one-on-one with those who report to you, describing the problem and asking for each person's advice and recommendations. The final decision, however, is yours alone.
	CII	You consult with those who report to you in a meeting, describing the problem and requesting their collective advice and recommendations. The final decision, however, is yours alone and may or may not reflect your subordinates' influence.
	GII	You share the problem with your subordinates as a group. Your goal is to help the group concur on a decision. Your ideas are not given any greater weight than those of others.

Why would you use this style?

CASE 4: THE PHARMACEUTICAL COMPANY

You are executive vice president for a small pharmaceutical manufacturer. You have the opportunity to bid on a contract for the Defense Department pertaining to biological warfare. The contract is outside the mainstream of your business; however, it could make economic sense because you do have unused capacity in one of your plants, and the manufacturing processes are not dissimilar.

You have written the document to accompany the bid and now have the problem of determining the dollar value of the quotation that you think will win the job for your company. If the bid is too high, you will undoubtedly lose to one of your competitors; if it is too low, you would stand to lose money on the program.

There are many factors to be considered in making this decision, including the cost of the new raw materials and the additional administrative burden of relationships with a new client, not to speak of factors that are likely to influence the bids of your competitors, such as how much they need this particular contract. You have been busy assembling the necessary data to make this decision, but there remain several "unknowns," one of which involves the manager of the plant in which the products will be manufactured. Of all your subordinates, only she is in the position to estimate the costs of adapting the present equipment to its new purpose, and her cooperation and support will be necessary in ensuring that the specifications of the contract will be met. However, in an initial discussion with her when you first learned of the possibility of the contract, she seemed adamantly opposed to the idea. Although she has been an effective and dedicated plant manager over the past several years, her previous experience has not particularly equipped her to evaluate the overall merits of projects such as this one. From the nature of her arguments, you inferred that her opposition was ideological rather than economic. You recall in this context that she is involved in the local nuclear freeze movement.

How would you go about determining the amount of the bid?

With a checkmark, indicate the style that most closely describes the action you would take.

	AI	You solve the problem or make a decision yourself, using whatever facts you have at hand.
	AII	You obtain any necessary information from those who report to you and then reach a decision alone. You may or may not tell them about the nature of the situation you face. You seek only relevant facts from them, not their advice or counsel.
	CI	You consult one-on-one with those who report to you, describing the problem and asking for each person's advice and recommendations. The final decision, however, is yours alone.
	CII	You consult with those who report to you in a meeting, describing the problem and requesting their collective advice and recommendations. The final decision, however, is yours alone and may or may not reflect your subordinates' influence.
	GII	You share the problem with your subordinates as a group. Your goal is to help the group concur on a decision. Your ideas are not given any greater weight than those of others.

Why would you use this style?

CASE 5: THE OIL PIPELINE

You are general supervisor in charge of a large gang laying an oil pipeline. It is now necessary to estimate your expected rate of progress to schedule material deliveries to the next field site.

You know the nature of the terrain you will be traveling and have in your records the historical data needed to compute the mean and variance in the rate of speed over that type of terrain. Given these two variables, it is a simple matter to calculate the earliest and latest times at which materials and support facilities will be needed at the next site. It is important that your estimate be reasonably accurate. Underestimates result in idle supervisors and workers, and overestimates result in tying up materials for a period of time before they are to be used.

Progress has been good, and your five supervisors and other members of the gang stand to receive substantial bonuses if the project is completed ahead of schedule.

How would you go about scheduling material deliveries?

With a checkmark, indicate the style that most closely describes the action you would take.

	AI	You solve the problem or make a decision yourself, using whatever facts you have at hand.
	AII	You obtain any necessary information from those who report to you and then reach a decision alone. You may or may not tell them about the nature of the situation you face. You seek only relevant facts from them, not their advice or counsel.
	CI	You consult one-on-one with those who report to you, describing the problem and asking for each person's advice and recommendations. The final decision, however, is yours alone.
	CII	You consult with those who report to you in a meeting, describing the problem and requesting their collective advice and recommendations. The final decision, however, is yours alone and may or may not reflect your subordinates' influence.
	GII	You share the problem with your subordinates as a group. Your goal is to help the group concur on a decision. Your ideas are not given any greater weight than those of others.

Why would you use this style?

TOPIC INTRODUCTION

To a manager, executive, or administrator, no other job function encapsulates the frustrations and joys of leadership more dramatically than decision making. It is in making decisions that managers most acutely feel the responsibilities, the power, and the vulnerability of their jobs. This central focus of decision making is illustrated in the autobiographies of political leaders, who characteristically organize their life stories around major decision points they faced, the dilemmas and pressures they experienced, and how in the end the "buck" stopped on their desks. Most of us in our life and work face decisions of less magnitude; nonetheless, from time to time we share the existential loneliness of making an important decision.

Yet there are two things wrong with using this admittedly powerful subjective experience of decision making as the focus for analyzing and improving the decision-making process in organizations. First, these experiences suggest that decisions can be thought of as independent, solitary events that are relatively unconnected to other decisions and the process that brought the decision point to a head. If there is anything to be learned from the Bay of Pigs fiasco or the Vietnam experience, it is that the organizational process of problem identification, information sharing, and problem solving, if mishandled, can undo the work of the finest, most logical, and experienced individual decision maker.

Second, these political memoirs suggest that decision making is an individual process and, therefore, the skills of logical analysis and problem solving (described in Chapter 10) should be sufficient to produce high-quality decisions. In reality, decision making in organizations is also a social process. Organizational functioning requires an unending stream of decisions great and small. These decisions are identified, made, and communicated by individuals and groups throughout the organization. As a manager, you depend on the decisions of others and the information they bring you. You also delegate decisions and share information about them with others. Part of a manager's role is determining who in the organization has the information, experience, and wisdom needed to make a particular decision. Another part is understanding who are the stakeholders in each issue who need to be involved because their acceptance of the outcome is crucial. Seeing decision making as a social process means that the manager is responsible for determining how the problem is to be solved, but not necessarily the solution. The sense that any decision is made alone in an organization is an illusion.

The focus of this unit is on managing the process of decision making as opposed to the problem-solving skills of making a specific decision. It underscores the social aspects of that process and the alternative ways of making decisions with other people: the costs and benefits and the appropriate application of these decision-making methods in different situations.

Studies of 356 decisions in Canadian and U.S. organizations revealed that half the decisions failed (were never put into practice, only partly used, or completely dissolved).[2] The primary cause of failure can be traced to poor managerial tactics rather than factors outside managers' control. Although two tactics are commonly used by managers, they are less likely to result in successful decisions: persuasion (selling expert opinions to convince employees about a decision) and edicts (directives that announce decisions on which employees have not been consulted). The repeated use of edicts depletes a manager's social credit (the store of goodwill created by honest dealings and positive accomplishments) and may result in sabotage, token compliance, delays, and outright refusals to comply.[3] Employees are more likely to overlook the merits of a decision made by edict and devote their energies to complaining about how the decision was made. Companies are forced to expend unnecessary time, money, and effort to counteract the employee resistance that is a natural outgrowth of many edicts. The managers studied were not aware of the high failure rates associated with edicts and persuasion. Nor were they aware that the following set of tactics has a higher success rate: (1) setting realistic objectives for the decision (e.g., lower costs, higher market share) before moving on to consider options, (2) intervention (pointing out performance gaps and the need for the decision, networking, calling attention to ideas that might work, and identifying and justifying new performance norms), (3) participation (task forces with key individuals), and (4) integrated benchmarking (studying several organizations to learn from their best practices). Decisions are also more likely to be successful if managers involve themselves in the implementation process.

MODELS OF DECISION MAKING

The Rational Decision-Making Process

The process of rational decision making is somewhat similar to the problem-solving model we studied in Chapter 10:

1. Recognize and define the problem.
2. Identify the objective of the decision and the decision criteria.
3. Allocate weights to the criteria.
4. List and develop the alternatives.
5. Evaluate the alternatives.
6. Select the best alternative.
7. Implement the decision.
8. Evaluate the decision.

By decision criteria, we mean the factors that a decision must satisfy. Cost, time needed for implementation, and fairness are examples of decision criteria. The model of rational decision making is an outgrowth of classical economic theory with its view of rational man (and woman). Although this model is useful in guiding our general approach to decision making, the circumstances surrounding most decisions are seldom so simple or so rational that this model works perfectly and predictably.

Bounded Rationality

With this in mind, Herbert Simon won a Nobel Prize for his theory of bounded rationality, which maintains that people are restricted in making decisions and settle for less than ideal solutions.[4] In other words, there are limits or bounds on rationality. Bounded rationality is based on these assumptions:

1. Managers select the first alternative that is satisfactory, which is called satisficing.
2. Both the available information and the definition of the situation are incomplete and inadequate to some degree.
3. Managers are comfortable making decisions without first determining all the alternatives.
4. Managers use judgment shortcuts to make decisions, which are called heuristics.

Managers *satisfice* (i.e., accept a decision that is "good enough") because the costs of maximizing are too great. Maximizing would be analogous to searching the Internet to find the very best Web site to help you write an assigned report; satisficing is searching the Web only until you find a site that provides enough information to allow you to produce an acceptable report. *Bounded discretion* is another constraint on the decision-making process—optimal solutions are not always best because they may involve unethical behavior. For example, when Beech-Nut sold adulterated apple juice for babies, it optimized its profit in the short term. However, this decision was viewed as unethical, and the company was penalized.[5]

Heuristics are rules of thumb based on past experience that managers use to simplify decision making. For example, when a stock drops a set number of points, some investors automatically sell rather than analyze a wide array of factors that influence the stock. People also tend to compare one decision against another in an incremental approach rather than carry out a comprehensive consideration of all possible decisions.[6]

Garbage Can Model

The garbage can model of decision making diverges even more radically than bounded rationality from the conception of decision making as a rational process.[7] In the garbage can model, four factors—problems, participants, solutions, and choice opportunities—all float randomly inside an organization, described metaphorically as a garbage can. If they connect, a decision results. The garbage can model assumes that decision making is haphazard, chaotic, unpredictable, and sometimes depends on sheer luck.

The following section explains some of the human factors that influence and sometimes distort the decision-making process.

FACTORS THAT INFLUENCE DECISIONS

Decisions are affected by individual differences and biases. For example, some people are more risk averse than others and have less tolerance of uncertainty. As a result, their decisions tend to be more cautious and conservative. Sometimes, however, people support riskier decisions in a group setting than they would individually. This is known as the *risky shift*.[8] Apparently, people are more comfortable with increased risk due to the diffused responsibility of a group. People sometimes make more cautious decisions in groups (*the cautious shift*) than they would individually. The risky shift is more common than the cautious shift. The determining factor is the premeeting position of the members. Group discussion seems to cause individuals to exaggerate their initial stance and move toward extremes.[9] For example, a cautious shift is more likely when group members are leaning toward a cautious decision before the group meeting.

These shifts in group decision making have been called a special form of groupthink. Groupthink refers to the tendency for members of a highly cohesive group to seek consensus so strongly that they fail to do a realistic appraisal of other alternatives, which may be more correct.[10] Ford's decision to produce the Edsel, President Kennedy and his advisors' decision on the Bay of Pigs invasion into Cuba, Morton-Thiokol's decision to recommend launching in the *Challenger* disaster, and Salomon Brothers' illegal purchases at U.S. Treasury auctions are all examples of decisions characterized by groupthink. In each case, individuals "went along" with consensus-driven group decisions that should have been questioned. When groupthink occurs, members censor their misgivings about a decision, or they pressure dissenters to stifle their opinions. Thus, there is pressure toward uniformity and an *illusion of unanimity* that does not really exist. There is also an *illusion of invulnerability* that makes the group overly optimistic and more likely to take high-risk decisions. The *illusion of morality* occurs when groups feel they are morally correct and should, therefore, not be criticized. They collectively rationalize their actions and often stereotype out-group members who may be likely to criticize their actions.[11]

The concept of groupthink focused attention on the need for constructive controversy in decision-making groups. Subsequent empirical research on groupthink has not always validated Irving Janis's original theory.[12] Groups may not manifest all the characteristics of groupthink, yet it is important to remember that cohesive groups can develop groupthink tendencies. To avoid groupthink, groups can (1) encourage all members to express their doubts, (2) assign a devil's advocate in each meeting who challenges assumptions and arguments, (3) adopt the perspectives of other constituencies with a stake in the decision, (4) bring in qualified outsiders to discuss decisions, and (5) after a tentative decision has been reached, schedule a "let's sleep on it one last time" meeting for final concerns and doubts. Group leaders have to demonstrate their own willingness to be criticized and should avoid laying out their own opinions first.

Groupthink usually occurs in the deliberation period before groups begin to receive feedback on their decisions. Surprisingly, negative feedback is not always enough to deter groups and individuals from continuing to support bad decisions. *Escalation of commitment* occurs when people continue to commit resources to a failing course of action.[13] In spite of evidence that a previous decision was a mistake, people sometimes focus on what they have invested in an effort and become even more committed. Countries that continue with wars they cannot win or people who persist in buying shares of a failing stock are examples of escalating commitment.

THE LEADER-PARTICIPATION MODEL

The decision-making alternatives you used in the premeeting section reflect a contingency theory of leadership. The continuum ranges from autocratic decision-making behavior (in which the leader decides alone) to participative styles, ranging from consultation to joint decision making.

The choice of style depends on the problem at hand. Once again, managerial effectiveness depends on having the skills required to analyze the problem in question and the ability to vary one's leadership behavior accordingly.

The leader-participation model is based on evidence that the choice of leadership style can affect these four outcomes of the decision making process.[14]

1. The *quality* or *rationality* of the decision, which is defined as the extent to which decisions influence employee performance and further the attainment of organizational goals.
2. The amount of *commitment* to the decision, defined as the degree of employee commitment to executing the decision effectively.
3. The length of *time* required to make the decision, in other words, *efficiency*.
4. The amount of growth or *development* of the group or team.

The extent to which these four outcomes of quality, commitment, time, and development are critical varies from one decision to another. For some decisions, particularly those you will implement yourself, acceptance is not critical, but high quality may be absolutely essential, as for example, in decisions about how to program the computer for inventory control. Other decisions have very little quality requirement but involve great acceptance. The decision about how the office support staff will cover the phones at lunch time is an example of this type of decision. The solution devised has little in the way of a logical requirement because any one of the support staff can do the job, but it must be acceptable to the people involved. Efficiency is usually an important consideration in everything we do in organizations, but other objectives, such as developing subordinates or encouraging organizational learning, sometimes take priority.

It is, therefore, important to be able to diagnose decision situations to determine the outcome requirements and the appropriate method of decision making. No single decision-making method or management style is appropriate for all jobs or even all decisions in a single job.

One of the situational contingencies that determines the appropriate leadership style concerns whether or not the problem is structured or unstructured. A problem is well structured if we know the current state of the problem, the desired state, and the alternative courses of action that can remedy it. Structured problems are repetitive and routine problems for which a definite procedure has been developed. In contrast, unstructured problems are novel, and no procedures have been developed to handle them because they occur infrequently and/or are very complex. For example, repairing an airplane is a structured problem; designing a completely new spaceship is an unstructured problem. Because a situation involving an unstructured problem requires more ideas and brains, a more participative leadership style is required.

Victor Vroom and his associates have developed a formal model that helps us to analyze specific decision situations and to determine the decision-making approach that is likely to be most effective.[15] The model is constructed in the form of a decision tree based on seven rules (shown in Table 15-2) that were derived from research on problem solving and decision making. It poses eight questions for managers to ask about a decision.

A. **Quality requirement** How important is the technical quality of this decision?
B. **Commitment requirement** How important is subordinate commitment to the decision?
C. **Leaders information** Do you have sufficient information to make a high-quality decision?
D. **Problem structure** Is the problem well structured?
E. **Commitment probability** If you were to make the decision by yourself, is it reasonably certain that your subordinate(s) would be committed to the decision?
F. **Goal congruence** Do subordinates share the organizational goals to be attained in solving this problem?
G. **Subordinate conflict** Is conflict among subordinates over preferred solutions likely?
H. **Subordinate information** Do subordinates have sufficient information to make a high-quality decision?

By answering these questions sequentially and tracing the answers through the model's decision tree (see Figure 15-1 on page 338), managers are led to the most effective leadership

TABLE 15-2   Rules Underlying the Leader-Participation Model

Rules to Protect the Quality of the Decision

1. **The leader information rule.** If the quality of the decision is important and the leader does not possess enough information or expertise to solve the problem by himself or herself, then AI (see Table 15-1) is eliminated from the feasible set.
2. **The goal congruence rule.** If the quality of the decision is important and subordinates are not likely to pursue the organizational goals in their efforts to solve the problem, then GII is eliminated from the feasible set.
3. **The unstructured problem rule.** In decisions in which the quality of the decision is important, if the leader lacks the necessary information or expertise to solve the problem by himself or herself and if the problem is unstructured, the method of solving the problem should provide for interaction among subordinates likely to possess relevant information. Accordingly, AI, AII, and CI are eliminated from the feasible set.

Rules to Protect the Acceptance of the Decision

4. **The acceptance rule.** If the acceptance of the decision by subordinates is critical to effective implementation and if it is not certain that an autocratic decision will be accepted, AI and AII are eliminated from the feasible set.
5. **The conflict rule.** If the acceptance of the decision is critical, an autocratic decision is not certain to be accepted, and disagreement among subordinates in methods of attaining the organizational goal is likely, the methods used in solving the problem should enable those in disagreement to resolve their differences with full knowledge of the problem. Accordingly, under these conditions, AI, AII, and CI, which permit no interaction among subordinates and, therefore, provide no opportunity for those in conflict to resolve their differences, are eliminated from the feasible set. Their use runs the risk of leaving some of the subordinates with less than the needed commitment to the final decision.
6. **The fairness rule.** If the quality of the decision is unimportant but acceptance of the decision is critical and not certain to result from an autocratic decision, it is important that the decision process used generate the needed acceptance. The decision process used should permit the subordinates to interact with one another and negotiate over the fair method of resolving any differences, with full responsibility on them for determining what is fair and equitable. Accordingly, under these circumstances, AI, AII, CI, and CII are eliminated from the feasible set.
7. **The acceptance priority rule.** If acceptance is critical and not certain to result from an autocratic decision, and if subordinates are motivated to pursue the organizational goals represented in the problem, then methods that provide equal partnership in the decision-making process can provide greater acceptance without risking decision quality. Accordingly, AI, AII, CI, and CII are eliminated from the feasible set.

Source: V. H. Vroom, "A New Look at Managerial Decision Making," *Organizational Dynamics, 2* (Spring 1973): 67.

alternative for the problem. The leadership styles are described in Table 15-1 at the beginning of the chapter. To summarize and understand how the model works, let's analyze an actual problem using the decision tree.

You were hired last month as vice president in charge of purchasing for a large manufacturing company that has thirty plants located in the East. For the last 20 years, the company operated in a decentralized fashion with corporate executives providing a minimal amount of control and direction to autonomous plant managers. Each local purchasing manager reports directly to the plant manager and makes his or her own purchasing decisions. There is little or no coordination among the purchasing managers in different plants, and relationships among them are best described as competitive rather than collaborative.

The president predicted that the company would have increasing difficulty in procuring certain essential raw materials and, as a result, created your position so purchasing decisions would be centralized. You were selected for this job due to your extensive background in corporate

QR Quality requirement: How important is the technical quality of this decision?

CR Commitment requirement: How important is subordinate commitment to the decision?

LI Leader's information: Do you have sufficient information to make a high-quality decision?

ST Problem structure: Is the problem well structured?

CP Commitment probability: If you were to make the decision by yourself, is it reasonably certain that your subordinate(s) would be committed to the decision?

GC Goal congruence: Do subordinates share the organizational goals to be attained in solving this problem?

CO Subordinate conflict: Is conflict among subbordinates over preferred solution likely?

SI Subordinate information: Do subordinates have sufficient information to make a high-quality decision?

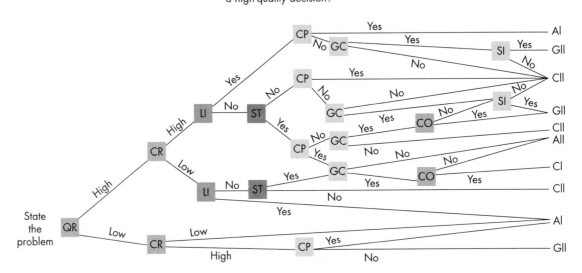

FIGURE 15-1   **The Revised Leadership-Participation Model**
Source: V. H. Vroom and A. G. Jago, *The New Leadership: Cases and Manuals for Use in Leadership Training* (New Haven, CT: Authors, 1987).

purchasing in a different industry. The president announced your appointment in last week's newsletter. Because the peak buying season is approaching, you want to quickly establish a procedure that will decrease the chance of serious shortages and maximize the advantages of centralized buying (greater leverage with suppliers, lower costs due to greater volume).

You are anxious to meet the purchasing agents and pick their brains about their purchasing practices. You have heard that they are a conscientious group that tends to resent interference from headquarters. They are likely to interpret a move toward centralized purchasing as a loss of power on their part. You will need both their input and cooperation for centralized purchasing to work effectively. Furthermore, any solution that does not receive the active support of the various plant managers is likely to fail.[16]

Answering the appropriate diagnostic questions and tracing them through the decision tree works as follows:

A. **Quality requirement?**	High. Running out of essential raw materials would threaten the company's performance.
B. **Commitment requirement?**	High. A solution that does not receive active support of the plant managers and the purchasing managers will not succeed.
C. **Leader's information?**	No. You need to pick their brains and get the purchasing managers' input and you came from a different industry.
D. **Problem structure?**	No. You don't know what the policy should be for this company with regard to their raw materials. The company has little familiarity with centralized solutions and policies.
E. **Commitment probability?**	No. You are an unproven newcomer trying to exert authority over employees who report directly to someone else.
F. **Goal congruence?**	No. The purchasing managers will probably resist giving up their power to make autonomous decisions, and their primary allegiance may lie with their plant than with Headquarters.

Therefore, the model predicts that CII, sharing the problem in a group meeting to obtain their ideas and suggestions and then making the decision alone, will be the most effective style for handling this situation.

 ## PROCEDURE FOR GROUP MEETING

The purpose of the group exercise is to provide an opportunity to practice using the decision tree and identify and discuss reasons for differences between what the model recommends and your own decision-making style.

STEP 1.   Each learning group should record its answers to the five cases on the chalkboard or flipchart so that all members can view the results. The following Case Analysis Record Form provides a format for recording the data.

STEP 2.   The learning groups should work through the decision tree on the preceding page for each case and arrive at a group recommendation (30 minutes). Trace your decision steps with a different color for each case or utilize a different tree for each one.

STEP 3.   Each group should post its recommended leadership style for each case on the board.

STEP 4.   The instructor takes the class through the cases using Vroom and Yetton's guide, answering the diagnostic questions for each case as they did. (See page 348.) Please pay attention to how your group's answers differ from the Vroom-Yetton model. At the end of each case, discuss how and why your group recommendations differed from the model. The point of this exercise is to learn from a comparison of your answers. (15–20 minutes)

STEP 5.   The class discussion should focus on these questions. (20 minutes)
   a.   Sometimes students end up with different answers than Vroom and his colleagues
        because of assumptions they have made about the decision. Can you identify any
        assumptions you made in the cases?
   b.   What assumptions does the model make?
   c.   What factors are missing from this model?
   d.   What did you learn about your natural decision-making style from this exercise?
   e.   What connections can you make with the readings?

Case Analysis Record Form

Participant Names	Case 1	Case 2	Case 3	Case 4	Case 5
Group recommendations after using the decision tree					
Vroom et al.'s recommendations					

FOLLOW-UP

A normative model, such as the leader-participation model, raises three questions: (1) When managers utilize this model, how likely are their decisions to be effective? (2) Do managers really make decisions in this manner? (3) If not, why not?

First, research has shown that when managers choose one of the alternatives within the feasible set, a greater percentage of their decisions was found to be effective.[17] In six studies, when managers used the leadership style indicated by the model, 62 percent of their decisions were effective; when they did not, only 37 percent of their decisions were successful.[18] Another study of 45 retail cleaning franchises revealed that managers whose leadership behaviors conformed to the leadership-participation model had more satisfied employees and more profitable operations than other managers.[19]

Second, research comparing the leadership-participation model with the actual behavior of managers has shown that there is a general correspondence between the model recommendations for a specific situation and a manager's behavior in that situation. Vroom and Jago report, "In approximately two-thirds of the problems, nevertheless, the behavior which the manager reported was within the feasible set of methods prescribed for that problem, and in about 40 percent of the cases it corresponded exactly to the minimum person-hours solution."[20] Thus, managers seem to be using an intuitive notion similar to the leader-participation model to manage the decision-making process in their organizations. In some ways, however, the *differences* between model recommendations and managerial behavior are more interesting, because they shed light on the assumptions on which the model is based and on particularly difficult issues in managing the decision-making process.

For example, when we have asked managers how they would solve the engineering work assignment case described in the prework for this unit, many of them chose an AI or AII decision. Most resisted strongly the idea of bringing the group together for decision making either in the CII or GII modes. Vroom et al.'s GII solution brought cries of "No way!" or "It will never work!" Further discussion of differences between individual styles and the GII decision recommendations raised some interesting comments and assumptions:

- "The group wouldn't be able to deal with a difficult problem like this."
- "I wouldn't know how to control the conflict this situation creates if it became a group decision."
- "In most groups the members would expect the manager to make this decision, and they would have to live with it."

These comments bring out some of the assumptions underlying the leader-participation model and, hence, define some of the problems in its application. These assumptions are:

1. Managers are equally skilled in using the different decision-making alternatives.
2. Groups are equally skilled in their adaptation to these decision-making alternatives.
3. Organizational history and the resulting organizational culture have no impact on a single decision analyzed by the model.

What the model does is analyze a specific decision dispassionately in terms of its outcome requirements without regard to the preceding assumptions about managerial and group skill or organizational culture. Yet in any specific situation, these issues must be considered to ensure that decisions are effective.

In conclusion, we suggest the following considerations in applying the leader-participation model to actual managerial situations:

1. Intuitive managerial decision-making models are more simplified than the leader-participation model. They do not account for some of the interactions among decision rules portrayed in Figure 15-1. This is supported by the research of Vroom and his colleagues.
2. Managers tend to underemphasize the importance of the acceptance and commitment components of decision effectiveness. This is also supported by Vroom and his colleagues' research.

3. Managers tend to use decision-making styles they are skilled at and avoid styles they feel uncomfortable with. For many, this means avoiding the more difficult group decision-making procedures.
4. Organizational history and culture will affect the decision-making method chosen, independent of the logical dictates of the situation. Organizational culture affects decision making in several ways:
   a. Group members will adjust to norms about "the way things are decided around here" and may have little experience or skill using other styles, such as group consensus.
   b. Managers may use a particular decision-making method because their boss uses it and be constrained in their flexibility of decision making by the style dictated from above. If your boss is autocratic with you, it may be more difficult to be participative with your own subordinates. The boss may neither understand or appreciate a style different from his or her own.

These considerations suggest that the leader-participation model is useful in determining how the decision-making process should be conducted, but the application of this ideal requires managerial skill training in all of the decision-making methods, team development in the various forms of group decision making, and organizational development to create norms that value quality, acceptance, and efficiency as the primary criteria for effective decision making. See Table 15-3 for realities in organizational decision making and suggestions for dealing with them.

TABLE 15-3 Some Apparent Realities of Decision Making in Complex Organizations

Some Things Individual Managers Cannot Expect to Do Much About	Some Things Individual Managers Can Do	Some Things the Organization Can Do
The fact that decision making in organizations is not a totally rational, orderly process	Exercise choices in the problems to work on, which battles to fight and where, and when to cut losses	Set values and tone to support problem solving and risk
The nature of managerial work: the juggling of problems and conflicting demands	Develop intimate knowledge of the business and good working relationships with the people in it	Design organizational structure, reward, and control systems to support action rather than bureaucracy
People are flawed: They are limited information processors, have biases and emotions, and develop vested interests	Know yourself: Know your strengths, weaknesses, and hot-buttons, and when to ask for help	Provide assignments in which decision-making skills can be developed
Fundamental forces in the business environment	Develop the diverse set of skills necessary to act in different situations	Keep business strategy focused on areas about which management is knowledgeable
Basic organizational components determined largely by the business one is in		

Source: M. M. McCall and R. E. Kaplan, *Whatever It Takes: The Realities of Managerial Decision Making* (Upper Saddle River, NJ: Prentice Hall, 1990) 120. Reprinted by permission of the publisher.

UPDATED VERSION

Vroom and Jago[21] developed a more sophisticated version of this theory that includes four new contingencies: time constraints, geographical dispersion (which acknowledges the difficulty of getting people together for a discussion), motivation to minimize the time needed to make the decision (so that time can be devoted to more pressing items), and motivation to develop subordinates. The new version utilizes a continuum ranging from 1 to 5 rather than a simple yes or no response to each question. It has four decision trees, two for group decisions and two for individual decisions. At the individual and group level there are separate trees for use when decisions must be made quickly and when time is not such an important consideration.

The new model allows for greater situational complexity and is designed to be used with a computer program. Neither the leadership styles nor the premises underlying the original questions have changed significantly, but the increased sophistication of the model makes it too complex for our teaching purposes in this course.

The leader-participation model gives us a partial answer to the question, "What are the pros and cons of group decisions?" The advantages are more complete information and knowledge, diverse views, increased commitment to the decision, and the increased legitimacy of a democratic decision. However, group decisions can also be time-consuming and overly influenced by conformity pressures or a dominant person or subgroup.

THE ZONE OF INDIFFERENCE AND CULTURAL DIFFERENCES IN DECISION MAKING

Chester Barnard, one of the first management writers, introduced the concept of the "zone of indifference."[22] Employees willingly accept decisions made by their boss on topics that fall within their zone of indifference (e.g., the font of the lettering on the new office stationery). Asking for participation on such topics wastes employee time and can even frustrate employees ("How can we get our work done if management keeps bugging us with stupid little decisions? Don't they get paid to make decisions?"). However, employees do want to have a voice in decisions that lie outside their zone of indifference. For example, a U.S. consultant redesigning a department in a Guatemalan agency repeatedly asked employees for their input on the new systems and processes. They rubber-stamped whatever she proposed to them and seemed more than content to let her make all the decisions. However, the employees revolted when she and the director surprised them by replacing their traditional desks with new workstations that inadvertently prevented them from being able to see and talk to other employees. Unlike the consultant's previous decisions, the new workstations did not fall into the employees' zone of indifference. She took measures to make the workstations more palatable for the employees, regaining some of the social credit she'd lost with the employees. However, it is always better to avoid causing rebellions in the first place—understanding what falls inside and outside the zone of indifference for one's employees is an important managerial competency.

In terms of the leader-participation model, the zone of indifference relates to the diagnostic question, "If you were to make the decision by yourself, is it reasonably certain that your subordinates would be committed to the decision?" This question will be answered differently in different settings as well as different cultures. For example, in high power distance cultures (e.g., Korea), employees are less likely to expect to influence decisions and more likely to expect bosses to make autocratic decisions. Their zone of indifference will be larger. Participative decision making is more likely in cultures with low power distance, as well as in individualistic cultures in which individual opinions are valued (e.g., the United States). As the global labor force becomes more educated, however, employees may expect to be consulted more frequently about decisions at work.

Japan is noted for *ringisei*, decision making by consensus. Proposals in document form are circulated for approval among employees before a decision is implemented. Thus, employees can voice an opinion before a manager makes the final decision. *Ringisei* is time consuming up front, but this participative process eliminates resistance to decisions, thereby improving implementation quality and speed.[23]

As we noted in the chapter on problem solving, cultures vary in terms of how accepting or proactive they are with regard to problems that may require decisions. Fatalistic cultures are more accepting of situations and, therefore, usually slower to make a decision to resolve a problem. The alternatives considered in the decision-making process are also affected by cultural values.

Source: Reprinted by permission of Tribune Company Syndicate, Inc.

Cultures oriented to the past (e.g., England) are more likely to make decisions in keeping with tradition and precedents. Present-oriented cultures (e.g., the United States) focus on short-term solutions. Future-oriented cultures (e.g., Japan) are more likely to focus on long-term solutions. Innovative solutions are generally welcomed and more accepted in cultures that are less tied to the past.

INTUITION AND DECISION MAKING

Cultures also vary in the way they search for information pertaining to a decision, which relates to the value given to rationality. In the United States, where rationality is highly valued, even intuitive decisions may be couched in rational terms so they are more readily accepted. Other cultures (e.g., Sweden) are more comfortable with intuitive decision making. Cultures that value rationality rely more on their senses (facts) while others rely on intuition (ideas, images, and possibilities). Before the Yom Kippur War in 1973, the U.S. experts, relying on facts, predicted that less than 8 million Israelis could not prevail against 100 million Arabs. The Israelis, who succeeded in spite of these odds, relied on their intuition and focused on the image of the continued existence of their country.[24]

There is a growing recognition that rational analysis has been overemphasized in U.S. business. Intuition is becoming more acceptable in the workplace. In a recent study, two-thirds of the professionals interviewed stated that intuition led to better decisions.[25] Intuitive skills are usually developed through experience or working with people who have intuitive qualities. Intuition is a "cognitive conclusion based on a decision maker's previous experiences and emotional inputs."[26] Thus, intuition and rational analysis are complementary aspects of good decision making.

LEARNING POINTS

1. Individual decisions are not independent, solitary events. Instead they are closely connected to previous decisions and are influenced by the process that brought the decision point to a head.

2. Although decision making at very high levels is frequently characterized as a lonely, individual struggle, decision making is also a social process. Decision making involves information sharing and interdependence among organization members. The manager's job is to manage the decision process by assessing which information and which players need to be involved.

3. The model of rational decision making is an outgrowth of classical economics, but the decision-making process is seldom completely rational.

4. The theory of bounded rationality maintains that people are restricted in making decisions and settle for less than ideal solutions. They satisfice, selecting the first alternative that is satisfactory.

5. In the garbage can model, four factors—problems, participants, solutions, and choice opportunities—all float randomly inside the organization, described metaphorically as a garbage can. If they connect, a decision results.

6. When people support riskier decisions in a group setting than they would individually, this is called the risky shift. When the group decision is more conservative than individual positions, this is the cautious shift.

7. Groupthink refers to the tendency for members of a highly cohesive group to seek consensus so strongly that they fail to do a realistic appraisal of other alternatives, which may be more correct.

8. Escalation of commitment occurs when people continue to commit resources to a failing course of action.

9. The leader-participation model is a contingency theory of leadership. The continuum of leadership styles includes autocratic, consultative, and group decisions.

10. The choice of leadership style affects these outcomes of the decision-making process:
    a. The quality or rationality of the decision.
    b. The commitment on the part of subordinates to execute the decision effectively.
    c. The amount of time required to make the decision.
    d. The development of the group or team.

11. Utilizing groups to make decisions involves more time but results in greater acceptance of the decision and more likelihood of successful implementation.

12. Structured problems are repetitive and routine problems for which a definite procedure has been developed. Unstructured problems are novel, with no procedures to handle them because they are infrequent and/or complex.

13. The leader-participation model helps managers analyze specific decision situations and determine which leadership styles are most appropriate by diagnosing these factors: quality and commitment requirements, source of necessary information, type of problem (structured or unstructured), commitment probability, and subordinate goal congruence and conflict.

14. Managers whose leadership behavior approximates the model are more likely to make effective decisions than managers whose behavior does not conform to the model.

15. Employees willingly accept decisions made by their boss on topics that fall within their zone of indifference. They want to participate, however, in decisions that fall outside that zone.

16. Intuition is a "cognitive conclusion based on a decision maker's previous experiences and emotional inputs." Intuition and rational analysis are complementary aspects of good decision making.

FOR MANAGERS

- One of the most important factors for a manager to bear in mind when decisions are being made is the concept of setting precedents. If you want to establish a reputation for fairness, it's worthwhile to consider whether you would want a given decision to be a guide for future ones. The criteria used for making any decision should reflect the cultural values you are trying to promote within the organization.
- Some decisions eventually become obvious with time. The trick lies in knowing which decisions (or which parts of them) can be postponed and which need to be made immediately. This is learned by experience.
- Because decision making is learned by experience, it's desirable to start employees out making decisions at the lowest possible level. Too often the first decisions employees get to make are when they are promoted to supervisor and find themselves overwhelmed. Teaching employees good decision-making techniques, explaining why you made the decision you did, asking what decision they would make in your shoes, and delegating as many decisions as possible are all ways to develop good decision makers before they find themselves in the hot seat.
- Decisions are only as good as the information on which they are based. Therefore, it's important to have reliable and accurate information sources. In some organizations the higher one goes, the more difficult it is to have accurate information because people are busy telling you either what they think you want to hear or information that reflects well upon them. Kotter found that the aggressiveness with which managers sought out information distinguished effective managers from less effective ones.[27]
- Test the water about possible solutions with carefully chosen people such as informal opinion leaders, greybeards (wise, older employees), and powerful people who are interested in the issue. Yes-men and -women and people with a narrow perspective or a self-serving approach are obviously not good choices.
- It is not uncommon to have second thoughts about decisions. Indeed, it's a natural cognitive phenomenon called cognitive dissonance. Knowing this can help you be more patient when employees (or even you) have second thoughts, even when a decision seemed to be final and everyone was in agreement.
- People can only process so much information because our brains have limited capacity. Furthermore, it is sometimes impossible to have all the information that is needed to make a good decision. Thus, there is often an element of ambiguity involved with decision making. People have different tolerance levels for ambiguity, which affects their decision-making process.
- Part of the psychological contract regarding employee input on decisions concerns the manager's response. When managers request input from employees, they "owe" them the courtesy of explaining what the final decisions were and why the employee suggestion was or was not used. When managers do not do this, employees are likely to say, "I don't know why I bothered; they just went ahead and did what they wanted to anyway." In the future, such employees may be less forthcoming with suggestions. However, when managers do explain how decisions were made and why an employee suggestion could not be used, they are both recognizing the employee's contribution and training him or her to make decisions in the future. Employees are not always aware of the broader contingencies their managers face. Sharing the rationale behind decisions is a way to develop employees.
- Don't let a disruptive debate over a decision drag on too long. When a group cannot come to an agreement after a reasonable amount of time, its members may be relieved if the manager steps in and makes the decision.

PERSONAL APPLICATION ASSIGNMENT

The topic of this assignment is to think back on a decision-making experience that was significant for you. Choose an experience that intrigues you and that you want to learn more about. One possibility is to analyze a previous decision using the leadership-participation model.

A. *Concrete Experience*

    1. *Objectively* describe the experience (who, what, when, where, how information). (2 points)

    2. *Subjectively* describe your feelings, perceptions, and thoughts that occurred during (not after) the experience. What did others seem to be feeling? (2 points)

B. *Reflective Observation*

    1. Looking back at the experience, what were the perspectives of the key actors (including you)? (2 points)

    2. Why did the people involved (including you) behave as they did? (2 points)

C. *Abstract Conceptualization*

    1. Relate concepts or theories from the assigned readings or the lecture to the experience. Explain thoroughly how they apply to your experience. Please apply at least two concepts or theories and cite them correctly. (4 points)

D. *Active Experimentation*
1. What did you learn about decision making from this experience? (1 point)
2. What did you learn about yourself? (1 point)
3. What action steps will you take to be more effective in the future? (2 points)

E. *Integration, Synthesis, and Writing*
1. Did you integrate and synthesize the four sections? (1 point)
2. Was the Personal Application Assignment well written and easy to understand? (1 point)
3. Was it free of spelling and grammatical errors? (2 points)

Decision-Making Case Answers

Case	QR	CR	LI	ST	CP	GC	CO	SI	Style
	Quality Requirement	Commitment Requirement	Leader's Information	Structured	Commitment Probability	Goal Congruence	Subordinate Conflict	Subordinate Information	
1	High	Low	No	No					CII
2	High	High	No	No	No	No			CII
3	Low	High			No				GII
4	High	High	No	Yes	No	No			CII
5	High	Low	Yes						AI

ENDNOTES

[1] This unit is based on the research of Victor Vroom and his colleagues Phillip Yetton and Arthur G. Jago. Cases used with permission of the University of Pittsburgh Press and the American Institute for Decision Sciences. Further information about training programs based on the model can be obtained from Kepner-Trego Associates, Inc.

[2] P. C. Nutt, "Surprising But True: Half the Decisions in Organizations Fail," *Academy of Management Executive 24*, no. 4 (1999): 75–89.

[3] E. Bardack, *The Implementation Game* (Cambridge, MA: MIT Press, 1977).

[4] H. A. Simon, *Administrative Behavior* (New York: Free Press, 1976).

[5] V. Haller, "Baby Juice Scam Nets Executives Fine, Prison Time," *Mesa Tribune* (June 17, 1988): A10, 3.

[6] C. E. Lindholm, "The Science of Muddling Through," *Public Administration Review* (Spring 1959): 79–88.

[7] M. D. Cohen, J. G. March, and J. P. Olsen, "A Garbage Can Model of Organizational Choice," *Administrative Science Quarterly 17* (1972): 1–25.

[8] J. A. F. Stoner, "Risky and Cautious Shifts in Group Decisions: The Influence of Widely Held Values," *Journal of Experimental Social Psychology 4* (1968): 442–59; N. Kogan and M. A. Wallach, "Group Risk Taking as a Function of Members' Anxiety and Defensiveness," *Journal of Personality 35* (1967): 50–63.

[9] D. G. Myers and H. Lamm, "The Group Polarization Phenomenon," *Psychological Bulletin 83* (1976): 602–27; M. E. Kaplan, "The Influencing Process in Group Decision Making," in *Group Processes*, ed. C. Hendrick (Newbury Park, CA: Sage, 1987).

[10] I. L. Janis, *Victims of Groupthink* (Boston: Houghton-Mifflin, 1972) and *Groupthink* (Boston: Houghton-Mifflin, 1982). See also G. Whyte, "Groupthink Reconsidered," *Academy of Management Review 14* (1989): 45–56.

[11] Janis, *Victims of Groupthink* and *Groupthink*.

[12] J. K. Esser, "Alive and Well after 25 Years: A Review of Groupthink Research," *Organizational Behavior and Human Decision Processes 73*, no. 2/3 (1998): 116–41; S. R. Fuller and R. J. Aldag, "Organizational Tonypandy: Lessons from a Quarter Century of the Groupthink Phenomenon," *Organizational Behavior and Human Decision Processes 73*, no. 2/3 (1998): 163–84; M. E. Turner and A. R. Pratkanis, "Twenty-Five Years of Groupthink Theory and Research: Lessons from the Evaluation of a Theory," *Organizational Behavior and Human Decision Processes 73*, no. 2/3 (1998): 105–15; and R. M. Kramer, "Revisiting the Bay of Pigs and Vietnam Decisions 25 Years Later: How Will Has the Groupthink Hypothesis Stood the Test of Time?" *Organizational Behavior and Human Decision Processes 73*, no. 2/3 (1998): 236–71.

[13] B. M. Staw, "Commitment in an Experimenting Society: An Experiment on the Attribution of Leadership from Administrative Scenarios," *Journal of Applied Psychology 65* (1980): 249–60.

[14] V. H. Vroom and A. G. Jago, *The New Leadership: Managing Participation in Organizations* (Upper Saddle River, NJ: Prentice Hall, 1988).

[15] V. H. Vroom and P. Yetton, *Leadership and Decision Making* (Pittsburgh, PA: University of Pittsburgh Press, 1973); and Vroom and Jago, *The New Leadership.* See also V. H. Vroom and A. G. Jago, "Situation Effects and Levels of Analysis in the Study of Leader Participation," *Leadership Quarterly 6*, no. 2 (1995): 169–81; and V. H. Vroom, A. G. Jago, D. Eden, P. W. Yetton, and J. F. Craig, "Participative Leadership," in F. Dansereau and F. J. Yammarino, eds., *Leadership: The Multiple-Level Approaches: Classical and New Wave 24* (Stamford, CT: JAI Press, 1998), pp. 145–89.

[16] A version of this case appears in Vroom and Jago, *The New Leadership*, pp. 166–168.

[17] R. H. Field and R. J. House, "A Test of the Vroom-Yetton Model Using Manager and Subordinate Reports," *Journal of Applied Psychology 75* (1990): 362–70.

[18] Vroom and Jago, *The New Leadership*, p. 79.

[19] C. Margerison and R. Glube, "Leadership Decision Making: An Empirical Test of the Vroom and Yetton Model," *Journal of Management Studies 16*, (1979): 45–55.

[20] Vroom and Jago, "Decision Making as a Social Process: Normative and Descriptive Models of Leader Behavior," *Decision Sciences 5* (1974): 754.

[21] Vroom and Jago, *The New Leadership*.

[22] C. Barnard, *The Functions of the Executive* (Cambridge, MA: Harvard University Press, 1938).

[23] W. Ouchi, *Theory Z. How American Businesses Can Meet the Japanese Challenge* (New York: Avon, 1989).

[24] N. J. Adler, *International Dimensions of Organizational Behavior.* (Cincinnati: South-Western, 1997).

[25] L. A. Burke and M. K. Miller, "Taking the Mystery Out of Intuitive Decision Making," *Academy of Management Executive 13*, no. 4 (1999): 91–98.

[26] Ibid., p. 93. For an interesting discussion of intuitive decision making, see G. Klein, *Sources of Power: How People Make Decisions* (Cambridge, MA: MIT Press, 1999).

[27] J. Kotter, *The General Managers* (New York: Free Press, 1982).

Chapter 16

▲▲▲

POWER AND INFLUENCE

OBJECTIVES By the end of this chapter, you should be able to:

A. Identify the three possible outcomes of an influence attempt.

B. Describe the various sources of power.

C. Identify the influence tactics people use at work.

D. Describe and utilize the four influence styles.

How to Manage the Boss

Most managers, including of course most chief executives, have a boss. Few people are as important to the performance and success of a manager as the boss. Yet while management books and courses abound in advice on how to manage subordinates, few if any even mention managing the boss.

Few managers seem to realize how important it is to manage the boss or, worse, believe that it can be done at all. They bellyache about the boss but do not even try to manage him or her. Yet managing the boss is fairly simple—indeed generally quite a bit simpler than managing subordinates. There are only a few Dos, and even fewer Don'ts.

The first Do is to realize that it is both the subordinate's duty and in the subordinate's self-interest to make the boss as effective and as achieving as possible. The best prescription for one's own success is, after all, still to work for a boss who is going places. Thus, the first Do is to go to the boss—at least once a year—and ask: "What do I do and what do my people do that helps you do your job? And what do we do that hampers you and makes life more difficult for you?"

THE CORRECT DEFINITION

This sounds obvious—but it is rarely done. For even effective executives tend to misdefine a "manager" as someone who is responsible for the work of subordinates—the definition of 50 years ago—and, thus, tend not to perceive that they have any responsibility for the boss's performance and effectiveness. But the correct definition of a manager—as we have known it for at least 40 years—is someone who is responsible for the performance of all the people on whom his or her own performance depends.

The first person on whom a manager's performance depends is the boss, and the boss is, thus, the first person for whose performance a manager has to take responsibility. But only by asking, "what do I do to help you or to hamper you?"—the best way to ask is without beating about the bush—can you find out what the boss needs and what gets in the boss's way.

Closely related is the need for awareness that your boss is a human being and an individual; no two persons work alike, perform alike or behave alike. The subordinate's job is not to re-educate the boss, not to make the boss conform to what the business schools and the management books say bosses should be like. It is to enable a particular boss to perform as a unique individual. And being an individual, every boss has idiosyncrasies, has "good days" and "bad days," and, like the rest of us, needs his or her own security blanket.

To manage the boss requires thinking through such questions as: Does this individual who is my boss want me to come in once every month—but no more often—and spend 30 minutes presenting the performance, the plans, and the problems of my department? Or does this individual want me to come in every time there is anything to report or to discuss, every time there is the slightest change, every time we make a move? Does this individual want me to send the stuff in as a written report, in a nice folder, complete with tabs and a table of contents? Or does this individual want an oral presentation? Is this individual, in other words, a reader or a listener? And does this boss require (as do, for instance, most financial executives) 30 pages of figures with everything as his or her security blanket—and should it be tables or graphs?

Does this individual need the information to be there when he or she gets to the office in the morning, or does this boss (as do a good many operating people) want it at the end of the day, say around 3:30 on Friday afternoon? And if there is disagreement among the management group, how does this boss want to have it handled? To have us iron it out and report our consensus (as did Gen. Eisenhower and President Reagan)? Or for us to report our disagreements in full detail and with complete documentation (as did both Gens. George Marshall and MacArthur)?

What are the things the boss does well? What are his or her strengths? And what are the boss's limitations and weaknesses—the areas in which the subordinate needs to support, to buttress, and to supplement the boss? A manager's task is to make the strengths of people effective and their weaknesses irrelevant—and that applies fully as much to the manager's boss as it applies to the manager's subordinates. If, for instance, the boss is good at marketing but uncomfortable with financial figures and analysis, managing the boss means to bring him or her into the marketing decision but to prepare the financial analysis beforehand and in depth.

Managing the boss means, above all, creating a relationship of trust. This requires confidence on the part of the superior that the subordinate manager will play to the boss's strengths and safeguard the boss against his or her limitations and weaknesses.

KEEP THE BOSS AWARE

The final Do: Make sure the boss understands what can be expected of you, what the objectives and goals are on which your own energies and those of your people will be concentrated, what your priorities are, and, equally important, what they are not. It is by no means always necessary that the boss approve—it is sometimes not even desirable. But the boss must understand what you are up to, must know what to expect, and what not to expect. Bosses, after all, are held responsible by their bosses for the performance of their subordinates. They must be able to say: "I know what Anne (or Joe) is trying to do." Only if they can say this will they be able to delegate to their subordinate managers.

And now two Don'ts:

Never expose the boss to surprises. It is the job of the subordinate to protect the boss against surprises—even pleasant ones (if any such exist). To be exposed to a surprise in the organization one is responsible for results in humiliation, and usually public humiliation. Different bosses want very different warnings of possible surprises. Some—again, Ike is a good example—want no more than a warning that things may turn out differently. Other bosses—President Kennedy, for example—demand a full, detailed report even if there is only a slight chance of a surprise. But all bosses need to be protected against surprises. Otherwise they will not trust a subordinate—and with good reason.

Never underrate the boss! The boss may look illiterate; he or she may look stupid—and looks are not always deceptive. But there is no risk at all in overrating the boss. The worst that could happen is for the boss to feel flattered. But if you underrate the boss, he or she will either see through your little game and will bitterly resent it. Or the boss will impute to you the deficiency in brains or knowledge you imputed to the boss and will consider you ignorant, dumb, or lacking in imagination.

But the most important thing is not what to do or what not to do. It is to accept that managing the boss is the responsibility of the subordinate manager and a key—maybe the most important one—to his or her own effectiveness as an executive.

Source: Peter F. Drucker. *The Wall Street Journal,* August 1, 1986. Reprinted with permission of *The Wall Street Journal*

PREMEETING PREPARATION

A. Read "How to Manage the Boss."

B. Answer the following questions:

1. Think about someone who handles power very well. How does he or she do it?

2. What differences in behavior have you observed between someone who has power and influence and someone who does not?

3. What do you want to learn about power?

4. What are the significant learning points from the *Readings*?

C. Complete the Influence Style Self-Diagnosis.

D. Read the Topic Introduction.

E. If your instructor has assigned the Robbins Self-Assessment Library, use "How Power Oriented Am I?" "What's My Preferred Type of Power?" and "How Politically-Oriented Am I?"

PERSONAL INFLUENCE STYLE DIAGNOSIS

The focus of this chapter is the effective exercise of power and influence. Before reading the Topic Introduction, do a simple self-assessment of your style of influencing others. Generally speaking, how descriptive is each of the following styles of your typical influence behavior? Using the key provided, record your rating (from 1 = not descriptive to 5 = very descriptive) in the space to the left of each paragraph. Then read the Topic Introduction.

1	2	3	4	5
Not at all descriptive of me		Somewhat descriptive		Very descriptive of me

INFLUENCE STYLE SELF-DIAGNOSIS

_____ I am direct and positive in asserting my own wishes and requirements. I let others know what I want from them, and I am quick to tell others when I am pleased or dissatisfied with their performance. I am willing to use my influence and authority to get others to do what I want. I skillfully use a combination of pressures and incentives to get others to agree with my plans and proposals, and I follow up to make sure they carry out agreements and commitments. I readily engage in bargaining and negotiation to achieve my objectives, using both tough and conciliatory styles according to the realities of power and position in each situation.

_____ I am open and nondefensive, being quick to admit when I do not have the answer, or when I have made a mistake. I listen attentively to the ideas and feelings of others, actively communicating my interest in their contributions, and my understanding of their points of view. I am willing to be influenced by others. I give to credit others for their ideas and accomplishments. I make sure that everyone has a chance to be heard before decisions are taken, even when I do not agree with their position. I show trust in others, and I help them to bring out and develop their strengths and abilities.

_____ I appeal to the emotions and ideals of others through the use of forceful and colorful words and images. My enthusiasm is contagious and carries others along with me. I bring others to believe in their ability to accomplish and succeed by working together. I see and can communicate my vision of the exciting possibilities in an idea or situation. I get others to see the values, hopes, and aspirations that they have in common, and I build these common values into a shared sense of group loyalty and commitment.

_____ I produce detailed and comprehensive proposals for dealing with problems. I am persistent and energetic in finding and presenting the logic behind my ideas and in marshalling facts, arguments, and opinion in support of my position. I am quick to grasp the strengths and weaknesses in an argument and to see and articulate the logical connections among various aspects of a complex situation. I am a vigorous and determined seller of ideas.

 # TOPIC INTRODUCTION

Power and influence have negative connotations for many people. They conjure up unpleasant images such as the misuse of power by politicians, the high-pressure tactics of some salespeople, and the destructive behavior occasionally exhibited by military dictators. We often see examples of poor organizational decisions that reflect the self-serving motives of powerful individuals or groups rather than a concern for the good of the organization. On the other hand, the ability to get things done is a crucial requirement for both personal and organizational success. Managers need a certain degree of power and influence to obtain the necessary resources for their units, to ensure that good ideas are heard and decisions are implemented, and to place competent people in key positions. Another advantage of having power is having access to top decision makers and receiving early information on decisions and policy shifts. Therefore, understanding and knowing how to manage power is a key skill for employees and managers alike.

In a comparative study of successful and unsuccessful executives, all the characteristics of the unsuccessful executives can be traced to an abuse or misuse of power. Their personal inadequacies were (1) insensitive, abrasive, and intimidating; (2) cold, aloof, and arrogant; (3) betrayed others' trust; (4) overly ambitious and political; (5) unable to delegate or build a team; and (6) overly dependent on others (a mentor, for example).[1]

In contrast, the personal characteristics of people who successfully obtain and exercise a great deal of power are (1) energy, endurance, and physical stamina; (2) the ability to focus their energy and avoid wasted effort; (3) sensitivity so they can read and understand others; (4) flexibility— the ability to consider different means to achieve goals; (5) personal toughness—a willingness to engage, when necessary, in conflict and confrontation; and (6) the ability to submerge one's ego and be a good subordinate or team player to enlist the help and support of others.[2]

The power and status differences that exist in hierarchies, between supervisors and subordinates, for example, are real and natural. They cannot be ignored or wished away. Indeed, in its simplest, most basic form, your role as a manager is to *make a difference* in the behavior of your subordinates. Your responsibility as a manager is to behave in ways that add to your subordinates' ability to do their jobs effectively and efficiently. The issue is not, therefore, whether or not managers have power, but how they choose to exercise the power demanded by the role and with what consequences. One does not "make a difference" without exercising power and influence.

Power is defined as the capacity to influence the behavior of others. Influence is the process by which people successfully persuade others to follow their advice, suggestions, or orders. In general, there are three possible outcomes to an influence attempt—*commitment, compliance*, or *resistance*. Whereas commitment implies internal agreement, compliance is merely going along with a request or demand without believing in it. Resistance occurs when a person's influence attempt is rejected. This can take the form of a flat refusal, passive—aggressive tactics (making excuses or pretending to agree while resorting to delaying actions or sabotage), or seeking out a third party or superior who has the power to overrule the request.

SOURCES OF POWER

Traditionally, managers have relied almost exclusively on the power inherent in their position. An extreme form of this sounds like "I'm the boss. I have the right and responsibility to tell you what to do, and if you don't perform, I retain the ultimate power of reward and punishment." Increasingly, managers are being forced to develop other influence skills. The greater need for different forms of influence is due to (1) a shifting value structure among younger generations who have less respect for traditional authority; (2) rapid organizational change; (3) the diversity of people, goals, and values; and (4) increased interdependence.[3] Many managers spend the majority of their time on interdependent lateral relationships with people who are neither subordinates nor superiors.[4] In the lateral relationships that we find in staff positions, self-directed work teams, and network organizations (see Chapter 19), power comes from *expertise, effort*, and *relationships*, rather than one's position or the ability to *reward* or *punish* others (*coercive power*). *Charisma* is another source of power, as is *referent power*, which is based on desirable personal traits or resources.[5] We admire and identify with people who have referent power, such as celebrities who endorse products.

Power also comes from "being in the right place." A good location is one that provides (1) *control over resources*, (2) *control and access to information*, in addition to (3) formal authority (*position*).[6] Units that cope with the critical uncertainties facing an organization also acquire a measure of power that they would not otherwise have. This is termed the *strategic contingency model* of power.[7] For example, John Zeglis, a corporate lawyer, became a powerful figure at AT&T, and eventually its president, because he helped lead the company through regulatory changes. "Chief counsels rarely rise so far in corporate America, but Mr. Zeglis... is a special case. AT&T's single most important operational concern remains regulation and how telecommunication laws might impede the company's ability to boost earnings and expand beyond its long-distance franchise. Nobody known these rules better than Mr. Zeglis, who helped write them."[8]

The more dependent people are on someone else, the more power that person has over them.[9] For example, if a person has a scarce skill or resource that is not easily substituted, he or she has power.[10] A highly valued and hard-to-replace employee has the power to negotiate a higher salary and perks than an employee who is less essential to the success of the organization. The former can always threaten to leave the organization; such a threat by a less essential employee is not a source of concern. Thus, it's important to understand the relationship between dependency and power.

INFLUENCE TACTICS

In addition to understanding the sources of power, effective managers need to know what influence behavior looks like. When people were asked to describe incidents in which they had influenced others at work, researchers identified nine generic influence tactics that appear in Figure 16-1.[11] U.S. managers prefer rational persuasion, consultation, and inspirational appeals over more coercive tactics. They often begin with the softer influence tactics and, if they are not successful, move to harder tactics, such as threats. Managers who use a variety of tactics tend to be more successful than those who rely on a single tactic.

Complex and vital influence attempts, such as those required for major strategies or new projects, always require multiple influence tactics. A successful attempt is likely to begin with gathering facts, citing parallel examples (who is doing this?), marshalling the support of others (perhaps

Rational Persuasion	The agent uses logical arguments and factual evidence to persuade the target that a proposal or request is viable and likely to result in the attainment of task objectives.
Inspirational Appeals	The agent makes a request or proposal that arouses the target's enthusiasm by appealing to target values, ideals, and aspirations, of by increasing the target's self-confidence.
Consultation	The agent seeks the target's participation in planning a strategy, activity, or change for which target support and assistance are desired, or is willing to modify a proposal to deal with target concerns and suggestions.
Ingratiation	The agent uses praise, flattery, friendly behavior, or helpful behavior to get the target in a good mood or to think favorably of him or her before asking for something.
Personal Appeals	The agent appeals the to the target's feelings of loyalty and friendship toward him or her when asking for something.
Exchange	The agent offers an exchange of favors, indicates willingness to reciprocate at a later time, or promises a share of the benefits if the target helps accomplish a task.
Coalition Tactics	The agent seeks the aid of others to persuade the target to do something, or uses the support of others as a reason for the target to agree also.
Legitimating Tactics	The agent seeks to establish the legitimacy of a request by claiming the authority or right to make it, or by verifying that it is consistent with organizational policies, rules, practices, or traditions.
Pressure	The agent uses demands, threats, frequent checking, or persistent reminders to influence the target to do what he or she wants.

FIGURE 16-1   **Definition of Influence Tactics**
Source: Adapted from Gary Yukl, *Leadership in Organizations* (Upper Saddle River, NJ: Prentice Hall, 1994): 225.

insured by an effective web of influence), precise timing and packaging of a presentation, and, in the case of initial resistance, persistence and repetition over weeks or even months. Less frequently, but sometimes successfully, managers may resort to manipulation, threats, or pulling rank.[12] When people are trying to obtain benefits or favors from others, they are more likely to use ingratiation or friendly behavior.

The organizational culture affects the type of influence tactics used. Norms and values determine which tactics are acceptable. For example, threats and sanctions are frowned on in informal, egalitarian cultures. New managers should carefully observe successful influence attempts rather than assuming that acceptable tactics in their previous job will work in a different organizational culture.

A common mistake is using influence strategies that fail because they are "too much too soon or too little too late."[13] Effective managers understand that there is a continuum of influence attempts, and they use the appropriate degree of "muscle" when influencing others. Generally, it works best if you begin with Level 1 in the following continuum and move up the scale if your influence target does not respond as you wish.

- Muscle Level 1 is a polite request: "I'd like you to let us know when you can't come to a steering committee meeting."
- Muscle Level 2 is a request that is stronger in word choice, voice characteristics, and body language: "When you don't let us know that you're going to miss a meeting, we sometimes end up meeting without a quorum, which is useless. I need to know when you can't make a meeting."
- Muscle Level 3 is a statement of consequences if the behavior doesn't change: "If you can't let us know when you'll miss a meeting, we will have to ask you to resign from the committee."
- Muscle Level 4 is the application of the consequences stated in Level 3: "Because you have not been keeping us informed about your attendance, I will have to ask you to leave the committee."[14]

If you escalate too quickly to the higher muscle levels, you can cause a backlash or ruin relationships. If you fail to escalate at all, the other person will simply continue with the unacceptable behavior.

INFLUENCE STYLES

In the group exercise, we will focus on the influence styles identifies by Berlew and Harrison that readily lend themselves to skill-based training and practice.[15] Effective managers need to develop the capacity to analyze a situation and determine which influence tactic will be most effective. Although people often use a combination of influence tactics, we tend to be predisposed to certain styles that feel more natural. In the premeeting preparation, you were asked to determine how much each style describes your influence behavior. These styles are described more fully in the following paragraphs. Two of the styles rely on "pushing" energy while the others utilize "pulling" energy.

ASSERTIVE PERSUASION

In the *assertive persuasion* style, we "push" others with our intellect. Assertive persuasion is considered the bread and butter of the business world. The essential quality of assertive persuasion as an influence style is the use of facts, logic, rational argument, and persuasive reasoning. While the influencer may argue forcefully with great élan and spirit, the power of assertive persuasion does not come from an emotional source. Facts and logic are, by definition, emotionally neutral. A person may react to a fact emotionally and thereby be persuaded to behave in a certain way. However, the feelings of the person using assertive persuasion should not enter into their argument. The facts are supposed to speak for themselves.

People using assertive persuasion to persuade others are usually highly verbal and articulate. They confidently present their ideas, proposals, and suggestions and can support their proposals with rational reasons. They structure their arguments and enumerate the points they want to make so listeners can follow their logic. Sometimes they are guilty of selectively listening to others' attempts at assertive persuasion, hoping to find a weak spot so that they can effectively reason against others' proposals.

This style is most appropriate when the issue in question is suited to a logical approach, which is not the case with emotional or value-laden issues. Assertive persuasion also works best when the person exerting influence is already respected and enjoys a certain prestige.

REWARD AND PUNISHMENT

The second "pushing" style is *reward and punishment*, in which we are "pushing our will" onto other people. Reward and punishment involves the use of bargaining, incentives and pressures, and demanding certain behavior from other people. People who use this style state their expectations for how others will behave and also evaluate that behavior.

Rewards may be offered for compliance, and punishment or deprivation may be threatened for noncompliance. Naked power may be used, or more indirect and veiled pressures may be exerted through the use of status, prestige, and formal authority.

This influence style is characterized by contingent, if-then consequences: "If you do X, then I'll do Y" or "If you don't do this, then Y will happen to you." At times, the consequence (Y) is left implicit or vaguely defined, but people using this style clearly state the behaviors or results (X) they want to see. They use negotiation, threats, and promises to influence others.

Both reward and punishment and assertive persuasion involve agreeing and disagreeing with others. The difference is that in assertive persuasion, one agrees or disagrees with another's proposal because it is more or less effective, correct, accurate, or true. In using reward and punishment, on the other hand, the judgment of right or wrong is an evaluation based on a moral or social standard, a regulation, or an arbitrary performance standard. The person making the evaluation usually sets himself or herself up as the judge instead of appealing to a common and shared standard of rationality.

People using reward and punishment are very comfortable, generally, in conflict situations. They are comfortable giving clear feedback—both positive and negative—and are very direct about prescribing their goals and expectations. They are comfortable evaluating the work of others and saying what they like and don't like about it. People who use this style should state their expectations clearly in a direct manner. They must be assertive rather than wishy-washy or tentative, so that it is clear what will happen if the other party does not do what the influencer is demanding. This style is not appropriate with individuals or group who have a strong need to be in control or not be controlled by a strong desire to others.

As you reflect on the description just given, it will be clear that any individual, regardless of formal position, can effectively utilize many reward and punishment behaviors. Anyone, theoretically, can make evaluative statements involving praise and criticism. Similarly, if a meeting were dragging, anyone could prescribe a goal and expectation ("We've got to finish our work by six o'clock"). However, not everyone can utilize the same incentives and pressures. The ability to follow through on an evaluation or a prescribed goal or expectation depends on one's access to and control of meaningful rewards and punishments (incentives and pressures). By withholding support, dragging their heels, and other forms of subtle "sabotage," subordinates demonstrate that bosses are not the only ones who have reward and punishment power.

PARTICIPATION AND TRUST

Unlike the first two styles that involve pushing energy, the use of the *participation and trust* influence style *pulls* others toward what is desired or required by involving them. By actively listening to and involving others, an influencer using participation and trust increases the commitment of others to the target objective or task. This is in sharp contrast to the reward and punishment style in which compliance (not commitment) must be monitored frequently.

People who use participation and trust are generally rather patient and have developed the capacity to be very effective listeners. They are very good at reflecting back to people (paraphrasing) both the content and feelings of what the person has said. They build on others' ideas and are quick to credit others for their contributions.

People who use participation and trust as an influence style also effectively use personal disclosure. By sharing personal information about themselves, others are encouraged to reciprocate, which is one of the first steps in developing a trusting relationship. People who use this style readily admit their own areas of uncertainty and mistakes. By openly acknowledging their own limitations and taking a nondefensive attitude toward feedback, they help others to feel more accepted for what they are.

On the surface, participation and trust may appear to some to be a weak and wishy-washy style of influence when contrasted, for example, with the toughness of assertive persuasion or reward and punishment. It is not. It can be very powerful by building the trust and commitment needed to implement actions and with it a willingness to be influenced. As with the other influence styles, participation and trust can be misused to manipulate others. For example, managers who involve subordinates in a consensus decision-making process even though they have already chosen a solution are treading on thin ice.

COMMON VISION

Another influence style that pulls rather than pushes is the *common vision* style. It aims to identify a common vision for the future and to strengthen the group members' belief that through their collective efforts, the vision can become a reality. This style appeals to people's emotions and values, activating their personal commitment to private hopes and ideals and channeling that energy into working toward a common purpose. People using this style clearly articulate goals and the means to achieve them. The well-known speeches of Martin Luther King, Jr. and John F. Kennedy are classic examples of the effective use of common vision, although it is by no means a style that is useful only in large-group or political settings. This style is especially important in organizations undergoing major change efforts.

Within the everyday world of organizations, there are numerous opportunities for the effective use of common vision. Many organizational meetings become exercises in competing assertions. In such situations, the ability to help the group to pull together around a common goal can provide a much needed spirit of collaboration and inspiration: "What we can accomplish *if* we work together."

People who use common vision are generally emotionally expressive. They are enthusiastic and skilled at projecting and communicating their feelings in an articulate manner. They talk in emotionally vivid imagery and metaphors. People using this style look for common ground and the synergy that can result from working together. People who use this style well are described as charismatic leaders.

Please return to the Influence Style Self-Diagnosis and determine which style is described in each paragraph.

THE VALUE ISSUES—POSITIVE VERSUS NEGATIVE POWER

None of these four styles is inherently right or wrong. The key to effectiveness is using them in the appropriate situation and paying attention to how others experience your use of power. For example, when people are uplifted by an inspiring vision or when their competence is recognized and rewarded, they are empowered and feel stronger. There are other times, however, when the use of power and influence makes others feel weak and powerless—put down by intimidating bosses, run over by autocratic people, or exploited by ambitious people.

The important distinction, therefore, has to do with how the exercise of power and influence is experienced: What is its impact? Assertive persuasion, reward and punishment, participation and trust, and common vision can be used in a way that results in other people feeling stronger. They can also be used to make people feel weaker—to feel like pawns in the hands of someone else. Common vision, for example, will result in people feeling weaker if it is used only to raise people's hopes and expectations without anything ever being realized or gained.

Conger has expanded the definition of persuasion to incorporate aspects of other influence styles—participation and trust, and common vision. The effective persuasion he observed in successful managers includes four steps:[16]

1. Establish credibility.
2. Frame goals in a way that identifies common ground with those you intend to persuade.
3. Reinforce your position using vivid language and compelling evidence.
4. Connect emotionally with your audience.

We learned in Chapter 4 that McClelland identified a need for power as a basic motivator, even though it is somewhat difficult in U.S. society to acknowledge this need because we are often suspicious of power. McClelland resolved this dilemma by referring to the two faces of power.[17] While a need for power always refers to a desire to have a strong impact on others, one face of power, personal power, is an unsocialized concern for personal dominance. It is characterized by an I win–you lose perspective and a need to dominate others. The second face of power is socialized. People motivated by a high need for socialized power show a concern for group goals, empowering others, and a win-win approach. This second face of power, the socialized version, is required for long-term success in organizations. In some cultures people maintain that "power corrupts" and even people who started out with a need for socialized power degenerate into a selfish concern for personal dominance. While this may not always be the case, it is essential for people to know themselves and their need for power.

It is important to remember that influence attempts have both content and relationship outcomes. You may be successful at winning what you want (content) from the other party, but if they resent being coerced or manipulated, you have harmed your relationship with them. In order to balance the content and relationship outcomes, it is helpful to plan out beforehand what it is that you want from the other party (content objective) and what impression you want the other party to have of you as a result of this influence attempt (relationship objective).

PROCEDURE FOR GROUP MEETING: INFLUENCE ROLE PLAY

The purpose of this exercise is to allow you to practice each influence style and increase your own behavioral flexibility.

STEP 1.   Divide into four-person groups and discuss the following. (20 minutes)

   a. Self-assessments. Which style(s) do you use most frequently? Do the descriptions in the Influence Style Self-Diagnosis accurately describe how you try to influence others?

   b. Which styles have you seen the other members in your four-person group use most often throughout this course?

   c. By which style(s) are you most likely to be influenced?
           Which style(s) are you least likely to be influenced by and most likely to resist?

STEP 2.   Preparing for role plays: individual work. (10 minutes)
           On the pages that follow you will find six potentially stressful influence situations.
              Individuals should read these situations carefully and select one (to start) that best meets the following criteria:

   a. It seems real to you (i.e., you have been in that situation and/or could easily imagine yourself being in that situation).

   b. You would expect yourself to experience at least a moderate level of stress in dealing with that situation.

   c. Pick a situation that calls for an influence style that you would like to develop.
           If none of these situations appeal to you, choose a real-life situation that you can quickly explain to your group.

           Jot down your response to questions (1) through (4) in each situation in the space provided following the situation you have chosen to work on.

STEP 3.   Conducting and critiquing the role plays. (minimum 1 hour)
           Each person in the group will have an opportunity to play all the following roles.

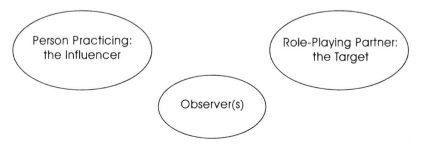

Please follow this sequence:

a. One person volunteers to go first. That person (the influencer) selects a partner (the target). The others are to be silent observers who can use the observation forms following each situation.

   Very briefly (2 to 4 minutes), the influencer tells his or her partner what the other person (boss, coworker, etc.)—the target—is like and how he or she is likely to act. Partners should behave in a way so as to produce the moderate stress level desired—neither outrageously stubborn nor a pushover.

b. Enact the situation. (5–6 minutes)

c. Feedback discussion. (8–10 minutes)

(1) The influencer begins by stating:

   (a) Which response style he or she was planning to use and which one(s) was actually used.

   (b) His or her content and relationship objectives. Were they achieved?

(2) The observers and the target person relate:

   (a) Which styles they thought the influencer was using based on the specific behavior they observed (e.g., "It looked like you were using trust and participation when you began talking about your previous personal experiences"—personal disclosure).

   (b) What influencer behaviors made the target feel stronger? Weaker?

   (c) What two or three specific suggestions would you offer the influencer to enhance his or her impact in a situation such as this?

The influencer should focus on listening to and understanding this feedback (i.e., use of participation and trust style) and *not* try to convince the others why their observations are wrong or misinformed (i.e., use of reward and punishment and/or assertive persuasion).

   Then repeat the procedure so that each person has at least one practice opportunity. (If time permits, select a second stressful influence situation and repeat the entire practice process, step 3.)

STEP 4.   General debriefing (15 minutes)

a. What did you learn about influencing other people from doing these role plays?

b. What connections can you make between this exercise and the readings?

Observations Category	INFLUENCE STYLES			
	Assertive Persuasion Logic, Facts, Rationality, Ideas, Proposals, Reasons For and Against	**Reward and Punishment** Evaluations, Use of Incentives and Pressures, Bargains, Stating Own Personal Goals and Expectations	**Participation and Trust** Active Listening, Recognizing Others' Contributions, Involving Others and Getting Their Contributions, Disclosing Own Areas of Uncertainty	**Common Vision** Building a Sense of Group Spirit, a We Feeling, Creating a Superordinate Group Goal, Shared Identity
Which styles did the influencer use most frequently? 1 = most frequently 4 = least frequently				
Examples of influence behavior that strength-ened the other person (positive power)				
Examples of influence behaviors that weak-ened the other person (negative power)				
Missed opportunities (i.e., example of where the style might have had a positive impact but was not used)				
Which style did the influencer use most effectively? 1 = most effective 4 = least effective				

SITUATION 1—PUSHING A CHANGE EFFORT

You are concerned that the other managers in your somewhat conservative company have not completely grasped the need to be more competitive. Even though the firm's profit and loss statement and other statistics have been slipping steadily, most of them do not yet perceive a need for change. You want to encourage them to reexamine the firm's strategy and implement a Customer Service program.

Planning Questions:

1. Which style(s) do you think would be most effective in this situation? Do you require compliance or commitment in a situation such as this?

2. What is it that you want the person you are trying to influence (the target) to do; that is, what is your content objective?

3. What kind of an outcome are you looking for in terms of your relationship with the other party; that is, what is your relationship objective?

4. Plan out how you will handle this influence attempt.

After the Role Play:

5. What were the content and relationship outcomes?

6. Is there any way this influence attempt might have been improved?

Observations Category	INFLUENCE STYLES			
	Assertive Persuasion Logic, Facts, Rationality, Ideas, Proposals, Reasons For and Against	Reward and Punishment Evaluations, Use of Incentives and Pressures, Bargains, Stating Own Personal Goals and Expectations	Participation and Trust Active Listening, Recognizing Others' Contributions, Involving Others and Getting Their Contributions, Disclosing Own Areas of Uncertainty	Common Vision Building a Sense of Group Spirit, a We Feeling, Creating a Superordinate Group Goal, Shared Identity
Which styles did the influencer use most frequently? 1 = most frequently 4 = least frequently				
Examples of influence behavior that strength-ened the other person (positive power)				
Examples of influence behaviors that weak-ened the other person (negative power)				
Missed opportunities (i.e., example of where the style might have had a positive impact but was not used)				
Which style did the influencer use most effectively? 1 = most effective 4 = least effective				

SITUATION 2—THE LESS-THAN-EXPECTED SALARY INCREASE

You and your boss had what you thought was a really great performance appraisal session last month. You were clearly led to expect a 6 percent salary increase and have begun to plan on it. Wham! Your increase notice comes through with only a 3 percent cost-of-living increase. You are about to enter your boss's office to "have a talk."

Planning Questions:

1. Which style(s) do you think would be most effective in this situation? Do you require compliance or commitment in a situation such as this?

2. What is it that you want the person you are trying to influence (the target) to do; that is, what is your content objective?

3. What kind of an outcome are you looking for in terms of your relationship with the other party; that is, what is your relationship objective?

4. Plan out how you will handle this influence attempt.

After the Role Play:

5. What were the content and relationship outcomes?

6. Is there any way this influence attempt might have been improved?

Observations Category	INFLUENCE STYLES			
	Assertive Persuasion Logic, Facts, Rationality, Ideas, Proposals, Reasons For and Against	**Reward and Punishment** Evaluations, Use of Incentives and Pressures, Bargains, Stating Own Personal Goals and Expectations	**Participation and Trust** Active Listening, Recognizing Others' Contributions, Involving Others and Getting Their Contributions, Disclosing Own Areas of Uncertainty	**Common Vision** Building a Sense of Group Spirit, a We Feeling, Creating a Superordinate Group Goal, Shared Identity
Which styles did the influencer use most frequently? 1 = most frequently 4 = least frequently				
Examples of influence behavior that strengthened the other person (positive power)				
Examples of influence behaviors that weakened the other person (negative power)				
Missed opportunities (i.e., example of where the style might have had a positive impact but was not used)				
Which style did the influencer use most effectively? 1 = most effective 4 = least effective				

SITUATION 3—SIGNING THE JOB CANDIDATE

It's taken you a few months, but you have finally located the perfect job candidate to fill the position of your assistant. This candidate, who will graduate with an undergrad/master's degree in business this June, has all the qualities you have been looking for. The candidate is highly skilled and has the service orientation and values that you need in your company, which prides itself on being a socially responsible company that focuses on the double bottom line. However, at least two other companies are also trying to hire this person. Convince the candidate to come to work for you.

Planning Questions:

1. Which style(s) do you think would be most effective in this situation? Do you require compliance or commitment in a situation such as this?

2. What is it that you want the person you are trying to influence (the target) to do; that is, what is your content objective?

3. What kind of an outcome are you looking for in terms of your relationship with the other party; that is, what is your relationship objective?

4. Plan out how you will handle this influence attempt.

After the Role Play:

5. What were the content and relationship outcomes?

6. Is there any way this influence attempt might have been improved?

Observations Category	INFLUENCE STYLES			
	Assertive Persuasion Logic, Facts, Rationality, Ideas, Proposals, Reasons For and Against	Reward and Punishment Evaluations, Use of Incentives and Pressures, Bargains, Stating Own Personal Goals and Expectations	Participation and Trust Active Listening, Recognizing Others' Contributions, Involving Others and Getting Their Contributions, Disclosing Own Areas of Uncertainty	Common Vision Building a Sense of Group Spirit, a We Feeling, Creating a Superordinate Group Goal, Shared Identity
Which styles did the influencer use most frequently? 1 = most frequently 4 = least frequently				
Examples of influence behavior that strengthened the other person (positive power)				
Examples of influence behaviors that weakened the other person (negative power)				
Missed opportunities (i.e., example of where the style might have had a positive impact but was not used)				
Which style did the influencer use most effectively? 1 = most effective 4 = least effective				

SITUATION 4—SEEKING DEPARTMENTAL COLLABORATION

You are one of five department heads in a software company. As the person in charge of production, you have no authority over the other department heads. However, you are worried that lack of collaboration among departments is costing the company business. Therefore, you have scheduled lunch with the head of marketing and sales because you think this department promises customers things that your department cannot produce.

Planning Questions:

1. Which style(s) do you think would be most effective in this situation? Do you require compliance or commitment in a situation such as this?

2. What is it that you want the person you are trying to influence (the target) to do; that is, what is your content objective?

3. What kind of an outcome are you looking for in terms of your relationship with the other party; that is, what is your relationship objective?

4. Plan out how you will handle this influence attempt.

After the Role Play:

5. What were the content and relationship outcomes?

6. Is there any way this influence attempt might have been improved?

Observations Category	INFLUENCE STYLES			
	Assertive Persuasion Logic, Facts, Rationality, Ideas, Proposals, Reasons For and Against	Reward and Punishment Evaluations, Use of Incentives and Pressures, Bargains, Stating Own Personal Goals and Expectations	Participation and Trust Active Listening, Recognizing Others' Contributions, Involving Others and Getting Their Contributions, Disclosing Own Areas of Uncertainty	Common Vision Building a Sense of Group Spirit, a We Feeling, Creating a Superordinate Group Goal, Shared Identity
Which styles did the influencer use most frequently? 1 = most frequently 4 = least frequently				
Examples of influence behavior that strength-ened the other person (positive power)				
Examples of influence behaviors that weak-ened the other person (negative power)				
Missed opportunities (i.e., example of where the style might have had a positive impact but was not used)				
Which style did the influencer use most effectively? 1 = most effective 4 = least effective				

SITUATION 5—SHAKING LOOSE THE LATE REPORT

One of your subordinates has been promising to finish a report for three weeks. Every time you inquire as to how it's going, what you get back is, "Oh, it's coming along. It's more complicated than either one of us imagined." The grapevine has informed you that your subordinate's marriage is going through some rocky spots. While you want to be fair, your boss is putting the screws on you to get the report in. The pressure on you is really mounting and something has to give. The "last recourse" meeting you called is about to begin.

Planning Questions:

1. Which style(s) do you think would be most effective in this situation? Do you require compliance or commitment in a situation such as this?

2. What is it that you want the person you are trying to influence (the target) to do; that is, what is your content objective?

3. What kind of an outcome are you looking for in terms of your relationship with the other party; that is, what is your relationship objective?

4. Plan out how you will handle this influence attempt.

After the Role Play:

5. What were the content and relationship outcomes?

6. Is there any way this influence attempt might have been improved?

Observations Category	INFLUENCE STYLES			
	Assertive Persuasion Logic, Facts, Rationality, Ideas, Proposals, Reasons For and Against	Reward and Punishment Evaluations, Use of Incentives and Pressures, Bargains, Stating Own Personal Goals and Expectations	Participation and Trust Active Listening, Recognizing Others' Contributions, Involving Others and Getting Their Contributions, Disclosing Own Areas of Uncertainty	Common Vision Building a Sense of Group Spirit, a We Feeling, Creating a Superordinate Group Goal, Shared Identity
Which styles did the influencer use most frequently? 1 = most frequently 4 = least frequently				
Examples of influence behavior that strength-ened the other person (positive power)				
Examples of influence behaviors that weak-ened the other person (negative power)				
Missed opportunities (i.e., example of where the style might have had a positive impact but was not used)				
Which style did the influencer use most effectively? 1 = most effective 4 = least effective				

SITUATION 6—STOPPING SEXUAL HARASSMENT

You have heard several accounts from reliable sources that one of your top performers, a man in his fifties, has been sexually harassing the young women in his department. You would hate to lose this employee, but you strongly disapprove of people who abuse their power in this fashion. You want him to stop this behavior before the company loses the young women as employees or is slapped with a lawsuit.

Planning Questions:

1. Which style(s) do you think would be most effective in this situation? Do you require compliance or commitment in a situation such as this?

2. What is it that you want the person you are trying to influence (the target) to do; that is, what is your content objective?

3. What kind of an outcome are you looking for in terms of your relationship with the other party; that is, what is your relationship objective?

4. Plan out how you will handle this influence attempt.

After the Role Play:

5. What were the content and relationship outcomes?

6. Is there any way this influence attempt might have been improved?

FOLLOW-UP

In their day-to-day work, managers are continually faced with a host of questions about the process of leadership. How can I get the job done most effectively? What is the "best" leadership style? How can I build commitment and loyalty among the members of my work team to the company and its objectives? When should I listen and when should I give orders? If I become too friendly with my subordinates, will I lose their respect? How can I get others to do their work well? These are all contingency questions—there is no one right or wrong answer for every occasion.

Some managers mistakenly believe that the more power they give to their employees, the less power they have for themselves. This is true only if you impose a win-lose framework on the situation and see power as a limited commodity. In fact, power is often paradoxical—the more one gives away, the more one has for oneself. Managers who work hard to develop and empower their employees are examples of people who accrue power by giving it to others.

Researchers have identified the steps that practicing managers use to establish sustained managerial influence:[18]

1. **Develop a reputation as a knowledgeable person or an expert. This is the most commonly reported form of gaining influence**. This requires keeping up-to-date in one's field or area. However, it is not sufficient to be knowledgeable; others must also be aware of this fact so it is sometimes necessary to market oneself or use impression management.
2. **Balance the time spent in each critical relationship according to the needs of the work rather than on the basis of habit or social preference.** Managers should spend their time where it will do the most good in advancing organizational goals. This may necessitate switching from a narrow focus upon subordinates or technical areas to developing both lateral and upward relationships and external relationships in order to have greater influence.

There are two interesting findings related to building relationships and personal advancement. First, women are more likely to assume that hard work will result in promotion whereas men tend to believe that political contacts within the organization are essential to their advancement.[19] Second, there is some research evidence, which is not gender related, that managers who spend time networking and trying to "look like a star" are more likely to win promotions in U.S. companies than effective, competent managers who devote their energies to their jobs and subordinates.[20] In organizations that allow this to happen, impression management and political skills rather than merit and performance are rewarded, and the people who make it to the top will be more dedicated to their personal career than to the company and, in some cases, less competent than others. Once again, the concept of the two faces of power helps us determine what type of networking and relationship building we want to encourage—networking for the good of the organization or unit (social power) as opposed to networking that only benefits the individual (personal power).

3. **Develop a network of resource persons who can be called upon for assistance.** In many cultures in Latin America, Asia, and Africa, things get done in organizations because of personal relationships. People who take the time to cultivate good relationships within the organization usually receive better service and cooperation than those who do not. Although this phenomenon is less striking in the United States, relationships are still extremely important. Luthans and his colleagues observed managers at work and identified networking as one of four key behavioral categories that emerged. He defined networking as "socializing/politicking and interacting with outsiders."[21] The other three categories were communication (exchanging routine information and processing paperwork), traditional management (decision making, planning, and controlling), and human resource management (motivating, disciplining, managing conflict, staffing and training).
4. **Implement influence tactics with sensitivity, flexibility, and adequate levels of communication.** As with any strategy, it is necessary to understand one's audience and do no harm to the long-term relationship with the other party—in this case, the target one wishes to influence. Therefore, good influencers analyze the target and use the communication style that will be most effective with him or her. Managers who are good at influencing others are also good listeners who can adapt their tactics to the responses they hear from the target.

There are contradictory findings concerning gender differences in the use of influence tactics; some studies find no differences between men and women[22] while others find that the only difference is that women are less assertive with their superiors[23] and more likely to appeal to altruism and rationale-based strategies than threats of punishment with their subordinates.[24] The longitudinal study of AT&T employees revealed these gender differences with regard to power. Women are more consensus oriented than men, which has been confirmed in many other studies. Women and men view and utilize power in different ways. Women see it as a "resource that can be used to influence outcomes on the job and to focus the competencies of the people who work for them. Men in the study, on the other hand, tended to think of power more as an end in itself, as something they can use to react against or take power away from others in authority. Men saw power as a way to supersede others in power, women rarely did."[25]

Sexual harassment is usually related to unequal power in the workplace. This term refers to unwelcome advances, requests for sexual favors, and other verbal or physical conduct of a sexual nature. Subjects of harassment, female or male, find themselves in especially difficult situations when their superiors, with their power to reward and punish them, are the ones doing the harassing. People sometimes fear that refusing to go along with sexual advances will result in termination, poor performance appraisals, and decreased promotion opportunities and salary. Therefore, power is often an aspect of sexual harassment. People in higher positions abuse their power to harass people in lower-ranking positions. Sometimes, however, the initiators are people in lower-ranking positions who offer sexual favors to obtain advantages at work from a powerful person. Sexual harassment is both illegal and unethical.

CULTURAL DIFFERENCES

Because of cultural values and history, power is perceived and exercised differently around the world. For example, power is one of the dominant values in Latin American cultures. It is the principal theme in the organizational literature indigenous to this region.[26] Therefore, the flagrant use of power is more acceptable in Latin America than in cultures with a more ambivalent view of power (e.g., the United States).[27] In high power distance cultures (e.g., Venezuela, Yugoslavia, and France), leaders are expected to behave differently from people of lower rank, and differences in rank are more apparent. In low power distance cultures, people are less comfortable with differences in power and there is less emphasis on social class distinction and hierarchical rank. Power is more likely to be shared in these cultures (e.g., Denmark, the Netherlands, and Israel).[28]

In any setting, it's important to decipher who has the power. Different cultures and organizations use various artifacts and symbols to designate power. Office size, private space (the executive restroom), large staffs, and immediate access to important people are symbols of power in many U.S. businesses. However, these objects may have no symbolic meaning whatsoever in other cultures, or even in specific organizational cultures in the United States. Thus, decoding the symbols and behaviors that indicate the location of power is an important skill. It is also wise to determine the norms and expectations about the exercise of power and influence in various cultures so you can adapt your behavior accordingly.

LEARNING POINTS

1. Power often has negative connotations for people, but it is a crucial part of leading and managing. A manager cannot "make a difference" without exerting power and influence over employees.
2. Power is defined as the capacity to influence the behavior of others.
3. Influence is the process by which people successfully persuade others to follow their advice, suggestions, or orders.

4. In general, there are three possible outcomes to an influence attempt: commitment, compliance, or resistance.

5. Managers traditionally relied on the power inherent in their position. Changes in both society and the workplace demand that managers be proficient in several influence styles.

6. Other sources of power are expertise, effort, and relationships, the ability to reward or punish others (coercive power), position, charisma, and referent power. People also gain power when they have control over resources, have control and access to information, and work in units that cope with the critical uncertainties facing the organization.

7. Nine commonly used influence tactics are rational persuasion, inspirational appeals, consultation, ingratiation, personal appeals, exchange, coalition tactics, legitimating tactics, and pressure.

8. U.S. managers prefer consultation, rational persuasion, and inspirational appeals over more coercive tactics.

9. Managers who use a variety of influence tactics tend to be more successful than those who rely on a single tactic.

10. Berlew and Harrison identified four influence styles:
    a. Reward and punishment
    b. Participation and trust
    c. Common vision
    d. Assertive persuasion

11. Power has two faces: a negative, unsocialized need to dominate others and a socialized concern for group goals and empowering others.

12. Effective managers diagnose the situation and determine which style will be most effective. This reflects a contingency approach to power and influence.

13. Power is paradoxical in that the more a leader empowers others, the more power he or she receives.

Tips FOR MANAGERS

- Naked ambition often generates distrust. Others sense that ambitious people will not let human considerations stand in the way of their quest for success.
- Some political behavior occurs when there is too much uncertainty in the organization. Managers can reduce political jockeying by establishing clear evaluation criteria that distinguish between high and low performers and reward them accordingly. Managers will be less likely to resort to political influence when organizational goals are clearly specified and when they do not have to compete for scarce resources.[29]
- Managers can deal with existing political fiefdoms by removing or splitting the most dysfunctional subgroups and warning individuals who are motivated by personal power. Top management should identify "an apolitical attitude that puts organizational ends ahead of personal power ends" as an important promotion criteria.[30]
- There are several ways to acquire power that are unrelated to one's position in the hierarchy within a system. Possessing a scarce expertise, serving as a liaison between two groups that have difficulty getting along, having access to information or people with hierarchical power, having a personal network that facilitates both tasks and information gathering, as well as being seen as an objective source of sound judgment are all ways to accrue power.
- People who are skilled at influencing others take pains to reduce the status gap that may exist between them. They communicate in ways that do not put the other person in a one-down position.
- Managers should convey orders or requests in a polite but confident manner.
- Don't give orders if you don't have the power to back them up. Instead, try another influence style.

PERSONAL APPLICATION ASSIGNMENT

The topic of this assignment is to think back on a significant experience involving power or influence. Choose an experience that intrigues you and that you want to learn more about.

A. *Concrete Experience*
1. *Objectively* describe the experience (who, what, when, where, how information) (2 points)
2. *Subjectively* describe your feelings, perceptions, and thoughts that occurred during (not after) the experience. What did others seem to be feeling? (2 points)

B. *Reflective Observation*
1. Looking back at the experience, what were the perspectives of the key actors (including you)? (2 points)
2. Why did the people involved (including you) behave as they did? (2 points)

C. *Abstract Conceptualization*
1. Relate concepts or theories from the assigned readings or the lecture to the experience. Explain thoroughly how they apply to your experience. Please apply at least two concepts or theories and cite them correctly. (4 points)

D. *Active Experimentation*
1. What did you learn about power and influence from this experience? (1 point)
2. What did you learn about yourself? (1 point)
3. What action steps will you take to be more effective in the future? (2 points)

E. *Integration, Synthesis, and Writing*
   1. Did you integrate and synthesize the four sections? (1 point)
   2. Was the personal application assignment well written and easy to understand? (1 point)
   3. Was it free of spelling and grammatical errors? (2 points)

ENDNOTES

[1] M. W. McCall, Jr. and M. M. Lombardo, "What Makes a Top Executive?" *Psychology Today* (February 1983): 26–31.

[2] J. Pfeffer, *Managing with Power: Politics and Influence in Organizations* (Boston, MA: Harvard Business School Press, 1992): 166.

[3] B. Keys and T. Case, "How to Become an Influential Manager," *Academy of Management Executive 4* (4) (1990): 38–51.

[4] L. Sayles, *Leadership: Managing in Real Organizations* (New York: McGraw-Hill, 1989). See the Bradford and Cohen article in the *Reader* for advice on influencing people over whom one has no authority.

[5] J. R. P French, Jr. and B. Raven, "The Bases of Social Power," in D. Cartwright, ed., *Studies in Social Power* (Ann Arbor, MI: University of Michigan, Institute for Social Research, 1959).

[6] Pfeffer, *Managing with Power*, p. 69. See also D. Mechanic's "Source of Power of Lower Participants in Complex Organizations," *Administrative Science Quarterly 7* (1962): 349–64.

[7] G. R. Salancik and J. Pfeffer's "Who Gets Power—And How They Hold Onto It: A Strategic Contingency Model of Power," *Organizational Dinamics 5* (Winter 1977): 3–21.

[8] J. K. Keller, "Who Is John Zeglis and Why Is a Lawyer on AT&T's Short List?" *The Wall Street Journal*, September 5, 1997, p. A-1.

[9] R. E. Emerson, "Power-Dependence Relations," *American Sociological Review 27* (1962): 31–41.

[10] H. Mintzberg, *Power In and Around Organizations* (Upper Saddle River, NJ: Prentice Hall, 1983).

[11] G. Yukl, *Leadership in Organizations* (Upper Saddle River, NJ: Prentice Hall, 1994): 225. These tactics are a modification of the exploratory work described in D. Kipnis, S. M. Schmidt, and I. Wilkinson, "Intraorganizational Influence Tactics: Explorations in Getting One's Way," *Journal of Applied Psychology*, 65 (1980): 440–52. See also D. Kipnis, S. M. Schmidt, C. Swaffin-Smith, and I. Wilkinson, "Patterns of Managerial Influence: Shotgun Managers, Tacticians, and Bystanders," *Organizational Dynamics* (Winter 1984): 58–67; and G. Yukl, H. Kim, and C. M. Falbe, "Antecedents of Influence Outcomes," *Journal of Applied Psychology 81*, no. 3 (1996): 309–317.

[12] Keys and Case, *"How to Become an Influential Manager,"* p. 47.

[13] B. McRae, *Negotiating and Influencing Skills* (Thousand Oaks, CA: Sage, 1998): 58.

[14] S. S. Drury, *Assertive Supervision: Building Involved Teamwork* (Champaign, IL: Research Press, 1984): 49–50.

[15] The ideas and materials here (with permission of Situation Management Systems, Inc.) are part of a series of training programs originally developed by David Berlew and Roger Harrison on positive power and influence. For more detail on the actual program, contact Situation Management Systems, Inc., Box 476, Center Station, Plymouth, MA 02361.

[16] J. A. Conger, "The Necessary Art of Persuasion," *Harvard Business Review* (May/June 1998): 85.

[17] D. C. McClelland, "The Two Faces of Power," in D. A. Kolb, I. M. Rubin, and J. McIntyre, *Organizational Psychology: Readings on Human Behavior in Organizations*, 4th ed. (Upper Saddle River, NJ: Prentice Hall, 1984): 59–72.

[18] Keys and Case, *"How to Become an Influential Manager,"* p. 43.

[19] M. Henning and A. Jardim, *The Managerial Woman* (New York: Anchor Press/Doubleday, 1977).

[20] F. Luthans, "Successful vs. Effective Real Managers," *Academy of Management Executive* (May 1988): 127–32; and F. Luthans, R. M. Hodgetts, and S. Rosenkrantz, *Real Managers* (Cambridge, MA: Ballinger, 1988).

[21] Luthans, "Successful vs. Effective Real Managers," p. 129.

[22] G. F. Dreher, T. W. Doughtery, and W. Whitely, "Influence Tactics and Salary Attainment: A Gender-Specific Analysis," *Sex Roles*, (May 1989): 535–50.

[23] A. Rizzo and C. Mendez, "Making Things Happen in Organizations: Does Gender Make a Difference?", *Public Personnel Management 17* (1) (Spring 1988): 9–20.

[24] N. L. Harper and R. Y. Hirokawa, "A Comparison of Persuasive Strategies Used by Female and Male Managers: An Examination of Downward Influence," *Communication Quarterly 36* (2) (Spring 1988): 157–68.

[25] D. C. McClelland and D. H. Burnham, "Power Is the Great Motivator," *Harvard Business Review* (January/February 1995): 138.

[26] G. Hofstede, *Culture's Consequences: International Differences in Work-Related Values* (Beverly Hills, CA: Sage, 1980).

[27] J. S. Osland, S. De Franco, and A. Osland, "Organizational Implications of Latin American Culture: Lessons for the Expatriate Manager," *Journal of Management Inquiry 8*, no. 2 (June 1999): 219–34.

[28] Hofstede, *Culture's Consequences*.

[29] D. R. Beeman and T. W. Sharkey, "The Use and Abuse of Corporate Politics," *Business Horizons*, (March–April 1987): 30.

[30] Ibid, p. 30.

▲▲

Chapter 17

EMPOWERMENT AND COACHING

OBJECTIVES By the end of this chapter, you should be able to:

A. Describe the characteristics of high-performance organizations.

B. Distinguish between the command-and-control and involvement-oriented approaches of management.

C. Define empowerment.

D. Explain the four aspects of empowerment.

E. Describe how managers can empower employees.

F. Identify four different types of coaching.

G. Distinguish between effective and ineffective feedback.

NOBODY'S AS SMART AS EVERYBODY

Monarch Marking Systems, now a unit of Paxar Inc., had been making price-marking equipment for more than a century, including the hand-held "guns" that spit out price tags. For a time, Monarch did a good job of keeping pace with technology as bar-code machines helped usher in the digital revolution in wholesaling and retailing. But Monarch was a cash cow and its former owners were content to milk it. By the mid-1990s product innovation had slowed to a crawl.

Even worse, the shop floor, with some five hundred workers, had become deeply hidebound at a time when many other plants were vaulting to new levels of efficiency. With employment stuck on a plateau very few new hires came aboard, causing the tenure of the production employee to reach an astonishing sixteen years on average; many had even been with the company twenty-five years. Management had assigned each of these people to a single machine and left them to perform the identical work, year in and year out. Job specialization was extreme, creating 120 different job descriptions, a modern-day version of Taylor's "you are not paid to think" syndrome. It was a small-scale version of the General Motors Lordstown plant.

"A mind is a terrible thing to waste," as they say, not just because society needs minds but because individuals need to use them. Through the years a deep despair took hold in the plant, not over money, since the money was pretty good, but over the mindlessness of the work. Management recognized the problem, but treated it with a Band-Aid instead of a cure—programs like "employee involvement" and "empowerment" that encouraged people to make suggestions that went into a black hole, which in the end only deepened the despair.

In 1995 Monarch Marking came under new ownership by private investors, who installed a turnaround artist named John Paxton as chief executive. Paxton was appalled when touring the plant for the first time—the workers blankly repeating the same motions, machinery bolted in the same location for decades. The manufacturing operation, he recognized, would be a ball and chain on whatever efforts the company launched to reinvigorate the product line and sales effort. "Without the shop floor behind us, we'd have limited success in everything else we did," he explained.

Paxton brought in a hard-charging, gravel-voiced production chief named Jerry Schlaegel, who, in turn, recruited a hyperkinetic quality assurance engineer he knew named Steve Schneider (who had spent much of his career steeped in the teachings of W. Edwards Deming). Their outward manners might have easily led one to mistake them for classic Industrial Age managers, Schlaegel with his gruffness, Schneider with his zealotry. But after spending several years on high-tech shop floors they had acquired a keen respect for the mind of the worker and for the combined mind of workers—and for the difficulty of unlocking them. Every program to put this knowledge into action seemed to fail miserably, not just at Monarch but just about every plant they knew of.

Schneider and Schlaegel resolved to involve the shop floor in ways that avoided problems, combining intellectual freedom with the kind of discipline demanded of a commercial enterprise. Although it had not occurred to them in precisely these terms, they needed "a small set of simple rules"—what the Canadian organization theorist Gareth Morgan calls "minimum critical specifications," or, better still, "min specs." "If a system is to have the freedom to self-organize it must possess a certain degree of 'space' or autonomy that allows appropriate innovation to occur," Morgan says. "This seems to be stating the obvious. But the reality is that in many organizations the reverse occurs because management has a tendency to over define and over control instead of focusing on the critical variables."[1]

Their first rule was an uncustomary one: Participation in the new exchange of knowledge would be compulsory, not voluntary. That simple rule altered the entire cast of the initiative. This was not a sop to employees, not a feel-good thing, not "empowerment." Indeed it was ridiculous to think that employees needed "power." They already had power! The power was in their heads! Schneider told people that Monarch was paying them to come to work and from that point forward they would be expected to bring along their brains. Every employee in the shop would receive training in problem solving and team communications, and anyone, at one time or another, might be required to sit on a team studying ways to improve the processes of the shop floor.

But how could they ground the process in meaningful business issues, in things that could be changed rather than merely talked about? Schneider and Schlaegel realized that every genuine problem in manufacturing can be measured. All told, Schneider identified 162 measurable variables—"metrics," he called them—involving everything from traditional quality and productivity statistics to such unusual indices as the number of unsolicited letters of commendation received from customers. Teams would form only with the intention of improving one or more specific metrics. There would be no open-ended, pie-in-the-sky committees.

There were just a few more rules. Teams not only had to come up with their own solution to a problem, they had to implement it as well. If other departments had to make changes, it was the team's duty to persuade them to do so. If vendors had to change how they served the factory, the team was charged with making the necessary arrangements. Combining ideas and implementation would motivate people to think hard for the most practical possible solution. "This is your job! This is your life!" Schneider told people. "Change it! Just go make it happen and tell us about it when you're through. In fact, you are required to make the changes and tell us when you're done."

The final rule: No project would last longer than thirty days, from the formation of the team to the implementation of the solution. "It's a project," Schneider told people, "not a process."

Those were the only rules. Anyone could create a team, management or labor. Anything and everything in the plant was fair game for review—so long as it could be measured. A team could come up with any solution at all—so long as it was willing to carry it out on the shop floor. Management forswore any and all veto rights. There were no limits on spending. Schneider and Schlaegel drew a deep breath, gulped, and rolled out the new rules.

---

[1] G. Morgan, *Images of Organizations* (Thousand Oaks, CA: Sage, 1997): 114.

An early test came from a group of a dozen workers who built Monarch's hottest product, a hand-held bar-code reader known as the Ultra. Monarch urgently wanted to reduce delivery times while cutting assembly costs. A group of Ultra assemblers was assigned to study whether there was a better way of putting the product together. And as if on cue, every one of them said, in effect, no way. They had no interest in participating. "I thought it was a big joke," recalled Effie Winters, who in her 20 years at the plant had seen one degrading and embarrassing episode of empowerment after another. "I wanted no part of it." Steve Schneider was facing an outright rebellion and went to his boss, Schlaegel, in a panic. So the raspy Schlaegel went before the group and declared in no uncertain terms, "You *will* do this." Recalls assembler Linda Viets: "We figured we would just go through the motions."

But when they found themselves alone with a deadline, the ideas came with startling ease. The dunderheads who used to run the company had installed a clunky, chain-driven assembly line for the assembly of the Ultra. Yet the product weighed two pounds! The workers knew they could easily pass it by hand from one station to the next, eliminating the oversize conveyor that actually limited their assembly speed. Then they realized that by getting rid of the mechanical equipment, they didn't have to sit in a row. They could sit in a large circle, facing one another, talking more easily, and tracking each other's progress. When anyone got ahead, she could help someone else catch up. The team not only changed the manufacturing process but soon realized that the new system exposed inefficiencies they had not seen before. This time, Effie Winters and the other team members launched a new round of investigations at their own initiative, inventing a way of moving parts in and out of the assembly area on rolling carts. In doing so they cut the time spent in switching to a new model from a few hours to a few minutes.

By the time it was all over they had reduced the square footage of the assembly area by 70 percent, freeing up space for new products. They had cut their work-in-progress inventory by $127,000. They had slashed past-due shipments by 90 percent. Best of all, they had doubled their productivity.

By the time of my visit Monarch had seen some one hundred teams form, create change, and disband. Before long Monarch's operating income hit an all-time high. The company's adroit application of knowledge received many commendations. Schneider and Schlaegel began freely teaching "practical process improvement," as they called it, to Monarch's suppliers and customers. Most interesting of all, a new culture emerged spontaneously within the workforce—a culture that did not permit but that insisted on brain work. Even those who were the most cynical to begin with became eager converts. "We're using our brains instead of sitting here like little robots," Effie Winters put it. "We're not just pieces of equipment anymore."

Source: Excerpted from Thomas Petzinger, Jr., *The New Pioneers* (New York: Simon and Schuster, 1999).

PREMEETING PREPARATION

A. Read "Nobody's as Smart as Everybody."

B. Fill out the Empowerment Questionnaire on the following page.

C. Read the Topic Introduction.

D. Practice building the spaceship *Enterprise* following the blueprints on pages 392–395.

E. If your instructor has assigned the Robbins Self-Assessment Library, use "How Willing Am I To Delegate?"

THE EMPOWERMENT QUESTIONNAIRE

The following questionnaire consists of managerial behaviors that promote empowerment. How frequently does your manager do each of the following? Please mark the response that best describes your manager's behavior.

My Manager	Very Infrequently	Infrequently	Sometimes	Frequently	Very Frequently
1. Lets me do my job without interfering					
2. Makes an effort to locate and remove barriers that reduce efficiency					
3. Encourages all of us to work as a team					
4. Clearly defines what is expected of me					
5. Provides me with honest feedback on my performance					
6. Openly recognizes work well done					
7. Keeps me focused on customer needs					
8. Encourages me to monitor my own efforts					
9. Makes sure I have the training I need to do my job					
10. Allows me to make decisions about my own work					
11. Listens to me before making decisions affecting my area					
12. Provides me with an environment conducive to teamwork					
13. Rewards me for meeting company goals					
14. Informs me regularly about the state of the business					
15. Encourages me to make suggestions					
16. Makes sure I have all the information I need to do my work					
17. Behaves in ways that demonstrate respect for others					
18. Explains how my job fits into the company objectives					

TOPIC INTRODUCTION

"Any company trying to compete... must figure out a way to engage the mind of every employee."

Jack Welch, CEO, General Electric

Companies that survive and flourish in today's business environment are those that focus upon high performance, which translates into the cost competitiveness, high-quality products and services, innovation, and speed that is necessary to gain a competitive advantage. Harris reported the following characteristics of high-performing companies.[1]

- Joint goal setting by managers and workers with objectives and targets that are always a bit beyond current levels to promote greater achievement.
- Employees reach a consensus upon norms of competence and high performance and standards of excellence that are incorporated into the corporate culture by means of logos and slogans.
- Continual reinforcement of positive behavior and accomplishment.
- Constructive feedback to redirect worker energies from ineffective to effective work habits and activities so that people learn from failure.
- Capitalizing on human assets and potential by giving individuals and work groups more flexibility, responsibility, and autonomy—while maintaining accountability.
- Encouraging and modeling a spirit of innovation and entrepreneurialism.
- Recruiting, selecting, promoting, and rewarding top performers, and identifying them as role models.
- Fostering synergy and collaboration so that individual competition is replaced by teamwork and group achievement.
- Using training, education sessions, and self-learning methods to develop people's potential for success and high performance.
- Eliminating underachievers who do not respond positively to demands for high performance.
- Altering organizational structure so that it is more decentralized, mission oriented, and responsive.
- Making work meaningful and fun by cultivating informality and fellowship in a context of achievement and accomplishment.
- Staying close to personnel, suppliers, and customers so that managers respond quickly to market and employee needs.
- Providing a mix of benefits, rewards, and incentives to encourage talented performance.

Creating organizations such as this, where people see themselves as businesspeople rather than employees, requires a different style of management.[2] There has been a gradual shift from a command-and-control model to an involvement-oriented approach centered on employee commitment and empowerment. The command-and-control model is based on the assumption that hierarchy and vertical relationships are the best way to organize. Managers working with a command-and-control mentality perceive their job as making decisions, giving orders, and ensuring that subordinates obey. The limited role of subordinates in this model ("Do what you're told") can result in passive workers with little commitment to organizational goals. When this occurs, management often finds itself shouldering the lion's share of the responsibility and prodding employees to get the work done. People talk in terms of "we and they" (workers versus management) rather than "us."

The involvement-oriented approach is based on the belief that the best way to organize is to give employees the freedom and responsibility to manage their own work as much as possible.[3] In addition to the work itself, employees also do the thinking and controlling aspects that only supervisors and managers do in the command-and-control model. In the involvement-oriented approach, employees are given both the information and the power to influence decisions about their work. Not surprisingly, high-involvement organizations require a special breed of employee—people who are capable and skilled at basic problem solving, communication, and quantitative techniques. They must also be responsible and willing to make a commitment to learning, to developing themselves, and to being a productive member of an organization. For their part, supervisors and managers in high-involvement organizations must be willing to share both power and information and listen to employees.

The command-and-control model worked fairly well for many years, but it is less appropriate for highly competitive, rapidly changing global businesses that employ highly educated workers. There are many U.S. companies that still operate in the command-and-control fashion, but it is harder for them to compete against companies that utilize their human resources more fully.[4] With a command-and-control approach, one can obtain satisfactory performance, but high performance only results when employees are truly committed to the success of the organization. Although the research has some limitations, the involvement-oriented approach is more productive than a control-oriented approach, except for companies that produce simple products or services in a stable environment.[5] High-involvement organizations also have less turnover because employees find them a more attractive place to work.[6] Listen to the differences in how these two employees talk about their managers.[7]

> *Down on the floor (in a GM plant), you can see the operation, and you know how it's supposed to be done. Up there, upper management's saying, "Nah, nah, we can do it cheaper and more efficient if we do it our way." So these people up there that are calling all the shots are not experiencing what really needs to take place on the floor. And they don't really care, because they're thinking, "Short-term dollars and cents, it looks real good" and we're here down on the floor thinking, "Long-term, it's our job." Plus we want to give a person exactly what they bought: a perfect vehicle for the price. Any auto worker would tell you that. ... They should not concentrate so much on quantity—and let us work on the quality. (GM worker)*
>
> *Honda's thing is, the guy on the line is the gut professional on his job, and he knows what is best for that process at that time. He knows best how to make it better. You give us an opportunity to have a say-so, and we can do a good job. (Honda worker)*

Management can be either a competitive advantage for a company or an obstacle to high performance. Most experts agree that to succeed in the current business environment, companies need managers who see themselves less as bosses and more as facilitators and coaches.

Rather than calling all the shots, the new breed of manager or supervisor focuses on developing subordinates and encouraging them to become involved and take responsibility for their own output. "The key assumption in the involvement-oriented approach is that if individuals are given challenging work that gives them a customer to serve and a business to operate they can and will control their own behavior."[8] The new managers talk about "working themselves out of a job" as subordinates are trained to take over duties formerly done by supervisors or middle managers. The involvement-oriented approach to managers relies heavily on self-control and self-management. This frees up management time to concentrate on areas that are more likely to ensure the organization's survival. For example, managers can utilize the time they formerly spent checking up on employees to focus on obtaining the resources subordinates need to do their jobs, adding value to the product, looking for and learning from problems, and creating the best possible environment for employees.[9]

EMPOWERMENT

Empowerment is the term that describes a large part of what the new breed of managers actually do. *Empowerment is defined as granting employees the autonomy to assume more responsibility within an organization and strengthening their sense of effectiveness.* We have known for many years that certain types of charismatic leaders, such as John F. Kennedy, empower their followers by making them feel stronger and more capable of taking action.[10] The term *empowerment*, however, has become popular only within the last 10 years and refers to an enabling process that increases the intrinsic task motivation for employees[11] and increases their self-efficacy, which is the individual's belief that he or she is capable of performing a task.[12] Higher self-efficacy is correlated with higher work performance.[13] Empowerment, which has been called an effort to "white-collarize" factory workers, has been adopted by an estimated 40 percent of U.S. manufacturers.[14]

Empowerment is a mind-set with these characteristics:[15]

1. **Meaning** People feel that their work is important to them. They care about what they do. There is often a connection between their personal values and the work they do.
2. **Competence** People are confident about their ability to do their work well; they know they can perform and, as a result, have a sense of self-efficacy.
3. **Self-determination** People are free to choose how to do their work; they are not micromanaged.
4. **Impact** People believe they can have influence on their work unit; others listen to their ideas.

Employees have to choose to be empowered, but organizations can encourage this mind-set by the following actions:[16]

- Reduce hierarchical and bureaucratic structures (e.g., design organic systems that emphasize flexibility, adaptability, and innovation).
- Increase access to sources of system power (e.g., access to strategic information, resources, and managerial support).
- Encourage an organizational culture that values the human assets of the organization.
- Establish direction and boundaries relating to empowerment.

Teams are often examples of organic systems that make organizations less bureaucratic. Employees at Frito-Lay have access to strategic information; they can log on to see the company's entire product development system and track the volume of each product line. The Levi Strauss mission statement provides an example of an empowerment culture: "We want our people to feel respected, treated fairly, listened to and involved. We want a company that our people are proud of and committed to, where all employees have an opportunity to contribute, learn, grow, and advance." Senior management has to agree on what they mean by empowerment and provide direction and boundaries. Unrestrained empowerment can do serious damage. The Barings Bank, for example, collapsed under a mountain of debt created by a young trader who worked without checks and balances. Many companies set limits on employee discretion so that mistakes cannot threaten the firm's survival.

The outcomes of empowerment are employees who are more effective, innovative, and capable of exerting upward influence than disempowered employees[17] and who have higher levels of job satisfaction and lower levels of stress.[18]

Empowerment is predicated on the beliefs reflected in both Theory Y (Chapter 2) and the Job Characteristics Enrichment model (Chapter 4) that people want to make a contribution and desire greater autonomy and meaning at work. Herbert Simon, Nobel Laureate, states that many people are motivated by a sense of altruism that translates into organizational commitment. However, not everyone shares these values or can break the old habits of the command-and-control model. Thus, it comes as no surprise that some employees and managers have found the transition to an "empowered" workplace exceedingly difficult.[19]

Not all workers enjoy being empowered. Being accountable, worrying about tasks that were formerly the concern of management, disciplining fellow workers or being disciplined by them is not for everyone. Of the managers who have made the shift, some did so because empowerment fits their own value system; others use empowerment simply because it is a more effective management technique.[20]

In addition to personal values and habits, another barrier to empowerment can be organizational cultures with norms that work against employee involvement. For example, at one university new faculty members are cautioned by senior faculty not to jeopardize their chances for tenure by making suggestions to the administration or getting involved in controversial topics. They are also told stories about professors who have been fired in the past for disagreeing with the administration on topics that fell within the professors' area of expertise. This perception of a closed-minded administration may no longer be true, but faculty members are still fearful of rocking the boat. Even when they believe the administration is making a serious mistake, they muzzle themselves and narrow their focus to their individual job or department. "I'll just teach my classes and let them stew in their own juices." Thus, the norms of silence and centralized decision making are perpetuated by the organizational culture. Faculty perceive themselves as a relatively powerless group. They complain about the administration, but they are not proactive about making improvements. This is an example of *learned helplessness*, which is passive behavior and a failure to exert effort even when success may be possible.

In contrast, high performance–high commitment work cultures have these characteristics: delegation, teamwork across boundaries, empowerment, integration of people and technology, and a shared sense of purpose.[21] Employees who have the most relevant information or the most appropriate work skills are delegated the responsibility for completing the work. Integrating people with technology signifies that employees control the technology rather than being controlled by it. A shared sense of purpose implies a common vision of the organization's purpose and the methods for accomplishing this purpose.

When organizations introduce the idea of an empowered workforce, they are changing the psychological contract that exists between management and employees. New behavior and expectations are required of both groups, but not everyone can adapt to these changes. Middle managers, who feel the pinch most personally in change efforts, sometimes find it difficult to relinquish their traditional ways of dealing with subordinates and carve out a new role for themselves. One tactic that has been used to prevent managers from micromanaging subordinates is to give them more direct reports than one person could ever supervise. Eventually, they realize that the only way to survive is to allow subordinates and teams greater autonomy.

Managers can use these strategies to encourage an empowerment mind-set:[22]

1. Solicit input from employees on a regular basis.
2. Ask for their help in solving problems.
3. Teach employees to make sound decisions by allowing them to gain experience with carefully selected decisions. As their judgement improves, let them make progressively more complex decisions.
4. Remove any bureaucratic obstacles that stop employees from taking initiative and responsibility. In many organizations, people feel powerless to fix things because both procedures and management practices promote the status quo and get in the way of positive changes.
5. Rather than automatically supplying answers to employees, ask questions that encourage them to come up with answers. "What would you do if you had to make this decision?" "What factors do we need to consider here?"
6. Provide workers with all the information they need to make decisions about the business.
7. Let employees know it's up to them to do whatever is necessary within reason to serve the customer, without having to request permission.
8. Provide a positive emotional atmosphere that promotes self esteem and self-development.
9. Reward achievements in visible and personal ways.
10. Serve as a role model for employees.
11. Coach people so they can successfully master tasks.

One of the common concerns supervisors and managers have about employee empowerment is whether it means relinquishing all their own authority. When managers share power with subordinates, their own power does not diminish as it would if power were a zero-sum commodity. When power is shared, it expands. Managers who practice empowerment are still responsible for setting the direction for their subordinates, or for seeing that a direction is set in a participative fashion. Furthermore, wise managers do not simply turn over power to subordinates without first ensuring that they have the necessary information and skills to make good decisions. Managers who empower their employees still have to:

- Know what is going on.
- Set or communicate the direction for the department or unit.
- Make decisions subordinates cannot make.
- Ensure that people are on course.
- Offer a guiding hand and open doors to clear the way.
- Make sure that employees have the necessary skills to assume greater autonomy and responsibility.
- Ensure that employees have the necessary information to make good decisions.
- Assess performance.[23]

Mary Parker Follett, one of the earliest management writers, noted, "Authority, genuine authority, is the outcome of our common life. It does not come from separating people, from dividing them into two classes: those who command and those who obey. It comes from the intermingling of all, of my work fitting into yours and yours into mine."[24]

Follett first proposed the idea of depersonalizing authority and adopting the law of the situation in which "the situation is the boss."[25] She observed that workers react to receiving orders by becoming more passive and taking less and less responsibility. However, by examining the situation, it becomes evident to almost everyone, regardless of their hierarchical position, what needs to be done. In this way, the situation becomes the boss. It is much easier to examine situations when employees have access to both information and data-analysis skills. When employees and managers engage in a "databased dialogue," the inherent tensions of a superior-subordinate relationship are reduced.[26]

There is a direct correlation between good people management and profits. High-commitment companies have a 30 to 40 percent higher productivity rate than other companies, according to years of research.[27] Wal-Mart, the Ritz Carlton, Whole Foods Market, and ServiceMaster have climbed to the top of their industries, distinguished from the competition by their people-centered management practices. More and more companies are realizing, as research shows, that the only way to ensure profits, and even survival, is to develop a work environment that attracts, focuses, and retains highly talented employees.[28]

COACHING

Empowerment implies a strong commitment to employee development. Managers see themselves as resource people who are responsible for developing their subordinates. One of the primary skills managers need for this task is coaching. *Coaching is defined as a conversation that follows a predictable process and leads to superior performance, commitment to sustained improvement, and positive relationships.*[29] Coaching generally takes place in a one-on-one conversation. Although it is usually performed by managers with subordinates, coaching can also be initiated by skilled coworkers or subordinates (e.g., the case of the young manager who is taught the ropes by an older subordinate).

There are four types of coaching.[30]

1. *Tutoring.* Tutoring is used to teach employees necessary job skills they have not yet learned. For example, when employees do not know how to run a team meeting, they must be taught the specific steps in the process and given both practice and feedback.
2. *Counseling.* In counseling sessions, the purpose is to help employees gain personal insight into their feelings and behavior. Counseling is appropriate for employees with attitude problems they themselves do not recognize. The focus in counseling is problem recognition and solution.
3. *Mentoring.* In mentoring sessions, the objective is to help employees gain a better understanding of the organization, its goals, and advancement criteria. This approach is used, for example, when employees ask why other employees have been promoted and they have not. In such sessions, managers try to make employees more politically savvy and warn them of possible traps. They also help employees live up to their full potential and encourage them to be more proactive in managing their careers.
4. *Confronting.* The purpose of confronting is to improve substandard employee performance. Confronting is used, for example, with an employee who is consistently late to work. Performance standards are clarified, the discrepancy between the standard and the employee's performance is pointed out, the cause of the discrepancy is identified, and both parties problem-solve to find a solution.

STEPS IN THE COACHING PROCESS

The tutoring process for teaching new skills consists of the following steps.[31]

1. Explain the purpose and importance of what you are trying to teach.
2. Explain the process to be used.

3. Demonstrate how it is done.
4. Observe while the person practices the process.
5. Provide immediate and specific feedback (coach again or reinforce success).
6. Express confidence in the person's ability to be successful.
7. Agree on follow-up actions.

The correct approach to take with employees who are not performing well depends on the cause. Unsatisfactory performance often has multiple causes, some of which lie within the control of the employee and some that do not. Fournies suggested that managers use the following guidelines to determine what action they should take.[32] When employees are unaware that their performance is unsatisfactory, the manager (or team) provides feedback. When poor performance occurs because employees are not really sure what is expected of them at work, the manager (or team) provides clear expectations. When employee performance is hampered by obstacles that are beyond their control, the manager removes the obstacles. When the employee simply does not know how to do a task, the manager provides training. The manager should also make sure that good performance is followed by positive rather than negative consequences, and that poor performance is not rewarded by positive consequences. If all these steps have been taken to ensure good performance, and the employee is still not able or willing to perform well, it is time for confrontation coaching. Although there are differences in counseling, mentoring, and confronting sessions,[33] the following steps can be used as a general guideline for all three.

Prior to the coaching session:

- Does the supervisor/manager have all the facts about the situation?
- What type of coaching does the situation require?
- How might the employee react and feel about the discussion?
- Think about the best way to present what you want to say to the employee.

During the session:

- Discuss the purpose of the session.
- Try to make the employee comfortable.
- Establish a nondefensive climate characterized by open communication and trust.
- Praise the employee for the positive aspects of his or her performance.
- Mutually define the problem (performance or attitude).
- Mutually determine the causes. Do not interpret or psychoanalyze the employee's behavior; instead, ask questions, "What's causing the lack of motivation you describe?"
- Help the employee establish an action plan that includes specific goals and dates.
- Make sure the employee clearly understands what is expected of him or her.
- Summarize what has been agreed upon in the session.
- Affirm your confidence in the employee's ability to make needed changes based on his or her strengths or past history.

After the session:

- Follow up to see how the employee is progressing.
- Modify the action plan if necessary.

PROCEDURE FOR GROUP MEETING: THE ENTERPRISE MERGER GAME

The Enterprise Merger game is designed to simulate the dynamics that occur when companies are merged or acquired. The class will divide into Enterprise Teams, which manufacture spacecraft, and Merger Teams, which have recently acquired Enterprise. The exercise focuses on the Merger Team's visit to the Enterprise production facility; the Merger Team's purpose is to improve Enterprise's productivity.

TABLE 17-1   Timetable for the Enterprise Merger Game

Step	Activity		Time
A	Select Game Coordinator; Form Teams Read Simulation Instructions		10 min.
B	**Merger Team** – Develop plan for helping Enterprise improve – Observe Enterprise's management and production process	**Enterprise Team** – Organize management and production process – Build spacecraft mockups – Buy materials – Prepare to produce	20 min.
C	Continue observation	First production period	5 min.
D	Coordinator evaluates and buys; teams compute profit		3–5 min.
E	Merger team consults with Enterprise Team		20 min.
F	Facilitator Team observes	Second production period	5 min.
G	Coordinator evaluates and buys; teams compute profit		5 min.
H	Teams average their evaluation scores in the consultation process and discuss Step 6 questions		20 min.
I	Class Debriefing		20 min.
		Total Time	105–110 min.

STEP 1.   Choose one or two game coordinators (instructors often play this role). The role of the game coordinator is to (1) act as a leader and timekeeper for the simulation; (2) function as the government inspector and buyer of Enterprise's products, and (3) guide the postgame discussion.

STEP 2.   The class should be divided in half to form two corporations—Enterprise and Merger. Teams of approximately five people from each corporation should be assigned to work together.

STEP 3.   Go over the timetable and game procedure shown in Table 17-1.

STEP 4.   The game coordinator and the Enterprise and Merger Teams should read their own instructions, which follow.

INSTRUCTIONS FOR THE GAME COORDINATOR

Read the instructions for the entire exercise. Your most important tasks are to:

- Keep to the time schedule described in Table 17-1 (or set by your instructor).
- Sell materials to the Enterprise Teams prior to production periods 1 and 2 so they are ready to begin construction at the exact moment the production periods begin.
- Inspect and buy acceptable spacecrafts from Enterprise Teams during production periods 1 and 2. *Don't buy the spacecraft unless they fully meet the quality criteria at the end of the blueprints.*
- Ask the Enterprise Teams to post the number of material sets bought and sold and their profit and loss after each production period on the blackboard. Use the Enterprise Team Accounting Form as a guide.

- Once the profit and loss figures have been determined after the second production period, ask each individual to evaluate the Merger Team's intervention, as shown in Step 5. Ask each team to average its scores, compare its average with that of the team assigned to work with it, and fill out the form in Step 6.
- Record the two team averages for each pair of Enterprise-Merger Teams on the blackboard and lead the discussion of the questions in Step 7.

INSTRUCTIONS FOR THE ENTERPRISE TEAM

Your previous successful experience in the aerospace industry has just won you a government contract to produce as many Enterprise spacecraft as your production facilities will allow during the next two months (represented in this exercise by the two 5-minute production periods). The government has just given you a set of blueprints for the spacecraft accompanied by a number of quality criteria. You must buy raw materials from the game coordinator as determined by the price schedule in Table 17-2. Your profit is determined by the number of spacecraft you sell to the government at a price of $5 million each minus the cost of materials (other factors, such as overhead, materials, and waste, have been eliminated for simplicity's sake). Only completed vehicles of acceptable quality can be sold. See the Quality Criteria at the end of the blueprints. No materials can be returned; nor can leftovers from period 1 be used in period 2.

TABLE 17-2 Costs of Enterprise Spacecraft Materials

Number of Sets Purchased	Cost Per Set
0–4	4,500,000
5–9	4,400,000
10–14	4,300,000
15–19	4,200,000
20–24	4,100,000
25–29	4,000,000
30–34	3,900,000
35–39	3,800,000
40–44	3,750,000
45–49	3,700,000
50–100	3,650,000
Over 100	3,600,000

Caution: The materials you buy may be slightly faulty. Apparently it is difficult to print the spacecraft perfectly. If you receive raw materials with nose cone lines that don't start at the exact corner of the paper, ignore the lines and make your fold from the true corner of the paper. We're sorry for the inconvenience, but we hear that real-life government contractors sometimes have the same problem.

In the 20-minute preparation time, you can organize your members in any way you wish to make purchasing and production decisions. During this time your team is allowed two free sets of materials *for each member* to use in any way the team wants to establish production techniques and time estimates. Any additional materials used during this time must be purchased at full cost. These materials cannot be used during the production periods.

Your agreement with the Merger Team is that it may observe your activities during this time, but it is not to interfere in any way.

When you have decided how many units you want to produce, tell the game coordinator how many sets of materials you want to buy and record that information on the Enterprise Team Accounting Form (page 390) and the blackboard.

INSTRUCTIONS FOR THE MERGER TEAM

Your task during the first 20 minutes is to decide how best to work with the Enterprise Team after the first production period to help it increase its profit during production period 2. You can organize yourself in any way you want (e.g., you can choose one or two members to act as consultants and feed information and ideas to them, work one-on-one with members of the Enterprise Team, or use any other model you may choose). During the 20-minute preparation period and the first production period, you can observe the Enterprise Team at work, but please do not intervene or speak to its members until Step E.

During the 20 minutes before production period 2 begins, help the Enterprise Team in any way you see fit. *Once the second production period begins, however, you are only allowed to observe.* During round 2, the Enterprise Team can have no more members than it had during round 1. Personnel transfers are, however, legitimate. In other words, the total number of people on the Enterprise Team during round 2 must be the same, but specific people can be shifted from the Merger Team to *replace* someone on the Enterprise Team.

Enterprise Team Accounting Form

	Material Sets Purchased	Cost Per Set	Total Cost	Number Of Units Sold At $5 million Per Unit	Total Receipts	Profit Or Loss
PRODUCTION PERIOD 1						
PRODUCTION PERIOD 2						
					total	total

ANALYSIS OF THE CONSULTATION PROCESS

STEP 5.   The Merger Team has just attempted to effect an improvement in a way in which the Enterprise Team produces spaceships. On the whole, how successful do you think the Merger Team was? (Enterprise Team members evaluate their Merger Team; Merger Team members do a self-evaluation.) Draw a circle around the number that most closely represents your personal opinion:

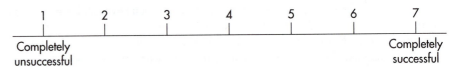

1   2   3   4   5   6   7

Completely
unsuccessful

Completely
successful

STEP 6.   Group Discussion.   Average the scores of your team (Enterprise or Merger) and compare it with that of the other team you worked with in the simulation. (e.g., the Enterprise Team's evaluation average for Merger Team compared to the self-evaluation average of the Merger Team). With them, discuss the following questions and choose a representative to report your findings back to the class as a whole.

(a) Did the two teams perceive the Merger Team's intervention in the same way?

(b) What did both teams do that either helped or hindered a successful collaborative effort? Use the following chart to record your answers.

Enterprise Team Actions That		Merger Team Actions That	
Helped	Hindered	Helped	Hindered

STEP 7.   Class Discussion.   After presenting the group findings, the class discusses the following questions.

a. What attributions did the Merger Team make about the performance of the Enterprise Team during the first production period? What was your opinion of them?

b. Was their definition of the problem the same as that of the Enterprise Team?

c. What was the Merger Team's strategy for helping the Enterprise Team? Did it work?

d. Was the psychological contract clarified between the two teams?

e. Did the Merger Team do anything to empower or disempower the Enterprise Team with regard to

(1) Meaning:

(2) Competence:

(3) Self-determination:

(4) Impact:

f. Can you draw any analogies between this simulation and real-life merger situations?

g. What connections can you make between this simulation and the readings?

DIRECTIONS FOR MAKING THE SPACESHIP ENTERPRISE

The following are directions for making the spaceship. After each step, there is a picture showing what to do and another picture showing what it should look like. Make sure you check this before going on to the next step. There are 11 steps.

1. You should have a piece of paper that has one blank side, and one side that looks like this:

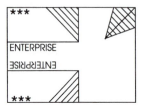

2. Turn the paper over so that the blank side is facing up and the word *ENTERPRISE* is on the left-hand underneath side. It should now look like this:

3. Fold corner A to B at the bottom of the paper.

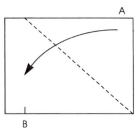

It should now look like this:

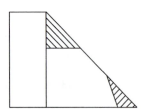

4. Fold corner C to D.

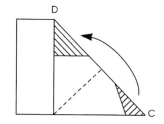

It should now look like this:

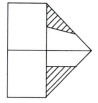

5. Fold E to E.

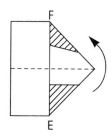

It should now look like this:

6. Fold on GH by starting with the part with the stars (***) on it and folding down so that the fold comes along the printed solid line. *There are three thicknesses of paper— make sure you only fold the first layer.*

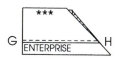

It should now look like this.

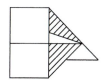

7. Make a fold (up direction) about 1 inch from the bottom along JK.

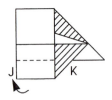

It should now look like this:

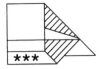

8. Turn the spaceship over and round so that L is on the left side.

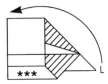

It should now look like this:

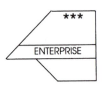

9. Fold on MN by starting with the part with the stars (***) on it and folding down so that the fold comes along the printed solid line. *There are two thicknesses of paper— make sure you only fold the top one.*

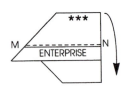

It should now look like this. *Make sure this sticks up in the center.*

10. Make a fold (up direction) about 1 inch from the bottom along OP to make wingtips.

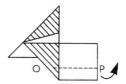

It should now look like this:

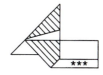

Read all of step 11 and then go back and do it part by part.

11. a. Hold spaceship in hand.

   b. Open up Q with finger and flatten the lined area (/ / / / /) by bringing central point R toward the main body of the plane.

   c. Fold along ST to keep it flat.

   d. Make wings level so that plane can fly.

   e. Make the OP fold a 90° angle so the wingtips point straight up.

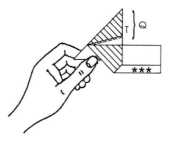

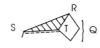

Finished plane should look like this:

top view

side view

front view

Quality Criteria

1. Printed lines should be in the position shown on the diagram (unless your materials are defective).
2. The wingtips must be 1 inch tall and point straight up.
3. The "pilot's cabin" (step 11) must be puffed out noticeably. Skinny cabins crowd the astronauts. Cabin folds must be creased on printed lines wherever possible.
4. The two wings must be even with each other (i.e., the entire wing deck should be perfectly level).
5. The nose of the spaceship should be pointed.

   The game coordinator will buy only those spacecraft that meet these quality control standards.

Effective coaching utilizes the communication skills we have studied in previous chapters—active listening, empathy, creating a nondefensive climate, response styles, assertive communication, the use of I-statements, and understanding the role of perception in communication. Communication has to be supportive so employees can absorb the message.

Another crucial coaching communication skill is providing effective feedback. Feedback helps individuals to keep behavior "on target" and, thus, better achieve their goals. Achievement-oriented people, in particular, want and need frequent and specific feedback to continue performing at optimal levels. The purpose of feedback is to provide people with information that they may or may not choose to utilize. In a work setting there may well be consequences for not utilizing the information, but feedback offered in the spirit of helpful data is less likely to arouse defensiveness. Before offering feedback, check with others to make sure your perceptions are valid and unbiased. Effective feedback has the following characteristics:

1. Effective feedback is descriptive as opposed to evaluative. For example, to tell a person "When you interrupt and don't let me finish my statements (description), it makes me feel as if you don't value my ideas (personal reactions)," it has a very different impact from the evaluative statement, "Boy, you sure are a power-hungry s.o.b." The latter is bound to cause a defensive reaction. While the former may not be totally pleasant, it is nonetheless easier to hear because it is more descriptive than evaluative.

2. Effective feedback is specific rather than general. To be told that one is "not performing well" will not be as useful as being told "your last three shipments were sent without the proper paperwork." Vague feedback based on fuzzy impressions is generally very hard to translate into the specific developmental goals that are so important to improvement.

3. Effective feedback is directed toward behavior that the receiver can control. To be told that "short people don't get ahead very fast in this company" is frustrating (as well as of questionable legality!).

4. To the extent possible, it is better for feedback to be solicited rather than imposed. If people can formulate the questions they feel a need to explore, their motivation to listen carefully is significantly enhanced. While this is the ideal circumstance, particularly in nonwork situations, giving an employee unsolicited feedback is an important aspect of any supervisory or managerial job. Even in this instance, however, you can share the control and provide the employee with an opportunity to participate by saying, for example, "I've noticed a few things I think it would be good for us to talk about. Is now a good time to talk? If not, when would be a good time for you?"

5. As seen in the preceding example, effective feedback is well timed. Feedback must be offered when the receiver can best accept it. For example, the end of a hectic day or when an employee is worried about a family-related problem are not the most propitious times to give feedback.

6. Feedback should be immediate and continual rather than delayed and sporadic. It does the receiver little good to find out that six months ago he or she did something "wrong." Feedback is generally most effective at the earliest opportunity after the behavior in question has occurred.

7. Good feedback suggests rather than prescribes avenues for improvement. Demanding that other people change their behavior in a certain way is similar to the control-oriented communication that provokes a defensive reaction and disempowers people.[34] Furthermore, we lose sight of the crucial role of self-determination in behavioral change. This means that people must decide for themselves what they want to do and take responsibility for their own actions.

8. Effective feedback is intended to help. Feedback is ineffective when the person giving feedback seems driven to do so for his or her own needs (e.g., venting one's personal frustration on an employee). Feedback is not punishment, although ineffective feedback may feel that way. It simply provides information that the receiver's behavior is off target.

In summary, the eight rules of thumb for giving effective feedback in a way that increases productive discussion and decreases defensiveness are:

- Descriptive rather than evaluative.
- Specific and data-based rather than general.
- Directed toward controllable behaviors rather than personality traits or characteristics.
- Solicited rather than imposed.
- Close to the event under discussion rather than delayed for several months.
- Occurs when the receiver is most ready to accept it.
- Suggests rather than prescribes avenues for improvements.
- Is intended to help, not punish.

There are also guidelines for receiving feedback. The most important is to take feedback as helpful information that warrants serious consideration. If the feedback is not clear, request more information or examples. If the feedback does not seem accurate, which is a possibility given what we know about perception, seek a second opinion by asking others how they perceive your behavior. Feedback is worthless if (1) we automatically deny its validity; (2) rationalize our behavior; or (3) assume the manager is only telling us this because he or she does not like us or is trying to manipulate us.

POSITIVE REGARD

Coaching and developing employees is a type of helping relationship. Carl Rogers, the famous psychologist, discovered the importance of unconditional positive regard in his own helping relationships.[35] "I feel that the more acceptance and liking I feel toward this individual, the more I will be creating a relationship which he can use. By acceptance I mean a warm regard for him as a person of unconditional self-worth—of value no matter what his condition, or his feelings....This acceptance of each fluctuating aspect of this other person makes it for him a relationship of warmth and safety, and the safety of being liked and prized as a person seems a highly important element in a helping relationship." Positive regard for employees is also one of the competencies of high-performing managers.[36] Assuming that employees want to do a good job, rather than assuming the worst about them, creates a self-fulfilling prophecy when they try to live up to their boss's good opinion.

ORGANIZATIONAL BACKUP FOR EMPOWERMENT

Some organizations, such as Cadillac, have turned their organizational chart upside down to form an inverted pyramid. This communicates that management's primary purpose is to serve the employees who are serving the customers. Federal Express not only has an inverted structure, but management reinforces it by having employees fill out yearly Survey/Feedback/Action (SFA) forms on their managers. The form includes items such as those found in the Empowerment Questionnaire you filled out before class. Upper management at Federal Express is evaluated on its openness to ideas and suggestions, its fairness, and whether or not it keeps employees informed. The survey results affect the managers' bonuses and future with the company. Thus, Federal Express has modified its structure, evaluation system, and rewards to encourage managers to empower their employees.

Dick (Sethi) Depak, assistant director of executive education at AT&T, uses this "seven R" model to develop a culture of high performance and high self-esteem among today's knowledge workers.[37]

1. **Respect** Not platitudes but a sincere belief that people at all levels of the organization have unique contributions to make. Too often, only people at the top of organizations can get a hearing for their ideas.
2. **Responsibility and Resources** Employees perform best when they have a discrete and well-defined area of responsibility and the resources needed to make it successful. In contrast, micromanaging implies a lack of trust in employees.
3. **Risk Taking** In order to promote innovation, employees have to learn to take risks—some of which will inevitably result in mistakes. Mistakes have to be viewed as opportunities for lessons rather than career-ending triggers.

4. **Rewards and Recognitions** Talented, hardworking employees should receive both monetary rewards and recognition for a job well done. The major reasons good people leave corporations are lack of recognition, lack of involvement, and poor management.[38]

5. **Relationship** "When people on all levels get to know one another in a respectful and benevolent way and get to understand one another's strengths, shortcomings, hopes, dreams, and fears, a context is established in which trust can flourish, as mutual and meaningful feedback is given and received."[39]

6. **Role Modeling** Managers "walk the talk" by acting, rather than "speechifying," in accordance with these values. Senior executives serve as inspiring role models.

7. **Renewal** A culture that promotes organizational learning at all levels results in the expanded consciousness needed for renewal.

LEARNING POINTS

1. Companies that survive and flourish in today's business environment are high-performance companies characterized by cost competiveness, high-quality products and services, innovation, and speed.

2. The command-and-control model is giving way to an involvement-oriented management approach in high-performance organizations because committed workers are more productive.

3. In the command-and-control model, managers make decisions, give orders, and make sure they are obeyed.

4. In the involvement-oriented approach, managers develop employee commitment by sharing both power and information, and developing the employee skills needed to plan and control their own work.

5. Empowerment is defined as granting employees the autonomy to assume more responsibility within an organization and strengthening their sense of effectiveness.

6. The four aspects of empowerment are meaning, competence, self-determination, and impact.

7. The characteristics of high performance–high commitment work cultures are delegation, teamwork across boundaries, empowerment, integration of people and technology, and a shared sense of purpose.

8. Empowerment does not imply that managers and supervisors relinquish all their own authority. They are still responsible for setting the direction, knowing what is going on, removing obstacles, ensuring that employees are on course, ensuring that employees have the necessary skills and information, and assessing performance.

9. Coaching is a conversation that follows a predictable process and leads to superior performance, commitment to sustained improvement, and positive relationships.

10. There are four types of coaching: tutoring, counseling, mentoring, and confronting.

11. Effective feedback is objective rather than judgmental, descriptive rather than vague, directed toward controllable behavior, solicited rather than imposed, and well timed. It is immediate rather than delayed, suggests rather than prescribes avenues for improvements, and is intended to help, not punish.

12. Positive regard for others is a characteristic of both effective helper/coaches and high-performing managers.

FOR MANAGERS

Based on surveys of 80,000 managers in 400 companies, the following questions identify the levers management should use to engage good employees and make them more productive and less likely to quit and work elsewhere. Ideally, all employees should be able to answer yes to these questions:[40]

- Do I know what is expected of me at work?
- Do I have the materials and equipment I need to do my work?
- Do I have the opportunity to do what I do best, every day?
- In the past seven days, have I received recognition or praise for good work?
- Does my supervisor, or someone at work, seem to care about me as a person?
- Is there someone at work who encourages my development?

    Other tips for managers follow.

- Some organizations purposefully give managers so many subordinates that it is impossible for them to micromanage. By default, employees are given more autonomy and responsibility.[41]
- Encourage employees to call meetings when they think an issue requires attention.
- Avoid being the source of all wisdom, satisfying though it is to your ego. Instead, use the Socratic method and ask questions that model for employees the thought processes needed to make good decisions.
- Manager-employee relationships can be mutually helpful. Managers model the receiving end of coaching when they themselves are open to feedback and coaching from subordinates.
- Developing employees sometimes means giving up tasks that one enjoys and does very well (at least in your own eyes) and turning it over to someone who will perhaps do a worse job until he or she has mastered it. Or the employee may do it differently, which can also be hard to accept. Letting go of tasks and delegating is an investment that should pay off in the future with competent employees who free up your time to look at the broader picture.
- Many new managers are shocked by the amount of time they must spend counseling or developing employees. It is an important part of the job, but employees with serious personal problems should be referred to professional counselors.
- Active listening is a key part of coaching because people often determine what is bothering them or what decision they want to take by talking things out with another person. In presenting their story to a listener, many people imagine how the listener is reacting and this provides the speaker with another perspective.
- The leader's behavior determines the level of trust within a group. When leaders micromanage or fail to delegate, employees assume they are not trusted—and, in return, their trust in the leader diminishes. Employees who trust their immediate supervisor are more likely to be high performers.[42]

PERSONAL APPLICATION ASSIGNMENT

The topic of this assignment is to write about a significant experience that involved coaching or empowerment, or the lack thereof. Choose an experience that intrigues you and that you want to learn more about. Alternatively, you may want to experiment with the skills taught in this unit and write about the outcome.

A. *Concrete Experience*
   1. *Objectively* describe the experience (who, what, when, where, how information) (2 points)
   2. *Subjectively* describe your feelings, perceptions, and thoughts that occurred during (not after) the experience. What did others seem to be feeling? (2 points)

B. *Reflective Observation*
   1. Looking back at the experience, what were the perspectives of the key actors (including you)? (2 points)
   2. Why did the people involved (including you) behave as they did? (2 points)

C. *Abstract Conceptualization*
   1. Relate concepts or theories from the assigned readings or the lecture to the experience. Explain thoroughly how they apply to your experience. Please apply at least two concepts or theories and cite them correctly. (4 points)

D. *Active Experimentation*
   1. What did you learn about empowerment and coaching from this experience? (1 point)
   2. What did you learn about yourself? (1 point)
   3. What action steps will you take to be more effective in the future? (2 points)

E. *Integration, Synthesis, and Writing*
   1. Did you integrate and synthesize the four sections? (1 point)
   2. Was the Personal Application Assignment well written and easy to understand? (1 point)
   3. Was it free of spelling and grammatical errors? (2 points)

ENTERPRISE

ENTERPRISE

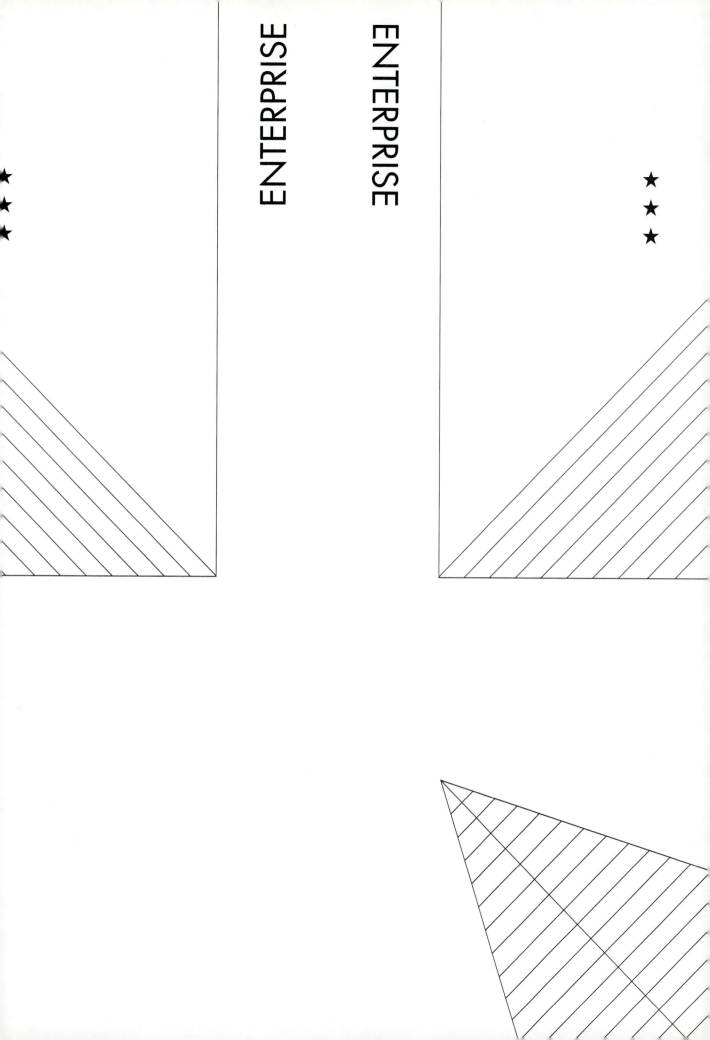

ENTERPRISE

ENTERPRISE

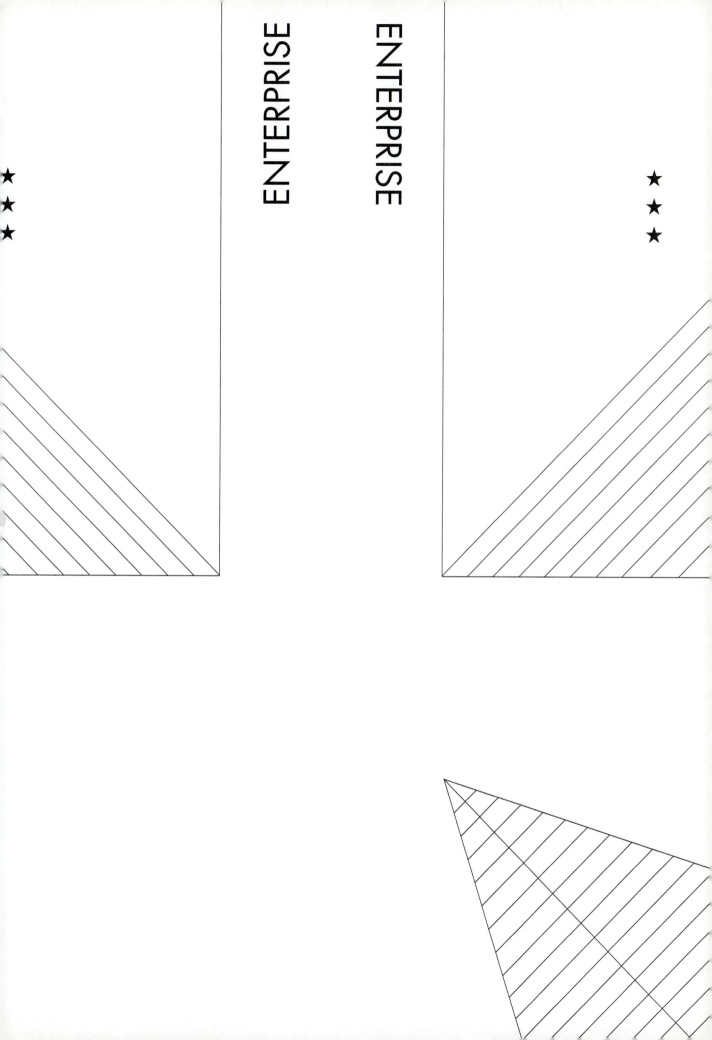

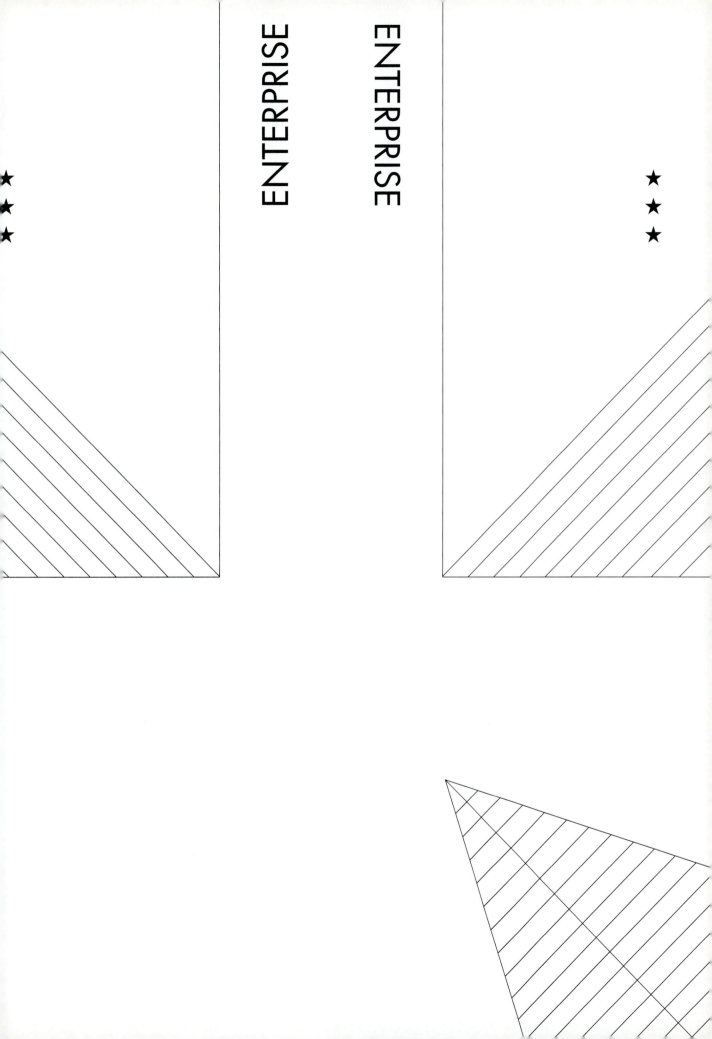

ENTERPRISE

ENTERPRISE

★
★
★

★
★
★

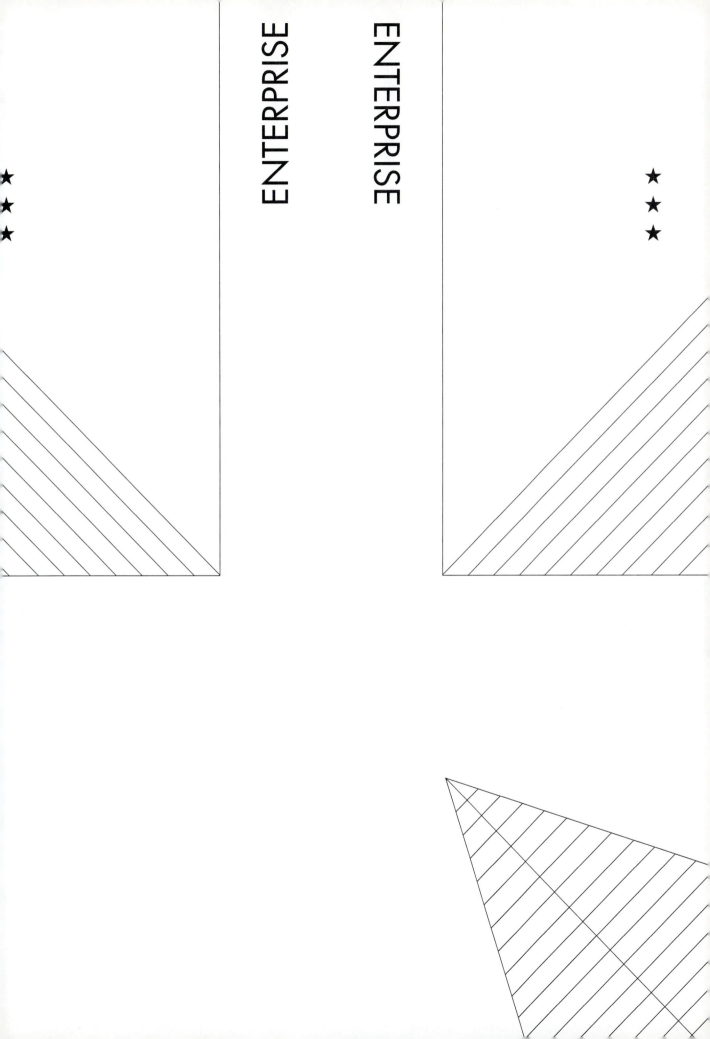

ENTERPRISE

ENTERPRISE

ENTERPRISE

ENTERPRISE

★
★
★

★
★
★

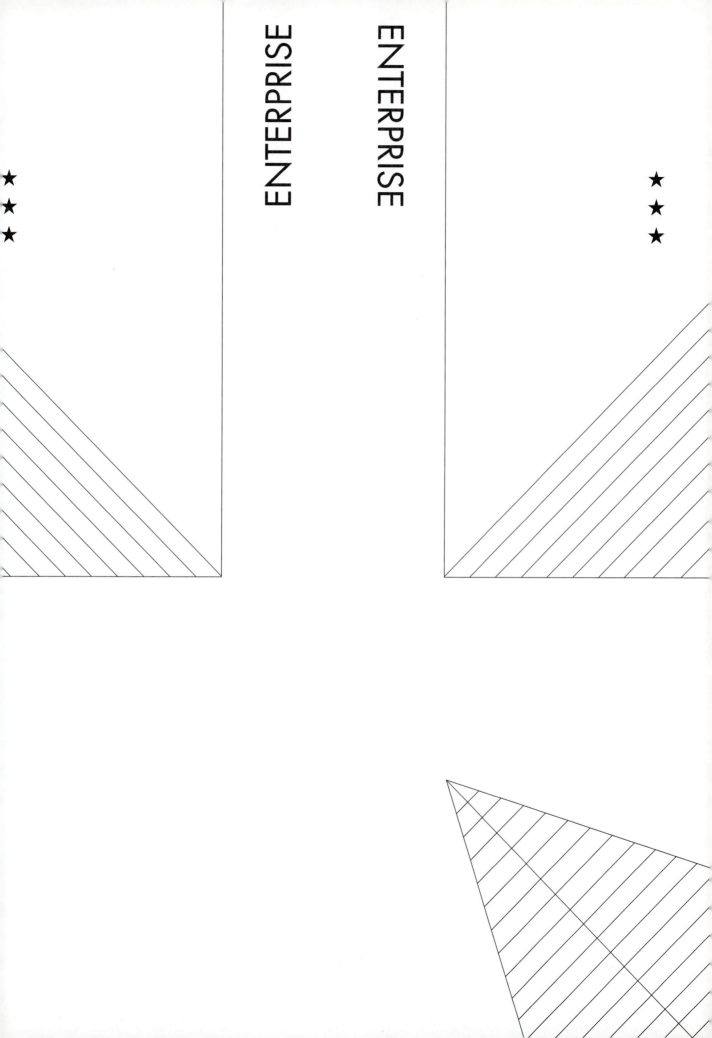

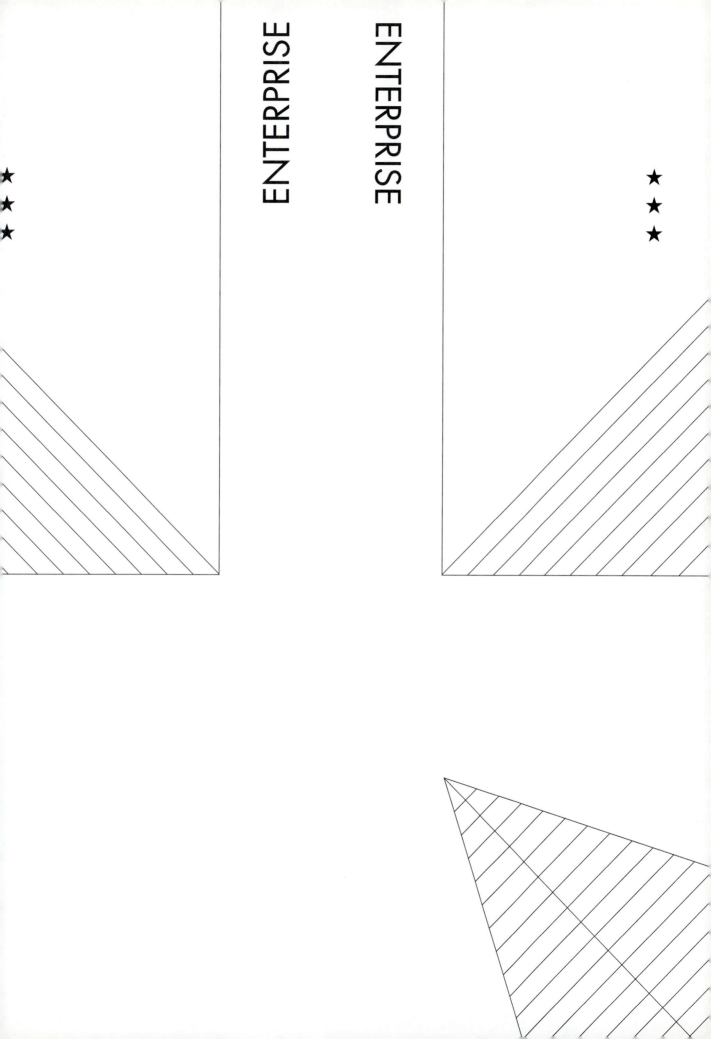

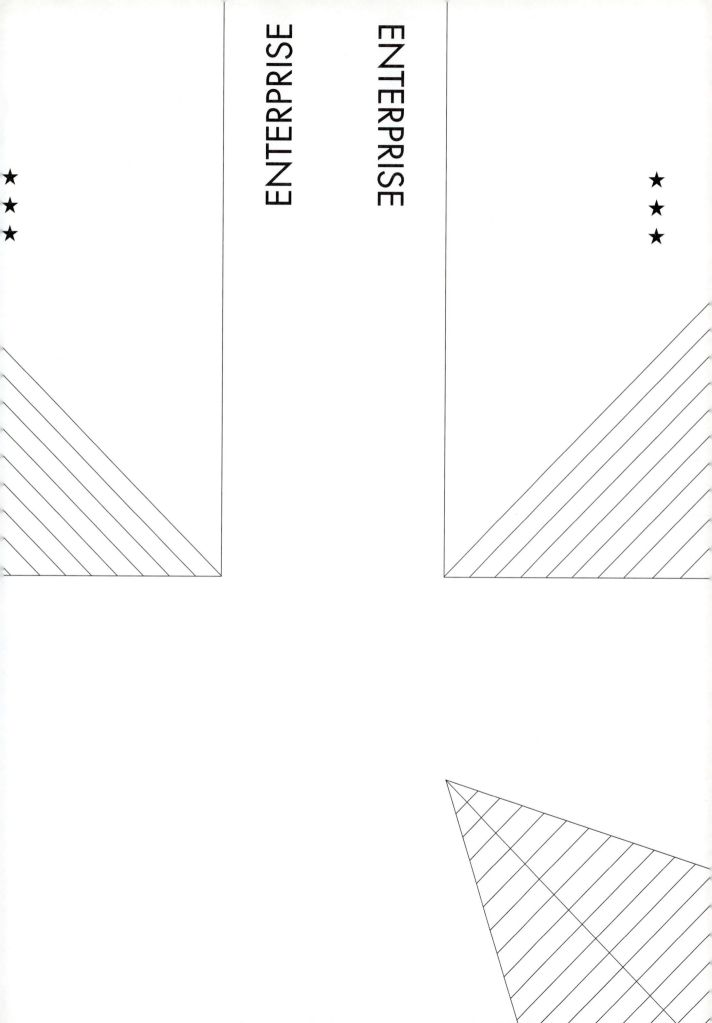

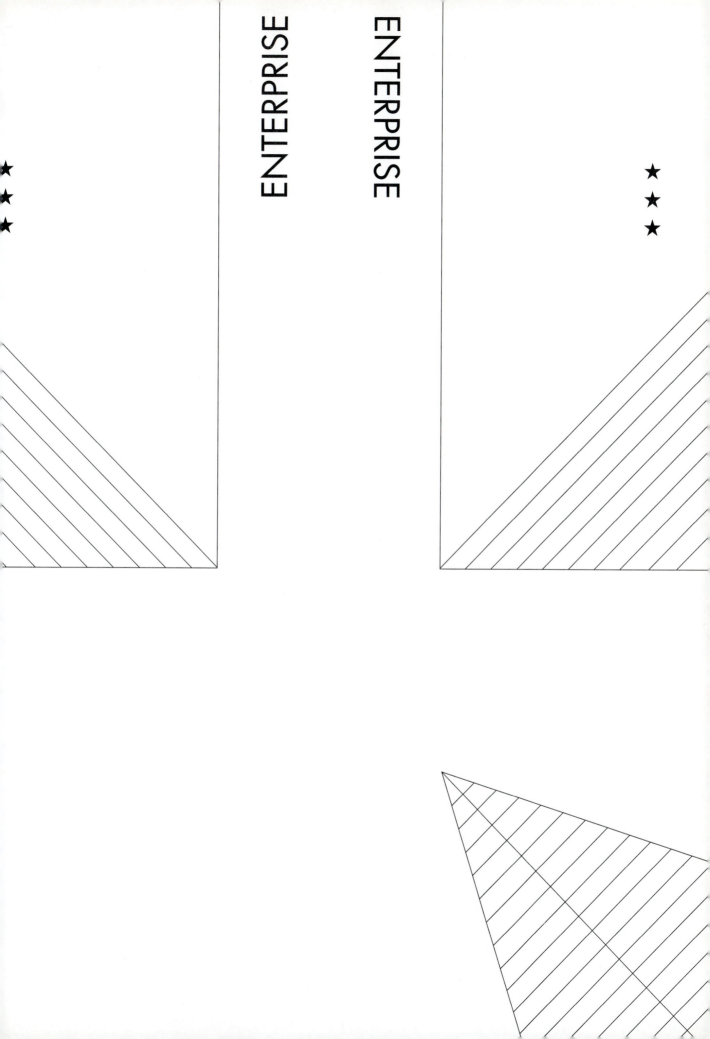

ENDNOTES

[1] This list is paraphrased from P. R. Harris, *High Performance Leadership* (Glenview, IL: Scott, Foresman and Company, 1989): 14–15.

[2] T. Peters, *Liberation Management* (New York: Alfred A. Knopf, 1992).

[3] E. E. Lawler III, *The Ultimate Advantage* (San Francisco: Jossey-Bass, 1992): 28–29.

[4] R. E. Walton, "From Control to Commitment in the Workplace," *Harvard Business Review* (March–April 1985): 76–84.

[5] Lawler, *Ultimate Advantage*, p. 44.

[6] Ibid, p. 41.

[7] M. Magnet, "The Truth about the American Worker," *Fortune*, May 4, 1992, pp. 58 and 64.

[8] Lawler, *Ultimate Advantage*, p. 29.

[9] W. H. Schmidt and J. P. Finnigan, *The Race Without a Finish Line* (San Francisco: Jossey-Bass, 1992), p. 46. Although these authors are writing about managers in TQM programs, which are not synonymous with high-involvement companies, this statement holds true for any manager who has empowered workers.

[10] D. C. McClelland, *Power: The Inner Experience* (New York: Irvington, 1975) and J. A. Conger and R. N. Kanugo, "The Empowerment Process: Integrating Theory and Practice," *Academy of Management Review 13* (1988): 471–82.

[11] K. W. Thomas and B. A. Velthouse, "Cognitive Elements of Empowerment: An Interpretative Model of Intrinsic Task Motivation," *Academy of Management Review 15* (October 1990): 666–81.

[12] A. Bandura, "Self-efficacy: Toward a Unifying Theory of Behavioral Change," *Psychological Review 84* (1977): 191–215; and A. Bandura, *Self-Efficacy: The Exercise of Control* (New York: W. H. Freeman and Company, 1997).

[13] A. Stajkovic and F. Luthans, "A Meta-Analysis of the Effects of Organizational Behavior Modification on Task Performance," *Academy of Management Journal 40* (1997): 1122–49.

[14] T. Appel, "Not All Workers Find Idea of Empowerment as Neat as It Sounds," *Wall Street Journal*, September 8, 1997, p. A-1.

[15] R. E. Quinn and G. Spreitzer, "The Road to Empowerment: Seven Questions Every Leader Should Consider," *Organizational Dynamics* (Autumn 1997): 41; G. M. and Spreitzer, "Toward a Common Ground in Defining Empowerment," in W. A. Pasmore and R. W. Woodman, eds., *Research in Organizational Change and Development 10* (Greenwich, CT: JAI Press, 1997).

[16] G. M. Spreitzer, "Social Structural Levers for Workforce Empowerment," *Academy of Management Journal 39* (1996): 483–504.

[17] G. M. Spreitzer, "A Comprehensive Model of Interpersonal Empowerment in the Workplace" *American Journal of Community Psychology 23* (1995): 601–29.

[18] K. W. Thomas and W. G. Tymon, "Does Empowerment Always Work: Understanding the Role of Intrinsic Motivation and Personal Interpretation," *Journal of Management Systems 6*, no. 2 (1994): 1–13.

[19] C. Argyris, "Empowerment: The Emperor's New Clothes," *Harvard Business Review* (May–June 1998): 98–105; J. Gandz and F. G. Bird, "The Ethics of Empowerment," *Journal of Business Ethics 15* (1996): 383–92; and T. Appel, "Not All Workers Find Idea of Empowerment as Neat as It Sounds."

[20] See R. Frey's "Empowerment or Else," *Harvard Business Review* (September–October 1993): 80–94, for a vivid description of one manager's experience in empowering his workers; and K. Blanchard, J. P. Carlos, and A. Rudolph, *The Three Keys to Empowerment* (San Francisco: Berrett-Koehler, 1999).

[21] J. J. Sherwood, "Creating Work Cultures with Competitive Advantage," *Organizational Dynamics*, (Winter 1988): 5–27.

[22] These suggestions come from a variety of sources including Bandura, "*Self-Efficacy*;" and W. C. Byham with J. Cox, *Zapp! The Lightning of Empowerment* (Pittsburgh, PA: DDI Press, 1989).

[23] Adapted from Byham, *Zapp*, p. 108.

[24] M. P. Follett, *Freedom and Coordination: Lectures in Business Organization* (London: Management Publications Trust, 1949): 46.

[25] E. M. Fox and L. Urwick, eds., *Dynamic Administration: The Collected Papers of Mary Parker Follett* (New York: Hippocrene Books, 1982).

[26] A. Osland, "The Role of Leadership and Cultural Contingencies in Total Quality Management in Central America," *Journal of Business and Management 3* (1996): 64–80.

[27] J. Pfeffer, *The Human Equation: Building Profits by Putting People First* (Cambridge, MA: Harvard Business School Press, 1999).

[28] J. Heskett, W. E. Sasser, and L. Schelsinger, *The Human Profit Chain* (New York: Free Press, 1997).

[29] D. C. Kinlaw, *Coaching for Commitment* (San Diego, CA: Pfeiffer & Company, 1993), p. 31.

[30] Ibid.

[31] Byham, *Zapp*, p. 129.

[32] F. Fournies. *Coaching for Improved Work Performance* (New York: Van Nostrand Reinhold, 1978).

[33] Kinlaw provides more detailed instructions for each type of coaching in *Coaching for Commitment*.

[34] J. Gibb, "Defensive Communication," *Reader*.

[35] C. Rogers, *On Becoming a Person* (Boston: Houghton Mifflin, 1961) p. 34.

[36] R. E. Boyatzis, *The Competent Manager: A Model for Effective Performance* (New York: John Wiley, 1982).

[37] S. Deepak, "The Seven R's of Self-Esteem," in Hesselbein, Goldsmith, and Beckhard, eds., *The Organization of the Future* (San Francisco: Jossey-Bass, 1997), pp. 231–238.

[38] M. Goldsmith, "Retaining Your Top Performers," in Hesselbein, Goldsmith, and Beckhard, eds., *The Organization of the Future*, p. 262.

[39] Deepak, "The Seven R's of Self-Esteem," p. 235.

[40] M. Buckingham and C. Coffman, *First, Break All the Rules* (New York: Simon & Schuster, 1999).

[41] P. Block, *The Empowered Manager* (San Francisco: Jossey-Bass, 1990) 66–71.

[42] L. R. Offermann, "Leading and Empowering Diverse Followers" in G. R. Hickman, ed., *Leading Organizations: Perspectives for a New Era* (Thousand Oaks, CA: Sage, 1998): 397–403.

Chapter 18

▲▲▲

PERFORMANCE APPRAISAL

OBJECTIVES By the end of this chapter, you should be able to:

A. Explain the importance of performance feedback.

B. Describe the process of performance appraisal.

C. Identify the components of effective appraisals.

D. Demonstrate the skills required for a good appraisal.

E. Describe 360-degree feedback.

F. Explain the opposition to appraisal systems.

LEADER AS DEVELOPER

During the conference when we were discussing difficult subordinates, I realized that I had completely written Mike off and had stopped any effective communication with him. Mike was a 53-year-old sales representative who had been with the company for over 12 years. He was well liked by the central office staff but had not met his sales plan for five of the last six years. Furthermore, I was starting to hear complaints about him from some of our clients.

I first tried to put myself in Mike's shoes. What must it be like to be near the end of one's career and starting to go downhill? If I were Mike, how receptive would I be to criticism? I might then be able to understand one of his habitual behaviors that had been particularly annoying to me: his tendency to look only to external factors for his failures, to blame "bad luck," the market, competitors who used unfair tactics, and the like.

Still, before meeting with Mike, I did two things. I considered what would be a reasonable goal for him in six months—what exactly did I expect of him in terms of sales level, generating new business, and the like. Then I thought, "What is it in Mike's behavior that would cause him trouble in making sales? Is it something in his style or is some knowledge lacking?"

I then sat down with Mike and began by acknowledging that our relationship had deteriorated, that I had been dissatisfied with him but hadn't confronted him before, and also that I probably hadn't helped him as much as I could have. Mike immediately blamed me for everything that had gone wrong. It was fortunate that I had thought this out before, because my first response was defensive, to attack back. What helped was that I had already thought about why Mike must be hurting—clearly his pain was greater than anything I was now feeling about his comments.

After Mike had vented his feelings, I repeated that I wanted to change our relationship so that I could be more helpful. In return, we needed to get agreement on some specific goals for Mike. Although I would help him, it would be his responsibility to meet certain objectives. He was to be accountable for them, and if he failed to meet or substantially reach them in six months, he would be placed on probation. We mutually negotiated these goals. When I felt he was setting them too low, I pointed out what other sales personnel would do. We ended up with my original list modified, but in a way both of us could live with.

I then asked Mike what he thought might cause him difficulty in going about reaching his goals. In what areas did he need more training, and were there ways he behaved that caused problems? (I also asked him to discuss what he thought was easy for him—what his especially strong areas were.) As he shared his self-perception, I also shared my perception. I tried to point to specific behaviors at specific times that illustrated the problem areas I saw. At one point, he got very defensive and offered external reasons why the problems I identified were not his fault. I used his response as an illustration of what I was pointing out in his behavior.

In this discussion, we agreed to specific areas in which he could benefit from training. I sent him to a training program to work on his time-management problem. Also, we set up regular meetings (every two weeks) when we would review progress. I said that I was always available if he had a question, but that the initiative was up to him.

Mike did not meet the goals at the end of six months. I placed him on probation, with notice of termination in three months. I again met with him on a regular basis to offer assistance and coaching. Seven days before the end of his probation, Mike came in and said that the fit between him and the job was not right and quit.

As a result of this process, there was minimal reaction by the office staff (who had very much liked Mike). There was neither a decrease in morale nor a rise in paranoia among the others. Mike found another job in an area both of us had discussed as being more in line with his skills. Perhaps most gratifying to me, he expressly thanked me for my concern. He is doing well in his new position and is much happier.

Source: David Bradford and Allen R. Cohen, *Managing for Excellence* (New York: John Wiley, 1984): 157–58.

 PREMEETING PREPARATION

A. Read "Leader as Developer."

B. Think back on the best performance appraisal you ever received regardless of where it occurred (work, school, or extracurricular activity). Write down what was good about it.

C. Think about the worst performance appraisal you ever received or gave. What made it so ineffective?

D. Write a list of the conditions you think are necessary for an effective performance appraisal.

E. What were the significant learning points from the reading?

F. Consider your performance in this course and write your answers to these questions. Bring them to class:
    1. What have you done so far that has contributed to your own learning and that of your learning group?
    2. What have you contributed to the general atmosphere of the class?
    3. Are there extenuating circumstances that have affected your performance in the course?
    4. What have your weaknesses and strengths been so far?
    5. What would you like to improve in your performance?
    6. How do you plan to do it?

G. Read the Topic Introduction.

H. If your instructor has assigned the Robbins Self-Assessment Library, use "How Good Am I At Giving Feedback?"

 TOPIC INTRODUCTION

Performance appraisals are often one of the least favorite activities of managers. Yet they can be a valuable managerial tool for maintaining and improving performance and reinforcing what's important in an organization. Without such systems personal decisions about promotions, raises, and terminations might have little objective basis.

Performance appraisal systems attempt to evaluate employees fairly using a standardized model, but because humans operate these systems we cannot guarantee total objectivity. Given what we know about the correlation between feedback and high performance,[1] it is surprising that some organizations still do not evaluate employees in a systematic fashion. Even when organizations have systems in place, many managers fail to comply. In such instances employees often interpret skipped or late reviews as an indication that their manager is not concerned about them and does not appreciate their work. It is not uncommon to find organizations in which reviews hold great significance for employees but are perceived as little more than a waste of time by their managers.

Why the difference in opinion about performance reviews? At the organizational level, some appraisal systems are outdated and cumbersome and seem to measure only that which can be quantified. It's difficult for managers to take such systems seriously and see how they have any positive results. On the personal level, some managers resent the time consumed by appraisals and feel uncomfortable sitting in judgment on another person. McGregor argued that the conventional approach to performance appraisal

> unless handled with consummate skill and delicacy, constitutes something dangerously close to a violation of the integrity of the personality. Managers are uncomfortable when they are put in the position of "playing God." The respect we hold for the inherent value of the individual leaves us distressed when we must take responsibility for judging the personal worth of a fellow human being. Yet the conventional approach to performance appraisals forces us, not only to make such judgements and to see them acted upon, but also to communicate them to those we have judged. Small wonders we resist![2]

Those systems that force managers to compare and rank all their employees go against the values some hold about the importance of valuing people in their own right and not creating "losers" merely to comply with a bureaucratic requirement. Many people are uncomfortable giving negative feedback to people and fear that doing so may make a bad situation even worse, maybe even prompt them to go "postal."

In contrast to these reasons why managers tend to avoid appraisals, we know that managers who see appraisals as a useful tool can utilize their human resources more effectively. Research has shown that monitoring and providing feedback on performance is one of the most effective ways to improve performance.[3] Appraisals allow managers the opportunity to give feedback on performance and set goals for future performance, which are highly effective ways to motivate employees.

In addition, performance feedback serves a variety of functions for employees.[4]

1. Contributes to the development of employees' self-concept.
2. Reduces uncertainty about whether their behavior is on track and how it is perceived by others.
3. Signals which organizational goals are most important in relation to others.
4. Helps individuals to master their environment and feel competent.

An awareness of these functions may help managers to realize that a performance appraisal session means more to employees than just finding out what their salary will be for the next year.

Let's return to McGregor's statement that managers feel uncomfortable when they are put in the position of "playing God." To an extent, this is determined by the attitude the manager has toward appraisal. If the manager's underlying approach is to help the employee develop, his or her feedback is more likely to be effective and well received. The theory-in-use that underlies this approach is one that acknowledges the role of enlightened self-interest. In other words, if employees understand what is required of them and what they need to do or stop doing to be promoted or receive good performance ratings, they will do it. Managers utilizing this approach see their function as presenting employees with objective feedback about their performance and career plans. A less successful managerial approach to appraisal is the judgmental "gotcha," which is more likely to result in defensiveness than in the behavioral changes the manager desires. The performance appraisal activity requires leaders and managers to switch into a coaching role.

Although the specific mechanics of implementation will vary across organizations, the "ideal" performance appraisal system is designed to achieve five basic objectives:

1. Provide feedback to subordinates to facilitate their ability to achieve organizational (and personal) goals.
2. Provide management with data to make salary and promotional decisions.
3. Identify needed professional development.
4. Motivate employees to be more effective workers.
5. Comply with equal opportunity regulations and ensure fairness.

Depending on how this process gets implemented, managers often find themselves in a role conflict. On the one hand, they are asked to be helper-coaches in the feedback process; on the other hand, they serve as judges, linking performance assessment to salary and promotion decisions. Some research on the performance appraisal process points strongly to the need to separate these roles.[5] In addition to mastering the coaching skills described in the last chapter, it's important for managers to understand the unique aspects of the performance appraisal process, which are presented in the next section.

PERFORMANCE APPRAISAL PROCESS

Too often managers see appraisals as a once-a-year event. In reality, appraisal is a process that begins long before the appraisal interview and consists of the following steps:

1. Review legal requirements.
2. Translate organizational goals into individual job objectives or requirements.

3. Set clear expectations for job performance and communicate both expectations and instructions clearly.
4. Provide employees with the job training or coaching they require to meet the expectations.
5. Supply adequate supervision, feedback, and coaching throughout the year.
6. Acknowledge employee accomplishments, diagnose employees' relative strengths and weaknesses, and present all of these objectively during the appraisal interview.
7. Use the appraisal interview to establish performance goals and a development plan with the employee, which includes an action plan for improved performance or further education and the efficient future use of the employee's abilities.

Framing performance appraisal as a process rather than an annual interview means that appraisal is better integrated with the rest of the organization's functions. For example, if promotions are closely tied to appraisals, managers are more likely to give them the attention they require to have an impact on performance morale. We know that people generally focus their energies on that which is evaluated. If the leaders measure only tangible factors (such as financial and output figures), the intangibles (such as service orientation, ability to get along with coworkers, organization building, etc.) are given less importance. The same phenomena can be observed with performance appraisal systems. Organizations that evaluate managers on how well they develop and evaluate their subordinates are more likely to have managers who give the appraisal process the attention it requires to be effective.

There are four common responses to appraisals that wise managers seek to avoid:

1. "I never knew that's what the boss expected me to do!"
2. "Why didn't they tell me before that they weren't happy with my work?"
3. "I wish I had known all along that they liked my work. I wouldn't have wasted so much time worrying about it or looking for other jobs!"
4. "I got a poor review because my boss doesn't like me."

By clarifying expectations carefully, giving immediate feedback throughout the year, and demonstrating a concern for fairness, managers can avoid some of these reactions. Providing immediate feedback has several advantages. First, it offers an opportunity to improve performance. Second, it gives employees an idea about how their supervisor sees them so that the appraisal does not come as a shock. Third, it can keep the channel of communication open between managers and employees. Often new supervisors see an employee doing something incorrectly but are not sure how to give feedback. Instead, they become more and more angry with the employee and either "dump" the feedback when they can no longer contain themselves or save it for the appraisal interview. This is sometimes referred to as "gunny-sacking." In the meantime, their relationship with the employee usually suffers, and they may have rounded out the employee's character with negative attributions that are inaccurate. The feedback given during the appraisal interview, be it positive or negative, should never come as a total surprise to employees.

The fairness issue with appraisals relates to the necessity for managers to know themselves and their personal tendencies. The research on similarity and attraction indicates that people prefer those who are similar to themselves. They also tend to give higher ratings to subordinates who are similar to them.[6] The result can be what Moore termed a "bureaucratic kinship system" based on "homosexual reproduction," in which men with the power to hire and promote reproduce themselves.[7] It is not uncommon to look around a table of senior managers and discover that they resemble one another, either physically or socially. Thus, it is easy for managers to perceive an employee they like more positively than that person really deserves. The opposite can occur with employees whom managers either dislike or perceive as different than themselves.

When certain appraisal conditions are met, the potential sources of bias such as age, race, sex, and being different are less likely to have a negative effect on performance appraisals. These conditions are:

1. when employees make their work visible to the appraiser;
2. when appraisers and appraisees together clarify objectives and task responsibilities; and
3. when the appraiser uses the behaviorally based appraisal scales,[8] described in the Follow-Up section.

Attribution theory maintains that we make attributions about the causes of behavior of both others and ourselves to understand what we see occurring.[9] We guess or infer the causes of people's behavior and base our reactions to their behaviors on these inferences rather than on the way they really behave. A practical example of attribution theory might be the "golden boys or girls" who surface, to the puzzlement of their peers, in some organizations. Although such people usually possess a certain degree of talent, they are seldom as outstanding as their superiors apparently need to believe.

Perhaps this is explained by the finding that managers are more likely to attribute excellent performance to internal causes (effort, ability) in the case of people who are members of their in-group than if they are members of their out-group.[10] Attributions, like perceptions, sometimes have more to do with the observer than with the person being observed. Appraisals are yet another instance when managers have to step back and ensure that their decisions and evaluations are not overly biased, either positively or negatively, by their personal values and preferences. If you recall, the chapter on perception and attribution contains examples of perceptual biases that can affect performance evaluation (stereotyping, halo effect, central tendency, contrast effects, projection, and perceptual defenses).

PROCEDURE FOR GROUP MEETING: PERFORMANCE APPRAISAL ROLE PLAYS

CLASS PERFORMANCE APPRAISALS

(Time allotted: 1 to $1\frac{1}{2}$ hours)

This exercise provides you with an opportunity to practice the "consummate skill and delicacy" required in a performance appraisal. The class should divide into three-person teams, consisting of members of their learning groups. The exercise stimulates a performance appraisal interview between two team members who will take on the roles of supervisor and employee, while the other member acts as an observer. Roles will be rotated so each person has a chance to perform every role. The performance to be evaluated is your performance in this course. Class participants prepared for the employee role by answering the questions in the Premeeting Preparation (section F).

STEP 1.   Decide whom each person will evaluate so that everyone has an opportunity to both evaluate and be evaluated once in the three rounds of the exercise.

STEP 2.   Take 10 minutes alone to plan the appraisal interview for the person you will evaluate. Use the following questions to help you prepare for the supervisor role.
   a.   What has the employee done so far that has contributed to his or her own learning and that of your learning group?

b. What has the employee contributed to the general atmosphere of the class?

c. Are there any extenuating circumstances that have affected the employee's performance in the course?

d. Is there anything you are doing that has hindered the employee's performance in the class? What could you do to help the employee improve his or her performance? Is there anything you could suggest that might utilize the employee's talents better in the classroom or learning group?

e. What are the employee's weaknesses and strengths so far?

f. Choose at least one strength and one weakness that you have observed in the employee's performance in class to discuss during the 5-minute interview. Base your choice on which behaviors could make a significant difference if they were to be changed. Write down how you could phrase the employee's weak point to him or her in case it's not brought out in his or her self-evaluation.

STEP 3. Read the Performance Appraisal Interview Guidelines that follow.

STEP 4. The supervisors should conduct a 5-minute performance appraisal interview with the employee while the observer watches and fills out the Observers' Worksheet on page 431.

STEP 5. After each interview all three participants should talk about how it went and what, if anything, could have been done differently.

STEP 6. Perform the interviews with the other two dyads and critique them.

STEP 7. Class debriefing session:
   a. What did you learn about performance appraisal interviews from this exercise?
   b. What did you learn about yourself in this process?
   c. Will the appraisal affect your future performance in this course? Why?
   d. What connections can you make between this exercise and the readings?

PERFORMANCE APPRAISAL INTERVIEW GUIDELINES

Prior to the interview

1. Fix a time and date for the interview that allows the employee enough time to prepare the self-appraisal.
2. Ask the employee to prepare the self-appraisal and provide an outline for doing so.
3. Don't postpone the interview or come late to it. Employees interpret these actions as a lack of interest in them and the appraisal process. To do any good, appraisals have to be taken seriously by managers.
4. Choose a private location where you will not be interrupted.
5. Set aside enough time (1 to 2 hours) so that you will have time to complete your discussion.
6. Gather all the materials and relevant information about the employee's performance. Some managers also give copies of this information to the employee.
7. Choose which parts of the employee's performance should be included in the interview. Decide how to phrase these points.

During the interview

8. Explain the format and purpose of the performance appraisal interview:
   a. To discover the employee's opinions regarding his or her performance and career goals.
   b. To provide the supervisor's appraisal of the employee's performance.
   c. To problem solve together about performance if necessary.
   d. To plan for the next period.
9. Ask the employee to present his or her self-appraisal.
10. Respond to the employee's self-appraisal and convey feedback. First, tell the employee the parts of the self-appraisal with which you agree and then identify parts with which you disagree, if there are any. Next, provide other feedback that would impact performance. In doing this,
    a. Be appreciative of the employee's accomplishments.
    b. Support the employee even when you are criticizing his or her behavior.
    c. Avoid defensiveness (on both your parts).
    d. Encourage participation.
11. Ask if there are any conditions or problems that have been hindering the employee's work.
12. Problem solve with the employee regarding what both of you could do to improve the employee's performance.
13. Together set objectives and design a plan for the next period.
14. Discuss the employee's long-term career goals and the training and experience needed to reach them.

After the interview

15. Fill out the performance appraisal form *after* the interview so the employee sees that his or her input was included.
16. Follow up on training and coaching needs identified in the interview.[11]

Observers' Worksheet

1. Did the supervisor explain the purpose of the appraisal interview?

2. Did the supervisor give the employee sufficient time to present his or her self-appraisal?

3. Did the supervisor do a good job of presenting his or her feedback?

4. Did the supervisor use active listening, or did he or she do most of the talking?

5. Did the supervisor create a nondefensive climate and refrain from becoming defensive himself or herself?

6. Did the supervisor take a problem-solving approach, or did he or she spend too much time giving advice or orders to the employee?

7. Did the supervisor jointly set goals and an action plan for the future with the employee?

8. Other comments:

FOLLOW-UP

Doing appraisal interviews may be uncomfortable in the beginning, but it is a skill that can be mastered with practice. The opening vignette is an example of a successful performance appraisal process with a problem employee. Managers who use performance appraisals well can utilize their human resources more fully. It is a mechanism for increasing the communication and dialogue that is so crucial to high performance. One of the truisms that is repeatedly mentioned when we discuss this topic is that the appraisal instrument itself is only as good as the people who use it. Therefore, it is important that supervisors be trained in appraisal techniques.

There are different ways to measure performance; some of the more common forms follow. Early appraisal instruments often focused on employee *traits* (diligence, appearance, initiative). Compared with other forms of appraisal, this approach has proved to be less effective and less likely to stand up in a court of law. Trait measures are often vague and lead managers into a murky ethical quagmire—what right do managers have to ask employees to change their personality? The answer is none. However, managers do have the right to demand performance and the behaviors that add up to high performance outcome.

Appraisal systems that measure *results* or outcomes are more effective than trait-based appraisals. For example, MBO programs (management by objectives) are examples of this type of system. Under this system, employees and supervisors jointly set goals, and then supervisors validate whether employee goals were completed satisfactorily and on time. Although this type of appraisal system has the advantages of clarifying goals and often motivates employees, it has been subjected to many criticisms. For example, results-oriented systems usually focus only on factors that can be easily quantified, they encourage a "results at all costs" mentality that may work against other company values, they fail to take into consideration factors that may be outside the person's control, and they fail to tell the employee how to improve performance.[12]

Other appraisal systems measure *behavioral* criteria (e.g., "distributes overtime equally," "explains job requirements to new employees in a clear manner"). Behaviorally anchored rating scales (BARS) describe the specific behavior that managers observe in subordinates in an effort to clarify expectations for employees and make the instrument as objective as possible. Each point on a continuum is a different behavior rather than the Likert scale numbers (low 1 to 5 high) used to measure traits. Instruments that utilize some form of behavioral criteria lend themselves more to coaching and developing employees because they focus on specific behaviors.

Appraisals can be made by any combination of the following appraisers: supervisors or managers, peers, subordinates, customers, and employees themselves. Peer reviews are becoming more common in companies that are moving to a team approach. They have to make sure their appraisal systems do in fact reward teamwork rather than individual accomplishment.

INNOVATIVE APPRAISAL SYSTEMS

One of the most popular innovations in performance appraisal is 360-degree feedback, defined as multirater assessment or multisource feedback (MSF). Supervisors, peers, subordinates, and sometimes customers evaluate the person being rated. The person then compares these ratings with his or her own self-ratings, sometimes with the help of a consultant or performance coach. This full-circle feedback is assumed to be more valid and reliable than assessment by a sole source or supervisor. It is also based on the assumption that greater self-awareness will lead to behavioral change. The various purposes for which 360-degree feedback is utilized follow.[13]

- Performance appraisal and/or performance management systems
- Leadership and management development
- Measuring client and customer-related behaviors and perceptions
- Succession planning
- General cultural assessment
- Organizational change initiatives

The Basic Industry Division of Nalco implemented a 360-degree feedback program to solve its turnover problem. Managers estimated that it cost $50,000 to replace a sales representative who has been with the company for six months and $250,000 to replace a seven-year veteran. After they cleaned up some pay and career path issues, they discovered that the primary reason people still quit was problems with the boss. Thus, the goal of their multisource performance appraisal system was to improve the leadership skills of their district sales managers. As a result, the company decreased its turnover rate from 15 to 18 percent to 8 to 10.5 percent.[14]

The various sources that evaluate an employee in 360-degree feedback perceive the employee in different ways and, therefore, their evaluations are not always similar. Effective managerial behavior is often in the eye of the beholder.[15] Differences in evaluations should be expected and analyzed.

A meta-analysis of feedback interventions found that feedback generally improves performance, but it can also diminish performance.[16] Appraisals that are used for developmental rather than administrative reasons are more likely to produce positive reactions.[17] The impact of multisource feedback is limited when:[18]

- Ratees are not held accountable for using the feedback
- Raters are not accountable for the accuracy or usefulness of their feedback
- Management does not accept accountability for providing resources to support behavioral change of those evaluated.

Like any program, 360-degree feedback has to be tailored to the particular organization, supported by and integrated with other organizational processes, and effectively implemented. The ratees have to be willing to change, and this does not happen without confidence, trust, and an understanding of 360-degree feedback and a strong belief in its importance. Such programs require both time and money to do well.[19]

In addition to 360-degree feedback, another innovative approach to appraisal was developed by the Air Force Research Lab in Dayton, Ohio. When managers there were pressed to cut staff, they discovered that virtually all their 3,200 scientists and engineers received uniformly positive performance ratings. Only one employee was judged marginal, and none were rated as unsatisfactory. Because this system failed to distinguish among employees, a group of lab scientists was assigned the job of designing a new system. Their solution was to assume that all employees are performing well and evaluate them on the contribution their particular job makes to the lab's mission. "They naturally gravitate toward the toughest jobs they can competently perform, and their pay is based on the value of those jobs to the lab."[20]

The move toward team-based work has resulted in different appraisal systems such as the one described here.

If knowledge work depends on teams, it makes sense to reward them, not individuals. People who move from project to project cannot be paid according to the number of direct reports they have .... Top industrial-design firm Ideo Product Development (it designed the mouse for both Apple and Microsoft, and the snazzy housing for Silicon Graphics computers) is a good example. It has several "vice presidents" who awarded themselves the title to get the free subscriptions some magazines give VPs. Ideo's performance reviews used to be done by a person's boss and two peers of the employee's own choosing, but that system, offbeat though it was, had to be scrapped a couple of years ago when the company realized that for many employees (more than one in ten) it was impossible to identify a boss. Now people pick two peers plus one from a slate of six "management types." According to Tom Kelley, people tend to pick demanding evaluators: "The culture says don't pick softies, because this is about improving performance, not about getting ahead."[21]

Appraisal systems should fit the organizational mission, culture, structure, and type of employees.

CRITICISM OF PERFORMANCE APPRAISAL SYSTEMS

New ways of doing business and managing people require appraisal systems that fit and complement new organizational goals. Two practices have received a good deal of criticism because they sometimes make good employees feel like losers. Forced ranking systems (every employee in a unit is compared to the others and ranked accordingly) and forced distribution in performance categories (e.g., only 20 percent can be superior performers, 30 to 40 percent good performers, etc.) encourage competition, require difficult judgement calls that may or may not be accurate, and can demotivate the employees who don't come out on top. Eastman Chemical Company, winner of the 1993 Malcolm Baldrige National Quality Award, decided that its old appraisal system no longer fit an organizational culture that emphasized teamwork and more open and trustworthy communications. Therefore, a team designed a system that responded to these employee suggestions: eliminate forced distributions, eliminate performance categories, obtain performance input from sources other than the supervisor, enhance coaching and development, minimize individual performance and teamwork conflicts, identify only extremes in performance (the superstars and the below-average employees), and separate the systems for handling selection (promotion, transfer, and layoffs), compensation, and coaching. The design team concluded that self-esteem is critical to motivation and that employees like to believe, not only that they are above average performers but that they are growing and improving from year to year.[22]

Deming, the total quality guru, was very opposed to performance appraisals and referred to them as one of the seven deadly diseases plaguing U.S. management. He and his disciples criticize appraisal systems for the following reasons.[23] Appraisals usually lack objectivity and attribute variations in performance to employees rather than crucial factors that are outside their control. Appraisals encourage an individual focus rather than a team orientation. When appraisals are based on measurable goals, they promote both short-sightedness and a short-term focus. Furthermore, employees come to see the boss as their "customer" rather than the real customer (the next person in the process, be they external or internal). When the main goal of employees is to gain the approval of their superior, fear, rivalry, and politics can result. Deming criticized merit rewards for rewarding people for doing well "in the system" rather than rewarding attempts to improve the system.

So how do we measure performance in a total quality program? TQM writers suggest that outstanding performers should receive recognition and poor performers should be coached. Groups should gather continuous data on their own performance and should receive coaching whenever necessary. Companies should base compensation on market rate, seniority, or the company's prosperity. However, U.S. companies that implemented total quality programs have been slow to relinquish their performance appraisal systems.

CULTURE AND PERFORMANCE APPRAISAL

Deming's opposition to performance appraisal may stem from his exposure to the Japanese system, which is very different from the U.S. approach. Japanese reviews tend to be informal, ad hoc, and based upon continuous feedback. Their objective is to find out why the employee's performance is not in harmony with that of the group. In Arab cultures, appraisals are also generally informal and held on an ad hoc basis. Their purpose is to set employees on track or reprimand them for bad performance.[24]

The individualism-collectivism dimension affects performance appraisal practices.[25] Individualists are geared more toward personal goals whereas collectivists focus more on group goals. Individualistic cultures emphasize individual achievement, individual incentive schemes, formal appraisal processes with feedback on performance, and merit-based hiring and promotion. In contrast, collectivist cultures emphasize group achievement, group incentive schemes, informal appraisals, and they hire and fire based on loyalty and seniority.[26] Formal appraisal systems are more prevalent in the United States than in collectivist countries such as Japan and Korea due to the emphasis placed on individual rather than group performance.[27] We cannot assume that an appraisal system that functions well in one culture (or one company) can be easily transferred to another.

LEARNING POINTS

1. Performance appraisals are intended to improve performance and motivate employees.
2. Feedback serves the following functions for employees:
   a. Helps to form their self-concept.
   b. Reduces uncertainty about whether their behavior is on track.
   c. Signals which organizational goals are most important.
   d. Helps them master their environment and feel competent.
3. The attitude managers bring to performance appraisal determines the effectiveness of that appraisal. Managers who are sincerely trying to develop their employees and provide them with objective feedback are more successful than those who take a judgmental approach.
4. Performance appraisal requires that managers take on the role of coaches.
5. The "ideal" performance appraisal system is designed to achieve five basic objectives:
   a. Provide feedback to employees to facilitate their ability to achieve organizational and personal goals.
   b. Provide management with data to make salary and promotional decisions.
   c. Identify areas for improvement to facilitate employee career development.
   d. Motivate employees to be more effective workers.
   e. Comply with equal opportunity regulations and ensure fairness.
6. Performance appraisal is a process that begins with translating organizational goals into clear expectations for each individual, training people to do their jobs, providing effective supervision and coaching, determining strengths and weaknesses, and developing plans for each employee. It is not a once-a-year event but an ongoing activity.
7. Providing immediate feedback gives the employee an opportunity to improve, ensures that the appraisal is not a surprise, and keeps the employee-manager channel of communication open. Saving up negative feedback and "dumping" can cause a defensive reaction.
8. Fairness is always a matter of concern with appraisals because people tend to rate those who are similar to themselves more highly than those who are different.
9. Attributions or inferences about why people behave the way they do can also bias the appraisal process.
10. Effective appraisal instruments measure results or behavioral criteria.
11. Multirater or multisource feedback, such as 360-degree feedback, has been gaining popularity.
12. Total quality experts suggest that companies stop doing performance appraisals and focus more on continuous feedback and coaching.

FOR MANAGERS

- A major purpose of an appraisal interview is to provide the interviewees with data that will allow them the opportunity to change negative behavior. You cannot always make them change their behavior, but you can outline the likely consequences of their behavior in an objective fashion.
- The appraisal interview can be an occasion of great anxiety for some individuals. This means that their ability to take in information may be impaired, so verbal or written summaries of what has been said are useful. People with low self-concepts may hear only the negative feedback, whereas others will hear only positives and completely miss the improvements you would like to see made.
- Being evaluated evokes authority issues for many individuals and results in defensive communication. Taking care to posture yourself more as a counselor than a judge and creating a nondefensive climate by the way you communicate are two ways to decrease defensiveness.[28]
- When people succeed, they are likely to attribute their success to the internal qualities they possess (e.g., tenacity, intelligence). When they fail, some are likely to blame external conditions (e.g., their boss, the company's policies). Assigning blame is not as important as trying to figure out ways to improve performance in the future.

- Managers are sometimes guilty of keeping their employees from performing well. For that reason, this issue should be addressed by managers. Employees are less likely to bring this subject up, though it may well be on the tip of their tongue. Sessions involving mutual feedback are usually more effective than one-way feedback. If you give feedback, you should also expect to receive it.
- No matter how objective managers try to be, there is always a possibility of bias or misperception. Incorrect evaluations are very demotivating. There are two ways to avoid making incorrect evaluations. One is to collect robust data and check out your perceptions with other colleagues. The second way is to allow employees the opportunity to present their self-evaluation first and then carefully consider the employees' viewpoints. This does not mean that managers should back down from their opinion if an employee disagrees. There are times when people cannot agree because of perceptual processes or ego defenses. The message here is to beware of possible biases or lack of information and collect enough data to ensure an evaluation's validity.
- Some managers focus more on what employees do wrong than on what they do right. If you think you have this tendency, force yourself to sit down and compile a list of the positive contributions made by employees and/or seek a different perspective from someone else in the organization who picks up on positives.
- When employees publicly set specific rather than general goals for the future, their performance is more likely to improve.

PERSONAL APPLICATION ASSIGNMENT

Please write about a significant experience that involved performance appraisal. Choose an experience that intrigues you and that you want to learn more about.

A. *Concrete Experience*
   1. *Objectively* describe the experience (who, what, when, where, how information) (2 points)
   2. *Subjectively* describe your feelings, perceptions, and thoughts that occurred during (not after) the experience. What did others seem to be feeling? (2 points)

B. *Reflective Observation*
   1. Looking back at the experience, what were the perspectives of the key actors (including you)? (2 points)
   2. Why did the people involved (including you) behave as they did? (2 points)

C. *Abstract Conceptualization*
   1. Relate concepts or theories from the assigned readings or the lecture to the experience. Explain thoroughly how they apply to your experience. Please apply at least two concepts or theories and cite them correctly. (4 points)

D. *Active Experimentation*
   1. What did you learn about performance appraisal from this experience? (1 point)
   2. What did you learn about yourself? (1 point)
   3. What action steps will you take to be more effective in the future? (2 points)

E. *Integration, Synthesis, and Writing*
   1. Did you integrate and synthesize the four sections? (1 point)
   2. Was the personal application assignment well written and easy to understand? (1 point)
   3. Was it free of spelling and grammatical errors? (2 points)

ENDNOTES

[1] G. P. Latham and K. N. Wexley, *Increasing Productivity Through Performance Appraisal* (Reading, MA: Addison Wesley, 1993). This book is a good compendium of knowledge on performance appraisal.

[2] D. McGregor, "An Uneasy Look at Performance Appraisal," *Harvard Business Review 35*, no. 3 (May–June 1957): 89–94.

[3] D. A. Nadler, C. Cammon, and P. Mirvis, "Developing a Feedback System for Work Units: A Field Experiment in Structural Change," *Journal of Applied Behavioral Science 16* (1980): 41–62; and D. R. Ilgen, C. D. Fischer, and M. S. Taylor, "Consequences of Individual Feedback on Behavior in Organizations," *Journal of Applied Psychology 64* (1979): 359–71.

[4] S. J. Ashford and L. L. Cummings, "Feedback as an Individual Resource: Personal Strategies of Creating Information," *Organizational Behavior and Human Performance 32* (1983): 370–98.

[5] H. H. Meyer, E. Kay, and T. R. P. French, Jr., "Split Roles in Performance Appraisal," *Harvard Business Review 43*, no. 1 (1965): 123–29.

[6] E. D. Pulakos and K. N. Wexley, "The Relationship among Perceptual Similarity, Sex, and Performance Ratings in Manager-Subordinate Dyads," *Academy of Management Journal 26*, no. 1 (1983): 129–39.

[7] W. Moore, *The Conduct of the Corporation* (New York: Random House, 1962): 109.

[8] Latham and Wexley, *Performance Appraisal,* p. 152.

[9] J. Jaspars, F. D. Finchman, and M. Hewstone, *Attribution Theory and Research: Conceptual Developmental and Social Dimensions* (London: Academic Press, 1983).

[10] R. L. Heneman, D. B. Greenberger, and C. Anonyo, "Attributions and Exchanges: The Effects of Interpersonal Factors on the Diagnosis of Employee Performance," *Academy of Management Journal 32*, no. 2 (1989): 466–76.

[11] This list is adapted from Patricia King's helpful book, *Performance Planning and Appraisal* (New York: McGraw-Hill, 1984): 73–74, 88.

[12] Latham and Wexley, *Performance Appraisal,* pp. 52–55.

[13] A. H. Church and D. W. Bracken, "Advancing the State of the Art of 360-Degree Feedback," *Group and Organization Management 22*, no. 2 (June 1997): 149–61.

[14] B. Flannigan, "Turnaround from Feedback," *HR Focus 74*, no. 10 (October 1997): 3–4.

[15] S. Salam, J. F. Cox, and H. P. Sims, Jr., "In the Eye of the Beholder," *Group and Organization Management 22*, no. 2 (June 1997): 185–209; and A. Fumham and P. Stringfield, "Congruence in Job-Performance Ratings: A Study of 360-Degree Feedback Examining Self, Manager, Peers, and Consultant Ratings," *Human Relations 51*, no. 4 (April 1998): 517–31.

[16] A. N. Kluger and A. DeNisi, "The Effects of Feedback Interventions on Performance: A Historical Review, a Meta-analysis, and a Preliminary Feedback Intervention Theory," *Psychological Bulletin 119* (1996): 254–84.

[17] K. L. Bettenhausen and D. B. Fedor, "Peer and Upward Appraisals: A Comparison of Their Benefits and Problems," *Group and Organization Management 22*, no. 2 (June 1997): 236–63.

[18] M. London, J. W. Smither, and D. J. Adsit, "Accountability: The Achilles' Heel of Multisource Feedback," *Group and Organization Management 22*, no. 2 (June 1997): 162.

[19] W. Tornow and M. London, eds., *Maximizing the Value of 360-Degree Feedback: A Process for Successful Individual and Organizational Development* (San Francisco: Jossey-Bass and Greensboro: Center for Creative Leadership, 1998).

[20] D. Grote, " Performance Appraisal Reappraised," Harvard Business Review (January–February 2000): 21.

[21] T. Stewart, "The Great Conundrum—You Vs. the Team," *Fortune 134*, no. 10, November 25, 1996, p. 165.

[22] R. C. Jines, S. Quisenberry and G. W. Sawyer, "Business Strategy Drives Three-Pronged Assessment System," *HRM Magazine* (December 1993): 68–72.

[23] W. E. Deming, *Out of the Crisis* (Cambridge: MIT Press, 1986). Other sources on this topic are M. Walton, *Deming Management at Work* (New York: Putnam, 1990); P. R. Scholtes, *An Elaboration on Deming's Teachings on Performance Appraisal.* (Madison, WI: Joiner Association, 1987); and W. M. Fox, "Improving Performance Appraisal Systems," *National Productivity Review* (Winter 1987–88): 20–27.

[24] F. Elashmawi and P. R. Harris, *Multicultural Management* (Houston: Gulf Press, 1993): 152.

[25] H. C. Triandis, *Individualism and Collectivism* (Boulder, CD: Westview, 1995); and G. Hofstede, *Culture's Consequences* (Thousand Oaks, Sage, 1980).

[26] S. J. Carroll and N. Ramamoorthy, "Individualism and Collectivism Orientations and Reactions Toward Alternative Human Resource Management Practices," *Human Relations 51*, no. 5 (May 1998): 571–89.

[27] K. Kim, H. Park, and N. Suzuki, "Reward Allocations in the United States, Japan, and Korea: A Comparison of Individualist and Collectivist Cultures," *Academy of Management Journal 33* (1990): 188–98. See also L. R. Gomez-Mejia and T. Welbourne, "Compensation Strategies in a Global Context," *Human Resource Planning 14* (1991): 29–41.

[28] See Chapter 7, Interpersonal Communication, and Jack R. Gibb's article, "Defensive Communication," the *Reader.*

Part 4

▲▲▲

MANAGING EFFECTIVE ORGANIZATIONS

In this section of the book, we're going to make a more obvious transition from micro-level topics in organizational behavior dealing with individuals and groups to macro-level issues that effect the entire organization. In addition to a thorough grounding in the topics we have already covered, organization design and change are heavily dependent on systems thinking and analytical skills. These final chapters examine how managers can design and change organizations to make them more effective and successful.

Chapter 19

▲▲

ORGANIZATION DESIGN

OBJECTIVES By the end of this chapter, you should be able to:

A. Distinguish between mechanistic and organic structures.

B. Describe the three traditional types of organizational structures and their advantages and disadvantages.

C. Describe horizontal and network structures and their advantages and disadvantages.

D. Distinguish between formal and informal organizational structure.

E. Describe the boundaryless organization.

F. Explain the differentiation-integration issue in organization design.

PERMEABILITY IN ACTION:

CASE STUDY OF A BOUNDARYLESS ORGANIZATION

Retailer Financial Services (RFS) is one of GE Capital's approximately two dozen businesses. Headquartered in Stamford Connecticut, it provides private label credit card services to various retail chains in the United States and overseas, and through its "bank," it offers its own credit card programs. RFS customers include such retail chains as Macy's, Burton, Filenes' Basement, Harrods, IKEA, and hundreds more. Seeing this level of success, few people remember that less than a decade ago, GE was trying desperately to sell Retailer Financial Services, then named Private Label. It had been in business for fifty years, yet its market share was a mere 3 percent. To make matters worse, its own strategic planners did not believe it had much of a future. "Why," they reasoned, "would consumers want to carry multiple credit cards when they could carry just one or two? And if that's the case, we don't have a business here!"

Holding fast to his pledge to sell off businesses that could not become the number one or two performers in their industries, GE Chairman and CEO Jack Welch put the company on the block. Fortunately for GE, potential buyers agreed with GE's assessment that Private Label was a dying business. They stayed away. With little choice other than to make the best of it, GE Capital promoted David A. Ekedahl, who had spent his whole carrer in Private Label, to run the business. His mission: keep it going as long as you can without losing money. Ekedahl did better than that. He created a successful boundaryless corporation.

REFORMULATING EXTERNAL BOUNDARIES

As Ekedahl describes it, the initial objective was to keep the wolves at bay by aggressively adding new customers. However, Ekedahl and his managers first had to decide who the customers were and how to win their business. That analysis led them to an important insight—the company needed to concentrate not just on the consumer (the end-user of private label cards) but on the retailer as well.

By changing the longstanding external boundary that defined the customer, Ekedahl began a transformation that was to take Private Label light-years forward. He realized that fast and flexible processing would be the critical success factor for retailers. If Private Label could get the retailers on-line quickly, manage the volume of business efficiently, provide error-free processing, maintain balances and credit information accurately and manage customer databases, it would have tremendous leverage with retailers. But at this time, both putting systems in place for a new retailer and keeping them going for an existing one was an incredibly cumbersome process.

LOOSENING HORIZONTAL BOUNDARIES

To achieve fast and flexible processing, Dave Ekedahl had to open up another boundary.

We had just signed up a new company to do their private label credit cards, and I wanted to go through the process of getting that client on board. I found that in order to do that, I had a lot of people in the room, but none of us had any idea what to do by ourselves. We needed dozens of other people. So I figured if this was what it took to get something done, I might as well organize around these kinds of processes. So we began to recreate our own organization around the major processes that needed to get done rather than just do it ad hoc all the time.

Making organizational structure mirror the way work actually got done, Ekedahl gradually transformed Private Label, leveling horizontal boundaries between systems and other business functions. The change was especially difficult because the systems resources were all part of GE Capital's corporate organization, a centralized organization well defended by solid functional walls.

Early in 1989, Ekedahl tried to bridge the functions by sponsoring a joint working conference between his business people and the central systems organization. At a rancorous concluding meeting, the systems people complained that they were not consulted in the early stages of new customer conversions and were given unrealistic requirements and deadlines. On the other side, the marketing people accused the systems professionals of not delivering on their promises. Ekedahl found himself caught in the middle, wanting to create a cross-functional team yet forced to arbitrate between disagreeing sides.

Ekedahl did not give up. First, he influenced the head of GE Capital's systems to dedicate a particular group of systems professionals to his business. Then he insisted that the systems and marketing people find new ways of working together, and he encouraged them to rethink their basic work processes.

In 1990, Rich Nastasi, head of the group of systems people, began a process of working with the other business functions to radically reduce the time required to bring a new retailer on-line as a customer, an average of eight weeks. Nastasi then brought together a group of systems, marketing, finance, and customer service people and challenged them to complete new customer conversions in a matter of days, not weeks.

Over the next few months, as the solutions were implemented, customer conversion times began to drop dramatically, to less than a week for all but the largest new customers. Equally significant, the different functions put the solutions in place together.

Less than a year later, Nastasi and his people were reporting directly to Dave Ekedahl, as full-fledged members of business team for what was now called Retailer Financial Services.

FLATTENING VERTICAL BOUNDARIES

As RFS organized around key processes, a different organization gradually took shape. Essentially, the company shifted from a centralized model, in which such functions as systems, credit, marketing, and customer service were all run out of Stamford, to a hybrid model with both centralized and decentralized processes. The guiding idea was that processes to support specific customers should be managed in the field, close to those customers. Processes requiring consistency and control across all customers—financial reporting, credit scoring, systems processing, and telecommunications—should be handled by the head office. Additional head office roles were to facilitate the sharing of best practices, the movement of key personnel, and the allocation of investment resources.

To shift processes to the field, RFS created "regional business centers." The business processes they managed for the retailer customers in their regions included training of retailer staff in systems and procedures, developing mailing and promotional programs with the retailers, providing management information for the retailers, and handling the whole range of customer service for cardholders, both through the mail and on the phone. The key and single focus of these centers was to help retailer customers become more successful.

Setting up regional centers, however, was expensive. Ekedahl was under pressure to reduce costs by increasing productivity. So the cost-cutting pressure led to a radically different way of organizing the regional business centers. As Ekedahl explains: "We originally came at it from a productivity point of view. We figured maybe we could save costs by not having so many management levels. So we asked a group of our associates how to do this. The exempt and the nonexempt people got together for a week and went way beyond what we had been expecting. They recommended that we organize around teams, with no managers whatsoever. I said, 'what the heck, let's try it.' So we did, starting with one business center in Danbury."

The dissolution of hierarchical boundaries within the business centers represented a fundamental revolution. And as in any revolution, there were casualties—managers who could not adjust, supervisors who were no longer needed, and in particular, frontline associates who were not willing or able to handle increased accountability. For the first few years, an abiding issue in several centers was a high level of associate turnover.

Eventually, by involving everyone in the center in a dialogue helped along by a few outside experts in team processes, a pattern for success emerged. Teams were set up to service all the needs of one large or several small retailers and the retailers' customers. All team members were cross-trained in all the skills needed to provide effective service, including handling billing problems and collections, changing credit lines, and changing customer data. The more senior or experienced people (in most cases, former supervisors) became roving trainers, documenters of procedures, and problem solvers.

Gradually, the teams learned to police their own performance against an agreed-upon set of goals, setting up performance improvement programs for team members not performing up to standard. In essence, the teams were given all the same levels of authority as managers had held in the past.

The payoff from the first boundaryless business center was so great that Ekedahl and his team never seriously considered going back to the traditional vertical organization. Even with high levels of turnover, productivity was still many times greater and overall costs far lower. More importantly, the customers loved the service they were now getting from a dedicated team that knew the customers' business, their consumers, their systems, and their issues. They began to see the business teams as extensions of their own companies and not just as service providers.

RFS became a true boundaryless corporation, consciously evolving ways to function across different boundaries with speed, flexibility, integration, and innovation. RFS journeyed successfully from the traditional structural paradigm to the boundaryless paradigm of the twenty-first century. But that journey took a full decade. At times, it was marked by internal pain, struggle, and doubt. And any organization that intends to become boundaryless must prepare itself for resistance, both from within and without.

Source: Excerpted from R. Ashkenas, D. Ulrich, T. Jick, and S. Kerr, *The Boundaryless Organization* (San Francisco, CA: Jossey-Bass, 1995): 13–21.

PREMEETING PREPARATION

A. Read "Permeability in Action: Case Study of a Boundaryless Organization."

B. Analyze your organization (e.g., work setting, team, church, academic department, university, etc.) using the 7-S Model.[1] All seven components are important; they are interconnected and should complement one another. This "fit" among the components is a major source of organizational effectiveness. Describe the following components of your organization and analyze their fit.

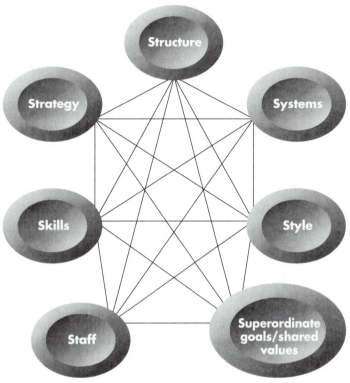

The 7-S model

1. **Strategy** The goals and objectives to be achieved as well as the values and missions to be pursued, the basic direction of the company. The strategy lays out the projects or services to be provided, the markets to be served, and the value to be offered to the customer. Strategy also specifies sources of competitive advantage.

2. **Structure** The anatomy of the organization that shows the formal reporting relationships and how job tasks are formally divided, grouped, and coordinated. The organizational chart is a representation of structure.

3. **Systems** The formal and informal procedures that make the organization work: capital budgeting systems, recruitment systems, training systems, compensation systems, cost accounting procedures, planning, reports, etc.

4. **Style** The way managers behave to achieve the organization's goals; how they generally interact with employees.

5. **Staff** A demographic description of important personnel categories. What types of people work in the organization (e.g., software designers, new immigrants whose limited language skills prevent them from working in their own fields, Ph.D. research scientists, part-time college students)?

6. **Skills** The distinctive capabilities of key personnel or the competencies for which the firm is noted.

7. **Superordinate Goals/Shared Values** The guiding concepts of the organization, the values and aspirations that are taught to members. These are the fundamental principles around which the organization is built (e.g., innovation, customer service, integrity).

C. Read the entire chapter.

D. What are the significant learning points from the readings?

E. If your instructor has assigned the Robbins Self-Assessment Library, use "What Type Of Organization Structure Do I Prefer?"

TOPIC INTRODUCTION

Peter Senge regularly asks groups of managers to imagine their organization as an ocean liner and themselves as the "leader." "What is your role?" he asks them. Most answer, "The captain." Some reply, "The navigator determining the direction" or "the helmsman." Others see themselves as "the engineer stoking the fire, producing energy" or "the social director communicating with and involving everyone." Rarely do they mention the role of ship designer. Senge, however, maintains that "no one has a more sweeping influence than the designer. What good does it do for the captain to say, 'Turn starboard 30 degrees,' when the designer has built a rudder that will only turn to port, or which takes six hours to turn to starboard? It's fruitless to be the leader in an organization that is poorly designed."[2]

This chapter addresses the essential skill of organizational design. There are various models, such as the 7-S model, that portray the basic organizational building blocks. Galbraith, an expert on organizational structure, proposed the star model, which consists of the following five components. He suggests managers begin by determining the strategy and then move to processes, people, rewards, and motivation.[3] Although the components in design models may be slightly different, all of them emphasize the importance of fit and complementarity among interconnected aspects. And none of them view structure as the only aspect of an organization that needs to be designed. However, because some design aspects have been covered in previous chapters or in other business courses (organizational theory, strategy, human resources), this chapter will focus primarily on structure.

Organizational design is a challenge that must be revisited again and again as companies grow and other conditions change. At present many corporations are restructuring to respond more quickly and with greater flexibility to changing environments and customer demands.[4] Large companies worry about becoming rulebound bureaucracies and losing the entrepreneurial spark that fueled their early growth. For example, Sony, with 170,000 employees, recently underwent restructuring "so that a small venture capital spirit can be brought into management."[5] The corporation was divided into four divisional companies organized around different technologies.

In general, we can categorize organizational structures as either mechanistic or organic. *Mechanistic organizations* are rigid bureaucracies with strict rules, narrowly defined tasks, top-down communication, and centralized decision making. They are best suited to routine functions within stable environments. A banana plantation is mechanistic because everyone has assigned jobs, and the work is very predictable. McDonald's is another example of a mechanistic organization. There are rules to ensure that customers receive a more or less standardized product all over the world, and the work is broken down into specific, standardized tasks. Walk into any McDonald's, and you will find employees performing the same tasks in the same way.

In contrast, *organic organizations* are flexible, decentralized networks with broadly defined tasks. One example of an organic structure is a new start-up firm in which employees do whatever needs to be done at a given moment rather than follow a fixed job description. They also communicate directly with anyone in the company rather than limiting their communication to their direct superior or subordinates and unit coworkers. Organic structures are most appropriate for complex, changing environments that require flexibility. A "skunkworks" where a relatively small, multidisciplinary group of employees sequesters itself until it comes up with a new computer design is another example of an organic organization. One seldom finds organizations that are

Mechanistic	Organic
1. Tasks broken down into specialized, separate parts	1. Employees contribute to the common task of the unit
2. Rigidly defined tasks	2. Broadly defined tasks
3. Centralized authority and control	3. Decentralized authority and control
4. Vertical communication	4. Horizontal communication
5. Rigid departmentalization	5. Cross-functional teams
6. Clear chain of command	6. Cross-hierarchical teams
7. Narrow span of control	7. Wide spans of control
8. High formalization	8. Low formalization

FIGURE 19-1   **A Comparison of Mechanistic and Organic Structures**

totally mechanistic or totally organic. For example, although a skunkworks is organic, other parts of the same company may be mechanistic. Figure 19-1 depicts the differences between mechanistic and organic structures.[6]

THE LANGUAGE OF STRUCTURE

Organization structure refers to the pattern of roles, authority, and communication that determines the coordination of the technology and people within an organization.

To discuss structure, we need to equip you with definitions of the key terms, found in Figure 19-2.

TRADITIONAL ORGANIZATIONAL STRUCTURES

There are various forms of organizational structure, each with a particular focus and unique advantages and disadvantages. We'll describe some of the more common forms in this section. Organizational charts represent structure; in particular, they illustrate how employees have been

Hierarchy	Distribution of authority among organizational positions. The power to influence and direct others resides in the higher levels of a hierarchy.
Centralization	Authority to make decisions is concentrated at the top of the organization.
Decentralization	Authority to make decisions is granted to those closest to the situation.
Complexity	Number of levels in the hierarchy (vertical differentiation) and the number of departments or jobs (horizontal differentiation). Large organizations, therefore, tend to be more complex than small organizations.
Specialization	Degree to which organizational tasks are subdivided into separate jobs. If specialization is high, employees perform a narrow range of tasks. If it is low, they perform a wide range of tasks.
Standardization	The extent to which similar work activities are performed in a uniform manner.
Routine technology	Technology characterized by little task variety and formalized, standardized tasks (assembly lines). Nonroutine technology has high task variety and involves problem analysis based on experience and technical knowledge (strategic planning, basic research).
Formalization	Extent to which explicit rules, regulations, policies, and procedures govern organizational activities.
Span of control	Number of employees who report to a single supervisor or manager.

FIGURE 19-2   **Organizational Design Terms**

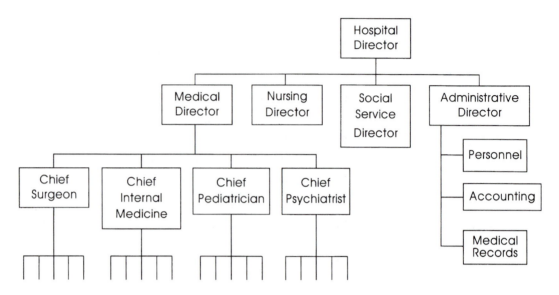

FIGURE 19-3   **Functional Structure**

grouped, who has authority over whom, and how certain forms of communication are directed. We'll use organizational charts from hospitals as an example for the first three traditional types of structure: functional, divisional, and matrix.

Functional Structure

In this model the organization is differentiated primarily by the functional specialties (e.g., nurses, physicians) required to accomplish the organization's mission. Each organization member, throughout the chain of command, reports to his or her functional superior (e.g., a nurse reports to a head nurse who reports to a nursing director). A health care delivery system may be functionally organized as shown in Figure 19-3.

Functional structures have various advantages. They enable the system to develop and maintain higher levels of expertise in the various functional areas or specialties. Organization members' loyalties are to the function, or specialty, and its standards of performance. In addition, each functional department can maintain subspecialists in various areas and allocate their time across the various services (e.g., inpatients, outpatients) being performed by the organization. One cardiologist, for example, could serve inpatients, outpatients, and the operating room. Thus, duplication of resources is reduced with functional designs. They promote standardization; with everyone doing similar work, it is easier to work in a uniform fashion. Functional designs also allow companies to centralize purchasing and facilitate buying leverage.

On the other hand, under a functional structure, it is often very difficult to perform the integration and coordination of services and inputs required by the organization. Problems in different services areas become difficult to manage since the various functional representatives in that department often do not have a strong direct reporting relationship to the service director. For example, pediatricians in the outpatient department under a functional structure may hold themselves more responsible to the chief of pediatrics than to the outpatient director. If coordination of doctors, nurses, and social workers is important in the outpatient department, and each health professional is responding to a different functional director, then coordination becomes difficult and problems may develop. These problems may take the form of inability to agree on schedules to ensure proper coverage, difficulty in developing work responsibilities for each function in a given service, problems in developing procedures for coordinating activities in the service, or even trouble agreeing on the goals and objectives of the service.

Other disadvantages of the functional structure relate to slow decision making. Because decisions are sent up the hierarchy to the top of functional areas, sometimes called functional silos,

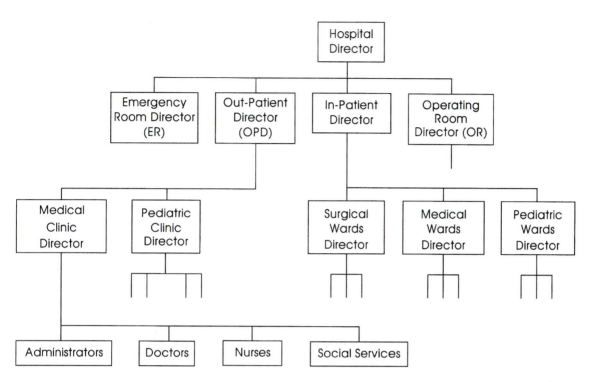

FIGURE 19-4   **Divisional Structure**

decision making may be slow. The priorities of the functional silos may assume greater importance than those of the organization as a whole. The barriers between different functions inhibit cross-functional collaboration, coordination, and information sharing.[7]

A functional structure is appropriate when the organization is small, when there is a single product line or service, when the number of markets served is limited, and when product life and development cycles are long. This type of structure is becoming less popular because survival depends on responsiveness to variety and speed. Functional structures are being replaced by product, market, or process structures and by lateral cross-functional processes.[8]

Divisional Structure

As shown in Figure 19-4, the divisional structure is differentiated by its outputs—usually its products or services. This structure is also referred to as a product structure or strategic business units. As an organization grows in size and adopts a strategy of product diversification, many companies switch from a functional to a divisional structure. Each department or division contains representatives from the various functional areas. Each organization member in this system reports directly or indirectly to a manager in charge of a particular product or service (e.g., a pediatric nurse reports to the director of the pediatric clinics). In larger companies, divisions can consist of business divisions, businesses, or profit centers.

Divisional structures have several advantages. The concentrated focus on one area often results in improvements as well as increased customer satisfaction. Because customers deal directly with the unit, there is a stronger possibility that their customized needs will be met and their suggestions incorporated into product design and service procedures. Changes in the environment or in customer taste can be speedily addressed. Ideas for improvements and adaptations do not have to compete internally for attention with all the company's other products or services and wait for a decision to come from on high. The product development cycle is most easily speeded up in divisional structures divided into product units.[9] This structure allows for coordination across functions and decentralized decision making. Decisions that are best for the product or service can be made closer to the customer.

Divisional structures also have their disadvantages. Because each department or division has representatives from each functional area, there is duplication of effort and resources. There may not be enough work for each department to have full-time specialists. Each unit may need equipment for functional specialists that could be shared in a functional structure. Divisions may buy their materials from different vendors rather than consolidating their orders. Therefore, various economies of scale are lost with divisional structures. Different divisions sometimes reinvent the wheel. Furthermore, because specialists no long work only with people in their own field, there is decreased opportunity for in-depth competence and technical specialization. Standardization across product lines is also more difficult. It is not uncommon, for example, to find departments using different procedures with customers or using different computer systems and software that eventually create compatibility problems. Coordination across the boundaries of different departments or divisions is difficult, so opportunities for shared learning and collaboration are often lost. And finally, customers who want to buy more than one product from the company cannot do "one-stop shopping" and deal with only one department or division. This is less efficient for the customer. Finally, employee loyalty may be to the division rather than to the company as a whole.

Divisional structures are appropriate when the company has several products or services, when the environment is rapidly changing and unpredictable, when the technology is nonroutine and depends on several functional areas, when the organization's goals are external effectiveness, adaptation, and customer satisfaction, and when organizations are large.[10]

A variation of the divisional structure is a *geographic* structure, divided into regions. For example, Bestfoods International, one of the largest global food companies, has four geographic divisions: Europe, Asia, Latin America, and North America. Divisions can stay close to their customers and reduce travel and distribution costs. The company understands that different regions (and countries) have different tastes in food and, therefore, allows a great deal of local autonomy. In yet another variation, *market structures*, the most rapidly increasing type of structure, divide the company into units that serve particular customers, markets, or industries.[11]

Many companies have adopted hybrid structures, which are combinations of different structures, because they are better suited to their needs and avoid the disadvantages of the pure structures.

Matrix Structure

Matrix structures, like hybrids, allow companies to have more than one focus. They evolved out of the need to provide both the advantages of functional specialization and the coordination of products or service activity. The structure is differentiated by both product and function as shown in Figure 19-5. For example, a nurse working in the pediatric ward would report to the pediatric clinic director and to a nursing director for the hospital in general.

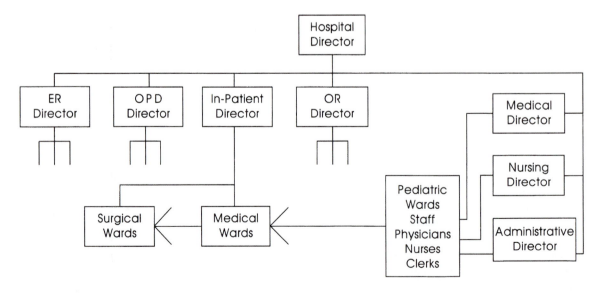

FIGURE 19-5 **Matrix Structure**

By maintaining the functional organization, the subspecialists can be retained and allocated where needed in the organization. The functional director can provide for in-service education and screening to maintain professional standards. At the same time, the product or service managers' authority over the functional representatives when they are in their service areas allows for better coordination. Unfortunately, the existence of two or more bosses for the various organization members involved can lead to confusion and conflict. Matrix structures require unique skills in both managers and employees to be successful.

Matrix structures have the advantages of facilitating the communication and coordination required to meet dual demands from the environment. The organic nature of the matrix (e.g., project groups) makes it flexible and adaptable to environmental changes. They allow for flexible and efficient sharing of human resources across products, which avoids duplication of resources. They provide the opportunity for both functional and product skill development.

The disadvantages of matrix structures are rooted in the dual structure. Matrices are time-consuming because employees attend meetings in both areas and sometimes have to resolve conflicts. The dual authority is confusing for some employees, and if organizational members do not develop the special skills required by a matrix structure (e.g., handling ambiguity, competing demands, and shared authority), this structure does not work. As a manager once noted, "The challenge is not so much to create a matrix structure as it is to create a matrix in the minds of our managers."[12]

Matrix structures are only appropriate under very specific conditions:

1. Pressure exists to share scare resources (people and equipment) across product lines.
2. Environmental pressure exists for two or more critical outputs (e.g., new products and high technical specialization and quality).
3. The organization's environment is both complex and uncertain. There are frequent changes that require both vertical and horizontal coordination and information sharing.[13]

Matrix structures are appropriate when the technology is nonroutine and interdependent or when the strategy has a dual focus, such as product innovation and technical specialization.[14] Matrix structures work best in medium-sized organizations with multiple, but not too many, products.

NEW ORGANIZATIONAL FORMS—HORIZONTAL AND NETWORK ORGANIZATIONS

Galbraith contends that organizations need to develop *lateral capability* in today's environment.[15] This term refers to the coordination of different functions without communicating through the hierarchy. He identifies three types of lateral capability:

1. coordination across functions
2. coordination across business units in a diversified corporation
3. international coordination of activities across countries and regions

Both horizontal structures, sometimes called process structures, and network structures are organic structures that increase lateral capability. Both are gaining in popularity.

Horizontal Structures

Horizontal structures, as shown in Figure 19-6, focus on a complete flow of work, which means managing across rather than up or down a hierarchy. Horizontal corporations are flat structures with minimal layers of management and self-managing, multidisciplinary teams organized around core process. Their primary goal and benefit is customer satisfaction, which is attained by reducing the boundaries with suppliers and customers alike and empowering employees.

Any work that does not add value is eliminated. Teams are the central organizational building block, and to reduce the need for supervisors, they manage themselves. Employees are trained to make their own analyses and decisions and then share the raw data. Employees are rewarded for skill acquisition and team performance. The use of multidisciplinary teams means that companies can decrease the number of "disconnects" and "handoffs" that occur whenever work is passed from one functional area or department to another.[16] Chrysler used a horizontal structure

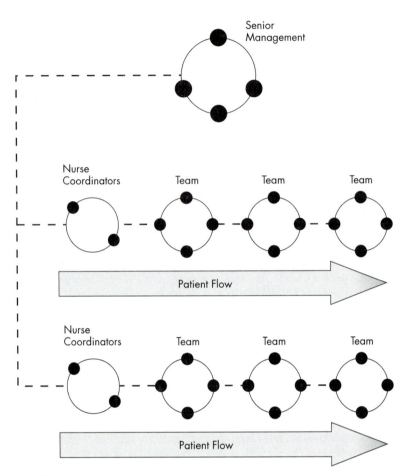

FIGURE 19-6   **Horizontal Hospital Structure**
Source: Karolinska Hospital in Stockholm, Sweden, as described in R. Rao, "The Struggle to Create an Organization for the 21st Century," *Fortune* (April 3, 1995): 90–99; and J. A. Byrne, "The Horizontal Corporation," *Business Week* (December 20, 1993): 76–81.

with the Neon car, thereby reducing both development time and costs. Examples of units within a horizontal structure might be new-product development process, order fulfillment process, and customer acquisition and maintenance.

Because horizontal structures are a fairly recent innovation, there is less research on their advantages and disadvantages. In general, the benefits of leaner, flatter structures are lower management costs, more widely shared communications and decision making, and greater employee involvement. The advantages of horizontal structures are customer satisfaction and the potential redesign and improvement of processes, resulting in increased efficiency, speed, and reduced costs. Because one manager is responsible for the entire process, the resistance to improving the process sometimes found in functional departments is reduced. It is easier to measure entire processes and hold process units accountable than to determine what bits and pieces of functional units have contributed to a process. Horizontal structures eliminate duplication of effort across functions. Because many tasks are delegated to self-managed teams, administrative overhead is reduced. Decentralized decision making in the teams makes for rapid decisions. Empowered, involved employees report improved morale. Administrative overhead is reduced because of the teams. By coordinating functions across the process, cycle times can be reduced, making some companies more competitive.[17]

One disadvantage of horizontal structures is figuring out how to define the numerous processes in most large organizations. Employees have to be trained to work in self-managed teams, and managers have to work as coaches rather than bosses. More time may be spent in meetings.

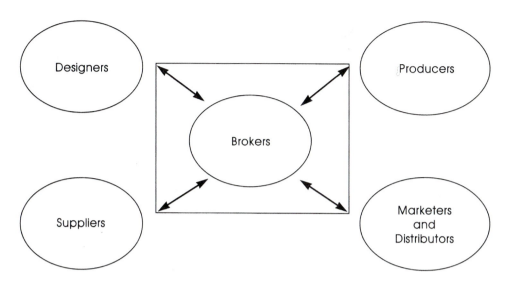

FIGURE 19-7   **Network Organization Structure**

Horizontal structures are appropriate in companies with short product life and development cycles, when customer satisfaction is the goal, and when the environment is uncertain.

Few companies are making a total transition to a horizontal structure, perhaps because there will always be a need for some managers with functional expertise.[18] In the future, we can expect to see more hybrid structures that organize multifunctional teams around core processes whenever possible.

Network Structure

Network structures are found in network organizations, sometimes called modular or virtual corporations. Shown in Figure 19-7, they made their appearance in the 1980s. *Network organizations consist of brokers who subcontract needed services to designers, suppliers, producers, and distributors linked by full-disclosure information systems and coordinated by market mechanisms.* These organizations are also referred to as hollow corporations because some activities are farmed out to other companies that form the network. For example, Nike, Apple Computer, Reebok, and Emerson Radio do virtually no manufacturing. Some employees never touch their company's product. Instead, these brokers form relationships with other companies that are responsible for manufacturing, selling, and transporting their products. Their contribution, as the center of the network, is the design, marketing, advertising, and integration of the network.[19]

The characteristics of networks are:

1. *Vertical disaggregation* Functions normally performed within the organization are carried out by independent organizations.
2. *Brokers* Networks of designers, suppliers, producers, and distributors are assembled by brokers.
3. *Market mechanisms* The key functions are tied together by market mechanisms rather than plans and controls.
4. *Full-disclosure information systems* Broad-access, computerized information systems substitute for extensive trust-building processes based on experience.[20]

Benetton has 8,000 franchises and 350 factories manufacturing the company's clothing that interact via an extensive, worldwide telecommunications network. Benetton's core is modern information technology that tracks each purchase from the cash registers in every franchise, so they can reportedly respond to market changes in 10 days' time. Benetton is relieved of the headaches of the manufacturing work that is subcontracted out to companies that work exclusively for Benetton and are guaranteed both work orders and a set profit margin.[21]

Network organizations have given rise to new ways of collaborating with other companies. Network partners must agree to ground rules that result in trustworthy relationships and transactions. Companies develop close and helpful relationships with several suppliers and customers so they do not become overdependent on one particular relationship.

The primary benefit of network structures is that they allow organizations and managers to concentrate on what they do well and subcontract activities that lie outside their specialty. Network structures help companies deal with complex relationships both within and outside the organization in rapidly changing environments. For example, when labor costs become too high in one country, Nike simply looks for subcontractors in countries with lower labor costs (a practice that disturbs critics of globalization).

Network structures are also lean with few administrative overhead costs. They make it possible to break into a market without incurring prohibitive start-up costs.[22] Network structures can be large (centralizing purchasing at the lead company) and small (subcontracting to small flexible shops) when it is to their advantage.[23] Companies in rapidly changing industries can avoid investing in factories and technologies that will quickly become obsolete because sourcing is flexible.

One of the disadvantages of network organizations is limited control over subcontractors. For example, how do you ensure quality and acceptable worker conditions in a company owned by a subcontractor? Brokers are vulnerable to allegations of human rights abuses committed by subcontractors. Subcontractors have been known to raise their prices once a broker has become dependent on them. Brokers also risk losing proprietary knowledge to companies that become competitors. "Apple taught independent software vendors about the Macintosh's operating system so that they could write application programs that would run on the Mac. One of those vendors was Microsoft. Microsoft did, indeed, write programs for the Mac, but it also incorporated what it learned into its own operating system, Windows. Once Windows 3.0 appeared, Apple had lost its competitive advantage."[24] Networks have limited loyalty because contractors can be replaced at any time in favor of a better deal. Network organizations are especially appropriate for fast-paced, changing industries in uncertain environments.

BOUNDARYLESS ORGANIZATIONS

Boundaryless organizations work at eliminating or diminishing the boundaries between both internal and external entities in order to be more effective. Good ideas are welcomed whatever their source whether inside or outside the company. People should collaborate and make things happen without waiting for permission from a central authority.[25] For example, Daimler Chrysler and Ford use cross-disciplinary teams that include designers, engineers, plant managers, and people from finance, marketing, and human resources. In the past, the plans for a new car would have been passed sequentially and bumpily from department to department, taking a great deal of time. Some companies also include customers in the product phase. Others, such as Johnson and Johnson, have computers located within their customers' facilities that keep them abreast of inventory. Honda believes that helping its suppliers become better companies makes Honda a better company. To this end, Honda assigned a team of engineers to work with and train employees at Parker-Hannifin. The benefits to Parker-Hannifin were cost savings and faster production time.

The Informal Organizational Structure

The points just discussed focus on the formal organizational structures. An organizational chart, as we have noted, specifies the nature of the formal organizational authority and communication patterns. However, these charts do not always reflect the reality of life within an organization. For example, a young boss may not have the necessary technical expertise so employees turn to an older employee as the real source of authority in their department. Employees and managers typically leave people out of the communication loop who are not respected or powerful. The in-groups in companies in collective cultures (e.g., Latin America) often call the shots and share information, regardless of where these members appear on the organizational chart. All these examples of variations from the formal structure reflect the organization's social system. Thus, organizations have both a formal structure and an informal structure that determine how both authority and communication really function.

The importance of understanding the distinctions between formal versus informal organizations and the problems that can arise if the two are not understood is at no time clearer than when one attempts to introduce a technical change into an organization. In Trist's famous study of an attempt to change the process by which coal was mined, the anticipated production increases from the new method were not being realized.[26] Upon investigation it was observed that the new technology substantially altered the social system that had developed within this mine. The men were used to working in close-knit teams characterized by loyalty and mutual help. The new technology involved factorylike, individualized workstations that disrupted the informal group patterns that had made their jobs satisfying. Whereas a formal organizational chart can be redrawn to account for the effects of a technological change, the informal social system, which does not appear on an organizational chart, is also influenced by the technological change. Both must be taken into account.

DIFFERENTIATION AND INTEGRATION

A key design issue, called differentiation and integration, was identified by Lawrence and Lorsch.[27] Organizations divide up their tasks among employees. As employees focus more and more on their particular tasks, differentiation occurs. Differentiation is "the differences in cognitive and emotional orientations among managers in different functional departments, and the difference in formal structure among these departments."[28] For example, accountants develop a particular mind-set toward their work that is quite different from that of salespeople. Departments differ from one another, as shown in Figure 19-8, due to the nature of their work. They develop particular goals, time horizons, interpersonal orientations, and levels of formality. Sometimes these differences are the source of intergroup conflict. When organizations have complex tasks and operate in dynamic environments, they become more differentiated than when their tasks are simple and their environments stable. The natural result of high differentiation is the difficulty in coordinating the work of the various units. Therefore, organizations have a variety of integration mechanisms that promote collaboration. Some examples are coordinators, committees, liaison positions, and task forces.[29]

Characteristic	R&D Department	Manufacturing	Sales Department
Goals	New developments, quality	Efficient production	Customer satisfaction
Time horizon	Long	Short	Short
Interpersonal orientation	Mostly task	Task	Social
Formality of structure	Low	High	High

FIGURE 19-8   **Differences in Goals and Orientations Among Organizational Departments**
Source: Based on P. R. Lawrence and J. W. Lorsch, *Organization and Environment* (Homewood, IL: Irwin, 1969): 23–29.

"And so you just threw everything together?...
Mathews, a posse is something
you have to *organize*."

 # PROCEDURE FOR GROUP MEETING: STRUCTURE, INC.

The purpose of this exercise is to develop a good understanding of different organizational structures and experience what it is like to work within them.

STEP 1.   Divide into groups of 10 to 12 students (unless your instructor decides otherwise). These groups will form different companies whose product is the transfer of knowledge to their customers, in this case, your classmates. Each group will be assigned one of the following structures: functional structure, horizontal structure, or network structure.

The groups have two tasks: (60 minutes)

a.   Prepare a 15- to 20-minute class presentation with the following minimum components. If you want to exceed these requirements, please do so.

1.   Explain how your assigned structure works. (If you were assigned this project ahead of time, please try to obtain an organizational chart from a company using this structure.)

2.   Describe the strengths and weaknesses of the structure.

3.   Under what conditions is a structure such as this most appropriate?

4.   Prepare a one-page handout for your classmates (to be copied and distributed as instructed).

5.   Make your presentations as interesting and creative as possible—the goal of your group (a service business) is to transfer knowledge about your structure to your audience.

b.   Carry out the preparation for the presentation by organizing your group using the type of structure you were assigned. For example, if your group has the network structure, two of you might constitute the core organization and the rest of the members will be subcontractors who produce different services. Please adhere strictly to this requirement so we can compare afterward what it was like to work in the different structures.

Depending on your structure and the type of presentation you choose, some of the specialized tasks in your company might be research, writing, design, graphics (Power Point, overheads, posters), talent (presenters or actors), and management.

STEP 2.   Each group makes its presentation.

STEP 3.   As a class, discuss the following questions. (30 minutes)
   a. How did you organize your group?
   b. What effect did your structure have on your preparation phase?
   c. Were there any differences in the presentations that might be traced back to different structures?
   d. Did any other design-related issues surface in this project?
   e. Did you like working with the type of structure you were assigned?
   f. What did you do to ensure communication? Coordination? Quality control?
   g. What connections can you make between this exercise and the readings?

FOLLOW-UP

Choosing the most appropriate structure is a matter of making trade-offs, because all structures have advantages and disadvantages. A starting point for determining the right structure for a particular organization is the design principle: "Form follows function." The task (function) should determine the structure (form). This explains why departments or divisions with very diverse tasks are usually structured in different ways. Champy suggests this principle be modified to "form follows customers." In his opinion, structures should mirror the customers and cater to their specific needs.[30]

There are other contingencies that affect the choice of structure: the company's strategy, the environment, technology, size, national culture, and the people and their shared values. The Quaker religion, for example, is predicated on a direct relationship to God and personal conscience. These beliefs translate into a highly developed form of participative decision making in most Quaker organizations and a predisposition toward decentralized structures.[31]

Galbraith recommends setting strategy first and then choosing the structure most likely to make that strategy a reality.[32] For example, if the company's competitive advantage is fast cycle times, a horizontal, process-oriented structure is more appropriate than a functional structure.

The Environment and Structure   The environment has a major effect on the choice of structure. Two dimensions are used to analyze an organization's environment: the simple-complex dimension and the stable-unstable dimension. Both concern the elements in an organization's domain, such as customers, competitors, suppliers, government regulators, unions, financial resources, and so on.

The *simple-complex dimension* refers to environmental complexity, the heterogeneity or the number and dissimilarity of external elements relevant to an organization's operations. Small, family-owned businesses usually have a simple environment—few, fairly similar, external elements that influence the organization. In contrast, global corporations have complex environments.

The *stable-unstable dimension* gauges whether the elements in the environment are dynamic. Stable environments remain the same for a relatively long period. Unstable environments change quickly.

Environmental uncertainty is high when information on environmental factors is insufficient and it is difficult to predict what will happen. The more uncertain the environment, the more information the organization needs about the environment. People in *boundary-spanning roles* often gather information on the environment as well as represent the interests of the organization to the

TABLE 19-1   Environmental Characteristics and Recommended Organizational Designs

	Simple	Complex
Stable	**Low Uncertainty** Formal, centralized mechanistic structure with few departments	**Low-Moderate Uncertainty** Formal, centralized mechanistic structure with many departments and integration roles
Unstable	**High-Moderate Uncertainty** Decentralized, organic structure with participation and teamwork Few departments Boundary spanning roles	**High Uncertainty** Decentralized, organic structure Participation and teamwork Numerous departments and boundary spanners

ENVIRONMENTAL RATE OF CHANGE

Simple   **Complex**

ENVIRONMENTAL COMPLEXITY

Source: Based on R. B. Duncan, "What Is the Right Organization Structure? Decision Tree Analysis Provides the Answer," *Organizational Dynamics* (Winter 1979): 59–80.

environment. Two examples of boundary spanners are people engaged in market research and corporate lawyers who specialize in government regulations.

A matrix of the simple-complex and stable-unstable dimensions, shown in Table 19-1, provides more guidance about organizational structure.[33]

Low uncertainty environments exist when the environment is both stable and simple (e.g., beer and soft-drink industry). The most appropriate structure for this type of environment is a formal, centralized mechanistic structure with few departments.

Low-moderate uncertainty environments exist when the environment is stable and complex (e.g., chemical companies and universities). The most appropriate structure for this category is a formal, centralized mechanistic structure. The complexity of the environment makes it necessary to have more departments along with integration roles to coordinate them.

High-moderate uncertainty environments exist when the environment is unstable and simple (e.g., cosmetics and toy industries). The most appropriate structure is a decentralized, organic structure characterized by participation and teamwork. Because there are few elements in the environment, few departments are necessary; however, boundary-spanning roles are prevalent to keep on top of information and changes in the environment.

High uncertainty environments exist when the environment is both unstable and complex (e.g., computer firms, airlines, telecommunications). The most appropriate structure is a decentralized, organic structure characterized by participation and teamwork. Due to the complexity of the environment, however, numerous departments and boundary spanners are necessary.

Technology and Structure   Changes in technology have had a far-reaching impact on organizational design. Successful Internet companies may have organizational charts with only three full-time employees. Geographical location ceases to matter when people make their purchases on-line.

Telecommuting and groupware mean that many colleagues are no longer physically grouped, even though they work "together." Flexible manufacturing processes ensure that factories produce a greater variety of products and provide more customization for customers. E-mail makes it easier for subordinates to gain access to decision makers; hitting "send" on your keyboard is simpler than trying to get past the executive secretary guarding the president's office in many companies. Automation and information technology make possible wider spans of control, resulting in flatter hierarchies.[34] Advanced information technology has been credited with broader participation in decision making, faster decision making, and better organizational intelligence.[35]

In some cases, information technology has revolutionized industries. Before Wal-Mart, most small-town retail stores in the United States were "mom and pop" operations in which the owners made business decisions without knowing what was happening in stores outside the area. Sam Walton of Wal-Mart changed this scene forever by centralizing pricing, buying, and promotional decisions on a national level, thanks to the company's state-of-the-art electronic ordering and inventory control systems. As a result, Wal-Mart was able to deliver better-quality products at lower prices, and many of its competitors were forced out of business. Wal-Mart has, however, designed in some decentralized decision making. Local managers have some latitude on decisions about ordering stock and allocating space. There are also 500 to 600 price-sensitive items for which local store managers can determine their own prices, depending on the local competition (if there is any left).[36] As Wal-Mart's CIO (Chief Information Officer) said: "I think the challenge...is to enable a chain as big as Wal-Mart to act like a hometown store, even while it maintains its economies of scale."[37]

International Structures

Expanding the business into a foreign country for the first time often means entering a highly uncertain environment. Companies may choose to minimize the risk and uncertainty via a range of strategic alliances. Some *license* their products to foreign companies that have access to global markets and distribution channels. Other companies enter into *joint ventures* with companies that are well established in the target country or region. Joint ventures are separate business entities designed to enter new markets, formed by two or more firms that share development and production costs. Other companies join consortia—groups of independent companies (e.g., suppliers, customers, and competitors) that join together to share skills, resources, costs, and access to one another's markets.

Corporations that have established a presence abroad may use some variation of the structures described in the chapter. Their choice of structure may depend partly on the stage of their international development, how many products they sell internationally, and the importance of their international sales.[38] Bartlett and Ghoshal recommend an integrated network model for transnational corporations.

> In such companies, key activities and resources are neither centralized in the parent company, nor decentralized so that each subsidiary can carry out its own tasks.... Instead, the resources and activities are dispersed but specialized, so as to achieve efficiency and flexibility at the same time. Furthermore, these dispersed resources are integrated in an interdependent network of worldwide operations.[39]

Integrated network models consist of (1) distributed, specialized resources and capabilities; (2) large flows of components, products, resources, people, and information among interdependent units; and (3) complex processes of coordination and cooperation in an environment of shared decision making.[40] They can be illustrated as a network (no top or bottom to denote authority) with interconnecting lines to all units.

CULTURE AND STRUCTURE

Family businesses are the most common form of business organization throughout the world. As a general rule, they are characterized by paternalistic, centralized decision making—the male leader or owner makes the decisions—and decisions are often based on kinship considerations rather than rational business judgment. For example, providing jobs for relatives may be more important than maximizing performance and profit. Family businesses may or may not follow bureaucratic rules.

In Chinese family businesses, the dominant values are patrimonialism, which includes paternalism, hierarchy, mutual obligations, responsibility, familialism, personalism, and connections. With the exception of Chinese businesses that employ nonfamily members and operate as a clan or extended family, many businesses remain small and, therefore, have simple structures. They do not have systematic sets of rules, systems, or roles. Workers do not specialize and are switched from task to task at the owner's whim. Given the absence of formal structure, cliques occasionally form as a substitute; intergroup conflict sometimes results, an indication of the factionalism found in Chinese family businesses.[41]

The Japanese *keiretsu* and Korean *chaebols* are structures that originated in family businesses and have played a major role in the economic development of these countries. *Keiretsu* are complex interfirm networks that combine market exchange and noneconomic social relations. Each member firm buys a small percentage of stock in the other firms in the group. They generally participate in a large number of industries and have a bank at their core. *Keiretsu* networks, such as Mitsubishi, reduce costs and risks and safeguard member firms by ensuring trusting, reliable business dealings and a certain degree of protection from competition with nonmember firms.[42] Korean *chaebols* are "a business group consisting of large companies owned and managed by family members or relatives in many diversified business areas."[43] Hyundai, Samsun, and Daewoo are *chaebols*.

National culture affects the choice of structure. High-power-distance cultures tend toward organizational structures with centralized decision making. Low-power-distance cultures prefer decentralized decision making. The uncertainty avoidance dimension relates to the degree of formalization—the need for formal rules and specialization. High uncertainty avoidance cultures will prefer formalized structures. Matrix structures were not widely accepted in France because they go against the French respect for the hierarchy and unity of command.[44]

 LEARNING POINTS

1. Mechanistic organizations are rigid bureaucracies with strict rules, narrowly defined tasks, top-down communication, and centralized decision making. They are best suited to routine functions within stable environments.

2. Organic organizations are flexible, decentralized networks, with broadly defined tasks, horizontal communication, and cross-functional teams. They are most appropriate for complex, changing environments that require flexibility.

3. Organizational structure refers to the pattern of roles, authority, and communication that determines the coordination of the technology and people within an organization.

4. The functional form of organizational structure centers around the functional specialties required to accomplish the organization's mission. It allows for greater development of functional expertise but may make organizational coordination more difficult.

5. The divisional structure is organized around outputs such as products or services, business divisions, businesses, or profit centers. The concentrated focus and decentralized decision making improve the chances of customer satisfaction and rapid adaptation and change.

6. Matrix structures have a dual focus, usually products and functions. It is an attempt to profit from the advantages of both functional and product structures. However, having both a product boss and a functional boss can cause confusion and conflict.

7. Horizontal corporations are flat structures with minimal layers of management and self-managing multidisciplinary teams organized around core processes.

8. Network organizations consist of brokers who subcontract needed services to designers, suppliers, producers, and distributors linked by full-disclosure information systems and coordinated by market mechanisms.

9. A guiding rule in design is "form follows function." Therefore, different parts of the organization may have different structures.

10. Boundaryless organizations work at eliminating or diminishing the boundaries between both internal and external entities in order to be more effective.

11. The informal structure refers to natural formations, informal leadership, and communication patterns that evolve in an organization and run parallel to the formal structure.

12. Because they do different tasks, employees become differentiated and develop dissimilar goals and orientations; therefore, organizations need mechanisms for integrating various units.

13. Organizational design is influenced by these contingencies: strategy, environment, technology, size, national culture, and the people and their shared values.

14. The simple-complex dimension (environmental complexity) and the stable-unstable dimension (rate of environmental change) can be used to determine the level of environmental uncertainty organizations face.

15. Corporations may gain access to foreign markets via strategic alliances such as licensing agreements, joint ventures, and consortia.

16. Family businesses are the most common form of business structure throughout the world.

TIPS FOR MANAGERS

- Match the internal organizational structure to the external environment.
- As always in management, balance is important. Some companies go overboard with bureaucracy busting. Organizations need enough bureaucracy to facilitate the work and avoid reinventing the wheel and enough chaos to promote initiative and creativity.[45]
- Looking at an organizational problem, it's important to ask, "What is the problem, not who?" Unless managers are sophisticated about design issues, they are likely to see individuals, rather than structure, as the problem.
- When a succession of people fail in a position, it is often a signal that the position or the organizational design is at fault. Some jobs and even departments are simply doomed to failure by poor designs, and it's a manager's job to determine that and rectify it.
- There is a saying, "When in doubt, reorganize." Don't reorganize, however, unless you have undertaken a thorough analysis and are fairly certain that the design issues are really the culprit. Above all, don't choose a structure simply because it's in fashion.
- Make sure the informal structure is well understood before any changes are made. Some organizations succeed in spite of their structure because the informal structure is stronger than the formal structure.
- It's difficult to forecast the unanticipated consequences that will result from new structures. Without doubt there will be some. Therefore, it makes sense to brainstorm possible consequences and leave some room for later modifications.
- A change in organizational design often results in resistance. It is upsetting to most people to participate in reorganization. Getting employee participation in the process of developing a new design is one way to reduce resistance.

PERSONAL APPLICATION ASSIGNMENT

"Leaders in highly layered organizations are like people who wear several sweaters outside on a freezing winter day. They remain warm and comfortable but are blissfully ignorant of the realities of their environment."

Jack Welch, CEO, GE

In this assignment you are to write about the design of an organization you know well by answering the following questions:

1. How would you diagram the formal structure of your organization?

2. How would you describe the communication and coordination among different departments?

3. How would you diagram the informal structure of your organization?

4. How does your organization deal with the differentiation-integration issue?

5. What are the strengths and weaknesses of your organization's design?

6. What improvements could you suggest?

ENDNOTES

[1] R. T. Pascale and A. G. Athos, *Art of Japanese Management* (New York: Simon & Schuster, 1981).

[2] P. Senge, "The Leader's New Work: Building Learning Organizations," *Sloan Management Review* (Fall 1990): 10.

[3] J. R. Galbraith, *Designing Organizations* (San Francisco: Jossey-Bass, 1995): 11–17.

[4] Charles Handy, *The Age of Unreason* (London: Hutchinson, 1988).

[5] Y. Nakamura, in "Sony's Yoshihide Nakamura on Structure and Decision Making," interviewed by P. W. Beamish, *Academy of Management Executive 13*, no. 4 (November 1999): 13.

[6] T. Burns and G. M. Stalker, *The Management of Innovation* (London: Tavistock, 1961) was the original source describing

organic and mechanistic structures; a few additional descriptors included in the chart are taken from G. Zaltman, R. Duncan, and H. J. Holbeck, *Innovations and Organizations* (New York: Wiley, 1973): 131.

[7] The advantages and disadvantages of the functional, divisional, and matrix structures are described in R. B. Duncan, "What Is the Right Organization Structure? Decision Tree Analysis Provides the Answer," *Organizational Dynamics* (Winter 1979): 59–80; and R. L. Daft, *Organizational Theory and Design* (Cincinnati, OH: SouthWestern, 1998).

[8] Galbraith, *Designing Organizations*, p. 27.

[9] Ibid.

[10] Daft, *Organizational Theory and Design*, p. 218.

[11] Galbraith, *Designing Organizations*, p. 30.

[12] C. A. Bartlett and S. Ghoshal, "Matrix Management: Not a Structure, a Frame of Mind," *Harvard Business Review 68*, no. 4 (1990): 45.

[13] S. M. Davis and P. R. Lawrence, *Matrix* (Reading, MA: Addison-Wesley, 1977).

[14] Daft, *Organizational Theory and Design*, p. 228.

[15] J. R. Galbraith, *Competing with Flexible Lateral Organizations* (Reading, MA: Addison-Wesley, 1994).

[16] J. A. Byrne, "The Horizontal Corporation," *Business Week* (December 20, 1993): 76–81.

[17] Galbraith, *Designing Organizations*; and Daft, *Organizational Theory and Design*, p. 253.

[18] Byrne, "The Horizontal Corporation."

[19] E. E. Lawler, III, *The Ultimate Advantage* (San Francisco: Jossey-Bass, 1992): 69–70.

[20] R. E. Miles and C. Snow, "Organizations: New Concepts for New Forms," *California Management Review 28* (1986): 62–73; R. Johnston and P. R. Lawrence, "Beyond Vertical Integration— The Rise of the Value-Adding Partnership," *Harvard Business Review 66* no. 4 (1988): 94–101; C. C. Snow, R. E. Miles, and H. J. Coleman, Jr., "Managing 21st Century Network Organizations," *Organizational Dynamics 20* 3 (1992): 5–19; see also R. E. Miles, C. C. Snow, J. A. Mathews, G. Miles, and H. J. Coleman, Jr., "Organizing in the Knowledge Age: Anticipating the Cellular Form," *Academy of Management Executive 11*, no. 4 (November 1997): 7–35.

[21] S. R. Clegg, *Modern Organizations* (London: Sage, 1990); T. Waterstone, "Benetton—the Family, the Business, and the Brand," *Management Today* (April 1999): 48.

[22] R. E. Miles and C. C. Snow, "The New Network Firm: A Spherical Structure Built on a Human Investment Philosophy," *Organizational Dynamics* (Spring 1995): 5–18.

[23] Galbraith, *Designing Organizations*.

[24] Ibid., p. 130.

[25] R. Ashkenas, D. Ulrich, T. Jick, and S. Kerr, *The Boundaryless Organization* (San Francisco: Jossey-Bass, 1995).

[26] Eric Trist as reported in W. G. Bennis et al., *The Planning of Change*, 2nd ed. (New York: Holt, Rinehart and Winston, 1969): 269–81.

[27] P. R. Lawrence and J. W. Lorsch, *Organization and Environment* (Homewood, IL: Irwin, 1969).

[28] J. W. Lorsch, "Introduction to the Structural Design of Organizations" in G. Dalton, P. R. Lawrence, and J. W. Lorsch, eds., *Organizational Structure and Design* (Homewood, IL: Irwin and Dorsey, 1970): 5.

[29] J. W. Lorsch and P. R. Lawrence, "Environmental Factors and Organizational Integration," in J. W. Lorsch and P. R. Lawrence, eds., *Organization Planning: Cases and Concepts* (Homewood, IL: Irwin and Dorsey, 1972): 38–48.

[30] J. Champy, "Management Strategies: Form Follows Customers," *Forbes* (March 8, 1999): 130–131.

[31] M. J. Sheeran, *Beyond Majority Rule: Voteless Decisions in the Religious Society of Friends* (Philadelphia Yearly Meeting, 1983).

[32] Galbraith, *Designing Organizations*, p. 12.

[33] Duncan, "What Is the Right Organization Structure?"

[34] Galbraith, *Designing Organizations*.

[35] Daft, *Organizational Theory and Design*, p. 144.

[36] M. Stevenson, "The Store to End All Stores," *Canadian Business Review 67* (May 1994): 20–29.

[37] T. W. Malone, "Is Empowerment Just a Fad? Control, Decision Making and IT," *Sloan Management Review* (Winter 1997): 26.

[38] J. M. Stopford and L. T. Wells, *Strategy and Structure of the Multinational Enterprise* (New York: Basic Books, 1972).

[39] C. A. Bartlett and S. Ghoshal, *Transnational Management* (Boston: Irwin McGraw-Hill, 2000): 13.

[40] C. A. Bartlett and S. Ghoshal, *Transnational Management*. See also C. A. Bartlett and S. Ghoshal, *Managing Across Borders: The Transnational Solution* (Boston, Harvard Business School Press, 2000) and G. Hedlund and D. Rolander, "Action in Hetarchies: New Approaches to Managing the MNC," in C. A. Bartlett, Y. Doz, and G. Hedlund, eds., *Managing the Global Firm* (New York: Routledge, 1990): 15–46.

[41] M. Chen, *Asian Management Systems: Chinese, Japanese, and Korean Styles of Business* (New York: Routledge, 1995).

[42] R. Lincoln, M. L. Gerlach, and C. L. Ahmadjian, "Keiretsu Networks and Corporate Performance in Japan," *American Sociological Review 61*, no. 1 (1996): 67–88.

[43] S. Yoo and S. Lee, "Management Style and Practice of Korean Chaebols," *California Management Review 24*, no. 4 (1987): 97.

[44] A. Laurent, "The Cultural Diversity of Western Conceptions of Management," *International Studies of Management and Organizations 13*, no. 1-2 (1983): 75–76.

[45] P. S. Adler, "Building Better Bureaucracies," *Academy of Management Executive 13*, no. 4 (November 1999): 36.

Chapter 20

▲▲

MANAGING CHANGE

OBJECTIVES By the end of the chapter, you should be able to:

A. Describe the nature of change.

B. Explain the essential components in the change process.

C. Understand the leader's role in the change process.

D. Define resistance to change and its function.

E. List tactics for dealing with resistance to change.

How to Live in a Fad Culture

Every so often a guy like Kip Breen descends from corporate Mecca, all teeth and gray twill, to spread ultrasenior management's latest instant credo with beamish zeal and a steel fist. That year it was something called Negative Task Evaluation, and it made us dance like Saint Vitus before it disappeared into the mists of corporate time, as fads do.

"It's pretty simple," Kip said benignly, easing a glossy, user-friendly packet across my blotter. "We want each manager to break down his or her ongoing activities, then derive the amount of time each chore requires as a percentage of the total workweek. Then you just work out a couple of simple graphs to see who is spending an inappropriate amount of time on matters of minor importance."

And then fire them, I thought.

In the coming months, I filled out more graphs than an infertile couple. People were evaluating one another all over the place, and relationships grew formal. We needn't have worried, though, because while middle management was diddling with its new Tinkertoy, the big guys were seized by a more terrible trend then careening around the horn: decentralization. Out of the window went the assiduously kept charts. With them flew 400 nice folks, willy-nilly. Nothing has been heard of Kip since, except over booze, when we survivors haul out his memory just for a hoot. Then we get back to work.

You'll have to excuse us guys on the inside if we get a little giggly each time the next new dogma comes along. We've converted before, after all. We've managed in a minute and Theory Z'd, spotted megatrends, spun matrices, woven grids; we've hammered ourselves into hardnetworking intrapreneurs, and sat in stupefaction before lanky preachers nagging us to Be Excellent! Some of us, thank God, have even found Wellness. We're willing to give each new creed a chance, until its hasty priests begin torturing the innocent into false confessions. The damned thing is, when the right idea is given the chance to mellow, spread, and ooze deep into the culture, it can actually do some good. But don't hold your breath.

Even when the idea is right—which it rarely is—most corporations still get it wrong. "You can go back to Management-by-Objective, Son of Management-by-Objective, Management-by-Objective meets Appraisal-and-Counseling," says E. Kirby Warren, professor at Columbia University's Graduate School of Business. "Most of these fads would have some real value if senior management took the time to ask themselves: (1) How do I adapt the idea to our culture and business? (2) What has to be changed to reinforce that thing we're talking about? and (3) Are we committed to staying with it long enough to make it work?"

But in today's overheated environment, most firms are too desperate to wait for results. "When we're facing intense competition from Asia, and money is relatively expensive, and technology is available and moves rapidly, it's not surprising that people reach out for what you call fads," says Joseph Bower, professor at Harvard Business School. "If you take almost any of them and discuss it with the author, it's a perfectly qualified view of how a set of ideas can run a company. But if it's treated as a kind of cookbook, as a single tool carried to an extreme, you get nonsense."

Still, when the guys with liver spots get that nutsy gleam in their eyes, you may have to snap to. Here are some pointers on how to survive.

It must be an autocracy, because democracy doesn't squeeze like that. The guys put in charge of forging the new culture aren't usually the Mother Teresa type. They take things personally, and they're not long on patience. Don't be fooled by warm and fuzzy verbiage designed to win your heart. This is a full blown drill. Get out on deck and run around.

Keep your mouth shut. Yes, the anal graphs and rah-rah lingo may seem absurd, but develop some instant naivete—I've seen more than one astute critic mailed overnight to the Elmira office for being a party pooper. "It's a religion," says a friend currently being strangled in the noose of a Quality circle. "To openly question or be cynical about it—you're more than grumpy, you're an apostate."

Charts are not enough. The need to play with neat fad gewgaws doesn't call off your actual job. "I had this subordinate who insisted on spending six months doing a PERT chart, while completely ignoring his other duties," recalls Wes, strategic-planning director at a multinational. "I love the memory of Frank pouring over a chart as big as a barn door that was supposed to govern our actions for the next year. He finally finished it, and we never looked at it again." Frank is out on the Coast now, by the way, teaching people how to do PERT charts.

General Pinochet! I had no idea you were dropping by. There's a healthy whiff of authoritarian zealotry in many fads, and some big boosters may think they've been named Ayatollah. Push them gently off your back. Unostentatious resistance to excess—even excess orthodoxy—is rarely questioned. "One of the darker moments last year was when the Productivity Czar asked everyone to sign a *Petition of Commitment*," recalls my friend Andy, a marketing manager at a retail firm. "It was invasive and ridiculous. I tried to kid him out of it. It turns out a lot of other people did, too. He was even advised against it by some of his peers, who felt it was sort of like reading the Bible in the office." The loathed petition now resides on the czar's wall, half full. Not one of the missing was punished.

Dare to be sold. A little credulity can be a beautiful thing. Several years ago I worked for a manufacturing company that decided to dedicate itself to Excellence. The propaganda campaign we inflicted on our workers was fierce. Management spent actual money to improve service. Worker initiative was rewarded. And, unbelievably, the elephantine organism began to lumber forth, to feel pride and a determination to succeed. It was corny and inspirational. We were a team, suddenly, and felt it. I wouldn't have missed it for the world.

A year into the program, the corporation was abruptly sold to a group of midwestern investors who broke it down and resold its body parts for cash. So long, Excellence. Hello, Leverage. What the hell: One good fad deserves another.

Source: By Stanley Bing. Reprinted from *Esquire* (August 1986). With permission of publisher and author.

Rate Your Readiness to Change

Executives say that as many as two-thirds of total quality management efforts flop. Michael Hammer and James Champy, authors of the best-selling *Reengineering the Corporation*, estimate that well over half the radical change programs they advocate fade into similar oblivion. Take a bittersweet tour of your own company's failed attempts to shape up: Walk down to the galley and check out the slogans on the mugs on the shelf above the coffeemaker—"No. 1 in '91," "A team's for you in '92," "Qual-i-tee in '93," and this year's "Try once more in '94." They're almost enough to make you feel young again, like songs from the fifties.

If it's any comfort, the problem isn't new. According to the very first management consultant, Niccolo Machiavelli, "There is nothing more difficult to take in hand, more perilous to conduct, or more uncertain in its success than to take the lead in the introduction of a new order of things." Yet some companies do take to change readily, if not always painlessly. Think of Motorola, which grabbed TQM in a bear hug early in the 1980s and hasn't let go, continuously raising its standards and its profits. Or General Electric, which uses a set of management tools—maps of its processes, the study of other companies' best practices, and its bureaucracy-subverting Work Out program—to build a machine that churns out change the way a turbine makes electricity.

Why does one organization thrive on change while another sulks like a teenager? For Andrea Sodano, who holds a Ph.D. in psychology, the question is of more than academic interest. A consultant at Symmetrix, a firm in Lexington, Massachusetts, that specializes in reengineering, Sodano fretted as she saw some jobs go smoothly while others bogged down. Says her boss, Symmetrix CEO George Bennett: "Some places, we've gone in with our best people and broken our picks. That's a waste of our resources and those of our clients."

People and culture—the human systems of a company—are what make or break any change initiative. Last year the Wyatt Co., an actuarial and human resources consulting firm in Washington, DC, surveyed executives of 531 companies that had restructured their operations. It found that the most-often-cited barriers to change were employee resistance and "dysfunctional corporate culture." A dysfunctional culture, says Wyatt's John Parkington, is one whose shared values and behavior are at odds with its long-term health: For example, a high-tech company might celebrate individual star performers even though teamwork produces the innovation on which its future depends.

Sodano and several colleagues at Symmetrix have studied signs of change readiness and resistance. They looked for specific characteristics that tend to keep things in place and fuel resistance to changing behavior, as well as the common traits of companies that adopt new business practices successfully.

The quiz that follows is an adaptation of their work. Its first aim is to assess your company's or your business unit's versatility. The higher you score, the better able you are to change when change is needed. Conversely, says Bennett, "trying to reengineer a company that scores low is like sending troops into battle against superior forces." The old culture will rise up and overwhelm you.

The quiz serves a second, equally important purpose: Because it reveals likely causes of failure, it creates an agenda, a list of ways to make a big restructuring or reengineering more likely to take. Says Sodano: "The problem with the 'soft side' of management is getting good data, numbers that business people are willing to accept. This quiz gives you specifics." Last autumn, Sodano used the quiz with a British chemical company, a potential client. Afterward, the company's reengineering head realized that she needed more public support from top management if the project was to succeed, and she used the findings to get it.

Now to see how you measure up, pull out your pen or pencil. Ready? Begin.

A Quiz

The left-hand column lists 17 key elements of change readiness. Rate your organization on each item. Give three points for a high ranking ("We're good at this; I'm confident of our skills here"); two for medium score ("We're spotty here; we could use improvement or more experience"); and one point for a low score ("We've had problems with this; this is new to our organization"). Be honest. Don't trust only your own perspective; ask others in the organization, at all levels, to rate the company too. The consultants at Symmetrix believe—no surprise—it helps to have an outsider do the assessment with you.

Category	**Score**

Sponsorship

The sponsor of change is not necessarily its day-to-day leader; he or she is the visionary, chief cheerleader, and bill payer—the person with the power to help the team change when it meets resistance. Give three points—change will be easier—if sponsorship comes at a senior level; for example, CEO, COO, or the head of an autonomous business unit. Weakest sponsors: midlevel executives or staff officers.

Leadership

This means the day-to-day leadership—the people who call the meetings, set the goals, work till midnight. Successful change is more likely if leadership is high level, has "ownership" (that is, direct responsibility for what's to be changed) and has clear business results in mind. Low-level leadership, or leadership that is not well connected throughout the organization (across departments) or that comes from the staff, is less likely to succeed and should be scored low.

Motivation

High points for a strong sense of urgency from senior management, which is shared by the rest of the company, and for a corporate culture that already emphasizes continuous improvement. Negative: tradition-bound managers and workers, many of whom have been in their jobs for more than 15 years; a conservative culture that discourages risk taking.

Direction

Does senior management strongly believe that the future should look different from the present? How clear is management's picture of the future? Can management mobilize all relevant parties—employees, the board, customers, etc.—for action? High points for positive answers to those questions. If senior management thinks only minor change is needed, the likely outcome is no change at all; score yourself low.

Measurements

Or in consultant-speak, "metrics." Three points if you already use performance measures of the sort encouraged by total quality management (defect rates, time to market, etc.) and if these express the economics of the business. Two points if some measures exist but compensation and reward systems do not explicitly reinforce them. If you don't have measures in place or don't know what we're talking about, one point.

Organizational Context

How does the change effort connect to other major goings-on in the organization? (For example: Does it dovetail with a continuing total quality management process? Does it fit with strategic actions such as acquisitions or new product lines?) Trouble lies ahead for a change effort that is isolated or if there are multiple change efforts whose relationships are not linked strategically.

PROCESSES/FUNCTIONS

Major changes almost invariably require redesigning business processes that cut across functions such as purchasing, accounts payable, or marketing. If functional executives are rigidly turf conscious, change will be difficult. Give yourself more points the more willing they—and the organization as a whole—are to change critical processes and sacrifice perks or power for the good of the group.

COMPETITOR BENCHMARKING

Whether you are a leader in your industry or a laggard, give yourself points for a continuing program that objectively compares your company's performance with that of competitors and systematically examines changes in your market. Give yourself one point if knowledge of competitors' abilities is primarily anecdotal—what salesmen say at the bar.

CUSTOMER FOCUS

The more everyone in the company is imbued with knowledge of customers, the more likely that the organization can agree to change to serve them better. Three points if everyone in the work force knows who his or her customers are, knows their needs, and has had direct contact with them. Take away points if that knowledge is confined to pockets of the organization (sales and marketing, senior executives).

REWARDS

Change is easier if managers and employees are rewarded for taking risks, being innovative, and looking for new solutions. Team-based rewards are better than rewards based solely on individual achievement. Reduce points if your company, like most, rewards continuity over change. If managers become heroes for making budget, they won't take risks even if you say you want them to. Also: If employees believe failure will be punished, reduce points.

ORGANIZATION STRUCTURE

The best situation is a flexible organization with little churn—that is, reorganizations are rare and well received. Score yourself lower if you have a rigid structure that has been unchanged for more than five years or has undergone frequent reorganization with little success; that may signal a cynical company culture that fights change by waiting it out.

COMMUNICATION

A company will adapt to change most readily if it has many means of two-way communication that reach all levels of the organization and that all employees use and understand. If communications media are few, often trashed unread, and almost exclusively one-way and top-down, change will be more difficult.

ORGANIZATIONAL HIERARCHY

The fewer levels of hierarchy and the fewer employee grade levels, the more likely an effort to change will succeed. A thick impasto of middle management and staff not only slows decision making but also creates large numbers of people with the power to block change.

PRIOR EXPERIENCE WITH CHANGE

Score three if the organization has successfully implemented major changes in the recent past. Score one if there is no prior experience with major change or if change efforts failed or left a legacy of anger or resentment. Most companies will score two, acknowledging equivocal success in previous attempts to change.

MORALE

Change is easier if employees enjoy working in the organization and the level of individual responsibility is high. Signs of unreadiness to change: low team spirit, little voluntary extra effort, and mistrust. Look for two types of mistrust: between management and employees, and between or among departments.

INNOVATION

Best situation: The company is always experimenting; new ideas are implemented with seemingly little effort; employees work across internal boundaries without much trouble. Bad signs: lots of red tape, multiple signoffs required before new ideas are tried; employees must go through channels and are discouraged from working with colleagues from other departments or divisions.

DECISION MAKING

Rate yourself high if decisions are made quickly, taking into account a wide variety of suggestions; it is clear where decisions are made. Give yourself a low grade if decisions come slowly and are made by a mysterious "them"; there is a lot of conflict during the process, and confusion and finger pointing after decisions are announced.

TOTAL SCORE

IF YOUR SCORE IS

41–51: Implementing change is most likely to succeed. Focus resources on lagging factors (your ones and twos) to accelerate the process.

28–40: Change is possible but may be difficult, especially if you have low scores in the first seven readiness dimensions. Bring those up to speed before attempting to implement large-scale change.

17–27: Implementing change will be virtually impossible without a precipitating catastrophe. Focus instead on (1) building change readiness in the dimensions above and (2) effecting change through skunkworks or pilot programs separate from the organization at large.

Source: T. A. Stewart, "Rate Your Readiness to Change," *Fortune 129,* no. 3 (February 7, 1994): 106–08.

PREMEETING PREPARATION

A. Read "How to Live in a Fad Culture" and evaluate your organization in "Rate your Readiness to Change."

B. Please answer the following questions:

1. Think back on a time when a major change effort took place within your organization or group. What was the change? What preceded it? What happened when the change occurred? How did people react to it? Was it successful?

2. What theories do you have about organizational change? What factors might determine success or failure?

3. What skills are necessary for instituting change?

4. What do you want to learn about organizational change and development?

5. What are the significant learning points from the readings?

C. Read to page 487.

D. If your instructor has assigned the Robbins Self-Assignment Library, use "How Well Do I Respond to Turbulent Change?"

TOPIC INTRODUCTION

Change is a way of life in today's business environment, and the ability to manage change is a key factor in organizational survival.[1] Foreign competition, deregulation, and rapid technological advances are some of the common triggers for change in business. As a result, organizations are merging, restructuring, reengineering, revitalizing, and rethinking how they do business in an effort to keep pace with the changes they confront. Therefore, managers and employees alike need to understand the nature of organizational change.

In spite of environmental pressures for change and the amount of resources devoted to change efforts, they are not always successful. Large organizations are notoriously hard to change. There are several common roadblocks to organizational change.[2]

- Changes often upset the political system in organizations and come into conflict with the vested interests of people who prefer the status quo.
- Managers are limited in their power to make changes in part because complex systems resist change.
- Changes are hard to sustain; some innovations succeed initially but conditions eventually revert to their previous state.
- What works in one part of an organization cannot always be transferred successfully to another area, so standardized change efforts may not be possible.
- Sometimes when organizations most need to change, they may lack the resources (will, energy, trust, slack time) to do so.
- In some U.S. companies, top management looks for quick fixes and suffers from a short attention span. Change programs are not given time to work before the next change fad comes along. This results in employee cynicism about management's commitment to change.

THE NATURE OF CHANGE

Organizational change is usually categorized in terms of magnitude as either incremental or transformative. Incremental change, also known as first-order change, is linear, continuous, and targeted at fixing or modifying problems or procedures. Transformative change, also called second-order change or gamma change, modifies the fundamental structure, systems, orientation, and strategies of the organization.[3] Transformative change is radical and tends to be multidimensional and multilevel. It involves discontinuous shifts in mental or organizational frameworks.[4] Whereas incremental change is analogous to rearranging the furniture in a room and making it more comfortable, transformative change means asking whether this is even the room or floor where we should be.[5] Organizational transformation implies not only new behaviors but also new ways of perceiving and thinking by members. The current trend toward organizational learning is based on a model of continuous change and adaptation.

Change is usually neither easy nor fast, except when there exists a strong consensus about what the organization needs to change and a pent-up demand for change among employees. Although a successful change effort generally requires top-management support, that alone is not sufficient to change a large system. There must be a critical mass of people who support the change. *Critical mass is defined as the smallest number of people and/or groups who must be committed to a change for it to occur.* Successful changes often begin at the periphery of the organization with dedicated general managers who focus energy on work improvements rather than abstract principles such as participation or organizational culture.[6] Their success then moves to the core of the organization as other units imitate their example.

Another requirement for successful change efforts is a sufficient level of trust within the organization so that people are willing to give up the known for the unknown and question some of their basic assumptions. Change almost always requires reexamining and rethinking the assumptions people hold about the environment, the way the organization functions, and their working relationship with other people. People often undergo a mourning period before they can let go of previous ways of behaving, psychological contracts, conceptions of their organization, and relationships. Change requires both new behaviors and organizational learning, which must eventually be institutionalized so that the change can endure. Previously, it was assumed that changes in attitudes led to changes in individual behavior. In reality, the opposite is more likely to occur. Behavior is shaped by the roles people are expected to play within organizations. Therefore, new roles, responsibilities, and relationships force people to develop new attitudes and behaviors.[7]

The study of human behavior reveals that people do not easily change long-term behaviors. Anyone who has tried to give up a cherished "bad habit" understands that behavioral change can be tricky, if not downright difficult or impossible. Lewin described the process of change as unfreezing, moving, and refreezing.[8] *Unfreezing* is accompanied by stress, tension, and a strong felt need for change. The *moving* stage refers to relinquishing old ways of behavior and testing out new behaviors, values, and attitudes that have usually been proposed by a respected source. *Refreezing* occurs when the new behavior is either reinforced, internalized, and institutionalized or rejected and abandoned.

There are some aspects of companies that should never be changed, such as their core values. Figuring out what should not change is just as important as figuring out what to change.[9] Furthermore, too much simultaneous change is disturbing. There has to be some stability for people to hang onto so that they can cope with the seeming chaos of large complex changes.[10]

Based on the preceding lessons, it should be obvious that change is a process rather than an event or a managerial edict. Furthermore, it is a process that is somewhat unpredictable since it is difficult to foresee how all the actors and interconnected parts of a system will react. Once we start tweaking a system, there are usually unanticipated consequences that require some modification in the change plans. Although there may always be a few surprises in a change effort, managers can avoid many problems if they are careful not to move immediately from a superficial diagnosis of a problem to the action steps. There will be more effective results and fewer tensions if a more thorough diagnosis is made of the situation to be changed and if the change process is managed systematically.

THE CHANGE PROCESS

There is no exact blueprint for change that works in every situation, but the essential components in this sequential process are described next and illustrated in Figure 20-1. As with most models of behavior, the steps may blur into one another, but the articulation and recognition of them can help steer a clearer course through a change effort.

Determining the Need for Change

The first step is to determine the organization's readiness for change. Is a change really necessary and who perceives this need? Changes have a greater likelihood of success when people with

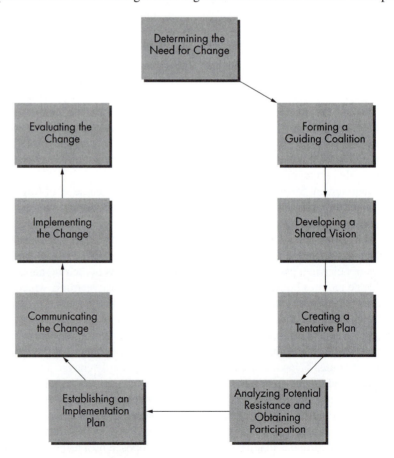

FIGURE 20-1   **Steps in the Change Process**

power believe the status quo is no longer good enough and when there is a critical mass that supports the change.

In this stage, potential change agents consider the costs and whether conditions are favorable for change. This formula helps change agents determine whether it's worthwhile to "rock the boat."[11]

$$C = (D \times S \times P) > X$$

where

C = change
D = dissatisfaction with the current state of affairs or status quo
S = an identifiable and desired end state
P = a practical plan for achieving the desired end state
X = the cost of change to the organization

As Beckhard states: "For change to be possible and for commitment to occur, there has to be enough dissatisfaction with the current state of affairs to mobilize energy toward change. There also has to be some fairly clear conception of what the state of affairs would be if and when the change were successful. Of course, a desired state needs to be consistent with the values and priorities of the client system. There also needs to be some client awareness of practical first steps or starting points toward the desired state."[12]

It is possible to increase the level of dissatisfaction with the status quo by sharing productivity information about competitors with employees or by survey-feedback techniques that present employees with the aggregated results of their individual opinions. In this manner, more people perceive the need for change and form the necessary critical mass.

Diagnosing the situation carefully is another way to ascertain whether there is a real need for change. As any consultant can tell you, it is not uncommon for managers to attribute organizational problems to the wrong source. For example, a hospital administrator received complaints about customer service in the emergency room. He identified the problem as poor communication skills among the nurses and hired a consultant to train them. In the beginning of the seminar, she asked the nurses what they hoped to get out of the training. They erupted and quickly let her know that, in their opinion, nothing was wrong with their communication skills—the real problem was understaffing and poor management. Managers (and consultants) have to poke around and talk to several people at different levels to find the root causes of problems. Otherwise, changes may not address the real issues. Furthermore, diagnosis should be a collaborative effort involving as many people as possible. When people participate in data gathering and diagnosis, they have greater ownership of the results and more commitment to making change happen.

Lewin saw change as a dynamic balance of forces working in opposite directions.[13] He devised the "force field analysis," which assigns pressures for change and resistance to change to opposite sides of an equilibrium state. For example, several years back Ford found itself pressured by foreign competition, declining market share, and stakeholder complaints to change the company. These were some of the forces that promoted change at that time. However, within Ford there were also forces that inhibited change such as an entrenched adversarial union-management relationship, and both managers and workers who were accustomed to a way of working that was less efficient and innovative than much of their competition. Eventually a critical mass of employees became convinced of the need to change in order to keep their jobs. The pressures for change were stronger than the resistance, allowing the company to make major innovations in a fairly short period of time. Identifying the major forces for and against change is a useful aid in diagnosing the situation. Managers have three choices: to increase the strength of a pressure(s) to change, to decrease or neutralize the strength of a resistance(s) to change, or to try to convert a resistance into a pressure for change. The key point here is the conception of change as a dynamic process in which a state of equilibrium is reached.

Many change efforts utilize the principle of creative tension.[14] Creative tension results from perceiving the gap between the ideal situation (the organization's vision) and an honest appraisal of its current reality. The natural tension that results from the gap between the vision and current reality can be resolved by either changing the vision to reflect reality or by improving current conditions so they match the vision. Most change efforts focus on the latter; understanding the gap often motivates people to change the current reality. The nominal group technique found on page 317 is often used in change efforts to diagnose the vision and the reality and then determine how to close the gap.

Organizations sometimes suffer from the Boiled Frog Phenomenon.[15] A frog placed in a pan of cold water fails to notice that the water temperature is gradually rising. The frog continues to sit in the pan and ultimately boils to death. Don't go home and experiment with your own frog, but do remember that organizations that don't pay close attention to environmental changes end up in hot water.

Some leaders raise the heat in their organizations by creating a sense of urgency. Peter Lewis, CEO of Progressive Insurance, paid attention to the finding that customers who bought his high-risk insurance were unhappy with high premiums. Convincing his employees that "our customers actually hate us," they significantly reduced the time it took to process claims and improved customer service.[16] Progressive was not doing poorly prior to this "crisis," but Lewis wanted to counteract complacency and spur his company on to greater improvements.

Like boiled frogs, successful companies can easily become complacent. John Kotter suggests these methods for turning up the heat.[17]

- Create a crisis by allowing a financial loss to occur or an error to blow up.
- Eliminate obvious examples of excess such as corporate jet fleets and gourmet dining rooms (that lull people into seeing only success).
- Set targets such as income, productivity, and cycle time so high that they can't be reached by doing business as usual.
- Share more information about customer satisfaction and financial performance with employees.
- Insist that people talk regularly to unsatisfied customers, unhappy suppliers, and disgruntled shareholders.
- Put more honest discussions of the firm's problems in company newspapers and management speeches. Stop senior management happy talk!

Not all change efforts are problem driven. Appreciative inquiry is a change approach, developed by David Cooperrider, that focuses on "the best of what is."[18] Members identify when their organization is working at its best, create a vision to reflect that state, and work toward making the vision an even greater reality.

Forming a Guiding Coalition

Change efforts are more likely to be successful with a powerful leadership coalition at the helm.[19] Coalition members should be carefully chosen for characteristics such as expertise, good relationships, powerful position, access to information, respected reputation, and dynamic nature and ability to get things done.

General Motors was considering closing a factory when its newly promoted manager asked for another chance. He was convinced that the factory could improve its performance if workers were involved in making decisions and recommendations. The consulting team he hired to design an employee involvement training program insisted on working with a steering committee composed of factory workers. Its members met many of the criteria mentioned earlier—they were dynamic, informal leaders and respected workers. One of them was vociferously opposed to this change effort; his inclusion on the team was an attempt to coopt him. By involving him in the project, the consultants believed he could voice his concerns and have an impact on the design; at the same time, greater exposure to the project and the consultants might lead him to develop more trust and confidence in both. This gamble paid off, and he became a valuable member of the committee and an active champion of the program. The consultants had the steering committee envision an ideal program and its immediate and long-term effects on the factory. Based on the needs and hopes they identified, the consultants designed a tentative training design and presented it to them for their approval. The consultants then incorporated the committee's suggestions into the final design. The committee funneled information about the program to the rest of the factory employees and generated enthusiasm for the initial training workshop. The employee involvement program was highly successful, due primarily to the manager's vision and support and the guidance of the steering committee. The factory's performance increased so significantly that it became a benchmark for other factories and was taken off the closure list.

Developing a Shared Vision

Creating a shared vision makes people more committed to the change. Any major change means asking people to leave the known for the unknown. That won't happen unless there is a clear and compelling vision pulling them away from the status quo. Their participation in shaping what the desired end state should look like gives them a greater sense of control and makes the change less threatening. Successful visions often contain a persuasive idea or an inspiring metaphor. Visions have to be communicated over and over again so people don't lose sight of where they are headed.

Creating a Tentative Plan

Once a vision is established, it must be operationalized into a plan. People need as much certainty as possible about what will happen in the change. However, plans should not be completely *precocinado* or "precooked," as they say in Latin America. It's important to let organizational members have an opportunity to tweak the plan and put their imprint on it. They may be able to see with greater clarity what will or will not work and point out other aspects the planners may not have considered. In the GM example, the consultants presented a tentative training design to the steering committee so the design could be improved by their input. The final plan is created after employees have a chance to provide their input.

Analyzing Potential Resistance and Obtaining Participation

Whenever there is change, some form of resistance to change is likely to appear. Analyzing possible sources of resistance ahead of time means that preventive measures can be taken. Including a resistant informal leader on the GM steering committee was an example of proactively managing resistance.

Because participation is the quick answer to the question of how to deal with resistance to change, change agents try to involve everyone who will be affected by the change. Their input almost always improves the plan. Formal meetings, focus groups, asking for written comments or e-mail responses are all vehicles for employee participation. When resistance is systemic (embedded in the overall system), changes must be made to align other areas of the organization.

Establishing an Implementation Plan

Having a time line with a set schedule for each component of a change process eliminates some of the uncertainty caused by change. Nevertheless, few large-scale change programs play out exactly as planned because complex human systems are somewhat unpredictable. Unforeseen crises, delays, and factors outside the change agents' control will require flexibility. Implementation generally takes more time than anticipated.[20]

Communicating the Change

The general rule of thumb for disseminating changes is to communicate at least three different times in three different ways. Because of the anxiety change evokes, perception sometimes prevents accurate listening. Managers should assume that misunderstandings will occur, no matter how carefully they explain what is to happen. Therefore, communication should be frequent and honest. In-depth communication helps counter the ubiquitous rumors that accompany change projects. There should some vehicle for two-way communication, whereby employees can get their questions answered and their suggestions heard.

Change announcements should:[21]

- Be brief and concise.
- Describe where the organization is now, where it needs to go, and how it will get to the desired state.
- Identify who will implement the change and who will be affected by it.
- Address timing and pacing issues regarding implementation.
- Explain the change's success criteria, the intended evaluation procedures, and the related rewards.
- Identify key things that will not be changing.
- Predict some of the negative aspects that people should anticipate.
- Convey the leader's commitment to the change.
- Explain how people will be kept informed throughout the change process.
- Capitalize on the diversity of the communication styles of the audience.

Implementing the Change

There are numerous pitfalls that may occur during the implementation stage. Some are inevitable and outside the change agents' control, such as industry- or government-related conditions that impede implementation. However, some problems can be avoided by building strong support for the change, clearly defining the expectations and goals, providing sufficient training for employees who are expected to take on new behaviors and skills, involving everyone affected by the change, listening respectfully to complaints, and carefully coordinating implementation activities.[22]

Begin by targeting "low hanging fruit"—highly visible projects that are easily achieved—and then work up to more difficult targets. Once the change looks as if it will succeed, more people will jump on board. To sustain the momentum of the change effort, organizations have to provide resources, build a support network for change agents, help employees develop new competencies and skills, and reinforce new behaviors.[23] When employees act in ways that support the change, they should be rewarded with bonuses, recognition, praise, and so forth.

Evaluating the Change

An evaluation of the change provides another opportunity to ensure the change is accomplishing its purpose and has been institutionalized. Evaluations can be done via surveys, focus groups, large-scale meetings, and so on. Sometimes external evaluators are used in this stage to ensure objectivity. It is not uncommon to find areas that need further improvement or alignment.

If the steps so far outlined have been followed, a great deal of effort will have gone into the change, excitement about reaching change goals will have been high, and the natural tendency will be to experience a letdown once the change has been implemented. Institutionalization should not mean a rehardening of the organization's arteries but a new way of working that combines stability and flexibility. If the change is seen as "complete," those arteries will harden. If it is seen as "continuous," there will be mechanisms in place for continuing to flex and change as situations demand. Some of these conditions necessary for the maintenance of the change are as follows:[24]

1. Management must pay conscious attention to the "continuous transition."
2. Explicit process or procedures for setting priorities for improvement should be instituted.
3. There should be systematic and continual processes of feedback.
4. The reward system should reward people for time and energy spent on these processes.

Leading a Change

Change agents are people who act as catalysts and assume the responsibility for managing change activities. Managing change can be exhilarating, exasperating, and exhausting, which is why it's important to create a supportive network for change agents.

How people feel about a change often depends on their position in the hierarchy and what they stand to lose or gain. For top-level managers, change is viewed as an opportunity "to strengthen the business by aligning operations with strategy, to take on new professional challenges and risks, and to advance their careers. For many employees, however, including middle managers, change is neither sought after nor welcomed. It is disruptive and intrusive. It upsets the balance."[25] Therefore, change agents seek first to understand and respect the different views people have toward a change.

According to Beer and his colleagues, top-down mandated change seldom works. The manager's role in the change process is a series of six steps that they call the critical path.[26] The steps are sequential and their exact timing is of critical importance:

1. Mobilize commitment to change through joint diagnosis of business problems.
2. Develop a shared vision of how to organize and manage for competitiveness.
3. Foster consensus for the new vision, competence to enact it, and cohesion to move it along.
4. Spread revitalization to all departments without pushing it from the top.
5. Institutionalize revitalization through formal policies, systems, and structures.
6. Monitor and adjust strategies in response to problems in the revitalization process.

Tichy identified three similar roles for transformational leaders who are attempting to make fundamental organizational change:[27]

1. **Envisioning** Executives must articulate a clear and credible vision of the new strategic orientation. They also must set new and difficult standards for performance and generate pride in past accomplishments and enthusiasm for the new strategy.
2. **Energizing** Executives must personally demonstrate excitement for the changes and model the behaviors that are expected of others. They must communicate examples of early successes to mobilize energy for change.
3. **Enabling** Executives must provide the resources necessary for undertaking significant change and use rewards to reinforce new behaviors. Leaders must also build an effective top-management team to manage the new organization and develop management practices to support the change process.

Organizational culture, with its well-entrenched norms and beliefs, can be a serious obstacle to change. Therefore, leaders and change agents need to thoroughly understand the culture and use it to leverage change efforts. They can emphasize the aspects of the organizational culture that fit with a proposed change. For example, a traditional value of excellent service might be refocused on the current definition of service rather than an outmoded definition. An in-depth understanding of the culture allows leaders to know what resources to use and how hard to push for a change. It also guides them in gaining participation and knowing how best to implement the change. When cultural norms and assumptions lie in direct opposition to the goals of a change program, determining a way to change the norms has to be part of the implementation plan.

RESISTANCE TO CHANGE

Resistance to change is a natural reaction to change and part of the process of adaptation. This resistance, when it occurs, is often treated as an irrational negative force to be overcome by whatever means necessary; yet, in some cases, resistance to change can be functional for the survival of a system if it helps us perceive the potential problems of a planned change. If an organization tried every new scheme, product, or process that came along, it would soon wander aimlessly, flounder, and die. The positive function of resistance to change is to ensure that plans for change and their ultimate consequences are thought through carefully.

Resistance may occur immediately in the form of criticism about the change or the process, or it may surface months later. Some resistance is passive—people go along with the motions to avoid trouble but don't really support the change, or they quietly sabotage it. Change agents should expect resistance and carefully analyze its sources, which can be categorized as inadequate change goal, inadequate process, personal resistance, political resistance, and systemic resistance.

Inadequate Change Goal   A successful change requires a high-quality idea or goal (e.g., a technical solution to an organizational problem, or a strategic mission that fits the environmental demands and provides competitive advantage) and acceptance by organizational members. People become resistant when they believe the proposed change is a poor idea—they know it won't do what planners say it will accomplish, or they know it will cause other problems.

Inadequate Process   People also resist changes, actively or passively, when the process is not carefully managed. For example, when change is decreed from on high without employee input or when the members of a system do not fully understand why a change is necessary or how it will play out, resistance will be strong. Unfortunately, an inadequate change process can overshadow and engender resistance to the most brilliant idea for change. More changes fail due to a poorly managed process than to technical flaws in the suggested change.

Kanter identified the following sources of resistance that occur when the change process is inadequately managed: (1) feeling out of control, (2) excess uncertainty from not knowing where the change will lead, (3) lack of time to mentally adjust to changes, (4) stress caused by too many changes and forced attention to issues that were formerly routine, (5) feeling compelled to defend the status quo because doing otherwise would involve a loss of face, (6) concerns about future competence when the ground rules seem to be changing, (7) ripple effects to personal plans that will be affected by the change, (8) greater work and energy demands necessitated by the change, (9) past resentments prevent people from supporting the change, and (10) the real threat posed by a change in which some people will be winners and others will be losers.[28]

Personal Resistance   Individual resistance results not from a considered opinion that the proposed change or the process is inappropriate but from personal discomfort with change. Some people fear the unknown and dislike change of any kind. Others worry about whether or not they can learn the new skills a change may require of them. Employees who can readily find work elsewhere if the change does not turn out as they hope may be less resistant than people who feel trapped and insecure about their jobs.

Political Resistance   Political resistance occurs when change threatens people who hold power. Resources (including employees) are often allocated differently as a result of changes; therefore, some people win power while others lose power in the aftermath of change. Furthermore, the status quo is generally the result of past decisions made by people in power. When change agents insist that the status quo is no longer acceptable, those responsible for former decisions may feel insulted and become defensive. One solution to this problem is emphasizing that former innovations or decisions were appropriate when they were made; because times have changed, however, new decisions and directions are necessary for organizational success.[29]

Systemic Resistance   At the organizational level, resistance often occurs due to habit ("This is the way we've always done things"), sunk costs invested in the status quo,[30] and problems caused by internal congruence. Changes hit a roadblock when only one aspect of the system is changed without modifying the other components.

To implement most changes, we also need to modify the performance review system, recruiting, compensation policies and systems, career planning, and human resources planning systems.[31] For example, when a chemical company decided to adopt a global strategy, it was not enough to change its production standards and capacity. It also started recruiting employees with international backgrounds and foreign language skills. The company established a policy that overseas experience was a prerequisite for senior management positions. These complementary changes in the system removed any obstacles that may have prevented employees from adopting an international focus.

In the preceding chapter, we wrote that fit among the components of an organization promotes effectiveness. Internal congruence among strategy, structure, culture, and people is responsible for short-term performance.[32] When major changes occur in the environment and organizations are forced to adapt or fail, however, that same congruence may turn into systemic resistance. Changing an organization that is meticulously aligned to an obsolete strategy or product takes on mammoth proportions. The solution, according to Tushman and O'Reilly, is to seek congruence during stable, evolutionary periods when change is primarily incremental but be willing to destroy that alignment and start over again when confronted with discontinuous, revolutionary change.[33] This is easier said than done because organizations, particularly successful organizations, cling to traditional ways.

Tactics for Dealing with Resistance

Resistance to change is not irrational, and managers who understand the reasons for resistance are better able to deal with it constructively. Managers often resent and become angry with employees who resist change. However, this reaction does nothing to reduce the resistance and often exacerbates an already difficult situation. Empathy is the starting point for dealing with resistance—trying to understand how others view the change without judging their reactions. Other effective tactics for dealing with resistance to change are:[34]

1. **Education and Communication** Help people understand the reasons for the change, the form it will take, and the likely consequences. This clears up misunderstandings that often cause resistance.
2. **Participation and Involvement** Encourage others to help with the design and implementation of the changes. This creates commitment to the change and usually improves the quality of the change decisions. The disadvantages of this tactic are the time it consumes and, if the participants lack the necessary expertise, their solutions may be inadequate.
3. **Facilitation and Support** Provide encouragement, support, training, counseling, and resources to help the people who are affected by the change.
4. **Co-optation** Co-optation occurs when the leaders of the resistance are "bought off" by allowing them a role in the change process. This is positive when previously unrepresented factions are given a voice, as in the GM example. Co-optation is sometimes used manipulatively to simply silence critics.
5. **Negotiation and Agreement** Offer incentives in return for decreased resistance to the change.
6. **Manipulation** Manipulation usually takes the form of distorting or withholding information or starting false rumors so that employees agree to a change. For example, one multinational wanted their employees to switch to a less expensive retirement plan. HR staff presented only the attractive features of the new plan and suppressed the information that employees would fare worse under the new plan. When people realize they have been manipulated, they lose the trust that is so essential to the change process and can become even more resistant.
7. **Coercion** When people are threatened with negative incentives (e.g., unwanted transfers, denial of promotion and pay raises, negative performance evaluations, etc.) if they do not accept a change, this is called coercion. Most people resent coercion, and its use may irreparably harm relationships. However, at times there is no other alternative to reduce resistance.

The first three tactics, although more time-consuming, are more likely to result in commitment to the change. The last three tactics may yield compliance with the change but not commitment. The result of co-optation depends on the intentions behind it.

Johnson & Johnson devised a method for decreasing resistance to change. Although size is a competitive advantage in maintaining financial strength and market leadership, the company was concerned that its size (170 distinct operating companies) could prevent rapid adaptation to emerging opportunities and environmental changes. Its nine-member executive committee devised a management process called FrameworkS because they wanted "frameworks" to better understand issues that cut across the company's decentralized structure, such as markets, customer expectations, and new opportunities. The capital S helps remind them that there are multiple frames through which they must view the diverse businesses in their global organization. The company forms FrameworkS teams—task forces comprised of members from various companies, countries, and functional areas who extensively research topics important to the company's future. Their findings are presented to and discussed by all the other FrameworkS teams and the executive committee. After including this input, the teams develop action plans, which are then implemented. The FrameworkS program has paid off in tangible results, such as setting up new businesses and entering new markets. However, the intangible results are equally impressive. The executive committee is more in touch with how employees and customers think, operating has learned it can push ahead to take advantage of opportunities without waiting for edicts from the top of the hierarchy, and "there is a greater receptivity to deal with change that did not exist five years ago."[35]

PROCEDURE FOR GROUP MEETING: THE HOLLOW SQUARE EXERCISE[36]

Materials: Each group should bring one pair of scissors and four envelopes unless the instructor will provide the necessary materials.

This exercise is designed to simulate the stage in the change process when the planners of a change must communicate it to the people who will implement the change. (Time allotted: 95 min.)

STEP 1. The class divides into groups of eight people. These groups will then further subdivide into 4 planners and 4 implementers. If there is an odd number of students, place three to five people on the planning team. The implementation teams, however, should always consist of exactly 4 people.

STEP 2. Once the groups have decided who will be planners and implementers, the implementers will wait in a separate area until the instructor has given the planners their instructions. Please do not read the instructions for the other team.

STEP 3. The instructor reads the planning teams their instructions (page 490) and either provides them with the materials they need to perform the exercise or explains how to obtain them.

STEP 4. The planning teams have 30 minutes to plan how they will communicate the instructions to their implementation team.

STEP 5. The instructor reads the implementation teams their instructions (page 483).

STEP 6. All implementation teams begin the 15-minute assembly period at the signal of the instructor. The first team to complete the assembly wins. During this time, the planning team can only observe and refrain from making any noises that might distract or influence the implementing team.

STEP 7. When the assembly period is completed, each participant should complete both sections of the evaluation that follows. Then each subgroup should average its scores for each question (i.e., the implementation team comes up with its own team average and the planning team does likewise).

STEP 8. *Group Discussion.* The two subgroups that worked together compare their evaluation scores. Discuss the following questions and choose a representative to present your answers to the class during the plenary session. (15 min.)
1. Are there any differences in the way the planning and implementation teams perceived and evaluated each other? Why or why not?
2. What did the planning team do that helped the implementation team? Did they do anything that hindered the implementers? Use the following chart to record these factors.
3. What did the implementation team do that helped it succeed in this exercise? Did the team do anything that hindered its success?
4. What can you learn about organizational changes from this exercise?

EVALUATION OF THE IMPLEMENTATION TEAM

a. How well was the puzzle completed?

1   2   3   4   5   6   7

Not at   Very
all well   well

b. How faithfully did the implementers follow the planning team's instructions?

1   2   3   4   5   6   7

Not at   Very
all well   well

c. How well organized was the implementation team?

1   2   3   4   5   6   7

Not at   Very
all well   well

d. How well did the implementation team understand the planning team's instructions?

1   2   3   4   5   6   7

Not at   Very
all well   well

e. To what extent did the implementation team try to clarify the planning team's instructions (e.g., asking questions, paraphrasing instructions, etc.)?

1   2   3   4   5   6   7

Not at   Very
all well   well

EVALUATION OF THE PLANNING TEAM

a. How clear (explicit, unequivocal) were the instructions given by the planning team?

$$1 \quad 2 \quad 3 \quad 4 \quad 5 \quad 6 \quad 7$$

Not at   Completely
all clear   clear

b. How well organized was the planning team?

$$1 \quad 2 \quad 3 \quad 4 \quad 5 \quad 6 \quad 7$$

Not at   Very
all well   well

c. To what extent did the planning team involve the implementation team in their strategies?

$$1 \quad 2 \quad 3 \quad 4 \quad 5 \quad 6 \quad 7$$

Not at   To a
all   large degree

STEP 9. *Plenary Session.* Each group presents its findings. (15 min.)

Analysis of the Hollow Square Exercise

Planning Team Actions That		Implementation Team Actions That	
Helped	Hindered	Helped	Hindered

The class as a whole discusses the following questions: (15 min.)

1. What feelings and thoughts did the implementation teams experience while awaiting the instructions for an unknown task?
2. How did the implementation teams organize to accomplish this task?
3. How much time did the planning teams devote to figuring out how to transmit their message to the implementation teams?
4. Did the time at which the planners brought the implementers into the process (early on or just before the assembly period) have an effect upon the proceedings? If so, what was the effect and why did it occur?
5. What parallels can you draw between this simulation and organizational change efforts you have observed or experienced?
6. Look at Figure 20-3 for lessons about communicating changes.

INSTRUCTIONS FOR THE IMPLEMENTATION TEAMS

1. You have the responsibility for carrying out a task for four people in accordance with the instructions given to you by your planning team. Your planning team can call you back to the classroom to receive these instructions at any time during their 30-minute preparation period. However, if they have not called you by _____ (five minutes before you are scheduled to carry out your task), you should report to them. Your task is programmed to start exactly at _____. Once you begin, your planning team cannot provide you with any more instructions.
2. Your mission is to complete the assigned task as quickly as possible.
3. While you are waiting for the planning team to call you in to receive your instructions, please discuss and take notes on the following questions. Your notes will be useful during the debriefing session.

    a. What feelings and thoughts are you experiencing as you await the instructions for an unknown task?

    b. How can the four of you organize yourselves as a team to accomplish this task?

FOLLOW-UP

Organization development (OD) is a specialized area of organizational behavior focused on planned change. It is a "system-wide process of data collection, diagnosis, action, planning, intervention, and evaluation aimed at: (1) enhancing congruence between organizational structure, process, strategy, people, and culture, (2) developing new and creative organizational solutions, and (3) developing the organization's self-renewing capacity. It occurs through collaboration of organizational members working with a change agent using behavioral science theory, research, and technology."[37] Many change agents are external consultants, but large corporations employ internal OD consultants. OD emphasizes organizational effectiveness and health and tries to improve organizational capacity to solve problems and cope with changes in the external environment.[38] Unlike traditional consulting, which involves diagnosis and recommendations by outside experts, OD consultants facilitate a process in which organizational members participate in diagnosing the system and agreeing on the changes that should be made. The rationale is that greater participation and involvement increase the likelihood that change will actually happen.

    There are numerous OD interventions; we'll describe some of the more commonly used interventions.[39] In *survey feedback*, organization members are surveyed or interviewed, the results are often shown first to top management (to avoid surprising them and give them time to prepare a constructive response) and then fed back to the surveyed group. The group discusses its diagnosis and decides on action steps to pursue. Survey feedback raises employee expectations that improvements will be made once the data are presented. Therefore, managers have to commit beforehand to implementing suggested changes and perhaps changing their own managerial style if that is identified as a problem.

    In *process consultation*, a process facilitator observes a work group or a manager in action and provides insight about what is occurring around, within, and between people. For example, a process facilitator may point out to a management team how it handles disagreement and coach team members so they have more skills to deal with differences in the future.

    In *team-building interventions*, consultants usually take work team members to a retreat location where they can get to know one another better and establish a more effective way of working together. Consultants often provide performance data that show why change is necessary and guide them through discussions and clarifications of the team's goals, roles, procedures for working together, and interpersonal norms.

    OD programs do not always work, but when implemented correctly, they can have positive effects on performance. Their success depends, among other factors, on management commitment, organizational readiness for change, the skill of the change agents involved, the appropriateness of the intervention for the specific organization, and enough slack to devote time and resources to the change. Using multiple methods in change interventions (e.g., team building, survey feedback, and skill training in the same change program) is more successful than using a single method.[40]

CULTURE AND CHANGE

The values that underlie OD are:[41]

- Respect for people
- Trust and support
- Equality and power sharing
- Candor and confrontation
- Participation
- Collaboration

These values naturally reflect those of the U.S. culture where OD was developed. One could argue that, more accurately, they reflect the values of a humanistic, democratic U.S. subculture—otherwise, we would not require special programs to encourage companies to adopt behaviors more in keeping with OD values. Whereas participation is the best way to allow U.S. employees to feel some sense of ownership of the change process, other cultures (e.g., the Philippines) expect their leaders to make decisions without their input. OD values fit low-context cultures characterized by low power distance, individualism, masculinity, and moderate levels of uncertainty avoidance.[42] However, OD is used successfully all over the world, primarily in developed nations, but it has to be adapted to the local culture.

Cultures vary in terms of their comfort with change. Few countries value change more than the United States. "In the Old World respect came from a valuable heritage, and any change from that norm had to be justified. In America, however, the status quo was no more than the temporary product of past changes, and it was the resistance to change that demanded an explanation. A failure to change with the times was more than just a private misfortune; it was a socially and organizationally subversive condition. This attitude still persists in America, particularly in the corporate world."[43] Cultures with a stronger value for the past and tradition (e.g., England, China) are generally more resistant to change. In such cultures, managers will tend to be less proactive about making changes, and change processes are likely to take more time. The same is true of cultures that believe more in fate than in human control of one's destiny.

Cultures also vary in their beliefs about how change occurs. U.S. companies often assume that modifying the organizational structure results in organizational change. This line of thought presupposes that a new structure causes changes in interpersonal relationships and processes, which leads eventually to changes in individual attitudes and mentalities. Most European and Japanese companies, however, have opposite assumptions about change. When they want to make a change, they begin by trying to change the attitudes and mentalities of their key people. Next, they modify the flow of communication and decision-making processes. Finally, they consolidate the changes by realigning the structure to mirror the changes that have already occurred. Bartlett and Ghoshal note, however, that these different national biases seem to be disappearing as global companies learn different approaches from one another.[44]

Managers in cross-cultural or multicultural settings need to understand the various cultural values about change and recognize that change interventions that work in one country may not succeed elsewhere.[45]

TOTAL QUALITY MANAGEMENT (TQM)

The *quality movement* was started by Edward Deming, an American management consultant who taught his famous 14 principles to the Japanese in the 1950s; where at the time, the "Made in Japan" label was synonymous with poor quality.[46] Japan's current reputation for producing goods of extremely high quality is credited in large part to Deming. Is there a cultural reason why TQM was so readily adopted in Japan? Several theories have been advanced to answer this question. Japan had a long history of fine craftsmanship among artisans that was transferred to the factory floor and technicians via TQM. Furthermore, Japan's scarce natural resources and cultural orientations of collectivism and harmony with nature created a belief that technology was a resource to be used frugally and carefully to obtain the maximum value. This resulted in systems thinking as well as an internal focus on productivity and manufacturing operations. The resulting organizational structures and mind-set made Japanese companies fertile soil for TQM.[47]

In addition to improving quality, other basic goals of quality programs are to lower costs; speed up the flow of information, materials, and products; increase flexibility; reduce inventory; and improve customer satisfaction. Quality programs focus on managing the process of the work rather than people and give workers the challenge of constantly trying to improve the quality of the work processes, placing primary emphasis on the customer. This provides workers with a sense of meaning. Such programs teach statistics as a common language that is used to measure variances from the perfect quality standard. Each employee is taught to inspect his or her own work so that defects and reworks are reduced or even eliminated. This emphasis on immediate feedback on quality stimulates needs for achievement. Quality programs generally involve group problem-solving efforts, which meet people's need for affiliation. Quality programs focus on the requirements of the task, but their manner of doing so also meets the motivational needs of employees.[48]

Continuous improvement, *kaizen* in Japanese, is a key factor in total quality programs. This term is sometimes used interchangeably by companies to describe their total quality effort. Continuous improvement programs are designed to take advantage of employee experience and commitment to improving the products, services, and work practices of the organization.[49] In recognition of the importance of quality in global competition, the U.S. government initiated the Malcolm Baldridge Quality Award to honor organizations that attain "world-class" quality in their products, services, and operations. The competition criteria are:

- A plan to keep improving all operations continuously
- A system for measuring these improvements accurately
- A strategic plan based on benchmarks that compare the company's performance with the world's best
- A close partnership with suppliers and customers that feeds improvements back into the operation
- A deep understanding of the customers so that their wants can be translated into products
- A long-lasting relationship with customers, going beyond the delivery of the products to include sales, service, and ease of maintenance
- A focus on preventing mistakes, rather than merely correcting them
- A commitment to improving quality that runs from the top of the organization to the bottom[50]

TQM is a good example of a program that was treated like a fad in some companies and later dropped while it produced (and is still producing) impressive results at other organizations. Even though some of its technical practices have fallen into disuse, TQM's core ideas, particularly its emphasis on quality and continuous improvement, are still visible in many companies.

 LEARNING POINTS

1. Managing change has become a crucial skill for both managers and employees.
2. Incremental change is linear, continuous, and targeted at fixing or modifying problems or procedures. Transformative change is radical, discontinuous, multidimensional and multilevel, and modifies the fundamental structure, systems, orientation, and strategies of the organization.
3. Critical mass is defined as the smallest number of people and/or groups who must be committed to a change for it to occur.
4. Successful changes often begin at the periphery of the organization with dedicated general managers who focus energy on work improvements rather than abstract principles.
5. Lewin described the process of change as unfreezing, moving, and refreezing.
6. Change is a process rather than an event or a managerial edict.

7. The essential components of the change process are determining the need for change, forming a guiding coalition, developing a shared vision, creating a tentative plan, analyzing potential resistance and obtaining participation, establishing an implementation plan, communicating the change, implementing the change, and evaluating the change.

8. Change agents are people who act as catalysts and assume the responsibility for managing change activities.

9. According to Tichy, the role of a transformational leader consists of envisioning, energizing, and enabling.

10. Resistance to change is a natural reaction and part of the process of adaptation.

11. Managers should seek to understand the source of resistance and listen carefully to concerns employees have regarding proposed changes rather than seeing those who resist as adversaries.

12. Resistance to change can be caused by inadequate change goals, inadequate change processes, personal resistance, political resistance, and systemic resistance.

13. Tactics for dealing with resistance include empathy, education and communication, participation and involvement, facilitation and support, co-optation, negotiation and agreement, manipulation, and coercion.

14. Organization development (OD) is a systemwide process of data collection, diagnosis, action, planning, intervention, and evaluation aimed at enhancing organizational fit, problem solving, effectiveness, health, and self-renewal.

 **FOR MANAGERS**

- Don't make changes just for the sake of making change. Too much change in a system is just as frustrating to employees as the feeling that any change is impossible. Think through the pros and cons of any change very carefully before taking action. For some people, making changes has more to do with their own need to impact the system than with the needs of the system.

- Trust is an important aspect of any change effort. Employees do not believe management's sense of urgency or new visions for the future unless their trust has been won. Clients seldom make significant movement until they trust their OD consultants. Trust allows people to unfreeze and move forward. Making promises regarding a change that cannot be kept or promising too much diminishes trust.

- Almost all organizations should focus energy on innovation and change on a regular basis. But not everyone in the organization needs to be involved in this. Some organizations utilize parallel or collateral organization structures. Parallel organizations have the freedom and flexibility to do the innovating and problem solving, while the "maintenance organization" carries on with business as usual. People who dislike uncertainty and who cherish a fondness for the status quo are more satisfied in maintenance organizations, while the creative, entrepreneurial types prefer the parallel organization. Managers who point out that both of these structures and types of employees are equally valuable to the organization can avoid potential conflict between these groups.[51]

- The more people have been allowed to participate in the change effort, the more committed they will be to its success.

- New programs require careful attention and nurturing. Having the head of a new program report directly to the CEO until the program is well established is one way of ensuring its survival.

- Change is not always a rational, linear process. Where major organizational transformation is required, change involves a leap of faith to move the organization to another plane that cannot always be seen from the point of departure. For this reason, such changes require shared values and symbolic gestures by managers.

- People often go through a period of "mourning" in large-scale change projects. Accepting this difficulty, acknowledging it with employees, allowing them to vent their feelings, and planning ritual celebrations like farewell parties help people to get through this period more easily.[52]

PERSONAL APPLICATION ASSIGNMENT

"How are you supposed to change the tires on a car when it's going 60 miles per hour?"

—Epitaph of a change agent

The topic of this assignment is to think back on a significant experience involving organizational change. Choose an experience that intrigues you and that you want to learn more about.

A. *Concrete Experience*
   1. *Objectively* describe the experience (who, what, when, where, how information) (2 points)
   2. *Subjectively* describe your feelings, perceptions, and thoughts that occurred during (not after) the experience. What did others seem to be feeling? (2 points)

B. *Reflective Observation*
   1. Looking back at the experience, what were the perspectives of the key actors (including you)? (2 points)
   2. Why did the people involved (including you) behave as they did? (2 points)

C. *Abstract Conceptualization*

1. Relate concepts or theories from the assigned readings or the lecture to the experience. Explain thoroughly how they apply to your experience. Please apply at least two concepts or theories and cite them correctly. (4 points)

D. *Active Experimentation*

1. What did you learn about change from this experience (1 point)
2. What did you learn about yourself? (1 point)
3. What action steps will you take to be more effective in the future? (2 points)

E. *Integration, Synthesis, and Writing*

1. Did you integrate and synthesize the four sections? (1 point)
2. Was the personal application assignment well written and easy to understand? (1 point)
3. Was it free of spelling and grammatical errors? (2 points)

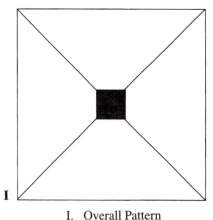

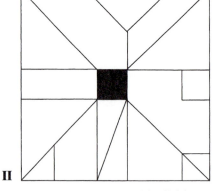

I. Overall Pattern

II. Detailed Assembly Guide

FIGURE 20-2 **Hollow Square Key**

INSTRUCTIONS FOR THE PLANNING TEAMS

Unless your instructor provides you with different materials, each member should cut out the shapes on either the A, B, C, or D pages found at the end of the chapter. Please do not mix these pieces up (keep all A pieces separate, etc.). Thus, each of the four members of the planning team will have a separate group of four shapes in front of them as we read the following instructions. (If there are five members on the team, two members can share one set of shapes.) These sets, when properly assembled with pieces from other participants, will make a hollow square design.

During the next 30 minutes, your task is to:

1. Plan how these pieces, distributed among you, should be assembled to make the design shown in Figure 20-2.
2. Instruct your operating team on how to implement your plan so as to complete your task ahead of the other teams. You may begin instructing your operating team at any time during the 30-minute planning period—but no later than 5 minutes before they are to begin the assembly process at _____ .

General Rules

1. You must keep all your four pieces in front of you at all times.
2. You may not touch the pieces of other planning team members or trade pieces with other members of your team during the planning or instructing phase.
3. You may not show Figure 20-2 to the implementation team at any time. Nor may you provide them with written instructions or drawings.
4. You may not actually assemble the entire square at any time (this is to be left to your operating team at the moment the assembly period begins).
5. You may not number or otherwise mark the pieces at any time during the exercise.
6. **Members of your operating team must also observe the preceding rules until the signal is given to begin the assembly.**
7. Just before the assembly time starts, place your four pieces into an envelope and give the envelope to an implementer. This will allow the implementers on each team to start from an equal position.
8. When time is called for your operating team to begin assembling the pieces, you may give no further instructions. Just step back and observe the implementation team at work without making any noises that might distract or influence the implementers.

A

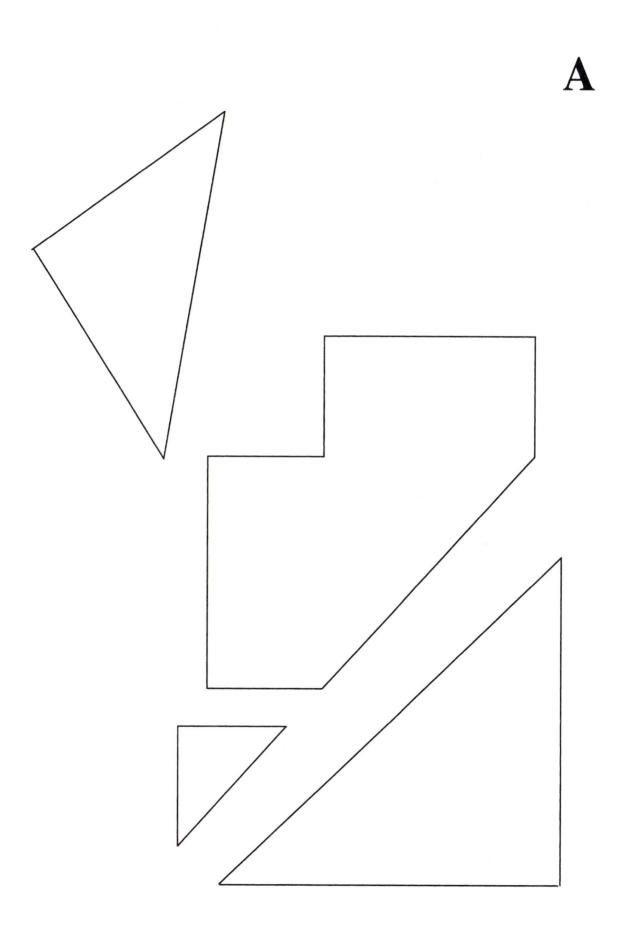

B

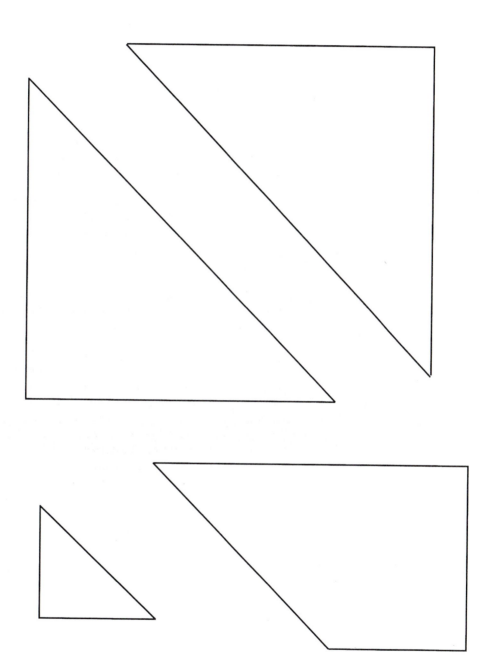

C

D

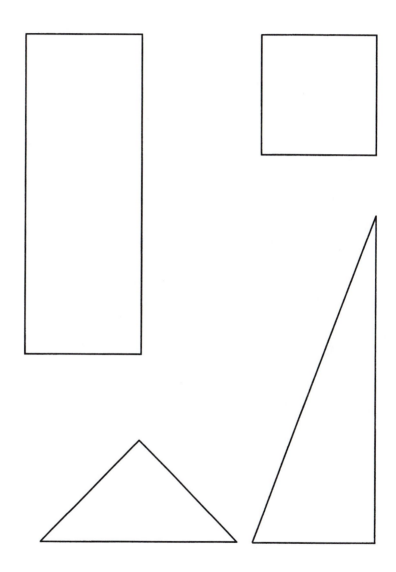

Problems that may occur when one group makes plans that another group is to carry out:

1. Planners sometimes impose restrictions on themselves that are unnecessary.
2. It is sometimes difficult for planners to see the task from the point of view of the implementers.
3. Sometimes in planning, more attention is given to details while the larger clues and possibilities go unnoticed.
4. Planners sometimes fail to apportion their time wisely because they plunge into the act of planning before they think through their entire task and the amount of time available to them.
5. Planners sometimes have different understandings of their task and the boundaries in which they must operate.
6. When members of a planning team fail to listen to one another, time is lost in subsequent efforts to clarify what each party meant.
7. Sometimes planners fail to prepare a proper physical setup for the implementation team.
8. Sometimes planners become so involved in the planning process that they do not plan their method of instructing the implementers.

Common problems when planners instruct implementers:

1. Sometimes the planners do not consider the implementers' anxieties when they orient them to the environment and task.
2. Planners may not allow enough time for instruction and fail to help the operators feel prepared and comfortable about doing their job.
3. Planners may not encourage questions from the implementers and, therefore, assume greater understanding on the part of the implementers than really exists.
4. The planners' own feelings of anxiety or insecurity are likely to be transmitted to the implementers.
5. Planners sometimes give detailed instructions before giving the implementers an "overall" feel for the task.
6. Planners sometimes stress minute problems instead of more important points.
7. The instructions may be given in a way that discourages members of an operating group from working as a team.

Common problems when operators carry out the plans of others:

1. If instructions are confusing, implementers tend to display irritation toward each other and the planners.
2. If instructions are unclear, considerable time will be spent in clarification.
3. Members of an operating team will often have different perceptions of their instructions.
4. The factor of pressure will influence different implementers in different ways—the efficiency of some will go up and the efficiency of others will decline.
5. If members of an operating group do not feel themselves to be a team, they will usually perform less efficiently.

FIGURE 20-3   **Lessons About Communicating Changes**
Source: Adapted from B. Bass, "When Planning for Others," *Journal of Applied Behavioral Science 6*, no. 2 (1970): 151–71. Used with permission.

ENDNOTES

[1] "The Nimble Giants: Hard-Learned Lessons in the Art of Change Are Paying Off at Last," *Business Week* (March 28, 1994): 64–69.

[2] Some of these pitfalls appear in R. M. Kanter, B. A. Stein, and T. D. Jick, *The Challenge of Organizational Change: How Companies Experience It and Leaders Guide It* (New York: The Free Press, 1992): 5–8.

[3] W. W. Burke and G. H. Litwin, "A Causal Model of Organizational Performance and Change," *Journal of Management 18* (1992): 523–45.

[4] Gamma change is described in R. Golombiewski, K. Billingsley, and S. Yeager, "Measuring Change and Persistence in Human Affairs: Types of Changes Generated by OD Design,"

Journal of Applied Behavioral Science 12 (1975): 133–57. First- and second-order change is discussed in A. Levy, "Second-Order Planned Change: Definition and Conceptualization," *Organizational Dynamics* (Summer 1986): 4–20.

[5] This analogy was created by Ken Wilbur, *A Sociable God* (New York: McGraw-Hill, 1983).

[6] M. Beer, R. A. Eisenstat, and B. Spector, "Why Change Programs Don't Produce Change," *Harvard Business Review* (November–December 1990): 158–66.

[7] Ibid., p. 159.

[8] K. Lewin, "Frontiers in Group Dynamics," *Human Relations 1* (1947): 5–41.

[9] J. C. Collins, "Change Is Good—But First Know What Should Never Change," *Fortune 131*, no. 10 (May 29, 1995): 141.

[10] L. D. Goodstein and W. W. Burke, "Creating Successful Organization Change," *Organizational Dynamics 19*, no. 4 (1991): 5–17.

[11] This formula was originally developed by D. Gleicher of Arthur D. Little and later modified by M. Beer, *Organization Change and Development: A System View* (Glenview, IL: Scott, Foresman, 1980). See also A. Armenakis, M. Harris, and K. Mossholder, "Creating Readiness for Large-Scale Change," *Human Relation 46* (1993): 681–703.

[12] R. Beckhard, "Strategies for Large System Change," in D. A. Kolb, I. M. Rubin, and J. S. Osland, *The Organizational Behavior Reader* (Englewood Cliffs, NJ: Prentice Hall, 1990).

[13] K. Lewin, *Field Theory in Social Science* (New York: Harper & Row, 1951).

[14] R. Fritz, *The Path of Least Resistance* (New York: Ballantine, 1989) and *Creating* (New York: Ballantine, 1990).

[15] N. M. Tichy and S. Sherman, *Control Your Destiny or Someone Else Will* (New York: Harper, 1994). This book describes the principles and actions Jack Welch used to make major changes at General Electric. The appendix contains a "Handbook for Revolutionaries," a step-by-step guide to change.

[16] B. Dumaine, "Times Are Good? Create a Crisis," *Fortune* (June 28, 1993): 123–30.

[17] J. P. Kotter, "Kill Complacency." *Fortune 134*, no. 3 (August 5, 1996): 170.

[18] C. Cooperrider and S. Srivastva, "Appreciative Inquiry in Organizational Life," in *Organizational Change and Development 1*, eds. R. Woodman and W. Pasmore (Greenwich, CT: JAI Press, 1987): 129–70. The Woodman and Pasmore annual series is an excellent source of current research in this field.

[19] J. P. Kotter, "Leading Change," *Harvard Business Review* (March–April 1995): 59–67.

[20] L. Alexander, "Successfully Implementing Strategic Decisions," *Long Range Planning 18*, no. 3 (1985): 91–97.

[21] T. D. Jick, "Implementing Change," in his book *Managing Change: Cases and Concepts* (Boston: Irwin, 1993): 200.

[22] Jick, "Implementing Change," p. 194; and Alexander, "Successfully Implementing Strategic Decisions."

[23] T. C. Cummings and C. G. Worley, *Organization Development and Change* (Cincinnati, OH: South-Western, 1997).

[24] R. Beckhard and R. Harris, *Organizational Transitions: Managing Complex Change* (Reading, MA: Addison-Wesley, 1987).

[25] P. Strebel, "Why Do Employees Resist Change?" *HBR* (May–June 1996): 86.

[26] Beer et al., *"Why Change Programs Don't Produce Change,"* pp. 161–65.

[27] This quotation is taken from T. C. Cummings and C. G. Worley, *Organization Development and Change*, p. 478; however, the primary source of this information is D. Nadler and M. Tushman, "Organizational Framebending: Principles for Managing Reorientation," *Academy of Management Executive 3* (1989): 194–202.

[28] R. M. Kanter's *The Change Masters* (New York: Simon & Schuster, 1983).

[29] Ibid.

[30] Cummings and Worley, *Organization Development and Change*.

[31] R. Beckhard and W. Pritchard, *Changing the Essence* (San Francisco: Jossey-Bass, 1992).

[32] D. Nadler and M. Tushman, *Competing by Design* (New York: Oxford University Press, 1997).

[33] M. Tushman and C. A. O'Reilly, "Amibidextrous Organizations: Managing Evolutionary and Revolutionary Change," *California Management Review 38*, no. 4 (1996): 8–30.

[34] J. P. Kotter and L. A. Schlesinger, "Choosing Strategies for Change," *Harvard Business Review* (March–April 1979): 106–14.

[35] R. S. Larsen, "FrameworkS: Turning the Challenges of Change into Opportunities for Growth," *Chief Executive 144* (May 1999): 12.

[36] This exercise was developed by Dr. Bernard Bass, Director, the Center for Leadership Studies, SUNY Binghamton, and is used with his permission.

[37] M. Beer, *Organization Change and Development* (Santa Monica, CA: Goodyear Publishing, 1980).

[38] W. L. French and C. H. Bell, Jr., *Organizational Development: Behavioral Sciences Interventions for Organizational Improvement* (Upper Saddle River, NJ: Prentice-Hall, 1999).

[39] See French and Bell, *Organizational Development* and Cummings and Worley, *Organization Development and Change*, for comprehensive descriptions of interventions. See S. Schein, *Process Consultation II: Its Role in Organizational Development* (Reading, MA: Addison-Wesley, 1987) for an in-depth review or process consultation. For team building, see W. Dyer, *Team Building: Issues and Alternatives* (Readings, MA: Addison-Wesley, 1987) and J. Katzenbach and D. Smith, *The Wisdom of Teams* (Cambridge, MA: Harvard Business School Press, 1993).

[40] J. B. Nicholas, "The Comparative Impact of Organization Development Interventions on Hard Criteria Measures," *Academy of Management Review* (October 1982): 531–42; and J. I. Porras and P. O. Berg, "The Impact of Organization Development," *Academy of Management Review 3* (1978): 249–66.

[41] Cummings and Worley, *Organization Development and Change*.

[42] K. Johnson, "Estimating National Culture and O. D. Values," in *Global and International Organization Development*, eds. P. Sorenson, Jr., T. Head, K. Johnson, N. Mathys, J. Preston, and D. Cooperrider (Champaign, IL: Stipes, 1995): 266–81; and A. Jaeger, "Organization Development and National Culture: Where's the Fit?" *Academy of Management Review 11* (1986): 178–90.

[43] W. Bridges, "Managing Organizational Change," in ed. W. W. Burke, *Managing Organizational Change* (New York: American Management Association, 1995): 20.

[44] C. A. Bartlett and S. Ghoshal, *Transnational Management* (Boston: Irwin McGraw-Hill, 2000).

[45] This article describes the various forms of organizational change efforts that emerge in different cultures—C. Faucheux, G. Amado, and A. Laurent, "Organizational Development and Change," *Annual Reviews of Psychology 33* (1982): 343–70. See also K. E. Weick and R. E. Quinn, "Organizational Change and Development," *Annual Review of Psychology 50* (1999): 361–86.

[46] M. Tribus, "Deming's Redefinition of Management," *The Organizational Behavior Reader* D. Kolb, J. Osland, and I. Rubin (eds.) (Upper Saddle River, NJ: Prentice-Hall, 1995): 654–64; M. Walton, *Demings Management at Work* (New York: Putnam, 1990); J. M. Juran, "Made in U.S.A.: A Renaissance in Quality," *Harvard Business Review 71* (1993): 42–50; and A. V. Feigenbaum, "How Total Quality Counters Three Forces of Internal Competitiveness," *National Productivity Review 13* (1994): 327–30.

[47] A. Bird and S. Kotha, "U.S. and Japanese Perceptions of Advanced Manufacturing Technologies: Revitalizing the Convergence/Divergence Debate," *Research in International Business and International Relations 6*, S. Beechler and A. Bird (eds.) (1994): 73–102; J. Liker, *Engineered in Japan* (New York: Oxford, 1995); W. M. Fruin, *Knowledge Works: Managing Intellectual Capital at Toshiba* (New York: Oxford, 1997).

[48] D. A. Garvin, *Managing Quality: The Strategic and Competitive Edge* (New York: Free Press, 1988) and W. H. Schmidt and J. Finnigan, *The Race Without a Finish Line* (San Francisco: Jossey-Bass, 1992) provide a good starting place for reading about the quality movement.

[49] D. M. Scrodoeder and A. G. Robinson, "America's Most Successful Export to Japan: Continuous Improvement Programs," *Sloan Management Review*, Spring 1991, 67–81; L. S. Vansina, "Total Quality Control: An Overall Organizational Improvement Strategy," *National Productivity Review*, (Winter 1989/1990): 59–73.

[50] See Schmidt and Finnigan, *The Race Without a Finish Line* op. cit. for lessons from the Baldrige Award winners.

[51] For more information on parallel organizations, see B. A. Stein and R. M. Kanter, "Building the Parallel Organization: Creating Mechanisms for Permanent Quality of Work Life," *Journal of Applied Behavioral Science 16* (1980): 371–88; and G. R. Bushe and A. B. Shani, *Parallel Learning Structures* (Reading, MA: Addison-Wesley, 1991).

[52] Bridges, op. cit., 20–28.

[53] Adapted from B. Bass, "When Planning for Others," *Journal of Applied Behavioral Science 6* no. 2, (1970): 151–71 and used with permission.

Integrative Cases

▲▲▲

The Donor Services Department*

Joanna Reed was walking home through fallen tree blossoms in Guatemala City. Today, however, her mind was more on her work than the natural beauty surrounding her. She unlocked the gate to her colonial home and sat down on the porch, surrounded by riotous toddlers, pets, and plants, to ponder the recommendations she would make to Sam Wilson. The key decisions she needed to make about his donor services department concerned who should run the department and how the work should be structured.

Joanna had worked for a sponsorship agency engaged in international development work with poor people for six years. She and her husband moved from country to country setting up new agencies. In each country, they had to design how the work should be done, given the local labor market and work conditions.

After a year in Guatemala, Joanna, happily pregnant with her third child, had finished setting up the donor services department for the agency and was working only part-time on a research project. A friend who ran a "competing" development agency approached her to do a consulting project for him. Sam Wilson, an American, was the national representative of a U.S.-based agency that had offices all over the world. Wilson wanted Joanna to analyze his donor services department because he had received complaints from headquarters about its efficiency. Since he had been told that his office needed to double in size in the coming year, he wanted to get all the bugs worked out beforehand. Joanna agreed to spend a month gathering information and compiling a report on this department.

WHAT IS A DONOR SERVICES DEPARTMENT IN A SPONSORSHIP AGENCY ANYWAY?

Sponsorship agencies, with multimillion dollar budgets, are funded by individuals and groups in developed countries who contribute to development programs in less developed countries (LDCs). Donors contribute approximately $20.00 per month plus optional special gifts. The agencies use this money to fund education, health, community development, and income-producing projects for poor people affiliated with their agency in various communities. In the eyes of most donors, the specific benefit provided by sponsorship agencies is the personal relationship between a donor and a child and his or her family in the LDC. The donors and children write back and forth, and the agency sends photos of the child and family to the donors. Some donors never write the family they sponsor; others write weekly and visit the family on their vacations. The efficiency of a donor services department and the quality of their translations are key ingredients to keeping donors and attracting new ones. Good departments also never lose sight of the fact that sponsorship agencies serve a dual constituency—the local people they are trying to help develop and the sponsors who make that help possible through their donations.

The work of a donor services department consists of more than translating letters, preparing annual progress reports on the families, and answering donor questions directed to the agency. It also handles the extensive, seemingly endless paperwork associated with enrolling new families and assigning them to donors, reassignments when either the donor or the family stops participating, and the special gifts of money sent (and thank you notes for them). Having accurate enrollment figures is crucial because the money the agency receives from headquarters is based on these figures and affects planning.

The Cast of Characters in the Department

The Department Head

Joanna tackled the challenge of analyzing the department by speaking first with the department head (see the organizational chart in Figure 1). José Barriga, a charismatic, dynamic man in his forties, was head of both donor services and community services. In reality, he spent virtually no time in the donor services department and was not bilingual. "My biggest pleasure is working with the community leaders and coming up with programs that will be successful. I much prefer being in the field, driving from village to village talking with people, to supervising paperwork. I'm not sure exactly what goes on in donor services, but Elena, the supervisor, is very responsible. I make it a point to walk through the department once a week and say hello to everyone, and I check their daily production figures."

Like José, Sam was also more interested in working with the communities on projects than in immersing himself in the details of the more administrative departments. In part, Sam had contracted Joanna because he rightfully worried that donor services did not receive the attention it deserved from José, who was very articulate and personable but seldom had time to look at anything beyond case histories. José never involved himself in the internal affairs of the department. Even though he was not considered much of a resource to them, he was well liked and respected by the staff of donor services, and they never complained about him.

The Supervisor

This was not the case with the supervisor José had promoted from within. Elena had the title of departmental supervisor, but she exercised very little authority. A slight, single woman in her thirties, Elena had worked for the organization since its establishment 10 years earlier. She was organized, meticulous, dependable, and hardworking. But she was a quiet, nonassertive, nervous woman who was anything but proactive. When asked what changes she would make if she were the head of the department, she sidestepped the question by responding, "It is difficult to have an opinion on this subject. I think that the boss can see the necessary changes with greater clarity."

Elena did not enjoy her role as supervisor, which was partly due to the opposition she encountered from a small clique of longtime translators. In the opinion of this subgroup, Elena had three strikes against her. One, unlike her subordinates, she was not bilingual. "How can she be the supervisor when she doesn't even know English well? One of us would make a better supervisor." Bilingual secretaries in status-conscious Guatemala see themselves as a cut above ordinary

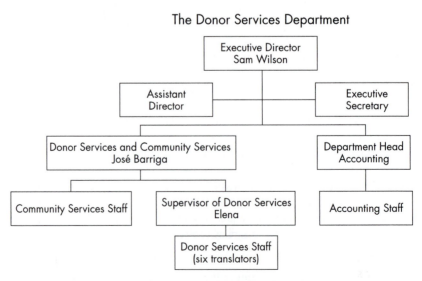

The Donor Services Department

FIGURE 1   Organizational Chart—Donor Services Department

secretaries. This group looked down on Elena as being less skilled and less educated than they were, even though she was an excellent employee.

Second, Elena belonged to a different religion than the organization itself and almost all the other employees. This made no difference to Sam and José but seemed important to the clique who could be heard making occasional derogatory comments about Elena's religion.

The third strike against Elena was her lack of authority. No one had ever clarified how much authority she really possessed, and she herself made no effort to assume control of the department. "My instructions are to inform Don José Barriga of infractions in my daily production memo. I'm not supposed to confront people directly when infractions occur, although it might be easier to correct things if I did." ("Don" is a Latin American honorific used before the first name to denote respect.)

This subgroup showed their disdain and lack of respect for Elena by treating her with varying degrees of rudeness and ignoring her requests. They saw her as a watchdog, an attitude furthered by José who sometimes announced, "We (senior management) are not going to be here tomorrow, so be good because Elena will be watching you." When Sam and José left the office, the clique often stopped working to socialize. They'd watch Elena smolder out of the corner of their eyes, knowing she would not reprimand them. "I liked my job better before I became supervisor," said Elena. "Ever since, some of the girls have resented me, and I'm not comfortable trying to keep them in line. Why don't they just do their work without needing me to be the policeman? The only thing that keeps me from quitting is the loyalty I feel for the agency and Don José."

THE WORKERS

In addition to the clique already mentioned, there were three other female translators in the department. All the translators but one had the same profile: in their twenties, of working class backgrounds, and graduates of bilingual secretarial schools, possessing average English skills. (As stated earlier, in Latin America, being a bilingual secretary is a fairly prestigious occupation for a woman.) The exception in this group was the best translator, Magdalena, a college-educated recent hire in her late thirties who came from an upper-class family. She worked, not because she needed the money, but because she believed in the mission of the agency. "This job lets me live out my religious beliefs and help people who have less advantages than I do." Magdalena was more professional and mature than the other translators. Although all the employees were proud of the agency and its religious mission, the clique members spent too much time socializing and skirmishing with other employees inside and outside the department.

The three translators who were not working at full capacity were very close friends. The leader of this group, Juana, was a spunky, bright woman with good oral English skills and a hearty sense of humor. A long-time friend of José's, Juana translated for English-speaking visitors who came to visit the program sites throughout the country. The other translators, tied to their desks, saw this as a huge perk. Juana was the ringleader in the occasional mutinies against Elena and in feuds with people from other departments. Elena was reluctant to complain about Juana to José, given their friendship. Perhaps she feared Juana would make her life even more miserable.

Juana's two buddies (*compañeras*) in the department also had many years with the agency. They'd gotten into the habit of helping each other on the infrequent occasions when they had excessive amounts of work. When they were idle or simply wanted to relieve the boredom of their jobs, they socialized and gossiped. Juana in particular was noted for cutting sarcasm and pointed jokes about people she didn't like. This clique was not very welcoming to the newer members of the department. Magdalena simply smiled at them but kept her distance, and the two younger translators kept a low profile to avoid incurring their disfavor. As one of them remarked, "It doesn't pay to get on Juana's bad side."

THE ORGANIZATION OF THE DEPARTMENT

Like many small offices in Latin America, the agency was located in a spacious former private home. The donor services department was housed in the 40 by 30 foot living room area. The women's desks were set up in two rows, with Elena's desk in the back corner. Since Sam and

José's offices were in former back bedrooms, everyone who visited them walked through the department. Inevitably they stopped to greet and chat with the longtime employees (Elena, Juana, and her two friends). Elena's numerous visitors also spent a good deal of time working their way through the department to reach her desk, further contributing to the amount of socializing going on in the department.

Elena was the only department member who had "official" visitors since she was the liaison person who dealt with program representatives and kept track of enrollments. The translators each were assigned one work process. For example, Marisol prepared case histories on new children and their families for prospective donors while Juana processed gifts. One of the newer translators prepared files for newly enrolled children and did all the filing for the entire department (a daunting task). Most of the jobs were primarily clerical and required little or no English. The letter translations were outsourced to external translators on a piece-work basis and supervised by Magdalena. Hers was the only job that involved extensive translation; for the most part, however, she translated simple messages (such as greeting cards) that were far below her level of language proficiency. The trickier translations, such as queries from donors in other countries, were still handled by Sam's executive secretary.

Several translators complained that: "We don't have enough opportunity to use our English skills on the job. Not only are we not getting any better in English, we are probably losing fluency because most of our jobs are just clerical work. We do the same simple, boring tasks over and over, day in and day out. Why did they hire bilingual secretaries for these jobs anyway?"

Another obvious problem was the uneven distribution of work in the office. The desks of Magdalena and the new translators were literally overflowing with several months' backlog of work while Juana and her two friends had time to kill. Nobody, including Elena, made any efforts to even out the work assignments or help out those who were buried. The subject had never been broached.

The agency was growing at a rapid pace, and there were piles of paperwork sitting around waiting to be processed. Joanna spent three weeks having each department member explain her job (in mind-numbing detail), drawing up flow charts of how each type of paperwork was handled, and poking around in their files. She found many unnecessary steps that resulted in slow turnaround times for various processes. There were daily output reports submitted to José but no statistics kept on the length of time it took to respond to requests for information or to process paperwork. No data were shared with the translators, so they had no idea how the department was faring and had little sense of urgency about their work. The only goal was to meet the monthly quota of case histories, which only affected Marisol. Trying to keep up with what came across their desks summed up the entire focus of the employees.

Joanna found many instances of errors and poor quality, not so much from carelessness as from lack of training and supervision. Both José and Sam reviewed the case histories, but Joanna was amazed to discover that no one ever looked at any other work done by the department. The employees were very accommodating when asked to explain their jobs and very conscientious about their work (if not the hours devoted to it by the clique). However, they were seldom able to explain why things were done in a certain way because they had received little training for their jobs and only understood their small part of the department. Morale was obviously low, and all the employees seemed frustrated with the situation in the department. Nevertheless, with the exception of Magdalena who had experience in other offices, none of them could offer Joanna any ideas about how the department could be improved.

THE DONOR SERVICES DEPARTMENT CASE— DISCUSSION QUESTIONS

1. What was Joanna Reed's diagnosis of the situation in the donor services department?
2. What should she recommend to Sam Wilson?
3. Describe the managerial styles of Sam, José, and Elena. What is the impact of their styles?
4. How can motivation be improved in the department?
5. How should Juana be handled?
6. What are the cultural factors that influence this case?

Custom Chip, Inc.*

INTRODUCTION

It was 7:50 on Monday morning. Frank Questin, Product Engineering Manager at Custom Chip, Inc., was sitting in his office making a TO DO list for the day. From 8:00 to 9:30 A.M. he would have his weekly meeting with his staff of engineers. After the meeting, Frank thought he would begin developing a proposal for solving what he called "Custom Chip's manufacturing documentation problem"—inadequate technical information regarding the steps to manufacture many of the company's products. Before he could finish his TO DO list, he answered a phone call from Custom Chip's human resource manager, who asked him about the status of two overdue performance appraisals and reminded him that this day marked Bill Lazarus' fifth year anniversary with the company. Following this call, Frank hurried off to the Monday morning meeting with his staff.

Frank had been Product Engineering Manager at Custom Chip for 14 months. This was his first management position, and he sometimes questioned his effectiveness as a manager. Often he could not complete the tasks he set out for himself due to interruptions and problems brought to his attention by others. Even though he had not been told exactly what results he was supposed to accomplish, he had a nagging feeling that he should have achieved more after these 14 months. On the other hand, he thought maybe he was functioning pretty well in some of his areas of responsibility given the complexity of the problems his group handled and the unpredictable changes in the semiconductor industry—changes caused not only by rapid advances in technology, but also by increased foreign competition and a recent downturn in demand.

COMPANY BACKGROUND

Custom Chip, Inc. was a semiconductor manufacturer specializing in custom chips and components used in radars, satellite transmitters, and other radio frequency devices. The company had been founded in 1977 and had grown very rapidly. Most of the company's 300 employees were located in the main plant in Silicon Valley, but overseas manufacturing facilities in Europe and the Far East were growing in size and importance. These overseas facilities assembled the less complex, higher volume products. New products and the more complex ones were assembled in the main plant. Approximately one-third of the assembly employees were in overseas facilities.

While the specialized products and markets of Custom Chip provided a market niche that had thus far shielded the company from the major downturn in the semiconductor industry, growth had come to a standstill. Because of this, cost reduction had become a high priority.

THE MANUFACTURING PROCESS

Manufacturers of standard chips have long production runs of a few products. Their cost per unit is low and cost control is a primary determinant of success. In contrast, manufacturers of custom chips have extensive product lines and produce small production runs for special applications. Custom Chip, Inc., for example, manufactured over 2,000 different products in the last five years. In any one quarter the company might schedule 300 production runs for different products, as many as one-third of which might be new or modified products which the company had not made before. Because they must be efficient in designing and manufacturing many product lines, all custom chip manufacturers are highly dependent on their engineers. Customers are often first concerned with whether Custom Chip can design and manufacture the needed product *at all*, secondly with whether they can deliver it on time, and only thirdly with cost.

After designing a product, there are two phases to the manufacturing process. (See Figure 1.) The first is wafer fabrication. This is a complex process in which circuits are etched onto the various layers added to a silicon wafer. The number of steps that the wafer goes through plus inherent problems in controlling various chemical processes make it very difficult to meet the exacting specifications required for the final wafer. The wafers, which are typically 8 inches in diameter when the fabrication process is complete, contain hundreds, sometimes thousands of tiny identical

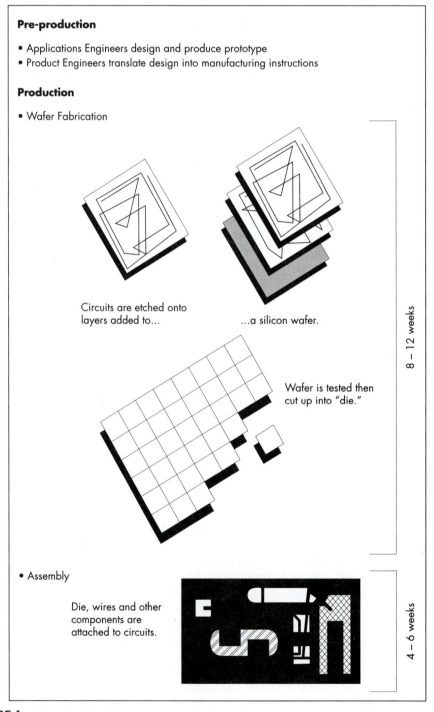

Pre-production

- Applications Engineers design and produce prototype
- Product Engineers translate design into manufacturing instructions

Production

- Wafer Fabrication

Circuits are etched onto layers added to...

...a silicon wafer.

Wafer is tested then cut up into "die."

8 – 12 weeks

- Assembly

Die, wires and other components are attached to circuits.

4 – 6 weeks

FIGURE 1   **Manufacturing Process**

die. Once the wafer has been tested and sliced up to produce these die, each die will be used as a circuit component.

If the completed wafer passes the various quality tests, it moves on to the assembly phase. In assembly, the die from the wafers, very small wires and other components are attached to a circuit in a series of precise operations. This finished circuit is the final product of Custom Chip, Inc.

Each product goes through many independent and delicate operations, and each step is subject to operator or machine error. Due to the number of steps and tests involved, the wafer fabrication takes 8 to 12 weeks and the assembly process takes 4 to 6 weeks. Because of the exacting specifications, products are rejected for the slightest flaw. The likelihood that every product starting the run will make it through all of the processes and still meet specifications is often quite low. For some products, average yield[1] is as low as 40 percent, and actual yields can vary considerably from one run to another. At Custom Chip, the average yield for all products is higher than 90 percent range.

Because it takes so long to make a custom chip, it is especially important to have some control of these yields. For example, if a customer orders one thousand units of a product and typical yields for that product average 50 percent, Custom Chip will schedule a starting batch of 2,200 units. With this approach, even if the yield falls as low as 45.4 percent (45.4 percent of 2200 is 1,000) the company can still meet the order. If the actual yield falls below 45.4 percent, the order will not be completed in that run, and a very small, costly run of the item will be needed to complete the order. The only way the company can effectively control these yields and stay on schedule is for the engineering groups and operations to cooperate and coordinate their efforts efficiently.

ROLE OF THE PRODUCT ENGINEER

The product engineer's job is defined by its relationship to application engineering and operations. The applications engineers are responsible for designing and developing prototypes when incoming orders are for new or modified products. The product engineer's role is to translate the application engineering group's design into a set of manufacturing instructions, then to work alongside manufacturing to make sure that engineering related problems get solved. The product engineers' effectiveness is ultimately measured by their ability to control yields on their assigned products. The organization chart in Figure 2 shows the engineering and operations departments. Figure 3 summarizes the roles and objectives of manufacturing, application engineering, and product engineering.

The product engineers estimate that 70 to 80 percent of their time is spent in solving day-to-day manufacturing problems. The product engineers have cubicles in a room directly across the hall from the manufacturing facility. If a manufacturing supervisor has a question regarding how to build a product during a run, that supervisor will call the engineer assigned to that product. If the engineer is available, he or she will go to the manufacturing floor to help answer the question. If the engineer is not available, the production run may be stopped and the product put aside so that other orders can be manufactured. This results in delays and added costs. One reason that product engineers are consulted is that documentation—the instructions for manufacturing the product—is unclear or incomplete.

The product engineer will also be called if a product is tested and fails to meet specifications. If a product fails to meet test specifications, production stops, and the engineer must diagnose the problem and attempt to find a solution. Otherwise, the order for that product may be only partially met. Test failures are a very serious problem, which can result in considerable cost increases and schedule delays for customers. Products do not test properly for many reasons, including operator errors, poor materials, a design that is very difficult to manufacture, a design that provides too little margin for error, or a combination of these.

On a typical day, the product engineer may respond to half a dozen questions from the manufacturing floor, and two to four calls to the testing stations. When interviewed, the engineers expressed a frustration with this situation. They thought they spent too much time solving short term

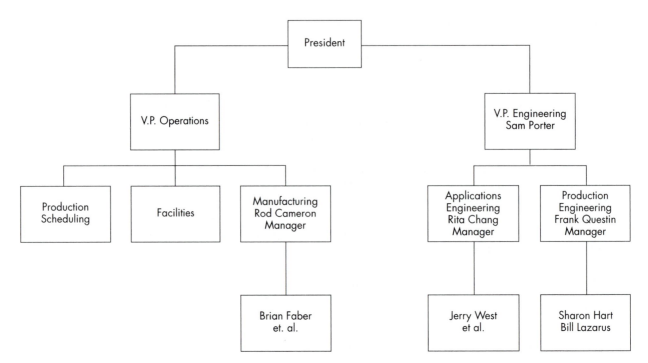

FIGURE 2   Custom Chip, Inc. Partial Organization Chart

Department	Role	Primary Objective
Applications Engineering	Design and develop prototypes for new or modified products	Satisfy customer needs through innovative designs
Product Engineering	Translates designs into manufacturing instructions and works alongside manufacturing to solve "engineering related" problems	Maintain and control yields on assigned products
Manufacturing	Executes designs	Meet productivity standards and time schedules

FIGURE 3   Departmental Roles and Objectives

problems, and consequently they were neglecting other important parts of their jobs. In particular, they felt they had little time in which to:

- **Coordinate with applications engineers during the design phase.** The product engineers stated that their knowledge of manufacturing could provide valuable input to the applications engineer. Together they could improve the manufacturability and thus, the yields, of the new or modified product.
- **Engage in yield improvement projects.** This would involve an in-depth study of the existing process for a specific product in conjunction with an analysis of past product failures.
- **Accurately document the manufacturing steps for their assigned products, especially for those that tend to have large or repeat orders.** They said that the current state of the documentation is very poor. Operators often have to build products using only a drawing showing the final circuit, along with a few notes scribbled in the margins. While experienced operators

and supervisors may be able to work with this information, they often make incorrect guesses and assumptions. Inexperienced operators may not be able to proceed with certain products because of this poor documentation.

WEEKLY MEETING

As manager of the product engineering group, Frank Questin had eight engineers reporting to him, each responsible for a different set of Custom Chip products. According to Frank:

> *When I took over as manager, the product engineers were not spending much time together as a group. They were required to handle operation problems on short notice. This made it difficult for the entire group to meet due to constant requests for assistance from the manufacturing area.*
>
> *I thought that my engineers could be of more assistance and support to each other if they all spent more time together as a group, so one of my first actions as a manager was to institute a regularly scheduled weekly meeting. I let the manufacturing people know that my staff would not respond to requests for assistance during the meeting.*

The meeting on this particular Monday morning followed the usual pattern. Frank talked about upcoming company plans, projects and other news that might be of interest to the group. He then provided data about current yields for each product and commended those engineers who had maintained or improved yields on most of their products. This initial phase of the meeting lasted until about 8:30 A.M. The remainder of the meeting was a meandering discussion of a variety of topics. Since there was no agenda, engineers felt comfortable in raising issues of concern to them.

The discussion started with one of the engineers describing a technical problem in the assembly of one of his products. He was asked a number of questions and given some advice. Another engineer raised the topic of a need for new testing equipment and described a test unit he had seen at a recent demonstration. He claimed the savings in labor and improved yields from this machine would allow it to pay for itself in less than nine months. Frank immediately replied that budget limitations made such a purchase unfeasible, and the discussion moved into another area. They briefly discussed the increasing inaccessibility of the application engineers, then talked about a few other topics.

In general, the engineers valued these meetings. One commented that:

> *The Monday meetings give me a chance to hear what's on everyone's mind and to find out about and discuss company wide news. It's hard to reach any conclusions because the meeting is a freewheeling discussion. But I really appreciate the friendly atmosphere with my peers.*

COORDINATION WITH APPLICATIONS ENGINEERS

Following the meeting that morning, an event occurred that highlighted the issue of the inaccessibility of the applications engineers. An order of 300 units of custom chip 1210A for a major customer was already overdue. Because the projected yield of this product was 70 percent, they had started with a run of 500 units. A sample tested at one of the early assembly points indicated a major performance problem that could drop the yield to below 50 percent. Bill Lazarus, the product engineer assigned to the 1210A, examined the sample and determined that the problem could be solved by redesigning the wiring. Jerry West, the application engineer assigned to that product category was responsible for revising the design. Bill tried to contact Jerry, but he was not immediately available and didn't get back to Bill until later in the day. Jerry explained that he was on a tight schedule trying to finish a design for a customer who was coming into town in two days and could not get to "Bill's problem" for a while.

Jerry's attitude that the problem belonged to product engineering was typical of the applications engineers. From their point of view there were a number of reasons for making the product engineers needs for assistance a lower priority. In the first place, applications engineers were rewarded and acknowledged primarily for satisfying customer needs through designing new and modified products. They got little recognition for solving manufacturing problems. Secondly, applications engineering was perceived to be more glamorous than product engineering because of opportunities to be credited with innovative and ground breaking designs. Finally, the size of the applications engineering group had declined over the past year, causing the workload on each engineer to increase considerably. Now they had even less time to respond to the product engineer's requests.

When Bill Lazarus told Frank about the situation, Frank acted quickly. He wanted this order to be in process again by tomorrow and he knew manufacturing was also trying to meet this goal. He walked over to see Rita Chang, head of applications engineering (see Organization Chart in Figure 2). Meetings like this with Rita to discuss and resolve interdepartmental issues were common.

Frank found Rita at a workbench talking with one of her engineers. He asked Rita if he could talk to her in private and they walked to Rita's office.

> *Frank:*   *We've got a problem in manufacturing in getting out an order of 1210A's. Bill Lazarus is getting little or no assistance from Jerry West. I'm hoping you can get Jerry to pitch in and help Bill. It should take no more than a few hours of his time.*
>
> *Rita:*   *I do have Jerry on a short leash trying to keep him focused on getting out a design for Teletronics. We can't afford to show up empty handed at our meeting with them in two days.*
>
> *Frank:*   *Well, we are going to end up losing one customer in trying to please another? Can't we satisfy everyone here?*
>
> *Rita:*   *Do you have an idea?*
>
> *Frank:*   *Can't you give Jerry some additional support on the Teletronics design?*
>
> *Rita:*   *Let's get Jerry in here to see what we can do.*

Rita brought Jerry back to the office, and together they discussed the issues and possible solutions. When Rita made it clear to Jerry that she considered the problem with the 1210A's a priority, Jerry offered to work on the 1210A problem with Bill. He said, "This will mean I'll have to stay a few hours past 5:00 this evening, but I'll do what's required to get the job done."

Frank was glad he had developed a collaborative relationship with Rita. He had always made it a point to keep Rita informed about activities in the Product Engineering group that might affect the applications engineers. In addition, he would often chat with Rita informally over coffee or lunch in the company cafeteria. This relationship with Rita made Frank's job easier. He wished he had the same rapport with Rod Cameron, the Manufacturing Manager.

COORDINATION WITH MANUFACTURING

The product engineers worked closely on a day-to-day basis with the manufacturing supervisors and workers. The problems between these two groups stemmed from an inherent conflict between their objectives (see Figure 3). The objective of the product engineers was to maintain and improve yields. They had the authority to stop production of any run that did not test properly. Manufacturing, on the other hand, was trying to meet productivity standards and time schedules. When a product engineer stopped a manufacturing run, he was possibly preventing the manufacturing group from reaching its objectives.

Rod Cameron, the current manufacturing manager, had been promoted from his position as a manufacturing supervisor a year ago. His views on the product engineers:

> *The product engineers are perfectionists. The minute a test result looks a little suspicious they want to shut down the factory. I'm under a lot of pressure to get products out the door If they pull a few $50,000 orders off the line when they are within a few days of reaching shipping, I'm liable to miss my numbers by $100,000 that month.*

Besides that, they are doing a lousy job of documenting the manufacturing steps. I've got a lot of turnover and my new operators need to be told or shown exactly what to do for each product. The instructions for a lot of our products are a joke.

At first, Frank found Rod very difficult to deal with. Rod found fault with the product engineers for many problems and sometimes seemed rude to Frank when they talked. For example, Rod might tell Frank to "make it quick, I haven't got much time." Frank tried not to take Rod's actions personally and through persistence was able to develop a more amicable relationship with him. According to Frank:

Sometimes, my people will stop work on a product because it doesn't meet test results at that stage of manufacturing. If we study the situation, we might be able to maintain yields or even save an entire run by adjusting the manufacturing procedures. Rod tries to bully me into changing my engineers' decisions. He yells at me or criticizes the competence of my people, but I don't allow his temper or ravings to influence my best judgment in a situation. My strategy in dealing with Rod is to try not to respond defensively to him. Eventually he cools down, and we can have a reasonable discussion of the situation.

Despite this strategy, Frank could not always resolve his problems with Rod. On these occasions, Frank took the issue to his own boss, Sam Porter, the Vice President in charge of engineering. However, Frank was not satisfied with the support he got from Sam. Frank said:

Sam avoids confrontations with the Operations VP. He doesn't have the influence or clout with the other VPs or the president to do justice to engineering's needs in the organization.

Early that afternoon, Frank again found himself trying to resolve a conflict between engineering and manufacturing. Sharon Hart, one of his most effective product engineers was responsible for a series of products used in radars—the 3805A-3808A series. Today she had stopped a large run of 3806A's. The manufacturing supervisor, Brian Faber, went to Rod Cameron to complain about the impact of this stoppage on his group's productivity. Brian felt that yields were low on that particular product because the production instructions were confusing to his operators, and that even with clearer instructions, his operators would need additional training to build it satisfactorily. He stressed that the product engineer's responsibility was to adequately document the production instructions and provide training. For these reasons, Brian asserted that product engineering, and not manufacturing, should be accountable for the productivity loss in the case of these 3806A's.

Rod called Frank to his office, where he joined the discussion with Sharon, Brian and Rod. After listening to the issues, Frank conceded that product engineering had responsibility for documenting and training. He also explained, even though everyone was aware of it, that the product engineering group had been operating with reduced staff for over a year now, so training and documentation were lower priorities. Because of this staffing situation, Frank suggested that manufacturing and product engineering work together and pool their limited resources to solve the documentation and training problem. He was especially interested in using a few of the long term experienced workers to assist in training newer workers. Rod and Brian opposed his suggestion. They did not want to take experienced operators off of the line because it would decrease productivity. The meeting ended when Brian stormed out, saying that Sharon had better get the 3806A's up and running again that morning.

Frank was particularly frustrated by this episode with manufacturing. He knew perfectly well that his group had primary responsibility for documenting the manufacturing steps for each product. A year ago he told Sam Porter that the product engineers needed to update and standardize all of the documentation for manufacturing products. At that time, Sam told Frank that he would support his efforts to develop the documentation but would not increase his staff. In fact, Sam had withheld authorization to fill a recently vacated product engineering slot. Frank was reluctant to push the staffing issue because of Sam's adamant stance on reducing costs. "Perhaps," Frank thought, "if I develop a proposal clearly showing the benefits of a documentation program in manufacturing and detailing the steps and resources required to implement the program, I might be able to convince Sam to provide us with more resources." But Frank could never find the time to develop that proposal. And so he remained frustrated.

LATER IN THE DAY

Frank was reflecting on the complexity of his job when Sharon came to the doorway to see if he had a few moments. Before he could say "come in," the phone rang. He looked at the clock. It was 4:10 P.M. Rita was on the other end of the line with an idea she wanted to try out on Frank, so Frank said he could call her back shortly. Sharon was upset and told him that she was thinking of quitting because the job was not satisfying for her.

Sharon said that although she very much enjoyed working on yield improvement projects, she could find no time for them. She was tired of the application engineers acting like "prima donnas," too busy to help her solve what they seemed to think were mundane day-to-day manufacturing problems. She also thought that many of the day-to-day problems she handled wouldn't exist if there was enough time to document manufacturing procedures to begin with.

Frank didn't want to lose Sharon, so he tried to get into a frame of mind where he could be empathetic to her. He listened to her and told her that he could understand her frustration in this situation. He told her the situation would change as industry conditions improved. He told her that he was pleased that she felt comfortable in venting her frustrations with him, and he hoped she would stay with Custom Chip.

After Sharon left, Frank realized that he had told Rita that he would call back, He glanced at the TO DO list he had never completed and realized that he hadn't spent time on his top priority—developing a proposal relating to solving the documentation problem in manufacturing. Then, he remembered that he had forgotten to acknowledge Bill Lazarus' fifth year anniversary with the company. He thought to himself that his job felt like a roller coaster ride, and once again he pondered his effectiveness as a manager.

ENDNOTE

1. Yield refers to the ratio of finished products that meet specifications relative to the number that initially entered the manufacturing process.

CUSTOM CHIP, INC.—DISCUSSION QUESTIONS

1. What are the key problems facing Frank?
2. What are the pros and cons of Frank's managerial style?
3. What is the source of conflict among the different departments? How could it be resolved?
4. What are the advantages and disadvantages of Custom Chip, Inc.'s organizational structure?
5. What steps should Frank take to improve this situation?

Rudi Gassner and the Executive Committee of BMG International (A)*

Rudi Gassner, CEO of BMG International, paused and glanced around the hotel suite at the members of his executive committee. They were not coming to any consensus on the issue at hand. It was May 1993 and the BMG International executive committee was gathered for one of its quarterly meetings, this time in Boca Raton, Florida, during the annual Managing Directors Convention.

Gassner had just congratulated Arnold Bahlmann, a regional director and executive committee member, on his recent negotiation of a reduced manufacturing transfer price for the upcoming year's production of CDs, records, and cassettes. Because business plans for the year had been established in March based on the assumption of a higher manufacturing cost, the new price would realize an unanticipated savings of roughly $20 million.

As a result of these savings, the executive committee now faced some tough decisions. First, they had to decide whether or not to change the business targets for each country to reflect the new manufacturing price. If they chose to alter the targets, they had to address the even more delicate matter of whether managing directors' bonuses, which were based principally on the achievement of these targets, should be based on the old or new figures.

Gassner had already discussed this issue with Bahlmann and CFO Joe Gorman, who had run calculations on the impact of the new price for each operating company. These had been distributed to the executive committee before the meeting. Through previous discussions and evaluation of the financial impact, Gassner had formulated his opinion about what should be done.

In his mind, the issues were clear. BMG International had achieved tremendous success and growth in its short lifetime of six years, and the regional directors (RDs) and managing directors (MDs)[1] had every right to feel good about their exceptional performance. (See Exhibits 1 and 2 for company organization charts.) But now Gassner wanted to guard against the company becoming a victim of its own success. He knew that they would have to carefully monitor the economics of the business and maintain their agility in order to meet the challenges of the future. In light of these concerns, Gassner felt that the MDs should be held accountable for the savings from the reduced manufacturing price. The executive committee needed seriously to consider not only adjusting the targets, but also the bonus basis. As he explained, "It seemed fair to me. These were windfall profits coming to the managing directors, and they didn't even have to lift a finger to get them. I didn't want them to become complacent during the year."

The executive committee, however, seemed unwilling even to entertain this possibility. Gassner suspected that some of the RDs were taking the "path of least resistance" because they did not want to return to their MDs and announce that the bonus targets had been changed. His frustration mounting, Gassner wondered if he should drop the issue for now or provoke them by saying what was on his mind: "Listen guys, you're thinking too much like MDs. You should be thinking about what is good for the whole company."

* Research Associate Katherine Seger Weber prepared this case under the supervision of Professor Linda A. Hill as the basis for class discussion rather than to illustrate either effective or ineffective handling of an administrative situation.

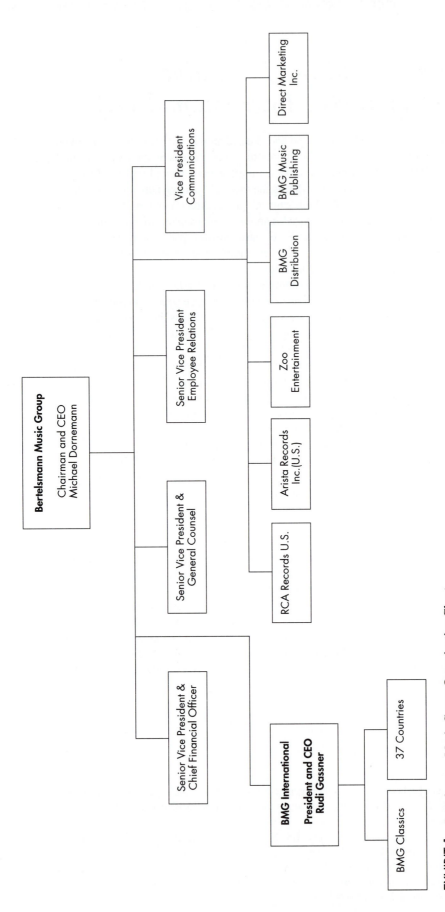

EXHIBIT 1   Bertelsmann Music Group Organization Chart

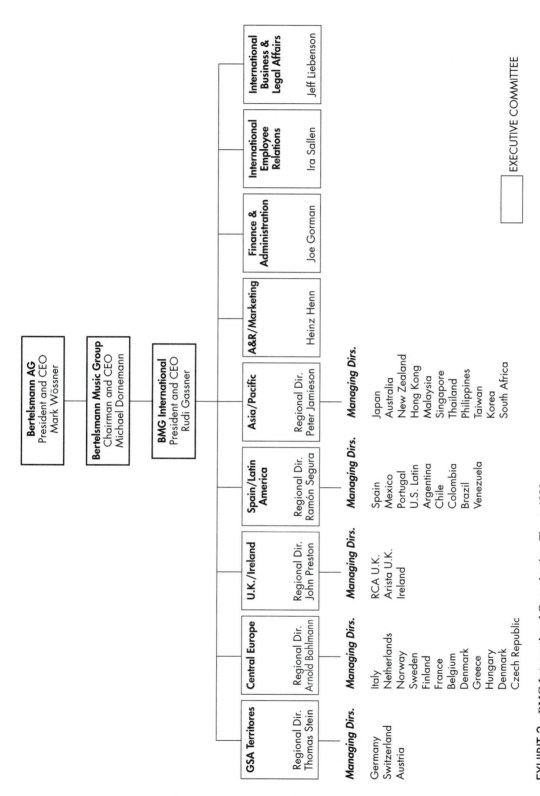

Bertelsmann AG
President and CEO
Mark Wössner

Bertelsmann Music Group
Chairman and CEO
Michael Dornemann

BMG International
President and CEO
Rudi Gassner

GSA Territores	Central Europe	U.K./Ireland	Spain/Latin America	Asia/Pacific	A&R/Marketing	Finance & Administration	International Employee Relations	International Business & Legal Affairs
Regional Dir. Thomas Stein	Regional Dir. Arnold Bahlmann	Regional Dir. John Preston	Regional Dir. Ramón Segura	Regional Dir. Peter Jamieson	Heinz Henn	Joe Gorman	Ira Sallen	Jeff Liebenson

Managing Dirs.

Managing Dirs.	*Managing Dirs.*	*Managing Dirs.*	*Managing Dirs.*	*Managing Dirs.*
Germany	Italy	RCA U.K.	Spain	Japan
Switzerland	Netherlands	Arista U.K.	Mexico	Australia
Austria	Norway	Ireland	Portugal	New Zealand
	Sweden		U.S. Latin	Hong Kong
	Finland		Argentina	Malaysia
	France		Chile	Singapore
	Belgium		Colombia	Thailand
	Denmark		Brazil	Philippines
	Greece		Venezuela	Taiwan
	Hungary			Korea
	Denmark			South Africa
	Czech Republic			

☐ EXECUTIVE COMMITTEE

EXHIBIT 2   BMG International Organization Chart, 1993

517

COMPANY BACKGROUND

BMG International was a subsidiary of Bertelsmann AG, a German media conglomerate with over 200 companies and 50,000 employees operating in 37 countries. Founded in 1835 as a lithographic printing company in Guetersloh, Germany, Bertelsmann's interests had grown to include businesses in music, film, television, radio, book, magazine, and newspaper publishing and distribution, as well as printing and manufacturing operations. Still headquartered in the small rural town, Bertelsmann had become the second-largest media enterprise in the world, with 1992 sales of $9.7 billion.

Bertelsmann's corporate charter mandated autonomous business divisions and entrepreneurial operating management, and emphasized respect for the cultural traditions of each country in which it operated. Each business unit had its own, usually local, entrepreneurial management with operating control over its business plan, the development of its assets, its human resources, and its contribution to overall profitability. Delegation of responsibility and authority was supported by performance-linked compensation for managers and profit-sharing by all employees.

In 1986, Bertelsmann entered the U.S. market with its purchases of Doubleday and Dell, two large publishing houses, and RCA Records, which had made music history with Elvis Presley in the 1950s. On acquiring RCA, Bertelsmann organized its worldwide music holdings—which also included the American record label Arista, the German label Ariola, and various smaller labels and music publishing and marketing operations—into the Bertelsmann Music Group (BMG). With RCA, BMG entered the ranks of the "Big Six" record companies—CBS, Warner, BMG, Capitol-EMI, PolyGram, and MCA—which supplied 80 percent of worldwide music sales.[2]

BMG was headquartered in New York under German Chairman and CEO Michael Dornemann, who split the company's operations into two divisions: the United States and the rest of the world. In the United States, BMG's priority was to stem the losses from RCA (which posted a $35 million deficit in 1987) and build market share for the flagging U.S. labels.[3]

With BMG's overseas holdings, Dornemann formed an international division and hired German-born Rudi Gassner, then executive vice president of PolyGram International, as president and CEO (see Exhibit 3). According to Dornemann, Gassner "had the right background in the music business and the right international experience. He best fit the leadership qualities we were looking for."[4] At its inception in 1987, the international division, also headquartered in New York, comprised operations in 17 countries across the globe. Gassner described the fledgling organization as "a patchwork of companies around the world. It had no mission, no goals, and in total, it didn't make any money . . . . The only way from there was up."[5]

In his first six years, Gassner led the company, which he named BMG International, through a tremendous period of growth. By launching new satellite companies, purchasing small labels, and forming joint ventures, BMG International's presence had expanded by 1993 to include 37 countries. Sales had increased an average of 20 percent annually, reaching $2 billion in 1993 two-thirds of BMG's overall revenue that year). International market share, which was near 11 percent in 1987, was a healthy 17 percent, and as high as 25 percent in some territories.[6]

Rudi Gassner
President and CEO, BMG International
German, 51 years old

1984-1987: Executive VP, PolyGram International, London
1983-1984: President, Polydor International (PolyGram), Hamburg
1980-1983: President, Deutsche Grammophon (PolyGram), Hamburg
Fall 1979: Harvard Business School Program for Management Development (PMD)
1977-1980: Managing Director, Metronome (PolyGram), Hamburg
1969-1977: Sales Manager, Deutsche Grammophon (PolyGram), Munich
1964-1969: Music Wholesaling, Munich

EXHIBIT 3   **Rudi Gassner Career Highlights**

Artist	Country of Origin	Units Sold 1992/1993 (in thousands)
Global Superstars		
Whitney Houston	United States	11,800
Kenny G	United States	2,200
Annie Lennox	United Kingdom	1,200
David Bowie	United Kingdom	700
SNAP	Germany	700
Dr. Alban	Germany	600
Regional Superstars		
Vaya Con Dios	Belgium	1,300
Juan Luis Guerra	Spain	1,100
Eros Ramazzotti	Italy	1,100
Die Prinzen	Germany	900
Take That	United Kingdom	700
Bonnie Tyler	Germany	500
Local Superstars		
B'z	Japan	5,700
Bronco	Mexico	1,300
Joaquin Sabina	Spain	500
José José	Mexico	400
Lucio Dalla	Italy	250

EXHIBIT 4   Selected BMG International Top-Selling Artists, 1993

BMG International was responsible for marketing and distributing top-selling U.S. artists such as Whitney Houston and Kenny G across the globe.[7] In addition, the company developed such artists as Annie Lennox and Lisa Stansfield (Britain) and Eros Ramazzotti (Italy) in their local territories to be marketed worldwide. On a local level, groups such as B'z (Japan) and Bronco (Mexico) were extremely successful, selling in excess of 1 million units in their respective countries. The company also had extensive classics and jazz catalogues, with artists such as James Galway and Antonio Hart. (See Exhibit 4 for roster of top-selling artists.)[8]

RUDI GASSNER AND BMG INTERNATIONAL

In 1987, at the age of 45, Gassner became the CEO of the newly-formed BMG International. "It was a once-in-a-lifetime opportunity," he reflected, "to build what I think a global company should look like." When he arrived at BMG, Gassner adapted quickly to the Bertelsmann culture. "My 17 years at PolyGram gave me the experience to run a global business; that was my know-how," he explained. "But on the other hand, I very much liked the Bertelsmann style. It was very close to my personal style." One of his colleagues at BMG described Gassner's transition:

Rudi came from PolyGram, which had a very different culture. The Philips PolyGram culture is highly politically charged; it is much more "stand by your beds when the senior management comes in." Rudi changed a lot when he came to BMG. He saw the value in the Bertelsmann managing style; he saw the freedom to do things, and he took it. He passed it on as well.

BUILDING BMG INTERNATIONAL

One of Gassner's first priorities was to instill this culture in the newly acquired companies. He reflected on what he inherited when he joined BMG:

> *My first step was basically to get to know the companies and the problems hands-on myself. RCA had been centrally managed out of New York, and the managers in the companies had the attitude that "I'm not doing anything unless somebody tells me what to do." I would find them hiding under tables. I spent the first two years preaching my gospel and saying to the managers, "You are responsible. I can give you advice, but don't send me a memo asking me to sign off here. You are in charge: you are Mr. Italy; you are Mr. France; you are Mr. Belgium."*

At the same time, Gassner also began to communicate his vision for BMG International. "There were basically two strategic targets in my mind," he explained:

> *One was globalization. Globalization allows you to serve a bigger world market. Every time we added a new country, we would increase our revenue accordingly. The other strategic target was domestic repertoire. I had a great fear of being too dependent on English-speaking repertoire. I made it clear to the managers that their foremost responsibility was developing domestic talent. Joint ventures and acquisitions were another way to add local repertoire.*

Gassner also instituted yearly business plans with each of his managing directors. He described the process:

> *We [Gassner and each MD] do a budget once a year. The budget is between you and me. I want to know where you are going and how much investment you will need. We talk about revenues and profits. I make a very aggressive bonus plan for them to be able to make a lot of money; if they exceed their targets significantly, they can make up to half their salary as a bonus. In America, this might not have been so sensational, but for those countries who were not used to that, it was pretty new.*

According to Gassner, "the majority of the guys came through with flying colors." For those who did not fit with the new program, Gassner held "career counseling sessions," as one colleague referred to them: "When Rudi conducts a career counseling session, it's pretty much over. But he's so smooth and so good at it, that it takes them about a week to figure out that they may have just been fired."

Gassner also turned his attention inward, focusing on his corporate management structure. "One advantage, obviously, was that nothing existed. I could do it any way I wanted. That was fantastic." He made Joe Gorman, who had been the senior finance executive for RCA's international arm, the chief financial officer of BMG International. During Gassner's first two years, Gorman accompanied him as he travelled around the world assessing each operating company.

Gassner's next corporate hire was Heinz Henn to coordinate global A&R marketing.[9] Henn had spent 17 years at EMI in international positions. He described his job interview with Gassner:

> *Rudi and I met for the first time on February 17, 1987, at the Park Lane Hotel and had breakfast together. What got me the job was that I ate two breakfasts—I was really hungry that day. He was impressed that somebody could eat two full breakfasts on a job interview.*
> *Seriously, Rudi asked me what I would do if he gave me the job, and I told him that I would do things differently than they had been done so far in the industry, particularly [the companies] where we had both come from. I wanted to cultivate local talent in individual markets*

to build hot acts which we could launch globally. He totally agreed with me. Ever since, he's let me do what I wanted to do.

Gassner described the need for Henn's role:

Heinz has a dual role: he not only has to break local artists worldwide, he also has to sell Whitney Houston to all the local companies. We need Heinz because the interests of the countries and the regions stop at the borders, and we need a global view on artists. This will give us the competitive advantage; there's more money to be made outside the borders if you do it right.

Henn added:

You have to have coordination between the regions as far as marketing and promotion activities are concerned because recording and marketing expenses are far too great these days for any one [local] company to be able to earn back its investment in one country only. It requires coordination between regions and also globally.

To round out his corporate staff, Gassner added a human resource executive, Ira Sallen, and legal counsel, Jeff Liebenson. Sallen would be responsible for negotiating and maintaining the managing directors' contracts, as well as for worldwide personnel and organizational policies. Liebenson would serve as in-house counsel, assisting in the intricate contracts that were part of operating a complex global enterprise.

Gassner also instituted an annual Managing Directors' Convention in which Dornemann, Gassner, the corporate staff, and all of the MDs and joint-venture partners (JVs) would converge from around the world. A major objective of the annual MD Convention was to provide a forum for the MDs and JVs to give repertoire presentations to each other in an attempt to sell their local repertoire to the other countries.

CREATING A REGIONAL STRUCTURE

As BMG International's number of operating companies continued to grow, it became impossible for Gassner directly to oversee them all. By 1989, he concluded it was time to aggregate the countries into five regions and hire a regional director for each, a plan he had had in mind from the beginning. (See Exhibit 2 for organization chart and Exhibit 5 for revenue and profit distribution by region.) The role of the RD would be "to provide leadership for the region; to oversee the strategic development of the region, in conjunction with the whole company; and to manage the managing directors." He explained:

I divided Europe into three different categories: the United Kingdom, German-speaking territories, and the rest of Europe. At that time, the German-speaking territories contributed about 50 percent of our profit, so they were a very important group unto themselves. I promoted Thomas Stein, who was the managing director of the German company, to regional director.

The United Kingdom, despite its relatively small profits, was our largest source of repertoire, a major supplier. I promoted John Preston, who was the MD of RCA Records U.K, to be the regional director of that region.

The MD for Ariola Spain, Ramón Segura, was an outstanding executive who also had, at that time, regional responsibilities for Ariola's Latin American companies. So I kept Spain/Latin America together as a region and made Segura the RD.

Net Revenue by Region

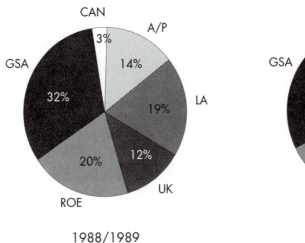

1988/1989

1992/1993

Operating Result (Betriebsergebnis) by Region

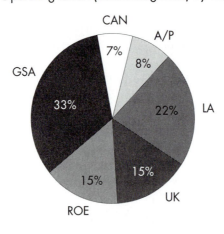

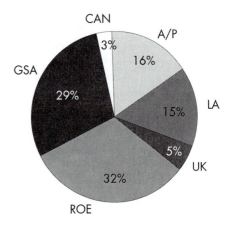

1988/1989

1992/1993

Legend: A/P = Asia/Pacific, Can = Canada, LA = Latin America
GSA = Germany/Switzerland/Austria, ROE = Rest of Europe, UK = U.K.

EXHIBIT 5   **BMG International Revenue and Operating Result Distribution by Region**

Now I needed someone for the rest of Europe. I hired Arnold Bahlmann, who was work-ing in strategic analysis for Michael Dornemann. He was not one of the music managers coming through the ranks. He had never had a line job in his life. Still, I thought, you don't necessarily need the detailed day-to-day experience of running a company to manage a re-gional territory. It was an organizational task, and I thought Arnold had very good people skills. I thought he was ideal, though it was a hell of a risk to put him in.

At the same time as I promoted John Preston to RD in the United Kingdom, I asked the chairman of the RCA U.K. label, Peter Jamieson, to go out and establish our Asia/Pacific market. I remember a British competitor in the industry joking with me that "wasn't I wor-ried about sending one of my best men out to the colonies?" I thought Jamieson was just the right person for the job. He accepted, and he's done a brilliant job building companies and repertoire in that region.

Gassner maintained the annual business planning system he had established with the MDs, but he now worked through the RDs. As Segura described it, "We are involved throughout the process, but Rudi has final approval." BMG International's fiscal year started July 1 and ran through June 30. In January, the MDs began to prepare their business plans, developing targets for critical measures such as revenue, *betriebsergebnis,*[10] return on sales, market share, revenue per employee, days inventory, and days sales outstanding. Gassner was as much interested in the assumptions used to arrive at the targets as the figures themselves; MDs were expected to include an in-depth analysis of the risks and opportunities they faced based on the current economic climate and market, new A&R releases, and their priority artists.

In February, the MDs met with the RDs to review their plans; the RDs then met with Gassner to discuss regional as well as local goals. Gorman described Gassner's stance in these meetings: "Rudi has a reputation for being tough—fair, but tough. One of the reasons he has that reputation is that he makes you do things which you know you should do, but which you don't want to do." One RD described these sessions as "the famous February meetings. Rudi and I dislike each other a lot in February. But by March we usually agree."

In March, the RDs returned to the MDs with a final plan and targets; Gassner and Gorman joined many of these sessions (see Exhibit 6). At this point, the MDs would have a final opportunity to discuss their plans and the targets would be agreed upon. Gorman described these meetings:

Location	Date	Review	
Munich	March 1	10:00 AM	Belgium
		11:30 AM	Netherlands
		2:00 AM	Italy
	March 2	10:00 AM	UK-RCA
		2:00 AM	UK-Arista
		4:00 AM	UK-Distrib.
	March 3	10:00 AM	GSA Overview
		11:30 AM	Munich Ariola
		2:00 AM	Germany Ariola
		3:45 AM	Hamburg Ariola
	March 4	10:00 AM	Germany Ariola
		11:30 AM	Austria
		2:00 AM	Switzerland
	March 5	10:00 AM	France Ariola
		11:30 AM	France Vogue
		1:30 AM	France RCA
		4:00 AM	European Regional Overview
New York	March 10	10:00 AM	Canada
		2:00 AM	Home Office
Hong Kong	March 16	10:00 AM	Australia
		3:00 AM	Hong Kong
	March 17	10:00 AM	Japan
		3:00 AM	Taiwan
	March 18	10:00 AM	South Africa
		3:00 AM	Malaysia
	March 19	10:00 AM	Asia/Pacific Regional Overview
New York	March 24	10:00 AM	Mexico
		2:00 AM	U.S. Latin
		4:00 AM	Portugal
	March 25	10:00 AM	Brazil
		2:00 AM	Spain
	March 26	10:00 AM	Latin America Regional Overview

EXHIBIT 6   **March 1992 Business Planning Meetings Attended by Rudi Gassner and Joe Gorman**

March is the critical planning month for us. We tell everybody, look, when the meeting is over, we all walk out of here with the same goals. Period. We can sit in the room an hour, or we can sit there for two days, but in the end nobody is going to leave this room disagreeing on what the goals are. In these meetings, MD bonus criteria are also defined, since betriebsergebnis is the primary criterion for bonuses.

One RD described Gassner's approach:

Rudi plays a different role with each MD, depending on their personality and where he wants the country to go. Sometimes he plays the good cop, and other times he plays the bad cop. He's very versatile, and very results-oriented. When necessary, he knows how to hit people's hot buttons and make them squirm.

According to one MD:

Rudi knows the business inside and out, and he has an amazing grasp of the details. When he is going through these plans, he will go into particular line items if he wants to. These business plans are like contracts between Rudi and me. Face-to-face with him, I am committing to try to make this target. It's like a moral imperative to get it done.

According to Bahlmann, "The business plans serve their purpose well. If you ask me if I enjoy them—no. It's not enjoyable. I hate the process. But it works." Stein concurred: "The business plans help me explain what I think should be done in my region. It's a fair process because it's based on an objective financial measure." Another RD, however, commented on the danger inherent in the system:

The business plan process is a necessary and effective tool. But the danger is that it becomes too inflexible. Instead of a jacket which guides, a sort of loose piece of clothing which shapes the way we operate, it becomes a straightjacket and restricts the way we operate.

Even with the addition of the regional directors, Gassner maintained close contact with the local companies around the world. "I emphasize what I call a very flat hierarchical structure," he explained. "I'm never too far removed from what's really happening." While he was primarily in contact with the RDs, Gassner always reserved the right to call the MDs directly, and they "feel absolutely free to call me about anything," according to Gassner. "But they all know that it is a two-way information system. Whatever they tell me, they know I will pass on to their regional director. And whatever they tell the RD, they know he passes on to me." When possible, Gassner made it a point to reach further into the organization by talking informally with local employees "just to double-check that my messages come through."

Gassner's style of running a global business was extremely demanding. Travel was a way of life: he and his corporate staff spent 50 percent or more of their time away from New York headquarters, and the regional directors traveled constantly throughout their regions. According to Gorman,

Rudi believes that you are not managing an international company unless you travel extensively, because it's all about people. The financial statements are fine, the statistics are fine. But in the end, you have to sit down with somebody in a room and talk to them to get a real sense for the people and for what's going on. There are things that always come out "by the way...." When you go out to dinner or you're at a concert until 4:00 in the morning, a lot of this comes out.

THE EXECUTIVE COMMITTEE AND THE ECMS

In 1989, after he had established his corporate staff and the regional structure, Gassner formally created an Executive Committee consisting of the five regional directors, the four senior staff members, and himself as the leader (see Exhibit 7). He recalled:

Regional Directors	New York Corporate Staff
Arnold Bahlmann Senior VT, Central Europe	**Heinz Henn** Senior VP, A&R/Marketing
• German, 41 years old. • Promoted from: Senior VP Operations, BMG. • 3 years strategic planning, Bertelsmann. • Doctorate in Political Science.	• German, 38 years old. • Promoted from: Director of International Division, Capitol/EMI America Records. • 17 years A&R/marketing, promotion, and management in record business.
Thomas Stein President, GSA Territories	**Joe Gorman** Senior VP, Finance and Administration
• German, 44 years old. • Promoted from: Managing Director, BMG Ariola, Munich. • 14 years sales, marketing, and management in record business.	• American, 50 years old. • Promoted from: Director, Operations Planning, RCA Records (U.S.). • 10 years finance at RCA Records. • 5 years Arthur Young & Company. • Master of Business Administration. • Military service, Captain, U.S. Army.
John Preston Chairman, BMG Records (UK) Ltd.	**Ira Sallen** VP, International Human Resources, BMG
• Scottish, 43 years old. • Promoted from: Managing Director, RCA Records, U.K. • 19 years retail, marketing, and management in record business.	• American, 39 years old. • Promoted from: VP, Human Resources, Clean Harbors, Inc. • 4 years corporate human resources. • 2 years Consultant, Arthur Young & Company. • 5 years research and clinical psychology.
Ramón Segura President, Spain and Sr. VP, Latin America	**Jeff Liebenson** VP, Int'l. Legal and Business Affairs, BMG American, 40 years old.
• Spanish, 52 years old. • Promoted from: MD, Spain, and VP Latin American Region, Ariola Eurodisc. • 31 years sales, A&R, marketing, and management in record business.	• Promoted from: Director, Legal and Business Affairs, SportsChannel America. • 15 years legal experience, including 12 in entertainment industry. • J.D. and LL.M. law degrees.
Peter Jamieson Senior VP, Asia/Pacific	
• English, 48 years old. • Promoted from: Chairman, BMG Records U.K. • 26 years marketing, sales, and management in record business.	

EXHIBIT 7   BMG International Executive Committee

I had always intended to have an executive committee. I always wanted to run a business on the basis of a European board system, like a vorstand:[11] although it is chaired by one person and members have their own portfolios [regions], the committee decides business issues jointly.

The way I see it, the board should decide about important issues strategically or from an investment point of view. And I wanted everybody to be involved in the process, despite the fact that some issues may not have a direct consequence for their region.

You cannot run a global organization without breaking it down into regions—it just becomes impossible. On the other hand, you have to have a global strategy. In our business, the regions are interlinked by artist agreements and by the exchange of repertoire. So it needs both a regional organization and a global vision.

Bahlmann recalled Gassner introducing the concept of an executive committee by describing it as "the group which will lead BMG International." Gassner decided that the committee would meet four times per year at the New York headquarters to discuss current operating issues, and once a year outside of New York to examine long-term strategy. Before each executive committee meeting (ECM), members were polled for agenda items; Gassner then, as he described it, "edited" the suggestions to create the agenda, which was circulated to the group.

Gassner described the first ECM:

We needed to define the limitations and boundaries of authority among ourselves and the MDs. What should we allow our MDs to do without our approval? What should they have to bring to your level? What should you then bring to my level? We needed certain regulations; it makes our lives easier. It was interesting because of the history of the group coming together—they had not been organized before in a way that had these limitations, and they didn't like it.

I also had to explain the role of the New York staff. There was a lot of theoretical discussion about, for example, Heinz's responsibility. What can Heinz say about my repertoire and my country? How can Heinz say I have to spend a certain amount of money on an artist that is not valid for my region? My answer to that was always that Heinz cannot say. He can only sit down with you and try to convince you that this is the right thing for you. You've got to see the staff as somebody helping you; it is not some governing body who tells you what to do. They have a dotted-line relationship with your people.

Preston described his perspective on the early meetings:

At first, there was no role for the RDs. Rudi had things he wanted to do; the agenda was laid out, and we would discuss ways of implementing the agenda. The staff people went into the meetings very well prepared and tried to establish a couple of policies with the help of Rudi in order to structure the business. It took us a certain amount of time to find a way of really working together.

Bahlmann echoed the same point:

Rudi needed to establish himself and the regional structure; it was like him telling us, via the agenda, what we're going to do. It was our "educational process." Although I think we sometimes found it frustrating, we were so busy with our own companies [regions], there was not a lot of resistance.

Gassner found this lack of "resistance" somewhat disconcerting. According to Gorman,

I remember after the first two ECMs, Rudi saying to me, "Everybody's too nice." He expects strong dissenting opinions. He doesn't want a bunch of people just sitting there mildly accepting anything. To him, a heated argument over an opinion is part of the fun of the job, I suppose. But if you're not used to this, and when I first started with him I wasn't, it jars you a little.

In time, however, the RDs became more vocal. According to Henn, "It took quite some time until the group felt comfortable enough with each other that they dared to say what they really wanted to say." According to the RDs, the shift in the ECMs was due to their growing confidence and success in running their regions. As Bahlmann noted:

About two years ago it turned around. The regional directors and the managing directors make the decisions about the operating businesses and acquisitions. Today in the ECMs, we go more into other issues. More and more, we are finally making decisions together and running the business as a team.

Preston also commented on this shift in emphasis: "In the beginning, the staff and Rudi were more dominant. But now, it's more balanced between Rudi and the RDs, and then the staff."

WORKING TOGETHER

By 1993, the executive committee and the ECMs had been in place for four years, and the meetings had fallen into a fairly regular pattern. Each agenda would include a presentation by Gorman on current financial results relative to targets; a discussion by Henn about A&R developments, new releases, and priority artists; a briefing by Sallen on significant worldwide human resource issues; and an update on each region by the RDs. Gassner described the importance of these regional reviews: "I want to give them room to explain to their colleagues what they're up to. Even though it's not relevant to somebody running South America, for example, he should listen, in my opinion, to what happened in Korea and how we do business in Korea. Here is where I try to get them involved in the global strategy."

Outside the ECMs there was frequent contact between Gassner and each RD. Contact among the RDs varied, and was most frequent among three of the European directors: Bahlmann, Stein, and Preston. Because they shared so many of the same circumstances and concerns, Gassner established a European subcommittee in 1991. As he explained,

> I created a European board because I didn't want to be in the middle of those discussions all the time. It seemed natural to make Arnold the chairman, since he is also the head of European-wide manufacturing and distribution. I told them: "You guys deal with European issues. Europe is your baby. If you cannot agree, I get the minutes and then I will make a ruling."

Since its inception, the European board had been very effective in achieving the purpose he had intended, according to Gassner:

> They deal with issues that are really not relevant to anybody else before they get to the ECM. They even discuss the ECM agenda before the meetings, and they sometimes come over with what I call a "prefabricated opinion." So now sometimes I have to work to break this group up a little bit.

Depending on their regional circumstances, the roles of the RDs varied significantly. Bahlmann, Preston, and Stein, for example, focused on continuing to carve out market share and bring costs down in their increasingly mature markets. Because of his region's importance as a repertoire supplier, Preston was seen as the "repertoire expert"; Bahlmann, on the other hand, was the "strategy expert." Segura and Jamieson were most concerned with establishing new companies and developing talent in the relatively undeveloped markets of Asia and Latin America. Jamieson commented on the satisfaction of being a "pioneer," as he called it: "Asia/Pacific is a huge, multicultural, diverse, economically varied region which is on exactly the opposite side of the world from America. It has the most growth potential and the most musical excitement, really. It's a very, very exciting place to be." Segura described the unique challenges in his region: "I am constantly battling against the terrible political and economic instability that affects some of the countries in my region. These situations cannot be solved with easy solutions or off-the-shelf business recipes."

Over time, the executive committee members developed a strong sense of mutual respect for one another. According to Henn:

> Everybody in that room is the best at what he does. The absolute best, and we all know it. It's pretty amazing. We're also total egomaniacs, the whole group of us. But in this company we still work as a team because we give each other the space to be the fool that everyone can be sometimes. Nobody's perfect.

Another RD commented, "I wouldn't necessarily choose these guys as my friends, but when we get together it's pretty awesome."

The group maintained a balanced mix of camaraderie and competition. Gassner, who himself used to play professional soccer, described the committee as "more like a soccer team than [an American] football team"; they frequently played heated games of golf or soccer when they were together. Stein remarked with a laugh, "It's all healthy competition—it's very healthy as long as I'm on top of the others. But seriously, it's a good sort of competitiveness. We are all ambitious people, but we respect each other; there is no jealousy."

Another executive committee member mentioned a different aspect of competition: "Rudi is only 51 [years old], far from the required retirement age of 60; but chances are good that he could move on to other things at Bertelsmann. As a result, there is a certain amount of jockeying for position within the executive committee, and people wonder if a non-German could ever be tapped to run this company."

As for Gassner's role in the ECMs, committee members had varying perspectives. Stein commented that "Rudi has a good relationship with the team. He knows when to be part of the team, and when to say yes or no. But he's always open-minded, and you can discuss things with him; it's like a partnership with him." According to Sallen, "Rudi does a lot of consensus-taking. He floats ideas by people, testing them on the group. He does impose his will, but not often. While he does not hand down many edicts, it is generally clear to all what his feelings are on most issues."

Jamieson, however, observed: "Debates in the ECMs are very rare. Rudi's not a man who needs or wants too many debates. I have never had an informal brainstorming session with him, a relaxed, almost agenda-less discussion. Rudi's management style is essentially autocratic." Henn commented:

> *Rudi's brilliant. He's a tyrant; no, not a tyrant, a dictator. He has to be. You don't have a leader if you don't have a dictator. If you don't have a dictator, you won't be successful. Show me a company run by democracy, and I'll show you a loser. There's always got to be one chief and plenty of Indians.*
>
> *He's very smooth. If he thinks we're coming to a conclusion that is not what his opinion is, he will make sure the whole thing will turn his way. He has the ability to make you feel it was your idea, and if that doesn't work, he'll tell you to go and do it anyway.*

Many committee members agreed that it could be difficult to change Gassner's mind. According to Stein, "To influence Rudi, you have to convince him. You have to be prepared properly with logical arguments." Preston added: "You have to be prepared to stand up for your argument. A lot of what he is testing is how much you really believe in what you are saying."

One RD noted that "Rudi usually does not allow himself in any way to be influenced by people who are not speaking directly about the areas for which they are responsible. In other words, he'll be very receptive to me for everything within my area, but when I stray into areas of the general good, I find him very unreceptive. I also find that I can influence him more one-on-one than I can in the ECMs."

Stein commented that he used the ECMs "as a tool to influence things in a way that I think they should go and to make the other RDs aware of things. Whether or not the committee agrees with me is another question." Preston agreed, explaining that he viewed participation in the ECMs as an important responsibility, even if it was sometimes hard to have much influence: "I believe that I have a job in the context of the group to say the things that I believe in order to get the group to behave in ways that I think are the right ones."

Bahlmann described the ECM as "an opinion-building exercise," explaining that:

> *Real decisions about who gets money for what acquisitions occur outside of the meetings. The other thing is that there has always been money there to do what we wanted. So for me, the*

group has never been tested to see whether we can really work as a team under pressure when it comes to a fight over who will get funds for what investment.

Jamieson commented:

Sometimes I feel that the main benefit of my coming all the way from Hong Kong to New York for the ECM is the ability (a) to meet my colleagues and chat with them from time to time, and (b) to have my separate meeting with Rudi, which is my best opportunity to influence him.

> *We have had some good meetings, and we have had some terrible meetings. Rudi occasionally runs them in an open way in which debate is invited and variations to policy are considered. In reality, there is not a team "working together" at the top; there are executives implementing predetermined policies in different areas. The enormous geography makes it difficult to manage by consensus. With Rudi, you know what you have to do, and you have the freedom to execute the policies in your own region with your own style. Nevertheless, you have to realize that Rudi's style works for him; the proof is his incredible success over the past six years.*

Gassner suspected these feelings and opinions in the group. "Many of them probably think I am influencing them more than I should," he commented.

Sometimes I hear grumblings and they say that they can't always express their long-term ideas at the meetings because the meetings are so focused. I think they feel a lot of things are a bit too prepared or precooked. It's true—they have a difficult time convincing me. I am a person who likes to win an argument.

> *But my opinions are not just invented on the spot. I usually discuss issues one-to-one with certain people beforehand. If I have a subject on the agenda, I almost always have an opinion of what I think the outcome should be. And then in the ECM, I see if my belief is confirmed. Occasionally, I may not go ahead with my original idea because I see that the entire group is going in another direction. In that case, I will take a step back and try to analyze it one more time, and I may change my mind. But if I see that they agree, or if it's just very important to me, then I obviously try to push it along.*

Reflecting on his original hopes for the role of the executive committee, Gassner commented:

It turned out to be a little bit different than I thought. I thought there would be more interface on strategic issues. I had hoped that they would contribute to problems which went beyond their ultimate responsibility.

> *In part, I guess it's because it's such a diverse group of people. Segura, for example, is an outstanding executive, but because he thinks his English is limited, he would rather discuss issues separately with me than in an open meeting. Bahlmann, on the other hand, is very interested in global strategy though sometimes he doesn't have as much impact as he would like to have. Stein and Jamieson are somewhere in the middle, and they are driven primarily by the success of their own regions. Preston is highly intellectual; he is also the biggest repertoire supplier, and sometimes he thinks we're not paying enough attention to his repertoire. It's a combination of very diverse people. That's probably why the results are still so much influenced by me.*

> *And it may very well have to do with me and the way I run things. I think I know what is good for us. Therefore, when I'm convinced that that's the right way to go, it takes a great effort to get me off that route. However, because it has been successful, it has been hard to say that I should change my style.*

THE MAY 1993 ECM

Gassner opened the May 1993 Managing Director's Convention in Boca Raton with a speech in which he stressed that the company's key success factor for the future was creating repertoire. "It's local artist development, it's joint ventures, it's acquisitions. That is the way we are going to grow. That is how we will reach our goal of becoming Number 1," he told the audience. He also congratulated them on another year of success in surpassing their business targets, but joked that "I am so naive; you must be lowballing your plans every time, because you have never missed them."

The week-long convention also included a session by Henn on developing A&R; a financial presentation from Gorman in which he emphasized the need to reduce costs and improve efficiency as markets matured and growth in the record business leveled off; a presentation about new recording and media technologies; and a speech by Dornemann about the future of the emerging Entertainment Group at BMG.[12] While the RDs attended, they played no formal role in the convention.

Whereas the focus in past conventions had been primarily on growth, the topics which formed the agenda for the 1993 MD Convention—global artist development, new technologies, BMG's expansion into new entertainment arenas, and cost control-emphasized disciplined management to position BMG International for the next phase. The MDs were excited about the important new role that BMG International could take on in the future. As Gassner told them, "We're the only company in Bertelsmann that is really global; we're the only ones in Japan, and we have over 300 people there. If Bertelsmann wants to sell film or video games globally, we are there. We have something Bertelsmann can build on."

On the other hand, many of the MDs expressed skepticism about Gassner's "conflicting messages." As one stated, "You can't grow market share unless you're willing to spend money, and you can't cut back on investing in new acts, because you never know who might be the next Rolling Stones." Gassner, however, did not see his goals in conflict: "Yes—it's inconvenient on the one hand to grow and on the other hand to control your costs. It's a difficult task, but I expect both. I cannot allow anyone to just charge ahead regardless of cost. I expect a balance; and I know they can do it."

These issues also figured heavily into Gassner's agenda at the May ECM, which took place during the convention. He knew that the future challenges would demand more cooperation and global strategic thinking on the part of the executive committee. They had all been extremely successful so far in their own regions, but a regional focus alone would no longer be enough to guide BMG International through the uncertain and ever-changing terrain of the next five years.

THE REDUCED MANUFACTURING PRICE

The reduced manufacturing price was a result of negotiations undertaken by Bahlmann with Sonopress, Bertelsmann's central manufacturing operation in Europe, which supplied product to the European countries. These countries were required to purchase a certain percentage of their CDs, records, and cassettes from Sonopress, and as part of his responsibilities as the head of central manufacturing, Bahlmann negotiated the transfer prices annually by comparing Sonopress's bid to those of outside vendors. Because the non-European countries did not source through Sonopress, they would not be affected by the new price.

As Gassner might have predicted, when he brought up the issue at the ECM by congratulating Bahlmann, Preston shot Stein a knowing glance. Preston was required to source his manufacturing through Sonopress even though he could get a better price by using a U.K. vendor. As he explained:

> *Because the United Kingdom is such a large repertoire supplier, I have volume benefits which I offer Arnold. He takes my volume, combines it with the other European countries, and negotiates a manufacturing rate with Sonopress in Munich, and then I buy the product back with the exchange rate working against me. Austria pays the same price as I do, getting the benefit of my volume scale.*

Gassner then raised the question of what to do in response to the new prices. There was a long pause at the table. Bahlmann responded first by suggesting that the "extra" profit from the regions be placed in investment funds for each territory. Stein argued that this was not necessary "since the money's always there if the investment is good anyway." The group agreed that the money did not need to be placed in a separate fund, but be left to each company to decide how to use.

"OK, so what about the targets?" Gassner asked. Looking down at his copy of the calculations that Gorman had distributed before the meeting, he continued, "There are significant variances here. An MD's *betriebsergebnis* in some cases could be increased by as much as 50 percent due solely to the price reduction."

Segura then spoke up: "This doesn't affect me in my region, so I can be objective.[13] We have never before changed targets once they have been set. Not for any reason. So I don't see why we should change them this time." Preston added: "I agree. Some years, I'm hurt by the transfer pricing and exchange rate, but our targets have never been eased to reflect this. So why would we change them now that it's working the other way? It doesn't seem fair."

Indeed, many of the executive committee members found the issue an unusual one for the ECM agenda. As Gorman explained,

> *To tell you the truth, I was a little surprised when Rudi asked me to calculate adjusted business targets to reflect the new manufacturing price. I know I'm the one who has been pushing reexamination of our cost structure. But we've never changed the targets. Whether you acquired a company, lost a company, lost a customer, had a major bankruptcy, an artist didn't release—we've had everything you can imagine happen, and I do not remember ever adjusting the targets for anybody, for any reason.*

Gassner said, however, that he was concerned that some of the MDs might become "complacent" because their *betriebsergebnis* target would be substantially easier to meet if it were not adjusted. "I want to maintain the challenge of an aggressive bonus target, I want the MDs to be held accountable for the savings. I want them to realize that it isn't just a Christmas gift," he explained to the group.

No one at the table responded or looked in Gassner's direction. Gassner then wondered how he could get them to address the question of changing the targets, a possibility they seemed unwilling even to consider.

NOTES

1. Managing directors managed local operations in a particular country; each MD reported to one of five regional directors.
2. Alan, Purkiss, "Let's Hear It for the Unsung Hero," *Accountancy,* June 1992, pp. 70-73.
3. Dannen, Frederick, *Hit Men: Power Brokers and Fast Money Inside the Music Business* (New York: Vintage Books, 1991), pp. 246-261.
4. "BMG's Five Year Man," *Music Business International,* Vol. 3, No. 1 (January 1993), p. 18.
5. Ibid.
6. According to Gassner, a 1% worldwide market share gain was worth around $250 million in revenue. ("Charting the Future" speech, May 1993, Boca Raton, Florida.)
7. The "prestige market" of the U.S. was the most important supplier of recorded music around the world, and BMG'S Arista, led by long-time music executive Clive Davis, had launched two global superstars, Whitney Houston and Kenny G, who reached No. I and 2 on the *Billboard* album chart. In 1993, Houston's soundtrack for *The Bodyguard* sold 20 million copies and became one of the top-selling albums of all time, fueling a significant portion of BMG's revenue in the U.S. and abroad. (Lander, Mark, "An Overnight Success—After Six Years," *Business Week,* April 19, 1993, pp. 52–54.)
8. In addition, BMG International had an agreement with MCA/Geffen to market and distribute that company's products outside the U.S. The MCA/Geffen deal gave BMG International access to such stars as Guns 'N' Roses, Nirvana, Aerosmith, Bobby Brown, and Cher.

9. *A&R* was a record industry term that stood for "artist and repertoire," record company products. In record companies, investing in A&R to develop talent was analogous to a manufacturing concern investing in R&D. "A&R marketing" was essentially product marketing.

10. *Betriebsergebnis* was a German accounting term roughly translated to mean profit plus interest costs. The official language at BMG International was English (German was never spoken if a nonspeaker was present); *betriebsergebnis* was the only German word the company used.

11. A *vorstand* was a German managing board consisting of full-time executive members who carried out the day-to-day operation of the company. It was distinguished from the supervisory board (*aufsichtsrat*), which consisted of shareholders and employee representatives. [Parkyn, Brian, *Democracy, Accountability, and Participation in Industry* (Bradford, West Yorkshire, England: MCB General Management Ltd., 1979)], p. 105; and Kennedy, Thomas, *European Labor Relations* (Lexington, Massachusetts: Lexington Books, 1980), p. 185.

12. In response to trends toward multimedia entertainment technology, Dornemann had begun to look toward expanding BMG's reach in the entertainment industry to include television and even film. Industry analysts speculated that Dornemann was interested in purchasing an independent film studio, but such a deal had not yet materialized. In September 1993, BMG announced a joint venture with Tele-Communications, Inc., the largest cable system operator in the U.S., to launch a hybrid music video/home shopping cable channel that would rival MTV and VH-1. (Robichaux, Mark and Johnnie L. Roberts, "TCI, Bertelsmann Join to Launch Music, Shopping Cable Channel," *Wall Street Journal,* September 17, 1993.)

13. Since the Latin American region included Spain and Portugal, Segura was affected minimally by the reduced price.

Rudi Gassner and the Executive Committee of BMG International—Discussion Questions

1. What should Gassner and the executive committee do about modifying the business plan and bonus targets of each country?
2. How should Gassner make this decision?
3. How effective has Gassner been in managing the executive committee?
4. What are his sources of power?
5. What is Gassner's influence style?

Women and Global Leadership at Bestfoods[1] *

Laura Brody had just finished analyzing the progress she'd made in her first two years as director of diversity and development for Bestfoods International, formerly known as CPC. Brody is a stylish woman in her forties, possessed of a droll sense of humor. She had begun working for Bestfoods 10 years earlier in management development. The position provided Brody the opportunity to meet and develop good relationships with many of the managers who were identified as having senior management potential and who were now in senior executive positions. Brody spent eight years coordinating the company's well-respected annual Senior Management Development Program. The program, taught by world-famous professors, was for managers who had been tapped to become leaders. She also had helped organize Bestfoods' global action-learning programs (where knowledgeable people were brought together from all parts of the company to tackle strategic, systemwide issues). These programs were often held at Arrowwood, an off-site corporate conference center just outside New York City.

Brody came to Bestfoods in 1988 and was surprised to find that the company seemed to be far behind most leading companies in promoting diversity, particularly in the company's proportion of women and minorities. She found herself revisiting what it was like to work with senior men who had limited experience working alongside high-level professional women. Corporate efforts to date had been limited primarily to diversity awareness training. When Brody was asked to take over the diversity function in 1995, she wanted to be sure that real, substantive change was possible. Brody explained to her prospective boss, Dick Bergeman, senior vice president of human resources, that she needed to be assured of the company's sincerity and willingness to support progress and changes in this area. Bergeman is an engaging, well-respected, 22-year veteran with Bestfoods who spearheaded the transformation of human resources from an administrative function to an integral part of the global strategy team. He replied, "I can't tell you I will automatically agree to everything you propose, but I will agree that it is your job to make change happen. And if I say 'no' the first time, then it is your job to figure out a different way to approach it or structure it and come back at me again and again and again." Since Brody was not expecting "carte blanche" up front, she was sufficiently reassured by his response and took the job. Brody's diagnosis of her new job was that the company supported diversity, but there were few specific strategies in place for her to implement. She saw her position as "a double-edged sword."

> It was a wonderful opportunity to stand out on my own, set an agenda and implement it. As this was a senior position, I was expected to establish the goals and strategies for the company-wide diversity function. If I was successful, I could be well positioned for future career progress. If not, like my two predecessors, I might have to look for future career growth elsewhere.

Bestfoods has had a diversity function since 1989. It evolved from traditional EEO[2] compliance reporting and had two previous directors, a male Hispanic and a male African American. Unlike Brody, both were disadvantaged by not having an established network throughout the organization, since one was brought in from outside the company and the other had experience only in the U.S. division in labor relations. Brody suspected that the climate had not really been ripe for change in the area of diversity until the last few years. Another advantage Brody enjoyed was the fit between her personality and the challenges of this particular job. In the early years of her career, she had received feedback that she was too direct and not easily deterred from pursuing a certain path. Brody was counseled to "go along to get along." Characteristics that had formerly been seen as weaknesses, however, were now perceived as her strengths:

In my current job, I am expected to be the conscience of the organization. Like an Old Testament prophet, I am frequently expected to preach fire and brimstone, nudging the company in a certain direction even though they may not want to go that way. For once my style and the type of person I am fit exactly with what my job demands and what my boss expects me to do. I love my job! As I told Dick Bergeman, "I can't believe you pay me to make trouble—I would have done that for free!"

COMPANY BACKGROUND

Bestfoods is among the largest global food companies, with annual sales in 1999 of $8.6 billion. Its most well-known brands include Hellmann's and Best Foods condiments and dressings; Mazola corn oil and margarine; Knorr soups, sauces, and bouillon; Skippy peanut butter; Thomas' English muffins; and Entenmanns's baked goods. Bestfoods also has a catering division that is known as Caterplan in most global markets. Bestfoods has operations in more than 60 countries and markets products in 110 countries. The 93-year-old company is well positioned internationally with over 90 years of operating experience in Europe, 70 years in Latin America, and more than 68 years in Asia. Although headquartered in the United States, the company earns 60 percent of its revenues from non-U.S. sources. The company projects future growth to continue to come primarily from outside the mature markets of North America and Western Europe. Africa, Asia, Eastern Europe, the Middle East, Latin America, and the countries of the former Soviet Union are projected to lead increases in twenty-first century revenue. At present the company has four geographic divisions: Europe, North America, Asia, and Latin America.

Bestfoods has a highly decentralized structure, which gives general managers and local management the autonomy to adapt and modify changes suggested by corporate headquarters. One of the company's strengths is its global strategic vision combined with a consistent local focus and decision making. CEO Dick Shoemate appreciates the difficult balance between giving the local divisions power to make their own decisions and integrating these units into a coherent whole. "It's our strength, but it's also a challenge when we try to make changes."

The company's vision (see Case Appendix A) is to be the best international food company in the world by building on the organization's core businesses, values, and strengths. Bestfoods has three global *core businesses*: savory products (e.g., soups, bouillon, sauces), dressings, and catering. The company's *core values* are:

- Growing (financial success, business growth, people development, and diversity)
- Caring (adherence to the law and highest moral and ethical standards, respect for individual worth and ability, satisfying customer and consumer needs, safe workplaces, and protecting the environment)
- Sharing (valuing teamwork, internal and external partnering, learning from experience and transferring learning with pride)
- Daring (courage, candor, conviction, pioneering and leadership, quick decision making, and aggressiveness in seizing new markets).

The company's identified *core strengths* are:

- A unique culture combining global strategic vision with local focus, decision making, and action.
- A proven ability to transfer and use products, skills, technology, and people from all parts of the world.

To best link employee actions with the company's vision, Bestfoods uses a strategic performance measurement system called the Balanced Scorecard. "The Balanced Scorecard provides a framework that helps shape our activities and measure our performance in four critically important areas (customer satisfaction, people development, business practices, and innovation and learning) which together result in a fifth critical area, financial performance, the ultimate measure of the best."[3] Instead of one uniform global measurement system, each division, affiliate, department, and functional group within the company creates its own Balanced Scorecard that identifies the key activities, or "strategic drivers," that will move its particular business closer to the company's goals. Nevertheless, the CEO may announce specific new goals to add to the Corporate Balanced Scorecard at WorldTeam Meetings, which the company holds about every three years. At the WorldTeam meetings, approximately 150 of the most senior executives from around the world spend several days together focusing on strategic issues, sharing innovative implementation plans, and learning together. The WorldTeam meetings are another way to coordinate the far-flung global company.

Dick Shoemate is chairman, president, and chief executive officer of Bestfoods. He joined the company in 1962 and held positions in manufacturing, finance, and business management in the consumer foods and corn refining businesses. Shoemate was president of the Corn Refining division before assuming the corporate presidency in 1988. Unlike many CEOs, Shoemate is not only bright but unassuming and down to earth. He is both approachable and an excellent listener. Shoemate is equally as impressive and comfortable dealing with board members as with the 60 children of employees he addressed on "Take Your Child to Work Day." Shoemate, in his late fifties, wants one of the marks he leaves on Bestfoods to be increased diversity worldwide and at the most senior levels.

DIVERSITY AT BESTFOODS

Of the corporation's 44,000 employees, two-thirds currently work outside of the United States. In the U.S. division, Bestfoods has 10 to 15 percent more minorities than the industry norm, but 5 to 10 percent fewer women. Bestfoods has been known as a company where people spent most of their career. Similar to many companies, however, a disproportionate number of women and minorities leave Bestfoods within their first three to five years. Historically, women at Bestfoods tended to hit the "glass ceiling" at the middle-management level. Women have succeeded primarily in staff positions, such as the corporate legal department, which has the highest representation of women. There are numerous entry-to-midlevel women in human resources, but the division-level executives are all male. There are women in marketing who have attained midlevel jobs and some who have been promoted into senior-level positions, but only one woman has successfully made the leap from marketing to a general manager position. The usual career path that men followed in Bestfoods to become senior executives has gone from general manager positions to operating division presidents to corporate officers. Women have remained a small percentage of the candidate pool for senior executive jobs because they tended to be scarce in the usual career pipelines to the top—line positions and high-level positions outside the United States.

Not surprisingly, the 1997 employee survey in the United States showed that minorities and women perceived less opportunity for advancement and career development than did whites or men. Similarly, they perceived their performance to be less linked to compensation than did whites or men. It surprised many at the company, however, that men ranked "workload and pace interfere with work/life balance" as the number one issue among the five diversity-related issues they would like the company to address. Although women ranked this issue last at number five, the work/life integration issue cut across gender and hierarchy. For example, while female administrative staff might worry about making it to a day care center by 5 or 6 P.M., some senior men grumbled that their wives were "threatening to divorce them" if they missed one more family event.

Retention analyses revealed that at every management level, women and minorities had more turnover than males and whites. As a result of these findings, Brody's objective within the United States was to have better retention and development of both women and minorities.

When Brody and her staff did a global analysis of female employees, they discovered that 15 percent of the employees who had been designated as "high potential" were women. They also found that there were more U.S. women in management positions when compared to other regions, although Europe appointed the first woman as a country general manager. Among the approximately 264 participants who attended the Senior Management Development Programs from 1988 to 1998, the company sent only 15 female managers. It wasn't until 1998 that a senior female manager attended who was not an American. Brody knew that attitudes toward promoting women varied widely throughout the company, from extremely supportive to indifferent—or even chauvinistic in a few cases. For the most part, she believed that although managers were well intentioned, they were uncertain about what improvements could be made regarding career advancement for women. The company was committed to advancing diversity as a key competitive element in its overall business strategy.

Bestfoods has a diverse board of directors. Of their 14 directors, two are female CEOs, one is an African American CEO, seven are white U.S. American male CEOs, and four are male CEOs from other countries. Bestfoods has three female corporate officers, one each from manufacturing, marketing, and public relations. By 1997, 14 percent of the members of the board of directors, 15 percent of the corporate officers, and 13 percent of directors and vice presidents were women.

THE REASONS BEHIND THE FIGURES

When Brody and her staff ponder the barriers that women face at Bestfoods, they think some attitudes and behaviors may be due to generational rather than gender issues. For example, most of the corporate officers are in their late 1950s and early 1960s and have stay-at-home wives. They have never watched their wives struggle to climb the corporate ladder or juggle the competing demands of work and home life. Nor have their own careers been affected by the demands of a dual-career marriage. As a result, Brody wonders how well some of the senior male executives really understand the barriers or challenges today's women often face.

For example, a common complaint among women is that men have the luxury of coming to work early and staying late if they want to attempt to impress the boss in this fashion. Because many women are responsible for dropping off and picking up children at school or day care and then supervising them at home while preparing dinner, they have to work more regular hours. This does not mean the women work fewer hours or less hard. However, to the extent that the corporate culture values time spent in the office (rather than actual time spent working and achieving results) as an indicator of loyalty and promotability, working mothers (and some fathers) are at a disadvantage. One division manager has the night watchman keep track of the time employees leave at the end of the day; accurately or not, his employees interpret this as a clear signal that, "If you want to get ahead, you must work late."

Another factor that could be hindering development and ultimately retention is that the company has few women at high enough levels to be selected for senior management development opportunities. The corporation's senior-level management training programs are offered to senior managers whom the company has already promoted up the hierarchy. Few women attain that level and, therefore, receive little in the way of company-sponsored, formal management and career development opportunities, or the executive-level exposure and visibility that such opportunities provide.

DIVERSITY AS A STRATEGIC ISSUE

While the number of senior women, corporate officers, and board members at Bestfoods is respectable when compared to many companies, neither Brody nor Shoemate think it is adequate to support the future they envision for Bestfoods. Consumer foods, not unlike many other industries, has become increasingly competitive; only the companies with top talent and top brands survive. Moreover, whereas many consumer foods companies used to be able to operate as loose confederations of fairly autonomous country operations, global competition is now forcing all members of the industry to more closely coordinate their worldwide operations.

To succeed in such an environment, Bestfoods needs to attract and retain the best talent available globally and have local employees from each country in which they operate reflect the consumer base. With women making more than 80 percent of purchasing decisions for Bestfoods' products, the company will suffer if it fails to understand women's perspectives, needs, and decision-making criteria. Shoemate sees promoting women into senior management positions not primarily as a matter of diversity but rather as an issue of strategic competitive advantage. On numerous occasions, he has explicitly expressed his commitment to developing the most highly talented women and men from around the world:

> We believe that one of Bestfoods' unique competitive strengths is a management team that delivers outstanding performance in the local marketplace and also works together to build the "Best International Food Company in the World." ... We actively seek to identify and to develop high performing Bestfoods' managers throughout the company, including men and women from all countries and ethnic backgrounds.

Shoemate knows, however, that words are not enough to change an organization. He personally appointed all three of Bestfoods' female corporate officers during his tenure as CEO. Nevertheless, he wants to see more rapid progress on the goal of including more women in senior management and leadership. He made a note to himself to discuss with Brody what form this change should take at Bestfoods.

MANAGING CHANGE AT BESTFOODS

No CEO can simply mandate change in a highly decentralized multinational that values local autonomy. Focusing on diversity further complicates change efforts because it is sometimes viewed as a "U.S. issue." Within some cultures, equity among women and men is not a well-publicized concern, and diversity is locally defined to refer to other groupings within the population. Therefore, for companies headquartered in the United States, the leadership has to tread carefully. Both within the food industry and within Bestfoods, employees tend to work their way up, and executives brought in from the outside often do not adjust to the informal norms and values of the company. This practice has the advantage of providing continuity and a strong organizational culture, but the downside is less new blood and fewer innovations. Bestfoods' U.S. employees tend to reflect "Middle America"—conservative, traditional people with "old-fashioned American values." Brody affectionately describes the company as a Norman Rockwell painting. While the pace and pressure has picked up in recent years, it is neither an industry nor a company with a prior reputation for being "fast-paced." Brody describes Bestfoods' culture as traditional, conservative, polite, "gentlemanly," and nonconfrontational. While the politeness contributes to the pleasant relations Bestfoods is noted for, it also makes face-to-face confrontations rare; criticism and dissent tend to go underground. The emphasis on tradition makes change slow and risky. Some executives are leery of being blamed if changes they initiate don't work. As a result, some managers use the "drip method" of change—small changes over time that eventually add up to progress.

While individuals may approach change somewhat cautiously, Bestfoods has developed a very effective group method for taking advantage of opportunities and resolving problems that affect all divisions. When the global action-learning task forces come together, they analyze situations and, toward the end of the meeting, present their recommendations to top management. The CEO and his direct reports immediately consider each recommendation and respond to the task force before the meeting ends.

As a result of all these factors, Brody's strategy has been to focus on getting the decision makers "on board" and then making incremental changes. Her style is to plant the seeds of ideas and provide information and options to the executive team so they can begin thinking about diversity more broadly and from different perspectives.

BRODY'S PHILOSOPHY ON HUMAN RESOURCE DEVELOPMENT

Brody has a very clear idea of the role of human resources, as seen in the following description of her job.

> *As an HR executive, I do not see myself as merely an ombudsperson for employees. I have always seen HR as a critical management responsibility. There are several aspects of HR in which one is required to be the conscience of the organization. I spent many of my formative years as a consultant working with clients on diagnostic and implementation issues to help make organizations more effective. So my focus is more proactive and action-oriented, trying to create programs that lead to long-term change rather than compliance. My goal has always been to "make a difference" at work. I've learned that everything has to be linked to the business. Line management has to have an itch they want to scratch, and it's my responsibility to make them feel that itch—whether they know it or not. So I don't see HR as an administrative staff function, but as an organization development function that needs to work with line managers. Although people like me are sometimes seen as mavericks, I think you have to understand the needs of the business, create effective relationships with line management, and bend rules to solve problems. Traditionally, HR has a reputation for writing the policies and then telling people why they* can't *do things.*

Brody went on to explain that the traditional HR roles are switched at Bestfoods. In most companies, corporate HR establishes policy and procedures and then administers them, while the operating divisions creatively try to bend the rules to meet the needs of local line managers. At Bestfoods, HR policies are frequently developed and implemented at the divisional level, while the corporate group often has more freedom to experiment and be innovative.

LAYING THE GROUNDWORK FOR CHANGE

Bestfoods already had a Diversity Advisory Council (DAC) when Brody took over. It continues today and is composed of 14 members—senior executives in the U.S. business, corporate staff, and the vice presidents of human resources from each unit. The council is chaired by the CEO and facilitated by Brody. Her predecessor met with the council a few times a year, and their primary achievement was coming to consensus on a common diversity training program for senior managers throughout North America. By contrast, Brody adopted a team-building approach with the council. She knew they had to establish a common vision, so Brody spent almost her entire first year working with them to craft a vision and to agree upon a definition of diversity. Brody worked to ensure that Bestfoods defined diversity very broadly (see Case Appendix B on page 547) for two reasons: (1) to avoid excluding white males; and (2) so that other countries would not see diversity only in light of U.S. EEO requirements. The council also developed a Balanced Scorecard for diversity that mirrors the Corporate Balanced Scorecard (see Case Appendix B). As Brody states,

> *In corporate life, you only make progress on things you measure, and you only measure things that are important—such as operating income, profitability, ROI, ROA, and market share. These things are all measured and tracked very, very frequently. So in terms of making progress on diversity, the measurable goal was increased career opportunity—promotions, salary levels, and representation at senior management levels—and not the "nice-to-haves," like calendars with every ethnic holiday posted or "feeling included"; it was in fact about* being *included. I preached that you could not have an effective diversity function without, at a minimum, having effective equal employment policies and actions in place.*

Brody and the council also linked diversity to the corporate vision.

> *It's very simple. We could not be the best food company in the world if we weren't recruiting and retaining the talented women and minorities who make up large proportions of current M.B.A. programs and who bring different perspectives and experiences from those of whites and men. Since the number of minorities we have is fairly good, one of the first things I did was to focus on the representation of women, an area in which our numbers were not so good. I had industry measures to justify doing this. I also had my own personal experience in the organization and the frustration at seeing a lot of diversity awareness training going on but not seeing many tangible results coming out of it.*

Consistent with the CEO's perspective, Brody sees diversity as a business issue and insists on promoting it as such. She does not see her job as reengineering society or changing societal attitudes; her primary focus is on behaviors and practices that will benefit the company. Brody's team building with the Diversity Advisory Council paid off. After about two years, the council wanted to raise the bar on diversity and chose to go forward in a proactive way. To learn what leading companies were doing about leveraging workforce inclusion to increase their business competitiveness, Brody invited outside practitioners who were involved in best-practice efforts to make presentations to the council. She also gathered a variety of benchmarking and best-practice studies and reports for council members.

In addition to the groundwork Brody was laying with the Diversity Advisory Council, she established a program called Cultural Connections, an employee-driven education and awareness program, and a peer coaching and mentoring program for new hires called SOS, "Sponsoring Our Success." Brody's new initiatives complemented Bestfoods' long history of involvement with INROADS (Bergeman is on the board of directors for the northern New Jersey chapter). INROADS is an internship program for high school and college-age minority students that had proven successful for the company in recruiting top talent, as many interns later joined Bestfoods. Brody's department, which consisted of one other professional and a secretary, coordinated entry-level diversity awareness training, sexual harassment prevention training, and diversity training for the most senior 300 managers and executives in the company. At her suggestion, Shoemate sent out an open letter to all employees in 1997 regarding the company's diversity initiative (see Case Appendix B) and another "state of diversity" letter to U.S. employees in 1998 (see Case Appendix C). Brody's job is made easier by both Shoemate's and Bergeman's sincere belief in the strategic importance of diversity.

While these efforts have been successful, Brody knows that still more has to be done, and she too would like to pick up the pace of change. Among others, she has been considering three alternatives that might have an even larger impact.

1. Conduct a survey that would compare the differences in perception between women and men regarding development and retention in the company and more clearly identify the unique barriers women face.
2. Hold a meeting modeled after the global action-learning programs to tackle the problem of retaining and promoting women.
3. Offer a leadership development program for midlevel women managers.

One day Brody was in Shoemate's office getting his signature on some letters. He was in the midst of reviewing the 1997 employee survey data and said, "Laura, if you could do one thing to improve things for women in this company, what would it be?" Brody knew this was a big opportunity. The mental Rolodex in her head started spinning as she quickly considered a variety of options she'd been pondering. Brody took a deep breath and pitched her best idea.

> *I really cannot speak for all women. But if I were the CEO, what I would want to do is to engage a significant number of women in this dialogue. What about sponsoring a global forum for high-potential and senior women representing all the businesses from around the world*

and bringing them to Arrowwood? They could help us better understand the environment and culture in the company and how it impacts women. We could do what we always do with a business issue that needs to be driven from the center—have an action-learning program with outside experts to design and facilitate it. We could receive both information and recommendations from participants on how to proceed and make progress, and we could also do some leadership training at the same time.

Shoemate asked a few probing questions and suggested she flesh it out with Bergeman. Brody and Bergeman prepared a position paper that Bergeman discussed with the Corporate Strategy Council (CSC) at its next meeting in April. The CSC is composed of the six most senior corporate officers, who are responsible for the four geographic divisions, the baking business, and the corporate staff. The CSC immediately approved the forum idea. Shoemate requested that it take place no later than the end of July. That meant Brody had only 90 days to organize her company's first-ever Women's Global Leadership Forum.

Brody and her staff dove into preparations, and the plans began to fall into place. The question that continued to nag Brody was how to ensure that the forum resulted in real organizational change. She worried that participants might leave feeling good, with raised expectations about what the company would do for women, only to be disillusioned if the recommended changes didn't materialize afterward. As it turned out, senior management shared Brody's concern about unrealistically heightened expectations. Some of them also wondered how they could participate and interact with the attendees so that neither group would feel threatened.

FORUM INVITATIONS AND REACTIONS

To create a comprehensive list of senior and high potential women, Brody solicited nominations from all division presidents, which she personally reviewed along with the corporate high-potential lists and succession plans. Next, the CEO sent a letter to all six members of the Corporate Strategy Council describing the forum and requesting that they rank order their nominees. As Bestfoods does with its Senior Management Development Program, the company allocated spaces at the Women's Global Leadership Forum according to the relative size of each division and geographical area to ensure balanced representation. Brody's goal was to invite 50 participants, of which at least half were to come from outside the United States. As an early indication of the high level of support, every division requested additional spaces. Brody responded by increasing the number of participants to 60 and choosing 10 of these as facilitators for small group sessions. Shoemate personally sent a letter of invitation to each participant. Fifty-five women from 25 countries were able to accept the invitation.

Brody knew that merely asking the division presidents to identity their high potential women, thereby adding them to the recognized and visible talent pool for the company's future leadership, was a significant intervention in and of itself. "Even if we'd never held the forum, it was a good exercise for the senior executives to stop and consider how many highly talented women managers they had and where they were in the company. One president promoted a woman a few months earlier than he had planned to as a result of thinking about whom he wanted to nominate for the forum!"

The reactions to the forum announcement were, for the most part, very positive. Several people commented that this was one of the most exciting and forward-looking initiatives the company had ever tackled. Many women were gratified to be identified as participants. Not all women, however, reacted positively. Some senior women, primarily Americans, worried that attending an all-women forum might encourage others to think their success was owed primarily to their status as women rather than to their competence; they had no desire to be at the forefront of women's issues. Some women who were not invited, from secretaries to directors, felt excluded from yet another "private club." Some invitees were also concerned about the potentially negative reactions from their male colleagues and bosses, including worrying about the likelihood of a male backlash.

There were sporadic dismissive and skeptical comments by both men and women who doubted that the forum would result in anything more than a "bitch session." One senior male manager told his female subordinate, "Have a good time at the koffee-klatch" as she left for the forum. Some men complained of discrimination because they were not invited. However, other men thought the forum was long overdue and emphasized their support. Brody kept Shoemate and Bergeman informed of the resistance she encountered so there would not be any surprises regarding this controversial program among the senior managers. At one point, Brody sent Shoemate a note saying, "You know how women get crabby and lose their sense of humor when they're left out? Well, guess what—it seems that men also get crabby and lose their sense of humor when they are excluded!" Given her strict deadline, Brody didn't feel she had enough time to deal with the backlash in depth, other than being aware of it and trying to deflect it with humor and an ongoing reiteration of the CEO's rationale and goals for championing the forum.

PLANNING THE FORUM

As far as Brody was aware, no other company had ever held a global meeting for its most senior and high-potential women with the intent of opening a dialogue on global leadership and organizational change. There were no models to follow, so she began searching for outside consultants to help design and implement the forum. One of the consultants she hired began by interviewing Shoemate, Bergeman, all corporate officers including the three female corporate officers, and one of the female board members to get a feel for the organization. She and Brody began designing a program to fit Bestfoods' needs and to meet the forum's goals:

- Increase the global competitiveness of Bestfoods.
- Develop the global leadership skills of Bestfood's most highly talented and senior women.
- Create an internal network among Bestfoods' women leaders to facilitate their global effectiveness.
- Develop both global and local recommendations for enhancing Bestfoods' ability to support the career advancement and success of an increasing number of highly talented and senior women.

Early in the process, Brody warned Bergeman that the cost of the program would be higher than the original estimate. His response was, "Spend whatever you need to put on an outstanding program." Bergeman was aware that some people who were ambivalent about the program might try to find reasons for it to fail. He, therefore, insisted that everything about the program be first rate. While Bergeman remained available when Brody wanted his support or advice, he allowed her to take full responsibility for the program.

PRE-FORUM SURVEY

Brody's team carried out a survey-feedback process aimed at producing data that would serve as a baseline and cause people to reexamine their thinking about the opportunities and barriers for women's career advancement. Brody was especially interested in surveying both senior women and men, so both groups' views would be visible at the forum. She developed a survey modeled after the Catalyst[4] report, "Women in Corporate Leadership: Progress & Prospects" (Wellington, 1996). A primary purpose of the survey was to determine whether there were significant differences of opinion between the views of women and men in Bestfoods regarding individual and corporate strategies that would most benefit women, common reasons preventing women from advancing, beliefs about women, and personal experiences in the company. Brody sent the survey to all corporate officers, the 125 most senior executives who were being invited to this year's WorldTeam meeting, and the 60 women who had been invited to the forum. The response rate for the survey was 70 percent. Brody understood quite clearly that for any significant organizational change to occur, the senior levels of management, almost exclusively male, had to be part of a coalition for change. For that to happen, they had to be included on the front end as part of the overall organizational change process. Brody sent the survey results to all the survey participants after the forum.

The survey data revealed the following key points:

1. Although women and men agreed on most of the barriers perceived to be inhibiting women's career advancement (women's lack of mobility for international assignments and lack of both general management and line experience), the women reported a number of barriers that appear to have been invisible to the men:
   - Senior men's discomfort with ambitious women
   - Senior men's negative stereotyping and preconceptions of women
   - Senior men's difficulty in reporting to a woman

2. While women and men agreed on the three most important strategies for women's career success at Bestfoods (consistently exceeding performance expectations; gaining line management experience; and seeking difficult and high-visibility assignments), they disagreed on other key strategies.
   - The majority of women believed that they had to "develop a style that men are comfortable with" in order to succeed, whereas men ranked this strategy next to last in terms of importance.
   - Women were more likely than men to believe they had to develop a relationship with an influential mentor in order to succeed.
   - More men than women stressed the importance of gaining international experience.
   - None of the men stated that they would consider changing companies to get ahead whereas 14 percent of the women stated that they would consider leaving Bestfoods for another company.

3. Men and women agreed on the five most important corporate strategies that would benefit women (more assignments managing people; include more women on divisional and global strategic task forces; include more women in the Senior Management Development Program, hold managers more accountable for identifying, developing, and advancing high potential women; and include a higher percentage of women in succession plans). However, women placed greater importance on each of these corporate strategies than did their male colleagues.

4. It was noteworthy that both women and men perceived the barriers facing women to be greater than the reality of what women actually experience. For example, although some men hold stereotypical assumptions about women in general, they reported that these assumptions usually disappear when they actually work with or for a women manager. However, the specific women they know and work with are typically viewed as "exceptions" to the rule.

Brody and her team worked long hours to analyze the extensive survey data and present then in such a way that both women and men in the company would be able to understand each other's different views of reality. She hoped the survey results would trigger more in-depth discussion at the forum, so more people would be motivated to eliminate the gap in perceptions and find new ways for women and men to work together.

THE WOMEN'S GLOBAL LEADERSHIP FORUM

Brody and the consultants wanted to ensure that the forum was more than just an effective leadership training seminar for women that developed recommendations for organizational change. They had confidence that the participants would develop recommendations that were appropriate for Bestfoods, but what would happen afterward? Much depended on the continued support of senior executives and their reaction to the forum. To encourage their growing support, the majority of Bestfoods' most senior executives (CEO, Corporate Strategy Council, Diversity Advisory Council, corporate officers, and a board member) joined the women participants at the welcome dinner, as well as at other sessions (at which their presence would not be inhibitive), and at the all-important presentation of recommendations on the final morning of the 4 1/2-day Women's Global Leadership Forum. The senior executives' inclusion allowed them to see the women participants in action, hear their opinions firsthand, and learn for themselves what the company needed to do, and to avoid doing, in order to succeed.

The design of the forum tried to enhance the women's preparation for proactive roles in the company's future leadership. The forum design included three types of sessions: (1) individual professional development sessions focusing on global leadership skills; (2) organization development sessions aimed at gathering information and making recommendations to the company on women's retention, development, and advancement; and (3) sessions facilitating the formation of a women's network. At the participants' request, the design was modified to allow more time in small groups to formulate recommendations for presentation to the senior executives at the final session. Leadership development activities included "herstories" about significant women who influenced the values and leadership styles of the participants, skill assessment, skill building and coaching, experiential exercises, a panel of female CEOs and Bestfoods' highest-ranking women, and another panel of Bestfoods' senior male executives who gave career advice, and Brody's presentation of the survey results.

As predicted, the forum had some intense and challenging moments as the widely diverse group of 55 women with differing goals, opinions, experiences, and communication and behavior styles met and discussed key corporate and personal challenges. Nevertheless, the participants judged the forum to be a resounding success.

FORUM RECOMMENDATIONS AND EXECUTIVE RESPONSE

A highlight of the forum was the participants' presentation to the CEO, Corporate Strategy Council, and the Diversity Advisory Council on the last day. The women stayed up late the night before, working in teams on the various recommendations. In an offer that reflected their skills as mentors and coaches, the senior American women graciously suggested that younger women from outside the United States do the actual presenting so that they could benefit more directly from the high visibility. Before the presentations began, Shoemate requested that the participants be candid and assured them that they could be totally honest in their feedback. All participants were visibly pulling for the presenters. At one point, a highly articulate and self-assured Chinese woman in her late twenties brought down the house when she assured Shoemate that "There's no need to feel threatened by us—we don't want your job. We want to be CEOs of bigger, better companies than Bestfoods!" Their specific recommendations (found in Appendix D) focused on three key areas: career development (enhancing career opportunities), diversity (increasing representation of women in senior and high-level positions), and work/life balance (enabling women to perform to their highest capabilities while recognizing their multiple roles). In addition to recommending what the company should do, the participants also identified what they themselves should do to enhance their own career opportunities.

While the women participated in a final small group session, Shoemate and the senior executives discussed the recommendations and planned their response. Shoemate suggested separating the recommendations into three categories:

- Current company initiatives—recommendations the company is already doing but which need to be accelerated and better communicated to employees.
- New corporatewide recommendations, which the Corporate Strategy Council could consider at its next meeting.
- New "local" recommendations best addressed within specific countries, regions, or divisions.

When the women rejoined the executives, Shoemate responded to each recommendation, some of which he immediately accepted. He was very open to feedback and did not argue with or become defensive about any points the women raised. He promised to look into existing programs and policies that were not consistently working to the benefit of women's development and retention. Shoemate eloquently referred to his belief that the company's strength lies in its local decision making and explained why he hesitates to mandate most policies from corporate headquarters. However, he also clarified what he could do as CEO to make change happen and assured the women that he would communicate to them the outcome of each recommendation as soon as possible. Shoemate's obvious sincerity and thoughtfulness made a positive impression, as did the response of other CSC members. Shoemate closed the session with an inspirational story about his first experience as a very young manager whose orders were obeyed because, like the women at the Forum, he had the backing and utter confidence of his boss. Shoemate and Bergeman then led a standing ovation for Brody and her staff.

Two hours later, after bidding goodbye to participants about to jet off to all corners of the globe, Brody gratefully collapsed on a lawn chair on Arrowwood's manicured grounds. She was delighted that the forum had ended on such a positive note. The immediate feedback at least seemed to indicate that it had indeed been the catalyst she was hoping for. Nevertheless, Brody still had that nagging question, "What next steps have to take place so that real change in the company and its leadership occurs and becomes institutionalized?"

NOTES

1. The development of this case was funded by the CIBER program at the University of Washington under a grant from the U.S. Department of Education.
2. Equal Employment Opportunity (EEO) laws, under the provisions of Title VII of the Civil Rights Act of 1964, were created in the United States to ensure work environments free from illegal discrimination on the grounds of race, color, religion, disability, age, national origin, or sex.
3. 1998 Vision and Policies pamphlet.
4. Catalyst, located in New York City, is a well-respected research and education institute that focuses on corporate women in senior leadership and management positions.

Case Appendix A

▲▲

The Bestfoods Vision

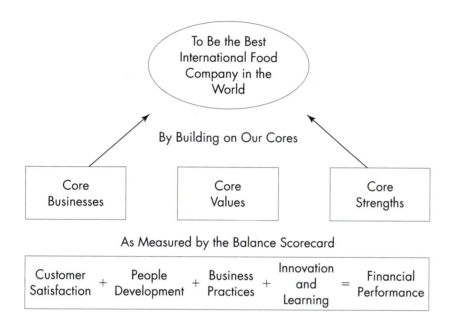

International

CPC INTERNATIONAL INC., INTERNATIONAL PLAZA, ENGLEWOOD CLIFFS, NEW JERSEY 07632

C.R. SHOEMATE
CHAIRMAN AND PRESIDENT   January 10, 1997

An open letter to all CPC Employees …

Subject: CPC's Diversity Initiative

CPC's strong culture and proud traditions are deeply rooted in our core values of honesty, integrity, fairness, and respect. They are also the best foundation on which to build our future. Our values have not changed over time but the way we demonstrate them continues to change. Our customers and consumers, business partners and investors, our own workforce and managers reflect a more diverse society in the growing global economy. Our World Team vision, To Become The Best International Food Company in The World, our core values and company policies challenge every one of us to help in our drive toward becoming the best. That is only possible when every one of us truly believes we will have the opportunity to fulfill our potential at CPC.

Our diversity initiative is an ongoing process that affects everyone in the company. In order to ensure a more inclusive environment that values the contributions of all, we need to engage every person in this effort. The diversity vision that follows highlights the business rationale for increasing and leveraging our diversity, so that CPC employees can develop a shared understanding of why this is a strategic imperative.

The diagram that depicts elements of diversity in the workplace clearly demonstrates our commitment to a broad spectrum of differences that go far beyond equal opportunity programs, which are often limited to race and gender.

The Diversity Advisory Council has embraced four long-term objectives for CPC: Preferred Employer, Balanced Workforce, Equitable Workplace, and Enhanced Business Results. The Balanced Scorecard that follows identifies the drivers and measures to which Corporate Staff, Corn Refining North America, Best Foods and the Baking Business are committed. Division Presidents will be reviewing their progress with me every year.

But progress throughout CPC is everyone's responsibility. Increase your own awareness of people who are different from you and understand how your own assumptions affect the way you treat others. Support our Diversity initiative by following and reinforcing equal treatment and respect for all. Challenge others and speak up if you see inappropriate behavior or hear derogatory comments or jokes and talk to other people about your concerns and suggestions.

On the back cover of this brochure are additional questions and answers about our progress in this important area.

I hope you join me in continued learning and self improvement to reach our vision for the future.

CM Shoemate

OUR DIVERSITY VISION FOR THE FUTURE

WE WILL VALUE, LEVERAGE, AND INCREASE VARIETY AND DIFFERENCE IN OUR WORKFORCE SO THAT OUR DIVERSITY IS THE PERPETUAL STIMULANT OF INNOVATION, CREATIVITY, AND EFFECTIVE PROBLEM SOLVING, PROVIDING US WITH A SUSTAINABLE COMPETITIVE ADVANTAGE THAT HELPS US REACH THE HIGHEST LEVELS OF QUALITY, PRODUCTIVITY AND PROFITABILITY IN ACHIEVING CPC'S VISION p TO BECOME THE BEST INTERNATIONAL FOOD COMPANY IN THE WORLD.

We envision a workplace where diversity is fully integrated into the organization to create an environment that encourages, values, and respects the uniqueness of the individual; fosters achievement; and optimizes business opportunities.

ELEMENTS OF DIVERSITY RECOGNIZED IN THE WORKPLACE

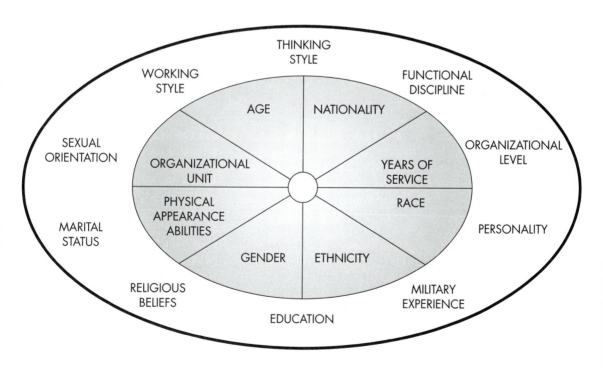

A myriad of characteristics make us who we are. The whole person contributes to the diversity of CPC International and to our success as a company.

LONG-TERM OBJECTIVES

- **PREFERRED EMPLOYER** ESTABLISH BEST PRACTICE STANDARDS OF EXCELLENCE THAT EARN THE CORPORATION INTERNAL RECOGNITION BY EMPLOYEES AND EXTERNAL RECOGNITION BY THE MARKETPLACE FOR BEING THE PREFERRED EMPLOYER TO ALL SEGMENTS OF THE POPULATION.

- **BALANCED WORKFORCE** ENSURE EVERY CPC ORGANIZATION'S WORKFORCE REFLECTS VARIETY AND DIFFERENCE AT ALL LEVELS.

- **EQUITABLE WORKPLACE** ENSURE AN EQUITABLE WORKPLACE IN WHICH OPPORTUNITIES AND REWARDS ARE SUPPORTED BY POLICIES AND PRACTICES BASED ON ACHIEVEMENT, FAIRNESS, AND EQUITY. OUR CORE VALUES DEMAND THAT WE TREAT ONE ANOTHER WITH RESPECT AND DIGNITY AT ALL TIMES, TAKING INDIVIDUAL RESPONSIBILITY FOR DEVELOPMENT AND PERFORMANCE IN AN ENVIRONMENT FREE FROM BIAS AND DISCRIMINATION.

- **ENHANCED BUSINESS RESULTS** ENSURE THAT VARIETY AND DIFFERENCE IN THE CPC WORLD TEAM IS LEVERAGED TO REACH THE HIGHEST LEVELS OF INNOVATION, CREATIVITY, EFFECTIVE PROBLEM SOLVING, AND PERFORMANCE FOR THE BENEFIT OF OUR CUSTOMERS, CONSUMERS, EMPLOYEES, AND SHAREHOLDERS.

DIVERSITY BALANCED SCORECARD

OBJECTIVES	DRIVERS	MEASURES
■ PREFERRED EMPLOYER	RECOGNITION BY EMPLOYEES	EMPLOYEE SURVEY RESULTS
	RECOGNITION BY EXTERNAL EMPLOYMENT CANDIDATES	TURNOVER/RETENTION RATES
		RECRUITING RESULTS
■ BALANCED WORKFORCE	REPRESENTATIVE OF CONSUMER BASE AND WORKPLACE AVAILABILITY	TRENDS IN CONSUMER AND WORKFORCE DEMOGRAPHICS
	REFLECTIVE OF CUSTOMER BASE	CUSTOMER DEMOGRAPHICS
	INCLUSIVE OF WORLDTEAM	VARIETY AND DIFFERENCE REFLECTED IN ALL ORGANIZATION LEVELS
	WORKFORCE DIVERSITY PLAN BY EACH OPERATING UNIT BASED ON PEOPLE DEVELOPMENT CHALLENGES FOR THE YEAR 2000	PEOPLE DEVELOPMENT COMPONENT OF THE BALANCED SCORECARD
■ EQUITABLE WORKPLACE	FREEDOM FROM BIAS AND DISCRIMINATION AS RECOGNIZED BY LOCAL EMPLOYMENT LAW AND OUR EMPLOYEES	EMPLOYEE SURVEY RESULTS (I.E., EMPLOYEE SATISFACTION WITH CAREER DEVELOPMENT COMPONENTS OF THE PERFORMANCE ENHANCEMENT PROCESS)
	EFFECTIVE POLICIES AND PRACTICES	LEGAL CLAIMS FILED AND (LITIGATED) RESULTS
■ ENHANCED BUSINESS RESULTS	BUSINESS GROWTH	SHAREHOLDER RETURN, NET SALES AND EARNINGS

SELECTED QUESTIONS AND ANSWERS

Q: **Why is CPC interested in diversity?**

A: A highly competent and motivated workforce that is characterized by variety and fully qualified to advance in the CPC WorldTeam is a critical element of realizing our vision, "TO BECOME THE BEST INTERNATIONAL FOOD COMPANY IN THE WORLD."

Q: **A new member of our department recently transferred from another unit of CPC. He is standoffish and makes me uncomfortable. Another team leader told me to join in making him feel more welcome, that this is part of diversity. I thought diversity referred to race and gender.**

A: People are unique individuals and "diversity" encompasses a wide range of things that make us different from others. Organization unit can be one of them. Share your department's "informal" rules with a newcomer. Make an extra effort to include a new employee in your lunch plans. Learning and growing is a two-way street. Ask about the unit he came from and what he sees as some differences. Take the opportunity to broaden your horizons by learning from him.

Q: **Sometimes at staff meetings my peers repeat ethnic jokes they've heard recently. I am uncomfortable with this type of humor. What can I do?**

A: Part of supporting diversity is challenging others when they make ethnic, cultural, gender-related, or sexually derogatory jokes. But sometimes we are hesitant to speak up in group because we think we are the only one with that concern. Often that is not the case. If you find something offensive, chances are others do too. You are not "off the hook" because you didn't tell the joke. Creating an inclusive environment at CPC means each of us has the responsibility to help educate others when certain behavior is objectionable.

Q: **Who can I talk to to find out more about our diversity efforts?**

A: Many people at CPC are actively involved and committed to these initiatives. A good place to start is with your immediate manager or your local Human Resources department. You can also contact the Workforce Diversity and Development Unit at Englewood Cliffs.

CPC'S U.S. EEO STATISTICS—1996

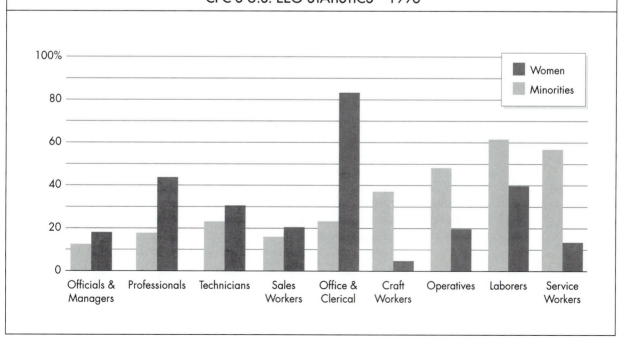

BESTFOODS

January 12, 1998

An open letter to all Bestfoods North American Salaried Employees . . .

Last year at this time, I introduced our Diversity Initiative and our diversity vision for the future. The Diversity Advisory Council, of which I am Chairman, defined a global diversity strategy. Our goal is to establish a workplace where diversity is fully integrated into the organization creating an environment and culture that encourages, values, and respects the uniqueness of the individual; fosters achievement; and optimizes business opportunities.

Our long-term objectives have four components: Preferred Employer, Balanced Workforce, Equitable Workplace, Enhanced Business Results. Each of our business units, as well as the corporate staff, has been engaged in specific actions this past year to ensure that Bestfoods benefits fully from the contributions, creativity, energy, and commitment of the broadest range of men and women representing different cultures, religions, ages, abilities, ethnic and racial backgrounds, and points of view. This is a competitive asset that every one of us must wholeheartedly embrace and actively foster if we are to achieve the outstanding growth that we seek. What are some of the specific accomplishments from this past year?

In order to measure our progress as **preferred employer**, we have committed to our second employee survey. Once again, there are a group of core questions that will be asked around the world. Several questions relate specifically to the amount of respect, inclusiveness, and fair treatment accorded to every Bestfoods employee.

We intensified our efforts to make faster progress in establishing a **balanced workforce** with more variety and difference reflected in all organization levels. We have begun breaking down glass ceilings and walls across the company. As a result of opening up our posting program globally for senior management positions, we have created more cross functional, cross divisional, and international moves than ever before.

We have made great strides in enhancing our career development practices resulting in a more **equitable workplace**. Our Performance Enhancement Process is being used worldwide. Every employee participating now has an individual development plan linked to our Bestfoods Leadership Competencies. And our WorldTeam Development Process, which drives our succession planning, has been revitalized.

All of these efforts are helping to reenergize the organization and are contributing to our **enhanced business results**. At a time when we must achieve more, often with fewer available resources, we are still meeting our financial targets. This was confirmed last year by Wall Street and our shareholders when our stock-price went above 100 for the first time ever!

Our Diversity Initiative is more than a training program, it is the way we do business and live our core values. It is hard work and sometimes frustrating. It requires full participation. Each one of us must be willing to act as a diversity change agent. This means acting as a role model and it often takes personal courage to do so.

In the past I have asked you to join me in continued learning and self-awareness. We are making progress and moving in the right direction. I now ask you to join me in becoming a change agent for the future.

[signature]

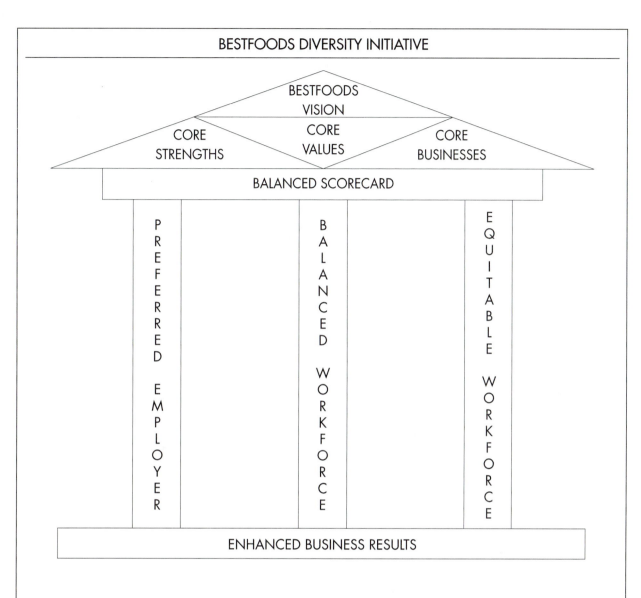

BESTFOODS DIVERSITY INITIATIVE

BESTFOODS VISION

CORE STRENGTHS   CORE VALUES   CORE BUSINESSES

BALANCED SCORECARD

PREFERRED EMPLOYER

BALANCED WORKFORCE

EQUITABLE WORKFORCE

ENHANCED BUSINESS RESULTS

1997 DIVISIONAL PROGRESS

■ **Corporate**
- Sponsoring Our Success
- Cultural Connections
- Revised EEO and Sexual Harassment Policies

■ **Bestfoods North America**
- Analysis and focus on recruiting/development gaps in Operations and Sales
- Enhanced INROADS participation
- Awareness and skill training for managers

■ **Baking Business**
- Mentoring Program
- Enhanced entry-level college recruiting and career development: Mfg; Sales; Fin; Mktg.
- 1st time INROADS participation: five interns

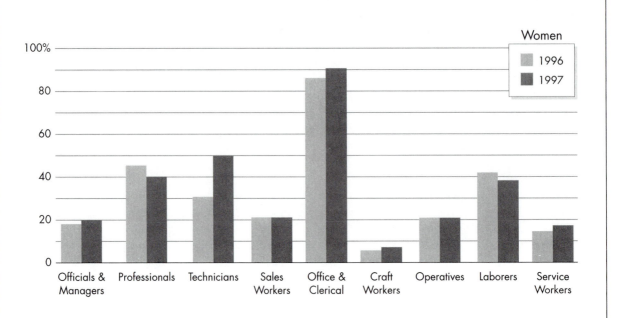

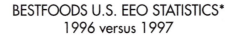

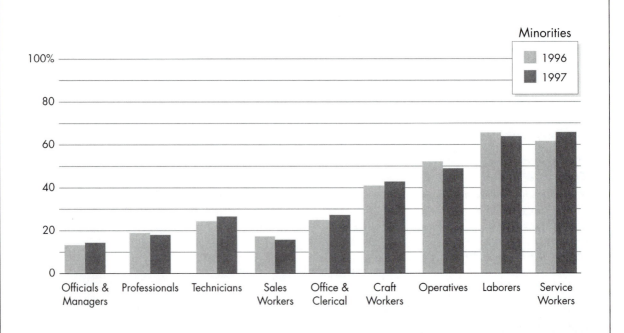

* These numbers include Corn Products North America.

SELECTED QUESTIONS AND ANSWERS

Q. **What are the critical factors that we need to address in order to be successful with our Diversity Initiative?**

A. The Conference Board recently conducted a survey with leading edge organizations in diversity. The companies identifying the greatest progress with diversity efforts had two things in common: active support
and involvement by their CEO and integrating diversity efforts into business and organizational objectives.

Q. **How do we compare to other companies that are implementing diversity programs?**

A. Although our Corporate initiative is fairly recent, Dick Shoemate's leadership on this issue has helped Bestfoods rapidly catch up with "best practice" companies. We have made great strides in integrating diversity into many of our business practices. Some of the key areas where this is occurring include: ongoing management and employee communications, employee awareness, education and involvement, management accountability measured by the balanced scorecard, the Performance Enhancement and Career Development Planning Process, community involvement and outreach, and divisional diversity action plans.

Q. **What impact has the recent restructuring had on minority representation in our workforce?**

A. There has been virtually no negative impact on minority representation despite a difficult year. In fact, we exceed the industry average for minority white collar workers by 5% and for blue collar by 10%.

Q. **Does Bestfoods think diversity is only an issue in the United States?**

A. We are deeply committed to extending our Diversity Initiative beyond the United States. Our definition of workforce diversity includes nationality, religion, age, and gender. These are just some of the elements of diversity that often resonate outside the United States. While legislation is increasing in many countries, our own U.S. heritage of equality and democracy tends to put emphasis on these issues here. However, the drivers of diversity are clearly universal. Ranked in order of importance they are customers and markets, global diversity, productivity, external workforce demographic trends, and internal workforce demographics.

Q. **How many international employees are there in Bestfoods? How many are women?**

A. Bestfoods has approximately 130 employees on international assignments representing 34 nationalities. China, Hong Kong, Spain, and Colombia each have a female expatriate on assignment. We expect this number to continue to grow. Of our global posting applicants, 17% were women.

Q. **Has Bestfoods ever had a class-action suit filed?**

A. We have never had a class-action suit filed against us in our 90-year history. In fact, the number of discrimination charges filed by our 17,000 U.S. employees is very small. Year-to-date, we have only had 10 charges of discrimination filed with the EEOC, three of which have been dismissed for "no reasonable cause."

EQUAL EMPLOYMENT OPPORTUNITY

Bestfoods is committed to prohibiting discrimination in all employment practices including recruiting, hiring, pay, training, promotion, discipline, and termination on the basis of race, color, sex, age, religion, national origin, sexual orientation, disability, or veteran status. The Company prohibits harassment, including sexual harassment of its employees, in any form. The Company is also committed to an affirmative action policy, which will promote and ensure equal opportunity for minorities, women, individuals with disabilities, and covered veterans.

Case Appendix D

Women's Global Leadership Forum Recommendations

CAREER DEVELOPMENT

To enhance career opportunities:

- Increase participation in high-visibility projects/assignments
  - Senior management development program
  - Task force assignments via posting and self-nomination
- Create flexible international assignments
  - Include assignment not involving relocation
  - Shorter-term assignment (six months to one year)
  - Job swapping/exchange
- Clarify career path and development opportunities
  - Provide honest, clear, consistent feedback
  - Full and consistent use of PEP (employee development program)
  - Management accountability for implementing action plans (PEP + employee interest)
- Take same level of risk with women as with men in promoting people
- Post all eligible job openings consistently

DIVERSITY

To increase representation of women in high-level positions:

- Have CEO communicate expectations to *all* global managers
- Create ombudspersons
- Appoint global representation on Corporate Diversity Advisory Council
- Share full results of Women's Global Leadership Forum survey with all divisions
- Benchmark with other companies and recognized experts
- Ensure appropriate measures in Balanced Scorecard

WORK/LIFE BALANCE

To enable women to perform to their highest capabilities, provide options for:

- Telecommuting
- Flexible work schedule, including maternity leave
- Job sharing
- Part-time opportunities

PERSONAL REPONSIBILITIES FOR CAREER DEVELOPMENT

- To take responsibility for your own personal career development
  - Identify goals
  - Communicate personal willingness for high-risk, challenging assignments
  - Self-nominate for those assignments as available
- Learn how to better develop personal networks to facilitate access to career opportunities

- To prepare for future opportunities
  - Develop leadership skills
  - Increase cultural sensitivities
  - Develop language skills
  - Maintain open-minded attitudes
  - Support, nurture, and develop career growth opportunities for those we manage

PERSONAL RESPONSIBILITIES FOR WORK/LIFE BALANCE

- Communicate personal needs and offer alternatives to meet those needs
- Set priorities and recognize the need for trade-offs
- Be sensitive to the needs of individuals we manage

WOMEN'S GLOBAL LEADERSHIP FORUM GROUP RESPONSIBILITIES

- Support diversity initiatives and share forum results
- Network on the basis of relationships developed at the forum
- Borrow with pride
- Share best-practice local learnings with other forum participants

WOMEN AND GLOBAL LEADERSHIP AT BESTFOODS—DISCUSSION QUESTIONS

1. Should the headquarters of U.S.-based multinationals promote diversity initiatives in their worldwide subsidiaries? If so, what's the best way to accomplish this?
2. Do you agree with Brody's idea to hold the forum? Why or why not? Can you suggest an alternative that would accomplish the same purpose or be even more effective?
3. What challenges and problems do Brody and Shoemate face in getting their diversity strategy implemented?
4. Prior to the opening session of the forum, what steps have Brody and her HR colleagues taken to promote diversity efforts throughout the company?
5. What actions or factors contributed to making this a successful change effort?
6. What else should Brody and Bestfoods do to institutionalize the changes begun at the Women's Global Leadership Forum?

Index